the complete design catalog

PETE CULLER'S BOATS

by John Burke

WoodenBoat BOOKS
BROOKLIN, MAINE USA

Published by
WoodenBoat Books
Naskeag Road, PO Box 78
84 Great Cove Drive
Brooklin, Maine 04616 USA
www.woodenboatbooks.com

ISBN 10: 1-934982-03-2
ISBN 13: 978-1-934982-03-7

Printed 2010

Previously published by International Marine, 1984

Book Design: Grace Bell
Cover Design: BasRelief Design

On the front cover: The 10½-foot wherry yawlboat *AF Chapman*, built for the wooden ketch *Stormsvalla*, was originally designed for the schooner *Fiddler's Green.* (Bart Hauthaway photo)
On the back cover: The 17-foot clipper wherry *Seaman's Friend* under sail at Mystic Seaport. (Mystic Seaport photo by Mary Anne Stets)
Author photo: Scot Bell

Printed in USA by Maple-Vail

10 9 8 7 6 5 4 3 2 1

To Captain R.D. (Pete) Culler

Sailor, boatman, boatbuilder, Master Shipwright, skipper, designer of wholesome craft; a unique man whose entire life was devoted to "messing about in boats."

Contents

Foreword

by George B. Kelley

I first met Captain Pete Culler when he came into Hyannis in Spray in 1947 or 1948. We soon became fast friends.

Soon after he bought his house, he built a shop, doing some general woodwork—furniture repair, odd carpentry—anything honest to supplement his income from chartering. Before long, somebody wanted him to build a skiff. First a half-model, then a plan, and soon the skiff was taking shape, with much looking on, on my part.

I soon developed a habit of looking in on the shop at the end of my workday, usually finding Captain Pete finishing up his day's work—whether it was a design job or a building job. I was at an age to be full of questions, and Captain Pete always had the time and patience to explain what he was doing. I soon learned that he had vast, self-taught knowledge of the fine points of boat design. I was forever intrigued by his understanding of the complexities and mathematics of things, such as calculating the center of gravity of a hull, and his knowledge of a cheap-and-dirty method of finding the same point by balancing a half-model on a draftsman's three-sided scale rule. I enjoyed his demonstration of the fact that the calculation method and the simple mechanic method gave the same answer within a very small degree of variation. Because of his great intellectual curiosity, he knew a lot of "rule of thumb" methods of calculation that are mostly unknown to many college-educated naval architects.

I looked over his shoulder at some point during the development of almost every design he did, and I thought it interesting that with his great knowledge of what he was doing he was always interested in my comments and questions on each design.

Some years ago he did a sharpie design, *Old Glory*, which I fell in love with. After a couple of years of agonizing over the thought of building such a boat, I decided it was really what I wanted, but a little too big for my needs. So I asked him one day if sometime when he had a little slack in his schedule he'd design me a sharpie similar to *Old Glory* but only

George Kelley surveys traditional craft from his dock in Hyannis, Massachusetts. In the foreground, Brian Kelley in his 11-foot sampan *Jade Arrow* is about to make a beachhead. Just behind him is Stefan Galazzi's version of the Culler Presto-type ketch. At right is the Kelley-designed and built sharpie ketch *Sparrow*. (David Hartman photo)

about 28 or 30 feet long. His immediate answer was a very blunt, emphatic, "No!"

By then we had become very close friends and were continually doing each other favors, so his "No!" was a shock. I was at a loss for words, and before I could think of just how to say, "Why?" he added, "I won't design your boat because you can do it yourself—and if you can, you should." When I completed the design, I suggested to him that before I committed all that lumber and labor, maybe he'd check the design over to see if he felt it was sound. He said, "Sure." Then he unrolled the plan, looked at it for about two minutes, and said, "Looks good. Looks good usually is good; why don't you go ahead and build it?" I did, and if I do say so myself, it worked out to be a pretty good boat.

I think this story illustrates a great deal about the measure of the man.

Preface

Once upon a time, when you found yourself needing a watercraft, large or small, the requirements would be met locally. Most communities, either inland or seashore had the talent at hand to design and produce what was sought. The craft would be a reflection of a tradition, built up over time that answered the needs of its customers, both commercial and pleasure. This system nurtured individual craftspeople in a time-honored evolution of apprentice to journeyman to master. Occasionally, one individual would have the requisite talent and skill to be both designer and builder.

Pete Culler was one who designed and built vessels, large and small, over a career spanning nearly fifty years. Beginning in the late 20's until his death in 1978, he was always 'messing about with boats'. This book is a design catalog of his work produced primarily from the twenty years prior to his passing. It comprises just over 100 designs ranging in size from 8' prams to 125' three-masted schooners. All were intended to be built of wood using traditional methods and all are derived from examples of American watercraft developed over time for regional users either doing work or pursuing pleasure.

The pillars of Pete Culler's design philosophy were simplicity, economy and ease of use. He believed that designs based on the working craft of the past could fulfill today's boating needs—and do so with style. His lasting contribution lay in his ability to refine and enhance these workboat types for pleasure use without losing their appealing qualities.

Pete Culler said "Anything good requires knowledge of its creators and money to do it right; this very much applies to boats, cruising boats as much or more than any. The fact that boats now (mid-1970's) cost 12 to 15 times what they did in my youth is beside the point; it's only dollars, yen, pounds, francs, etc. I found out long ago that a well-built and well-designed craft that you will keep a long time is the most economical, even though the first cost may seem high. Good workmanship and good materials are still around and it takes more or less the same time and effort it always did to turn out a nice craft."

Should you be looking for a boat to suit your needs take a moment to peruse the designs listed here. They have all stood the test of time and are sufficiently varied that one will likely fulfill your individual requirements.

Acknowledgments

I wish to thank my family, Jodi, Josh and Drew and especially my wife Joanne, for all the support given over the years and for their encouragement and good cheer.

At WoodenBoat Publications, Maynard Bray and Scot Bell have been instrumental in the production of this re-issue after many years out of print and I wish to thank them both.

Mystic Seaport Museum is now the repository of all things Culler including the designs in this catalog and they have graciously consented to our reprinting them here. Should you wish to build one of boats included here, and we hope that you do, we have included a listing with specific instructions on how to order plans in the appendix.

A man and his world; Pete Culler at the helm of *Spray*, off Cape Cod. The vessel's yawlboat, affectionately known as *'dink'*, hangs in the davits with *Spray's* lug rigged mizzen sail resting on top. The yawlboat was just under 11 feet and of traditional shape. Capt. Pete comments, "The *Spray's* yawlboat, though old and secondhand, and much rebuilt, could live in quite rough water, carry a water barrel, and run out the kedge and cable. If things were quiet, she could carry the bower (anchor) too, slung under her, warship style. Grub, ice and passengers were her daily cargoes, and even with all of that, she was a prime sailer. She carried a standing lug rig with two deep reefs, so she could make it back in a hard chance." (George Yater photo)

Introduction—Keep Them Simple

by R.D. Culler

The following essay appeared in National Fisherman, *December 1974 and January 1975.*

Much has been written in journals and books about the common sense approach, the easy and sensible ways, by very able and experienced boatmen and designers. All of it is very worthwhile and instructive reading. They described it in their era, and time marching on has dimmed the usefulness in only a few ways.

That I should bring up this previously well-covered subject again may seem a redundancy; however, I speak of now. The apparent world crises of various kinds are having, or will have, an effect on many phases of boating. They do now, only some are not quite aware of it.

Man adjusts to most anything. The day of the large steam yacht, and big ocean liners violently competing against one another, is past. The big diesel electric yachts, M-boats, and coastal steamers came to their ends. Few now own really large yachts, or even what used to be considered modest-size craft. Instead, we have hordes of small craft and, thanks to the Affluent Society, most anyone can own one.

Yet, not all at sea is small; the thirst for oil has brought about tankers of a size undreamed-of only a few years ago. These monsters have brought with them problems that in many cases are not yet understood.

The huge number of small and moderate-size craft has also brought about problems; most of these are brought on by the national mania for huckstering, aided and abetted by boating publications that rely for their income on the hucks that advertise on their pages. This in turn has brought about a strange set of customs, social mores, newfangled dogma, and befogged outlook. Most all of it costs a lot of money, with little real return, except to the hucksters' pockets.

If I seem to condemn the general boating scene, I intend to. I have no objection at all to a man gilding his boat in any way he sees fit. He can load her to sinking with all the goodies that are available to bait him. It does not matter, except to his creditors, whether he can afford it or not.

As indicated by many current publications, this

is the way it should be done. With that philosophy, however, I take noisy issue.

Many have been led to think this is the only way boating can be done—the proper way, the only safe way. Then they find it too expensive. Discouragement sets in and the craft is soon up for sale. It's a rich man's game, with the boat always in the shipyard. All because they have been conditioned *not* to think simple.

Without doubt, much of the new gear developed for boats has its uses on the right boat—and if the operator understands the item and its maintenance. It makes no sense to jam it on an unsuited craft, or one that does not need it. Take a boxy 20-footer, drawing all of 18 inches, with a depth sounder, gull chaser, radiophone (she never leaves the bay), gas stove, and a huge mill to pry her misformed hull along. Her owner cries about the cost of it all; this-and-that does not work, and now the head is stopped up! Last week his stove played out. Next week, although he does not know it yet, his stern drive will fold up, so he can join the ranks of those hauled up with a gaping hole in the stern. Boatyards seem full of them in midseason. This type of person does like to get afloat, so I have some feeling for him, but to get him to see the error of his ways is most difficult, for he has just read the last issue of *Putter Yacht*, and that grand publication cannot be wrong.

Having made this Joe's acquaintance, you are apt to see him around another season, if he has not given up in disgust. It sometimes dawns on him that you are having a lot of fun in a very simple craft, while he is not. His type sometimes comes alongside to see just what sort of craft you're really enjoying. Being the right sort, though very much misguided, he is interested. Things are discussed, and it's found the little craft is quite easy to look at, relies not at all on a shipyard (if you have a friend who controls some beach), and makes no noise, no smoke, and no stink. It is totally biodegradable and very simple to use, so it gets a lot of it, costs maybe a to-spot a year to keep up, and is smart enough to tax the senses and abilities pleasantly. Besides, she is a little personality, depending on the weather for her moods, which are seldom stubborn, and can be pure witchcraft, especially in little or what appears to be no wind at all.

Needless to say, I've not made a convert, for the road is long, but I have set a fellow to thinking, maybe sown the seeds of doubt.

This same philosophy applies to larger craft, both pleasure and, to maybe a lesser extent, recent commercial craft. If it can be afforded, well and good, but much can be omitted easily if the economics don't work. Many so-called modern hulls are not cheap to propel. Until recently, pushing a hard-driving hull through the water was not considered a drawback; possibly the desire for large capacity on a short length seemed more important. It may well be that in the future this whole approach will be reversed.

In the past, certain tonnage rules tended to encourage poorly shaped craft. Now, dockage by the foot works very much in favor of a short tub, and certain stability rules for some craft result in the design of vessels that are poor seaboats. With the rather certain interest in going back in the future to easily driven hulls, if only for economy's sake, some of these recent standards may be relaxed or changed. It's been my experience that the cost of any boat is based pretty much on her pounds of displacement, and very much on the amount of gear and dressing that is thought necessary. In other words, for a given displacement, a long, easy-lined craft is no more expensive than a short, boxy on—and often a bit less for the hull alone. Less power and fuel are needed to push her, and if she be a sailer, less area and lighter rig. The slimmer craft is usually better looking and an easier seaboat.

Excess freeboard and high houses absorb power, cause the craft to be awkward to handle in a wind, and raise the crew up where the motion is greater. The larger area costs more for materials to build, and for the most part is apt to be ugly. None of it makes sense. True, you can pack a lot of people in—and make them miserable.

Any boat should fit her intended use; otherwise, there is disappointment in her performance, even though the craft may not be basically poor. We have developed a throwaway economy and are almost on the threshold of the throwaway boat. However, there has been much jazz about a "no-maintenance boat"; this is neither sensible nor cheap. Part of boating is the proper care of your craft. If this does not appeal, you should not own a boat, for the simple reason that you do not really care enough about it to learn the craft in all ways. Or, the upkeep may seem just too much and too costly or the boat may be too big, too elaborate, or both.

To get the most out of any craft, you may have to develop some senses and powers of observation that have been dormant. Weather sense for local conditions a few hours in advance is acquired by

A rowing craft for sensible exercise: Captain Pete in his bateau *Otter*. (Richard White photo)

constant observation; it does not require a hook-up to the news media or the daily weather reports, which are helpful but often too general for very localized conditions.

I don't quarrel with the present-day methods of getting the usual weather information, but I do point out that a cultivated knowledge of local conditions is often more important, and it frees you from being a slave to some black box that, if you are off in the semiwilds in a tiny craft, you don't want to be cluttered with. Besides, if a box is along, you listen to the news, which is usually bad, and why spoil the day?

All this very much applies to the tides too; they can be very much against you, yet by proper planning, very much for you. A fine tide book is nice, costs money, and soon gets spoiled in an open craft. Most coastal newspapers carry tide table extracts, daily or weekly. At least one oil company puts them out; maybe several do. *The Old Farmer's Almanac* does just fine. Thing of it is, tide information is around free for the using and if you boat with any regularity, you find that you "get run" of the tides and know just about how they are each day, going for weeks without consulting a table.

This kind of outlook is true in so many facets of boating. I suppose it is sort of developing an awareness, a happy condition that the finest instruments and equipment can never really replace.

Some of the best boating, and often the only kind for some people, is in portable boats that live in the backyard when in home port. Usually they are man-propelled, although often with some sail. These can vary from skin boats to manufactured portables, double-paddle canoes, light pulling boats, or some combination. Whatever the type, they should be easy moving and easy to use. Often they are owner built, which is all the better, because they are apt to be loved more. This is mighty nice boating, and it's well worthwhile even if you own a larger craft for bigger water. Fortunately, the gadgets and gear for these boats are not much, and since it all has to be lugged at one time or another, the useless stuff is soon junked. The "navigation gear" is at most a small pocket compass (seldom used), while lunch and a water jug suffice for sea stores.

The wind is free, but it costs some to put it to work to move a boat properly. Yet sail has much attraction, one reason being that you have to work along with it, as much of the boat's performance depends on the ability of the one who sails her. This is not just being a good helmsman, but also having a good understanding of how to keep up such a craft, marlinspike seamanship to some degree, and a knowledge of tuning and trim. In the smaller open sizes, I've found the classic types, most with portable rigs, to be the most economical. These include peapods, dories, Whitehalls, wherries, sailing skiffs, sampans, garveys, and beach yawls.

Like all craft, none of these suit all waters and uses equally well, so a choice should be made with understanding. I favor classic small craft because they have stood the test of time and have had long and careful development for their particular use. Nearly all can be rowed or sculled, which is very simple and cheap auxiliary power. Most sail so well that there is little use for rowing except for the pleasure of it.

Many now think that the traditional rigs for these craft are inefficient and should be "modernized." If, in re-creating one of these craft and her original rig, she does not sail properly, it's the fault of those who made her or the lack of understanding of her use. The usual mistakes are: a lack of sense of proportion in making the spars and gear, making a nonturning mast when it should rotate, poor sheeting of the sails, and attempting to add "store-bought" fittings that don't suit the job. And now, sadly, there are the problems created by some sailmakers who know little of cutting sails for such craft. This lack is more bullheaded cussedness and an unwillingness to do anything except make modern racing sails. Fortunately, not all sailmakers are this way.

These little rigs are pure sticks and string, all material readily available, easily made, and not dependent on boatyards and marine supply catalogs. These classics don't take kindly to the tall, stayed-mast rig and may even be unsafe with them, and they all become very unhandy.

Some will say that these boats are now expensive and more or less hard to come by. My experience has been that it's not quite so; some builders turn them out, usually on order, and the first cost may seem much more than some factory-built craft. However, many find the boats so suitable that most owners hang on to them, while those using production boats always seem to be getting another, in a search for something that is really satisfactory. The result is that in five years these guys have often had four boats, spent far more than the cost of a new classic, and still have not found their dream.

I find that over a period of, say, five years, these nice little craft are by far the most satisfying, economical, and sensible of all small sailing utility boats. They seem to get a lot of notice and admiration, mostly because they seem so right and fit their surroundings.

I get noise about the cost of good small sailing craft, yet the most popular, apparently, by the numbers you see, is some sort of motor craft, which is now quite expensive—even a poor one—to say nothing of the cost of operation.

Yet, there is a place for the motor craft. Often it can be the only choice for many good reasons.

Who knows whether a world fuel shortage, real or contrived, will have some effect on powerboats. Regardless, the days of six gallons for a buck are long gone, and there seems no point at all in running an extravagant craft. Speed has always been costly, be it in boats or in other conveyances.

A rather long, easy-lined craft with a minimum of tophamper is, and always will be, cheaper to propel, although many boxy designs seem to flaunt this. Overloading any craft with gear and gadgets simply uses more fuel. The more alternators, compressors, and other stuff that is run off the engine, the less power there is to drive the boat. Or, to do so properly, a bigger engine is required. So much stuff on boats now is really not needed.

The popular planing boat is, at least in the smaller sizes, much misunderstood by many. The advertised speed of these craft sounds great; yet, in many waters the conditions suited for it are not often present. Any planing hull is fearfully rough riding in lumpy conditions. Some are worse than others, but all of them are bad, and they can be quite a danger if mishandled. As a whole, planing craft are not very good seaboats. A few that handle well when slowed down get along in rough going, but it's not pleasant or good. People tend to overload craft with gear and sometimes passengers. Then the boat won't lift out; more power and weight, including more fuel, are tried, and you are just where you were before—overloaded.

I feel that this very popular and available type is much misused. As a commuter, runabout, rescue craft, water taxi, etc., it has a lot going for it. As a general-use boat, especially in rather open water, the small powerboat has many failings. A properly designed one, not loaded, is maybe cheap on fuel by the mile; by the hour, along with first cost and upkeep, she is not. If the boat is used as a runabout joyrider, I can't see how anyone can be other than bored and uncomfortable after about an hour of it.

If I seem to downgrade these now-popular craft, and bring rage from the purveyors of them on account of my remarks, I wish to point out that in the now-distant past I bent the throttles on Uncle Sam's finest, and I have been designing and building planing boats for some time.

For larger power craft able to go farther afield and do some cruising, I find the planing hull even less suitable, for all the reasons previously given for smaller ones but compounded. The idea that you must make fast trips seems totally out of keeping with cruising. Aircraft and cars do it better.

In bigger motor craft, simplicity, easy-moving hulls, fairly comfortable seakeeping ability, modest fuel use, and simple maintenance are essential. Many of these craft today are so loaded mechanically that on a cruise they seem to run from boatyard to boatyard, and to ports where an electronic expert is on hand. There is so much stuff on them that something is always out of whack, and the whole lashup is so designed and built that often one simple failure clobbers the whole thing.

Spritsail boats are quick to set up and easy to stow: Captain Pete's *Seaman's Friend.* (John Burke photo)

A properly installed and maintained engine, well understood by its operator, seldom fails totally, and if its engineer is hep and on the ball, it's soon going again. A major failure of parts, such as broken cranks, busted pistons, etc., is almost unheard of. If such a thing does happen, there was something radically wrong with the setup to begin with. Strange as it may seem to the younger generation, it was about the same with engines 50 years ago, with the exception that they were then more simply installed, and usually quite accessible, so some minor failure could be repaired readily, even in a considerable seaway. Most of the new mills are so unreachable, especially in a hurry, that some small failure can totally cripple the craft.

I'm often appalled at some of the design and building I see, and I wonder if the men responsible have ever changed a belt, cleaned a filter, repaired a leaking hose, or done a host of other small things in a seaway—say, off Point Jude, with night coming on—or, if they know better, do they care?

Of course you can put your money in a black box, with the power to run it, so as to get the Coast Guard out in the wet, all on account of some simple thing you should be able to take care of. You become another statistic on the yearly roster—engine failure—possibly started by the designer, maybe compounded by the builder, and then helped out by you, who didn't know what you were getting into in the first place.

Tuck the heart of a powerboat away in a corner (usually poorly ventilated), taking care to use the very minimum of space in doing so in order to have a lot of "living space," cover with hatches (a menace when raised in a seaway), be sure to install a wall-to-wall carpet, then clutter it more with all the comforts of home. Later something really quite minor goes wrong below. No need to say more, except that the craft is "right up there" following the very latest style.

Cruising sailing craft appeal to so many, and with good reason. It's a very happy way to enjoy the sea. Captain Joshua Slocum remarked that the sea was made to sail on; I daresay he knew exactly what he was talking about.

To many, the mention of sailing craft, large and small, only means racing. Those who are experienced racers know some things not generally realized by many who have never done it. Racing is a very serious game to those who really go at it, and there is no point in racing if you don't go all out. And it's expensive—far more than the inexperienced ever realize. It always was, and always will be, both in money and effort, with a lot of discomfort and often plain misery.

Very small racing classes are financially within reach of many, and just fine if you take racing seriously. If you persist in starting with an even slightly dirty bottom, sails not just right, and other signs of the not completely dedicated, forget it and don't clutter up the scene. Instead, just daysail, although any craft designed mainly for racing will not be the easiest and most handy, having been produced to be totally competitive within her class limits, so that other things fall where they may.

Racing larger craft in open water or for some distance is where you really layout the cash. I speak from experience, having been a pro on a couple of these. The constant grooming, upkeep, and repair of these sleek money-eaters is what the pro does, besides any other dirty work the regular yachtsman does not care for or does not know how to do. This often includes everything from cooking or battling a spinnaker wrap, to mending a blown-out sailor batting the depth sounder in the side of the head to make it work, to putting up with the owner-skipper's moods and foibles. And, of course, a good and trusted pro authorizes most of the bills and does a lot of purchasing; he knows what most of it costs and can pretty well surmise the rest of the owner's expenses.

Campaigning a 40-foot racer all summer, fully and well enough to at least be a constant menace to the top competitors, takes big money. First, there's the home shipyard all winter, with work going on; then you must be ready for any emergency during the season. Often there's a call or two to a yard farther off; you have a racing reputation, so they lay it on. Often two sailmakers are on tap, besides other lesser suppliers. Purveyors of all kinds surround you, especially to sell grub, for a good racing crew likes the best food and lots of it.

The game is sometimes brutal to the craft, and on a gold-plater the finish suffers. She's taken out of the ring at every chance to mend things and, of course, give her another bottom job.

It's quite possible—or at least it was at the time I was in the game—to spend the first cost of the craft, built by the best builders of her kind, in two years of heavy campaigning. This assumes you have no big accidents or do not do the Southern Circuit. You play it very hard, supposedly within the rules of the game, but you take chances and heavy damage of some kind can well happen.

The craft I was in were extremely well built for their type, but if kept at hard racing, they aged quickly, and they were always undergoing changes (all expensive) in an effort to keep up with the younger set and the changes of rules that go along with the sport.

Finally, structural troubles can become big, and more is spent, for all you are really doing is trying to push the mast through the bottom for a small silver cup. I must say that the time we retired a cup for good (a little halfpint thing), three in a row in three years, the last round being a complete rout, was a small satisfaction to me, as the rig had held together long enough to do it. To the owner-skipper it was a really big occasion, and had been really worked for—I know, I did my share. There was a big blowout that night, and it must have cost the owner plenty—one of the lesser expenses of racing.

Most of these craft I now speak of are considered cruisers too, although my experience has been that they are so oriented to racing that nothing is really right for cruising, even to the position of the pot locker, for you cannot encroach one inch on the space allotted for stowing 15—yes, I said 15—light sails, most soaking wet.

But all things end, and the racer-owner had a nice cruising schooner built and took up a different way of life. If we were exposed to racing after his conversion, it was as occasional spectators and, as someone pointed out long ago, watching a yacht race is not interesting. The new cruiser was a fine craft that sailed on her bottom; no winches, no light sails except a fisherman. The topsail was a working sail as rigged. She had a fine galley, good ground tackle, and all the other stuff that makes a real cruiser. The little vessel took all the bad weather we wanted to face without fuss, required a very small crew, and though she had much more tonnage than the racer, her upkeep was less and life on board was no strain at all. The reason, of course, was that the craft was designed for cruising only. Her speed, if anything, was better than the racer's, especially in dusty going; she was definitely not a dull sailer. Being somewhat of a classic type, she was very handsome, and the details of her rig had long ago been worked out. A racer's rig is always in a state of change and development, so it always has bugs and growing pains of some sort. The little schooner's troubles had been worked out generations ago, and any wear, damage, or failure was readily repairable on board. Once properly fitted out, and with routine careful maintenance, she was

Simple boats to build, use, and maintain: Captain Pete in his *Otter* and Maynard Bray in his L. Francis Herreshoff double-paddle canoe. (Richard White photo)

a very self-sufficient little world.

Cruising should not be a wearing occupation. The craft should be suited to it and to the waters she will mostly use. Some think a cruising boat should have a huge amount of room in her. She should, to a point, have room to stow the required gear well, out of the way but readily accessible with room enough for the expected crew but not much more. I see no point and some unhandiness in a craft so roomy you rattle about in her. There is no reason to live in a shambles of gear and goods improperly stowed. It's not good seamanship either way.

Here again the more or less classic craft seems the most suited. The more the racer is developed, the less suited it is to plain cruising. I hear howls of "Not so!" but it's been one of the worries and a thorn in the side of some clubs who have worked long and hard in the past to encourage cruising.

Like powerboats and smaller dayboats, many a cruising sailing craft is now made difficult, complicated, and expensive, with little real return from the gadgets and what some think are now necessities. A well-known designer said to me long ago: "A tight deck and a good stove are the first two important things in a cruising boat."

This statement still holds true, and no doubt always will. A wet bunk, no matter how fancy, is no good; a warm, dry straw mattress on a wooden platform is something you can get used to even though this old-time donkey's breakfast has long been out of fashion on any craft. Good, well-cooked grub makes the world a bright place. If you're wet, cold, and hungry, fine woodwork, electronics, and other gadgets mean little.

This all applies to cool and temperate climates; similar mistakes and unsuitable craft are now seen in the tropics. The tight deck still applies; any kind of stove below is impossible at times. The charcoal box stove on deck is a pretty fine thing, but where are you going to put it on some of these modern boat layouts? Screens are far more useful than a Loran, and in many cases the old "summer cabin" construction should be used few now know what it is.

For some time *National Fisherman* has been running monthly articles by Roger Taylor on interesting boats of the recent past, most of them very sensible cruising craft for now. They are more or less classic in their way. I've known many of these craft, seen a couple built, and sailed on them. They were quite successful cruisers and many are still around.

As we look back on these boats, one thing stands out—they were quite simple compared to many craft today, some of them extremely so. Most were quite well built, so they are for the most part still with us. It's been said that craft of that kind can't be built now, but that's wishful something or other, because they can. It's also said that they are too costly—maybe so if you follow the modern custom of trading in every couple of years. This trading is to me an indication that a fellow is not happy with his craft, and that the latest thing, still smoking from the mold, will somehow answer his desires. The hell of it is, it's often worse than the one before.

Anything good requires knowledge of its creators, and money to do it right; this very much applies to boats, cruising boats as much or more than any. The fact that boats now cost 12 to 15 times what they did in my youth is beside the point; it's only dollars, yen, pounds, francs, etc. Good workmanship and good materials are still around, and it takes more or less the same time and effort it always did to turn out a nice craft. One thing is sure; it's all taxed more.

I found out long ago that a well-built and designed craft that you will keep a long time is the most economical, even though her first cost may seem high. This changing of boats, always looking for greener grass, is in the end most expensive. Keep the gear and gadgets to a minimum. You can always add 'em later, but usually, after doing without, you find you don't need them.

Most people's cruising time is limited, so they often set a schedule and work hard at keeping it. If you have much of a schedule, you are attempting too much. Beating through the Mussel Ridge, say, under good conditions, with a fair current under you, is far more interesting and you see more of the country than steaming through in a rush so you can make some predetermined port miles Down-Along.

And if there is the smell of wood smoke and a good chowder coming right aft while she's in stays, so much the better.

PART I

Round-Bilged Open Craft for Sail and Oar

Sharp Wherry

Length overall: 16 feet 11½ inches
Beam: 4 feet 2¼ inches
Molded depth: 1 foot 3 inches
Sail area: 61 square feet

Fast Gig

Length overall: 18 feet
Beam: 37 inches
Depth: 16 inches

Sharp Wherry And Fast Gig For Dr. Nicholas Freydberg

Pete Culler had a particular genius for designing traditional small craft that both rowed and sailed well. There was nothing new about this kind of performance. It was what was demanded every day before the age of power by the users of sailing workboats.

The Old Man stated many times that he was not presenting anything new. If there were any innovations in his design work, he often said, they lay in new combinations of old ideas. This is a most modest statement, but it is certainly true.

Many of us today do not have the need to haul home a quarter ton of cod or a dozen bushels of scallops or clams, although a few of each would be nice. Pete knew this, and adjusted accordingly. One of his genuine talents was the ability to "clipperize" the hull forms of working watercraft of the past. He made them less burdensome, sharper, and more suited to pure enjoyment and he did this without losing the essence of the design. This is most important. It reflects the core of truth suggested by his modesty.

The following two designs are fine examples of this capability. Both have workboat backgrounds. Each has been refined to meet the demands of today's boat user.

Both the 17-foot sharp wherry and the 18-foot fast gig were designed and built for Pete's friend and patron Dr. Nicholas Freydberg, himself an accomplished oarsman. In fact, Pete's own 17½-foot fast bateau, *Otter*, was sold to the good doctor after the Captain's first heart attack. The two men saw eye to eye on almost everything except where to put their butts when rowing. Pete preferred his stationary, while the doctor liked his to slide. That's why there is a sliding seat in the wherry.

The lines of the wherry are very nicely proportioned. The waterlines are sharp, with a nice hollow entrance forward. The lines then fair to a finely shaped tuck aft. On the waterline she is double ended. Her sections show a moderate rise of floor and a nice turn to the bilge. There is a slight hollow in the garboards. The buttock lines are well balanced with a long and very fine run. The bow profile is pleasing to the eye and the rake of the post has a certain rightness to it. The transom has the traditional wherry heart shape.

The sheer goes by various names: S-, compound, coble, and powderhorn have been applied. This was a particular trademark with the Captain; his designs always seemed to benefit from it. With this sheer, the gunwales were always tapered fore and aft, for this accented the line nicely.

Unlike the usual wherry construction, this boat was relatively easy to plank. Witness the well-balanced and fair diagonals. Part of the secret is the use of a glued-up deadwood skeg, stair-step fashion, which tapers aft. The rabbet is cut into this keel-skeg. This eliminates planking the tuck—a fearful-looking piece of construction to most amateurs, and some pros, too. Seven planks to a side do nicely. If lined off correctly, the fourth or middle plank should have no shape, just taper.

The rig is adjustable by the use of an ingenious mast gate in the partners. The heel of the mast lands in one of two steps bored in the stem knee. This built-in flexibility is a great aid in tuning the rig for varying conditions. When lofting, the boatbuilder should include step locations on the stem knee. After the knee is cut and fitted properly, but before assembling with stem and keel, the piece should be taken to the bench to bore the steps. This is common sense, but it is sometimes forgotten.

The rig is adequate, but somewhat modest. On

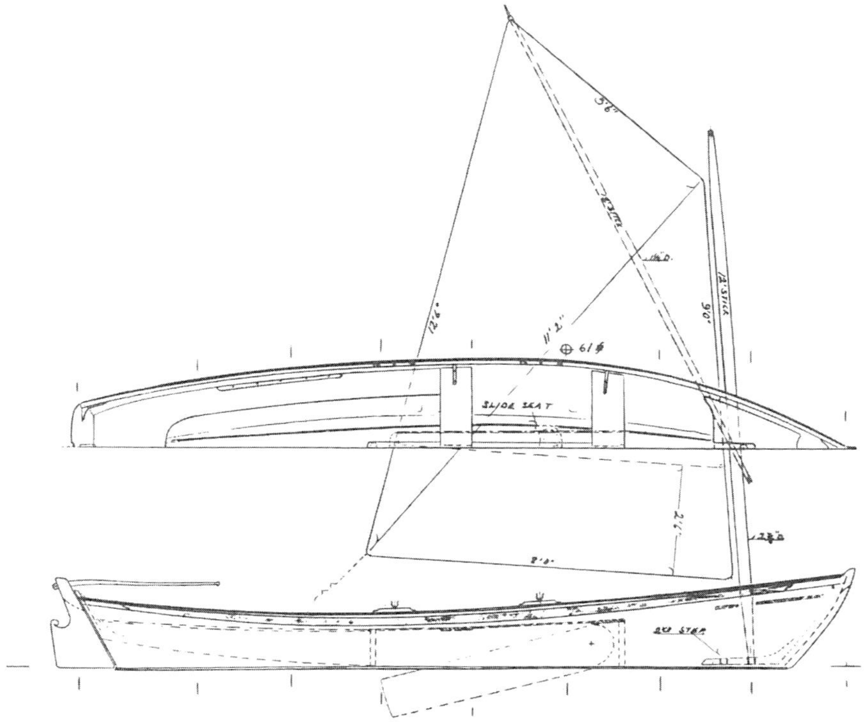

Above: Sail plan, profile, and half breadth of the sharp wherry. **Below:** Her lines.

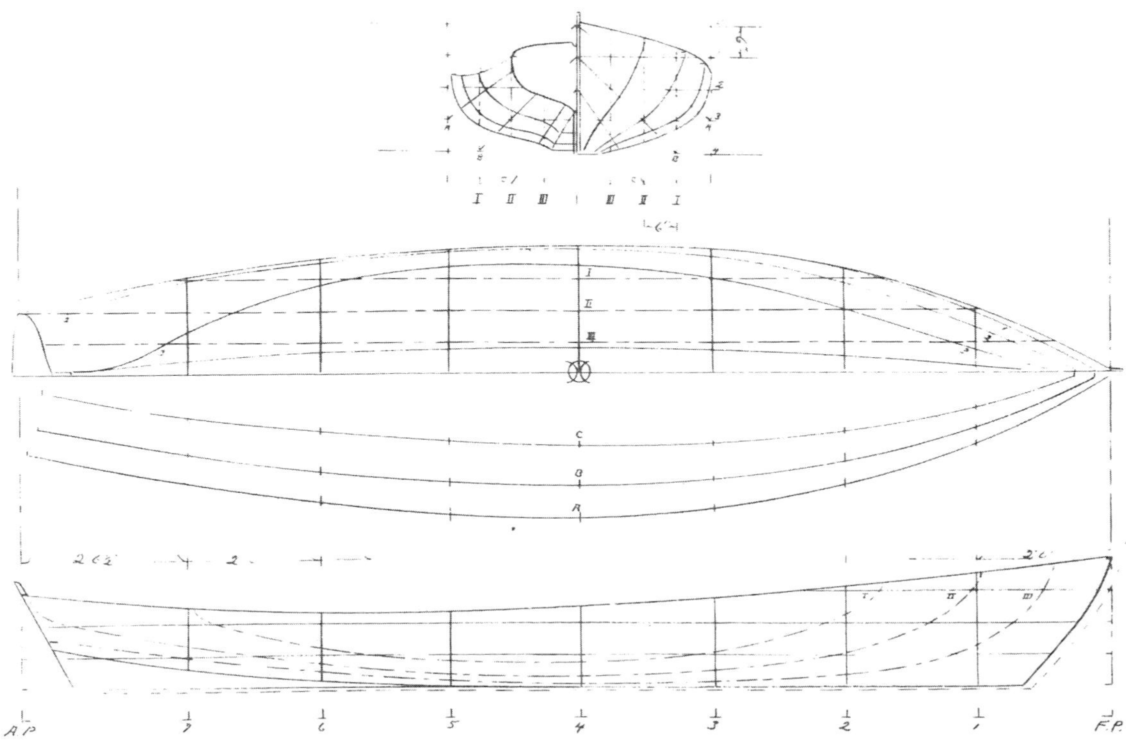

The wherry all ready for her stemhead to be carved. (Chuck Melcher photo)

Seaman's Friend, Pete's own boat of this design, the sail area is 74 square feet. With the spritsail rig, this seemed to do nicely. Pete also worked out a standing lug rig of 84 square feet. He felt that this was all the boat could handle, for at times "she would shake and shudder a mite." This sail had a step just forward of the box's king post. The partner was located directly above and fastened to either side of the box and under the forward thwart. In addition, it was necessary to brace the fore thwart on both sides, at the riser, with knees fore and aft.

The rudder area should be increased by extending the heel perpendicular to the transom rake. A picture of this is shown on page 86 in Captain Pete's book *Skiffs and Schooners.*

Both boats are fitted with rigs (not shown on the fast gig). The wherry provides good performance under sail. Indeed, she is very fast reaching or running. When beating to windward, however, much depends on the man at the helm. If he understands the rig and the boat, she is very responsive on this point also. Reaching in a fresh breeze on a measured-mile course, the boat has been clocked at 11 minutes. This boat can sail! Even with only an "ash breeze," the boat is quite able. Either loaded or light, her wake is flat and shows little disturbance. Two rowing positions allow for trim under different conditions, or for doubles, if two people wish to row. With two strong men at the oars and a light coxswain, the boat really moves. Having been designed for Cape Cod waters, she can take a lop of a sea. Also, with her flat plank keel, beaching the boat is a simple matter. This boat was one of Captain Pete's favorite designs.

Dr. Freydberg enjoyed the wherry in his home waters around Martha's Vineyard for a number of years. However, at 300 pounds, it got to be a bit heavy at layup time. The good doctor began to yearn for something about half that weight. Pete's answer was the fast gig.

The doctor's only design requirement was that the gig weigh just 150 pounds. After the boat was designed and built, Pete felt the need to make an apology. She weighed 151! His masterful touch is evident throughout. The boat is capable of a very high level of performance. "Sharp" hardly begins to describe her. The waterlines are markedly hollow, fore and aft. The buttocks are very sharp with a long, very fine run. The sheer is strong and graceful, with little rake in the posts. It hardly needs saying, but this boat is fast. To get the most out of her, outriggers and spoon oars are required. Nine-foot oars are about right.

There are three rowing positions to accommodate various circumstances. The rudder, as shown on the plan, uses steering lines. This, however, can be changed readily to a hinged tiller, Norse style, when using the sail rig.

Walt Simmons would have fun planking this boat. The planking run tucks to a most beautifully shaped transom. *Quitsa Pilot,* Dr. Freydberg's version, has nine strakes to a side. Leaving the sheerstrake bright accents the boat handsomely. Construction is very much Cornish gig style, with one

The 17-foot wherry *Seaman's Friend* under sail at Mystic Seaport. (Mystic Seaport photo by Mary Anne Stets)

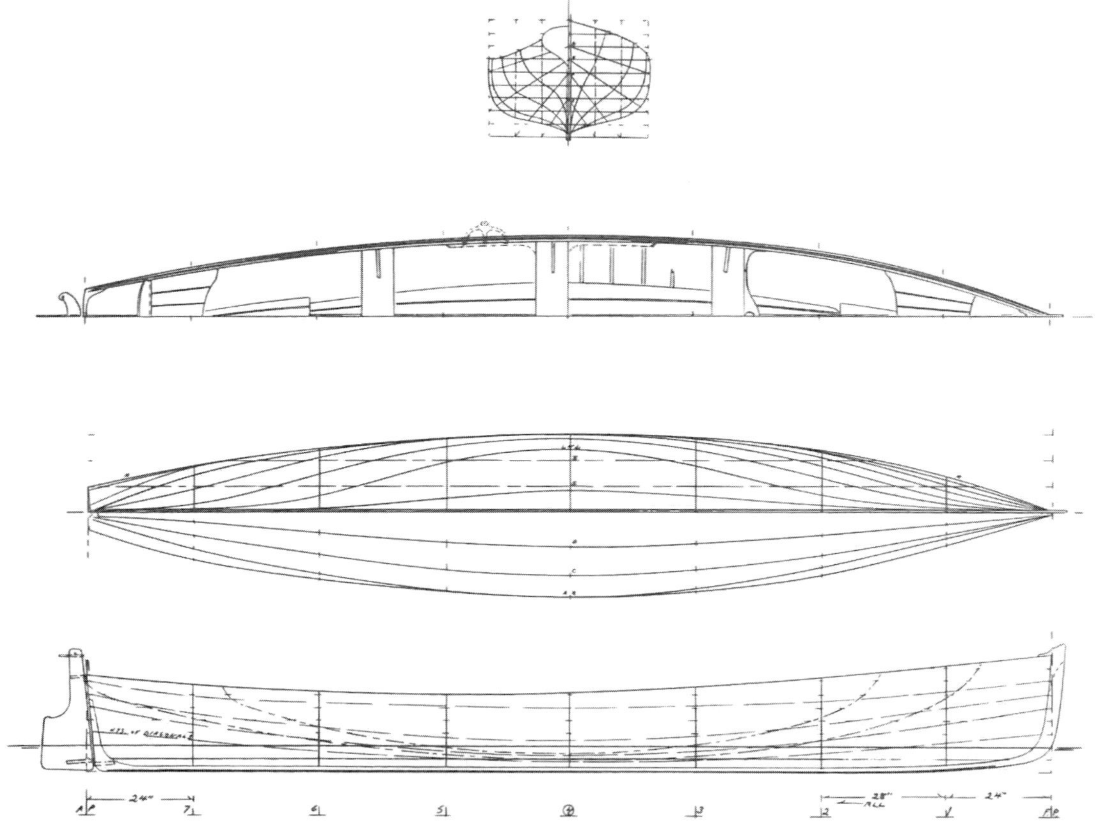

Lines of the l8-foot fast gig.

exception. The frames on *Quitsa Pilot* lap over the keel the width of the garboards, rather than being full length. This is a design idiosyncrasy of Pete's. He felt it was stronger. Floor timbers fitted between frames are an important part of the boat's construction. These extend across the first three strakes of planking. In the ends, where there is much shape, these floors are solid. Amidships, they can be steam bent.

The thwarts and seat riser are an integral part of gig construction. Note the placement of fore-and-aft and athwartships seat knees. The thwarts are crowned with turned posts underneath that land on the top of the keelson. The construction of this boat, as a whole, results in a light yet flexibly strong craft. During the boat's first summer, she parted her mooring during a gale and was pounded on the rocks for several hours before being rescued. The only damage was some scuffed planking. This is high testament to the boat's design and construction concepts.

True to her type, this gig is an able seaboat. When the course is downwind, a sailing rig can be employed. Never shun Mother Nature's gifts! Although not shown on the plan, a small spritsail about like that shown on Pete's Cornish yawl will do fine.

Dr. Freydberg's comparison of the two boats is interesting. The gig, of course, is faster. However, in a beam or quartering sea, the wherry is easier to handle. The flat plank keel of the wherry allows it to give some with such a sea, whereas the gig's straight scantling keel does not. An oarsman ends up working harder with one oar. Cornish gigs largely overcame this problem with a coxswain and large crews. With her centerboard and adjustable rig, the wherry is an outright sailboat. The ease with which the gig moves through the water, however, precludes the need for a sail, except when the wind is favorable.

Dr. Freydberg is to be envied for having played with both.

Above: Culler-designed and-made outriggers on the fast gig *Quitsa Pilot.*

Below: Pete Culler and crew take the *Quitsa Pilot* out for a row. (Benjamin Fuller photos)

Length overall: 18 feet 6½ inches
Beam: 4 feet
Molded depth: 1 foot 5½ inches

Punch, Pulling Boat For Glenn MacNary

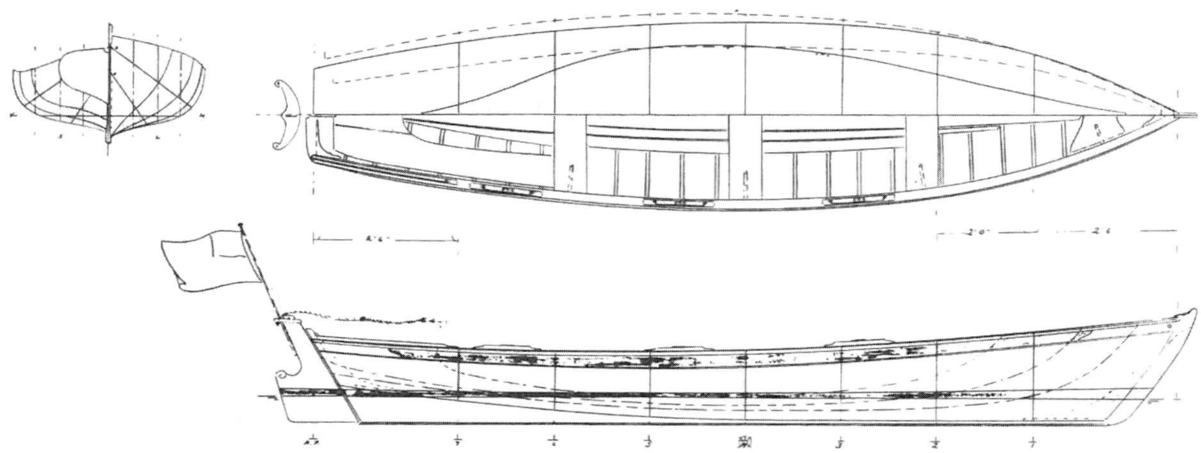

Lines of the pulling boat *Punch*.

Captain Pete always kept in mind what was successful in the past. Such design elements stood the test of time; they usually included much common sense. This approach occasionally was applied to his own past design work. If a client's requirements were similar to those met in the past, other things being equal, Pete would follow the same course previously found successful. Again, this was common sense, and it benefited the customer, too. All of Pete's design work was charged on an hourly basis.

Therefore, when Glenn MacNary came to him looking for a pulling boat of about 18 feet in length, the success of the clipper wherry as a rowing model was fresh in Pete's mind. It had been designed just two years earlier.

Pete took the wherry model and lengthened it to 18½ feet, making the lines sharper while retaining the long, fine run. This can be seen in a comparison of the buttock lines and waterlines. In addition, *Punch* has a sharper forefoot with more wood in her stem left noble to help the fine entry. The lengthening also makes the boat leaner. Her beam is just 4 feet.

Because it was a pure pulling boat, Pete opted for a scantling keel for *Punch* instead of the deadwood skeg and plank keel used for the wherry. The rabbet rises aft to end just above the waterline at the transom. A true keelson of 1⅝-inch-square spruce fits over frames and floors as in old naval pulling boats.

Pete said, "She's very fast, carries strong and powerful headway when one rests on the oars, and makes practically no waves at any speed. Though smaller, this craft is not much different from fast naval gigs built before 1850. A stylish boat, she should weigh in at about 250 pounds."

Punch has three rowing positions for versatility and trim. The thwarts are crowned with turned posts underneath that land on the keelson. Notice the handsome quarter rail. The pulling boat is higher sided with more flare than the wherry, and the hull is planked eight strakes to a side. Because *Punch* is strictly a rowboat, the extra freeboard makes sense.

With her bowstaff and stern pennants flying, *Punch* has the look of a smart classic. The only improvement would be a pretty girl with a parasol!

Left: *Punch* battened off for plank.
Right: *Punch* ready for finishing touches. (R.D. Culler photo)

Length overall: 19 feet 6 inches
Beam: 5 feet 5½ inches
Light draft: 1 foot 2 inches
Sail area (shallop rig): 172 square feet

Shallop For George Putz

Here is George Putz's shallop. She is a rather nicely styled craft with a very versatile sail arrangement. This shallop employs a lute stern, or double transom. That handsome quarter rail not only lends good looks, but also adds strength in the lute stern construction. This transom should be stoutly kneed with natural crooks.

The boat steers with a tiller through a port in the transom; the rudder is generously proportioned. With adjustments to the board and the rig to meet differing wind and sea conditions, this shallop should steer well.

The hull is burdensome, being long and somewhat beamy with ample draft. She was designed for the deep waters of Penobscot Bay, Maine, and thus required seakindliness and power. For this area, it was a good decision to use the ancient shallop as the starting point for a fair-sized dayboat. Shallops developed over many years as working coastal watercraft, for both fishing and transportation. The shallop is a direct descendant of the ship's boat used when this country was colonized.

Professor E.P. Morris, in his definitive work *The Fore and Aft Rig in America*, has this to say about the shallop: "Postponing for a moment the questions of rig, the other characteristics harmonize easily; the shallop, having come over as a ship's boat, had become a type, an open craft, probably square sterned, of a size between the small rowboat and the decked vessel."

Although a type, local conditions produced regional examples of shallops unique, both in hull and rig, to distinct areas. These include the Block Island cowhorn, the No Mans Land boat, the Kingston lobsterboat, the Hampton boat, and the Crotch Island pinky, to name a few. W.A. Baker, in *Colonial Vessels*, comments further: "It is generally agreed that by the middle of the eighteenth century the typical shallops were open boats propelled by oar and sail. Some had transom sterns while others were double-ended; both types were usually fitted with two masts."

The hull of Putz's shallop is sharp lined, with moderate rise of floor, hard bilges, and powerful quarters. The run is long and flat. She moves along nicely with her ample rig, under oars, or when a moderate size outboard engine is employed. The occasional use of an outboard is the primary reason for the lute stern. It hides the engine bracket best. Later shallops employed counter sterns, particularly when racing mania took over, so the style is in keeping.

Pete thought the British Seagull, with its long shaft, was the best engine for this application. Seagulls need plenty of air; with the lute stern they get it. They give the most thrust at moderate speeds, and although they stink and are noisy, my experience with them has shown these drawbacks to be an advantage—you use a Seagull only when absolutely necessary. The engine's most endearing quality comes into play at this time also—it almost always starts on the first pull.

With the shallop's ample and versatile rig, however, an outboard is needed only when the wind dies out completely and the course lies into a residual swell. Otherwise, I would opt for oars and peace and quiet. Oarlock location is not shown on the plan. It will depend on your thwart location. For the forward

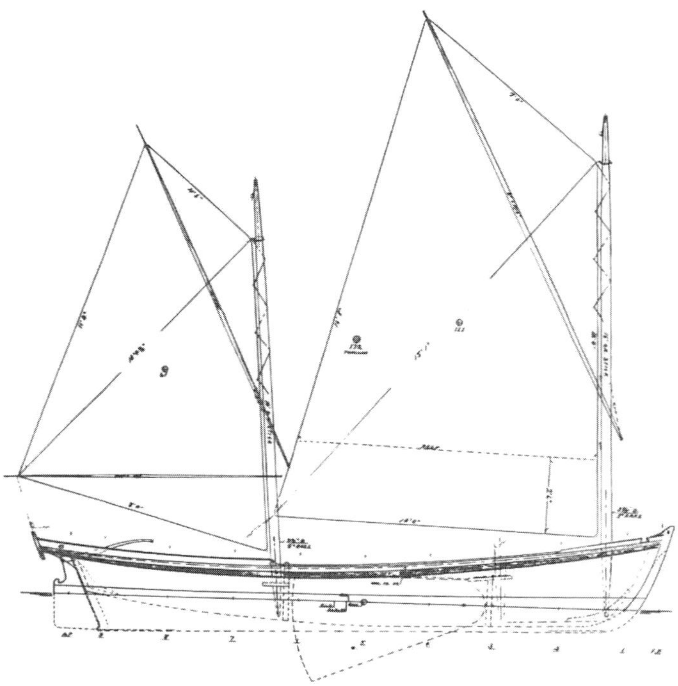

Pete gave her the typical shallop rig.

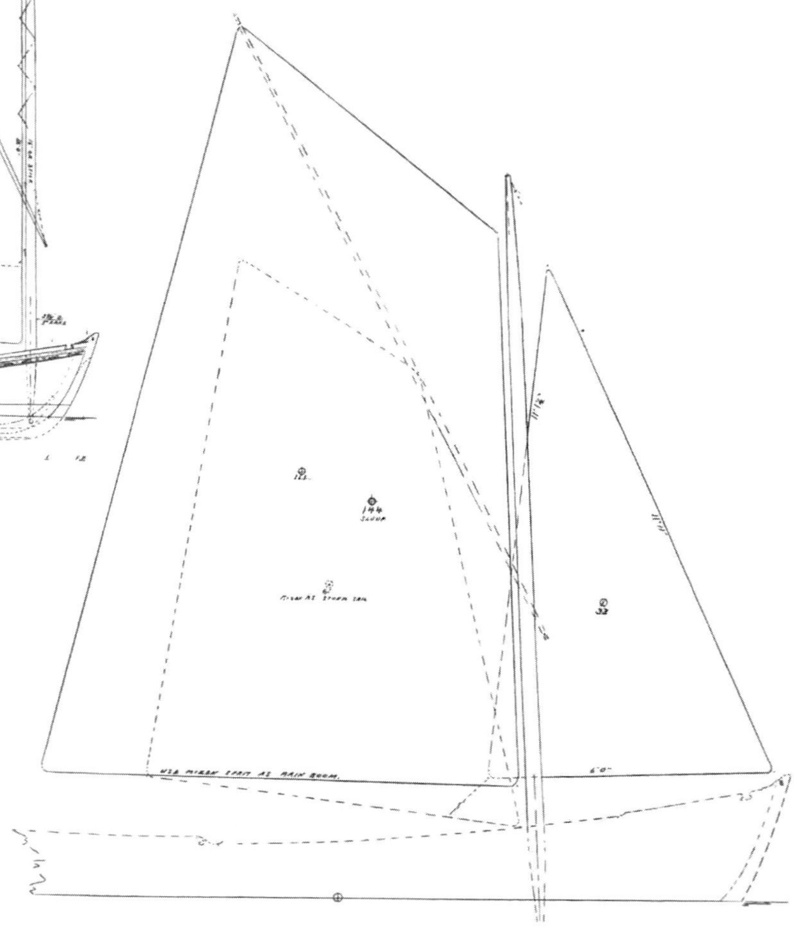

Alternate sail plan for the shallop.

A Putz-built model of the shallop. (George Putz photo)

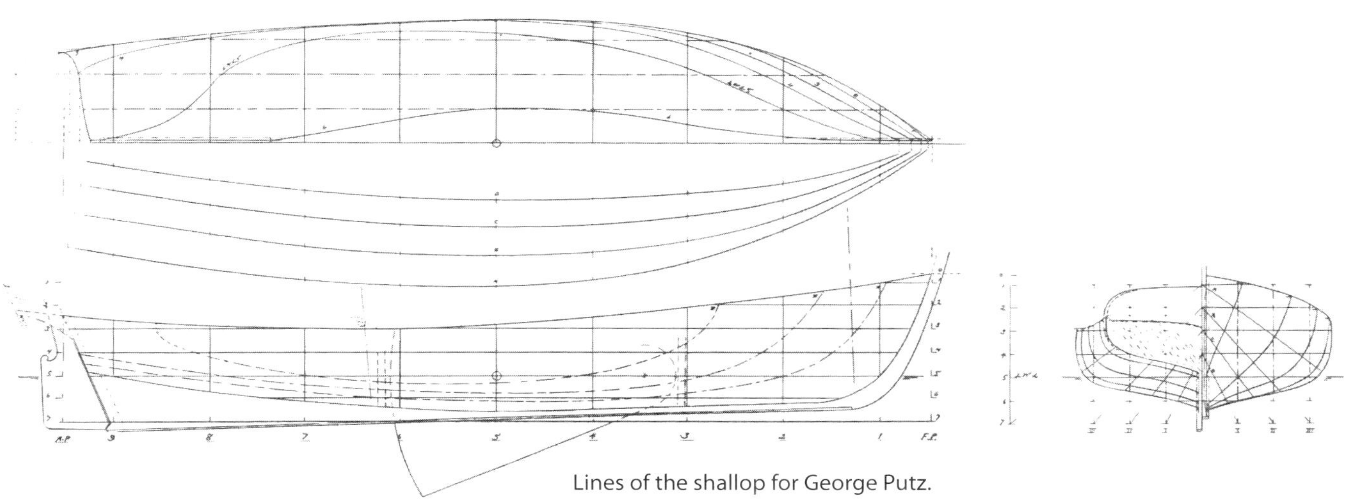
Lines of the shallop for George Putz.

thwart, it is no problem to locate oarlock pads. Fit a block to the coaming and washrail and tie into both. Because of the quarter rail, it takes some tinkering to fit oarlock pads aft. I would consider it worth the trouble, however.

In profile the shallop is handsome. Indeed, it is downright pretty! Her bow profile is quite proud. This helps her sharp entry. In addition, because the bow is partially decked, there is good reserve stability. Pete was a master at producing a good-looking bow.

Not too long ago I came close to building one of these shallops. I hope I get another chance.

Stern design and layout of the Putz shallop.

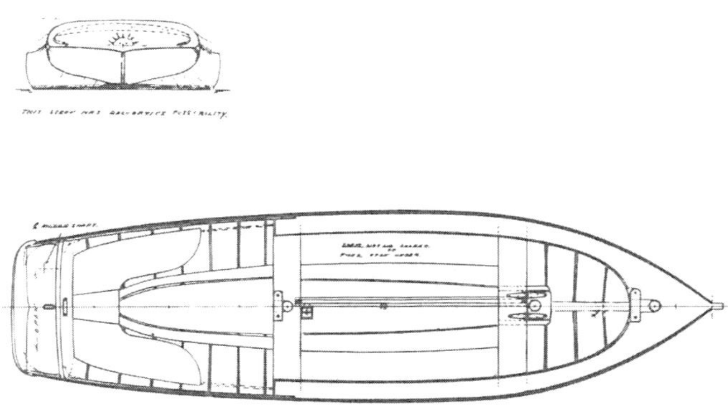

Length overall: 20 feet
Beam: 4 feet 1 inch
Depth: 1 foot 6 inches
Sail area: 51 square feet

Clipper Cornish Yawl For Clayton Lewis

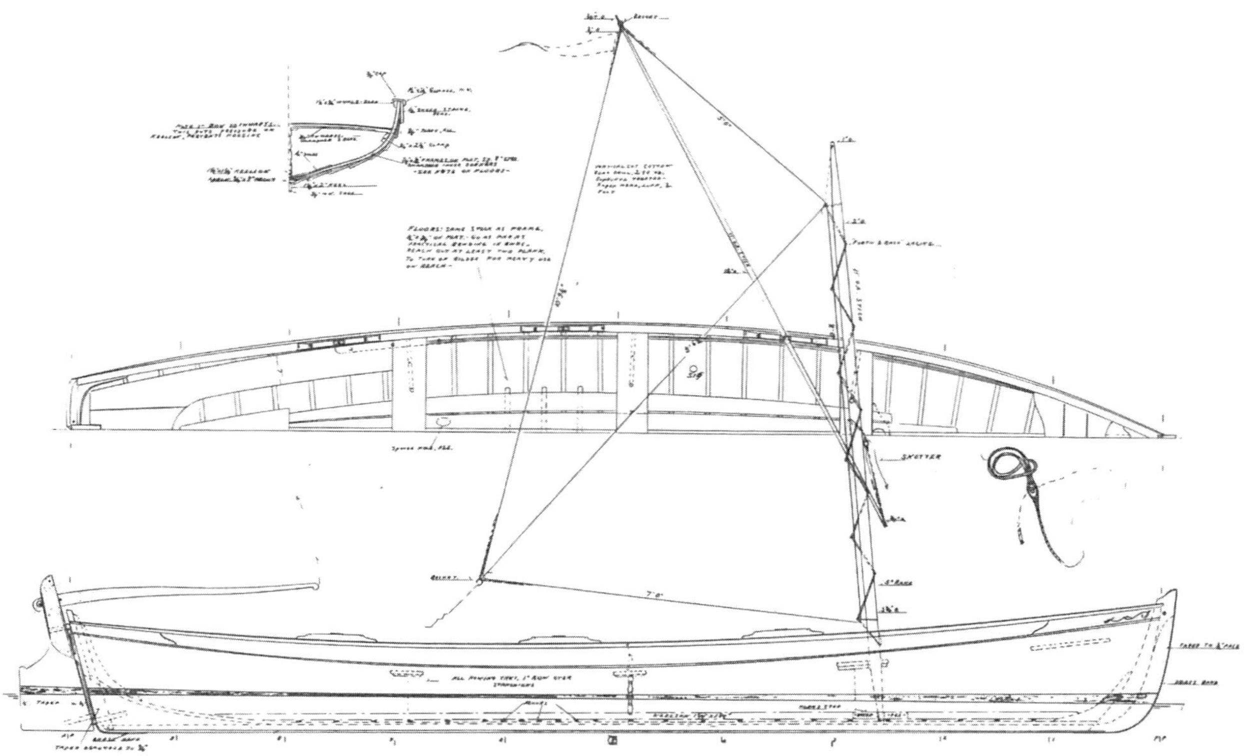

The clipper Cornish yawl with her auxiliary spritsail.

This Cornish yawl is a high-performance rowing craft fitted with an auxiliary sail. The hull is very sharp with much deadrise, and wineglass sections throughout, resulting in fair and easy diagonals. Her forefoot is thin and sharp, with much hollow in the waterlines fore and aft. On the load waterline she is double ended. The buttocks are extremely sharp forward, and the run is long and very fine. There is little rake to the posts, in keeping with Cornish style. There is a slight drag to the keel. The sheer is very pretty with slight reverse and some flare in the bows. This boat is a real clipper, and about as handsome as they come. She would be a joy to row.

There are three rowing positions for one and two oarsmen, or for two pulling with a coxswain.

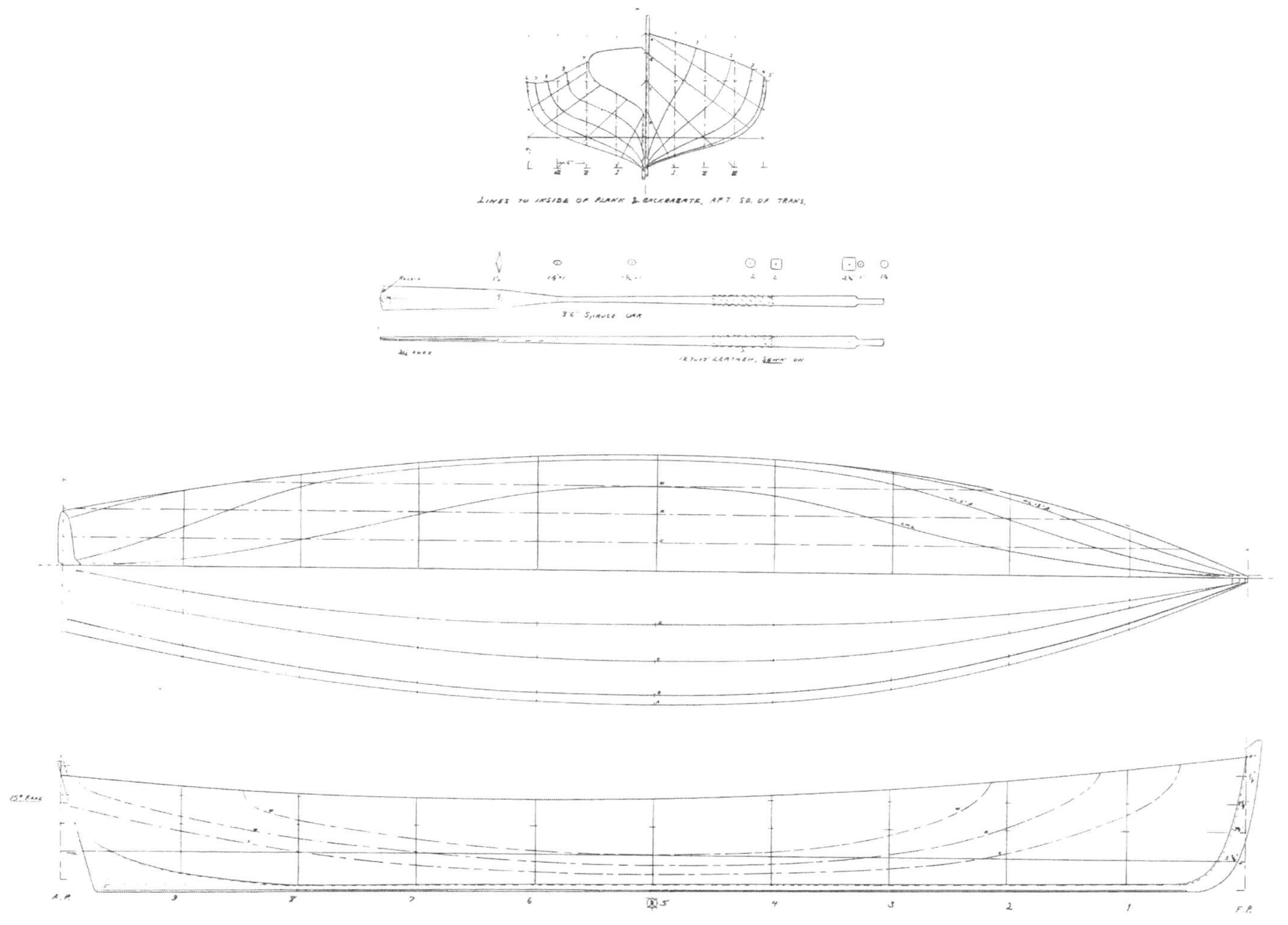

Lines of the Cornish yawl, plus plans for 8 1/2-foot oars.

The three positions allow for trim under varying conditions. There is a plan included for 8½-foot flat-bladed oars. I would include a pair of spoons, the same size, as part of her equipment. Captain Pete discusses making these oars in considerable detail in his fine little book *Boats, Oars, and Rowing.*

The boat's construction follows the strong yet lightweight and flexible style popular along the Cornwall coast of England. The principal components are light plank (⅜ inch) and framing coupled with capped rails and seat risers integrated with bowed or crowned thwarts with stanchions under set into a stiff keelson. All of this is well kneed, particularly at the thwarts. This is one of the best systems ever worked out for lightweight small craft.

The boat is fitted with an auxiliary loose-footed spritsail for the occasional favorable breeze or for when the spirit moves the skipper. There is no centerboard. The craft relies on her scantling keel and hull shape for lateral resistance. If I were building her, I would change the tiller to a Norse-style push-pull to permit steering with yoke and lines when a coxswain is aboard.

At 20 feet, this sharp-model clipper yawl should be very fast under oar and sail. If you can accommodate a vessel this size, give it serious consideration. She is a beautiful creation.

Concordia Sloopboat, Kingston Lobsterboat Buzzards Bay Sloop

Concordia SloopBoat

Length overall: 17 feet 8 inches
Beam: 5 feet
Draft: 1 foot 6 inches
Sail area: 172 square feet

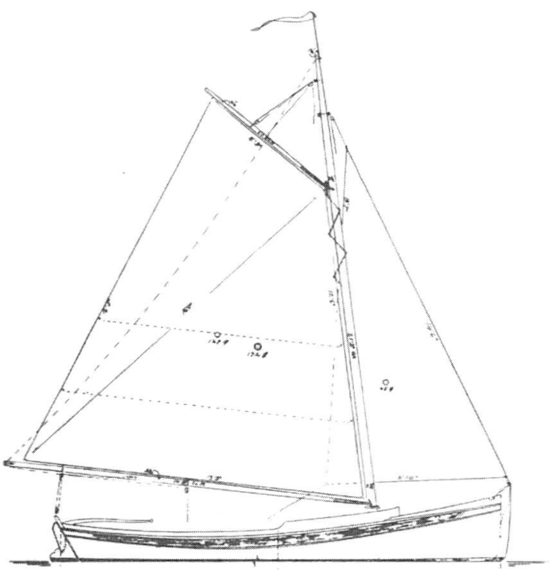

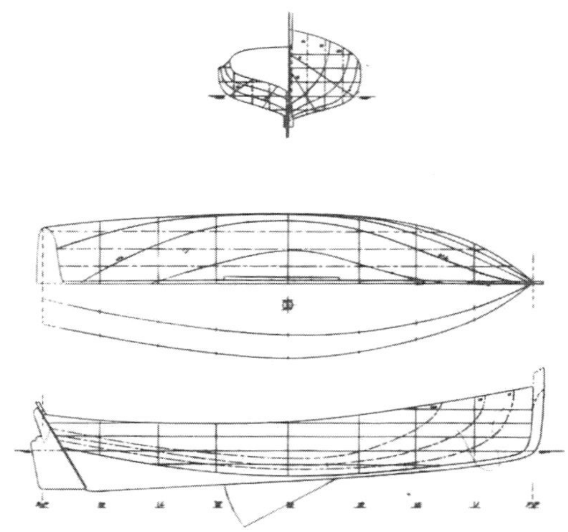

Sail plan and lines of the Concordia sloopboat.

The Concordia Company of South Dartmouth, Massachusetts, has produced some very fine wooden stock boats. The 40-foot Concordia yawl has achieved fame far and wide for its beauty and speed. The smart little 12-foot 4-inch Beetle Cat is deservedly popular, and is now into its second 50 years of continuous production. However, to the traditional small boat sailor, the 17-foot 8-inch Concordia sloopboat has to be the most appealing and useful.

In response to demand for a good small wooden daysailer, Waldo Howland of the Concordia Company decided to produce a boat that would fulfill that need. He had this to say: "Such a boat would have to be attractive to look at and shipshape in appearance. She would have to be well built with special attention to detail. For a number of reasons, wood seemed to be the best and only medium for construction. [This was a courageous statement during the early 1960s. — J .B.] Wood has natural virtues so far as appearance, sound, feel, smell, and flotation are concerned. Variations and modifications by its owner are easy. And it can be painted, polished, and puttered with. In short, it can be loved.

"In the search for a model I talked mainly with Captain Pete Culler and my friend Major Smyth. The former favored a boat having the general characteristics of a Scituate lobsterboat. The latter urged me to keep in mind a model like the Connecticut River shad boats. I myself have always liked the Bahama dinghies. We were all thinking along the same lines."

Captain Pete designed a sloop that incorporated the features that Howland was seeking. The design is based on the Kingston lobsterboat, and is similar to others used on the Connecticut River and

Chesapeake Bay.

The hull of this craft is one of the finest shapes Pete ever produced. He was especially fond of it. In profile, the hull has moderate drag to the keel, a nearly plumb stem, and ample rake to the transom, allowing a goodsized rudder that does not extend below the heel. This is important in shallow water, and, in addition, allows the boat to be beached without difficulty. The hull has an extremely well-shaped run. The waterlines are long and easy. The midsection shows a moderate deadrise with slight tumblehome. There is good bearing aft and flare forward. The transom is of particularly nice shape. The skeg and board provide good area for working to windward, which the boat does very well.

The rig for the Concordia sloopboat is unstayed. It uses lacings on the mast and jaws on gaff and boom. The main halyards can reeve either single or double. The jib clips into the stem iron, which allows it to be stowed under the foredeck when the boat is at anchor or moored. In profile, the rig is exceedingly handsome and well balanced. The boat will spin on her heels, and from experience, is "a witch in tight places."

There are many nice Culler details in this design that delight the eye. The shape of rudder and tiller, the beautiful sheer and cove line, proud stem and stemhead, buffalo rail and coaming, the wooden pump that empties into the centerboard well, smart pinrail, and liberal use of wooden cleats are just a few. All unite in a classic of lasting value.

With regard to the sloopboat's performance, allow me to quote from letters to Captain Pete and Waldo Howland from owners and users.

From Robert Kaufman, Stamford, Connecticut: "*Reliance* is everything you told me it would be and everything I had hoped for. In light airs, she carries her way from puff to puff and unlike lighter displacement hulls, does not come to a stop once the wind dies.

"In medium winds *Reliance* quickly comes to her waterline and by lashing the tiller will sail herself with a minimum of attention. I sailed over to Long Island this way, making only two adjustments for wind shifts.

"*Reliance* really comes into her own during heavy weather. Once when the radio predicted 10 to 15 knots out of the SW and I was halfway across the Sound, it backed to the NW and increased to 20-25, with gusts to 35. It was at this time that I learned how easily the sloopboat will lay to. Letting go the jib and lashing up the tiller, *Reliance* stood still waiting out what was thought to be a squall. After a short steep chop had built up abeam in the direction of Stamford, I pulled in the jib tightly and started the main, heading for home. It wasn't an easy go, for I dragged the boom a few times, but *Reliance* made her way inside the breakwater surprisingly dry and able."

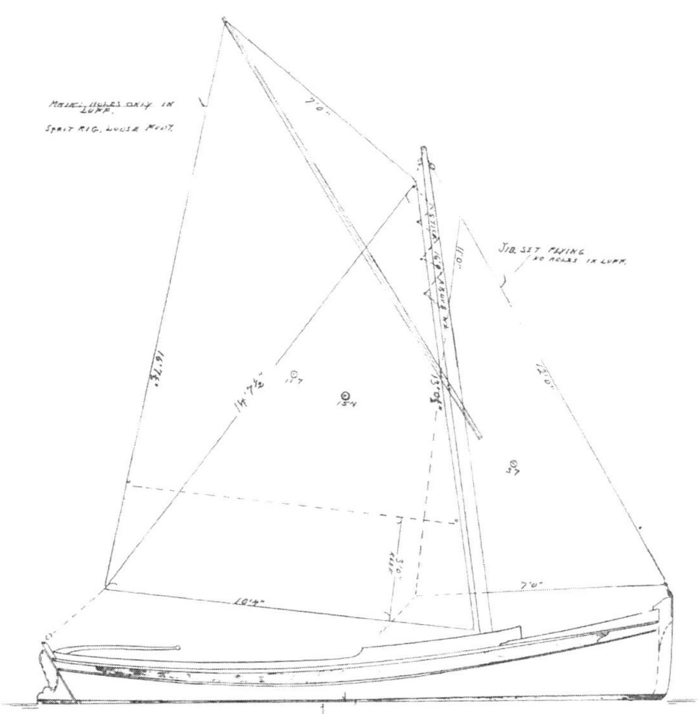

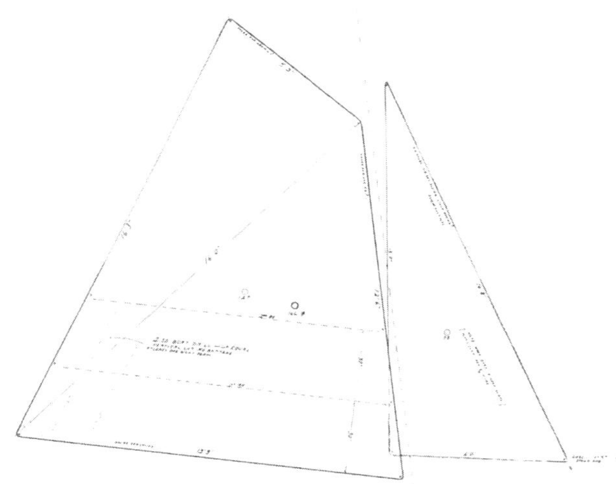

Above: A 1964 revision of the original gaff rig on the sloopboat
Left: Concordia sloopboat with sprit rig—a 1970 revision.

The sloopboat is a popular daysailer.

The sloopboat casts a classic silhouette during an evening sail. (R.D. Culler photo)

From Joseph Outerbridge, Princeton, New Jersey: "What I wanted to write you about was to tell you that I had a most happy and thoroughly satisfactory summer with *Patience*, and I'm looking forward to many more.... She has a quality and style all her own and on top of that she is just plain good fun to sail. Who could ask for anything more than that?"

From W. Knight Sturges, Nonquitt, Massachusetts: "In light weather Evening Star has proved to be a joy to sail. In a Buzzards Bay slop she is dry and comfortable. Her graceful sheer doubtless gives her this seagoing quality. What is more surprising is the speed with which she slips through the water and the ease with which she holds her course when off the wind. I have never known a boat to sail this way before the wind."

From Karl Metzenberg, Los Angeles, California: "The sloopboat attracts a lot of attention wherever she goes, which includes the island of Santa Catalina, about 35 miles south of Santa Monica. Did it in nine hours each way—a relaxed and relaxing weekend. As you state, the boat performs very well in the open sea."

From Lees S. Brown, Boston, Massachusetts: "It's been many years since I've had so much pure enjoyment and I feel personally beholden to you for the design and craftsmanship. The boat draws compliments like sugar draws flies, and I'm beginning to tire of saying 'Thank you.' I wish the admirers could put their money where their mouths are, but they've all made their commitments, generally to those short, fat, fiberglass sloops that seem to be popping up like mushrooms everywhere."

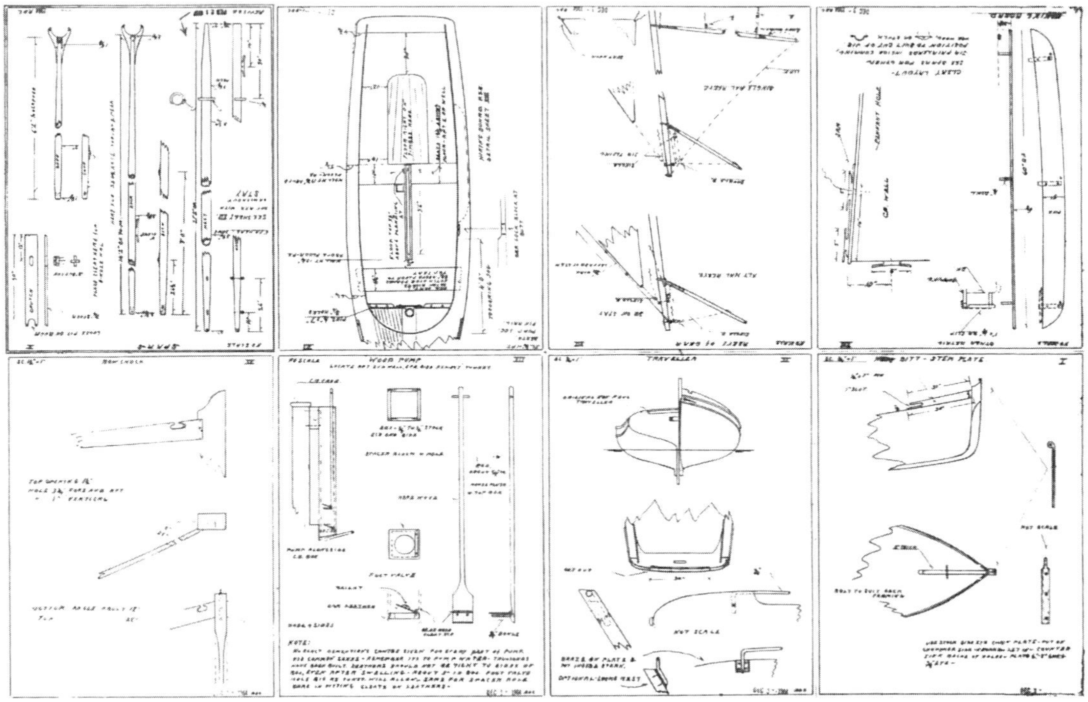

Culler details specified for the Concordia sloopboat.

Kingston Lobsterboat

Length overall: 17 feet 8 inches
Length on waterline: 16 feet 4 inches
Beam: 5 feet
Draft: 1 foot 3 inches, board up
Sail area: 141 square feet

As can be seen from the above, the Concordia sloopboat was well received. However, one client, Albert Bigelow of Bourne, Massachusetts, had for some time wanted a bona fide Kingston lobsterboat. Knowing of the origins of the sloopboat design, and realizing that it was true to the type and clipperized, Bigelow asked Captain Pete to convert a sloopboat back to a Kingston lobsterboat.

Primarily, this entailed designing a two-sail shallop rig for the hull. Captain Pete discussed this conversion as follows: "Things worked out very nicely. I could get good area in the rig. There is no point undercanvasing with all the shortening-down combination—and good area is needed for evening sailing, as a rule.

"Spar stowage seems no problem when rowing their short lengths and the straight sides of the craft allow them to stow in the wings, just as they were in the working boats.

"Reduced the skeg 3 inches aft, and lengthened the centerboard a bit forward, as I reduced the fin on the after end to make it come in plane with the thwarts. Also, centers on present rig are somewhat lower. With her docile nature, I think the balance will be as good as the sloop, and, once one gets used to her, even more sensitive to fine adjustments of trim and use of board.

"I suggest she be built with all the attention to detail for a pulling/sailing boat of this class—it pays off in the end.

"Sculling slot is offset to port (the traditional location) so one can use sweep with rudder in place and sail set.

"What it all boils down to is this. We have very light, small spars and practically no gear by modern standards. For the location (Buzzards Bay, Nantucket Sound) and use intended, this one has the average, present-day boat hopelessly outclassed. I feel she will more than hold her end up under sail.

"The reduced skeg, thin board rudder, and somewhat reduced upper weight should payoff under oars. I would call her quite a powerful boat, fit to go fishing, pilot work, crimping, or wrecking in the old way. She is not much different from a Goodwin Sands hoveller, only smaller. "One point I always stress: a couple of pairs of properly built oars are essential."

Right: The Kingston lobsterboat. Captain Pete preferred this rig.

Lower Right: Body plan and layout of the lobsterboat.

Below: The Kingston lobsterboat with her two-sail rig.

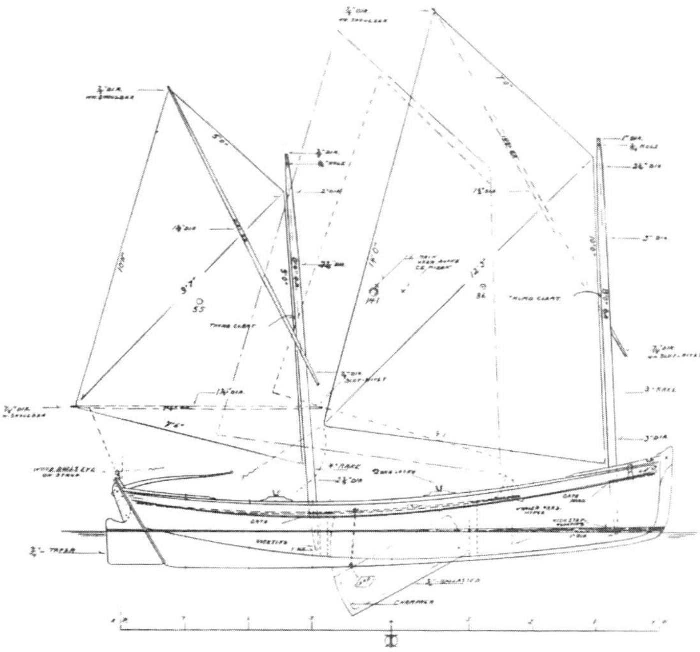

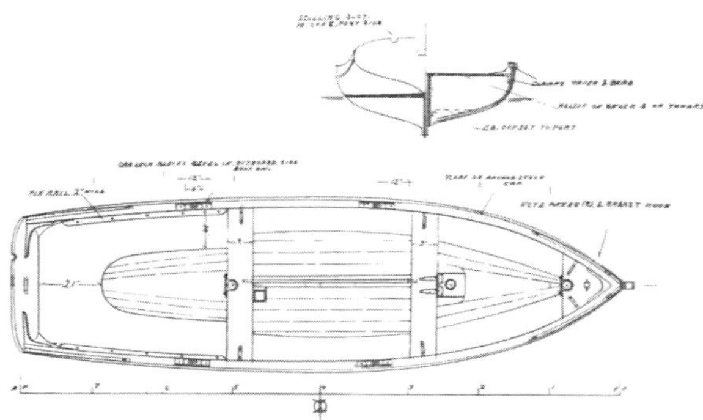

Buzzards Bay Sloop

Length overall: 18 feet 8 inches
Draft: 2 feet
Sail area: 177 square feet

The final evolution in this model's design occurred in 1977. Wyatt Garfield was familiar with Culler boats, having built the 21-foot fishboat *Long John.* He much admired the sloopboat also, but he felt the model needed more ability for the waters around his summer home on Cuttyhunk Island. For those who don't know, Cuttyhunk is a beautiful outpost. It is the last island in the Elizabeth Islands chain that separates Vineyard Sound and Buzzards Bay. The waters are characterized by strong tides and high winds most of the time. The island is exposed to the ocean on three sides.

Captain Pete lengthened the sloop to 18 feet 8 inches and added a foot of beam and six inches of draft, as well as outside ballast. He increased the sloop's sail area, and thus had to add a standing headstay and shrouds. The result of all this was a more powerful and able vessel whose lines are very similar to those of the smaller version. Pete called this new design a Buzzards Bay sloop.

The hull was designed for lapstrake construction, seeking strength with light weight, in line with Pete's noted preference for this type of planking. The garboards and sheerstrakes are ¾ inch, the remainder

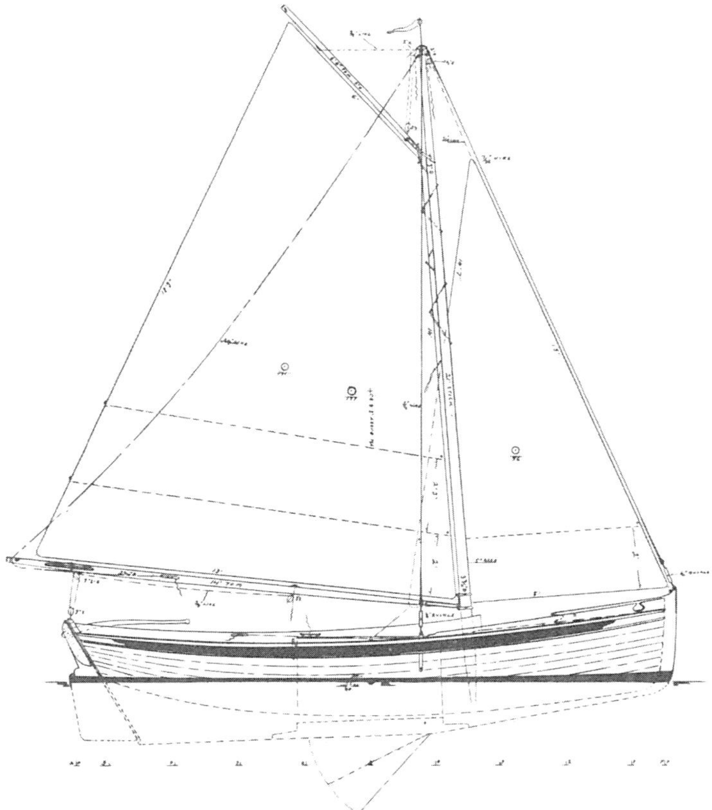

Sail plan of the Buzzards Bay sloop.

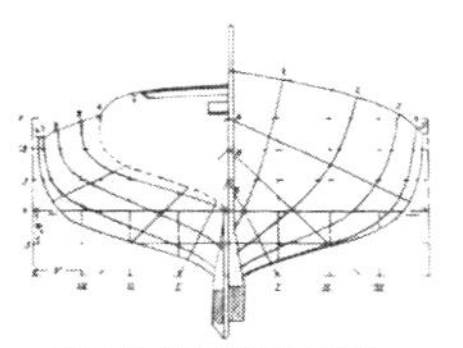

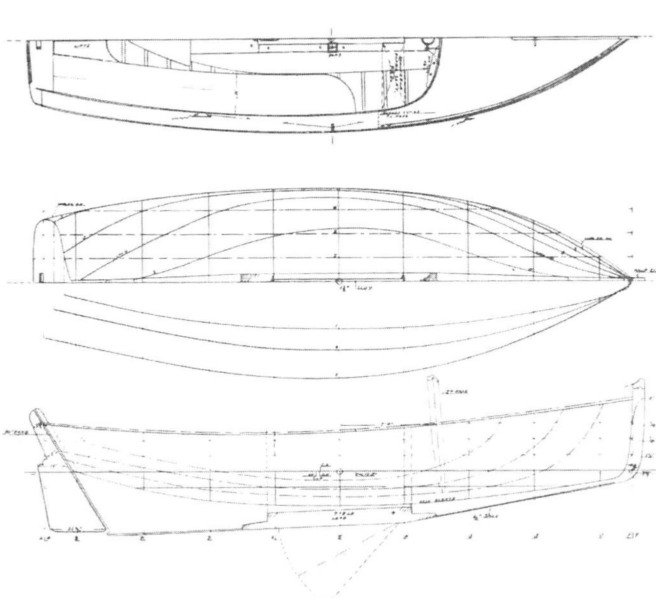

Lines and body plan of the Buzzards Bay sloop.

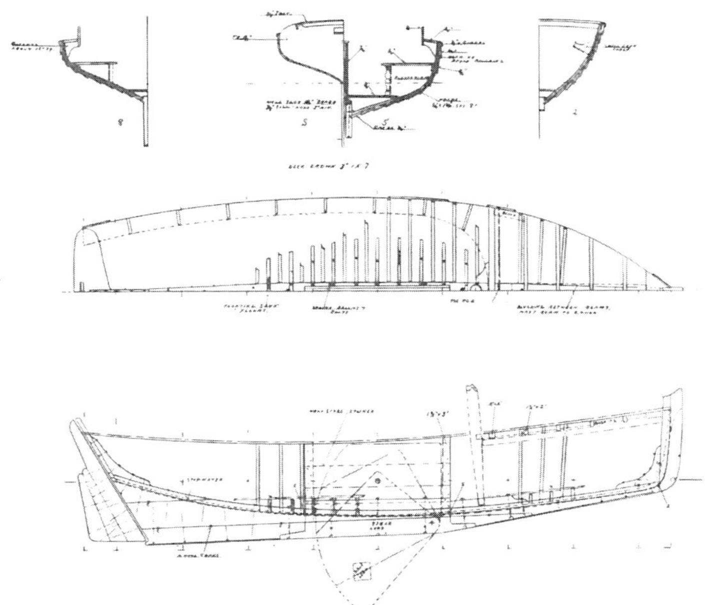

Construction plans for the sloop.

The Buzzards Bay sloop *Beaver*, built for Wyatt Garfield.

being ½ inch. Lapstrake planking certainly accents the hull's beautiful lines. In fact, the Old Man would approve even if you decided to build the two smaller versions lapstrake. Original construction was begun at the Clytie Corporation of Beverly, Massachusetts, and after that business folded, it was completed by the company's foreman, Grant Robinson, at his shop in Marblehead. Shortly before his death, Pete took his last trip off-Cape to view this boat under construction. He was impressed with the job. Garfield later wrote Pete's wife, Toni, and gave the boat high marks for performance and appearance. He said that he was very satisfied with the design. So there you have it. Three designs based on one of the fastest and handiest sailing workboats ever evolved, clipperized for today's pleasure use as smart little daysailers.

Staten Island Skiff For Richard Hovey

Molded length: 16 feet 7⅝ inches
Molded beam: 4 feet 11 inches
Molded depth: 1 foot 7½ inches
Sail area: 98 square feet

Until recent times, the body of water constituting Upper and Lower New York Bay supported various fisheries, largely shad and oysters. Over a period of time, certain working craft best suited to these fisheries evolved.

In his book *The Sea Bright Skiff and Other Shore Boats*, Peter J. Guthorn goes into considerable detail on the oyster skiffs of Raritan Bay. He refers to this oyster skiff as being similar in type to the nearby Staten Island variety. Both models were noted for their steadiness, either loaded or light. It was this quality that Captain Pete had in mind when he designed his version.

Richard Hovey had employed Pete earlier to design a beautiful fantail steamer. He was very happy with this boat, so he sought out the Captain when he desired a small skiff to row about the rocks of his hometown waters looking for fish and lobster.

It is not known how Pete knew of the Staten Island skiffs. The only reference to them that I know of is the one stated above. During his chartering days, Pete was a frequent visitor to New York Bay. Perhaps he came across an example during his travels. The skiff's combination of a stable, burdensome, and able hull and good performance under sail and oars was what was required, because Hovey was a large man. An examination of the boat's lines will show these qualities.

The waterline is a fair sweep; it gives an indication of the boat's immersed portions. This wetted surface is proportionately large, and, as can be seen in the body plan, is nearly carried the full width. A large portion of the bilge is submerged. These characteristics, along with generous depth and beam, give the hull her large capacity. The buttock lines are remarkably sharp, considering the above, and there is a long, fine run. The sections have some reverse down in the garboards. The transom is slightly immersed and is of good shape for bearing aft. Note the sailing lines.

There are three rowing positions for flexibility. The oars need to be longish due to the large beam

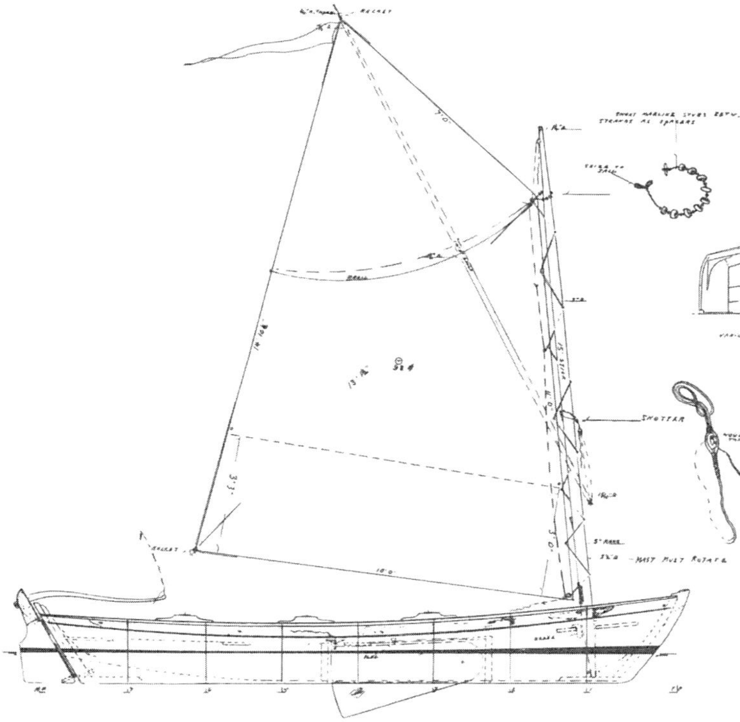

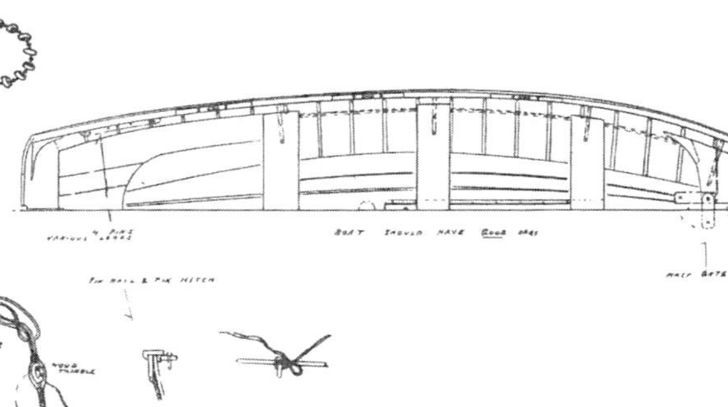

Plans of the Staten Island skiff.

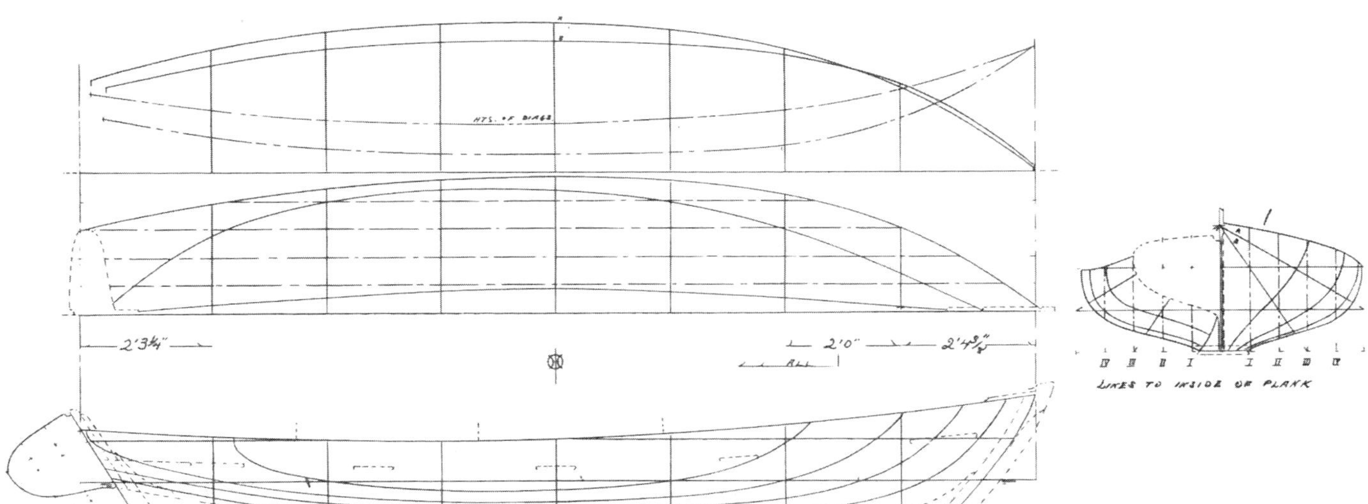

The Staten Island skiff shows Captain Pete's method of plank line-off: Use the diagonals as guides and sweep up the garboard to minimize hook in the remaining strakes. (With classic models having odd-numbered strakes lined off properly, the middle strake will have no shape, just taper.) (R.D. Culler photo)

Below: A Staten Island skiff built by Walt Simmons of Lincolnville, Maine. (Walt Simmons photo)

and burdensome hull, and perhaps a bit stiffer than usual. If glued up of spruce, a center piece of fir would work out nicely. The boat should move along easily under oars; once moving, she should carry well.

The rig is large because the hull can stand it. Moreover, she needs it with her wetted surface. A deep reef is provided for when it blows. There's a lot of sail up there! As designed, there is a brail. The ability to shorten sail quickly is an integral part of prudent seamanship. The swinging mast gate is clearly shown on the plan. There is a tapered chock for tuning the rig. It alters the rake of the mast.

A centerboard is provided. Its construction would be no problem with the plank keel. The skeg is built up stair-step-fashion, and tapered (see Appendix). The sternpost is fitted to the keel and skeg, kneed, and the transom is set into this post. This is a traditional form of construction with this model. The rabbet is then cut into the whole. Remember, the lines are to inside of plank and back rabbet. The outer rabbet and bearding line develop on the loft floor either by adding a keelson or adding wood to the keel-skeg assembly. Be careful. You can slip here.

Altogether, this craft is a handsome, able, and powerful boat, and a remarkable design achievement, considering the requirements.

Double-paddle canoe

Length overall: 12 feet 10½ inches
Molded beam: 27½ inches
Depth: 10 inches

17′ double-paddle canoe

Length overall: 17 feet 3½ inches
Beam: 28 inches
Molded depth: 12 inches

Double-Paddle Canoes

Pound for pound, you will get the most boating enjoyment for your money from a double-paddle canoe. L. Francis Herreshoff was a great admirer of the type. He was primarily responsible for a resurgence of interest in the craft around Marblehead in the 1930s, and he stated that the only thing that would come close to giving as much pleasure for the dollar would be a canoe yawl, such as his *Rozinante*.

Nowadays, many different kinds of stock canoes and kayaks are available in a variety of materials. The canoe we refer to here has come to be known as the Rushton type, after the famous New York builder. Pete was exposed to this light wooden lapstrake canoe late in his life by his good friend and neighbor George Kelley. Kelley had started canoeing by building Herreshoff's dory-style model, faithfully adhering to the plans. She was a fine canoe, but at 90 pounds, difficult to portage, in spite of the designer's statements otherwise. Kelley went looking for something lighter.

At this time H. Atwood Manley's book, *Rushton and His Times in American Canoeing*, came out. Rushton had pioneered the "go light" movement in canoeing, having been prodded by a Cape Cod shoemaker, George Washington Sears, whose pen name, "Nessmuk," was well known in *Field and Stream* magazine. As Kelley was gearing up to build a Rushton, he kept running into people who said he couldn't, that the skill to build those canoes had died with their builders. To which Kelley said "Baloney," and promptly built an exquisite Wee Lassie right from the book. Now that he has built three, in various sizes, he's considered an expert. The point is, if you think you can do it, you can!

Pete has said, "These little Rushton-type hulls are of an ageless shape, about as easy going for their size as man has ever developed." The double-ender is indeed an ancient form that has sired many examples. The Norse longboat is well known. The whaleboat, and in modern times, the *S.S. United States*, which is really a greatly stretched-out canoe, are additional examples.

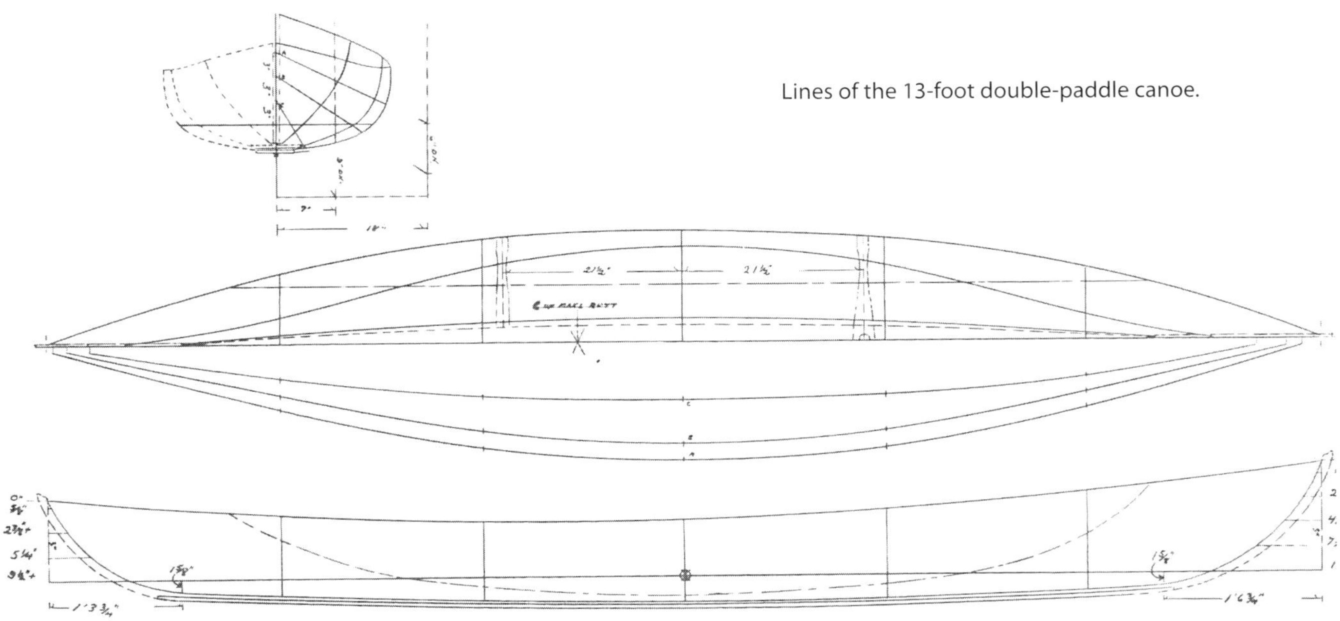

Lines of the 13-foot double-paddle canoe.

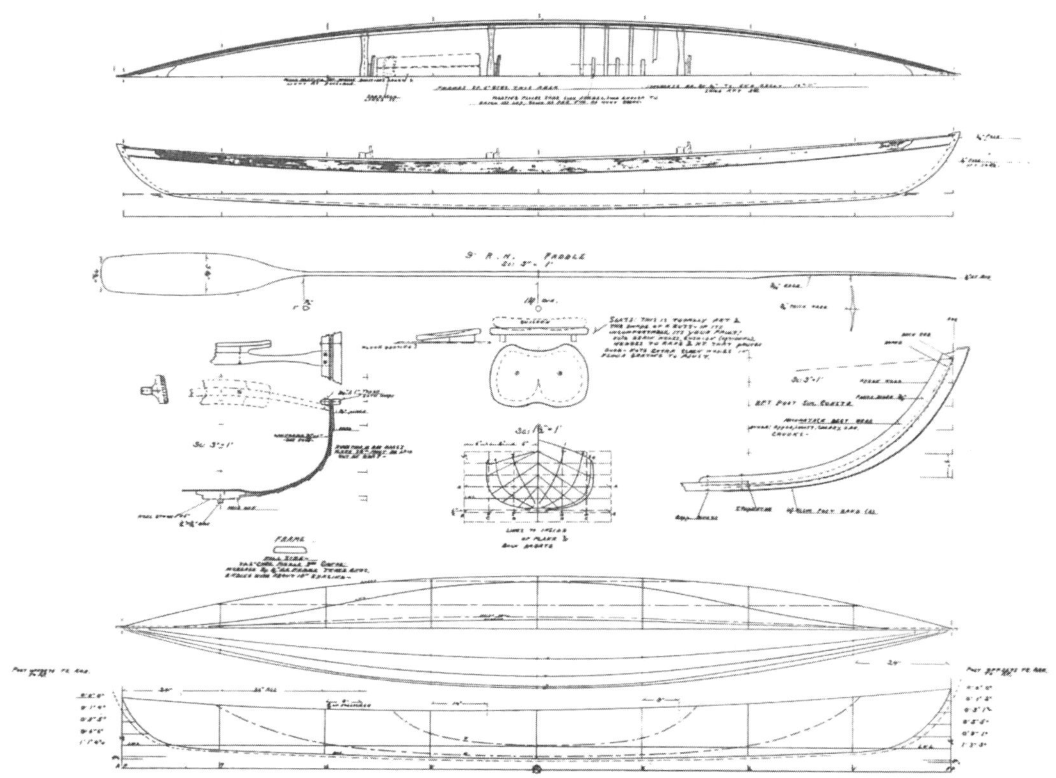

Plans of the l7-foot double-paddle canoe.

Right: The interior of *Butternut*.
(John Burke photo)

Below: Captain Pete and his 13-foot, 39-pound *Butternut* canoe under Chinese lugsail.
(John Sherwood photo)

A very nice amateur-built canoe. (Doug Hallock photo)

Two of Dr. John Roche's small craft: on the left is *Cymba*, a stretched-out version of *Butternut*, designed by Catain Pete to accommodate two persons. On the right is a Rushton Wee Lassie. (Benjamin Fuller photo).

The most often heard criticism of these small light canoes, frequently presented as a question, but meant to be a statement, is, "How long a trip can they make?" Bart Hauthaway, noted canoe and kayak builder from Weston, Massachusetts, turns the tables on such critics by asking, "How short a trip can your canoe make?" And then, "When was the last time you used it?" Most times the critic can't remember. The underlying point with these canoes is simplicity and ease of use. They are easy to transport and get in and out of the water, economical to build, maintain, and store, and a lot less difficult to build than one would first assume. For those who must get out into the wilds for extended periods, they are capable of this, too, with sensible planning. Kelley spent a week cruising the Connecticut River in his Rushton, and original Rushtons floated down the Missouri when it was a wilderness. The plans include a one- and a two-man version, being 13 feet and 17 feet, respectively, sold as a set, since scantlings work for both. Pete never understood why, but the longer version is only slightly faster, if at all. A plan for a double paddle is included. Pete summed up these little vessels best when he said, "I prefer rowing, and sailing if the boat is suited to it, but I would not be without a classic wooden double-paddle canoe."

Sailing, Paddling Canoe For William Pinney

Length overall: 17 feet
Beam: 27 1/2 inches
Draft: 11 inches
Sail area: 56 square feet

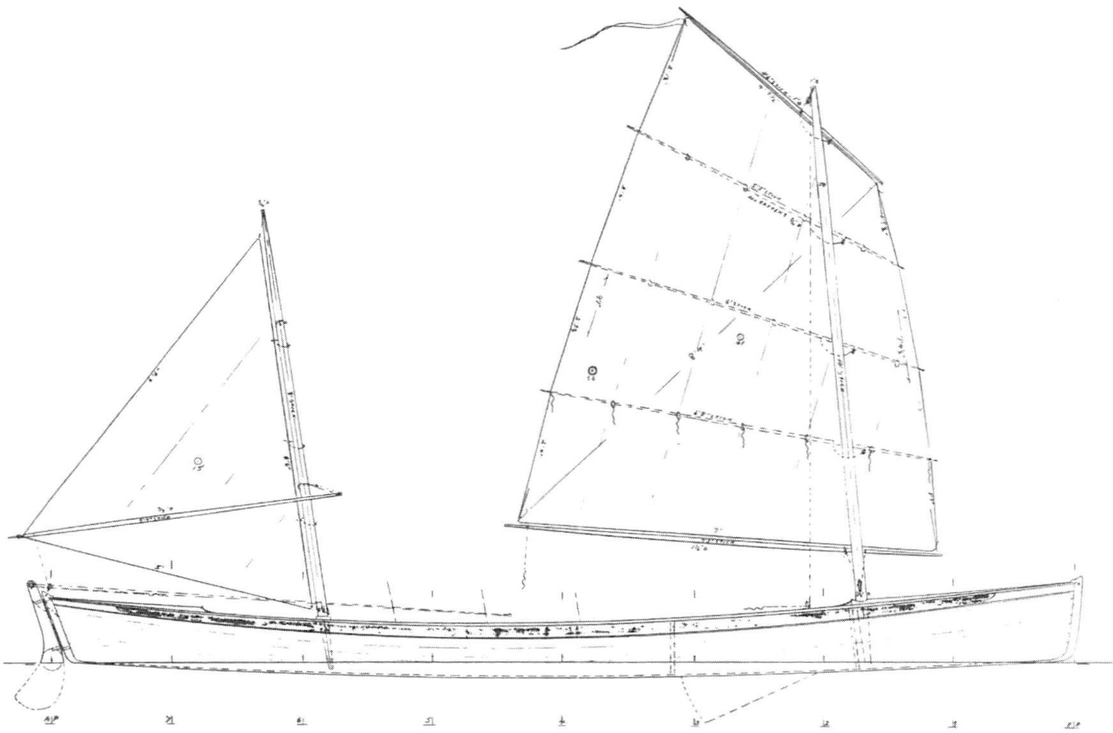

Sail plan of the sailing and paddling canoe.

This sailing and paddling canoe was designed for Captain Pete's employer, William Pinney, who as owner and president of Concordia Company had a close association with Pete for nearly 10 years. Most people who got to know Pete felt at some time or other the need to have him design a boat. His philosophy toward good wholesome watercraft was infectious.

Pete was all ready to build this fine little canoe for the Pinneys when deteriorating health kept him from doing so—and that is a real pity. With his special talents for building small craft, she would have been a jewel. The canoe's design is sharp, sweet lined, and daintily pretty.

After much experimentation with sail rigs on his own 13-foot *Butternut* canoe, Pete came to the conclusion that a fully battened Chinese lugsail fit these hulls the best. He had *Butternut* rigged with one slightly smaller, but of similar proportions, to the mainsail on this design. Of course, *Butternut* had no

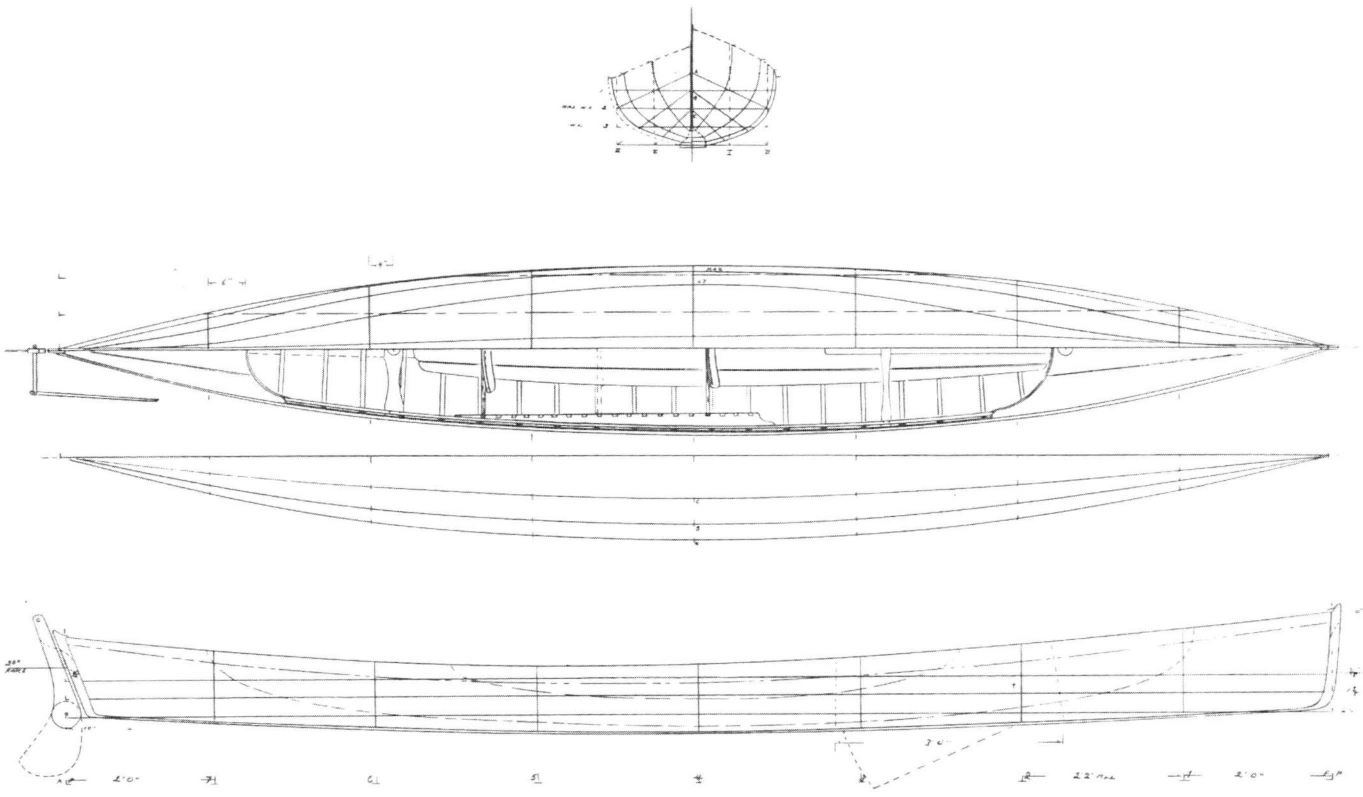

Plans of the 17-foot canoe.

rudder or centerboard. She relied on her keel for lateral resistance and a single paddle trailed over the lee side for directional control. The canoe described here incorporates all that he learned from his sailing trials with *Butternut*.

You will note that this canoe's shape is very similar to that of *Butternut*. The beam is the same, and the depth is only 1 inch more. Because she is a sailer, Pete gave this canoe more rocker. The keel is wider, a plank type, to land the centerboard box better. It's wider forward, because that's where he found that the rig and board balanced best. The sternpost is straight and slightly raked to accommodate the rudder, which must be weighted somewhat, because it will kick up if struck. The pintles and gudgeons are reversed so as to be self-tending if the rudder needs to rise. With these craft there is no leaning over the stern to make adjustments. When underway, the rudder must take care of itself; as designed, it will. By the same token, the sails, tiller, and board can all be handled with a minimum of movement by the skipper. You'll know what I mean when you find the need to shift the change from your leeward pants pocket to the windward one.

Although these Rushton-type canoes can be called "tiddly," it is not fair to imply that they are unstable. In experienced hands, they are anything but! A few years ago, during Mystic Seaport's small craft meet, the wind piped up to over 30 knots, driving most of the participants ashore. It was then that Captain Pete gave his good friend Chet Farrell a nudge and said, "Let's show 'em how it's done." They then rigged their canoes, and for the next hour zipped back and forth across the river—to the astonishment of many.

There's nothing mysterious about it, really. It is simply a matter of understanding and knowledge gained through experience. These canoes are very easy to use, very easy to look at, and, most important, easy on the pocketbook.

Length overall: 16 feet 4 inches
Beam: 5 feet
Depth: 2 feet 6½ inches
Sail area: 55 square feet

Yacht *America II* Yawlboats

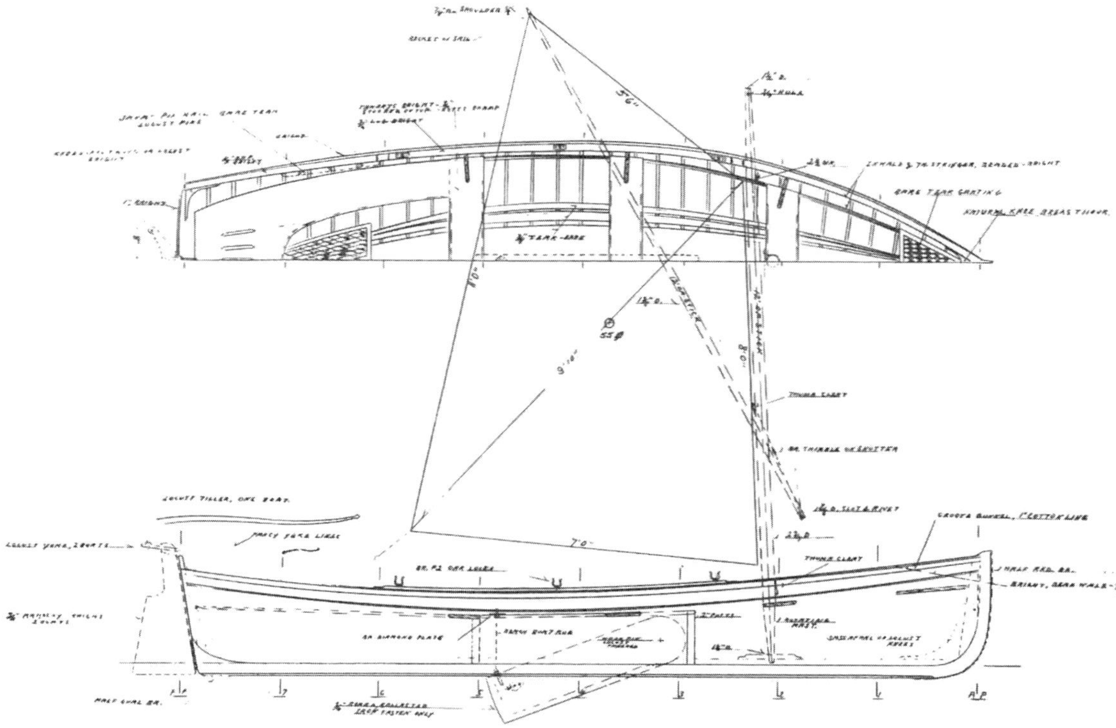

Sail plan of the *America II* yawlboat.

In 1966 Rudolf J. Shaeffer, a yachtsman of many years' experience, approached Waldo Howland with the idea of having Concordia Company build a replica of the original *America.* For reasons of size, Howland felt that Concordia was not the place to build the schooner. *America II* was eventually constructed at Goudy & Stevens in East Boothbay, Maine. Concordia, however, did accept the commission to build the vessel's two ship's boats. Captain Pete was given the task of designing them.

It was quite a chore, for Pete was saddled with the task of marrying two irreconcilable differences. He had to design a smart pulling yawlboat that was historically authentic for *America,* and the boat had to be powered by an outboard engine. As it turned out, *America II's* captain never intended to pull an oar. Eventually, the two yawlboats were replaced by those so-called Whalers from Boston. Most recent accounts have placed the *America II* in Spain. I have no idea what became of the yawlboats.

Some notes by Captain Pete give an indication of what was involved in designing them.

"It's understood that these boats must be in keeping with the yacht *America* and her period, yet adapt to modern use, and the outboard motor.

"A short discussion of ship's boats, as suited to small vessels used in the past, may be in order. Generally, small commercial vessels carried the ship's yawl, or jolly boat, which was burdensome, rowed fairly well with a stout crew and long oars, and was

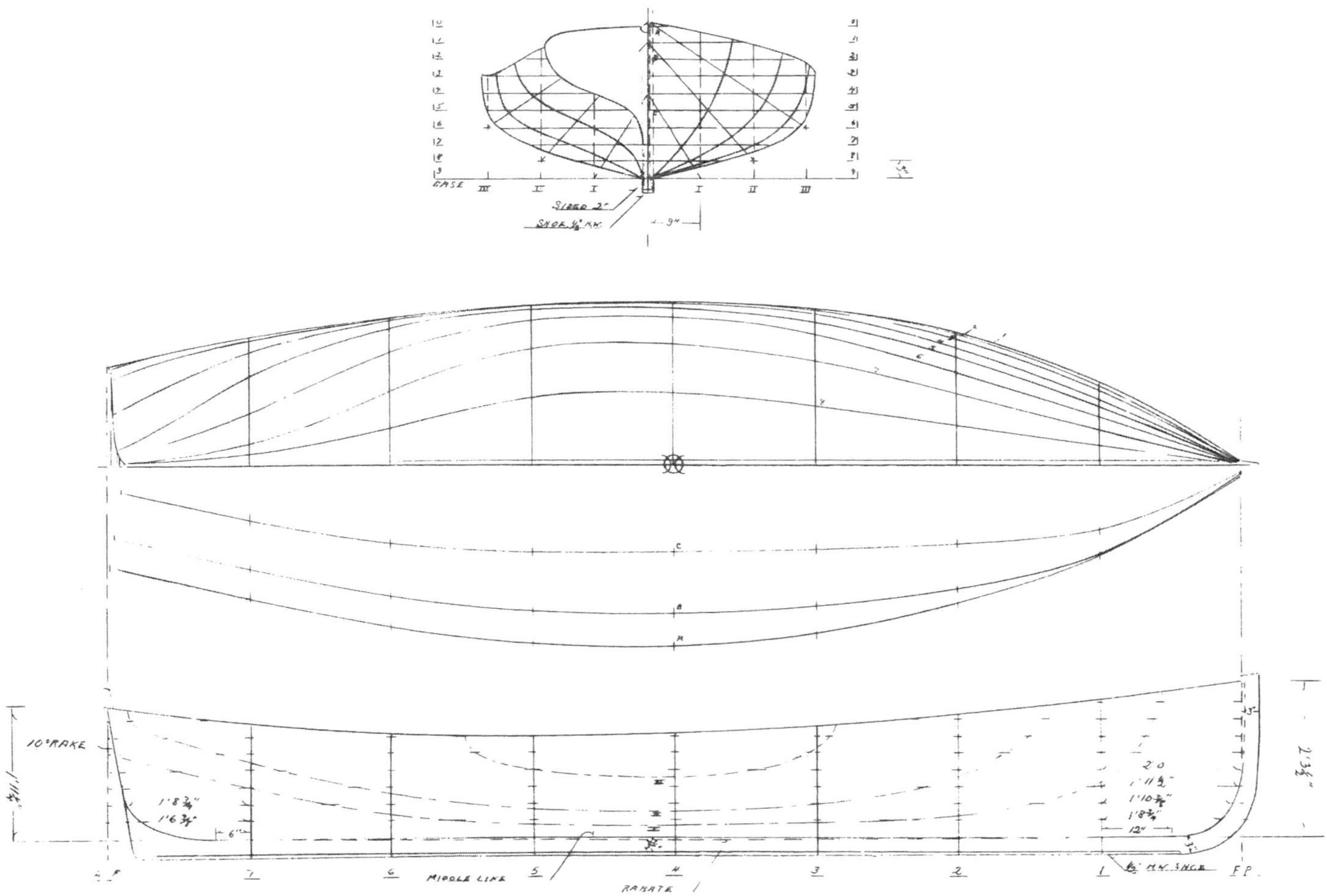

Lines of the *America II* yawlboat.

heavy to stand hard use. If the vessel carried two boats, the second was often a gig, or smart pulling boat, usually similar to a Whitehall, which rowed very well, was light, and had reasonable capacity. Actually, they were small in carrying capacity in deference to good handling under oars . In some cases, these craft became extreme in design—especially in larger yachts. Competition was keen to have a smart gig. One assumes the original *America* had at least one of these; it was the custom of the times.

"Suiting the present requirements, and using outboard engines, is a different matter. Outboard boats are no problem to design and build, nor are smart pulling gigs, for that matter. Combining the two, that is, providing an efficient outboard hull with the looks and style of our old-time gigs, is quite another matter. The two are not really compatible.

"One feels, with the use of outboards being a fixed item, that the real question is how much power and speed are required. Very small power will work fairly well on a hull somewhat modified from a Whitehall. Speed will be modest, and performance under oars not as good as it could be. More power and real speed call for radical changes in the model. If the boat works really well as an outboard, it's a real barge under oars. The two just don't go together."

With all of the above in mind, Pete took the 1876 Chandler's Whitehall model for inspiration, gave it more beam for capacity, then worked the diagonals until they were fair and somewhat slack for ease of planking. As Pete said, "The use of such diagonals in a wide hull produces a flaring bow, thin forefoot, and reverse section forward—more than was in the narrow gigs. This is of no matter and may be an advantage in an outboard-driven hull. Anyhow, it works well, and it was a feature in many bulky craft of the past. The plan seems to indicate the style we wish to have, without too much disfigurement by modern concessions."

The yawlboat popped off the molds. (R.D. Culler photo)

The finished boat ready for delivery. (Note that the gunwale is recessed to accept the rope rubrail.) (R.D. Culler photo)

It is obvious from the lines that Pete used his good judgment and produced a design that would row as well as possible, sail with distinction, and still be respectable under modest power with an outboard engine. The little vessel is still very much Whitehall.

When these boats were built in 1967, heavy construction was used and extras were added in the interest of ostentation. Each cost over $4,000. Pete always felt they should be built in the traditional manner using lapstrake construction—cedar, oak, and pine. Using these methods, they will always be affordable to anyone wishing to build a sensible ship's boat.

Ship's Yawlboats Whitehall Model For Yacht *America II*

Brief Construction Notes

1. Scantling keel, stem, sternpost: white oak.
2. Planking carvel: ½-inch native cedar, narrow planks. Sheerstrake with bead: Honduras mahogany ⅝ inch.
3. Frames: good-bending white oak.
4. Plank fastenings: copper rivets.
5. Seats, removable back: teak.
6. Floorboards: teak.
7. Oarlock sockets and horns: bronze.
8. Drain plug: bronze.

Brief Painting Schedule

1. Sheerstrake: varnished.
2. Topsides: painted. Color optional, but white would be most practical to prevent heat and shrinkage and much easier to keep looking shipshape. Black would look well, but would be hard on boat and crew. (Other colors probably not suitable.)
3. Bottom: antifouling. Green would be good for dirty harbors. White could look well.
4. Inside: painted white to reflect sun and prevent drying-out of planking.
5. Seats, grating, and floorboards: bare.

Length overall: 16 feet 8½ inches
Molded beam: 4 feet 4¾ inches
Molded depth: 1 foot 3 inches

Race Point Surfboat *Coskata*

Comments by Pete Culler

Everyone interested in the sea seems to be familiar with Coast Guard life and surfboats. Such boats, especially those worked off the beach, are fast passing from the scene as stations are closed and air, electronic, and other improvements in rescue methods make them obsolete. This obsolescence probably started with the passing of the sailing ship.

The record and exploits of Coast Guard beach stations are so impressive, many feel this history should be enshrined. Cape Cod National Seashore has done this well, and so have other places, notably Nantucket, where there is a long history of surf rescue work.

Robert Caldwell heads the Nantucket Lifeboat Museum, which is devoted to Coast Guard rescue work in the days of sail. An accurate presentation of just how this type of rescue work was done is displayed for those interested. Obviously, much thought, research, money, and hard work went into setting up this fine museum. I'm proud to have had a small hand in it.

Caldwell thought it would be nice to have a

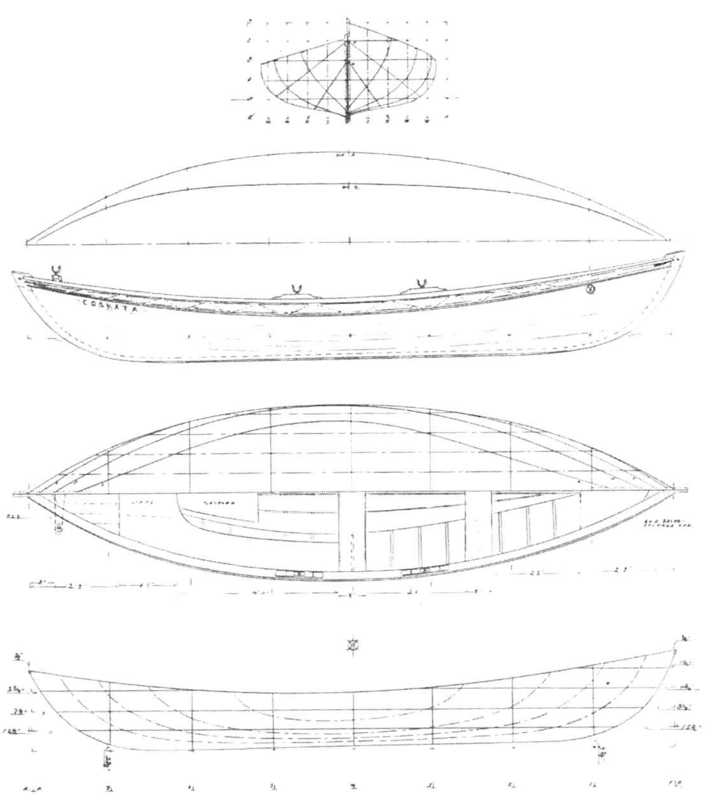

Lines of the Race Point surfboat.

Interior of the finished surfboat *Coskata*. Decked in the ends, she is rigged with sponsons, there is a yoke aft for a steering/sculling sweep, and there are drainholes at the low points, port and starboard. (R.D. Culler photo)

A version of the surfboat built in the winter of 1979-80 at the Maine Maritime Museum. (Lincoln Draper photo)

lifeboat to use in the harbor in good weather. Museum property, however, is holy, and therefore untouchable. Besides, a full-size lifeboat requires a crew, and is designed for bringing heavy loads in through the surf. This was not exactly the thing for a pleasant afternoon row, so the problem was turned over to me.

The boat desired was to live ashore on a cart in a miniature Coast Guard boathouse when not in use. Actually, the shed amounted to a two-car garage with a ramp to the water.

The boat designed looks like a lifeboat, and was built like one. The design concessions were that she's sharper for ease of moving, and though there are end decks, the bulkheads were left out for more stowage. The knees are grown apple (naturally), and she has a true keelson for stiffness. Aside from this, she's just about the same as such boats always have been, including sponsons. Because she is a light boat, the two pairs of oars are spruce, 9 feet long. In addition, there is an 11-foot steering sweep. The oars and sweep are of my own make.

Building such a craft is fun. Posts and keel are oak, as are the frames, with sprung "floating floors." That is, the floorboards go in the bays between the frames and fasten separately, keelson over all, with the thwarts bowed and stanchioned on top of the keelson—a rugged but lightweight construction.

Planking is ⅜-inch cedar; thwart stringer, floorboards, and end decks also are cedar. The thwarts are Eastern pine, as are the sternsheets, which are in the traditional oval in the interests of pleasure boating. Rails are oak as tradition requires, and she may have just a bit more brightwork than full-size lifeboats had.

The craft is named *Coskata*, after a well-known Nantucket station. She carries badges on her bows, using the old surfmen's insignia of life ring with crossed oars.

She's 17 feet long, with a 4-foot 6-inch beam and

very little draft when stark light. She weighs 263 pounds, a good weight for hauling out. This weight verifies that lapstrake planking is by far the lightest wooden boat construction method. Her colors are traditional: brightwork, buff inside, and all white outside.

I want to add a few remarks on her construction—which is traditional. She is bronze and copper fastened; I guesstimate that there are over 3,000 fastenings in her. I find that a round-bilge double-ender of this approximate shape is slightly easier to loft and set up than a transom-stern boat. And although slightly more trouble to plank, she is easier to frame aft.

She was set up on posts, upright, braced to a timber overhead in the Norse fashion, and was "on the stocks" almost to final finishing. This is a very rugged setup, with little chance for the hull to go out of shape. I think that on a boat of this size or bigger of this construction, that the time spent on one's knees, or more often on a small stool, in the early stages, is more than made up for by not having to reset and true again. This is a great advantage when working alone.

I realize that my views may be slanted, but I think she's sort of attractive.

Yawl For Stephen Forbes

Length overall: 10 feet 6½ inches
Molded beam: 4 feet 4 inches
Molded depth: 14½ inches

This little vessel has much of the old ways in her. Captain Pete called her a New England yawlboat, which suggests a throwback in time. This seems to fit, for the boat has an old-world look about her. Look in *Architectura Navalis* or Chapelle and you will find models of similar shape and line.

Many requirements had to be met in yawlboats of the past, some of them quite exacting. One was that the hull be burdensome. The ability to carry cargo, human or otherwise, between ship and shore or ship and ship was a high priority. Another requirement that came up frequently was the ability to work on and off a beach and to navigate shoal water.

This craft was designed and built for Stephen Forbes of Nashawena Island, Massachusetts. Nashawena is one of the Elizabeth Islands, which stretch between Buzzards Bay and Vineyard Sound. The topography of Nashawena is such that there is much pasture land ending at high, steep sand cliffs, which slide down to a narrow beach. A large flock of sheep is kept on the island and left to roam freely. It seems that in their grazing near the sand cliffs, the sheep have a tendency to lose their footing and slide down to the beach. Or so the story goes, in any event.

The yawlboat was designed to rescue the sheep and bring them to higher ground. Because of this, the boat has come to be known as the "sheep boat."

These requirements are met by the abilities of the old working yawlboats mentioned above. Thus, this design was used.

The vessel's construction too is in keeping with the old style, for she has a skeg and a fair amount of drag to the keel. Chapelle, in *American Small Sailing Craft*, says, "An apparently popular variant of the yawlboat was a boat built with a skeg instead of a planked-up deadwood. The skeg-hull seems to have been particularly popular in merchant ships that needed a burdensome yawl, or longboat, to work off beaches or in shoal water. The skeg construction appears to have been quite common because of its cheapness." If you build such a hull, be sure to allow enough deadwood in your lofting so the ends can be worked and kept thin and sharp. This means leaving enough wood noble in the stem so

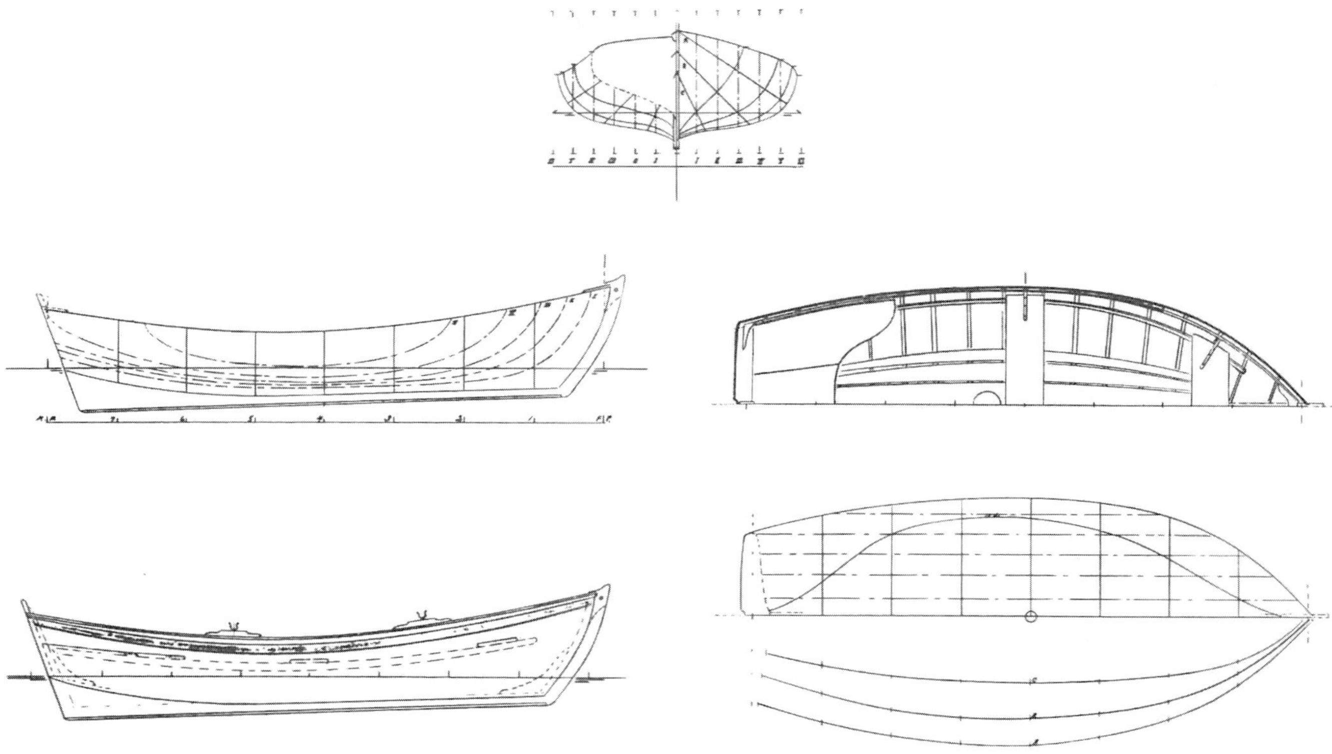

Plans of the yawlboat designed for Stephen Forbes.

The Forbes yawl planked up. The old standard was "a streak a day, clear round." This boat took Pete eight days to plank in his shop. (R.D. Culler photo)

it can be beveled back to the rabbet at a low enough angle, and having enough wood in the skeg so it can be tapered as it approaches the sternpost.

Although short and beamy, this boat has remarkably well-shaped sections. Captain Pete explained why. "Wineglass sections throughout the hull will give slack diagonals in a chunky boat. Now everyone thinks just the opposite (never having planked one), but the Norsemen knew a thing or two!" Although this is not an easy boat to plank, those slack diagonals will certainly help.

The waterline is a nice, fair sweep with hollow fore and aft. The boat's buttock lines are rather sharp forward, and there is a well-shaped run. With her turned-up ends, strong sheer, and stout-looking stem and sternpost, she appears all business and ready to go to work.

Although I never heard him say so, the Captain seems to have had a soft spot for this vessel, and for her very similar sister, the 10½-foot wherry yawl. Each is a small boat with a job to do and the ability to do it.

Length overall: 10½ feet
Beam: 4 feet 6 inches
Sail area: 47 square feet

Wherry Yawl For A Schooner

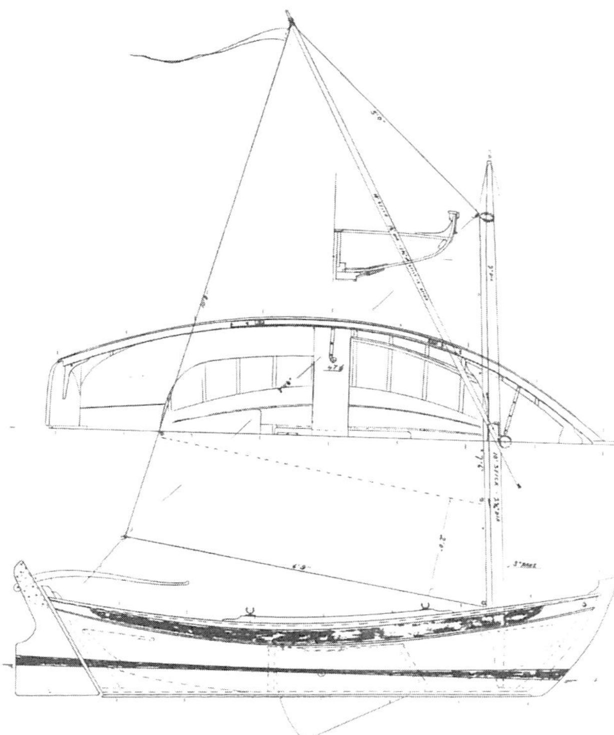

Sail plan of the wherry yawl originally designed for *Fiddler's Green*.

Comments by Pete Culler

In these days of small cruising craft, able to accommodate a small dink shaped like a bathtub, or at worst a rubber doughnut of some sort, it's not often that I get to build a proper ship's yawl—one intended to be used as such.

The design was originally made for the schooner *Fiddler's Green*, a vessel quite capable of carrying a good yawl. However, the owners of the wooden ketch *Stormsvalla* also liked the design, and commissioned me, through the Concordia Company, to build her.

Because she is a proper ship's yawl, her construction is in keeping. It is strong, but not overly heavy. The design closely follows that of working yawls of the distant past. Several people, observing her during construction, said, "She looks right out of Chapman *(Architectura Navalis)*." Thus, a backboard was fitted and inscribed to the English-Swedish naval architect of the 1700s. I must say that I find his designs most fascinating.

Above: The 10½-foot wherry yawl. **Below:** Lines of the schooner *Fiddler's Green's* yawl.
(Bart Hauthaway photo)

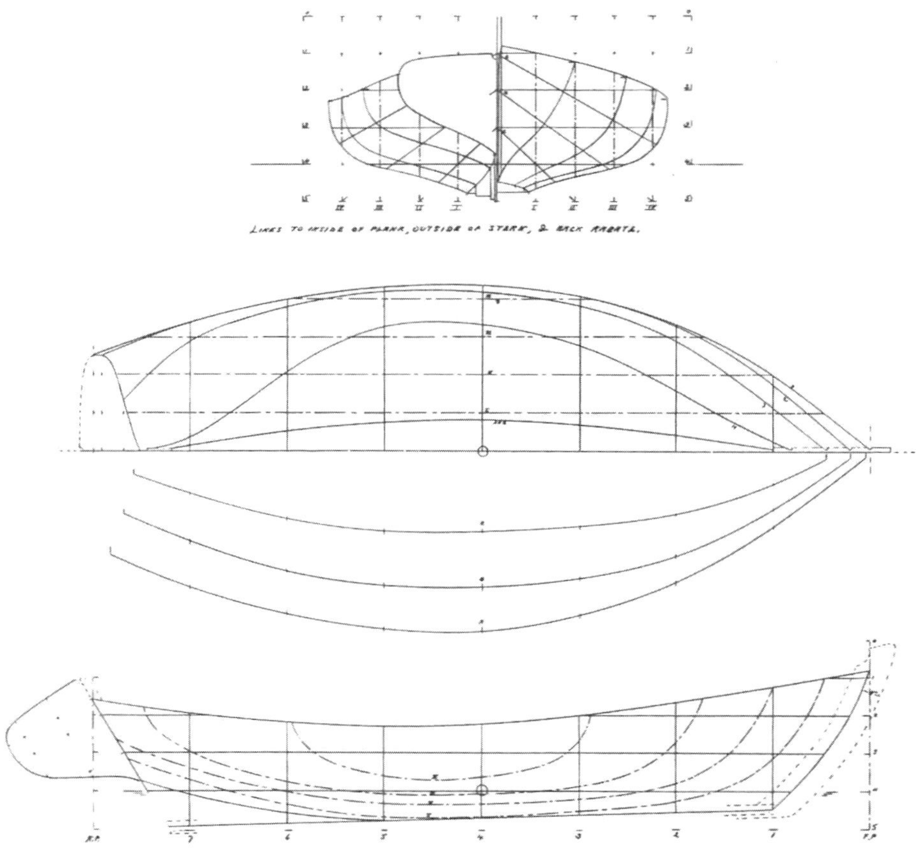

Sailing at Mystic Seaport's small craft meet. Pull in that dory strap!
(Bart Hauthaway photo)

Few may know today what was required of ship's yawls in the days of sail. They had to carry, be very able for their size, row well, and often sail considerable distances. Such boats had to carry stores and/or water barrels, and sometimes even tow them. They had to run out lines and anchors—once in a while a bower anchor, which took considerable skill. They fished for fun, or necessity. Often they were launched and hauled out in great haste. They often spent long periods of time hoisted up, and, of course, many went to war.

Obviously, requirements are not as stringent now, especially for pleasure use, yet the general design was so sound, nothing new can do any better.

This little craft was designed in the old way, to the inside of plank and perpendiculars of rabbets. By this method she's 10½ feet overall, with a beam of 4 feet 6 inches. Having built a similar working yawl for use on Nashawena Island, I had a good idea of what the weight would be. This one, having a sailing rig with centerboard, stout rudder pintles, mast partners and so on, could weigh more—perhaps too much. Thus, care was taken in the choice of stock—though one could not skimp on strength. In spite of the extra gear she weighs 178 pounds, slightly less than the previous yawl.

To accomplish this, I've made her a monument to all the woods it's said you can't get, all of them durable and rather light. The stem is a natural crook of sassafras. The sternpost is chestnut, as are the stanchions under the thwarts. The keel is Sitka spruce, a wood that is both light and stiff. Post knees are hackmatack, and oak is used for wear shoe, frames, and gunwale trim. Maine cedar is used for the planking. I selected Eastern pine for the thwarts, kneed with apple and pear, and locust for the cleats. The thumb cleats aft are apple, and for the hell of it, it's butternut for the centerboard well cap! Spars and oars are of Sitka spruce. Finally, the stern is Philippine wood, used because it was just right, very red and dense. The fastenings are copper and bronze.

Present thinking might consider this a hodgepodge of lumber, yet each wood was chosen for specific reasons—durability in its function, strength, and keeping weight within bounds. Many ask where I get such exotic stuff. It's around, underfoot; you stumble over it at times. It's just a matter of keeping one's eyes open. Small craft don't require much stock, so a little goes a long way. Though the hours putting them together always seem to mount up, there is great satisfaction in the work.

The design follows very closely the old yawls of very small size. The boat is burdensome, yet a good sailer using a traditional sprit rig of good area, with a reef. These little craft are extremely powerful for their size. They can sail in quite blowy conditions under short sail—this was one of the old-time requirements. The plank, sometimes called the wherry, keel was used to provide a good landing for the centerboard well, and also to allow the boat to sit upright on a beach. She uses wedge deadwood construction aft, and it is considerably shaped. I very much like to see a thin forefoot and heel in any craft—this is a matter of lofting and allowing enough deadwood to work with. So many boats now have stubby stems and sternposts. In this day and age it's difficult to understand why.

The little craft is finished with a green bottom, white topsides, black wale with varnished bead, bright thwarts and cap, and French gray inside. Her floorboards are oiled, and the bilge is red leaded. To suit present-day boating requirements, she has the usual dinghy fender, but I can't say that it helps her looks. It took as long, with leather ends, and so on, to put this fender on as it took to both frame her out and put in the floor timbers. And the material was far more expensive than oak. Somehow, you always pay more for yacht standards.

Length overall: 9 feet
Molded beam: 53 inches
Molded depth: 15 inches

Concordia Baeteka Pram

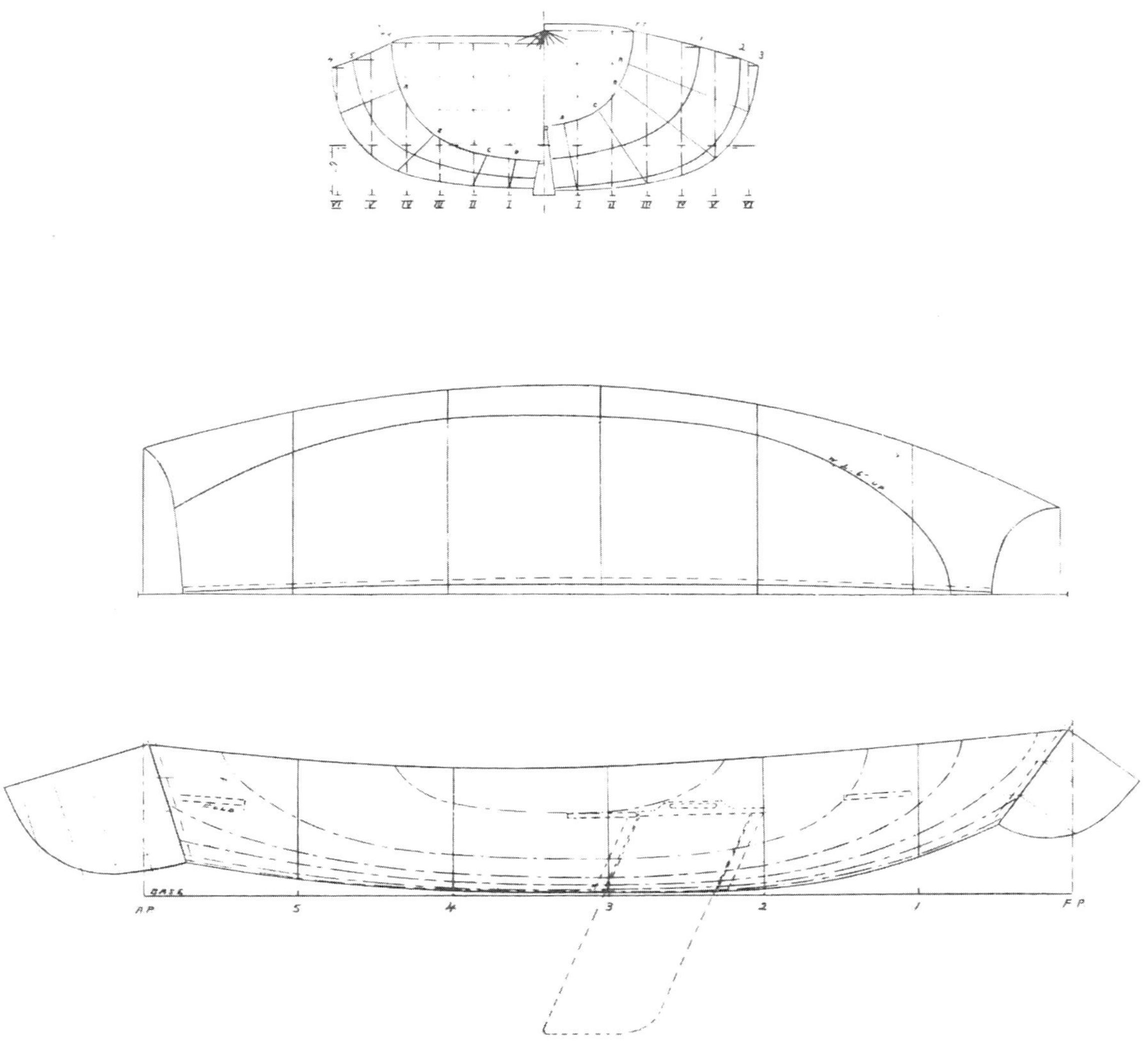

Plans of the Concordia Baeteka pram.

There are many requirements that a good yacht dinghy must satisfy. It must have the capacity to transport passengers and gear, be able in all types of weather (you may need one as a lifeboat), have good rowing ability, be stable in the ends for setting kedge anchors or picking up swimmers, and, if at all possible, be capable of pleasure sailing.

In construction, a dinghy must be light in weight, yet rugged enough to stand hard use. In this day and age, affordable yachts are small with little or no room on board to stow a dinghy. It is difficult to fulfill the requirements given above in a dinghy short enough to stow aboard. You can always tow, but this adds new requirements, and is not always the best solution. The sad fact is that most people consider the problem of the small boat as an afterthought. On the other hand, all honest designers, which Pete certainly was, feel that the problem of the small boat or dinghy must be solved early on in any design effort.

Although characterizing what passes for a dinghy today as "little better than the sliced-off top half of a

The 9-foot Baeteka pram. (R.D. Culler photo)

loaf of bread," Pete felt that the Concordia Baeteka pram was better than most. These little 8-footers came as standard equipment with every 40-foot Concordia yawl. They were designed to fit, bottom up, over the deckhouse. They were good to begin with, but Pete and Captain Hardy, a Deer Isle man and longtime skipper of a Concordia yawl, felt they could be improved. As Pete said, the "result was a longer, lighter, and abler boat; it was better looking, too."

This version is 9 feet overall, with a 53-inch beam and 15 inches of depth amidships. She draws a scant 6 inches. There is considerable rocker to the bottom and the run is long and fine. She rows very well and is very maneuverable. She is designed for one pair of oars, and a daggerboard can be fitted. As Pete said, "any practical rig will do." A loose-footed spritsail or standing lugsail would be my choice. The sternsheets can be flipped up when working aft or for more carrying capacity—a nice feature.

With this design, what you see is what you get—there is no table of offsets. This should be no deterrent, however. With a set of dividers and scale rule, these can be picked up from the plan. This way, you have no one to blame but yourself for any errors.

If your existing vessel or the dreamboat you are contemplating can handle it, I strongly suggest you consider this well-thought-out little pram.

PART II

Vee- and Flat-Bottomed Open Boats for Sail and Oar

Length between perpendiculars: 24 feet
Beam: 4 feet 9 inches
Depth:1 foot 4 inches
Sail area: 153 square feet

Revised Sharptown Barge

"Hey, Pete, do you remember that Sharptown barge that appeared in *The Rudder* a number of years ago?"

"Sure. Sure I do. Good boat," the Captain replied.

"Well, do you think you could build me a boat like that?" the Old Man's good friend Dick White asked one day.

"Why, of course. If that's what you want, that's what you'll get."

Pete had known and been friends with Dick White ever since they had become neighbors when the Captain moved ashore to Hyannis in 1948. Many years of talking about boats and their building and way of going cemented that friendship. Thus, when White asked Pete about a certain boat, he knew which one. No doubt they had discussed it earlier.

That night Pete went up to the attic and sifted through his back issues of *The Rudder* to find the copy in question. The Sharptown barge, a flat-bottomed utility skiff with an outboard engine, was designed for *The Rudder* by Robert M. Steward. The article appeared in the November 1952 issue.

The boat had been developed for the shad fishery on the Nanticoke River of Maryland's Eastern shore—a fertile breeding ground for good small craft designs. Pete made few changes in the original design. After all, it was what White wanted. He did, however, lengthen the boat to 22 feet 9 inches and give the transom less rake to better accommodate an outboard, and he rigged her for sail by installing a centerboard and short skeg aft. The rig consists of a sprit main, a leg-o'-mutton sprit mizzen, and a "balanced" jib. This makes her a real little ship!

The rig is low and well spread out, and pushes the long, lean hull right along even in a whisper. I

The Sharpto wn barge rigged for sail.

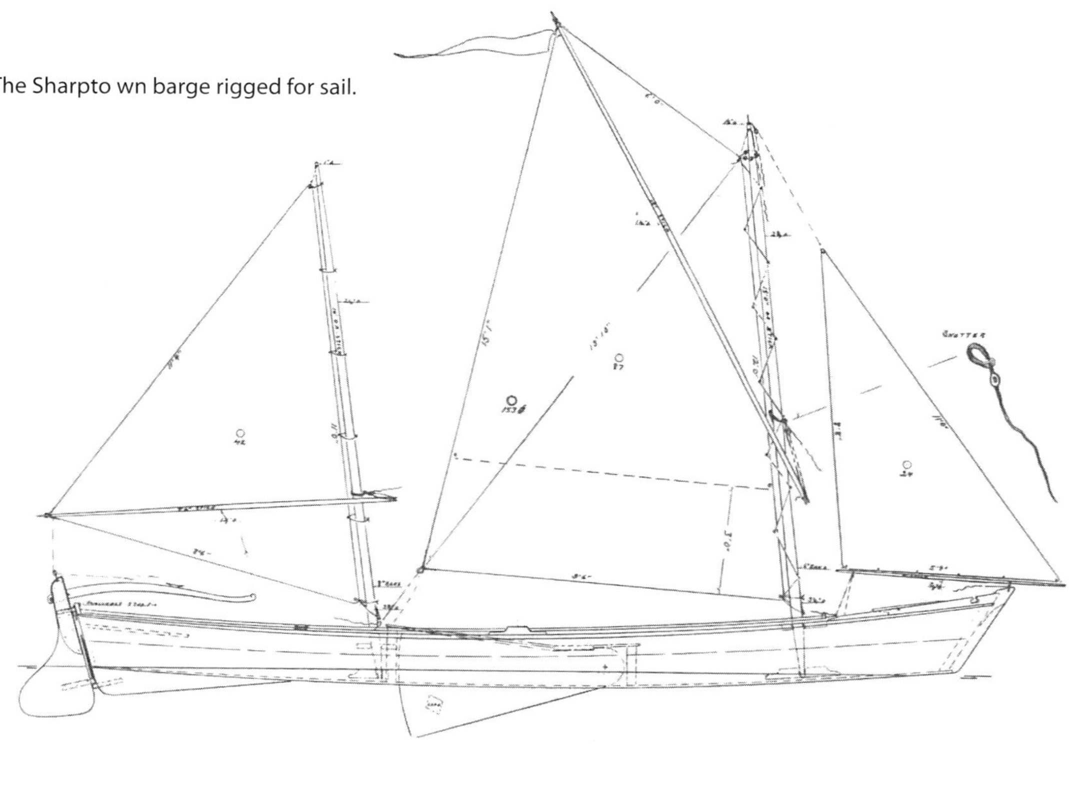

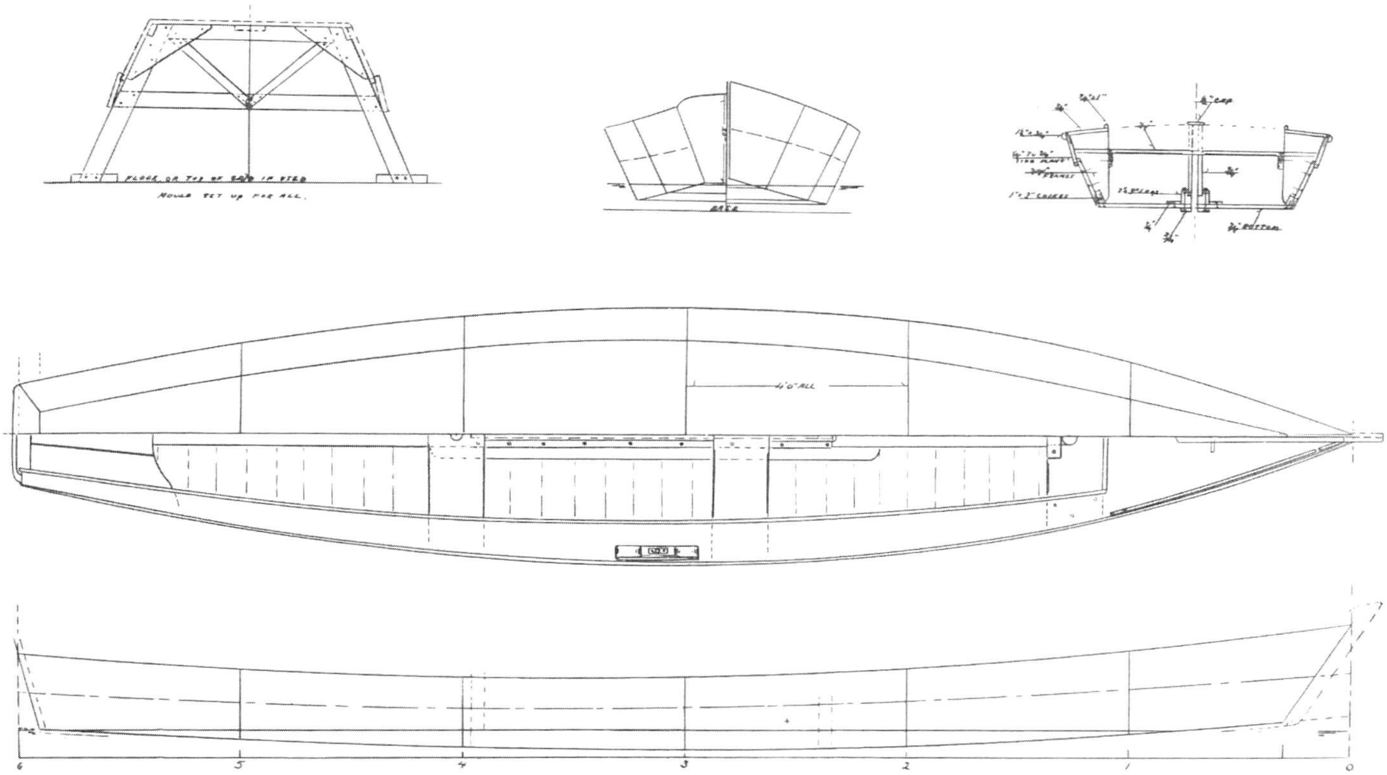

Plans of the Sharptown barge.

daresay she would be a good self-steerer once everything has been balanced. The mizzen sheets through a fairlead at the rudder head to a cleat on the tiller. The mainsheet is two part, reeving through bull's-eyes set up on either side of the coaming and back to cleats handy to the helmsman. With the jib and mizzen more or less selftending, the mainsheet is all that needs working when tacking. The whole rig stows easily in the boat.

The hull is easily pushed along with a 6 h.p. outboard. Most people overdo it and use a 10, but with gas prices where they are today, you would do well to stick with the smaller engine. Have an engine in mind before you cut the transom, and remember that the rudder must fit back there, too.

In an emergency, or if you're in the mood, oarlocks are provided. With her length, the boat will move along nicely under oars. The narrow beam, 4 feet 9 inches, allows normal-size oars. Nine-footers of ash will do fine.

With all this gear—engine, gas tanks, rig, and oars—plus the catch for the day, the possibilities for trim are endless. Even though narrow, this boat's considerable length makes for a very burdensome hull.

By all means build it and see how much fun you'll have!

The Sharptown barge on the stocks showing clearly by the method of framing for both side and washdeck. (R.D. Culler photo)

Length overall: 20 feet
Beam: 5 feet
Sail area: 104 square feet

Sharpie For John Parkinson

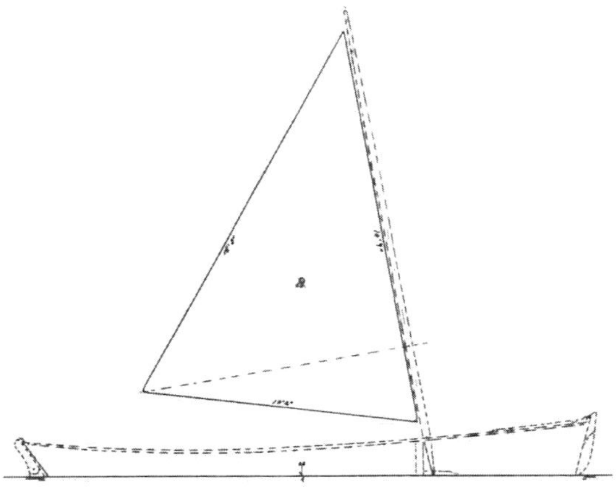

The sharpie's working or fishing rig.

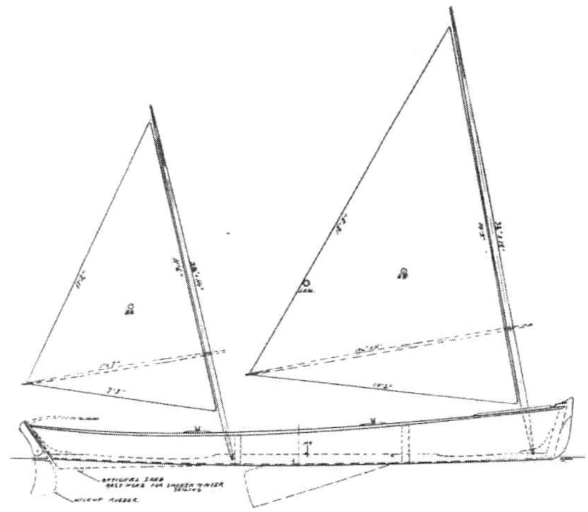

The typical two-sail sharpie rig (referred to by Captain Pete as the summer, or sporting, rig).

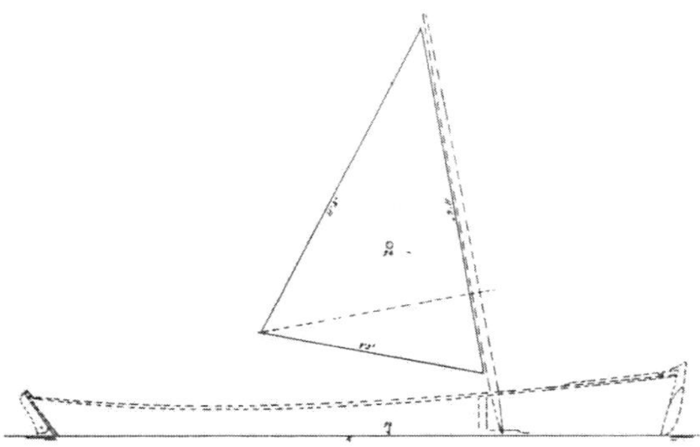

The sharpie's heavy-weather rig.

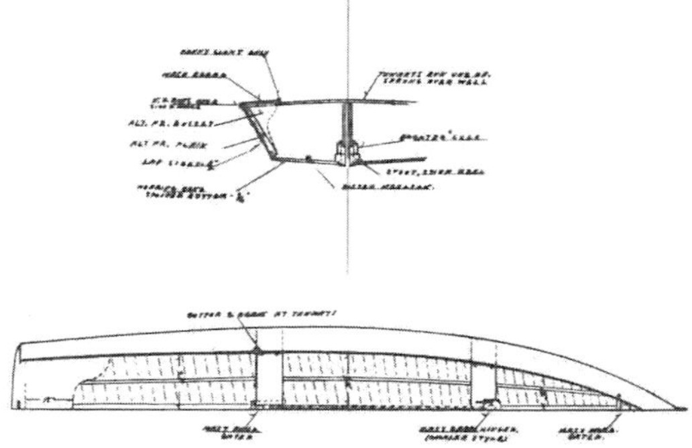

Construction plan of the 20-foot sharpie.

Small boats based on the sharpie model are, as a rule, fast; this one is no different. The hull is very much in the Chesapeake style—V-cross-planked herringbone bottom, with washboards reminiscent of the Sharptown barge. It has the sharp-headed, two-sail Chesapeake rig.

One very important factor in this style of construction is that the keel must be strong and stiff, since it is literally the backbone of the entire vessel. A centerboard slot cut in the middle of the keel makes this doubly important. Close-grained fir would be a good choice of material. Recognizing this as a possible weakness, Pete worked in sprung thwarts under the washboards and over the centerboard trunk. Tied into the washboards and thereby into the chines with a system of alternating frames and gussets, along with the sister keelsons, this results in a strong and relatively stiff hull. The washboards, in addition to being a good place to plop your fanny, give the boat good reserve stability. By the time you start taking water over the coaming, it's time to reduce sail. The boat will sail best on its bottom.

Under any sail combination (fore and mizzen, foresail alone, or mizzen alone stepped forward), the centers line up well. The rig is most versatile for any condition you might encounter. Essentially, this is really the ancient shallop rig, bay style. With this hull, weight aloft is critical, so keep it in mind when choosing spar stock. If you wish to use halyards, bore a hole in the masthead. Remember, this takes no maintenance and you're keeping weight down. About all I would add are a couple of pennants sewn to the sail peaks.

The centerboard has been kept long and shallow for good shoal-water ability. The rudder should be adequate with its deep leading edge, and it will kick up if struck. Make your gudgeons and pintles strong, for they are mounted quite close together. There is an optional skeg. In smooth-water areas, Pete felt it would be best to eliminate the skeg.

With its low, well-spread-out rig and long, lean hull, this boat has a light helm, yet it responds immediately. She would be a real ghoster in light air. If the wind gives out entirely, there are oarlocks. You'll have to make the oarlock pads somewhat high due to the thwart arrangement.

I'd like to see this boat skim across Lewis Bay on Cape Cod for an afternoon of clamming at Egg Island.

Swampscott Dory For Captain Charles Sayle

Length overall: 18 feet 8 inches
Molded beam: 4 feet 10 inches
Molded depth: 1 foot 6¼ inches
Sail area: 94 square feet

The dory is a deservedly popular small craft. Straightforward and economical to build and maintain, dories have been in use for centuries.

Until recent times, the dory has been primarily a working craft. It was in this area that the type's design reached a high degree of development. Universally known for their fisheries work, dories have also proven successful in the surf, on rivers, and anywhere else a stable, seaworthy, and burdensome working platform was required.

The North Shore of Massachusetts is well known as a breeding ground for the dory. Boatshops from the towns of Amesbury, Marblehead, Gloucester, Rockport, Salem, and others built dories to a high level of perfection. However, a special place is held for those that bear the name of the town of Swampscott. As John Gardner has said, they were known as the "aristocrats" of dories. With their round-knuckled sides, narrow bottoms, and fine ends, Swampscott dories were prized for their very impressive performance under oar and sail.

Captain Pete's version was designed and built for Captain Charlie Sayle of Nantucket. This gentleman, having sailed aboard the Gloucester fishing fleet in the 1920s, knew pretty much what he wanted. He gave Pete the length on the bottom and the length overall, and then allowed him to proceed.

The result is a handsome clipper dory of 14 feet 5 inches on the bottom and 18 feet 8 inches overall, with a beautiful sheer and 3 inches of rocker. The bottom was kept narrow for good performance, and the ends are fine, with a pleasing shape in profile.

The two-sail rig is most versatile. It is well spread out and low. As Captain Pete said, the idea is to have more than you need for light airs and yet be able to take in, reef, and adjust for hard blows. This is easily done once you learn how, and it's fun to boot. Fussing with small boat rigs is enjoyable. One young man is even toying with adding a sprit topsail. This seems a worthwhile experiment. It certainly would help in those light evening zephyrs.

Construction is standard dory. The boat can be built right side up, as Pete did it, or upside down as John Gardner has suggested. There are pros and cons each way. If you build upside down, however, please turn her right side up to hang the sheerstrake. You will note that apple knee gussets are indicated on the plan for the sawn frames. These will look better and last longer than metal clips. Captain Charlie's intention was to give this boat to his great-grandchildren. If clips are all you have, on the other hand, by all means use them.

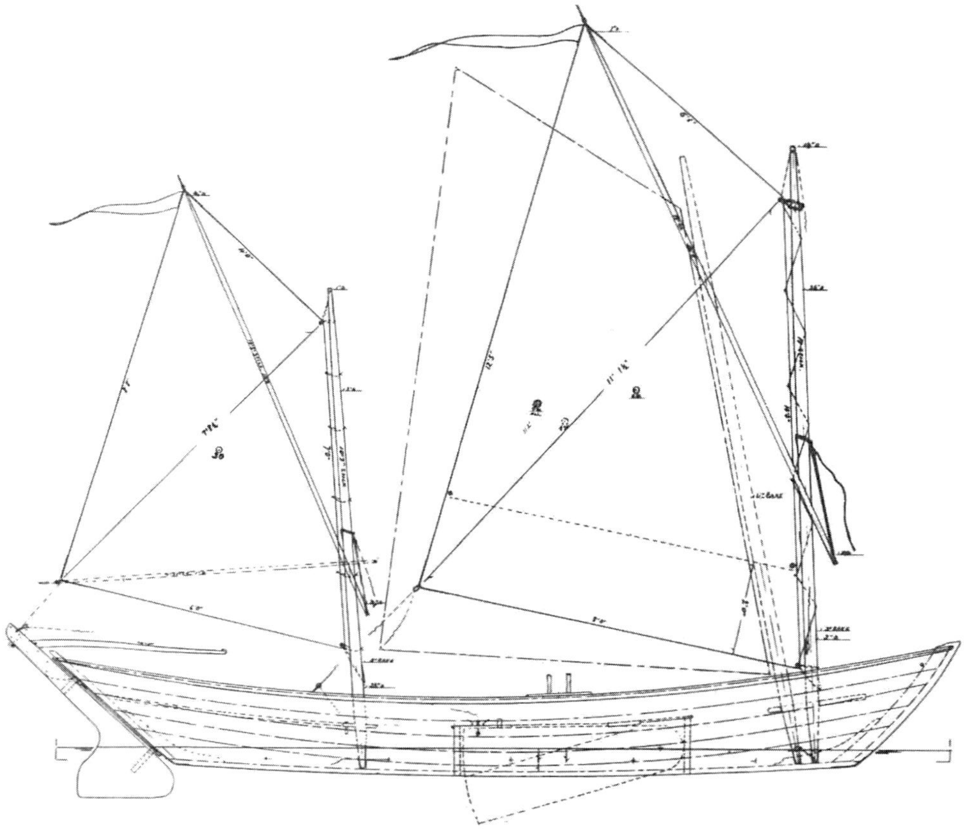

Plans of the Swampscott dory for Captain Charlie Sayle.

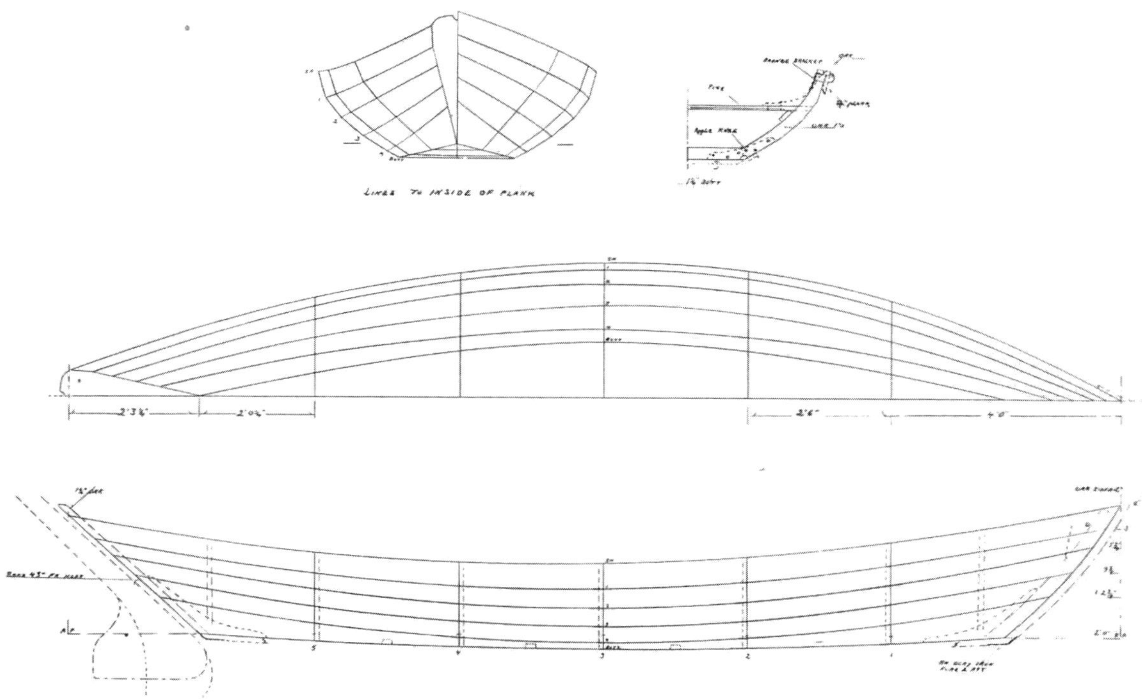

Charlie Sayle's Swampscott dory framed out in Pete Culler's shop. (R.D . Culler photo)

Charlie Sayle's Swampscott at anchor on Nantucket. (John Burke photo)

Since the need was for a long-lived boat, black locust was used for the transom, stem, and sawn frames. This wood is highly rot-resistant, close-grained, and easily worked, though somewhat heavy. This accounts for her weight of 399 pounds. The planking is ⅝-inch cedar, five strakes to a side.

The tholepins work well and certainly look appropriate for a dory. Depending on thwart arrangement, more can be added. A good set of oars is a must. Nine-footers of ash should do fine.

This vessel was finished out with a black hull, yellow wales, and light blue inside. The inside bottom is oiled and the outside bottom is green antifouling. Spars and rigging are tarred.

Captain Pete's Swampscott *Dancing Feather*, though 1½ feet shorter, consistently did the measured mile in 12 minutes. This one would be faster.

For those seeking a fine clipper dory for pleasure use under sail and oar, look no further.

Length overall: 17 feet 4 inches
Beam: 3 feet
Depth: 10 feet
Sail area: 31 square feet

Clipper Pulling Bateau *Otter*

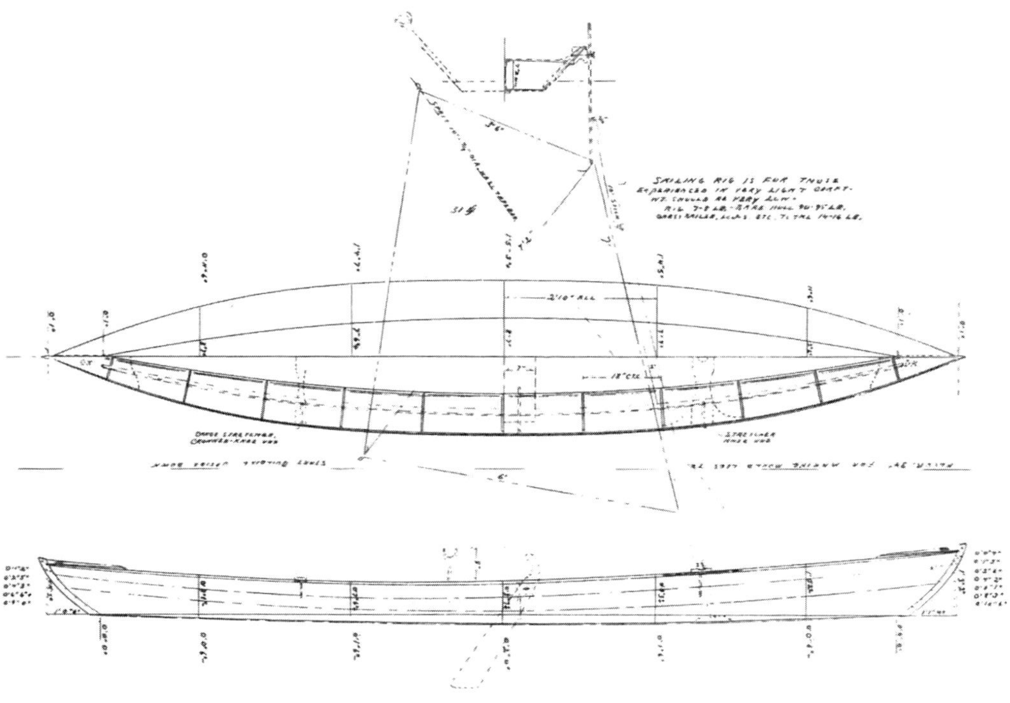

Plans of the bateau *Otter*.

Captain Pete stated that among flat-bottomed craft the bateau is tops for rowing. He had been mulling over this idea for a long time when in 1971 he took his first week's vacation in memory and built *Otter*. She is a simple, yet elegantly refined craft. Of all the rowing designs discussed in this book, *Otter* is the most unforgiving to the oarsman. One false move out of sync, and the boat screams out. All together—with body balance, oar entry, and pull and follow-through coordinated—*Otter* moves through the water with a slipperiness that would do her namesake proud. The boat is about as close as you can get to a racing shell with a traditional design.

We don't know whether historical craft of this type were cross-planked on the bottom. The only evidence found in existing artifacts and the few plans available shows bottom planking fore and aft, sometimes splined. According to Howard Chapelle, it is likely that crossplanking was used, however, for it is the easier, stronger way to go, and it was known to colonial builders. The plans for *Otter* call for a cross-planked bottom for the above reasons, and also because this method leaves the inside bottom free of framing, thus saving weight and space.

Above: George Kelley takes *Otter* for an early winter trial row. (Boatbuilders get their vacations in the offseason!) This photo clearlyshows the raising and spreading ofthe oarpivot with the unique oarlock design. (R.D. Culler photo)

Right: Interior details of *Otter*, rigged for sail. Note the bow and stern handles, the unique outrigger oarlocks, and the removable leeboard. (John Burke photo)

If the boat lives chiefly out of the water, and it should, it would be best to spline the bottom also. This will keep things tight. Some weight is saved here, too, because the bottom planking need not be as thick when splined. As designed, the boat should weigh somewhere around 90 pounds, finished. This lightness aids in portability as well as in rowing qualities.

The boat is moderately rockered on the bottom for easy rowing and maneuverability. Not truly double ended, she is slightly higher in the bow. The ends are decked with bow pieces, which have handles worked into them. The bow pieces accent the sheer. The sheer, which has reverse at both ends, is one of the sweetest lines you'll ever see. If you build one, by all means taper your gunwales. The posts have a pleasing shape in profile.

Otter is planked up three to a side; note that the sheerstrake is thicker. This is an important part of her construction. Also, instead of beveling the laps, pad out the molds the thickness of the plank. This will give the boat more flare and better shape (see Appendix).

Most of us are aware of the Coast Guard's regulations with respect to loading small craft. When these regulations were making the rounds for comment, Pete applied the formula to *Otter* and found that she could safely handle one-third of a person. Of course, his experience with the boat was otherwise (Pete was not a small man), but according to the formula, about-to-be-law, his experience would not mean a thing! This hit home at once. How many other traditional designs would be in jeopardy? Something had to be done.

At a small craft get-together held shortly thereafter, a dedicated group of enthusiasts held an impromptu meeting. The Captain voiced his concerns, which were shared by everyone present. From this meeting a political group, the Traditional Small Craft Association, was formed to persuade the Coast Guard of its erroneous thinking. The success of this effort, so far, has been less than totally satisfactory. The Coast Guard is rethinking its position and has assigned special consideration to traditional small craft.

But there is cause for hope. What once seemed preordained has been stopped. If *Otter* had anything to do with this, even indirectly, I say "God bless her."

Length overall: 20 feet
Beam: 4 feet
Draft: 3 inches

Clipper Pulling Bateau For Dr. James Eldredge

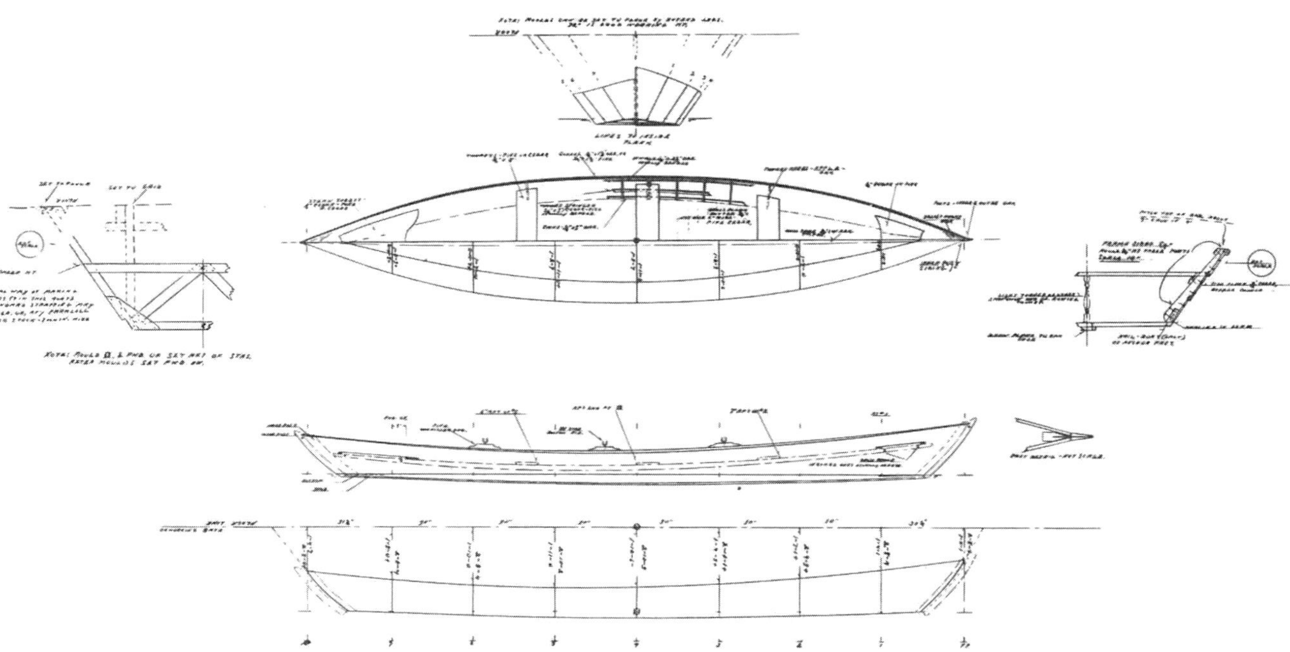

Plans of the 20-foot fast bateau for Dr. Eldredge. (*Otter* is a scaled-down version of this design.)

Captain Pete had a full stable of small craft at his Hyannis home. These included a 17-foot 6-inch Swampscott dory, *Dancing Feather*, until it was sold down-Cape. He purchased *Seaman's Friend*, a 17-foot clipper wherry, to join *Butternut*, a 13-foot double-paddle canoe, and *Otter*, the 17-foot bateau. During the year before his death, he was given a badly neglected 15-foot double-ended Rushton rowboat. This he restored—magically, it seemed—into *J. Henry*. But that's another story.

The Captain was very fond of early-morning rows in *Otter*. The air was usually light and the water calm. Pete enjoyed checking out new and interesting arrivals before the speed jockeys came out and destroyed the peaceful atmosphere. On these short cruises *Otter* never failed to elicit favorable comment, but many questioned her size. It usually went something like, "Gee, Mister, nice boat ya got there. Too bad it's not a little bigger so I could take along my wife (or girlfriend, mother, son, daughter, or whomever)."

Pete's reply was always, "I got the plans for that boat. Come on over and get 'em." In fact, *Otter* is a scaled-down version of this 20-foot fast bateau, which was designed for Dr. James Eldredge. The additional foot of beam and greater length provide extra capacity while retaining the same sweet lines and slipperiness of her smaller sister, *Otter*. This boat will safely accommodate two or three people. There is no rig on the larger version.

In making the boat more burdensome, it was possible to include regular oarlocks and pads. Spoon oars are needed to get the most out of her. Spruce or cedar oars, 8½ feet, do fine.

For any boat whose bottom is cross-planked it's best to start building upside down, either to a grid or a floor. Usually the first problem that arises, especially for amateurs, is fitting the chines. Because they are hardwood, they can be cranky, especially in a double-ender, where they must land against the stem- and sternposts. Most people try steam, but this can be unwieldy for a lone worker. Instead, spile them just as you would for plank in two or more pieces, joining them with slash scarfs, glued and riveted. It's much easier.

After you have the first two side strakes and the bottom on, turn over the hull to fit the sheer. It is nearly impossible to get a sweet sheer while standing on your head. This boat deserves the best you can muster, so do it right.

Considering all the apparent interest, it's surprising to learn that the 20-foot version has never been built. Who is going to correct this situation?

13½-Foot Skiff

Length overall: 13 feet 6 inches
Sail area: 70 square feet

The Good Little Skiffs

Most of Captain Pete's small boat designs and some of his larger ones are suitable for amateur construction. It all depends on one's abilities and pocketbook—more the latter than the former, it turns out.

Beginners have a tendency to get all worked up about boatbuilding. Curved wood, tight joints, and proper fastening mystify them. It shouldn't. A little study, a modest kit of tools—kept sharp, of course—and a willingness to go at it, are all that is required. Keep in mind that "experience starts when you begin," and you should do well.

For the serious learner, a flat-bottomed skiff is a good place to start. The three designs discussed here have come to be known as the Good Little Skiffs. They are sufficiently different in size and detail to satisfy anyone looking for a flat-bottomed skiff. Some folks even admit to liking them all.

John Gardner, the noted popularizer of traditional small craft, has said, "These shapely but simply built skiffs with their flat cross-planked bottoms and ample scantlings make ideal first boats for inexperienced builders, for there is nothing critical in their straightforward no-nonsense construction to stump the novice or discourage the diligent beginner with only moderate woodworking skill."

Now that we have convinced you to give one a try, which to choose? Perhaps a discussion of each design will help. The proper place to start is with the smallest. The 13½-footer has an interesting history, so please allow a digression. In the spring of 1970, Captain Pete received a notice from Mystic Seaport announcing a small craft workshop. This was the first of Mystic's now-famous annual event. Included was a request to submit a small boat design. The letter went on to list a lengthy set of requirements that, if fulfilled, would make the submitted design "the perfect boat." Pete knew firsthand that all boat design is a compromise, and that any craft purporting to satisfy everybody would be no good to anyone. However, the spirit of the request merited a response.

In discussing the problem with Waldo Howland, owner of Concordia Company, Pete decided that a small flat-bottomed skiff was the best design to submit. For ease of construction, economy, and general handiness, this type of small craft is hard to beat. That night Pete went up to the shop and drew the lines and some accompanying sketches. The next day Howland wrote in some pertinent comments and mimeographed about a half-dozen copies. They titled it "The Good Little Skiff." A very modest beginning for a most popular boat.

Once again, John Gardner's comments: "This rugged little 13½-foot flat-bottomed, cross-planked skiff with her more than 4 feet of beam is distinctive in several respects: for her able, seakindly performance, her jaunty good looks, and not the least, for her simple inexpensive construction that makes her especially attractive to the amateur builder. Here is a flat-bottomed boat with character in the real sense of that much-abused word. Her flaring clinker sides, raking stern, well-rockered bottom, and ample sheer unite to produce a striking craft,

Jodi Burke's 13½-foot skiff *Waterwings*. (John Burke photo)

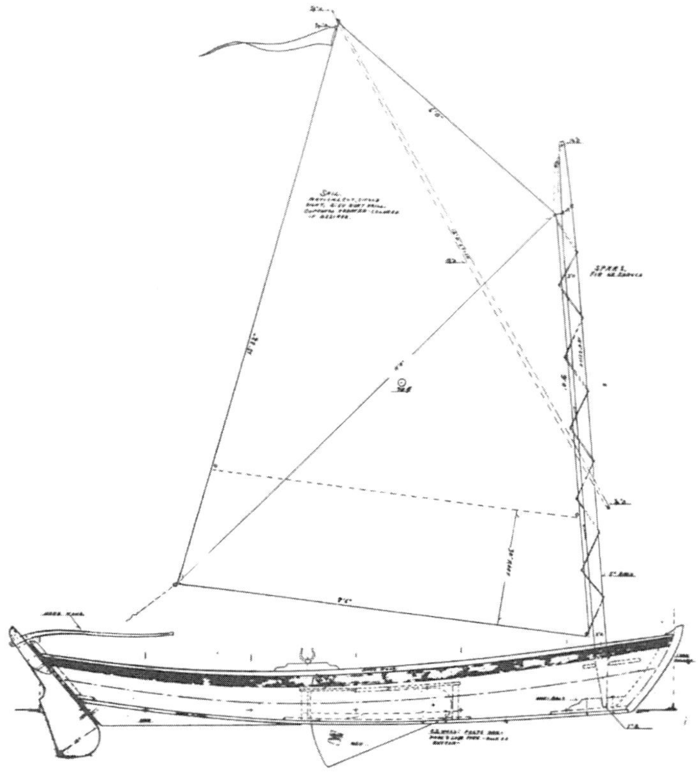

Sail plan of the 13½-foot Good Little Skiff.

Construction plans of the 13½-foot Good Little Skiff.

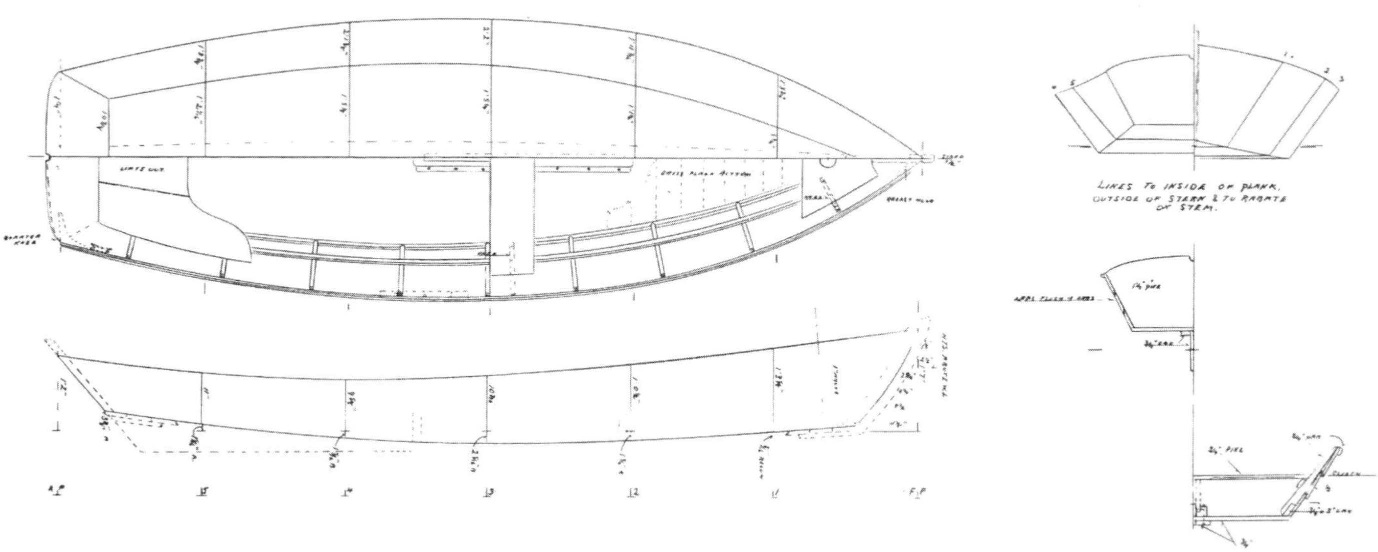

one that rows and sails equally well. The boat can navigate both in deep and shoal water and can run aground and sit upright on the beach without damage."

Construction, as stated before, is straight forward. However, some pointers learned the hard way by previous builders will be helpful.

Always lay down the lines full size, that is, loft. This is helpful in many ways. There are almost always some errors in plans. The place to fair things out is on the floor. This is also where you pick up templates for stem, knees, and other parts, full size.

Shape or spile the chines, plank, and thwart risers. It is much simpler and easier than attempting to steam or edge-set these members.

It is important to retain the flare in the sides. This flare complements the sheer, which has reverse, and gives good freeboard in the bow, where it's required. The flare also allows good capacity while keeping the bottom narrow. It makes 'em look good, too. The best way to build in this flare is to pad out the molds when planking instead of beveling the laps (see Appendix).

The centerboard on this skiff provides an ingenious way to get good area in a short length. Although not shown on the plan, it has been found that the entire board should be boxed. Otherwise, water tends to slop up through the well when the boat is underway. This requires caution in laying out, for the whole affair is between your legs when rowing; if it is built too high, your knuckles will take a beating. Even when built correctly, the box forces the oarsman to feather the oars properly.

15½-Foot Skiff

Length overall:15 feet 8 inches
Beam: 4 feet 8 inches
Sail area: 70 square feet

The 15-foot 8-inch skiff was a joint effort between the Captain and Robin Laggeman. The story of her building is wonderfully told by Captain Pete in the chapter on boatbuilding in *Skiffs and Schooners*. Because notes by Pete exist on this design, we think it best to let him do the talking. After all, who could be better qualified?

"This particular boat was designed and built for Robin Laggeman of West Barnstable, Massachusetts; she is based on the old West Coast skiffs. The history of the type is obscure; possibly they have some Italian origin. Not all were rigged to sail, as they were sometimes used as net boats. Those that were rigged sailed very well, and although the rigs did vary, the sprit or standing lug rig, loose footed, was the most popular one.

"The boats were quite able, good sail carriers, and excellent surfboats, these last having more bottom rocker, which was not so good for sailing. They also towed well astern of a seiner.

"Mr. Laggeman wanted a stable boat for use on the south side of the Cape and from protected beaches, suited to use alone or take a small child along, with the idea that the boy would soon be sailing the skiff himself. After experimenting with my two-sail Swampscott dory, he decided on what he wanted, and we worked up this design and built her.

"The thwart layout is largely the owner's choice; personally, I like another after thwart across her with sternsheets running in on it. Along this line, I put in a full capped gunwale to stiffen her, for the lack of another thwart. This is very strong, looks well, and is maybe the best way, but it does add somewhat to the cost. The boat was required to be light for transporting. She goes 303 pounds without her gear. We picked the lightest cedar available at Concordia. There is much of her construction of this cedar that in other craft is usually oak or pine. She is extremely well fitted and fastened, so she is quite strong. Except for the transporting angle, there is no point in building this light, as the boat needs some weight to carry way in a chop and in tacking. But a couple of sandbags can make up for it.

"I also feel that the boat is somewhat undercanvased, although the owner thinks it is enough. I did make the spars a bit longer so he could increase the area at a later date; one should plan a rig for local conditions. The boat has three steps and an

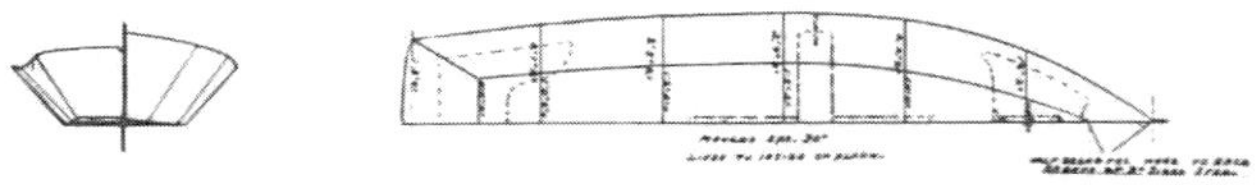

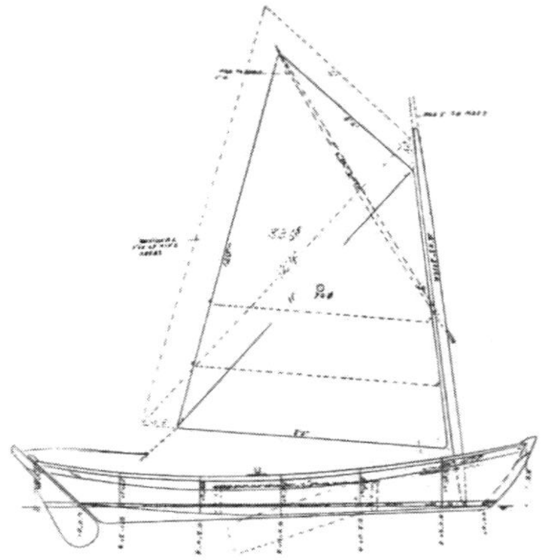

Plans of the 15-foot 8-inch Good Little Skiff.

Robin Laggeman's 15-foot 8-inch Good Little Skiff. (Pete Culler photo)

elongated mast partner with sliding block so the mast can be shifted to maintain balance under reduced sail.

"My own experience has been that the old two-sail sprit rig with a large foresail and small mizzen is the most versatile. My present clipper dory is rigged that way. It is most responsive in light going with the full rig, and is just right under fore alone in the usual afternoon breeze. In really heavy going, the little mizzen is placed in the after forward step and she is most manageable.

"The West Coast skiff is not necessarily the right boat for some uses, but advantages of draft and beaching, along with its general ability and moderate cost, make it worth considering. It will admit some variation of rig and shape—also size. However, the simple beachboat rigs that can easily be set up and struck, along with their low center of effort, always work best. This applies to the use of loose-footed sails especially; they seem to press the boats less when properly cut and have many advantages.

"The boats should not be built too short, not less than 15 feet, although they do well much longer. The beam should be kept modest and the great flare maintained.

"In the past I have incorporated a chine and deadrise in some models; it adds to the cost and seems to make them better in light going and a bobble. However, they are not as handy to beach. They do make a very handsome craft and are somewhat better in stays in the above-mentioned conditions."

The Old Man stated, "I never designed or built anything I could not improve on the next round, or at least have the desire to try." The previously mentioned 13½-foot skiff, which was designed after this one, has since become most popular.

A Good Little Skiff built at Mystic Seaport. (Russell Fowler photo)

18 ½-Foot Skiff

Length overall: 18 feet 6 inches
Sail area: 99 square feet

Plans for Waldo Howland's 18½-foot Good Little Skiff.

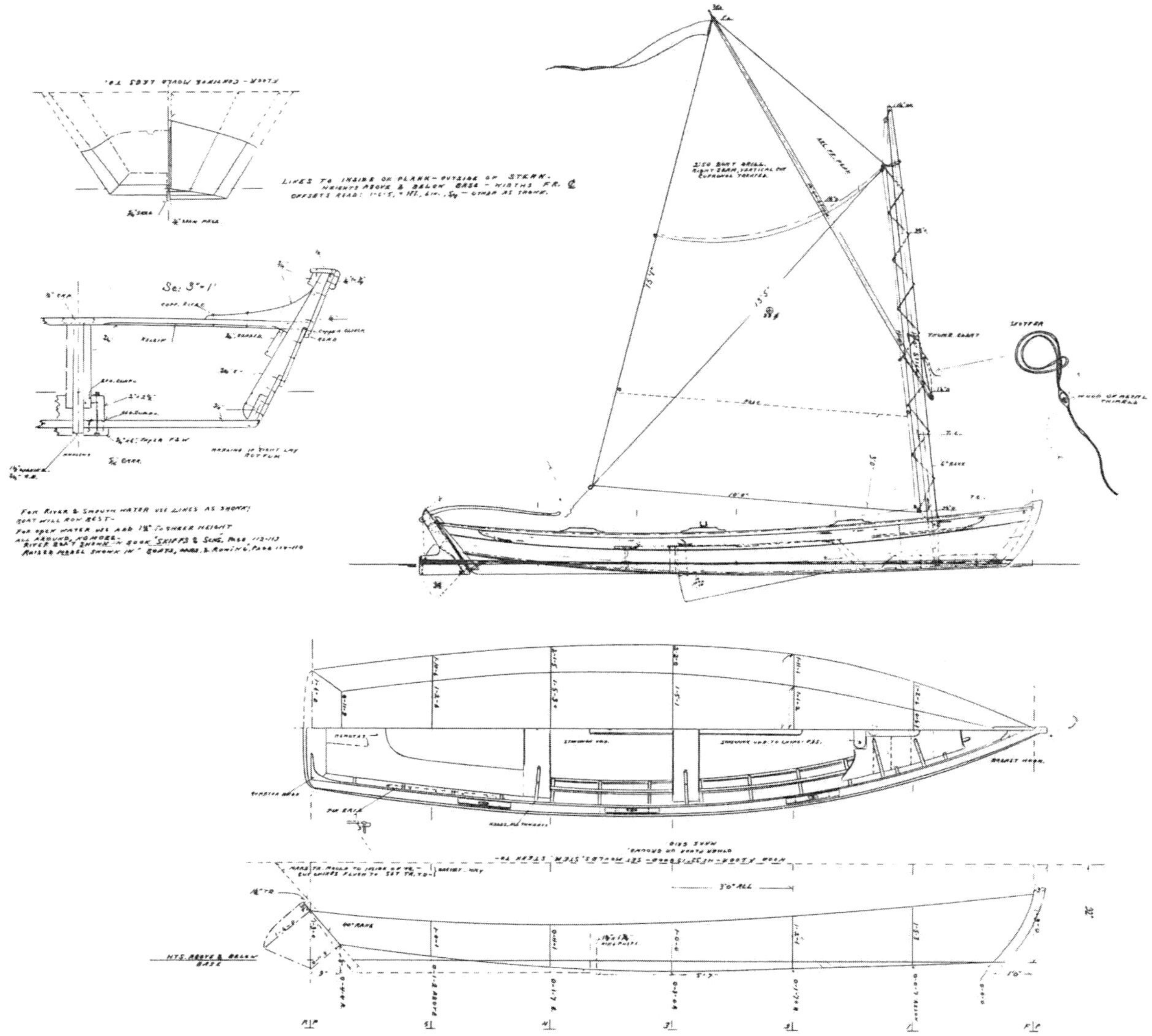

Waldo Howland was in need of a small skiff for use in the shallow bays and rivers around his winter home at Captiva Island, Florida. So the smaller model was lengthened out to 18 feet 6 inches, but the beam was kept the same. This made her a leaner and sharper boat and better with sail and oar due to the greater length. Her stability too was improved for the same reason. Howland is much enamored of *Dixie Belle.* In use, she has proved to be exactly what was required.

Some notable differences in the two boats in addition to length are the fully capped rail for stiffness, the three rowing positions, the two mast steps and the gate at the partners for sail balance, a brail fitted to the sail (this would work well on the smaller version, also), and a "centerboard rudder" for shoal water. This last should be included only where needed. Captain Pete commented: "Objections to it are: it's heavy, the boat will handle with the board up well enough but not real well; some

The 18½-foot Owl rows well.

A two-sail 18½-foot Good Little Skiff (R.D. Culler photos)

care must be taken in its building to allow for the swelling and distortion of the well part so the blade won't eventually jam, as the well hasn't the same support as one bolted in a boat. It's practical where very much needed; where it's not, there's no point at all in it, for it's not the most efficient."

With her extra length, the design really begins to show her Chesapeake heritage. I have often wondered how she would do with a two-sail rig. That's a lot of sail, as designed, and it might be interesting to split it up—say, using a sprit mizzen and main. There is no plan available for this, so you're totally on your own. It could, however, be a worthwhile experiment.

Remember, this boat was designed specifically for shoal waters. On a later example, built by Captain Pete for an owner on Cape Cod, the depth was increased by 1½ inches. The depth referred to here is the height from inside floor to top of gunwale amidships.

All together, these Good Little Skiffs are worthwhile craft for just "messing about." Whether it be sailing or rowing, clamming or fishing, or putzing with her maintenance on shore, you'll have fun with one of these boats.

Length overall: 16 feet 8½ inches
Molded beam: 5 feet 9½ inches
Draft: 1 foot 3¾ inches
Sail area: 182 square feet

Catboat For W.H. Hagan, Jr.

For anyone looking for a small daysailing catboat, this design should appeal. It was one of the last that the Captain laid down on paper before he died. This craft is one of the most sensible catboats I have ever seen, even though the V-bottomed construction is somewhat unusual. Pete was a lifelong proponent of the V-bottom style of construction. He felt it could be used successfully with a variety of hull forms; his design work is a testament to the success of this concept.

This little cat's length is 16 feet molded, 16 feet 8½ inches overall. Her beam is modest by present-day standards, being just 6 feet to the outside of the planking. The little vessel's draft is more than that of most cats today, and her molded depth is great for a Culler design, being nearly 2 feet. In fact, except for her V-bottom, this catboat conforms closely to the Old Man's requirements for a catboat in *Skiffs and Schooners*:

"Whether or not a person likes a cat is beside the point; he must admit the rig is fairly simple for the area it can spread. I think for present-day use, a cat can be greatly improved. I would give a catboat a fairly modest beam as cats go, more deadrise with some reverse in the sections, high, light quarters, and some overhang aft. I would give her generally sharp lines with some slight increase in hull depth and would use a fair amount of inside ballast, or

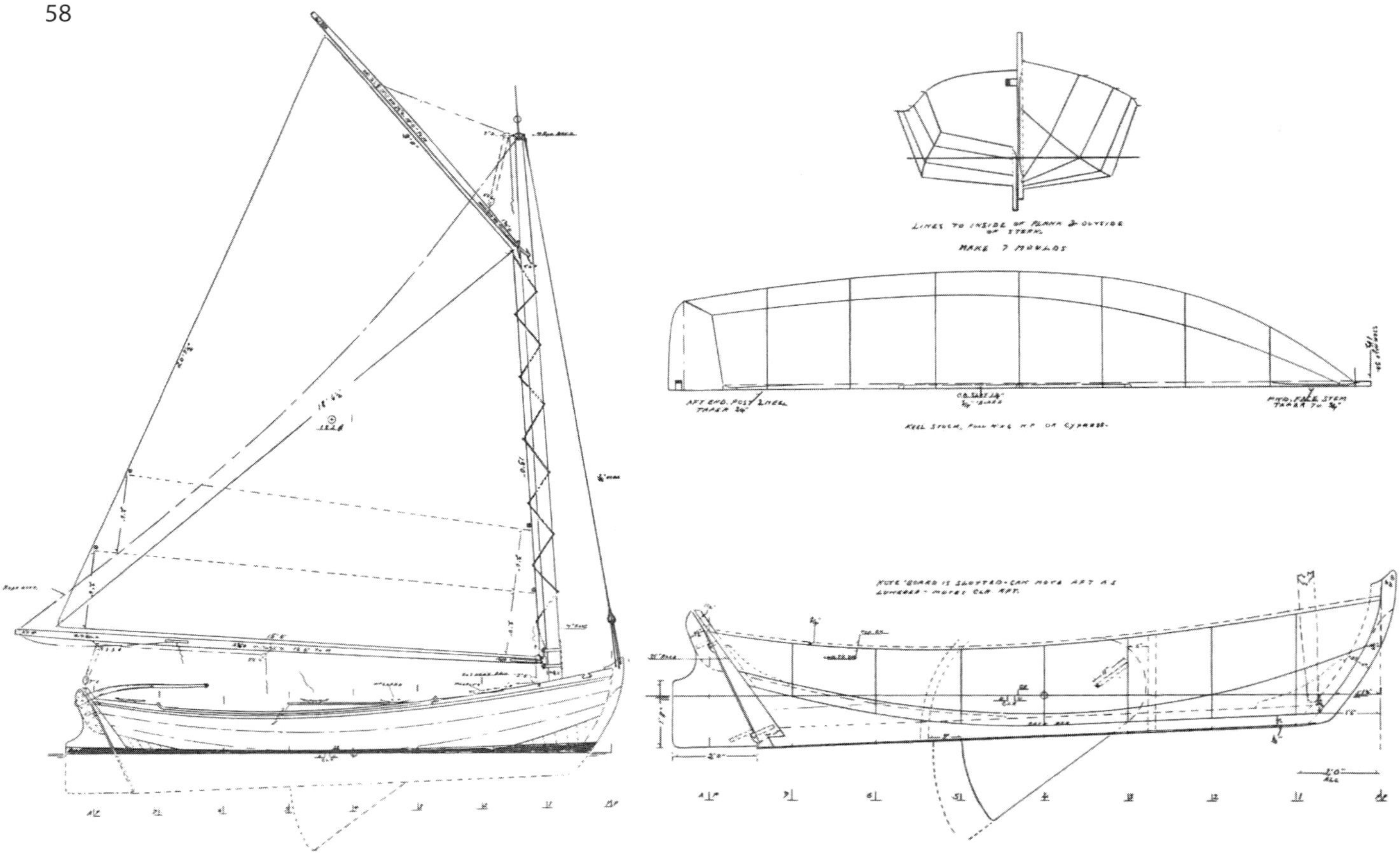

Sail plan, body plan, half-breadth, and profile of the 16-foot 8½-inch catboat.

outside ballast if expense were not important. I'd want a good amount of outside deadwood, and along with the sharper lines a somewhat smaller centerboard and a rudder that was not oversize. She would have a fairly sharp hull of modest displacement. Such a catboat would sail very well with a smaller rig. The gear would be a bit lighter. A lot of the brutishness of the overdeveloped cat would vanish, and if the designer had any art in his pen, the boat would be far better to look at than some of the cats now being built.

"Excuse my biased opinion, but I think Pete Culler had more than a little "art in his pen. "Anyone who studies this catboat design as a whole, and then in detail, will most certainly agree.

My eyes immediately focus on the general appearance of the boat—the nicely formed stem profile, sheer, and transom rake; the rudder shape; the way the rig "fits"; and the exquisite deadeye in the forestay. The rigging is all simple, and easily handled and maintained. The non-fouling traveler is efficient, strong, and good looking. The lapstrake planking adds much to the appearance of sheer, chine run, and the boat as a whole.

The details enhance the overall character of the design. The buffalo rails set off the sheer, and the generous deck, nicely crowned, gives good reserve stability and a fine place to plop your fanny, which the slight coaming allows without pain. The centerboard is small but more effective because of the slotted pin that allows the center of lateral resistance (CLR) to move aft as it drops down. The outside transom post is strongly constructed and thus allows a moderate rudder area. The V-bottom gives the hull a fine entry, good deadrise, and high quarters with a good form of run.

The boom has a gooseneck and the gaff has jaws. It's possible to either lace the luff or use hoops.

This little cat would not be cheap to have built professionally. There is much work with the bottom staves on both ends. And the deck, washrails, centerboard trunk, and bow section would take time to build. Her bow must be built stout. With the large rig set well forward, this is where cats go to hell first.

If you're an amateur, well, to heck with counting hours: go to it, take your time, step by step. Build her as she is designed and I'm sure you'll be pleased with the result.

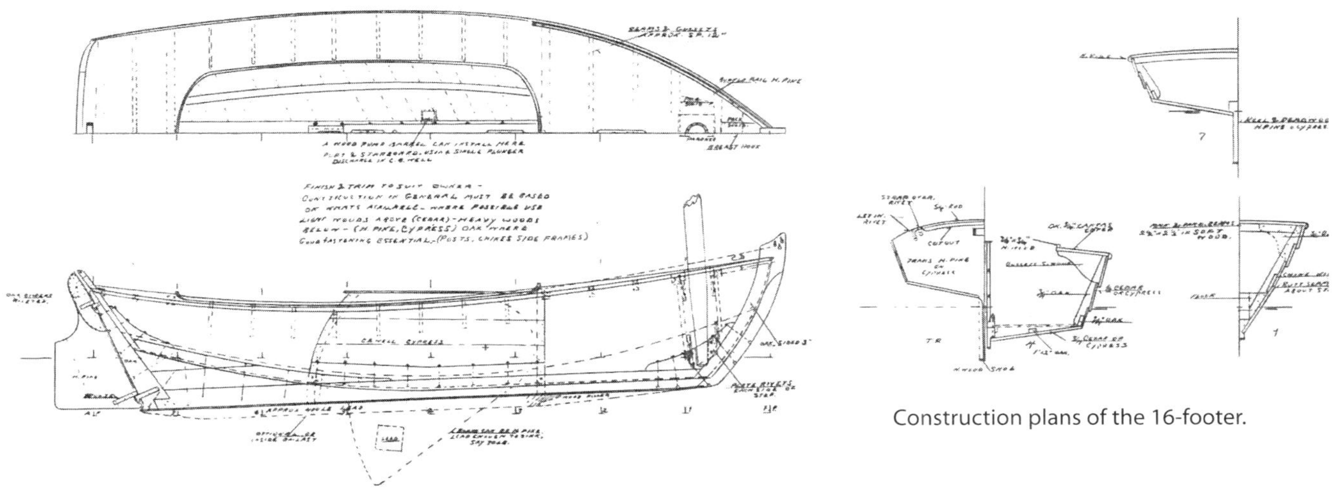

Construction plans of the 16-footer.

Beachboat *Java*

Length overall: 15 feet 9 inches
Beam: 4 feet 8 inches
Light draft: 8 inches
Sail area: 62 square feet

V-Bottomed Pod

Length overall:11 feet 6 inches
Beam: 3 feet 5 inches
Sail area: 38 square feet

Beachboat *Java*; V-Bottomed Pod For Paul Glaser

These two boats are essentially the same. They are both V-bottomed, double-ended beachboats. The smaller is a shrunken version of the larger. Both were developed early in Captain Pete's design career.

Among his papers and in the margins of his boating magazines there are numerous sketches of boat profiles, sail plans, and many construction notes. These go all the way back to the late 1920s, when he was building *Spray*. He started early to shape the ideas that would eventually become the body of work now known distinctively as "Culler."

On the list of boats built at Pete's Hyannis shop, the 11-foot version built for Paul Glaser is listed as #6. *Java,* the larger boat built for Waldo Howland, is #8. Both men were associated with the Captain during his seagoing career and, of course, Waldo Howland became his employer.

For a time, Paul Glaser and his family chartered *Spray* each summer season. The Cullers considered the Glasers good passengers, mostly because of Paul's sense of humor, which is indispensable on a boat. Prior to a cruise, the Glasers would busy themselves with inventive contraptions such as a toy duck that would walk up the side of a bulkhead and across the overhead upside down; or a full-size replica of a Banks anchor carved out of balsa wood and painted black that would be hoisted up the mainmast when entering port.

Later, the Glasers acquired a small Tancook schooner and found they needed a tender that could be stowed on deck. Eleven feet was the length limit. Remembering Glaser's puckishness, Pete designed and built him a pixie of a boat.

She is slight and dainty, but will still carry Ma, Pa,

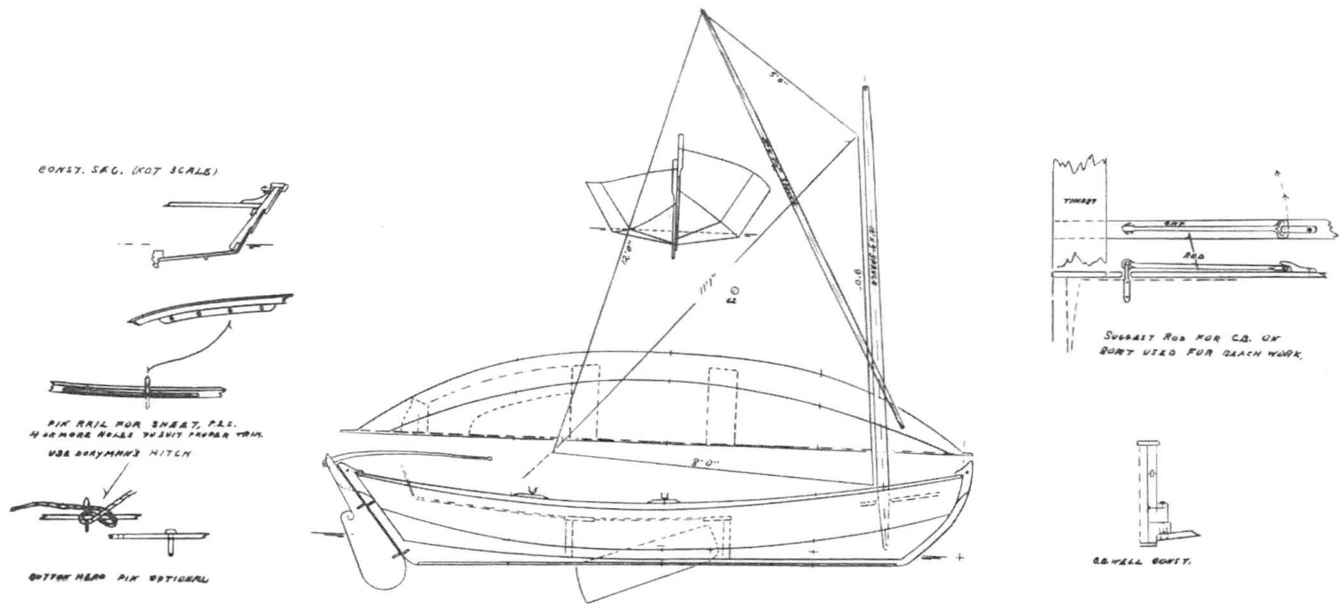

Plans of Waldo Howland's beachboat *Java*.

Junior, and the groceries for a cruise. Because she is very sharp underwater, she rows extremely well. With only one person aboard, she whisks along with a barely perceptible wake. Under sail the boat is surprisingly fast. Because of the long, deep rudder, a long tiller is required for an easy helm. A hinged Norse type could be used, for the sternsheets are confined and it's a bother lifting the tiller over your head when you wish to change helm. This applies also to *Java*.

When a cruise was over, the Glasers' toy contraptions were usually left behind and given to George Kelley's growing brood. Kelley remembered them very well when he recently built his version of the 11-footer and called her *Elf*.

Both of these boats are difficult to build as a result of their double-ended, V-bottomed construction. Of primary difficulty are fitting the chines and hewing the bottom staves in the ends. Recently, however, an amateur built the 11-foot version as his third boatbuilding project, and did a fine job of it. If you think you can do it, you probably can!

Here are some comments by Captain Pete on *Java*. "Here is a small boat built for Waldo Howland and called *Java*, after one of the ancestral whaleships. She is 15 feet 9 inches overall, with a 5-foot beam, and is very handy under oars and sail. She's about as dry as they come, and a fine seaboat. She's really a rowboat with auxiliary sail, but is quite fast and handy under canvas, being very sharp bottomed. She has a fair-size board and an extremely well-cut sail, cut by an old-time sailmaker who understands the sprit. With tanned canvas, green and colonial yellow, and trimmed out in barn red, she is a striking craft."

Indeed, she is striking to those who have seen her. Probably more people have seen this design than any other of Captain Pete's boats, although few realize it. In 1968 Pete built two for Miles Lane, the driving force behind Savannah's Museum of the Sea. These were to be used as ship's boats on the bark *Cruz del Sur*. One of them found herself carrying the Captain and crew ashore from the costumed slaver brig *Unicorn* in the first episode of the TV series "Roots." When one of Pete's friends, who knew of the upcoming scene, told the Old Man to watch his television that night to see one of his boats, the Captain responded, "What television?" Pete never owned one.

Interior details of a 15-foot 9-inch beachboat for the bark *Cruz del Sur*. (Pete Culler photo)

The 11½ -foot pod (beachboat) showing off her shape. Note the swelling of the chine log as it runs forward into the stem to give better landing for fastening the bottom staving. (Pete Culler photo)

Plans of the 11½-foot V-bottomed pod for Paul Glaser.

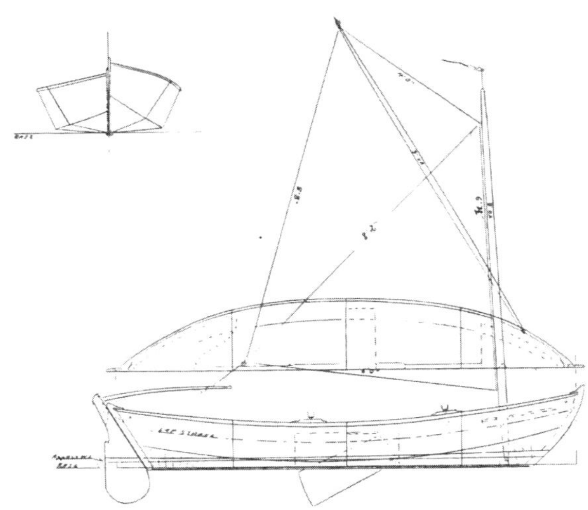

Skiffs For Maynard and Anne Bray

Maynard Bray Skiff

Molded length overall: 17 feet
Molded beam: 4 feet 9¼ inches
Molded depth: 14⅝ inches
Sail area: 96 square feet

Anne Bray Skiff

Length overall: 17 feet 9 inches
Molded beam: 4 feet 8¾ inches
Molded depth: 1 foot 5 inches
Sail area: 91 square feet

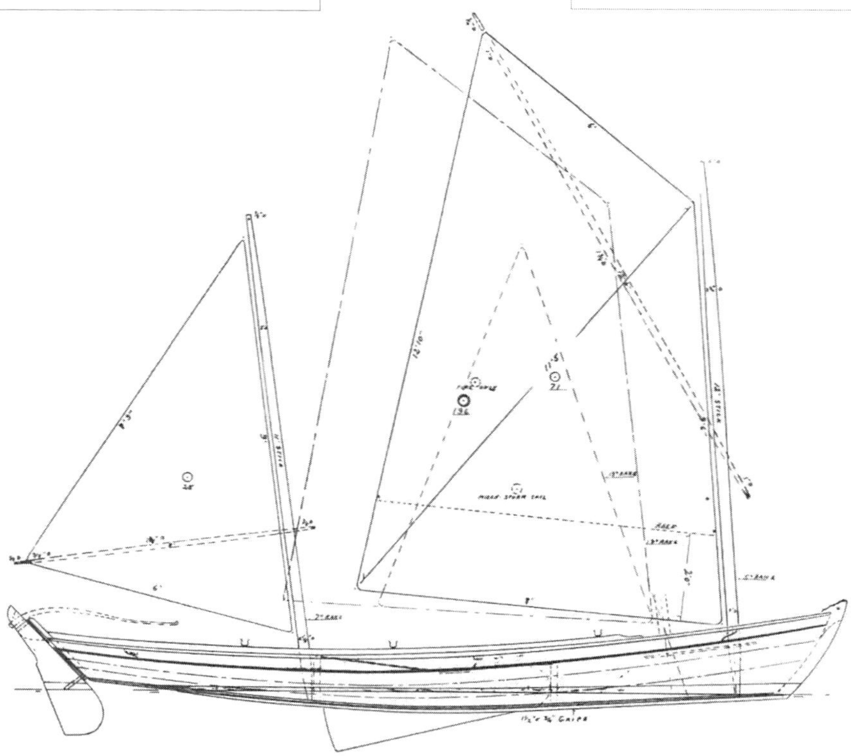

Sail plan of the skiff designed for Maynard Bray.

A great bugaboo for any boat designer is the client who does not know what he wants. Worse yet is the client who knows very well what he wants—but it is something that is completely unworkable from the standpoint of the designer's experience. Many designers who need the work will wade through such a job, cursing the whole time behind the client's back. Pete, a man of strong, principled integrity, and somewhat irascible too, usually showed such clients the door, sometimes at the end of his foot.

On the positive side, when a competent designer is handed a design problem within his specialty by a knowledgeable and experienced client, great things can happen. There is usually a give-and-take in the creative process, and the shared learning experience ends up benefiting both parties.

Such was the case with the two skiffs discussed here.

Maynard and Anne Bray are small-boat sailors of long standing. They needed small boats to act as tenders to their island camp in Penobscot Bay, Maine, which has no beach or dock. Loading and boarding from the stern of a skegless flat-bottomed skiff off the gently sloping granite ledges seemed the best solution. In addition, they planned much pleasure sailing in and around the rocky shores of this sheltered piece of water. To meet these requirements, the West Coast beachboat was used for starters, then quickly altered to suit.

The resulting boat is skegless in both versions for easy stern loading, with a gripe set on center for good directional control, and the centerboard

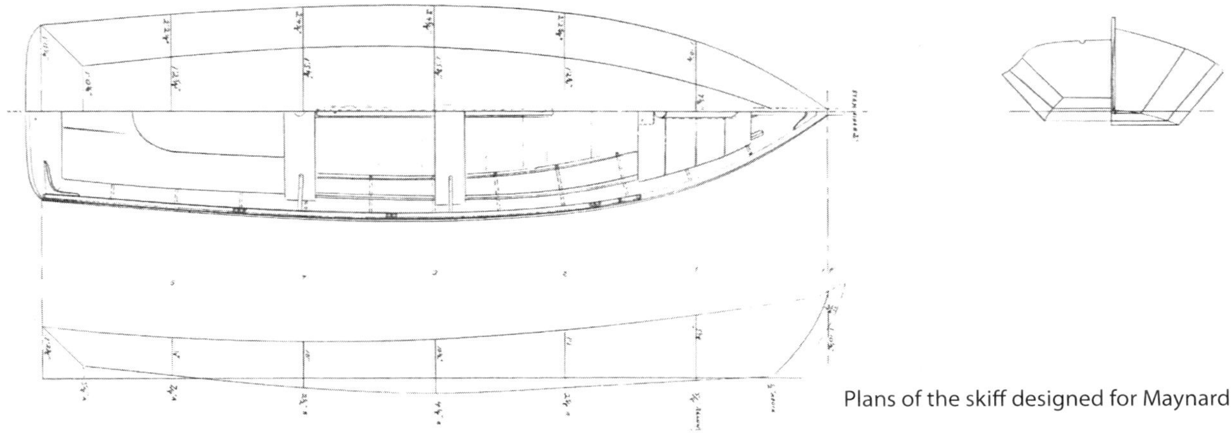

Plans of the skiff designed for Maynard Bray.

offset slightly to port. The sterns of both boats are quite wide and flared for such a slim craft. This is very buoyant and difficult to submerge when loading. The transom has good rake to "bring it closer to you" when boarding. In addition, the transom rake keeps the rudder from being pulled up by the mizzen when sailing; this sail is sheeted to the rudderhead. The most distinctive design feature is the tucked-up transom on one version. This was suggested by the Brays as a way to reduce the inherent abrasiveness of granite ledge. Such a transom would be constructed the same way as a punt-type bow. It would be no more difficult. Beyond that, it is standard skiff construction.

Flat-bottomed skiffs tend to be on the heavy side. Because of the intended use of the boats, however, and because they would be used primarily by Anne and the children, Pete worked out the following system to cut down on weight. These ideas apply to all skiffs for which weight is a factor.

- Reduce planking thickness from ½ inch to ⅜ inch and use four planks to a side instead of three.
- Use cedar or another lightweight wood instead of oak for the frames, and have more of them, spacing them 3 inches closer together.
- Use ⅝-inch bottom planks instead of ¾ inch and spline the seams—a simple operation on the table saw.
- Except for the chines, all other components normally made of oak or hardwood should be cedar or another lightweight durable wood. Hackmatack is a good choice.
- When reducing scantlings, a rough rule seems to be that more and lighter fastenings are required, spaced closer together.

It will do little good to follow the above suggestions unless you keep lightness in mind. Pick up two pieces of stock the same size and type of wood and invariably one will be lighter than the other. Try it at your local lumberyard with a dry stack of 2 x 4s. You'll be surprised at the differences you'll discover.

Pete found the rig, in general, to be most handy and versatile. The spar lengths are about the minimum for the sail area given. The spars will all stow easily in the boat. Pete felt "the Chesapeake mizzen to be the best of all mizzens to handle. The sheeting is not at all critical. Trim to a block on the rudderhead in this case. This sail sets well trimmed to the center of the boat, as it swings about like a barn door. The two steps for the foresail are essential, with the long, slotted partner and filler block. In the aft step is the working rig, the one that will most often be used, without mizzen. The third step, for using the mizzen as a storm sail, is optional, though I find it most useful on a rugged day when a reefed fore might be a little much. The lighter the spar stock the better. I have a weakness for little black spruce trees, about as tough as you can get for the weight."

The boats should row very easily with their narrow bottoms, low freeboard, and smooth run. The great flare gives them good capacity, stability, and dryness, and a good spread for the oarlocks. The oarlock-washrail is very handsome; it augments the low freeboard while keeping weight down. The rudder and centerboard are shallow to permit working around shallow rock ledges. The rudders are hung with the English beachboat system (see Appendix) and will kick up if they strike something. On the tucked-up

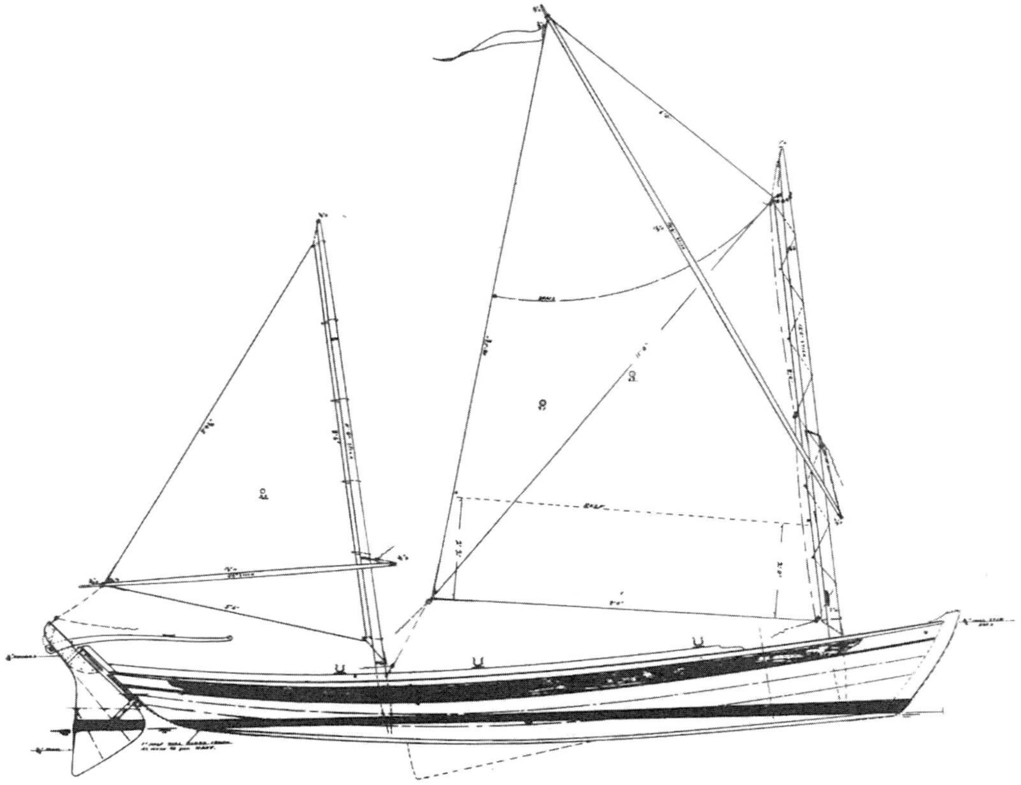

Plans of the skiff designed for Anne Bray.

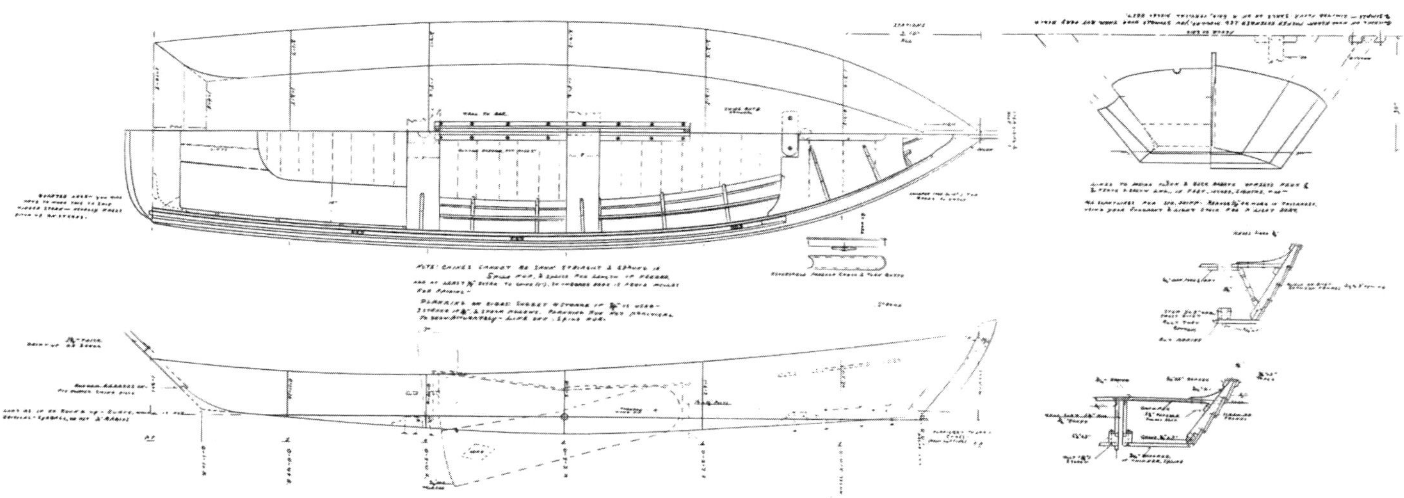

transom version, the rudder hardware will have to be strong, as the transom-mounted pieces are close together.

These boats are "specials," both in the requirements they were designed to fill and in terms of the design process that brought them about. If you have similar needs, by all means use them and take pride in ownership. If you feel the need for your own special boat, find yourself a competent designer who's willing—and have fun!

Length overall: 17 feet 7 inches
Molded beam: 5 feet 8 inches
Draft: 1 foot 2 inches
Sail area: 166 square feet

Daysailer For Dr. John Roche

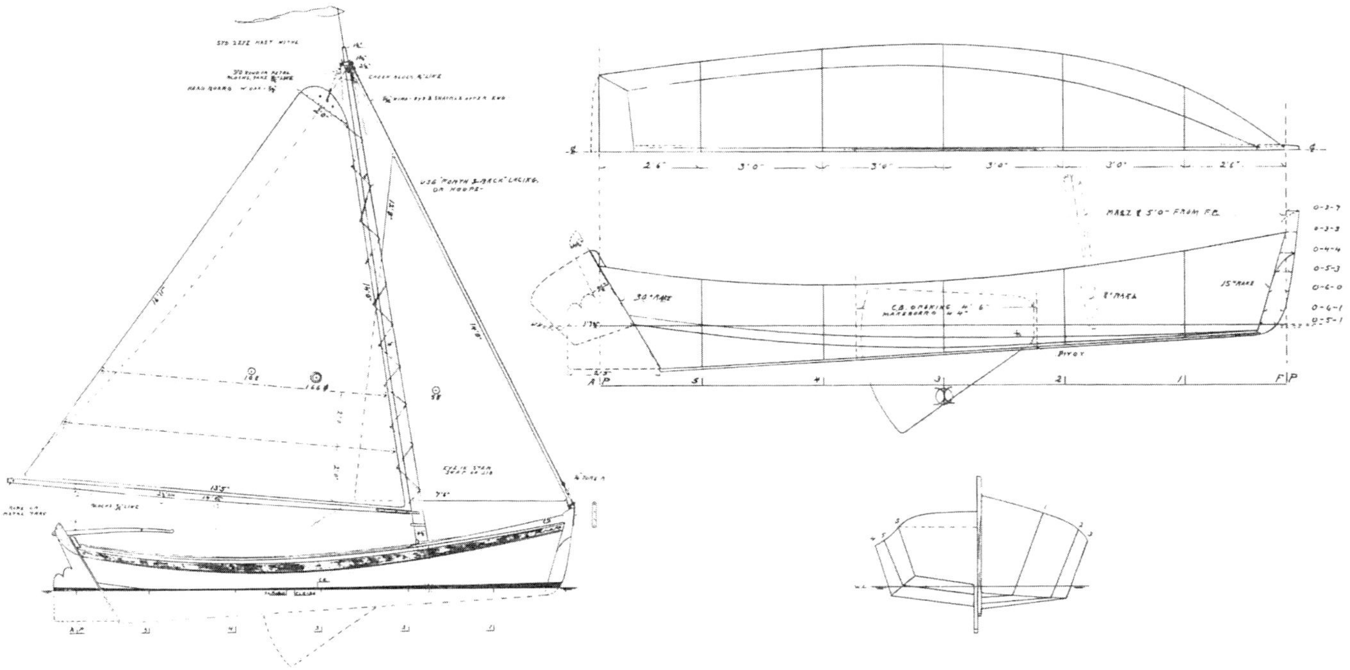

Plans of Dr. John Roche's l7-foot 7-inch daysailer.

This sturdy little daysailer was designed for Captain Pete's good friend Professor John Roche in 1963, for use in the waters of Pleasant Bay and Nantucket Sound.

At the time of her designing, Dr. Roche was a beginning boatbuilder, so there is a fair amount of detail included to meet his needs. This is an asset for anyone thinking about building the boat. It is a model that is eminently suited for an interested amateur.

The construction is "bay-style"—that is, the stiff keel, cross-planked, "herringbone" file bottom so ably developed by the Chesapeake Bay boatbuilders. Since Captain Pete discusses this type of construction with authority in *Skiffs and Schooners*, I'll quote him; his words have a timeless wisdom that I would not presume to improve on.

"The simple approach to building a file, or V-bottom, is only a modest variation from flat-bottomed skiff construction in that you can use the welltried, cross-planked, herringbone bottom. This is very strong, tough, and easy to repair. The only real trick in building it is—as in all boat carpentry—to get good fits, well fastened. It's often pointed out that the slight washboard effect on these bottoms slows a boat down. My own experience in rowing and sailing these craft is that if it does, it's not noticeable. Some folks think that the herringbone pattern is a benefit in a fast craft that planes—'lets her break out of it and get on top.' One can argue the point; my own feeling on it, based on designing and building this type, is that cross-planking does help.

"With the herringbone construction, a stout keel is a must, along with a couple of sister keelsons,

This little daysailer was inspired by the traditional Chesapeake Bay shrimpers. She is designed for shallow-water daysailing. (Photo courtesy Chesapeake Bay Maritime Museum)

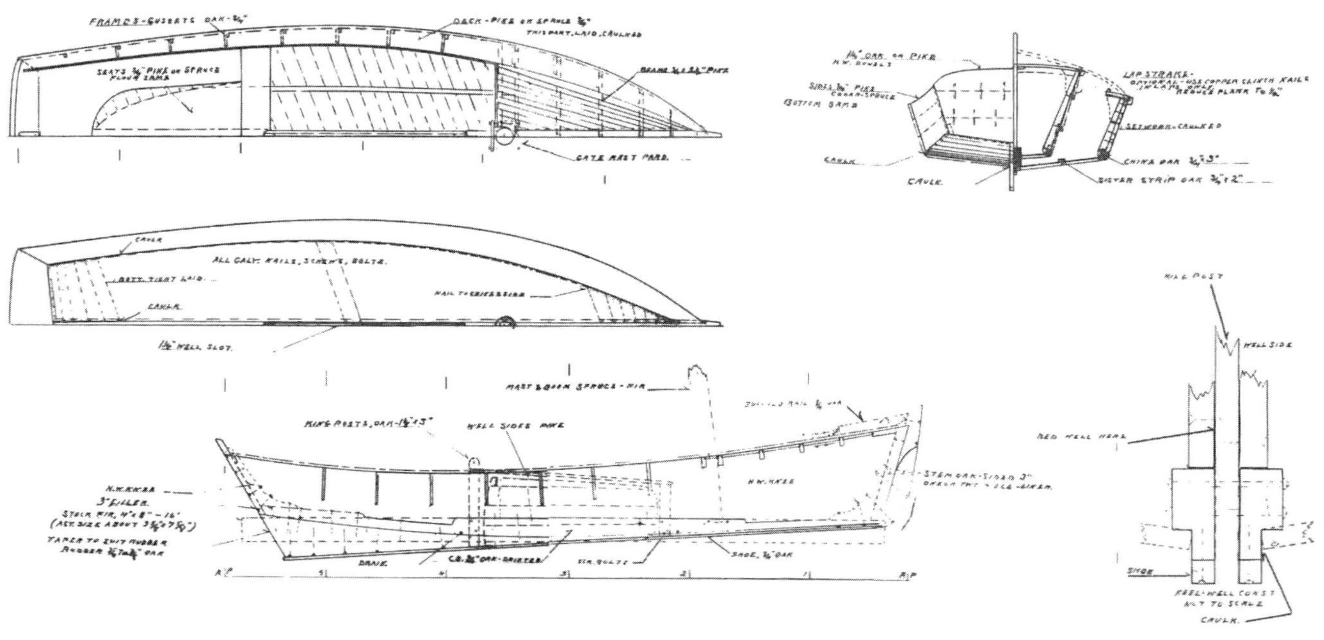

Construction plans for Dr. John Roche's 17-footer.

for there is no bottom framing unless the craft is of some size. On larger boats, two or more strongbacks are used; they are not true frames since they rest on the keelsons, chines, and, of course, on the main keel, being well bolted to all.

"In general, these craft, like the true flat-bottomed skiff, take only common sense and common care in their upkeep. Kept clean, well painted, properly stored and ventilated, they have a long life, even with much use, and seem to go on as long as any other type of construction, often outlasting more complicated hulls."

Although principally intended for Cape Cod waters, this model has proven equally effective in conditions as similar as Chesapeake Bay and as different as the lakes of Switzerland.

The sheer on this daysailer is particularly graceful, and is complemented by the buffalo rail forward, the slight coaming, the rake of the stem and transom and keel drag, which unite into a pleasing hull. Dr. Roche planked his version smooth, but the hull is eminently suited to lapstrake construction, and if you pad out your molds instead of beveling the laps, would make for a very shapely boat.

The centerboard area appears just right, coupled with the fair drag to the keel. This keel drag also allows good rudder area without extending the rudder below the boat's heel, which is of great advantage if you should ground out. The boat will beach easily, since she is primarily flat forward.

The rig is well balanced and uses the Bahama headboard and lacings. There are two reefs in the main; I would add one on the jib for versatility. With this ability to shorten sail and the reserve stability in her foredeck and washrails, she would be very able. The rig is basically handled from the cockpit.

The Professor used this boat for many years and was very happy with her. Her inspiration came from the old Bay shrimpers, and of course was modified to meet present-day requirements.

Dr. Roche, a respected Professor of Psychology at the local college in Hyannis, lives in the town of Harwich. His daily commute went right by Pete's shop and, more often than not, he would stop by at the end of the working day for a gam. To be sure, boats would be discussed, but Dr. Roche was always impressed by the depth and range of Pete's world view. The Captain would converse, knowledgeably, even within Dr. Roche's specialty.

It was in building this boat that the Professor learned a valuable lesson. Pete, of course, provided advice during those afternoon visits, and finally the boat was completed. At the first opportunity Pete stopped by to look over the finished boat. Naturally, Dr. Roche was anxious, with his pride held in check. Since it was late winter, the boat sat on sawhorses in the yard and was covered with canvas to keep out the elements. The Old Man walked over, lifted one corner of the cover, bent over, and looked at her bottom. "Looks good. Finest kind; she ought to sail well." That was the extent of his inspection. All you teak trim, varnish, and brass fanatics take note, and remember that the bottom is still the business end of any boat.

Daysailer For Dr. John Roche

Length overall: 14 feet 9 inches
Beam: 5 feet 3 inches
Draft: 1 foot 2 inches
Sail area: 100 square feet

This smart little daysailer is very similar to the 17-footer, both having been designed for the same gentleman, Dr. John Roche. The smaller one was designed a few years after the larger. It has more vee to its bottom, would foot and point better on that account, and has less capacity due to its shorter length. It would require less work to maintain, lay up, and launch for the same reason. For anyone who is excited by the 17-footer but requires less capacity and wishes to be challenged further by more vee in building, this plan should appeal. The boat would be easily trailerable. Striking and setting up the rig would be no chore.

This daysailer's inspiration lay in the fine Bahama dinghy model. The type's excellent sailing qualities were achieved by using a V-bottomed hull. She has a remarkably fine entry, good chine shape, and an excellent run. Dr. Roche reports that the sailing abilities of this 14-footer are impressive.

Perhaps the only item of the design that may give would-be builders pause is the V-bottomed construction, and of that, principally hewing and fitting the staves forward. As Pete said, this construction technique is "un-difficult." One clue is to "think airplane propellers"; that is, there is a twist to the staves that must be hewed out of thick stuff. Plywood won't work, because these curves are compound. Remember that the old way is the right way.

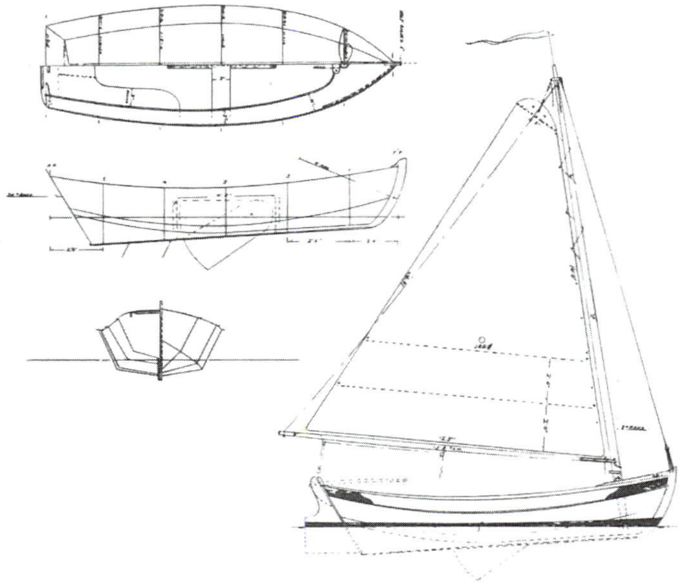

Above: Plans of Dr. John Roche's 14-footer.
Right: *Posy,* Dr. Roche 's V-bottomed daysailer, a Bahama dinghy type. (Pete Culler photo)

Rowing Skiff; Wheelbarrow Skiff For Dr. James Wallace

Rowing Skiff

Length overall: 14 feet 6 inches
Beam: 4 feet 6 inches

"I like to build rowboats for the sheer pleasure of rowing, but people will always ask you if you won't put a motor in them. I go out rowing just for the enjoyment of it, but most people hate physical exercise nowadays. I know all the clams and quahogs, and they put their horns up when I row by. But most people—I think sometimes my cat's got more sense than modern man!"

— Pete Culler in *A Yankee Way with Wood*

Here, first of all, is a flat-bottomed skiff designed just for rowing. She is very much along the lines of the Good Little Skiff. She is 14 feet molded, 14 feet 6 inches overall, with a narrow rockered bottom for good performance. Yet she has ample beam from her flaring lapstrake sides. This is an all-around handsome rowing skiff.

There are two rowing positions, with plenty of sternsheets for passengers. In addition, there is lots of room for gear, be it for fishing, clamming, or picnicking.

These flat-bottomed skiffs are very good designs for the backyard builder. It is no great chore to put them together. Build such a hull upside down to a grid or floor until the bottom and first two strakes are on. Then turn the hull over, reset and plumb, hang the sheerstrake, and finish out. To be fair, that's an over-simplification. There is much implied between those lines, but no mystery. Refer to standard works on boatbuilding for general information, and

Interior of the rowing skiff, which is very much on the Good Little Skiff model. Note the outboard sternpost. (R.D. Culler photo)

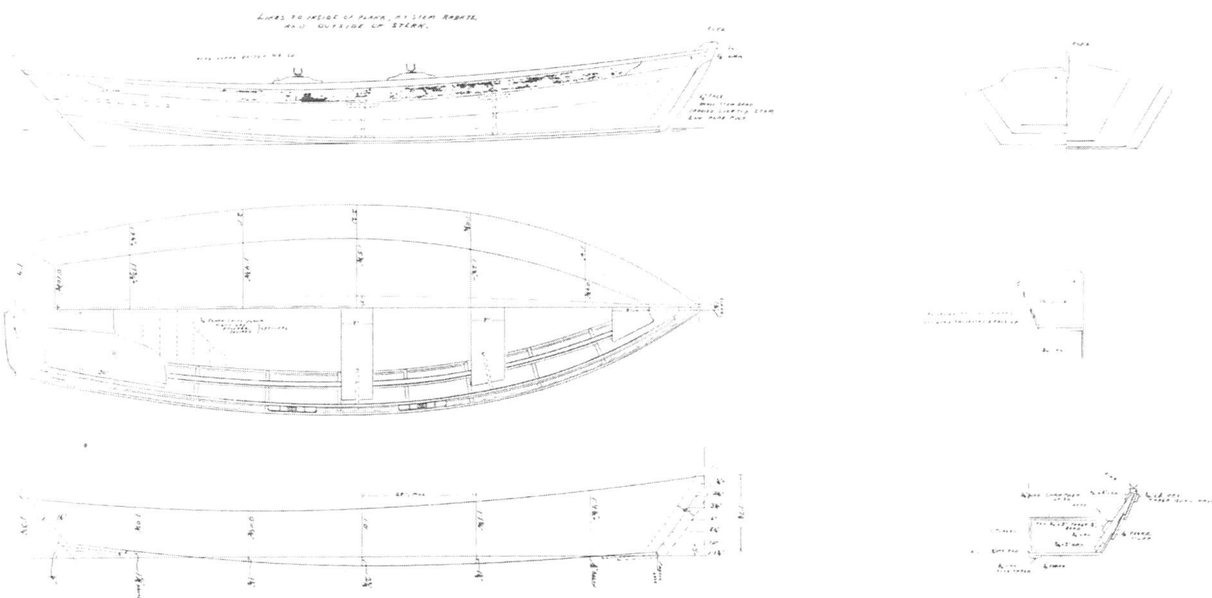

Plans of the 14½-foot rowing skiff.

above all else, use common sense. Being friendly with a local boatbuilder helps too.

Pete once referred to boatbuilding as a ritual, in that each step must follow the other, in continuity, until the job is finished. I prefer the analogy of climbing a mountain. You get to the top, step by step. Patience and some mental stamina are required, but believe me, the view from the summit is grand! Remember, too, that mountains come in all sizes. This little skiff is not Mount Everest.

Wheelbarrow Skiff

Length overall: 14 feet 6 inches
Beam: 4 feet 6 inches
Sail area: 63 square feet

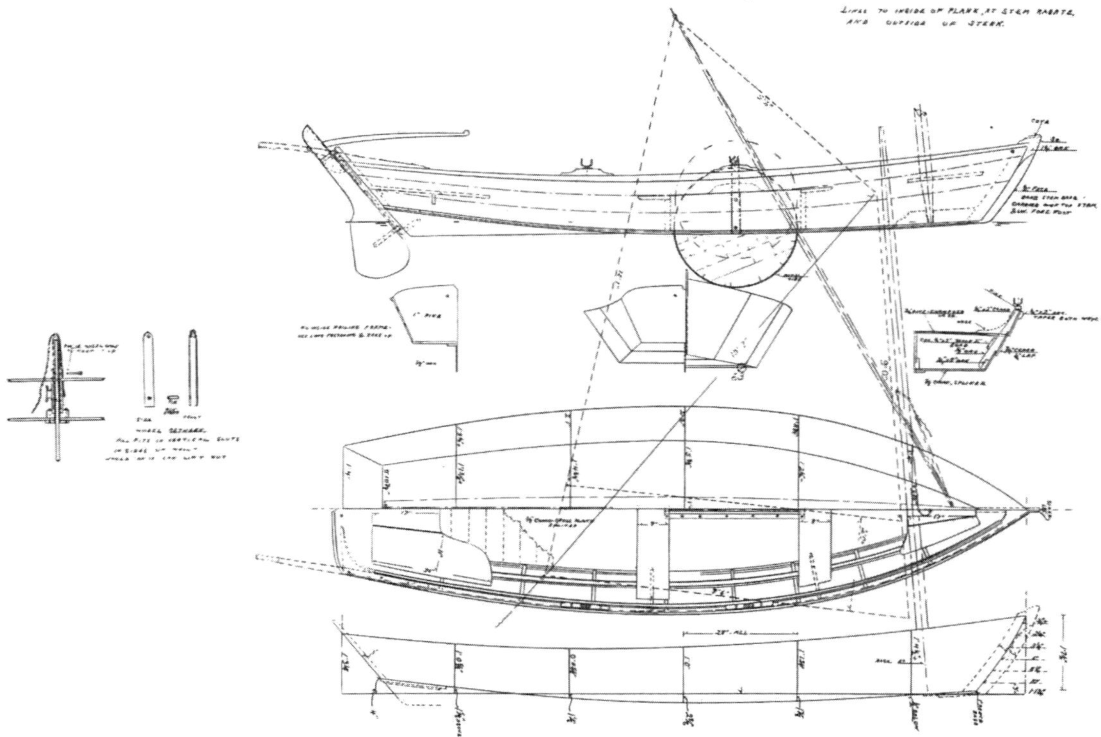

Plans of the wheelbarrow skiff.

With shorefront property at a premium and space in overcrowded anchorages becoming scarce, it is increasingly difficult for the sailor to get his boat in the water. To be sure, trailers have done yeoman duty for years and trailerable boats are very common. However, parking is often a problem, and maintenance costs and complexity are increased with a trailer.

The answer just might be the wheelbarrow boat. For those who live close to the water, say, a quarter to a half mile, such a boat would be a good choice.

This "boat with legs" is a 14-foot 6-inch rowing skiff fitted with a round centerboard that locks in position. The boat is wheeled about by grabbing the stern "handles" and pushing. The idea is not new. The concept was noted years ago when Howard Chapelle printed the plans for the *Farmer's Daughter,* an 8-foot Seal Cove skiff, in *Boatbuilding.*

The Seal Cove skiff had a non-removable wheel located just aft of the stem. This is fine for an 8-footer where weight doesn't amount to much, but 14 feet would be quite a lot to lift. Why not move the wheel aft where it will bear more weight, and in addition, use it for lateral resistance as a centerboard? This is just what Pete did in designing the wheelbarrow boat. The Seal Cove skiff was pictured in *The Mariner's Catalog, Volume 2.* It gave Pete an opportunity to discuss the concept, which intrigued him. *In The Mariner's Catalog, Volume 3,* he discusses the wheelbarrow boat. This led directly to Dr. James Wallace's commission of the design you see here. The following is excerpted from Pete's discussion of the craft.

"Though the Seal Cove skiff no doubt worked

fine for the intended use, I thought I could do better than have an iron or wood wheel in a rather turbulent well forward. Any boat should be designed for its intended use, and, since the boat is portable, the wheel enters into its design.

"The craft should be of fairly light construction say, lapstrake sides, modest oak frame, bottom splined, and cross-planked for tightness on shore, for she's an out-of-water, live-at-home boat. I would paint the bottom white, whatever colors are used elsewhere. The wheel should be about 2 feet in diameter, of ⅜-inch oak, drifted up like any centerboard and with a metal tire. The centerboard well should be built like any other, except that it has slotted sides to take the iron strap over the wheel. This strap should have a thimble seized on top. In practice, the strap (of, say, ¼-inch by 2-inch iron) rides in slots, free enough to move up and down. The rope lanyard carries the weight of the boat, acts somewhat as a shock absorber, and adjusts the height of the wheel. A pin or wedge of some sort will no doubt be needed if one wants to secure the board all the way up. Naturally, the amount of wheel exposed below the bottom to roll on can be adjusted.

"Here is where I borrow from the Chinese. A wheel with an axle well up in the boat, and well aft, should lighten the load and balance, like an Oriental wheelbarrow. The raked stern is to keep things clear of one's feet, as well as to make the boat dry and able aft. The barrow handles can be the subject of artistic tinkering. I think an iron rod across them will add strength, enable one to push with his body, and serve as a sheet traveler also. This last, though the sail should be loose footed, allows for a big rig in an attempt to smarten things up and overcome somewhat the other failings. I think little craft need a big rig, and can use it, as there is much human ballast for their size. You can always reef if it blows, but to be dull in light weather is no fun.

"How it will all work only trial can tell. I do know that if you hit the beach with the wheel well down under a press of sail, she might run out and capsize on dry land. That would be something new. You could possibly get cited for a motor vehicle violation."

Dr. James Wallace wheels his boat home. As an admitted experiment, the craft worked out very well in practice. (Jim Odell photo)

Jim Odell sculls the wheelbarrow boat out for a sail. (Joanne Burke photo)

Yawlboat For *Integrity*

Length overall: 12 feet 6 inches
Beam: 5 feet
Sail area: 67 square feet

Comments by Pete Culler

This design has proved to be a good carrier, is very able for her size, sails well, and rows far more easily than one would think, considering her bulk. She was originally designed to be a schooner's yawlboat. In terms of both design and construction, she is quite heavy. This seems to enhance her ability rather than detract from it. This type of craft is not suited to lightweight construction.

Considering the number built, very few of this general type; for sail, power, or rowing, ever got down on paper as formal plans. In fact, it's a hard type to present formally, though not extremely difficult to build, once one understands the many aspects not present in the usual hull. While now mostly forgotten, and never very well understood in some areas, these craft are, to some extent, connected to the log canoe, which they eventually replaced. That is, much is based on hewing and chopping, and fairing in by eye. Though having built and designed many cross-planked craft, I am still unable to present fully the methods on paper. Chapelle's *Boatbuilding* does it better than any, and should be referred to.

To begin with, these boats are 80 percent art, some skill with tools, and very little science, and this last of a crude, barnyard sort. What this seems to produce is a superior craft compared to the more modern type of V-bottomed boat—long lasting, economical, and often handsome. Just why this is so is hard to say. Possibly it is because the original developers of the type had a past of much experience. They just plain knew what they were doing.

Materials are not critical. It is possible to build these craft right out of a local lumberyard, plus a bit of poking around in the woods. In case one thinks there are no more woods left, assure him there are, with the same bullbriars, bugs, snakes, and all, along with some stuff very suited to natural knees.

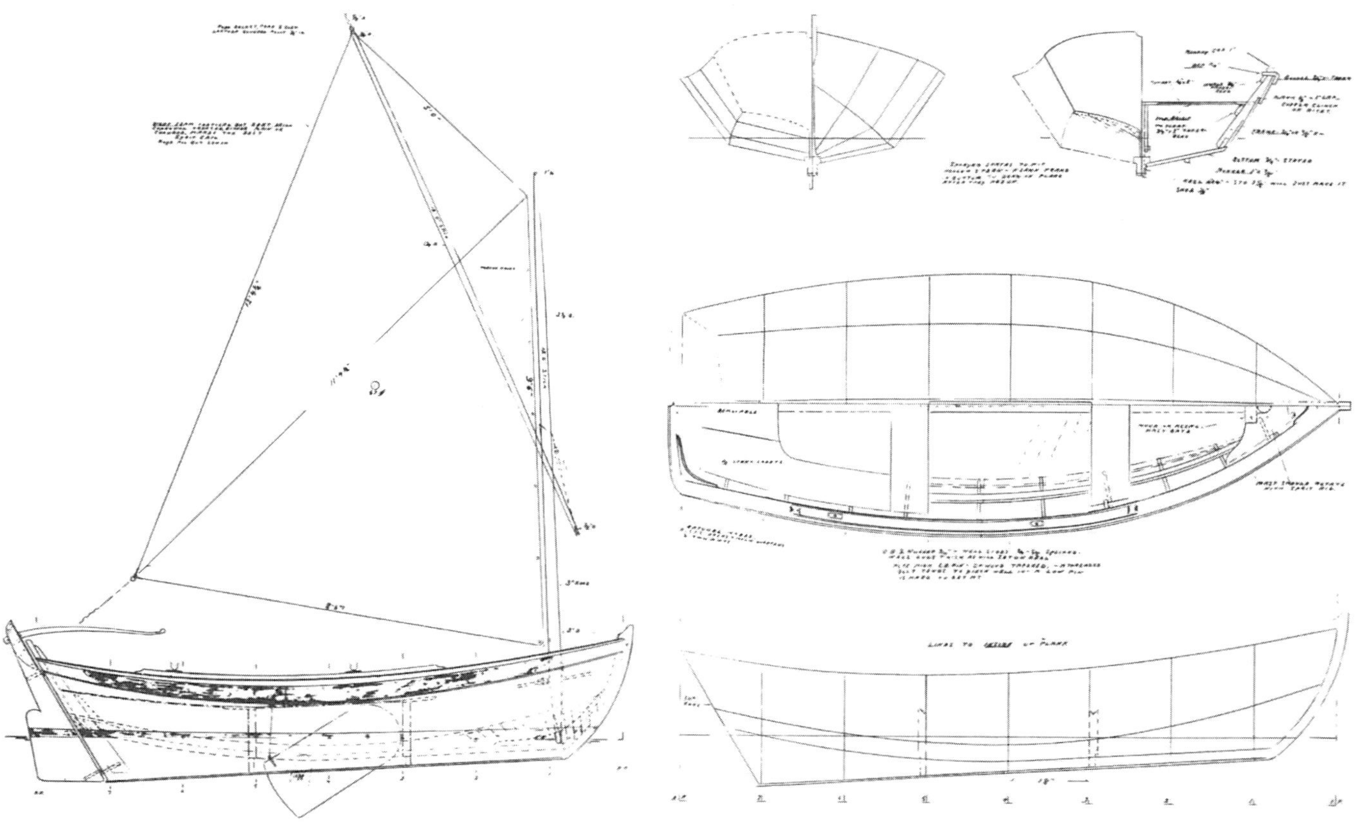

Plans of the 12½-foot ship's yawlboat.

Above: The 12½-footer built by Hornby Island Boatworks, in British Columbia, in 1977. (Hornby Island Boatworks photo)

Right: *Integrity's* little yawl, built by Captain Pete. (R.D. Culler photo)

Except for the lapped sides, which are copper fastened—I prefer lapped sides in a small craft, though carvel will do—galvanized iron fastenings are used throughout in craft of my build, unless others are requested. These last quite well and are very stiff. With the amount of wood in these craft, they can be readily refastened in their old age, if the wood is sound. My system is: "Nail where you can, screw where you must, and bolt where you have to."

One now hears nothing but stainless, Monel, and bronze as the fastenings. The economics of these is unsound in the type of craft being discussed. It's my experience that fastening troubles compound in direct proportion to the amount of electric gear on a boat. These small, open deadrises have at most a flashlight, and thus no other problems. Building a lightweight clipper pulling boat is another matter. Stock is very light, scantlings small, and fastenings small and many, a large part of which are not buried and thus subject to sandpaper abrasion. These craft are at best difficult to repair in their old age. Here non-ferrous fastenings make good sense.

Here are some hints learned the hard way. It always does pay to lay down full size. Personally, I use only four molds in boats this size and fullness—midship, two forward, and one aft—but more do no harm, and may be better. Staving of the bottom should start forward, never aft, as one loses the wedging effect. It's hard to say just when to change from butt to lap at chine with the bottom staves. It depends on the model and how one starts and manages the staves—usually somewhere around mold 2. These staves forward, and often aft with a hollow stern, must be shaped out of thick stuff. These staves can be laid tight, or with a caulked seam. Integrity's boat is tight seam. Fitting staves takes time, for there is much shaping, beveling, and final smoothing up. To some modern builders the procedure makes no sense; they think they know a better way. However, the right and traditional way makes a good boat.

These types require no steaming, though a little kerosene soaked into a plank limbers it wonderfully. One must be prepared to shape all planks, chines, thwart clamps, and so on. Spile and shape, then bend. The modern notion of edge setting makes these craft, or most any other type for that matter, extremely difficult. Again I say, do not edge set. Shape, and it will wrap right in place.

The stem rabbet is picked up from the floor keel rabbet until it dies out and becomes a bevel, and chine bevels are arrived at in fairing down the bottom. It is doubtful whether such things can be projected on paper with any degree of accuracy, which no doubt is why they never were.

Fairing down for bottom planking, doing bow staving, and in this particular case, a little of the bottom aft, are the most time-consuming parts of the whole building job.

If possible, get chines out of a matched pair of boards, or in some cases alongside each other in a wide board. There seems to be less fight to get them to lay alike than if they are out of widely different stock. This applies to a great extent throughout the boat—any boat, for that matter. Things go easy with matched stock—a point now more or less forgotten and not helped by mass-produced stock.

It will be noted that lines are to inside of plank and to back rabbet. There are no offsets shown, as the lines are simple and the scale is large, so they can be lifted directly from the plan. The more usual method was to lift directly from a half model. There will be some errors, which is what laying down full size is about, to get things fair. One must remember that some art and judgment are needed—small-craft building of this nature has yet to become a cut-and-dried science. Even in building several craft alike over the same mold, variations do creep in, for one is building with wood. This is just a part of boatbuilding.

A further word on bow staving. The more the builder keeps the staving upright after starting, and for a while going aft, the more hollow the forefoot he will have—a sought-after condition. The cross section here in the finished craft will not exactly follow a drafted section. The sooner and more the staves are raked aft right forward, the more bulbous the forefoot will be. This seems to be a disadvantage in sailing and rowing models. Getting a reasonably hollow forefoot takes some care.

Sailing Sampan

Length overall: 11 feet
Sail area: 52 square feet

The great seafaring tradition of the Orient, principally of Japan and China, has been with us for a long time thousands of years at least. Anything that has stood the test of time that long must be based on sound principles. Many Oriental designs that may at first appear odd to the Western eye soon reveal their subtlety and common sense to the observer with an open mind.

In recent years there has been a renewed interest in Oriental designs as cruising vessels. Some successful junks and sampans have been built, notably from the board of Tom Gillmer, who apparently understands their qualities. That they are able and seakindly in experienced hands is unquestioned by those who have observed them in action. Some World War II sailors remember all too well being battered about by a typhoon in their great warships, while alongside them a junk was calmly and peacefully riding it out with a cooking fire burning on deck!

What we have here is a smart little boat that draws on that centuries-old Oriental tradition. It's a sampan, or "butthead," as Pete would put it. She was originally designed for his good friend Hudson Baxter to be a yacht tender. Later, the boat was adapted for sail. As a tender, Captain Pete said, she "stowed well on deck, was a fine seaboat, a great carrier, and a good beachboat with her long snout, as one can step ashore dry." Once empty, the boat hauled up on the beach easily and sat upright on her flat bottom.

Although the Captain mentioned only stowing

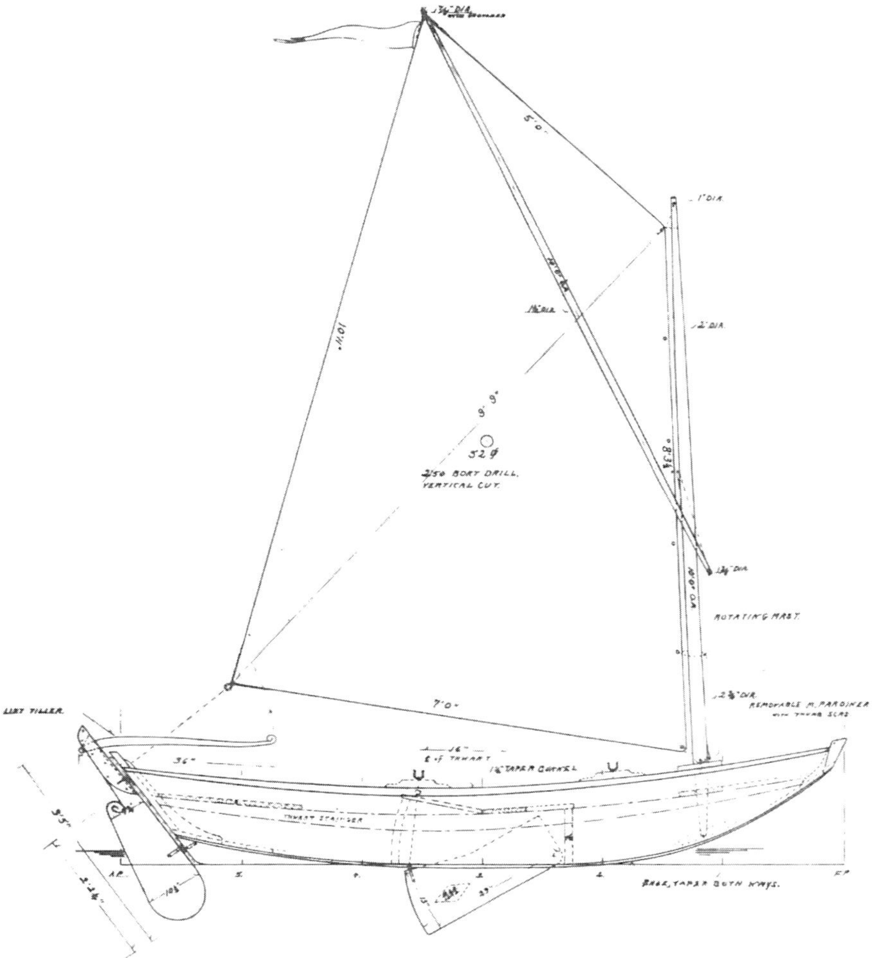

Sail plan and lines of the sailing sampan.

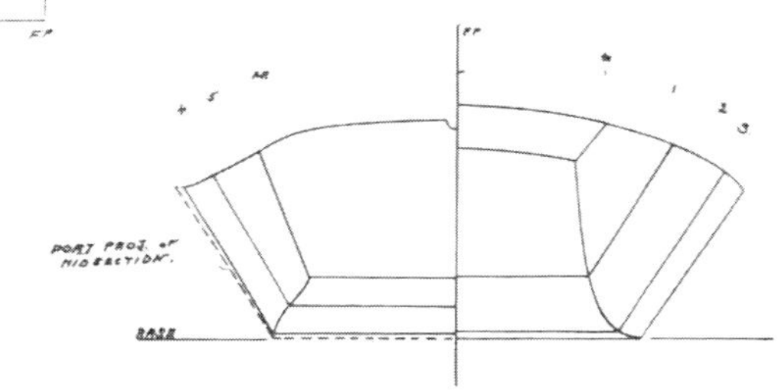

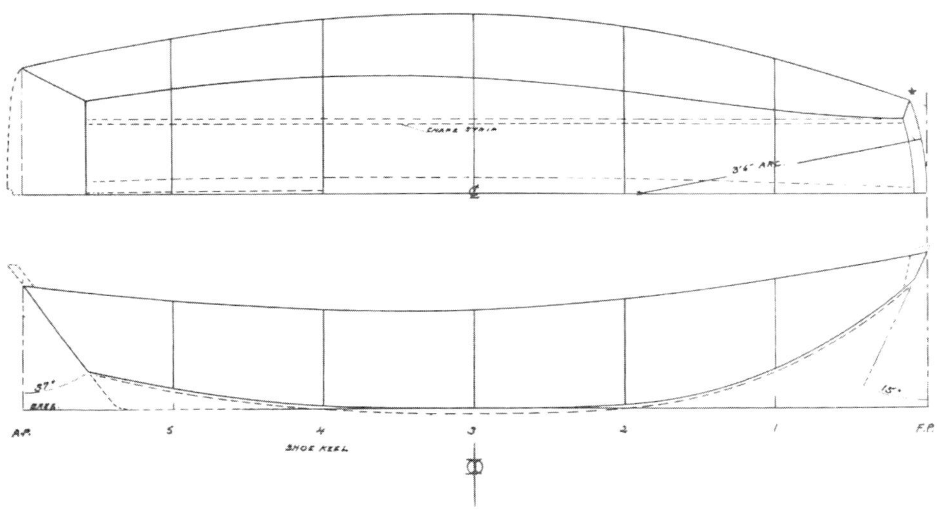

Right: Brian Kelley's I I-foot sampan *Jade Arrow* is built to sail. Note the shape 0f the chine log. (John Burke photo)

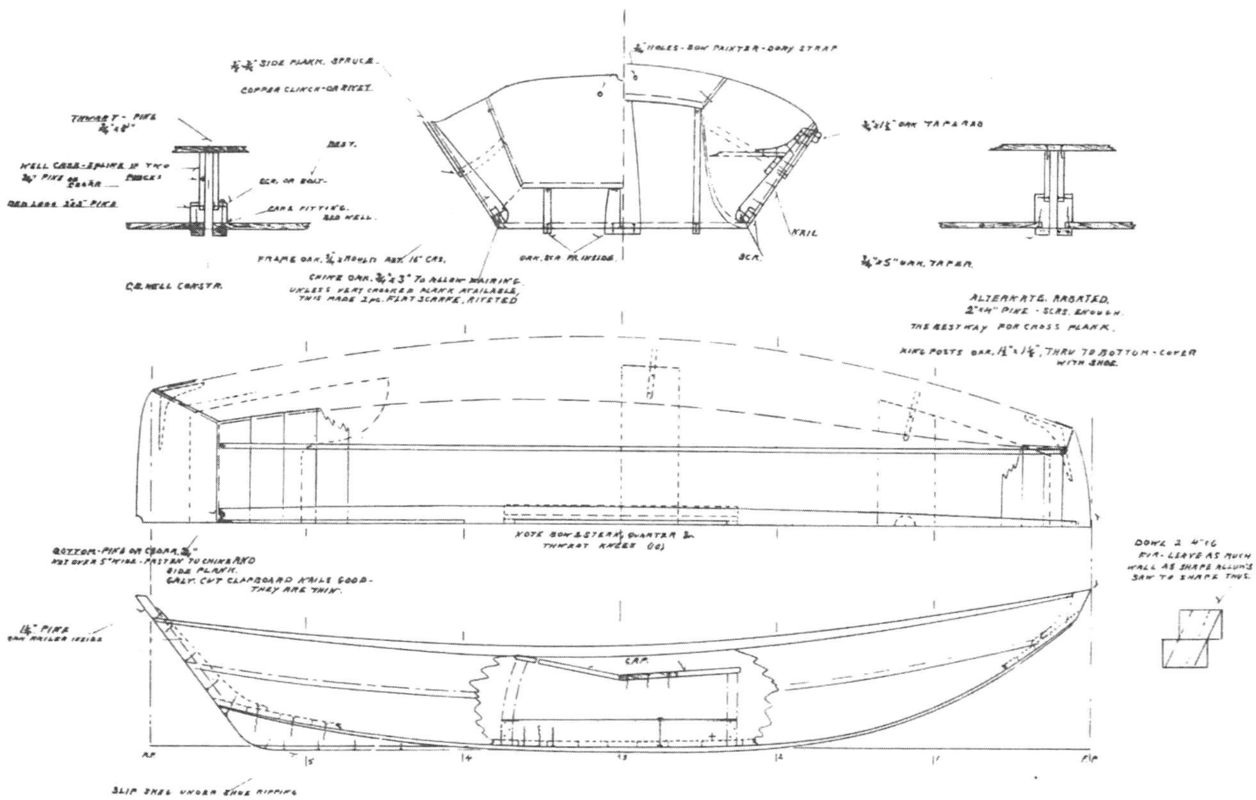

Construction plans of the I I-foot sailing sampan.

Interior details of a just-for-rowing version of the sampan. The lower frame ends are rounded up from the bottom of the chine log so as not to catch dirt or your toes, yet they are sufficiently strong to do the job. (R.D. Culler photo)

on deck, the boat is easily carried in stern davits. If, on the other hand, you can do neither of these, she tows very well too. Pete knew of one that was towed behind a bassboat at 30 knots. Of course, this is an extreme; it is certainly not recommended.

Under oars, the boat is very handy and quick. She will, quite literally, spin on her heels. There are two rowing positions, one for when you have a passenger in the sternsheets.

The rig, as drawn, has proven most adequate on a boat used in local waters. Contrary to what you might think, she sails very well except going into a chop in light air. Once heeled a bit, the boat presents her chine to the sea, which at that point is V-shaped. There is a lot less slapping and pounding than you would expect.

As stated, the rig has proven to be entirely satisfactory as drawn. In my mind's eye, however, I see it replaced by a fully battened Chinese lugsail, decorated to suit. With this rig the boat would really look appropriate.

The boat is well suited to amateur construction, for there is nothing overly difficult in her design, except perhaps fitting the chines. They have quite a lot of shape. However, if you spile them, then shape and scarf, they will bend right in and should be problem free. The rest is standard flat-bottomed skiff construction. Be sure to taper your gunwales and bottom shoe, both ways.

The local version, mentioned above, was built by a 14-year-old boy, Brian Kelley. And an excellent job he did, too!

Captain Pete liked this design so much for her intended use that no fewer than seven of them, with variations, were built in his Hyannis shop.

Length overall: 10 feet 2 inches
Beam: 4 feet

Concordia Yard Butthead

This is a sampan-style punt for serious work. Pete called her the yard butthead. The little skiff has very good capacity for her length. If built correctly, she would be quite light for hauling materials about. In the water she is stable, for the hull is proportionately wide on the bottom. Pete built one of these for Mystic Seaport. There she did yeoman work in the 'tween decks of the *Charles W. Morgan* while that vessel's hold was flooded.

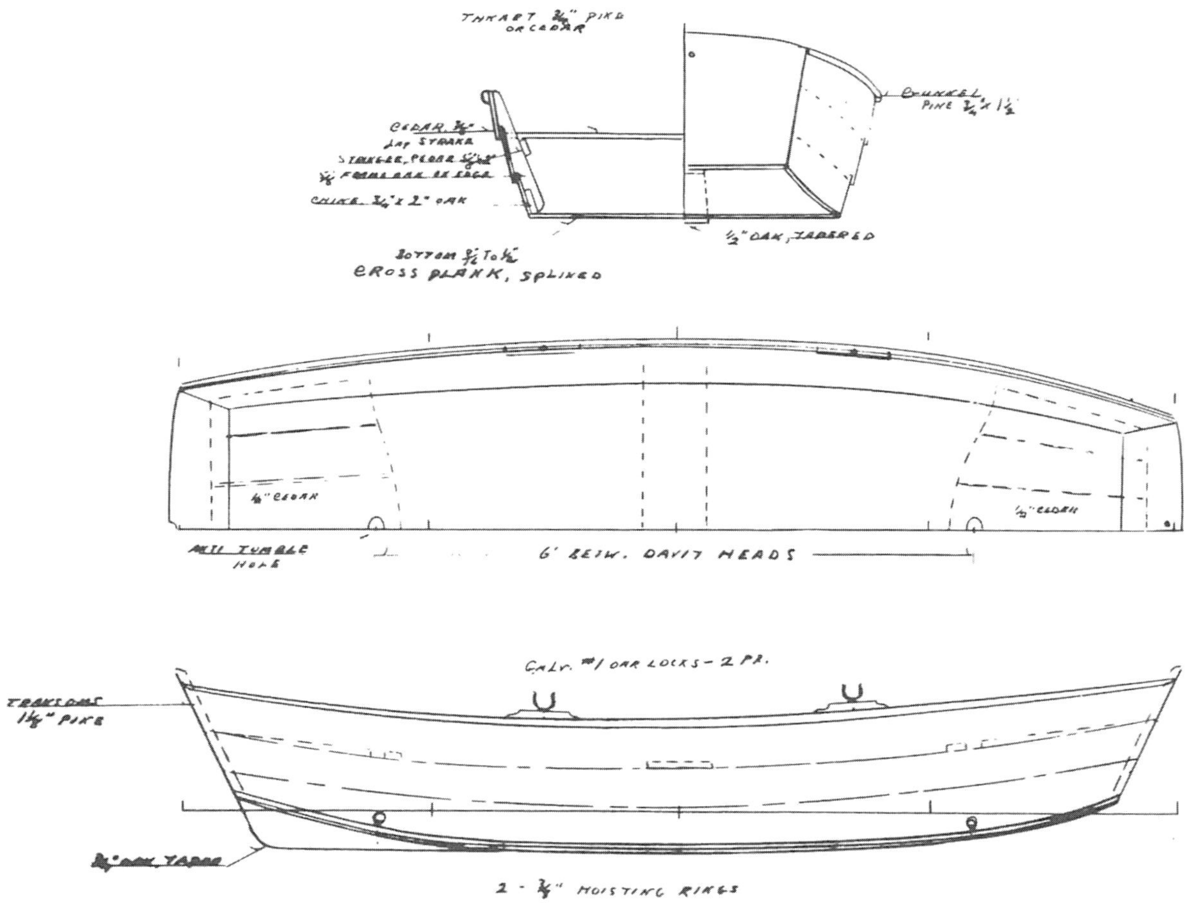

Plans of the Concordia yard butthead.

PART III

Power, Inboard and Outboard

Motor Vessel Proposal For Mrs. Brooks; Express Cruiser Proposal For Drayton Cochran

Motor Vessel

Length overall: 70 feet
Beam: 18 feet
Draft: 6 feet

Express Cruiser

Length between perpendiculars: 55 feet
Beam: 10 feet 6 inches
Draft: 4 feet 7 inches

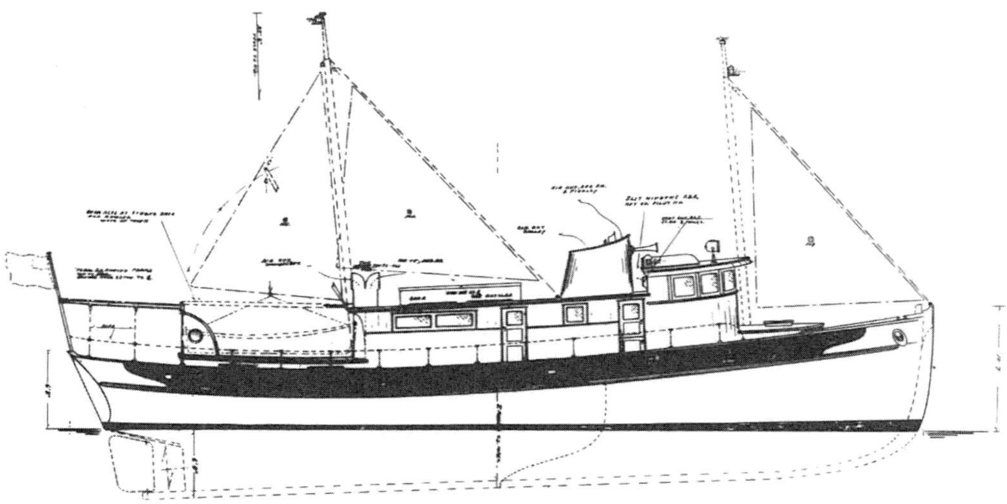

Profile of the 70-foot motor vessel proposal for Mrs. Brooks.

The vessels of these proposals are stylistically similar, but they fulfill different requirements. The 55-foot express cruiser was designed for speed under power. The 70-foot motor vessel was developed for comfort, with a cruising speed of about 10 knots. Most of today's powerboats can be classified the same way—either for speed or for comfort. Few, however, can compare with these two in style or appearance. Many modern powerboats are little more than molded, floating motel rooms.

The similarities in styling between the two lie in the bow profile and sternhead, the sheer stripe, wheelhouses placed forward for good visibility and appearance, excellent ventilation in both engine room and cabin areas, stern cockpits, and the deckhouses and equipment. The small-boat problem was solved in exactly the same manner on each design. On the 70-footer the boom also acts as the strongback for an awning while in port.

Proper masting on a motor vessel adds much to its appearance. On the 70-footer a steadying sail enhances comfort under certain wind and sea

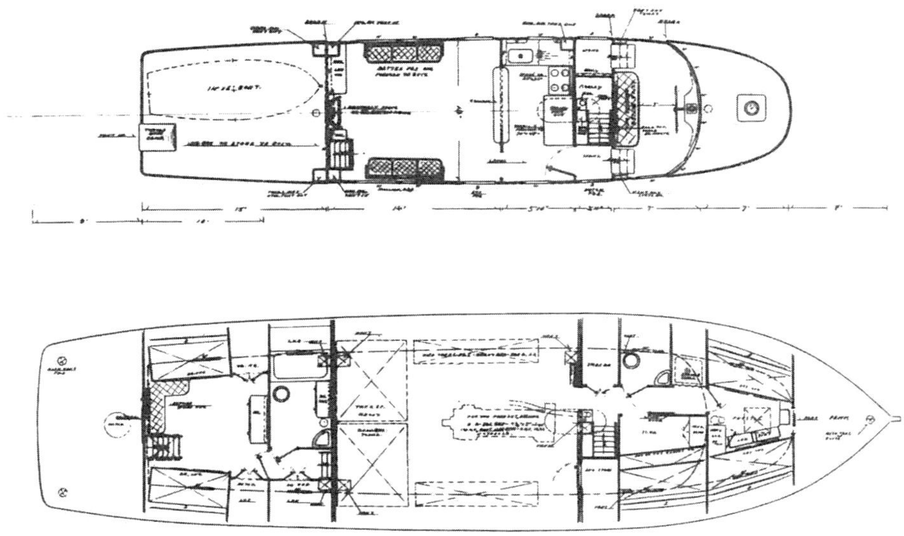

Engine room and cabin plans of the 70-footer.

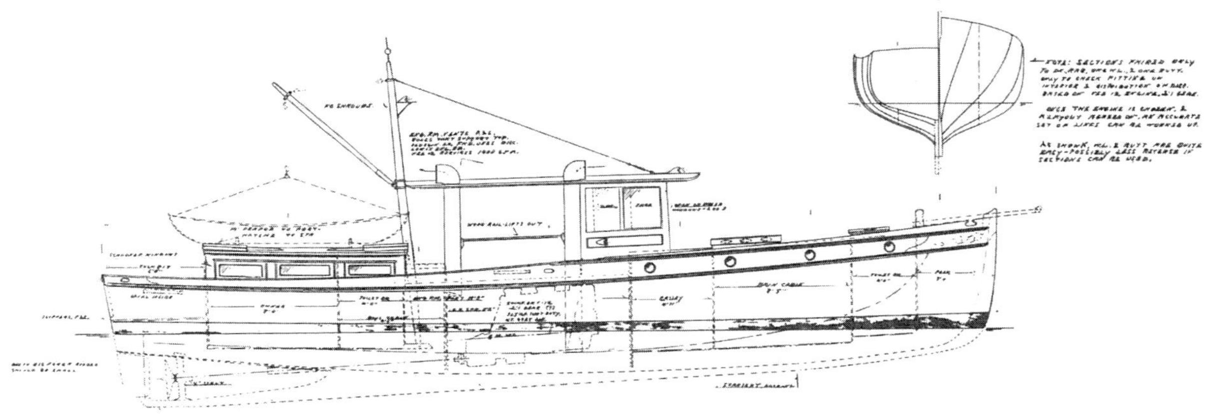

Above and below: Plans of the 55-foot express cruiser.

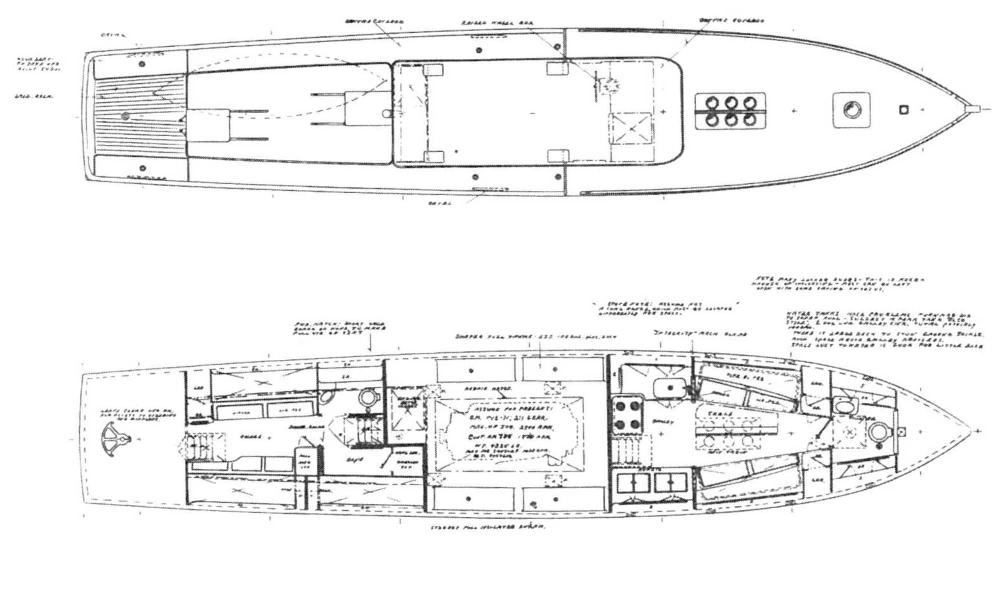

circumstances. The larger vessel has great range with its substantial fuel and freshwater capacity. Living aboard for extended periods would be no chore for me, for her layout is very well thought out and almost palatial, That fireplace in the main deck saloon would be very nice indeed.

After a sumptuous dinner in the warm glow of that stove, served from the nearby galley, I can picture myself ambling forward up the low companionway to visit with the Captain in the wheelhouse to see how the trip is proceeding. Or I might relax on the well-placed settee and sip a little brandy (in dinner jacket, of course) before retiring to the owner's stateroom aft. In the morning, I would wake up fresh and alive for all that the new day portends. Such dreams are easy with a vessel like this one.

The 55-foot express cruiser was designed with fast passages in mind. Boats of this type were developed during the 1920s to ferry the financial wizards of the time from their shoreside Long Island homes to the canyons of Wall Street, usually with a Deer Isle man at the wheel. Such a skipper would certainly understand the vessel's small boat.

Built for speed, the boat's comforts aboard are snug. They are entirely adequate for the intended use. Sleeping quarters are aft, with the main cabin and galley forward—accessible through the wheelhouse. There is a toilet in each area. As it should be on a vessel of this type, the greatest amount of space is devoted to the engine. The hull-and-engine combination is perhaps the most interesting aspect of this proposal. Diesel technology has evolved over the years to where it is an engineering marvel today. The number of pounds per horsepower has steadily decreased, and with this change, economy has increased. One persistent drawback with diesels is noise, which makes Pete's suggestion for a fully insulated engine room important. Fuel consumption for the Detroit Diesel 12 V-71 is about 12 gallons per hour at 1800 r.p.m. This vessel's service speed would be approximately twice that figure, so she would be very economical indeed.

Both vessels, with their long, lean hulls and flat runs, would move through the water with grace and little fuss compared with what is accepted as customary today. When necessary, both could be throttled down and still be able and seakindly.

In terms of traditional character and style, these two proposals have few peers. I would like to see the larger vessel wheel around Brant Point Light. There she would turn every head in Nantucket Harbor. Some might even give up their cherished Boat Basin slips out of embarrassment. I can envision the 55-footer steaming through Hell Gate and down the East River in New York. No doubt she would set off a chorus of melodious toots and whistles from towboats working the river. Tugboat men appreciate a proper vessel when they see one.

Albacore Troller For Wes Wickham

Length overall: 55 feet 5 inches
Beam: 15 feet 6½ inches
Draft: 8 feet
Sail area: 883 square feet

In recent years there has been considerable interest in sail-assisted fishboats. The ever-rising costs of fuel and engine maintenance make this idea economically attractive for those who must travel long distances to find and catch fish. This thinking has been successfully applied to trolling for salmon and albacore, longline fishing for swordfish, halibut, and cod, and in certain pot fisheries.

Wes Wickham, a successful albacore and salmon fisherman on the Oregon coast, was seeking a designer for his new 54-foot sail-assisted fishboat. A reading of the Old Man's *Skiff's and Schooners* convinced Wickham that Captain Pete was a designer who could put his ideas into form. From looking at Pete's design, I think Wickham made an intelligent choice.

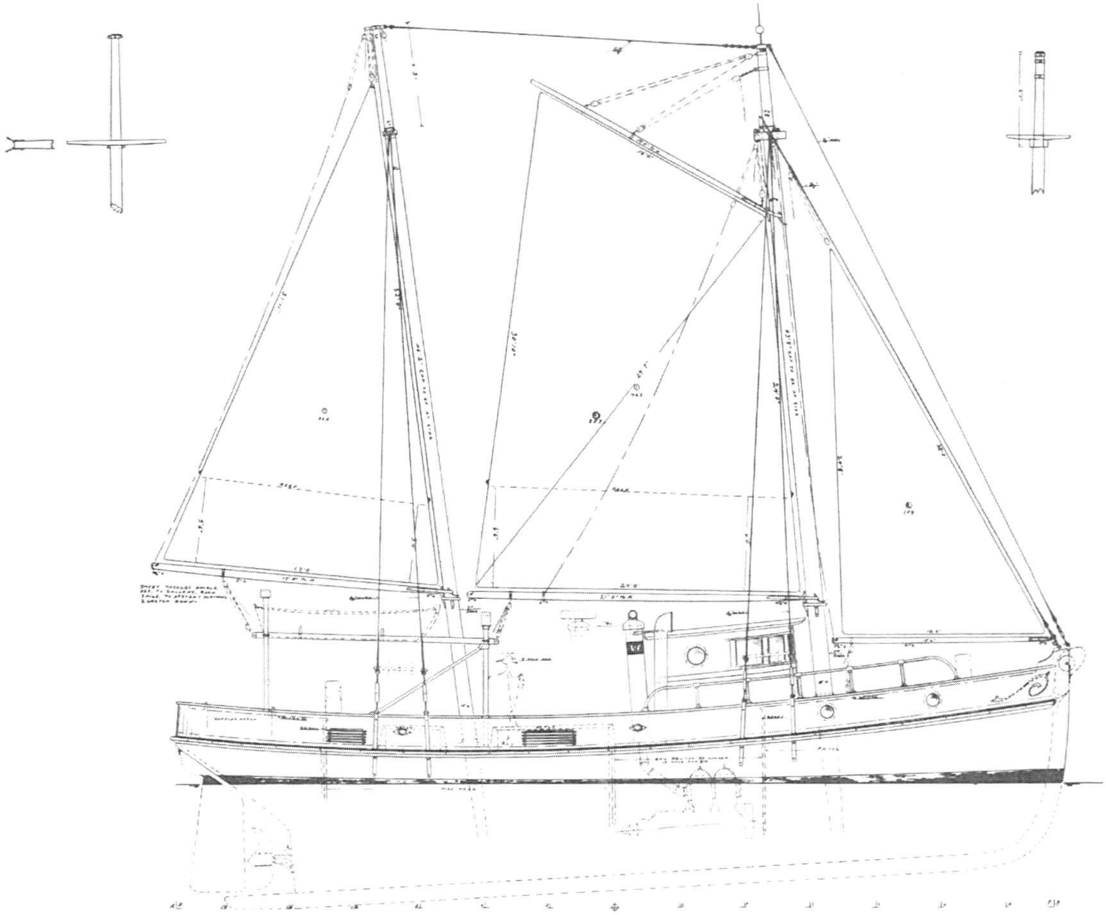

Sail plan of the 54-f oot sail-assisted workboat.

Wickham's requirements were:

• A capacity of ± 20 tons of fish in an insulated, refrigerated hold. [This might be a bit small, even for a Mom-and-Pop operation, but it's about all you can get in 54 feet. —J .B.]

• A range of from 25 to 30 days.

• Storage for a small boat, on board.

• Bulwarks on main deck, knee high, for safety and receiving fish.

• A break in the deck, fore and aft.

• An all-inboard rig, for maneuvering about docks, and the ability to sail the boat without interfering with the jigging poles while trolling. This is the reason why most of the sail area is in the foresail and headsails. The jibheaded main is lowered while trolling.

• Wheelhouse forward.

• A gaffing and killing pen, or hatch, aft.

Although Wickham was undecided about hull material before (and evidently after) the design was completed, Pete designed with wood in mind. There were a number of reasons for this. Captain Pete, besides being biased in its favor, felt that wood was the only realistic material for a fully molded hull of this type, if it was to be built in the United States. Fiberglass just doesn't hold up. Also, in order to profit from an expensive mold, the design would have to be a compromise that appealed to many, who would then be prodded to purchase by advertising hype. Raspberries to all that. A fully molded steel hull might be cost effective in Europe, but not on this side of the Atlantic.

Thus, the fisherman looking for a custom hull is faced with either the initial high cost of wood or some sort of chined steel box. I'm sure there are some who are quite satisfied with their steel fishboats,

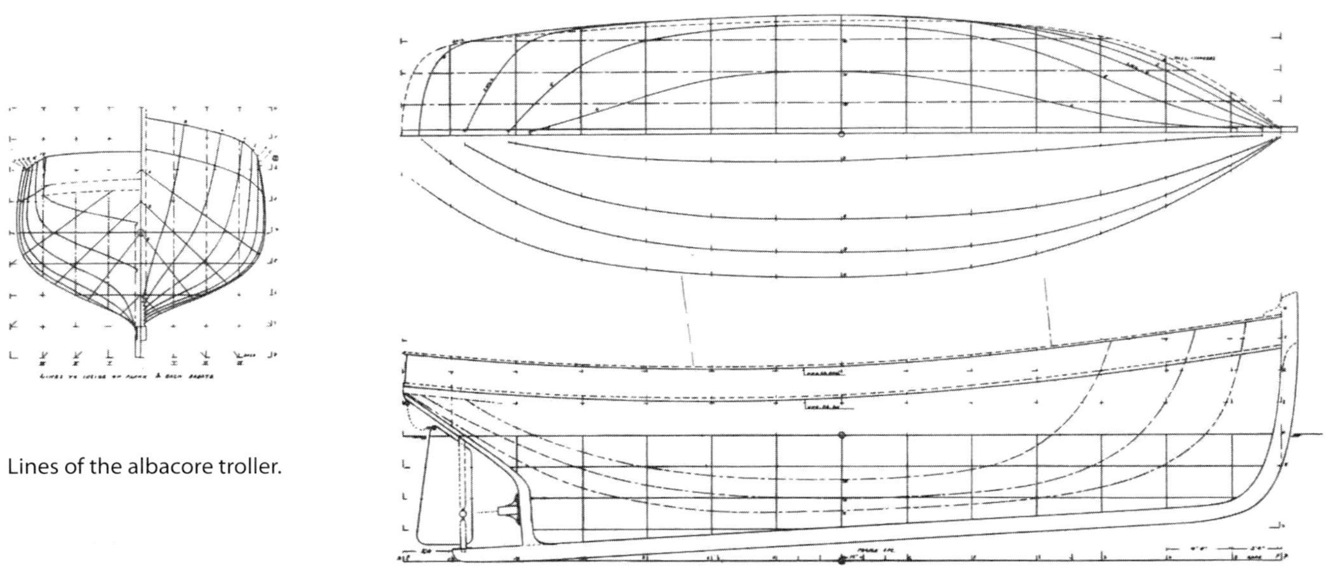

Lines of the albacore troller.

but it is very difficult to get a proper and able seaboat using developed surfaces. The main point in steel's favor is relative cheapness. However, closer inspection should reveal the illogic of going this route. The cost to build a hull is about 25 percent of the finished price of any boat. The cabin, decks, superstructure, propulsion, appointments, the rig on a sailboat, and the deck gear and electronics on a fishboat make up the remainder. Even with careful shopping, the savings one can accrue from those items other than the hull are slight. The great temptation is to slash costs in building the hull, for it is here that the widest disparity in prices is to be found. Any savings here, however, must be within the hull cost alone, and this is just 25 percent of total cost. Even more important, it is the quality of the hull that carries the *entire* investment. (If you are an owner/operator, that includes your hide!) It just doesn't make sense to cut corners with the hull. I suppose a skipper could insure a boat to the hilt, and hope the Coast Guard always got there in time. For the traditionally independent fisherman, however, this sort of thinking is completely alien to his character.

Considering the fishery the boat would be used in and Wickham's requirements, along with the philosophy about hulls just described, Captain Pete selected the old power halibut schooner as a basis for the design. As the Old Man said, "She is simply a small-size power halibut schooner. Built like a block, she will never drown you at sea.

"Michael Crowley, an intelligent commentator on today's marine scene, wrote a very informative article in *WoodenBoat* magazine on the excellent characteristics of power halibut schooners. Here are some of his comments.

"The durability of the halibut schooner can be traced to three things: first is the refusal to reject completely the influence of the earlier sailing schooners. The modern halibut schooners appeared at a time when sail had proven inefficient when matched against power. Yet power alone was viewed with skepticism and not completely trusted. The plumb stem and long, straight keel of the halibut schooner were the results of a powerboat model, but the slender hull, counter stern, and pleasing sheer allowed these craft to retain the easy, graceful, seakeeping lines and abilities of the earlier sailing schooners. Watch an old wooden halibut schooner and a modern, tubby steel boat run in a beam sea or plow their way through a head sea, but be careful that you do not watch the modern boat too long, for its motion could make you ill. Today sails are only used for stabilization, but a few years ago, her power lost, the schooner Grant was sailed across the Gulf of Alaska, as was the halibut schooner Wizard.

"Besides efficient design, a wooden boat—or any boat, for that matter—of over 50 years must be of good construction. For five years I fished from the

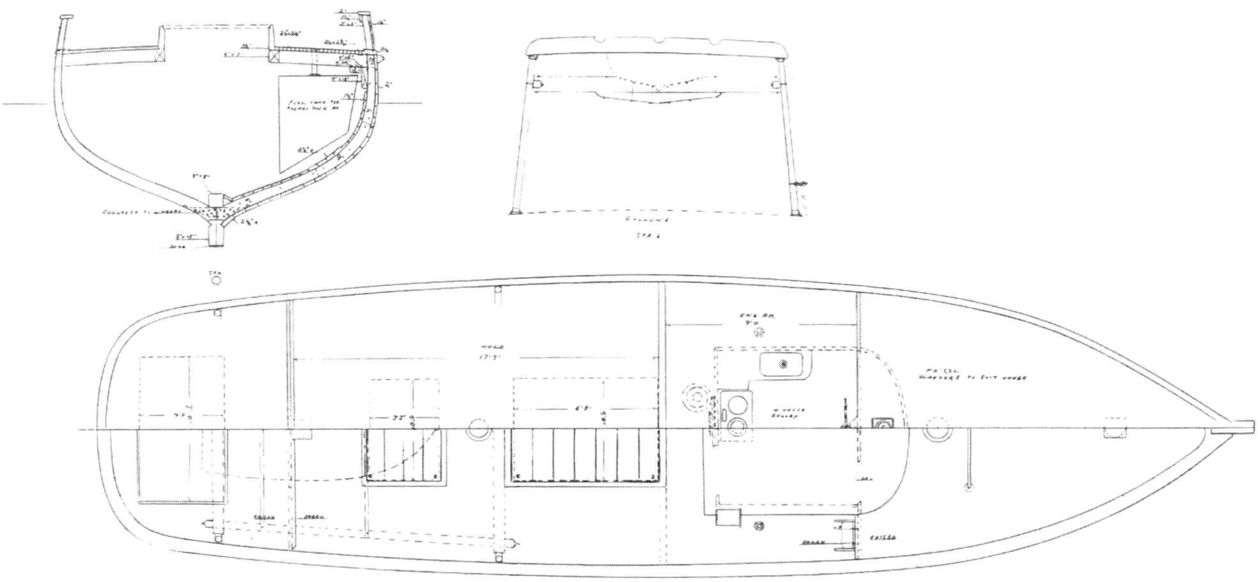

Above and Left: Construction plans and layout of the 54-foot fishboat.

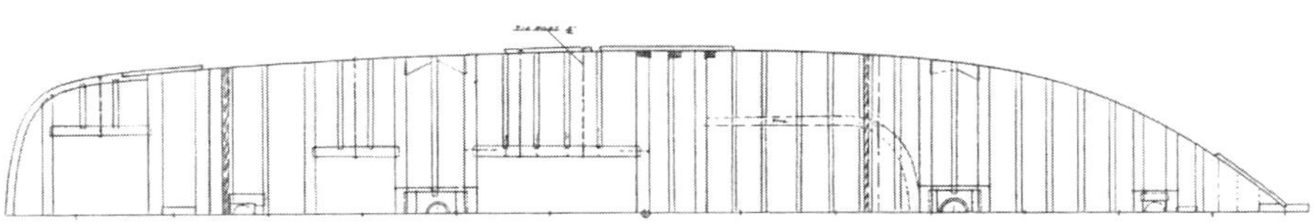

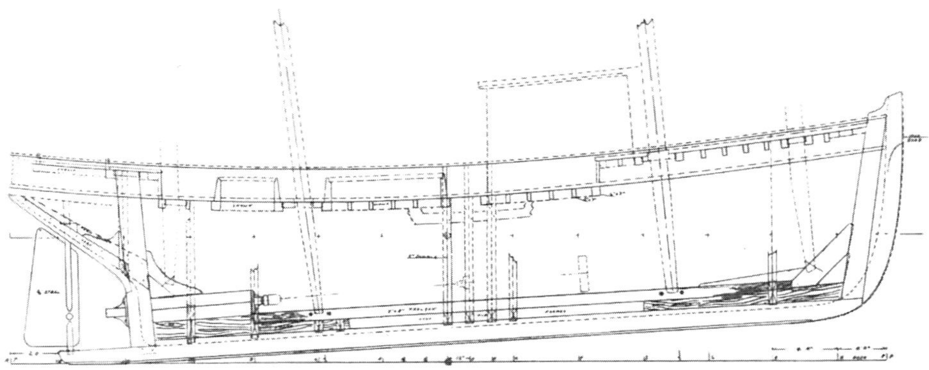

deck of the halibut schooner *Attu*—a boat of substantial construction. Built in 1924 by Matt Anderson of Olalla, Washington, the *Attu* is 74 feet overall with a 17-foot 4-inch beam and 8 feet 6 inches draft. The keel and keelson are 10 x 12, with sister keelsons 14 x 8 edge-bolted, and double-sawn frames sided 4 inches and molded 11 inches at the keel and 4½ inches at the sheer, spaced 18½ inches on center.

"The strength and durability of these vessels is indicated by a story I once heard in Kodiak and found later in *National Fisherman*. In 1972 'a schooner rammed a new steel crab boat, put an 18-inch dent in the crabber's side just aft of the bow, and buckled the deck like a tin can. The schooner backed off with no damage other than some chipped paint.'

"The third reason for this type of schooner's longevity is more intangible. It has something to do with pride and the idea that the schooners represent a timeless tradition, a tradition whose commitment has been to the sea 'since time out of memory.' It is a way of life, and oftentimes a question of life itself."

Length overall: 39 feet 8 inches
Beam: 12 feet
Draft: 3 feet

Concordia Novi Motor Cruiser

The Novi-type (Nova Scotia style) motorboats have a fine reputation in Downeast waters. As workboats, they are employed for lobstering, scalloping, and transportation. In addition, the type is the basis for some pilot boats. These boats are noted for their ability, seakindliness, and economy—all due to their easymoving hulls.

Considering this design's exemplary record of performance in all types of weather, it makes good sense to use it as the basis for pleasure motor cruisers. The design offers good carrying capacity, and is economical to propel, as long as you are satisfied with moderate performance. These boats can be put together with ease and efficiency, and thus relatively low cost, at least with a workboat finish. Such craft don't take to gilding anyway. They are simple, practical, and economical boats; this should not be forgotten.

With this design it is quite apparent that Pete kept these points firmly in mind. One of the nicer aspects of the design is the use of a raised deck forward and an extended cabinhouse for larger accommodations. This is about the only way to do that without greater length. It does not detract from the vessel at all. Besides adding room, it simplifies construction, will keep the deck tighter, and adds to the boat's looks.

Below decks, the feeling of practicality has been continued by including what's needed, and no more. The idea of keeping things simple has a lot going for it. Either arrangement shown should prove satisfactory.

Use of this design for a pleasure cruiser allows a large and roomy cockpit, especially if the steering house is open ended, as Pete shows it. This is standard practice with lobsterboats. A sliding curtain and snap-on dodgers can be used in foul weather. This is much cheaper and easier than closing in the after end permanently. The tank and rudder quadrant location are sensible. You can get at them, if need be, and there is plenty of natural ventilation for the tanks. Make the engine hatch just as large as

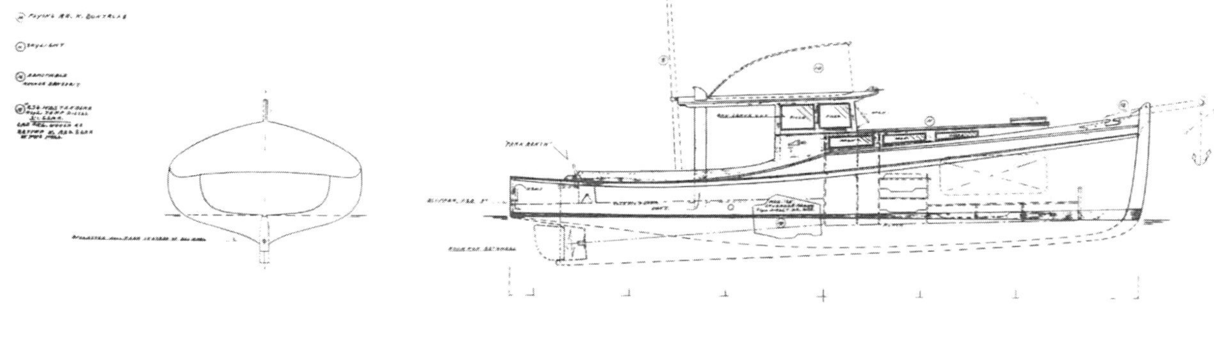

Profile and layout of the Novi launch proposal.

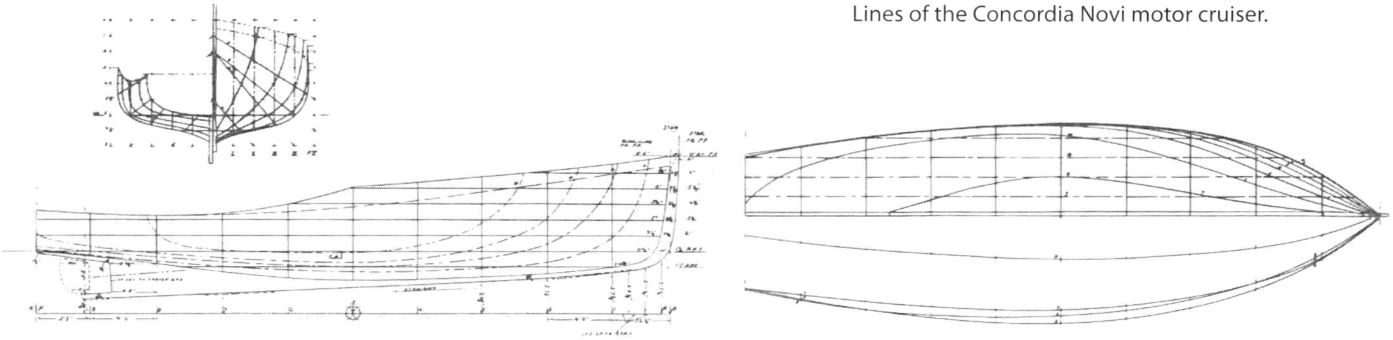

Lines of the Concordia Novi motor cruiser.

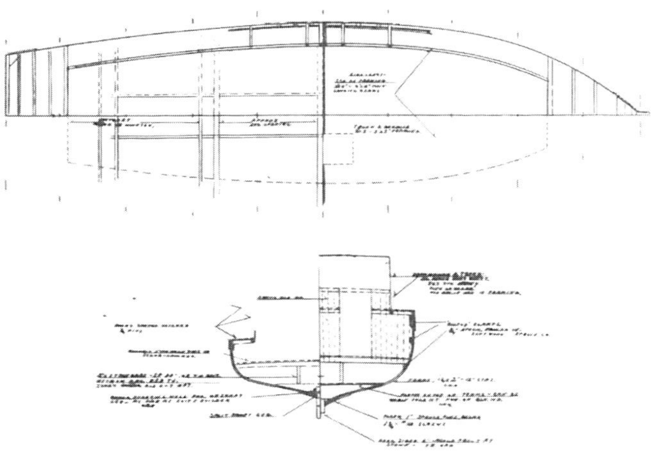

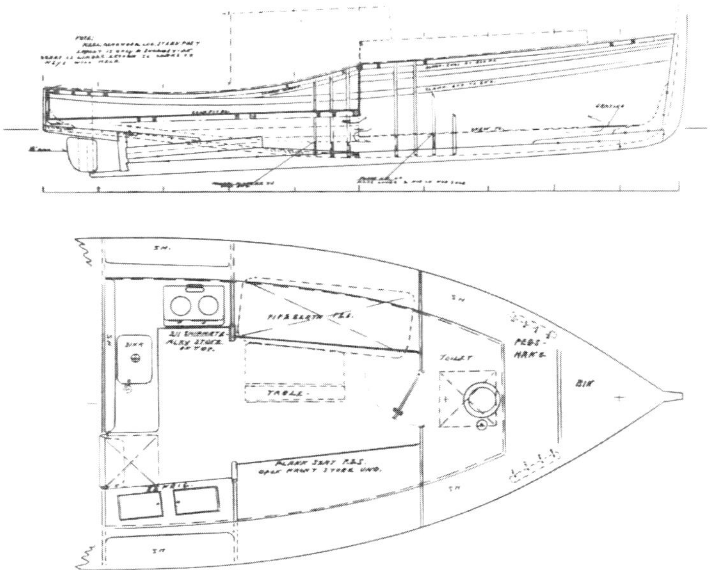

Above: Construction "suggestions" for the Novi launch.
Right: Alternate cabin plan.

you dare. Some day you may thank yourself for it.

Many builders opt for a flying bridge. If you do, it will mean doubling the controls. After many years of experience with power craft, I don't think a flying bridge is worth the trouble. An item that is worthy, however, is that bowsprit. If you don't have it, you will inevitably ding the topsides with the anchor.

A problem with a square stern in a boat with any pretensions to seakeeping is making the stern too large. This makes the craft difficult to handle in a following sea. I don't think there will be any such problem with this design. Pete has kept the stern area modest and tucked up a bit. With her nice run, skeg, and rudder position, the boat should steer well in a following sea.

Many people in this day and age are in too much of a hurry. Rush, rush, rush. Such folks run out, wolf something down, then later wonder why they have indigestion. I suggest you chew slowly on this design—in fact, on all of the designs shown in this book. Give the designer the benefit of the doubt. Think a bit about why this went here, that went there, and why this or that is so. A boat design is a kind of painted canvas. As such, there is much to be learned from the interrelationships shown.

As for this fine little motor cruiser, I think she would be a splendid, movable feast.

Steam Launch Proposal

Length overall: 32 feet 8 inches
Molded beam: 8 feet 9 inches
Molded depth: 4 feet 3 inches
Draft: 3 feet

Steam Launch

Molded length: 34 feet 2 inches
Molded beam: 8 feet 9 inches
Molded depth: 3 feet 8 inches
Draft: 3 feet 8 inches

Steam Launch Proposal, Steam Launch for Richard Hovey

Comments by Pete Culler

We hear much these days about how all boats are becoming production craft—no more individual ideas, no more one-of-a-kind, no more wood. Instead, it's all high speed, both through the water and in r.p.m.

To a great extent this is so. The new and inexperienced boatman has little else to choose from. If he stays with boating, however, this gentleman often seeks better things later on. At least, from the perspective of my shop, it appears that many come looking for classic craft. They want something that will do real work, a vessel that will go to sea in comfort and be a home afloat.

Often one of these seekers—a person with a love of small craft, a modest pocketbook, and the realization that just "messing about in boats" is what really counts—is exposed to a really good pulling boat, and says, "This is the way it should be." The same thing happens with powerboats and sailing vessels, too, for that matter. In *National Fisherman* one time, Bill Durham had an article on the joys of nice, easy-moving displacement launches using modest power. This naturally brought forth some further discussion. The exchanges soon got around to the old steam-launch hulls. Richard B. Hovey of Prides Crossing, Massachusetts—owner of a small steamer and an avid steam fan—liked what he read.

As a result, he commissioned me to see what we could do in the way of designing a larger steamer. Well, we submitted the usual proposal drawing, which looked practical. The boiler and engine we had not really nailed down, but there were several under consideration. You don't just rush out and

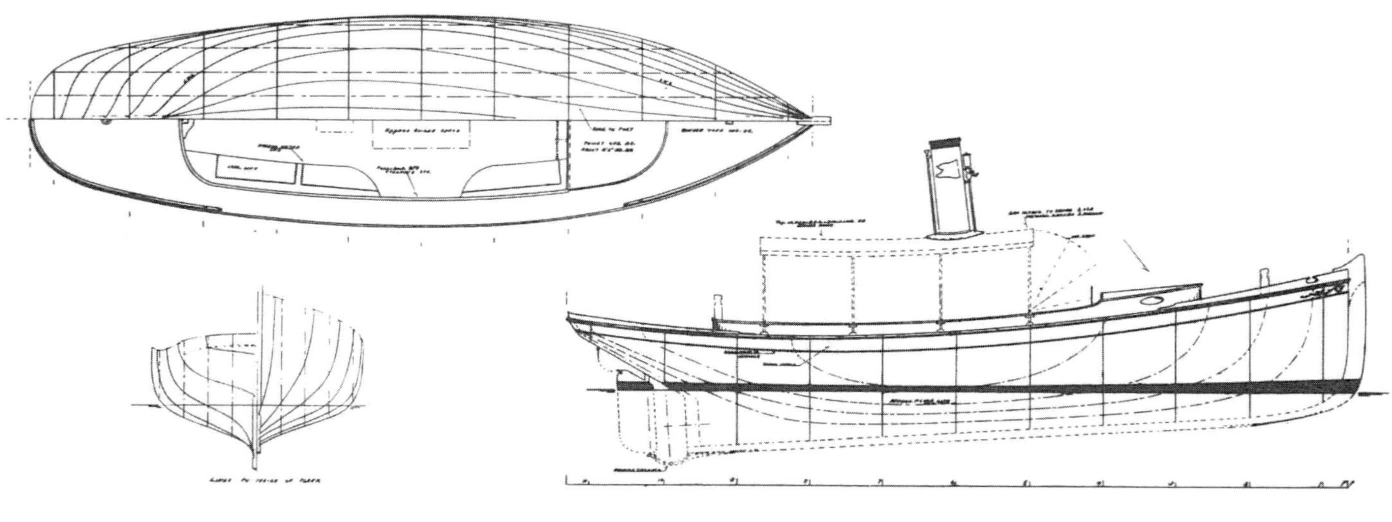

Plans of the original steam launch proposal for Richard Hovey.

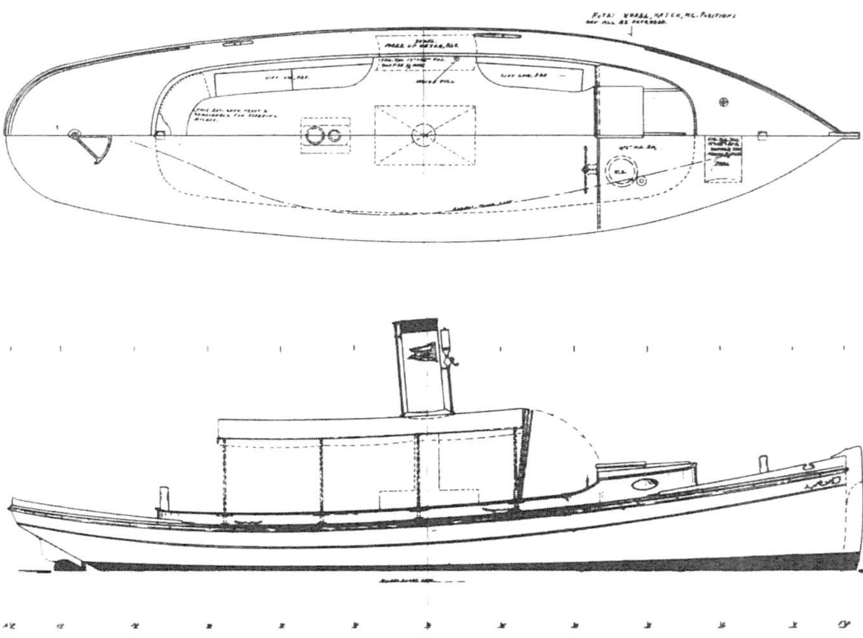

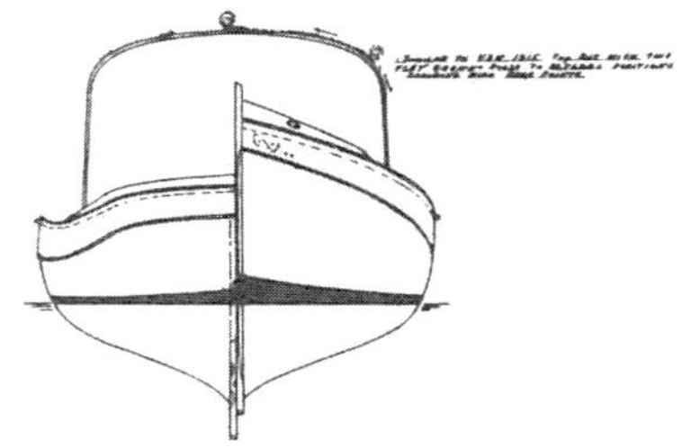

Final profile and layout plans for the Hovey steam launch.

buy an engine and boiler, like some machine made in Detroit. You have to know steam, and where this and that can be had, traded, swapped for, and even made. Good steam equipment—or even very poor stuff, for that matter—is not in junkyards today.

Anyhow, the project proceeded. It was decided that a bit more length would be better, so the design ended at 34 feet between the rabbets. It was a foregone conclusion that the boat would be traditional in model and build. As in all steamers, provision was to be made for a really large (by current standards) wheel.

Few today know that many small steamers of the past turned a screw with a pitch 1½ times or more greater than the diameter. Such wheels have real bite. The principle of their operation has little to do with the highspeed internal combustion engine.

Being a bit of a passive steam fan myself, having grown up when engine speeds of 300 r.p.m. were common, and also liking older hulls easily driven at modest speeds, I used the best small steamers of the past as a guide. I even referred to those of the U.S. Navy and other navies when naval small craft were steampowered.

Naval craft were specialized, so many of their requirements were not needed in a pleasure and fishing steamer. Some sort of canvas shelter was wanted, however. This very much follows U.S. Navy practice, although I hope it will be a better fit than some shown in Navy photos!

Bill Durham's book *Standard Boats of the U.S. Navy* has been a big help for details, including tables of construction, weights, and gear. Naval craft, then as now, were loaded down and very heavy. Such weight and displacement are not needed here, but you must keep in mind that a steam plant is very heavy—not so much the engine, for by present standards it seems way too small for the job. Horsepower rating has no relation to modern internal combustion practice. The boiler, its fuel, makeup water, hotwell, piping, and a host of other things in a steam engine are both bulky and heavy.

The cuddy is mostly to house a toilet, for at times ladies will be aboard, and also for use on the occasional overnight trip. This would be roughing it by some standards, but pretty good shelter, I say, in a snug cove after a day's fishing, with a portable stove and a simmering boiler for company (and to dry things out), and a pipe in the gloaming. There will always be plenty of hot water. You can even steam-clean the dishes if you wish.

Naturally, many will ask, "Why bother with a steamboat, with all that work, no speed, and no styling?" Such people are afraid of 'em! They often rush to their all-week-buttoned-up cruiser and hit the starter without even checking the engine space. Sometimes they take off faster than intended—straight up.

There are many very good reasons for owning a steamer. Just as with a lobster, you try one and like as not you are hooked. I can picture this craft all spic-and-span, blowing three long, melodious,

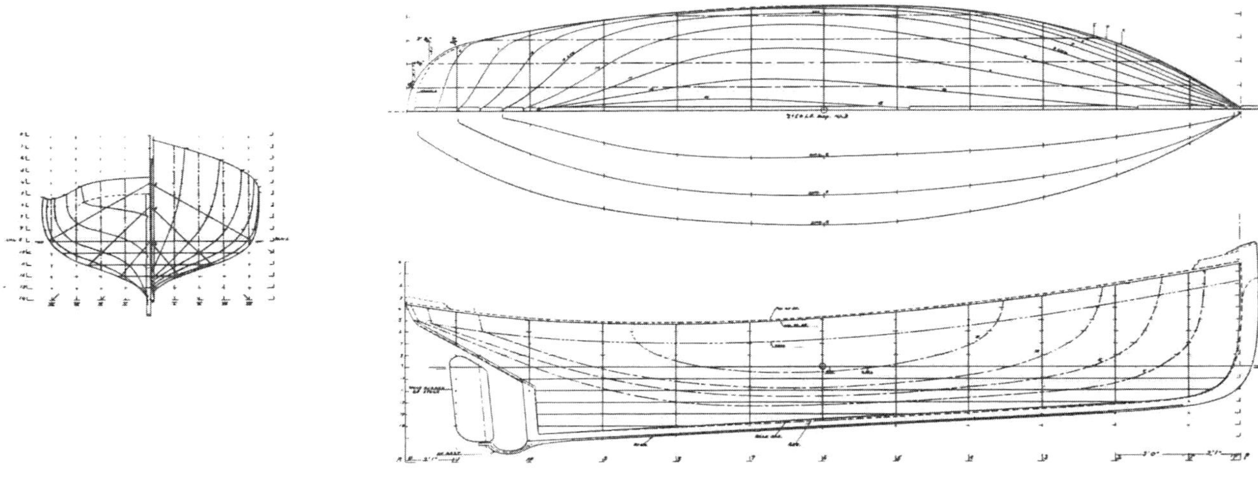

Above and below: Lines and construction plans of the Hovey steamer.

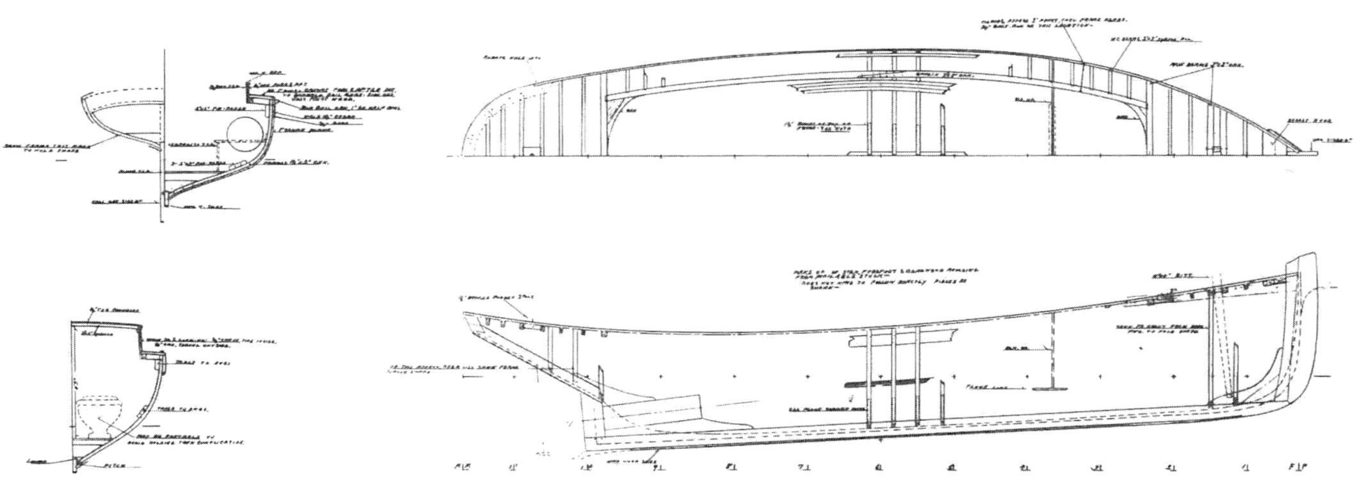

somewhat haunting blasts on her chime whistle—say, for the Annisquam bridge—for she has serious work with the fish off Plum Island. The bridge-tender will do a doubletake, and I bet he opens it some fast! He will gawk, unabashed, along with many others, and no doubt forget to lower the bridge until reminded to do it by some irate auto driver.

The craft drips with style, and there is that faint smell of steam oil. She is so quiet, you might even hear the slight beat of the screw. She's doing close to 7 knots, with a couple of knots of tide under her. Soon she's out of sight around the bend, leaving hardly any disturbance in the water.

Like people dedicated to guns, some are addicted to steam. Good guns are a lot of trouble. So is steam, but that's part of it, working with it. You don't learn it in a few minutes. It's not totally automatic and programmed for you. Fire and water are The Boss, and you learn to handle them, which makes you your own boss, in a way.

Real steam men usually do all their own machinery installation, or supervise it in detail. They then know their rig inside out, which is more than can be said for many internal combustion engine operators! Outlandish, you say, if not outrageous in these modern times? I don't think so. The owner of this steam craft knows the difference.

Length: 32 feet
Beam: 9 feet 8 inches
Draft: 3 feet
Displacement: 6,100 pounds

V-Bottomed Fantail Steamer

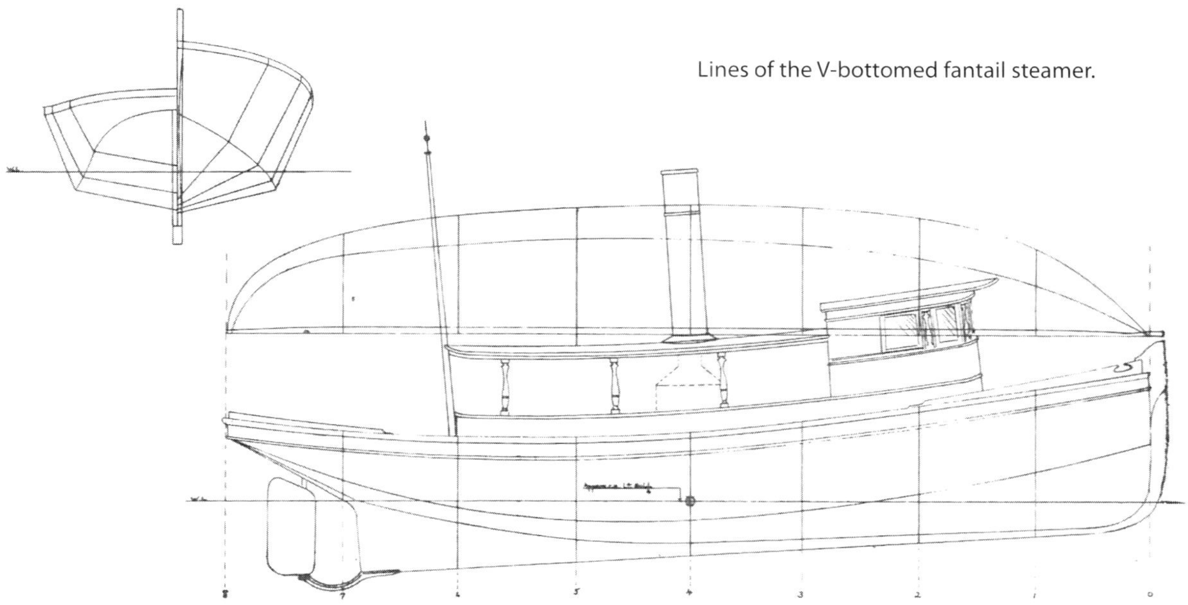

Lines of the V-bottomed fantail steamer.

This is a fine-looking steamer, and another example of Pete's ability to apply the V-bottom to practically any type of craft and have it turn out handsome and goodlooking. The Old Man was a master of this hull form, and I know of few others who have used it so successfully.

In the May-June 1962 issue of *Steamboats and Modern Steam Launches*, Pete had this to say about the boat: "She's 30 feet by 8 feet by about 3 feet. That is, the 8 feet is on top, and she's quite narrow on the water, which will vary somewhat with the load, as will the draft. Have done a lot of work with V-bottoms with great flare to the sides, and it certainly makes the boat, either power, rowing, or sail. Modest displacement under easy conditions or light load, but capable of great overload. Also very dry and goodlooking—not often the case in a chine boat. Along with a nice sheer, attention to traditional shape and detail suited to the type one may build, they can be very handsome craft."

Pete designed this little steamer for a man who had the design for some time before building the boat. When it was built, it was featured in a publication of the time, with the builder taking credit for the design. It seems he had drastically changed the topsides, leaving out that beautiful round house staving and other nice details. Well, this sort of upset Pete's good wife, Toni, but it didn't bother the Old Man a bit. He said, "Heck, I got paid, and the way it looks now, I don't want credit for it."

This may not have upset Pete, but it is an all-too-common practice that needs correcting. It is extremely difficult, if not impossible, to guard against design pirating. Some designers go to great lengths to thwart the theft of their work. Some have even been driven to drink. Copyrights do little good. All an unscrupulous designer or builder has to do is change some small aspect of the overall plan. Then he might say it's his (but not rightfully).

Pete was always respectful of those who went before him. He never failed to acknowledge his debt to them. The point I'm making is: Be honest. Acknowledge all your sources. When a designer or builder indulges in this sort of thievery, the only person being fooled is himself. With regard to this neat little V-bottomed steamer, build it as designed. I know you won't be disappointed.

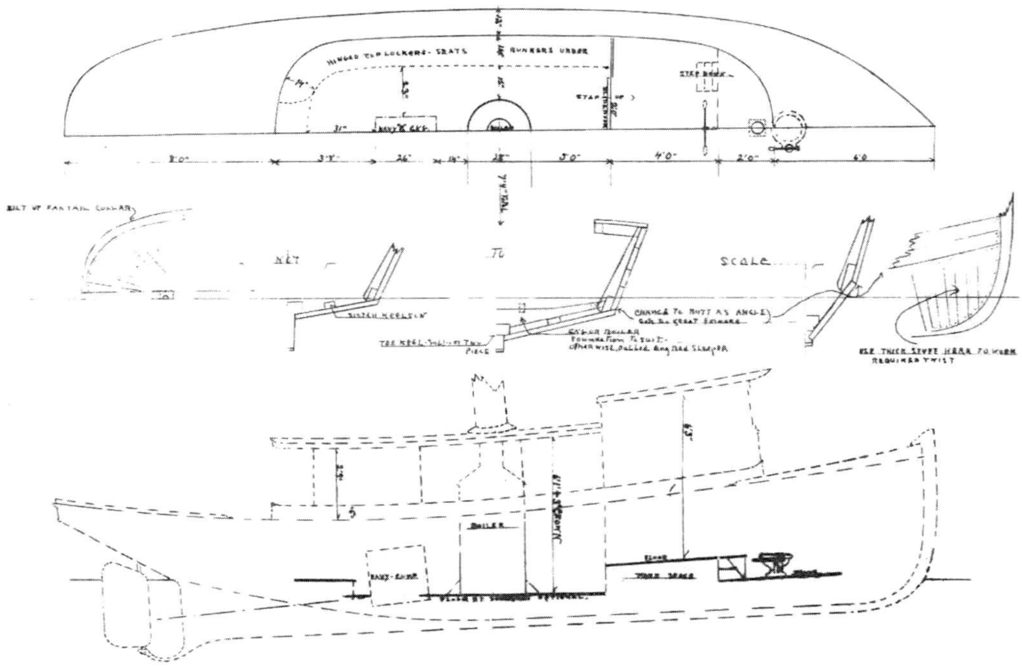

Above and below: Construction plans of the 32-foot V-bottomed steamer.

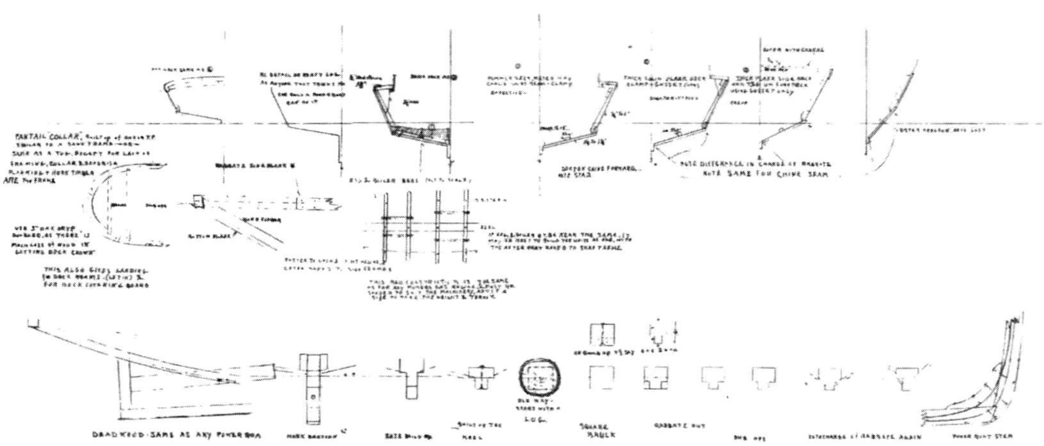

Length overall: 30 feet
Beam: 8 feet 6 inches

Fast Outboard Launch

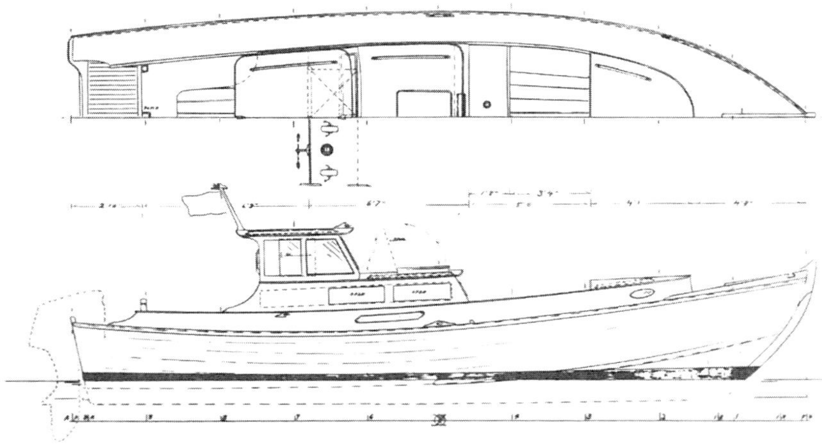

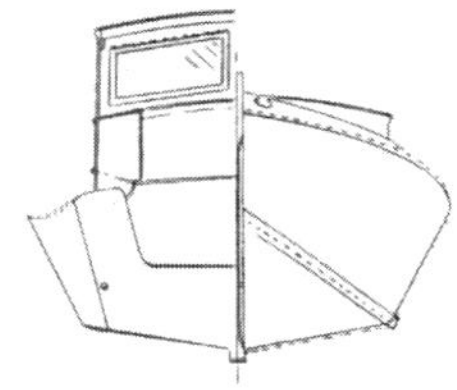

Left and above: Profile and plan views of the fast outboard for Commodore Chubb.

Below: Lines and offsets of the fast outboard.

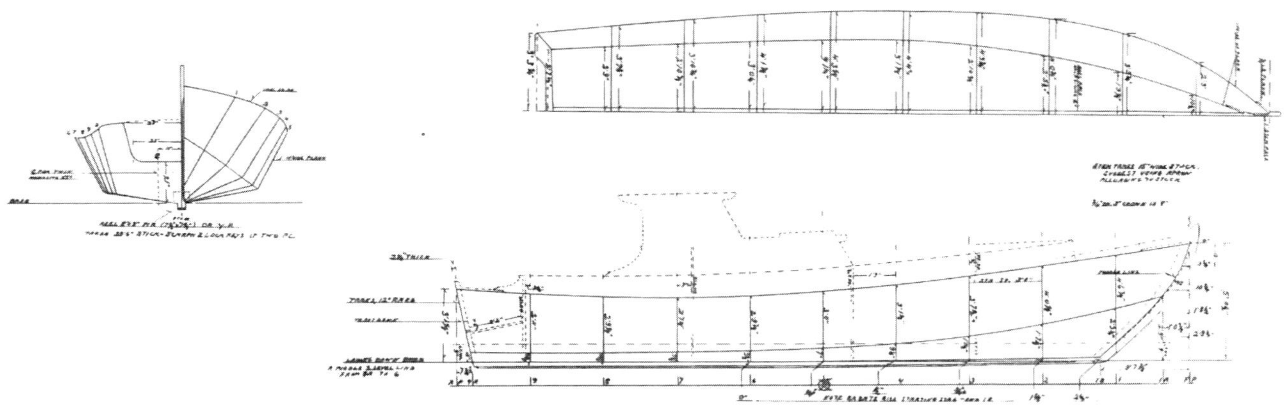

Comments by Pete Culler

Designed for Commodore Percy Chubb and Concordia Company. Built by Concordia in 1968.

Construction:
1. Keel: 8 x 8 fir.
2. Stem: white oak sided 4 inches.
3. Stern: double (inside vertical oak, outside horizontal cedar).
4. Planking, topsides: ¾-inch cedar, lapstrake, riveted laps.
5. Planking, bottom: 1¼-inch cedar, cross-planked and caulked, screw-fastened.
6. Shoe: ¾ x 3¾ yellow pine.
7. Coamings and house sides: Philippine mahogany.
8. Decks and house tops: marine plywood, canvas covered.
9. Deck and house beams: spruce; seats, floorboards, etc.: pine.
10. Fastenings: bronze and copper; hardware: brass, bronze, or wood.
11. Windows: lower house and trunk plexiglass, upper house safety glass.

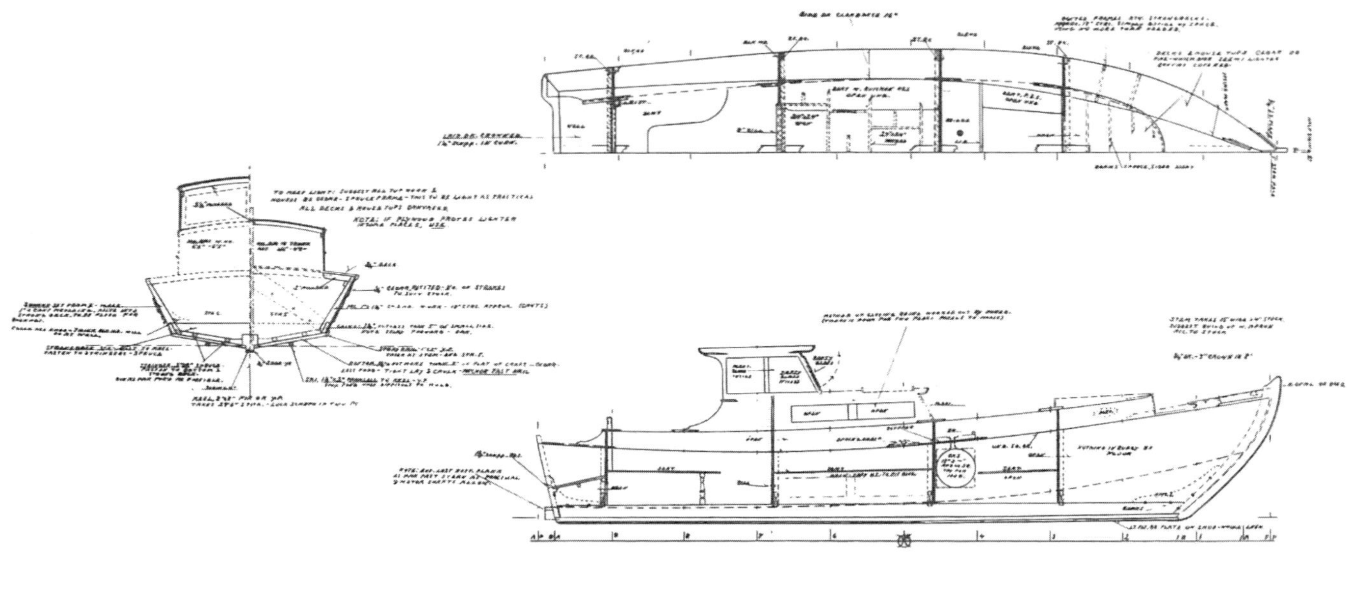

Above and below: Construction and layout revisions jar the 30-foot fast outboard.

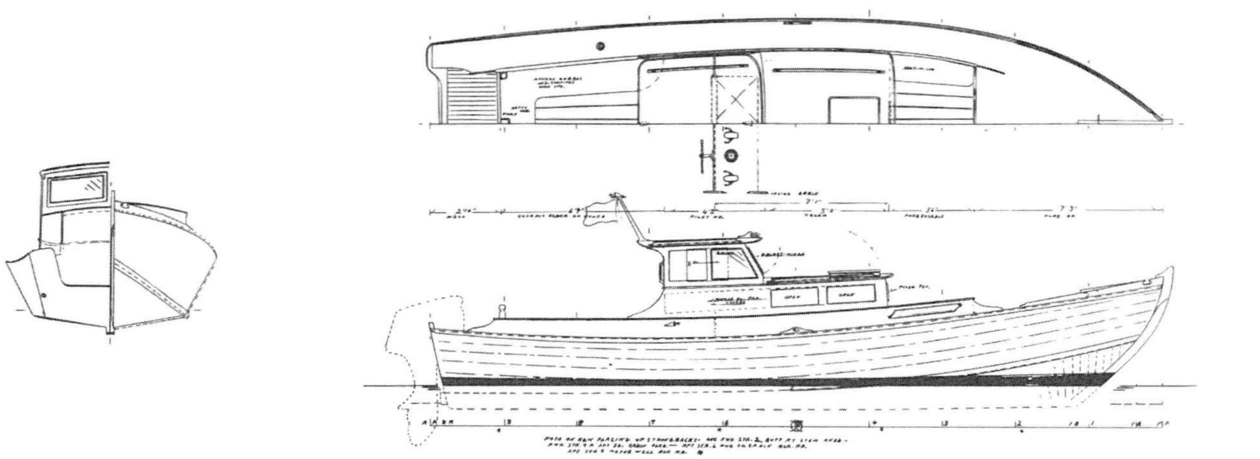

General Notes:

This little day cruiser may be of more than passing interest. As outboards go, she is a little larger than most. She operates very efficiently with what, in these days of great power, is a very modest set of machinery.

The design evolved over the years from small workboats used for alongshore shellfishing and other similar uses. These craft have been built in many smaller sizes—15, 16, 18, and 24 feet. All are very handy and able boats with a good turn of speed on modest power. The first question always asked is, "How fast are they?" The answers are that the little ones do 15 to 16 knots with 18 h.p.; the 24-footer, 20 knots with two 18s; and the 30-footer, 23½ knots with two 55 h.p. Bearcat outboards. To some, these speeds may not be impressive, but they are service speeds, in hulls built strong enough for working under modest power. A working craft must be able to carry and handle well at low speeds. These craft do this extremely well. The great flare forward and the shape of the bottom make them take very kindly to running as displacement hulls when the need arises.

There is no breakthrough of any kind in the design of these hulls. What you see is a matter of proper flare, deadrise, and chine run, all of which have been proven in use. These features vary slightly, depending on the size of the craft. The result is a boat that handles and banks extremely well, and has sufficient speed for most working purposes. As fast boats go, this is a type of hull that rides rather softly.

There's nothing new in construction either,

The key elements of lightness with strength are achieved by using lapstrake planking, a stout keel, sister keelsons, and strongbacks. Note the ready-to install washdeck frames. (R.D. Culler photo)

The 30-footer planing during trials. (R.D. Culler photo)

though several methods are combined, for they seem to give the required strength without too much weight. Weight is always the major stumbling block with planing hulls. The topsides are always lapstrake. Bottoms are old bay-style cross-planked herringbone. We are often questioned on this, and doubted too, but it works structurally, and in some other ways not readily apparent. The larger the craft, the more use is made of fore-and-aft stringers and strongbacks. The upper works are more or less standard practice with stress on light weight and durability. Keeping the design simple helps in this respect. Commodore Percy Chubb's requirements were for a simple but smart boat. He was quite willing to keep accommodations sparse rather than complicate or overload the boat. The result, using Concordia's methods and usual stock, is a nice-handling, long-lived boat, one that is easy to maintain and repair if damaged. She is a good seaboat, and we think quite nice looking.

We take considerable pains to turn out craft with a lot of style—ageless style that fits the sea. The next question is, how large an outboard can be used? I don't know. Greater outboard power is available. Fuel consumption, however, might become excessive. In addition, on hulls longer than 30 feet, there are engine shaft length problems. My feeling is that an inboard-outboard might work. This hull design is not suited to conventional inboard power.

Length overall: 27 feet 2 inches
Length between perpendiculars: 26 feet
Molded beam: 8 feet 10 inches
Draft: 4 feet 3 inches

Tug For Mark Marting

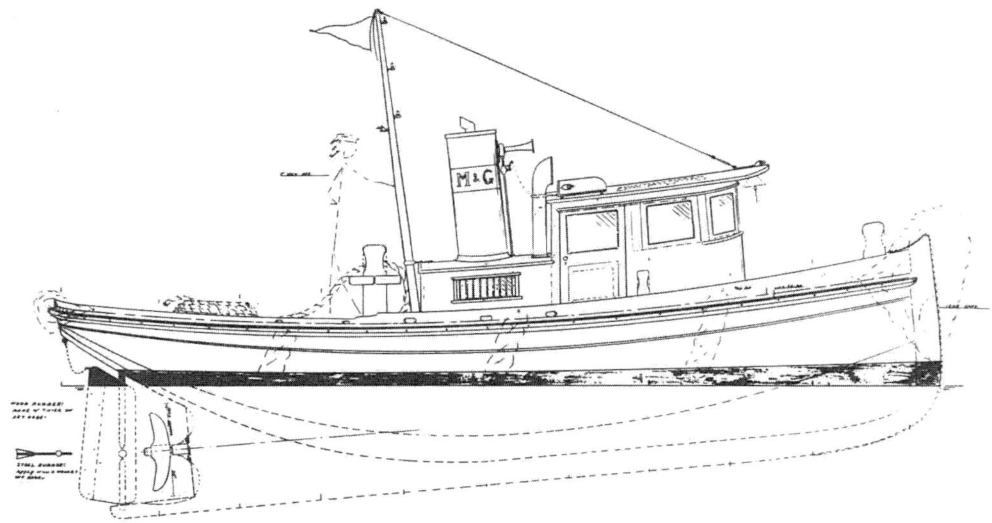

Profile and layout of the 26-foot tug.

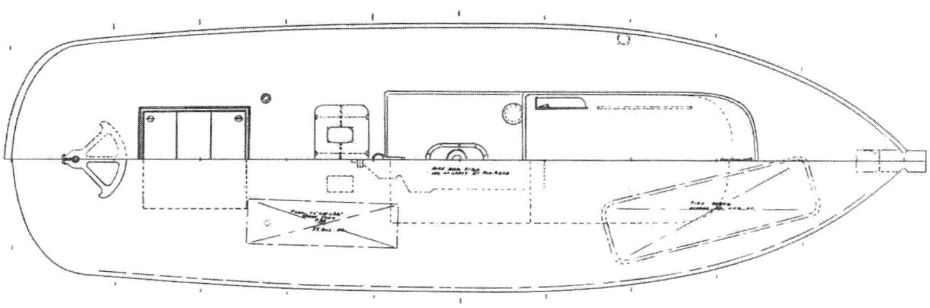

This jaunty little harbor tug is an enlarged version of *Gracie III*, which was designed for and built by Concordia Company.

Mark Marting was looking for a small tug for harbor work on and about San Francisco Bay. At the time, *Gracie III* was for sale. Her able good looks caught his eye. *Gracie*, however, was just too small for his requirements.

It proved no chore for the Old Man to enlarge *Gracie's* design to the 26 feet needed. He retained the smaller version's qualities that made her successful and able—the great drag in the keel, the full, strong quarters, the round transom and good deadrise to the bottom, with a chine line that enables a fine run and good entry. Once again, if you build, remember that this type of craft must be built stout; don't spare the wood.

With the extra length, there is room for a nice, efficient wheelhouse and a snug fo'c's'le with a berth for the off watch. The lazarette aft is very handy for stowing the hawsers, lines, and spare gear these marine Samsons require.

Ask any sailor who has had the pleasure of working on a tugboat; you will be told that these workboats endear themselves very quickly. The nature of the work, its variety and worthiness, and the joining of a man and a machine that responds as if it is an extension of the skipper, tend to engender purpose and peace of mind. That, my friend, is what life is all about.

When fitting out, remember the secret of Samson's strength and give the vessel plenty of thick, hairy fenders. These boats can't do proper work without them. To paraphrase Pete, "Here is a tugboatman's tugboat."

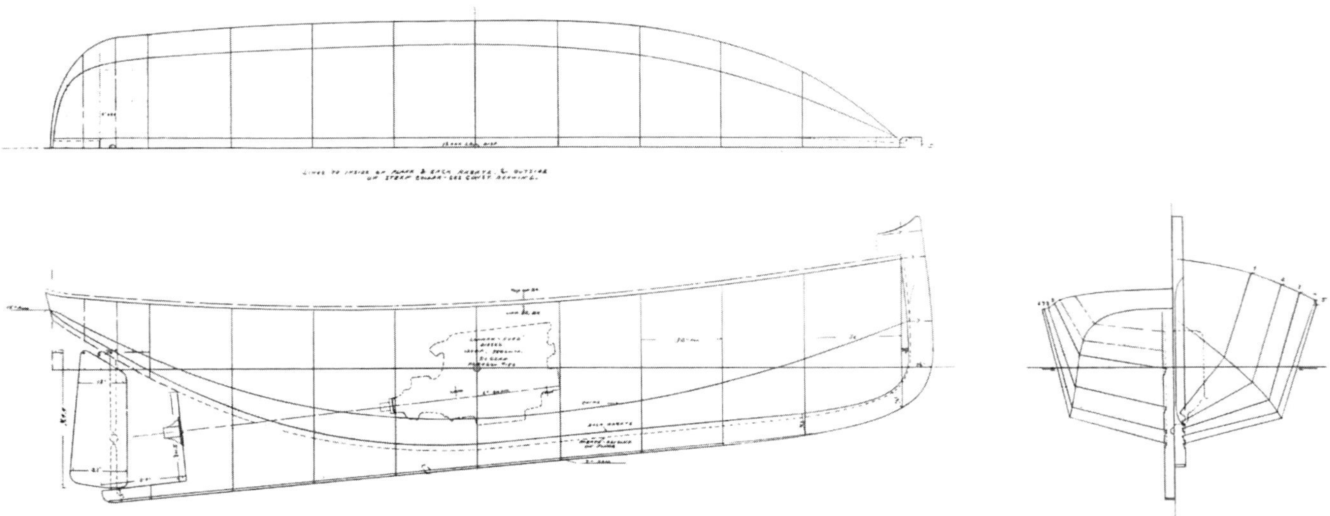

Above and below: Lines and construction plans of the tug for Mark Marting.

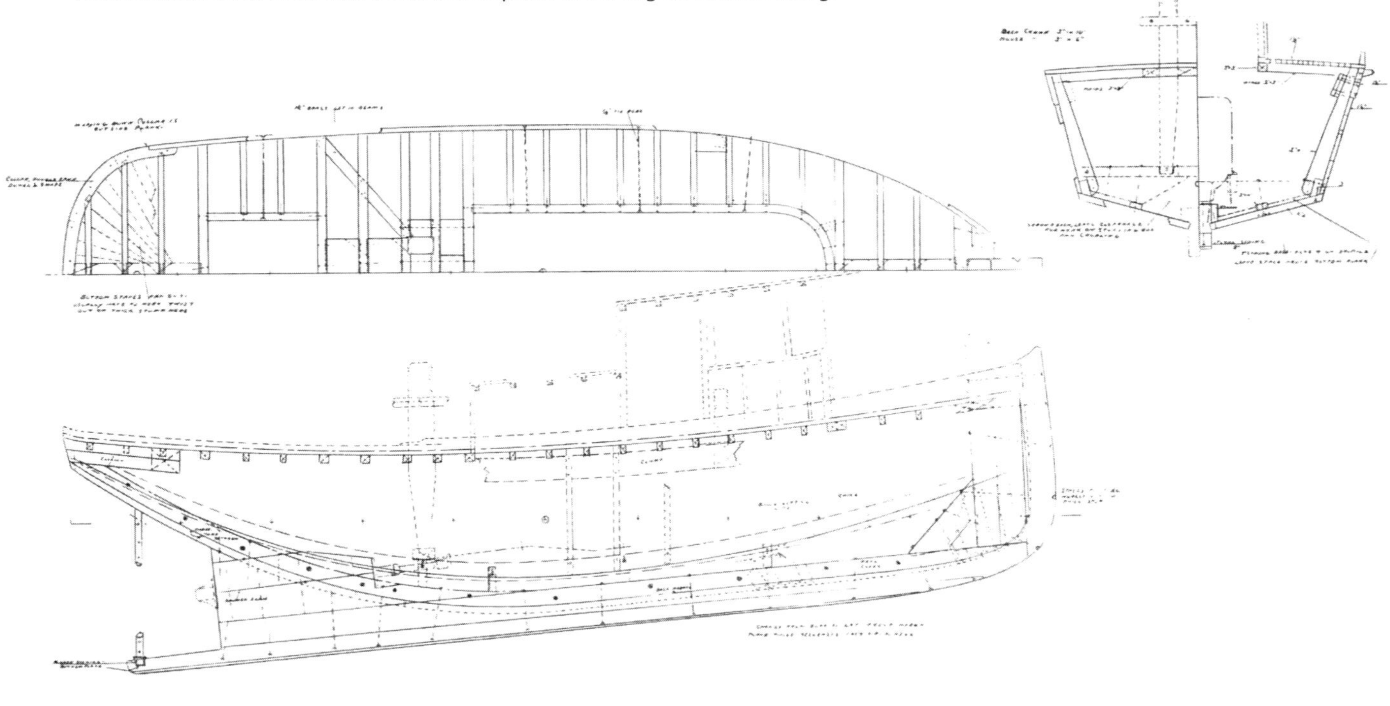

Length overall: 39 feet 10 inches
Beam: 9 feet
Draft: 2 feet 10 inches
Displacement: 4 tons

V-Bottomed Launch Proposal For Commodore Percy Chubb

This is a sleek, stylish, and handsome V-bottomed workboat proposal for Commodore Percy Chubb. She is somewhat along the lines of the Chesapeake Bay Deltaville deadrise design, using inboard power. Estimated displacement is 4 tons.

On any potential design commission, Pete would first rough out a sketch to solidify his thinking based on the client's requirements. Then he would work up a proposal drawing, including profile, body plan, and sometimes half-breadth, with accommodations sketched in. This is what you see here. Once the basic considerations were nailed down, he would cut a half-model, lift the lines, correct and fair them, and then flesh out the design with construction, accommodations, rig, and details. It was a process that allowed natural evolution and minimized unnecessary effort.

This 39-foot 10-inch V-bottomed boat and the 28-foot round-bottomed one discussed next were design proposals for a service launch for Peter Island in the British Virgin Islands. The boat was to make daily trips to Tortola, and occasionally a trip to St. Thomas, in the U.S. Virgins. For whatever reason, the boat was never built.

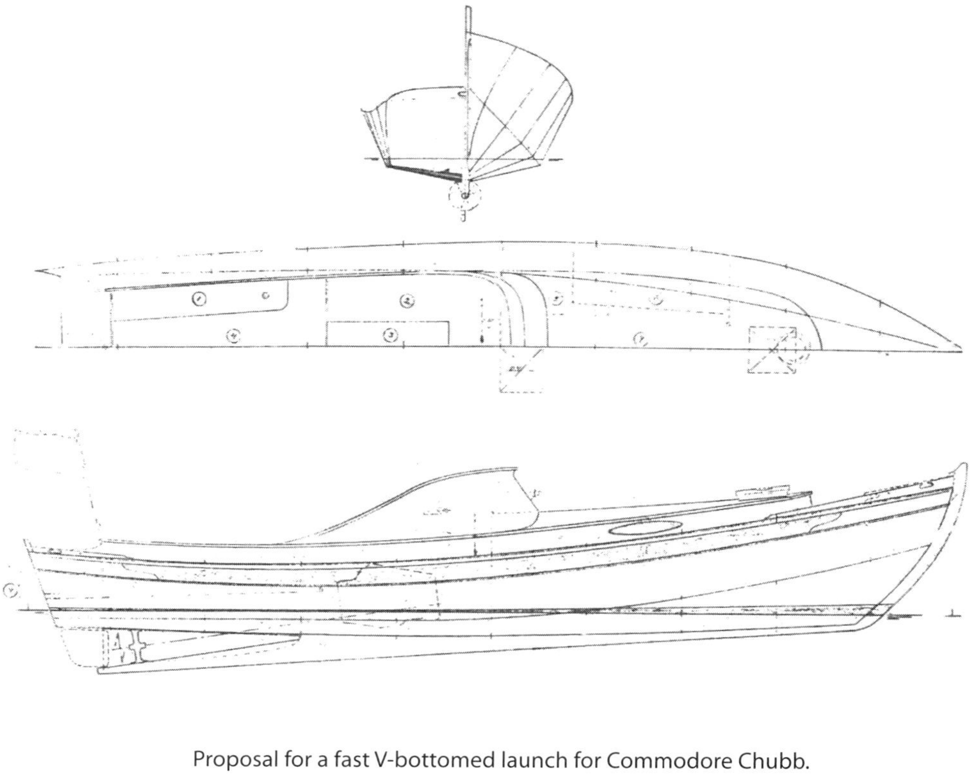

Proposal for a fast V-bottomed launch for Commodore Chubb.

Round-Bottomed Launch Proposal For Commodore Percy Chubb

Length overall: 28 feet 9 inches
Beam: 9 feet
Draft: 2 feet 9 inches

Comments by Pete Culler

This is a discussion of the proposed launch for Percy Chubb, and the thinking that developed the sketch this far. At this point I see no reason to make other than a simple sketch. When we see we are on the right track, it can be developed further, and a set of lines, construction requirements, and details worked up.

I feel that with the use of a diesel, the carrying capacity specified, and the waters used, that 28 feet is about the minimum we should consider. When one depends on a boat for supplies and transportation, it's very unhandy to be hung up because the craft is not up to wind and sea conditions. Also, there could be some emergency that would require making a trip, regardless of conditions.

To meet these needs, I'm considering a craft of good power and ability in the hull, with ample engine to handle her without working constantly at top r.p.m. Speed is not a problem, but ability as a working launch, modest upkeep, and a reasonable working lifespan are.

I suggest 28 feet by 9 feet by about 32 to 34 inches draft, depending on the size of the screw. I feel a 9-foot beam is on the fat side, and against the principles of Maine launch design. If that is what is decided, there will be cockpit space aplenty. On the other hand, I'd be more than happy to cut it down —say, to a bit under 8 feet—and increase the deadrise and draft a bit. The cockpit as shown is 11 feet long—about all one wants to expose to the weather in heavy going. Yet it is ample for the amount of cargo this craft should carry.

The engine presently being considered, a Westerbeke 4-cylinder, 236 cubic inches of about 60 continuous h.p., weighs about 1,000 pounds and will require a hull with some bearing forward. An engine of this cost is far better under shelter than in a cockpit box, which would spoil the cockpit for real carrying. Engine location is standard Maine practice, which makes for simple controls and installation—it should be quite open, with a pipe rail around it.

To my way of thinking, the rest of the cabin, with its very limited headroom, is just a place to stow light gear and to keep dry. It has been suggested that a toilet might be installed. There is room for one forward of the engine, but this is an added maintenance problem. Also, I doubt if anyone could stay on the toilet in a seaway, and for the short runs involved, it just isn't needed. In the tropics, I see this cabin as an engine house mostly, and partly a deck for the launch. It will be hot, noisy, and full of motion.

A diesel engine needs a lot of air. With a large cabin door, almost always open, and a really large Dorade vent, there should be no problem. The underside of the cockpit floor should be left open to the engine room and be vented from the quarters aft, and be left open at the sides, except for a high kickboard. What little rain and spray come in here do not amount to much—the air is more important. I think the Dorade should have a large decklight in it, along with the fixed side ports. Light discourages mold as well as air.

Using a windbreaker instead of the more common windshield is, I think, more practical, less liable to damage, and easy to keep in a workboat. These barbettes were common in naval steam launches. They are now coming back in favor.

The silly mast I don't like at all, but one must put the 20-point light out of reflecting distance of the helmsman. The reason for the high top transom (metal shod) is to catch the chafe of long objects that might be hauled. Also, it makes a very handy place to bury the stern light out of harm's way, yet it is reachable when it won't work. As shown, we can get in about a 42-gallon fuel tank, yet clear the quadrant, allow for floor vents, and provide a rather high exhaust.

This last is very important in a workboat. The usual exhaust near the waterline becomes submerged on loading the boat, and then the engine can't be started. There are very good reasons why workboat

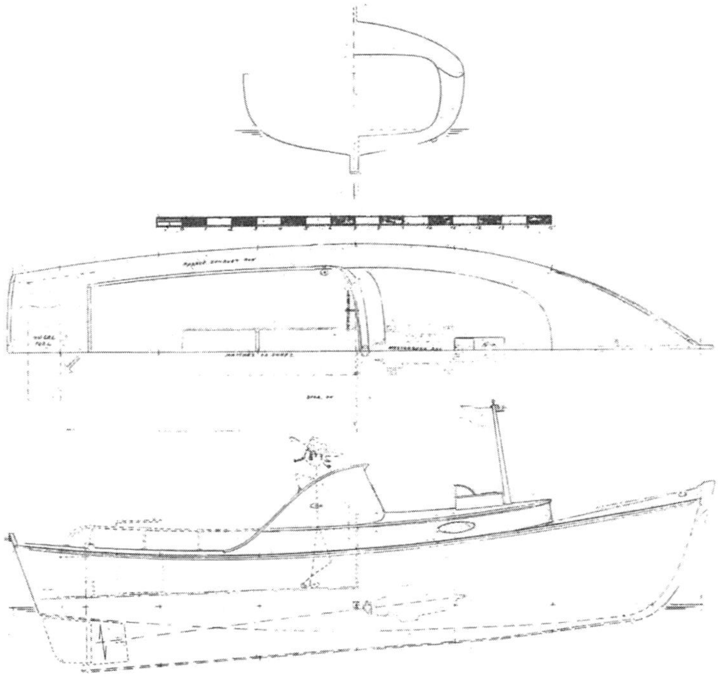

Proposal for a 28-foot 9-inch launch for Commodore Chubb.

exhausts are different from those of yachts.

A self-draining cockpit in a 28-footer always poses a problem, yet a rainy spell can produce much work, not to say danger, with anything that isn't self-draining. The one shown is 9 inches above the waterline forward, with a 4-inch drop. Possibly we can get a bit more drop when lines are developed. The scuppers aft, Maine style, have the same problem here that they have on other boats. They have to be plugged if the boat is to carry a heavy load. We can arrange these to be plugged conveniently.

To be reasonably safe and handy in a seaway, the cockpit floor should be at least 24 inches below the rail. This just does not work out in a small boat, unless she is so high sided as to be worthless. Hence, the stout pipe rails. I don't really care for them, but they work. They can be unhandy, depending on your loading and unloading methods. To accommodate passenger loading, one section is usually hinged. Such rails are worthwhile for keeping people and loose cargo in place, for small launches have a habit of slatting badly at times.

The 6-foot-tall pirate in the drawing is to give proportion—he does not come with the design.

About general fittings: I would have them stout and plain, and an iron wheel, with sprocket and cable steering. Nothing should be enclosed on the afterdeck or anywhere else. Instruments can be mounted within the cabin, with controls both manual and simple. The 14-inch dresser back of the barbette is intended only for a small compass and one's pipe. In other words, rig her out with simplicity and durability in mind.

Assuming that this launch might be built by Concordia, we must consider materials that this yard is able to get in good quality. I see no point in sending halfway around the world for exotic material in the hope that it will make the boat last longer. Good stuff, well put up—with more than the usual attention paid to light, ventilation, and the prevention of freshwater leaks—is better than all the teak in Burma poorly done and made airtight.

Maine launches, having developed over a long period of time, have a very good proportion of scantling. Personally, I much favor the flat-frame, clinched-plank construction, and the use of a stout harpin plank in the sides. This framing method is open to some question by those not familiar with it, and many do not agree with my views. However, it's a simple and lasting method. The plank harpin is needed. Boats of this type built otherwise are always subject to panting, no matter how good the work.

The bulkhead in such a craft offers little in terms of strength, for it's cut in two by a door. Thus, this is essentially an open, unsupported hull. This is standard, and common, but it requires a harpin to hold the shape. The house top and the decks aft of the cabin should be canvas covered. My feeling would be to avoid the use of plywood; it tends to sweat. Use good cedar instead.

I don't know just what your hauling and painting problems will be, but I can say that such work will have to be done often. Suppose the boat can be beached. Sheath the keel up to about 6 inches with copper, and put an ironwood or greenheart shoe below this, say, about 1 inch thick. At the turn of the bilge, it would be useful to have a short bilge keel of greenheart, so she could lie down, preferably on plank. Greenheart is resistant to worm, so if it's not painted just right, which is usually the case, it will get by. As you might expect, shoes are somewhat expendable; they won't last forever.

The lines I have in mind will have all the deadrise I can give her, which won't be much. With other considerations taken into account, she must have a rather short entrance, but as fine as possible. I want the low point of the bilge very near the center of the boat, and the shoal forefoot for best results in rough going. This seems to make a drier boat also. Many launches use a deep forefoot. All of these steer badly, impossibly running off. Nearly all are quite wet, and any bilge water running forward compounds the trouble. Water forward requires a long pipe for the pump to reach, which makes things worse, for there is a good chance the line will stop up. Because there are no speed problems, I propose that she should be somewhat more of a little vessel than most launches. I see a seakindly carrier that will run reasonably dry, and will not be a constant struggle to steer.

The proposal can be varied considerably to fit specific needs, if it does not already do so.

In considering the requirements of this design, I've assumed the usual fittings for rough work use. Items such as metal-shod guards and metal in the usual wear points are included, though not now indicated in the drawing. Such things as a thick cockpit floor that can stand the scuffing of drums and boxes, sides that can take some use, and so on, are included too. The barbette can well have a removable panel to allow carrying very long timber. I've not indicated any fittings for occasional towing, but this could be arranged.

Motor Skiff Proposals For Mr. Hankinwell

Light Skiff

Length between perpendiculars: 25 feet
Beam: 7 feet
Draft: 21 inches

Heavy Skiff

Length between perpendiculars: 25 feet
Beam: 8 feet
Draft: 2 feet 8 inches

Here are two proposals for inboard-powered motor skiffs using essentially the same hull. Due to the different arrangements, they can be classified as light and heavy (or simple and complex).

I think these two designs clearly delineate the philosophy Pete set down in the Introduction to this book. The heavier boat would be considerably more expensive, both in cost and operation. To my eye, at least, the gains achieved are dubious. I think the lighter craft is far more appealing. I suspect the primary objection would be the occasional need to bailout the lighter boat—open boat, inboard engine, you see.

I don't know! I suppose those who would beef about this simple duty also fear missing the umpteenth rerun of "Gilligan's Island"! Is that too harsh? Perhaps. With all the claptrap we hear today about maintenance, on the other hand, perhaps it isn't.

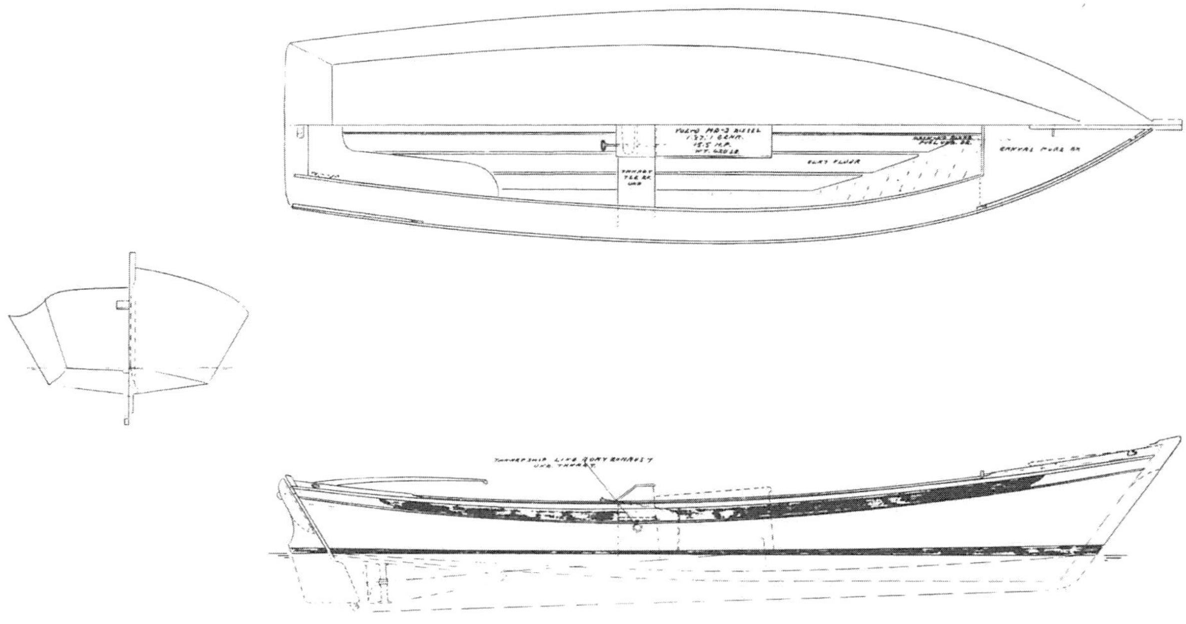

Above and below: Plans for the 2 motor skiff proposals for Mr. Hankinwell.

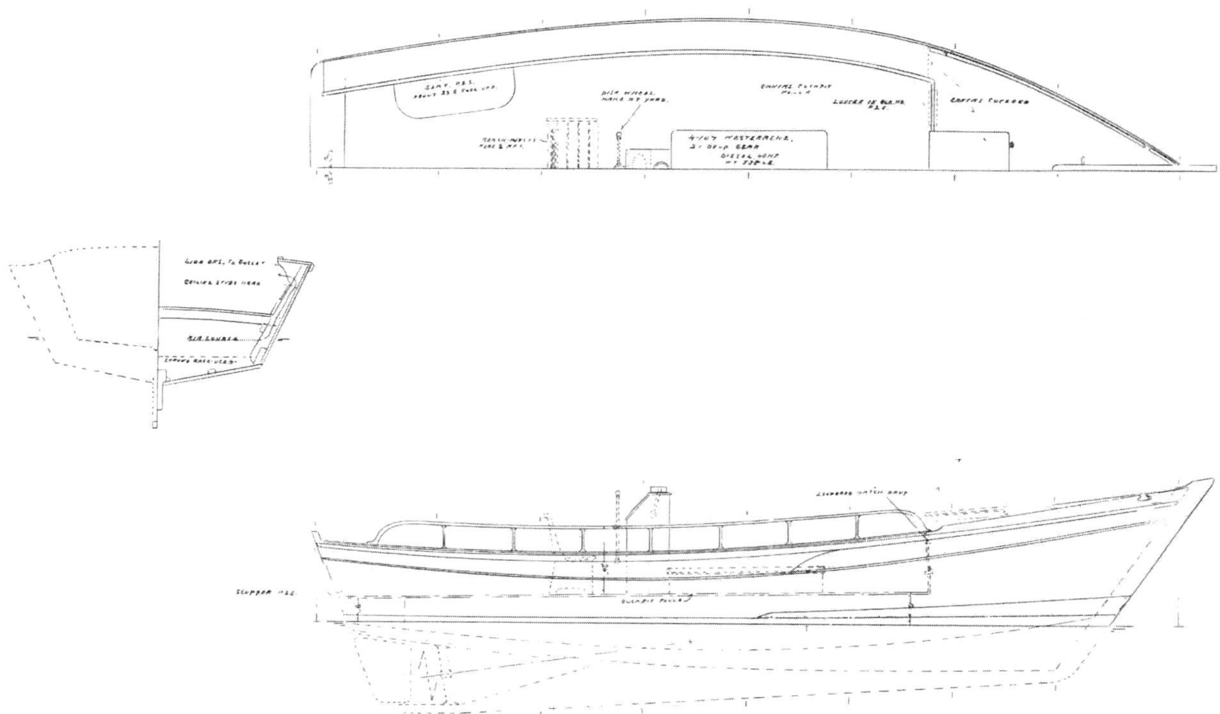

Fast Outboard For Commodore Percy Chubb

Length overall: 24 feet
Beam: 7 feet
Depth: 1 foot 11 inches

This fast outboard was initially designed and built as a service launch for Commodore Percy Chubb. Subsequent versions were built for Mr. Phalen of Falmouth, and Mr. Forbes of Naushon Island, Massachusetts, among others.

The same hull form is basic to the. 15-, 16-, 18-, and 30-foot versions. This hull is standard Chesapeake Bay file-bottom design and construction, and certainly nothing new. Captain Pete was primarily responsible for popularizing it in the waters of the Northeast. As the Old Man said, “It is all a matter of chine run, spray-rail placement, herringbone bottom, lapstrake sides, and keeping the construction light but strong.” Clearly shown on these plans is the technique for changing from butt to lap at the chine for the bow staving.

Outboard craft in the sizes mentioned above are today perhaps the most popular. Captain Pete stated, more than once, that a potential boat owner buys according to price, or by what he is brain washed into thinking is necessary by the advertising for mass-produced craft. Unless you build these outboards yourself, they are not cheap in initial cost. Beyond that, however, their advantages are many over mass-produced craft. Pete has mentioned some of these advantages, but one he did not mention is that these craft, being made of wood, are easily retrofitted to meet changes in requirements. Many will cry about maintenance. However, the no-maintenance boat does not exist. Besides, you get out of anything what you put into it.

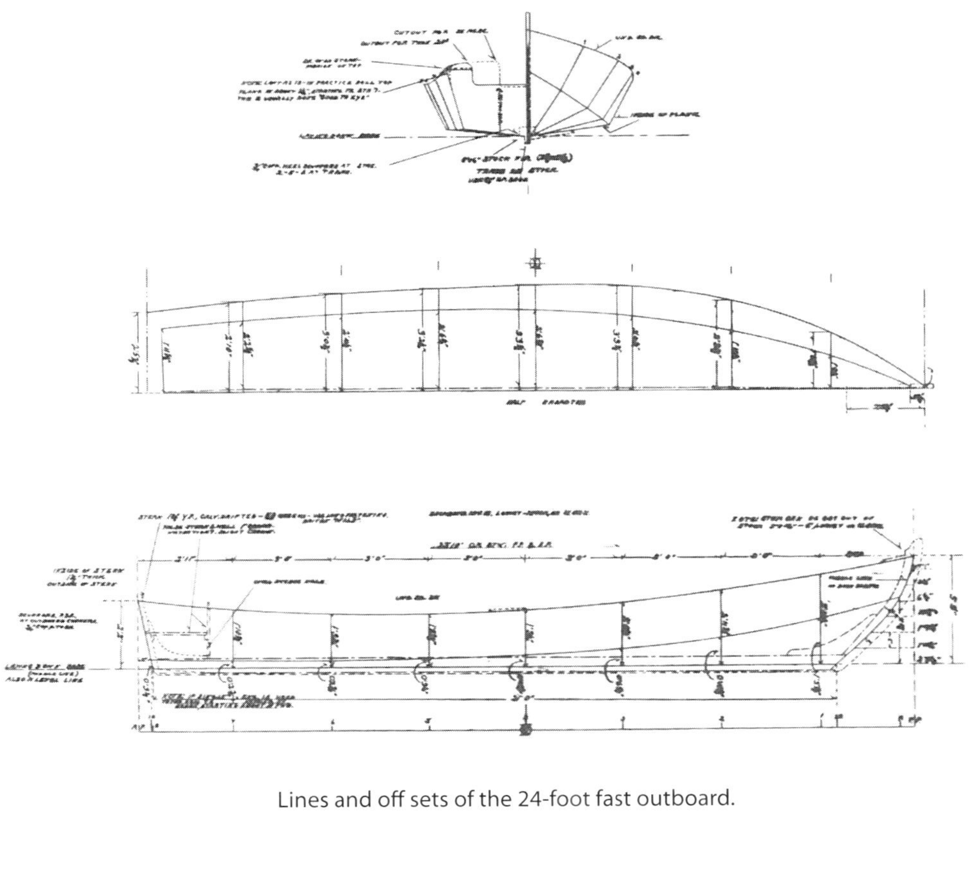

Lines and off sets of the 24-foot fast outboard.

Right: The 24-footer planing during trials. (Pete Culler photo)

Midde: Profile, half-breadth, and body plan of the 24-footer.

Bottom: Revised plan details ofthe 24-foot outboard launch.

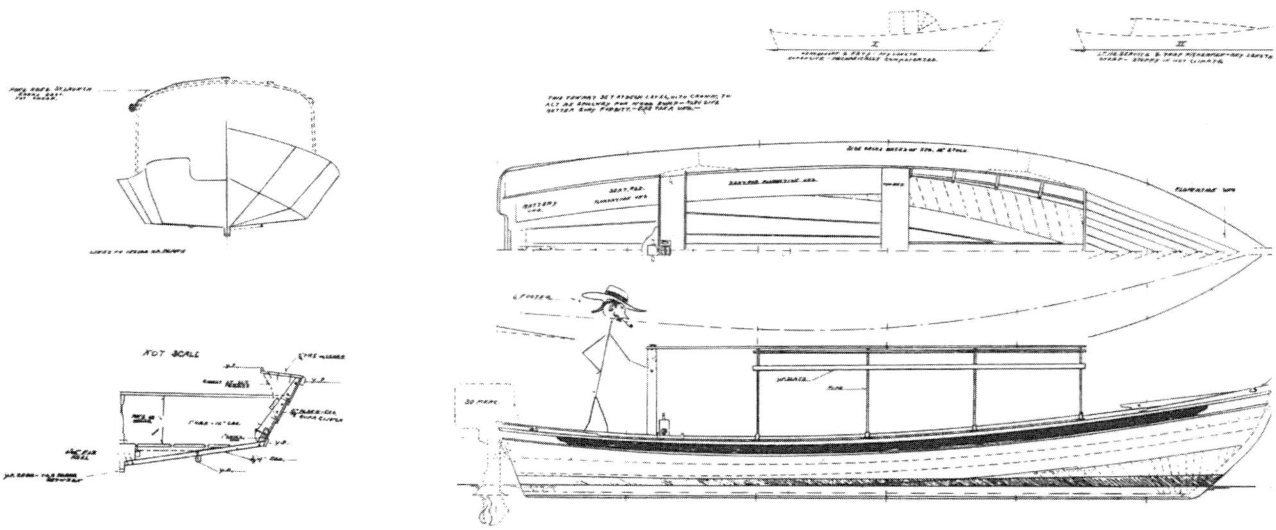

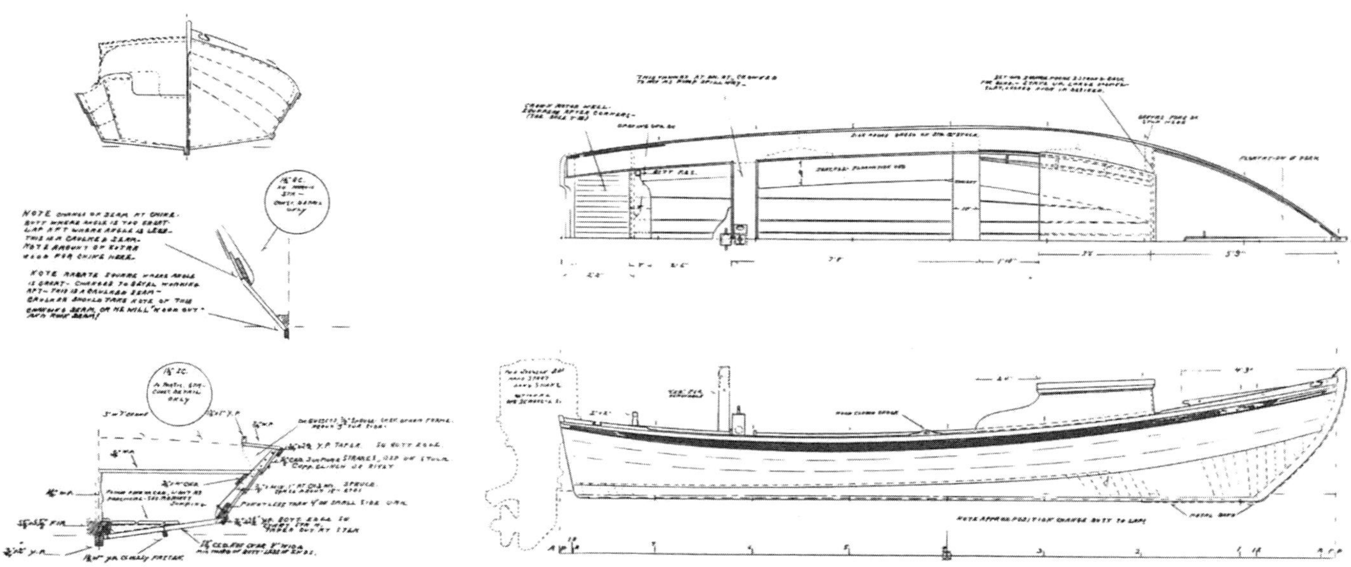

Mr. Forbes's Osprey. (Pete Culler photo)

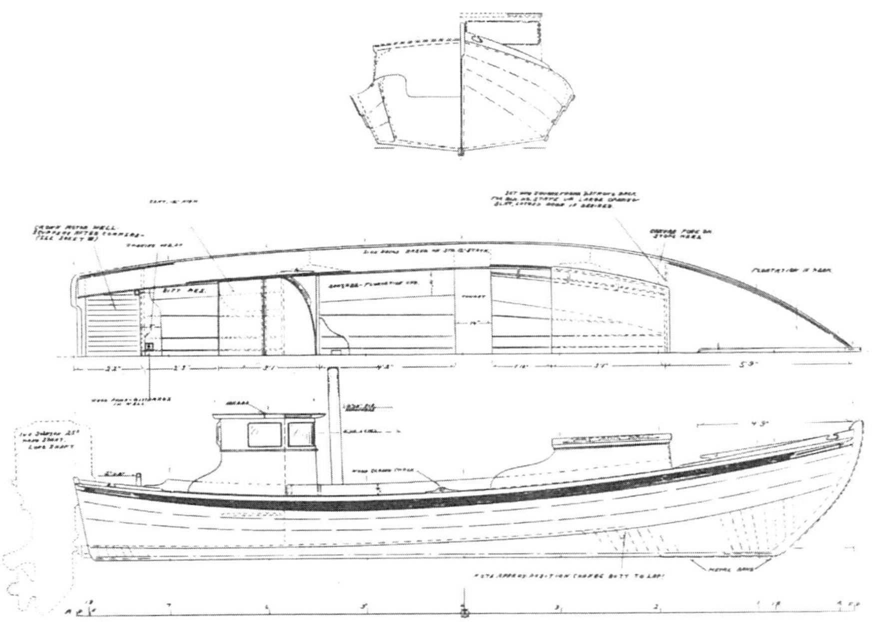

Revised plan of the 24-footer with "Rhode Island box."

Length overall: 24 feet 5 inches
Beam: 6 feet 2 inches
Draft: 2 feet
Displacement: 4,200 pounds

Fantail Motor Launch For Peter Burling

The fantail stern is deservedly appealing. In addition to good looks, it offers honest function in displacement hulls using modest power. Getting good capacity and bearing aft along with a fine run is no problem. In fact, it all seems to fall naturally in place once this design is chosen. The fantail stern is famous for steam applications, but it works equally well with other power options, as long as it's not overdone. I was once involved in putting together a 72-foot vessel of steamboat model; after the hull was planked up, it was unanimously agreed that a 5 h.p. outboard would push her along at 5 knots. The model is by nature very easy-moving.

On this launch, the topsides are very nicely styled. Fred Martin could not have done better.

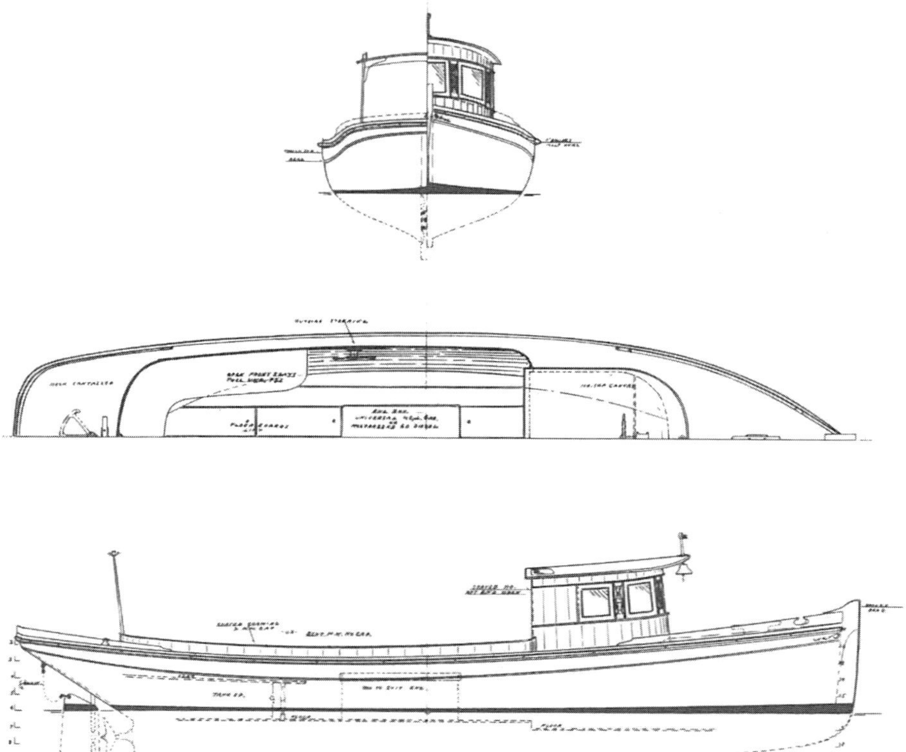

Profile, half-breadth, and body plans of Peter Burling's fantail launch.

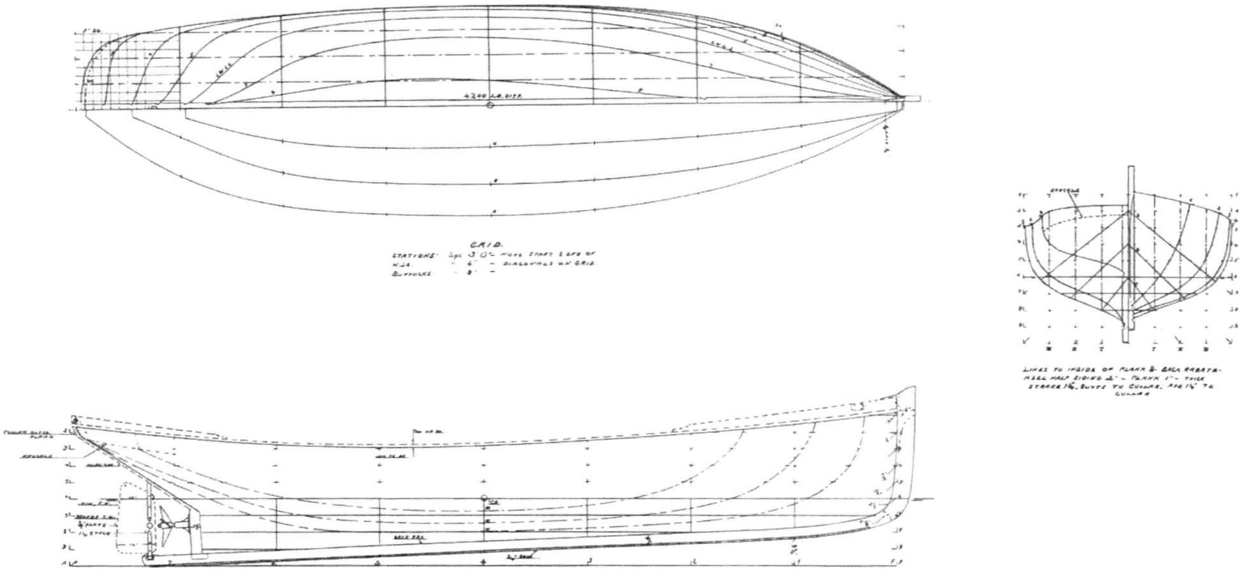

Above and below: Lines and construction plans of the Burling launch.

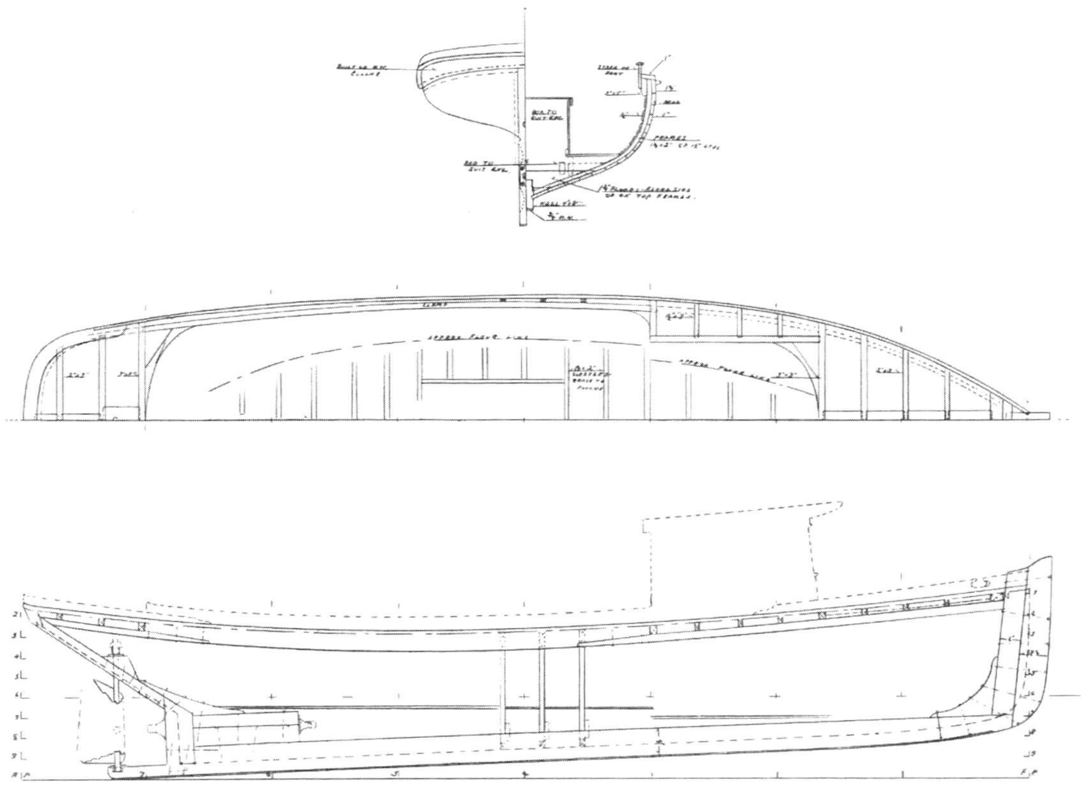

Length overall: 21 feet 9 inches
Sail area: 69 square feet

Outboard Fishing Workboat *Long John*

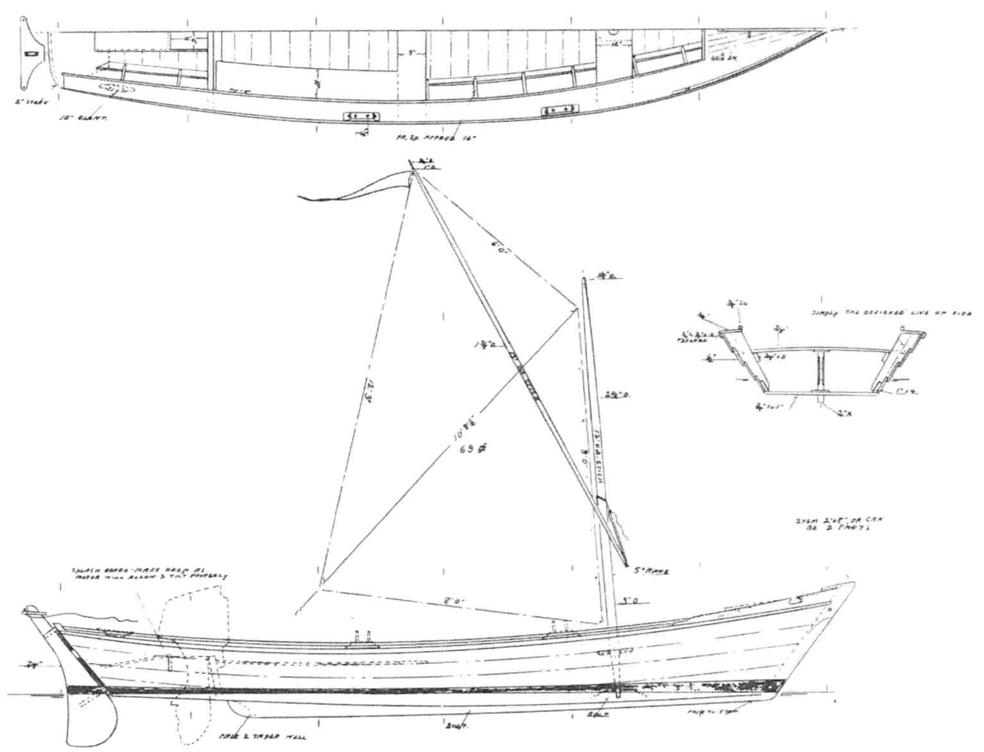

Sail plan, half-breadth, and section of the workboat *Long John*.

In 1974 Dave Getchell, the editor of *National Fisherman,* asked Pete to design a work/pleasure outboard boat that would be economical to build and use. The following comments by Captain Pete on the skiff's design, building, and use are reprinted from the July 1974 *National Fisherman.*

The editor, having had experience with a big standard dory with an outboard well in her, asked me to see what I could do in the way of turning out a design for an economical day fishing boat—economical both in operation and building, thanks to the high price of gas, big wages by professional builders, and all that.

We batted the idea around a bit; dories have some real advantages. Some time back I built a Sharptown barge that was well covered in the pages of NF at the time. This craft proved a very good one, and later when a full rig was added, she proved a very smart sailer. Both boats have some disadvantages, which to me at least seem very slight.

The editor had several "requirements" in mind; some of them jolt people a bit. After all, with expensive gas, maybe we need them. An outboard motor well was one; a weakness of many of these is the "gas," and the motor and operator both run poorly. I've used the open-end Carolina well, which gives a minimum of gassing. Oar propulsion was a requirement because you might have to have it, might want it, or might find it necessary for certain types of fishing. To confound things further, I've shown tholepins: you make 'em and they cost

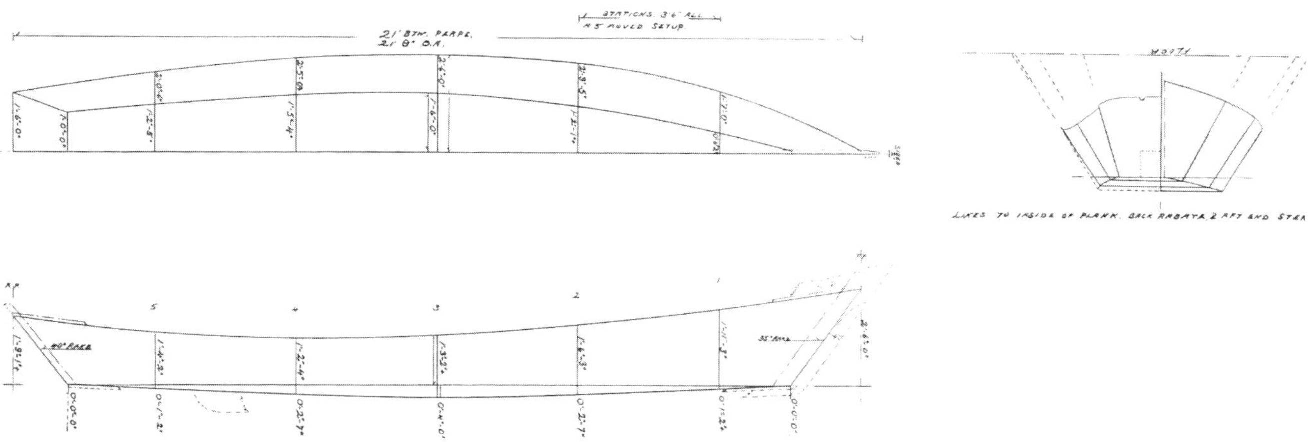

Lines and offsets of the workboat *Long John*.

nothing. I've heard many say they "can't row with tholepins." It's been my observation that those who can't use them have not yet really learned to row—besides, if you really don't like them, spend some money and get oarlocks.

Yes, the boat will row quite well in calms and flat water; she's fairly slim and has length. Don't expect to do it with 7-foot store-bought oars, however. She needs 10-foot narrow-bladers, properly shaped and balanced, which as far as I know can't be bought. You simply make them based on articles in NF, the works of Mystic Seaport, and such.

The sail is probably the most confounding of all—to have it on an outboard yet! In my young days there were motor dories about, and some carried just such a sail very useful reaching and running, and it steadies things in a seaway. One thing about it, if you can't stand the idea, it can be done without, along with the oars and tholes. But don't assume modern engines never fail; carry enough gas, or it's the Coast Guard to the rescue again because some fellow was not really prepared.

And will she sail? Yes, to an extent, a very good extent with started sheets and a good breeze, as the rig is purposely small. With a load of fish, fresh wind, and smooth water, she might even make to weather, full and by. Beat to windward? No, that's what engines are for in this case. There will be times when it pays to motorsail, motor and sail helping each other out—at today's fuel costs it's worthwhile.

The sail shown is simply the standard sprit rig, and is of a manageable size, not too big to stow in the boat handily. In spite of modern thinking, this rig should be done as shown, and as it always was—take it from one who uses this type of sail a lot.

No stays are needed, and it won't work right with them. The mast must rotate in the step for sail to set properly. Don't luff to take it in. It's better to payoff a bit, as the boat tends to anyhow, or even head downwind, letting the sheet payout. Stand to weather of the mast, take the sprit out, and roll the sail around it toward you, thus saving a flogging from it. Use a treated cotton sail, never Dacron. The latter flogs worse and is hard to stow. Dacron can be just fine for a racer's genoa, but for a working spritsail it's a flop. The sail should be well cut and made, for it will be at its best in moderate to stiff winds, and the hull can carry it. With a load in her and not too much sea, she might just carry it to the point of parting something.

As to the actual boat, you might say she is a cross between a dory and a Sharptown barge, using some very good points of each. The proud sheer, modified somewhat, great flare, and prominent bow are pretty much dory parentage. The general hull construction, side decks, and much deadwood in the stem (for a reason) are Sharptown barge, or more generally understood as plain flat-bottomed skiff construction.

This is not intended to be a how-to-build article. There are too many of these now, with full directions, paper patterns, and assorted precut parts. This is done on purpose, with malice aforethought on my part, and I think the editor's, too!

Many good boatbuilding books are around that need reading. I think maybe Chapelle's book does as good a job or better than any on flat-bottomed skiff building. Many may dream about having such

Long John under sail. (W. Garfield photo)

a craft, or something similar—a few just might build one. A rare person might take the project to a professional. I can say now that the boat can't be built for nothing. Doing it yourself, the cost will depend on how good a shopper you are; common sense helps too. Boating is expensive, but it's so much fun.

Though this isn't a how-to thing, I will pass on some tips that will help you over the rough spots—some of them dogma, many of them based on considerable experience, others simply common sense, and one or two not generally known. Along with this are some suggestions and options as to layout, and what I think will be gained or lost in doing so.

The side decks and simple, square, low coaming have worked out well on many boats. I find the usual high coaming much in the way in boats of this type. The side decks add much to the stiffness and strength of such hulls. I like them much wider than shown, but with the taper aft as indicated. Many feel that wide washboards cut down the room inside. Actually, you don't use much of the foot room beyond the chine line anyhow, so the decks can just as well be wide, and the boat picks up less rain and spray. The cuddy is slightly shorter than I like; it is dictated by mast position. Yet, it leaves about enough room to reach under. Too long a cuddy is not really useful either.

Bowed thwarts with stanchions under as shown add much to the stiffness of these hulls. The mast thwart might have two stanchions with mast going between, a system that I found works well. Note that the side framing also makes the deck frame. This is a strong and simple way—why it's not used more I can't say. A long flat-bottomed craft needs stiffness, and I say again, to build long makes an easy-moving boat.

Note that the rudder, which is intended mostly for sailing, is offset to clear the well and to keep the pintle low. The pintle and gudgeons are of the English beachboat type—different from what we usually see, and for good reason. The rudder can rise some on striking an obstruction without unshipping; even a tricing-up line can be rigged as on the beachboats. You can find the lower fitting easily in shipping the rudder, for its end is high up out of water. I often wonder why some of these old and tried methods, developed for tough use on a rugged coast, have been forgotten.

The craft will steer quite well with rudder offset. After all, it's more advanced than the old Norse steerboard. A tiller can be rigged, but on account of its length, stowage, and so on, I think the yoke and lines will do better. You can in theory steer anywhere in the boat, trimming her to most advantage. Just another device once much used that is becoming forgotten.

The tapered shoe, which should be through-bolted, adds much to a flat craft's directional stability in a breeze, especially coming alongside when light. The bow blowing off can be quite annoying. The shoe will also help her ability to "hold on" under sail, and further stiffen the hull. I even think it will add slightly to her speed made good on long

Long John at work.

hauls; less wandering and "the shortest distance" thing. There is no doubt that a craft that stays on a true course without much effort is, all other things being equal, the faster boat.

The outboard well is probably of the most interest. I've shown it for the short-leg motor, though I have no interest in these for a big boat—the 20-inch length is so much better. However, if you own a 15-incher, provision must be made to use it. In either case, the well dimensions allow some variation to suit various engines. I would run the part the motor clamps on clear across the boat as shown; it's strong and forms a pen board for the two spaces each side of the well.

I would scupper this inner transom near each chine with a round hole that could take a pine plug so that the after part of the boat will drain or can be used as a fish pen.

The depth of the splashboard is totally controlled by the amount that the motor needs to tilt. Where weed is a problem, some make the well top to open so the wheel can be cleared without unclamping the engine. My own feeling is that if the well is for a short motor, have the top fixed and watertight, for if the craft has a load in her, there is not much margin; hence my preference for a long-stemmer.

Many, or I might say nearly all, will want to build this well of plywood—go to it. Having had some experience building wells during The Big War, with government design and engineering, I long ago came to the conclusion that I would build one of my own out of boards. The same holds true for the materials for the rest of the boat—wood, and what you can get and afford—for you certainly can't build with what you can't get. Such a craft is very suited to galvanized fastenings, boat nails where possible, screws where needed, and bolts for the big stuff. The only exception is that I like copper rivets for laps of plank unless—and this is a big point—you have a helper to buck putting in galvanized clinch nails. These, I think, can still be had from Tremont Nail Works.

The point of it is, if you don't have a bucking pal, it's troublesome and time-consuming to set down the nail heads. If you leave them flush, chances are someone will sandpaper over them and ruin the galvanizing, and you will get rust weeps. If it is done properly, the weeps might not show up for 20 years. Myself, with no bucker, I like the copper-cut nail clinched, just hammered flush—a simple way. As far as I can see, it holds up just as well as any other method. One suggestion—don't attempt it with wire nails of any kind. The results are not good.

The number of side planks depends on stock available—three, four, or five—it does not matter. Laps should be about one inch, and the more plank the thinner it can be—three plank maybe ⅝ inch, four or more, say, ½ inch. Note that the lines are to the inside of planking.

As shown, there is no beveling of plank laps except near the ends. This is one of the little-known methods of skiff building. Plank, of course, must

Long John under construction at Kolin Boat Works, 1978.

be lined off for, and once the garboard is on, you fir out the mold with a piece of plank scrap or anything of the same thickness, spile for the next, and fir out again, doing it for each plank. I use the beveled shiplap in the ends on all my craft, although the various methods of flushing laps at the ends of a boat do quite well.

Sounds like treason maybe, by some building standards, but this lapping works in a straight-sided boat. Sure, she gains some beam and flare over "the designed lines," all up where you need it, and somehow the craft is always better looking. I've seen skiffs built from the same lines more than once, one being beveled, or "browsed off," in the laps so the planks hug the molds, and the other with no bevels and firred out. Assuming both builders are skillful and artistic, the latter craft is always better looking, but I don't know just why. On the other hand, when I do a round-bilged craft, I take pains with the browsing so that the planks hug the molds without mechanical help at all.

What appears to be an overly massive stem is done for a very good reason. It's not of big siding. The amount of wood inboard of the rabbet is to get good landing for the chines, which, the boat being sharp, will have a long bevel. There is no need for a stem knee in this type of construction (thousands have been built without it), since the chines and side plank make plenty of knee. The large amount of outboard stem deadwood serves to taper to about ½ inch on the stem face, making a sharp instead of a blunt stem. This tends to prevent a straightup plume of water leaving the stem, often seen in heavily loaded boats, which tends to blow on board in some conditions. The outside wood also allows for considerable stem damage without harm to the plank. After all, we do make a mess of docking at times.

I strongly suggest leaving the head of the stem square, ship style, to give a good landing for, and to protect the gunwale ends. Most craft now don't have this, and damage in these parts often shows the fallacy of not having it.

The Nova Scotia-type bitt and buffalo rails with wood chocks cut in can be left off, but I think they add much to the looks and usefulness. The foredeck is the highest point of the boat if you have to scramble ashore somewhere on a dock, and the rails are something to keep one's feet in place. Besides, in these days of trying to make a boat look like Lord-knows-what, it's refreshing to see one now and then that looks like she may just be a boat.

In the past it seemed to be the rule to attempt to make a craft look good, be she a simple punt, garvey, sharpie, or other uncomplicated hull. That you didn't always succeed was maybe beside the point, but at least you tried. Now so much of it seems just the other way around—spend a small fortune and create a monstrosity.

Just what you might expect from this design goes about like this: nothing is sure until tried out, although with the parentage of this craft, one can be pretty sure she will go with quite moderate power; that the speed will also be moderate (less than the editor probably hoped for). This is a displacement hull. The ability to plane has been swept under the rug. The lack of speed will make little overall difference in her coming and going. Just start a bit earlier, and if the going is a bit sloppy, you won't notice the lack of it at all. As to what power she will work best with, my own approach would be to borrow an engine or two and see what happens. A cruising speed with only modest wave making, the engine not going full bore, would be about right, the reserve power being saved for very heavy loads or strong head winds. This is not at all scientific; no graphs, power curves, prop figures, or slide rules were used simply tank testing full size!

The boat will be quite able and can take some bad going in experienced hands. For those with less experience, I say, remember that she's a small, open boat; they seem to get very small in big, lumpy water. With the flare and raking ends, she will also be fairly dry as open small craft go, and be capable of carrying a big load under proper conditions. But remember that any boat can be overloaded. Carefully joined, even of simple materials, she will be quite strong and reasonably easy to keep up. Upkeep is part of seaworthiness, in spite of the much touted so-called no-maintenance boat.

If, because of location, beach work is the only way you can come and go, I would leave off the deep shoe, using one of plank only, and a similar heavier one inside, bolted through. You might increase the bottom rocker somewhat, knowing this would slow her some and maybe increase bow pounding. There is no universal boat, perfect for all waters, so modification is often needed.

An example of this is the West Coast beach skiff, which is a miserable craft for my area, where the sea is very short and hollow. Yet off Cape Ann in the big swell, they are said to do fine. Of course, they are first class in their own waters. I'm often asked what's the best size of craft for these local waters, and I always say, start with 65 feet!

This being quite impractical, we put up with very much less, take a wetting and pounding, and say, "That's the way it is." In designing small craft for my local waters, I find I have very little to choose from as alternatives in making an able boat, because strong tides against the wind make it almost impossible for both operator and boat at times.

The exception is that if the boat is quite shoal, such as this one, handles well, and you have considerable local knowledge ("Yeah, I just bounced over that pile of sand."), you can work partial lees in: water so thin there is little current and a very modest sea. You can take other short cuts, while the deeper and sometimes abler craft not far from you is diving into a regular overfall and making very heavy weather of it.

For my own use, locally, I would do with the craft we are considering about like this. Try a 10 h.p. outboard of U.S. make, and a 5 h.p. such as the British Seagull, although its big square-tip prop is quite a weed catcher. The sail I would consider a useful bit of gear.

Build her of the traditional local materials for these parts; that is, oak, cedar, pine, and no doubt eke out with lumberyard spruce and fir. Galvanize-fasten throughout, except as mentioned for the plank laps. Try to give her some style when building. Do an attractive but not fancy and yachty paint job.

Outboard Workboats

Light Skiff	Length: 16 feet
Heavy Skiff	Length: 18 feet

Comments by Pete Culler

The plan of the 16-footer pretty well shows how it's done. This and the 18-footer work well with engines of 18 to 25 h.p. More power is a waste and cannot be used except in very smooth conditions. The point of these craft is that they work well with modest power, by present standards, and handle just as well slowed down. They simply become motor dories capable of carrying heavy loads. This, of course, is not always a trait of fast planing boats.

These boats should be well fitted and fastened as shown, for fast boats take quite a hammering. However, these two are said to hammer less than many other designs. During construction, weight should be watched closely. Too much weight is fatal to a fast boat in the same way it is lethal to an airplane. The 16-footer weighs about 417 pounds. Her range for good performance is between 400 and 425 pounds. The 18-footer goes about 450 to 469 pounds.

While I can't deliver full how-to-build details in the space allowed, I can provide a few important pointers. The shape of this craft cannot be produced with plywood, which simply will not take the shape of the forefoot. The boats are well suited to rather light wood of a floaty nature. The keel should be of very stiff wood. There have been a number of these craft built, from 15 to 30 feet, using the construction shown. It works. Most of the new notions

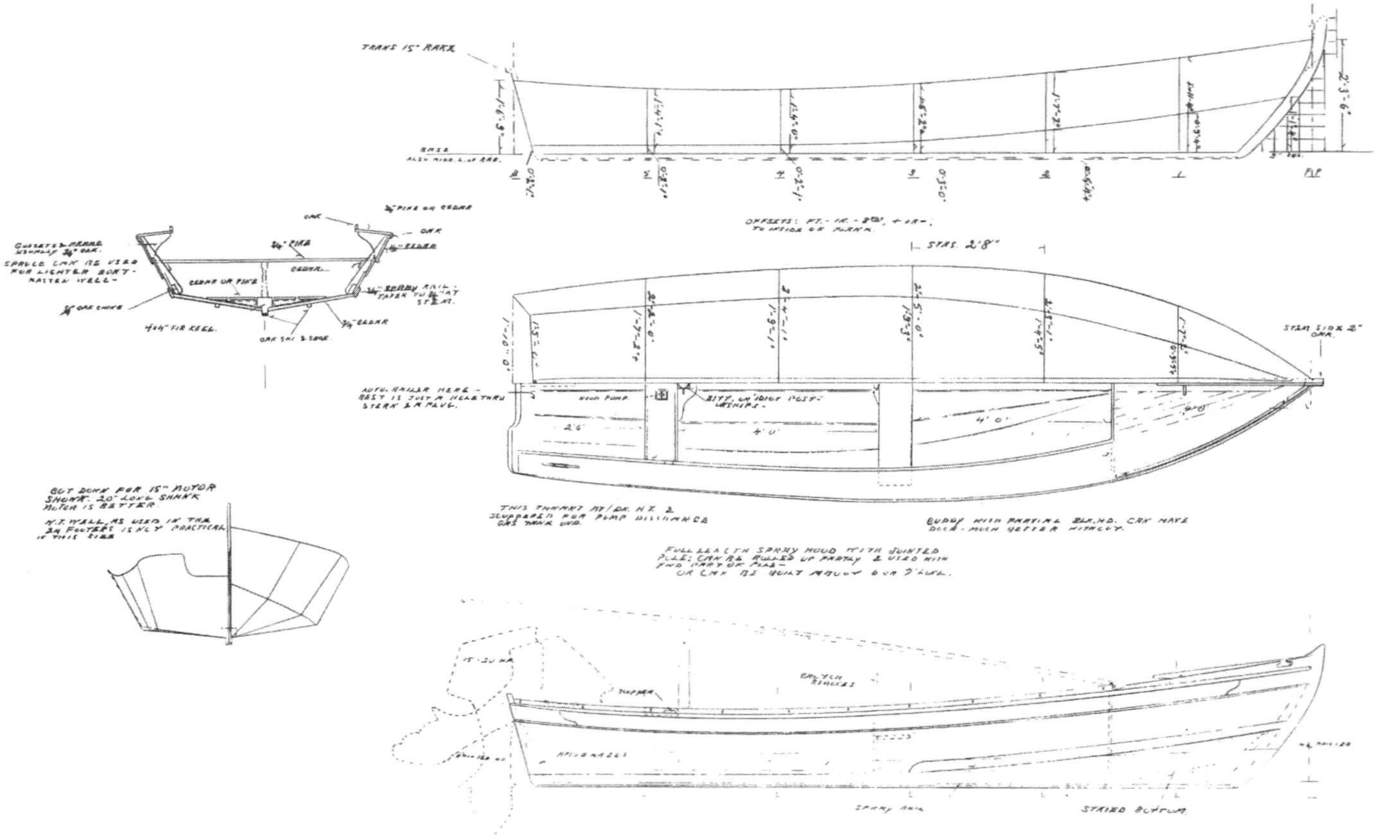

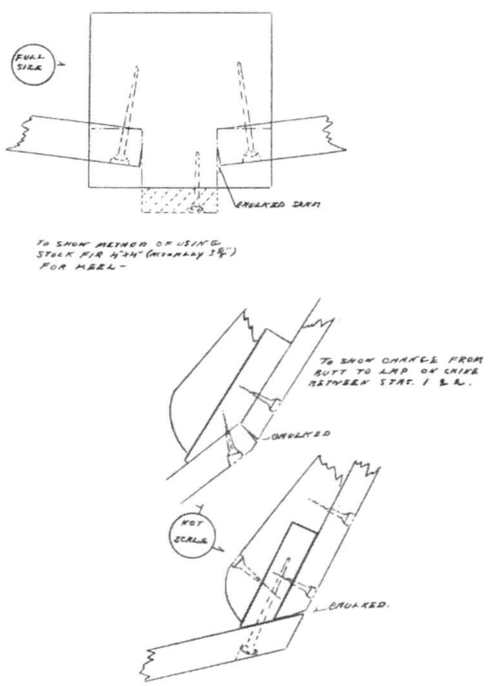

Above and below left: Plans ofthe 16-foot outboard workboat.

Below: Captain Pete at the helm of the 16-footer. (Pete Culler photo)

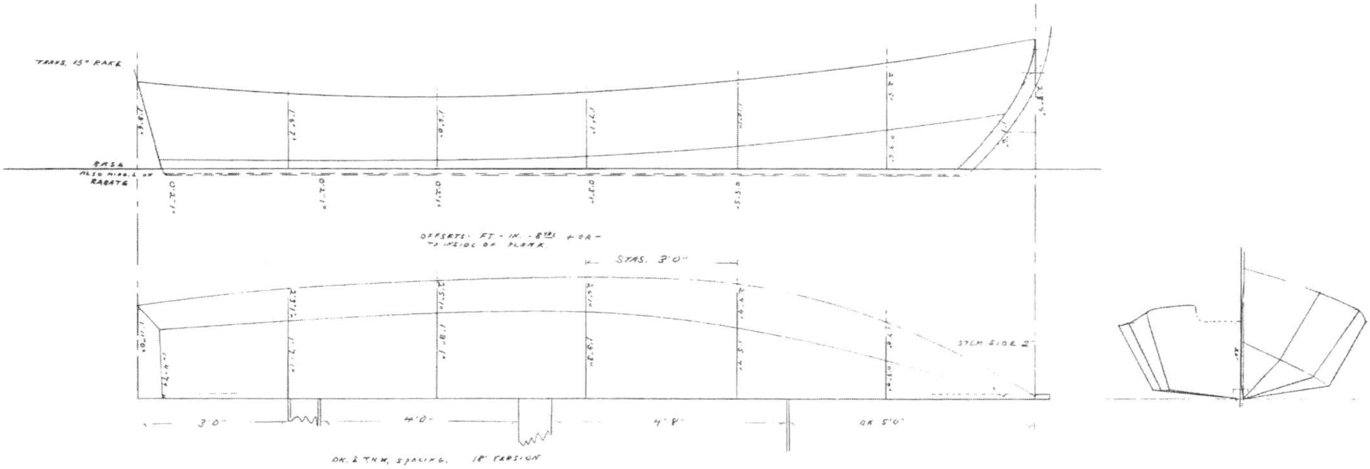

Lines and offsets of the l8-foot outboard workboat.

of construction just don't apply here.

After an 18-foot version was built, as expected it was more boat than a 16-footer, with more "reach" in a chop and more capacity. No new plans were drawn for the l8-footer. The plan of the l6-footer was used, the stations simply spaced 4 inches farther apart with the same offsets, which required slight fairing. The beam was *not* increased. This produced a slightly sharper boat. The sheer was raised about 1¾ inches forward and ¾ inch aft to make a pleasing line. The result is a handsome craft that performs very well. Of course, the 18-footer can carry more than the 16-footer, which was really the point of the enlargement—in addition to making her more of a seaboat.

It's very important to maintain the chine run as shown, and to place the skis parallel and in the position shown, as well as to place the spray rail as shown. This is where some builders go astray—they think they know better. Speed and dryness in these craft are very much controlled by these items.

Motor Yawlboat For a Schooner

Molded length: 15 feet
Beam: 5 feet 5¾ inches
Draf: 2 feet 5½ inches
Estimated displacement: 3,000 pounds

This is a very specialized design for a particular type of service. Her purpose was to be the sternboat on the windjammer cargo carrier *John F. Leavitt*, which was designed by Pete.

Power yawlboats came into being with the advent of the internal combustion engine. For existing vessels, conversion to inboard power was an expensive proposition, especially for anything as new and untried as power engines. Such engines were viewed with skepticism, and were employed conservatively by setting them in yawlboats. These could then be lowered away when needed from stern davits and put to use. Different designs evolved to do the variety of work intended. Some are essentially small tugs, used to push or pull. Such craft must be powerful.

This one, all 15 feet 6 inches of her, pushed around a 97-foot vessel of very heavy build and enormous windage in her tall schooner rig. This yawlboat was designed for an 80 h.p. diesel; it swings a 22-inch screw. The hull must be of a shape that can transmit all this power to the parent vessel and be stout enough not to fall apart in doing so. Look at the plan; it's obvious she was designed stout. Witness the molding in stem and sternpost, and the

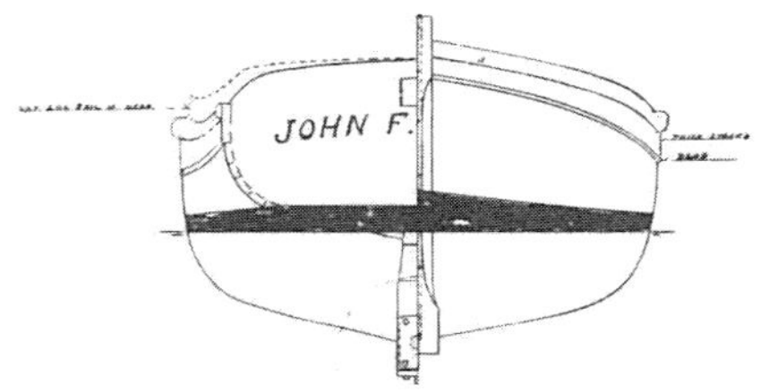

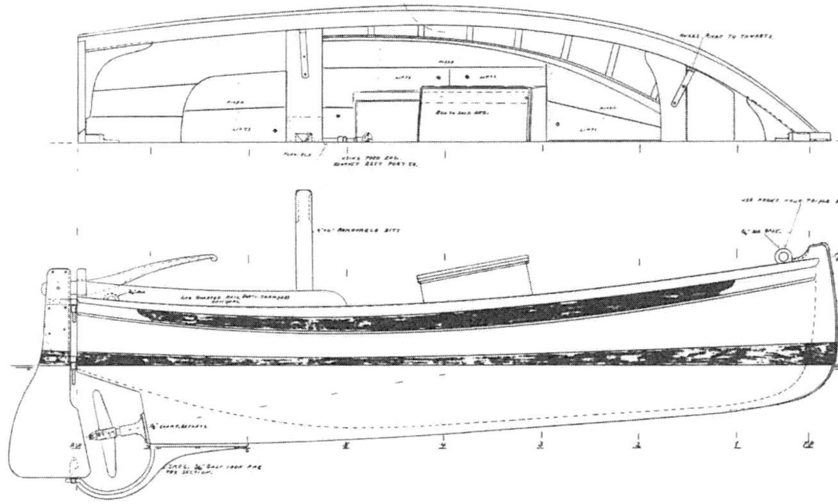

Profile, half-breadth, and body plan of the *John F. Leavitt's* yawlboat.

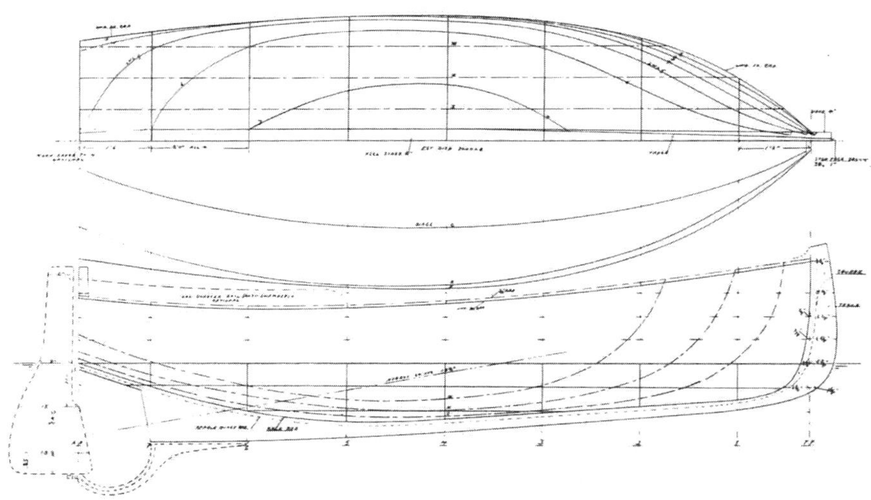

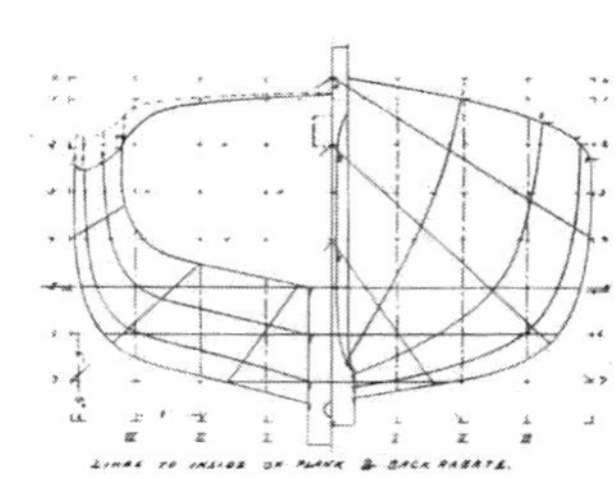

Lines of the motor yawlboat.

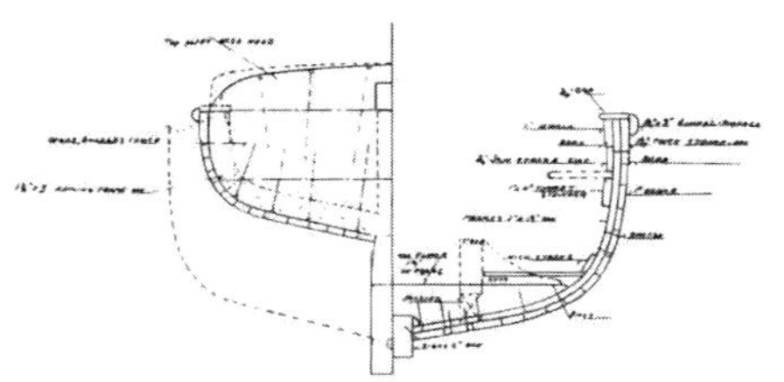

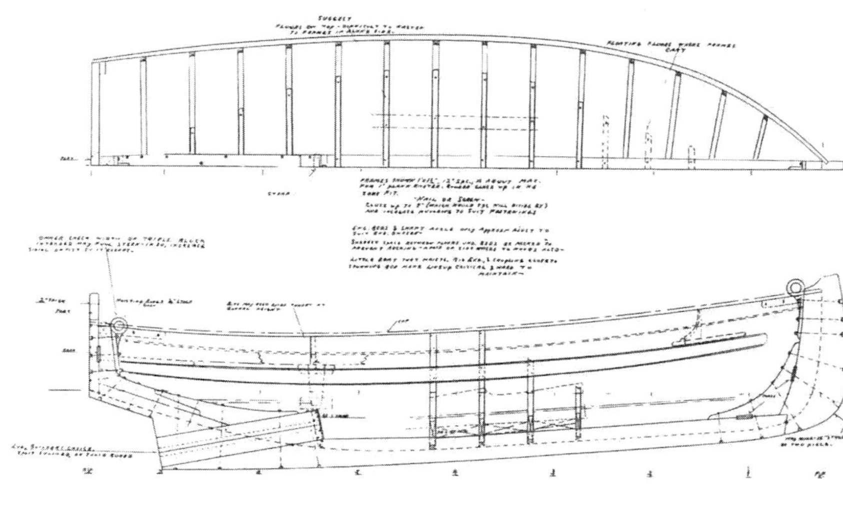

Construction plans of the *Leavitt 's* yawlboat.

"coaks" construction.

This boat was lost prior to the abandonment of the *John F. Leavitt* during the same winter storm in which the *Leavitt* was lost. The yawl filled with water while hanging from the davits. The captain decided that the little pushboat was jeopardizing the schooner, so he cut her away and allowed her to sink.

Today the use of power yawlboats is limited to a few specialized trades—the various passenger schooner fleets, the oyster dredging fleet on Chesapeake Bay, and entrepreneurs in sailing cargo carriers who wish to avoid certain regulations.

Molded length: 12 feet 6 inches
Molded beam: 6 feet
Draft: 2 feet 2 inches
Displacement: 2,600 pounds

Concordia Towboat *Gracie III*

Comments by Pete Culler

All boatyards these days seem to have some sort of workboat. Often it is just an outboard skiff, anything that is handy. Sometimes, however, one is built just for the work. Such craft are more rugged than the usual run, and better suited to the work. Such a boat may be called "the towboat." It will often serve quite well, depending on the amount and type of work the yard does, and very much on location and layout.

Concordia Company of South Dartmouth, Massachusetts, has a layout different from many. It is a large yacht harbor filled with moorings and boats, protected by a stone breakwater. Some heave sets in with certain winds, notably from the south and southeast. There is a drawbridge to the north, with a narrow passage. Occasionally strong currents run there. Next door there is a yacht club that is congested at times. A long stone dock, inherited from ancient schooner days, is on the other side. This forms the basin; it is, for the most part, well protected. Here there are floats, electric boxes, water taps, and all the gear we need for modern yachting. Larger craft moor here for service, and the bigger ones berth in winter, afloat. The craft moor all fours, stern in, and to buoys out ahead, as in harbors in Europe. Spar sheds and a crane are at the end of the dock. The railway and rigging loft are at the head of the basin—a nice but not very common setup in the United States.

Naturally, with this basin, the surrounding harbor, and other obstructions, a workboat was much used. For many years *Gracie I* was the boat of all work, along with a couple of tired but stubborn skiffs. The Towboat was a flat-bottomed thing of undetermined origin with a one-lung Falcon. Though underpowered, for years she did great work, mostly due to skillful handling. Like all things, she wore out, and a similar, slightly larger one was built, this time with a one-jug diesel in her. This is *Gracie II*. She's still working, though becoming outclassed. A trip down the harbor in her is an experience. The vibration points of the engine and hull totally agree, so anyone aboard sees everything double, and your jowls jiggle for a week thereafter.

Times change, and new men and boats appear. Boats with tall rigs, cutaway ends, light displacement, stocky houseboats, multihulls, and hordes of small stuff come along, most ailing at one time or another. A real towboat was needed, and it had to be in miniature for the crowded basin. I was asked to design one because I knew so much about conditions at the yard and in the basin and harbor.

There were some limitations: the craft could not be much over 15 feet in length, or have much over 5 feet beam; she had to be able to get into tight places; and she had to be able to pull. Having had experience with harbor towboats in the distant past, I felt I knew what makes a good tug, even if it had to be midget size. A tug is grossly overpowered by ordinary standards. She must turn a very large screw. This, along with great displacement, is more important than mere horsepower. Such a boat must be frightfully stout of build, not only to take the

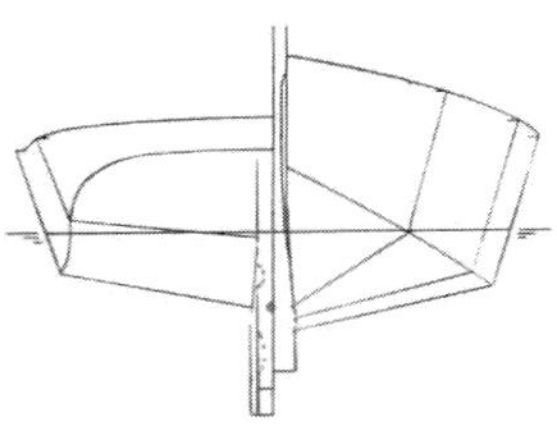

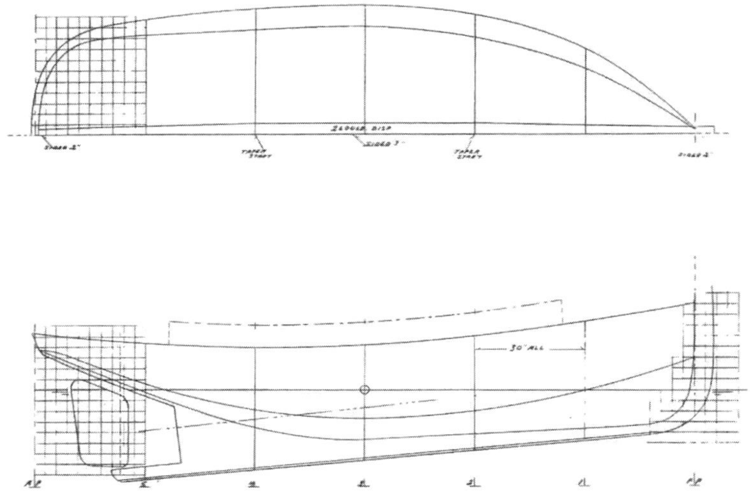

The *Gracie III's* lines.

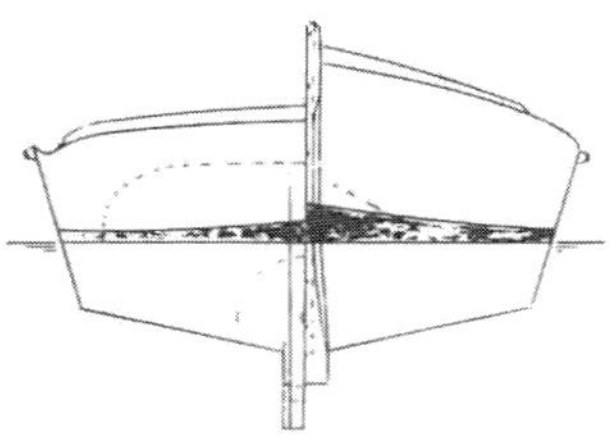

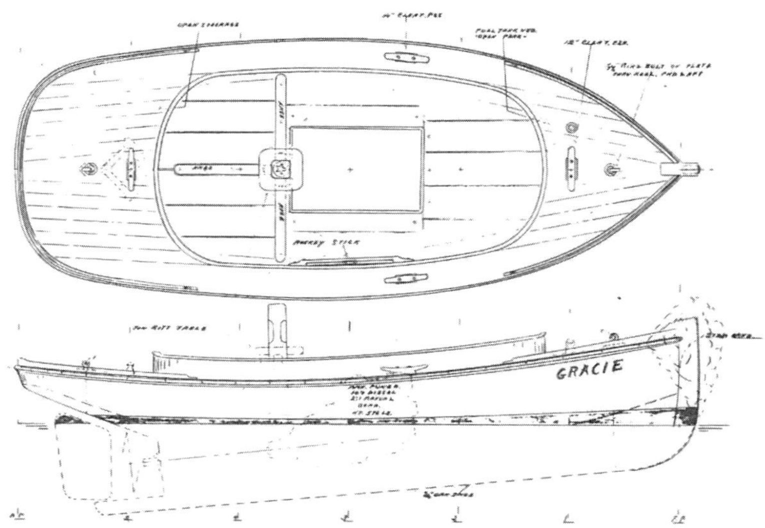

Profile and layout of the tug *Gracie III*.

pounding of an outsize engine, but also to take the hard knocks of her work. A tug can, and often does, get pinched by her charge. In other words, she often acts as an outsize fender; it's part of her work.

Besides having great displacement, the hull should squat to pull well, and handle in the extreme. In fact, a good tug's handling under an able skipper verges on the acrobatic. The towing bitt and controls must be arranged with understanding. The principles involved in towboating have not changed since the beginning of this art. Those who have violated these principles have turned out tugs "that couldn't pull, and wouldn't handle." Experienced towboatmen think such craft should be done away with, though their words for it are much more vulgar!

The engine having been decided on—a Westerbeke 107—the design and building went ahead. Fantail stern (so she could squat) with no corners to catch up. Crossplanked deadrise because it's durable, and easy to get big displacement in a short hull. Not at all for ease of building, for the craft has the scantlings of many a 40-footer. She is hard to build, with many curves. For taking a beating and standing up to the oversize engine, there is a fine snubbing bitt. She can take pinching to the point of turning up on her side and going down. I don't recall what the draft is; it was decided by the screw

The stoutly built *Gracie III* under construction. (R.D. Culler photo)

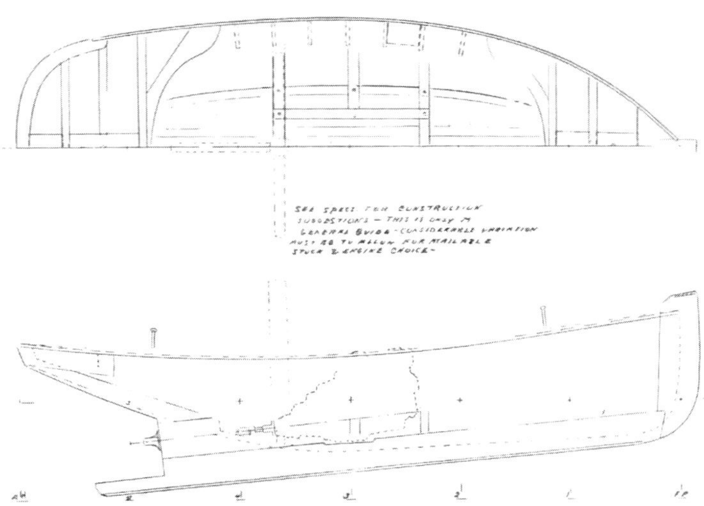

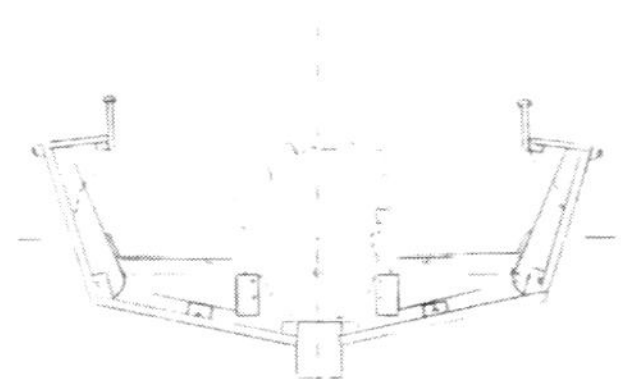

Construction plans of the *Gracie III.*

and shoe. The keel drag is great for handling. In addition, things were planned so there is little to hang up in, working among mooring lines.

Naturally, good fenders were a must; the great hairy Buffalo Nose does just fine. Being an ex-towboatman, I was assigned to make this item. After 30 years away from it, I found I had not forgotten how, only just how hard it was on the fingers! These noses just don't look right until there is an old grapefruit rind jammed in them! I say again that such a short, dumpy, full-lined, and heavy craft is not easy to build, no matter how you do it. Once at work, however, she has a lot of charm, for she is real, can do her work without effort, and with dispatch—a towboatman's towboat!

This is *Gracie III.* How well does she work? Just like a towboat, working most of the time at nearly closed throttle, with a touch of the gun now and then to start a tow turning or to snub her up. When you pour it on just a little, you get action right away. She can wheel right around and face her charge in an instant, and as mentioned, acts as an excellent snubbing post. She is not dragged along, screaming and protesting, by a tow that has taken charge—something often seen with light craft not built for the work. Like old-time schooner seamen who were "built to the decks," she's built to the water and can hang on to it. Her massive backbone and skeg

The *Gracie III* showing her stuffin tight quarters. (R.D. Culler photo)

are backed by a very thick rudder, with the traditional deep groove down the after side to give it bite. There is no rudder stalling while backing; she goes either way with dispatch. In this type of towing there is no time for the tug to back and fill, and then arrange herself for the next move. She must assume the position at once, usually hampered by lack of space.

When watching a good tug at work, I'm always struck by the similarity to certain very stout people on the dance floor. In spite of, or because of, in the tug's case, the apparent hampering bulk, they get around with ease and grace.

For those who might be considering a yard tug in the future, I point out again the most important aspects of designing one. Very great displacement, an upright stem, a fantail stern, and a large flat-pitch screw. Very great horsepower is not the main thing—an engine that will turn a large, slow-turning wheel is. And the engine must turn the screw at once, from a standstill. Occasional heavy but short belts of power are what do most of the work, along with a skilled operator. Brutally strong construction is needed; here I think there are only two suitable materials for tug building—wood for the smaller ones and steel for the larger ones.

Low freeboard is needed to keep the pull on the towing bitt low—many a tug has been rolled over by her charge. A layout that has a minimum of projections that might foul lines, and of course proper fenders, which should be of a material that gets soggy and stays put, are a must. A skilled operator too is needed; this comes with practice. In other words, do it just about the opposite from other power craft. Once you feel a good and responsive tug under you, and develop the skill to use her, it's a fine life—this is towboating! A proper tug, even of banty rooster size, is not cheap or easy to build.

PART IV

Cutters, Sloops, Yawls

Fishing cutter For Wayland Purmont

Length overall: 46 feet 5½ inches
Beam: 14 feet 4 inches
Draft: 6 feet 7 inches
Sail area: 1,178 square feet
Molded displacement: 43,600 pounds

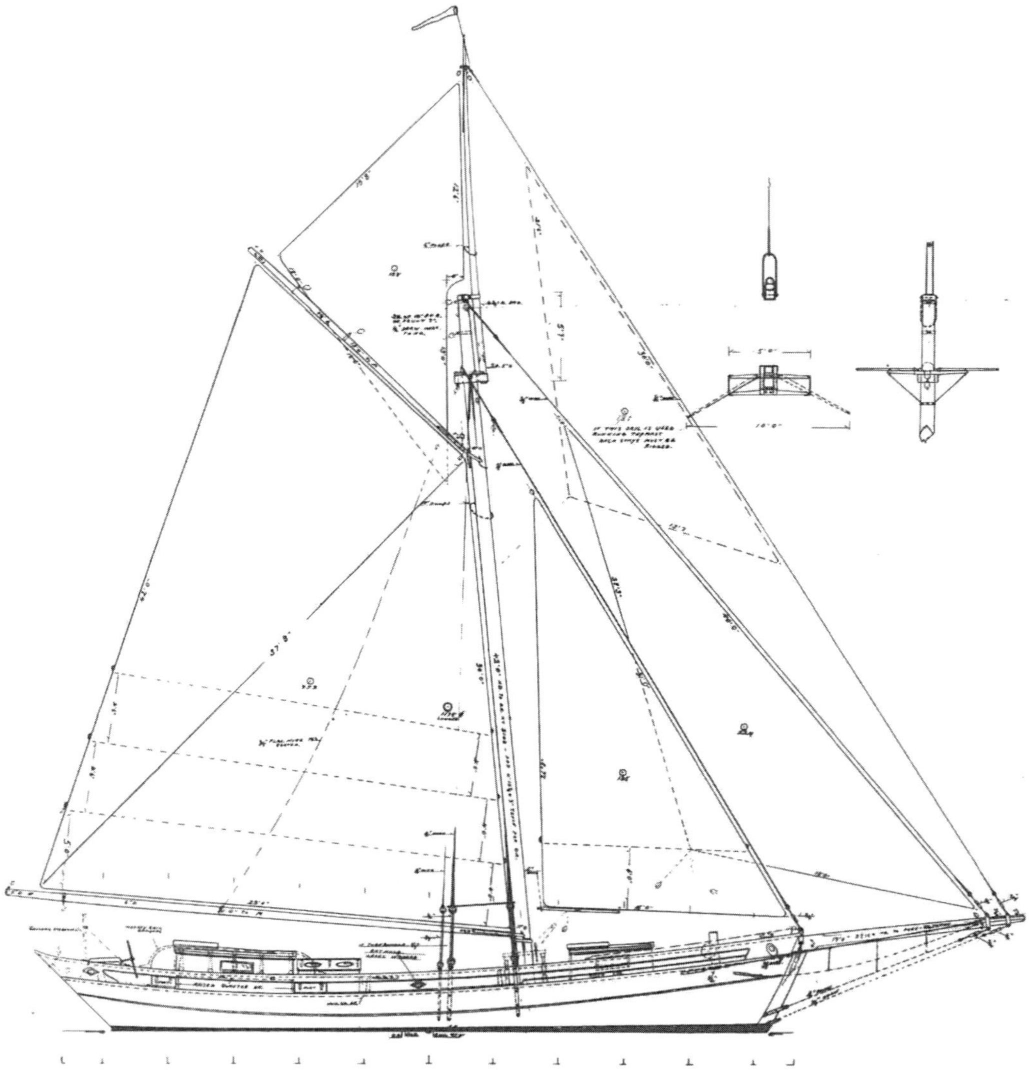

Sail plan of the 45-foot fishing cutter.

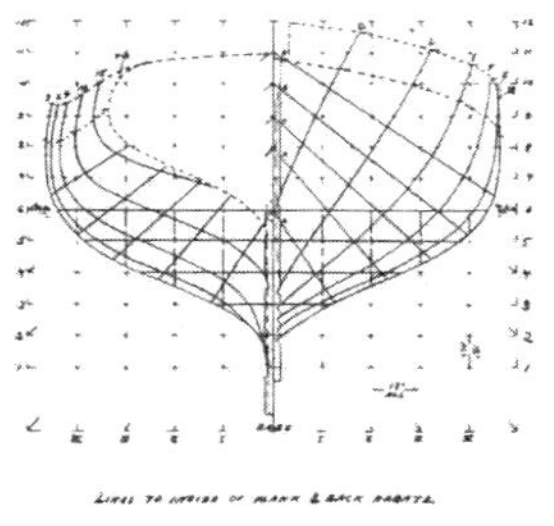

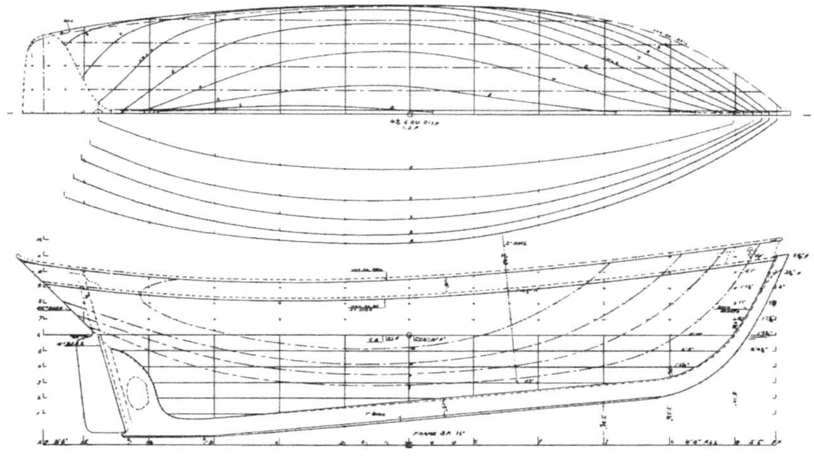

Right, above and below: Lines and accommodations plans of the Purmont cutter.

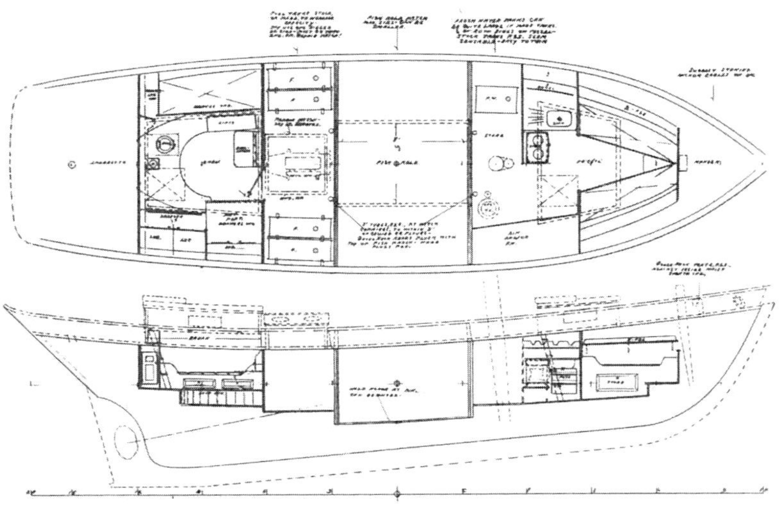

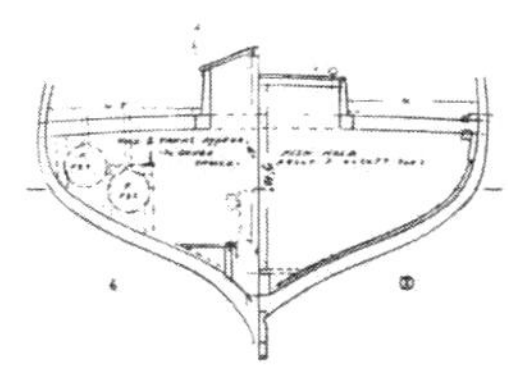

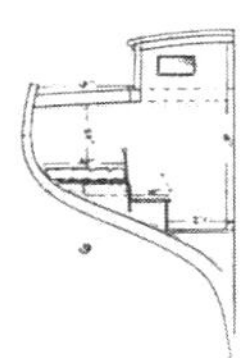

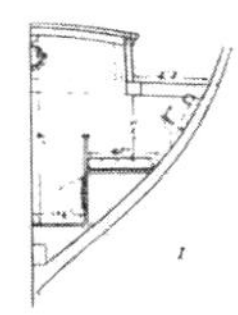

This wholesome-looking cutter with a 7-ton fishhold was designed for a gentleman involved in fisheries research in Florida, Costa Rica, and Honduras. The boat was to be built in Honduras.

The vessel incorporates a very powerful hull to accompany her high-hatted rig. The waterline is sharp, easy, and of nice shape. The keel is straight, with good drag. The buttocks are rather sharp, with a nicely shaped run. There is a fair amount of deadrise, in section, ending with high, hard bilges. With plenty of flare forward, the vessel's topsides tumble home aft, ending with powerful quarters.

Look for this cutter to be a very good sail carrier. I think she could stand up to more weather than most. With the versatile cutter rig, one could reduce sail to handle almost any conditions. Moreover, the vessel should trim well with the layout designed. Much thought and experience clearly went into the placement of engines, tankage, and weights.

Although that hold is not much more than a plaything, I very much like the idea of it. If nothing else, one could store all the Mount Gay rum ever needed. Because this craft is designed to be used primarily in the tropics, careful attention was given to ventilation. After many years of living afloat in southern climates, Pete felt that adequate ventilation was vital in a wooden boat.

There would be ample room to fit a small boat, bottom up, athwartship, over that cargo hatch.

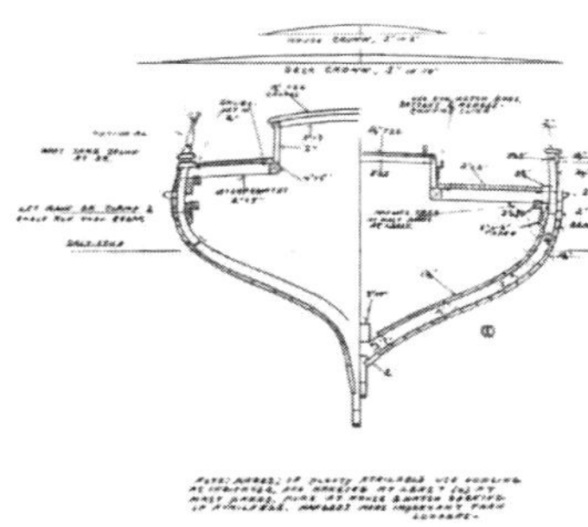

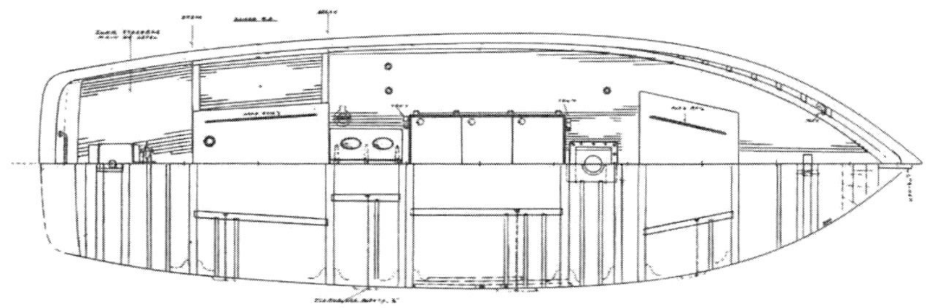

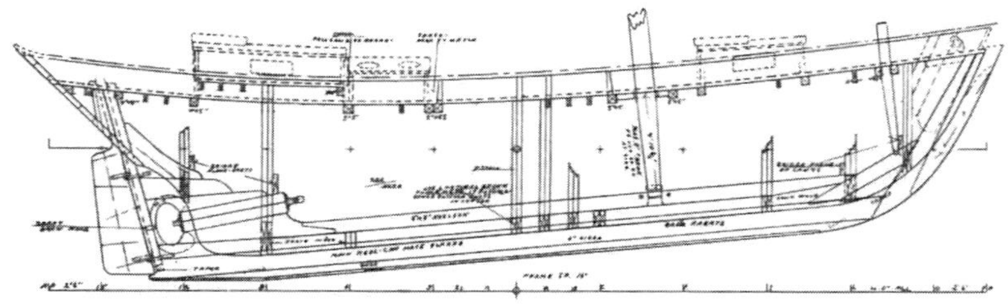

Construction plans of the fishing cutter.

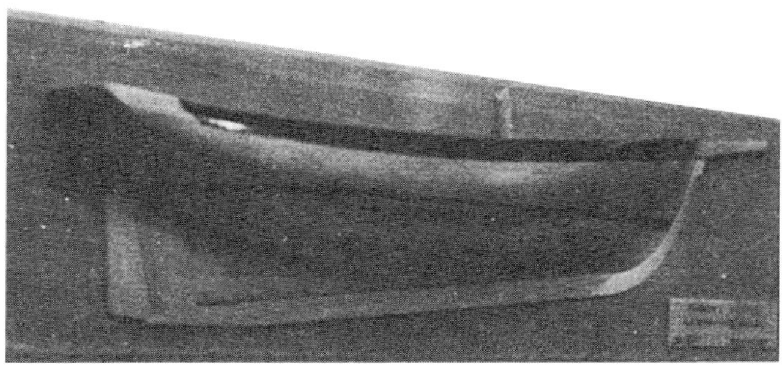

Half-model of the fishing cutter. (R.D. Culler photo)

Ballast required would be stowed inboard.

Construction is by traditional wood methods developed over the years and proved successful for the type—that is, sawn frames, keelson, stout floors, ample clamp and shelf, plenty of wood in the deck construction, backed by tie rods, and in way of the mast partners and hanging and lodging knees. The knightheads and hawse timbers are very important with that long nose post. When making the bowsprit, the bottom side is left flat and straight. All the crown (3 inches) goes on top. Naturally, it is eight-sided and rounded where indicated. With all the crown on the top edge, it will look correct when in place and hogged down by the bobstays to its proper steeve. This method is applicable to any bowsprit.

The bowsprit shrouds and footropes are required, for it is necessary to climb out there to secure jib and jib topsail, even with downhauls rigged to the foredeck. These headsails should be stowed and secure before it becomes too hazardous to do so. Be prudent.

There is much good to be said for the cutter rig. Good sail area can be had, essentially all inboard, with a single stick, which simplifies your standing rigging and thereby lowers cost and maintenance. Also, light sails are up high where they can catch any breeze and bring it down for the lowers. There's nothing more frustrating than wallowing in an ocean swell with whatever breeze there is just above your head, out of reach. After all is said and done, a gaff-rigged cutter with heads ails is a good-looking rig with a lot of charm.

This is a sensible craft as a working fisherman and sometime home afloat.

Length overall: 36 feet 9 inches
Length on waterline: 31 feet 3 inches
Beam: 14 feet 2 inches
Draft: 5 feet
Sail area: 604 square feet
Displacement: 13.71 long tons

Joshua Slocum's *Spray*

Ahhh, *Spray!* Ever since Captain Joshua Slocum and the *Spray* sailed alone around the world during the years 1895 to 1898, there has always been a *Spray* replica abuilding somewhere. In addition to those actually doing it, there must be untold countless numbers dreaming of seafaring adventure because of the *Spray's* odyssey.

As a boy and young man growing up around the docks and shores of San Pedro, California, Captain Pete too was smitten with "sea fever." He was, quite plainly, boat crazy. Early on, he showed uncommon maturity by realizing that boats and the sea would be his life's work. For role models he chose his physician father and Captain Joshua Slocum. Slocum was perhaps, at this time—the mid-1920s—the most well-known sailor in the world.

Captain Josh was gone, but the course he had steered was plainly marked for the young man to follow. In addition, Pete's father's thoroughness and exacting nature steered the young man clear of the many pitfalls that plague the building of a vessel like *Spray*. In fact, the contract to build the Culler *Spray* was signed by Pete's father, for Pete had not yet come of age (he was only 18) and could not legally do it. With *Spray* nearly completed at the Conley Yard at Oxford, Maryland, Pete's father

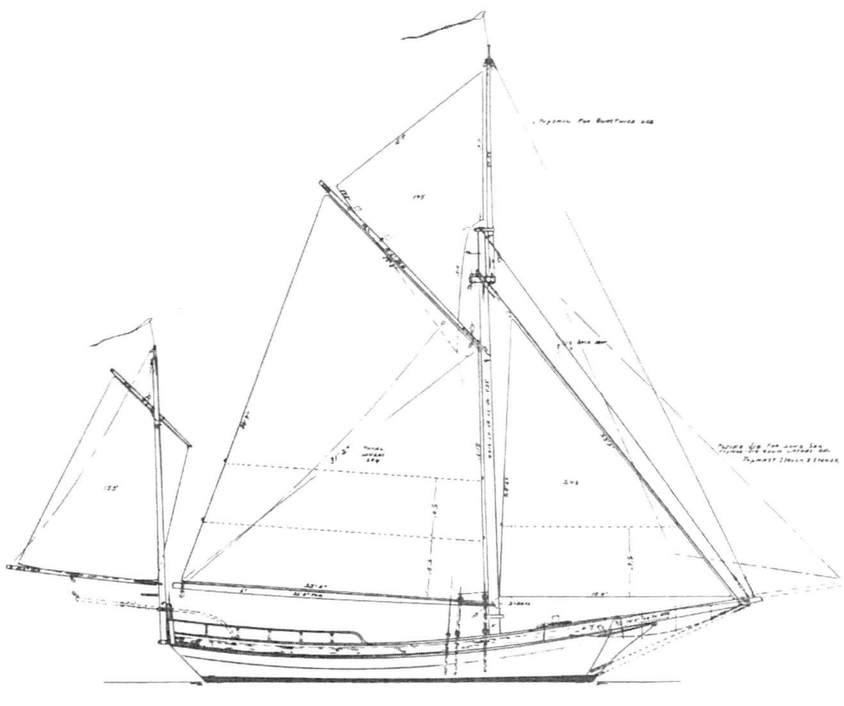

Sail plan of Pete's replica of Joshua Slocum's *Spray*.

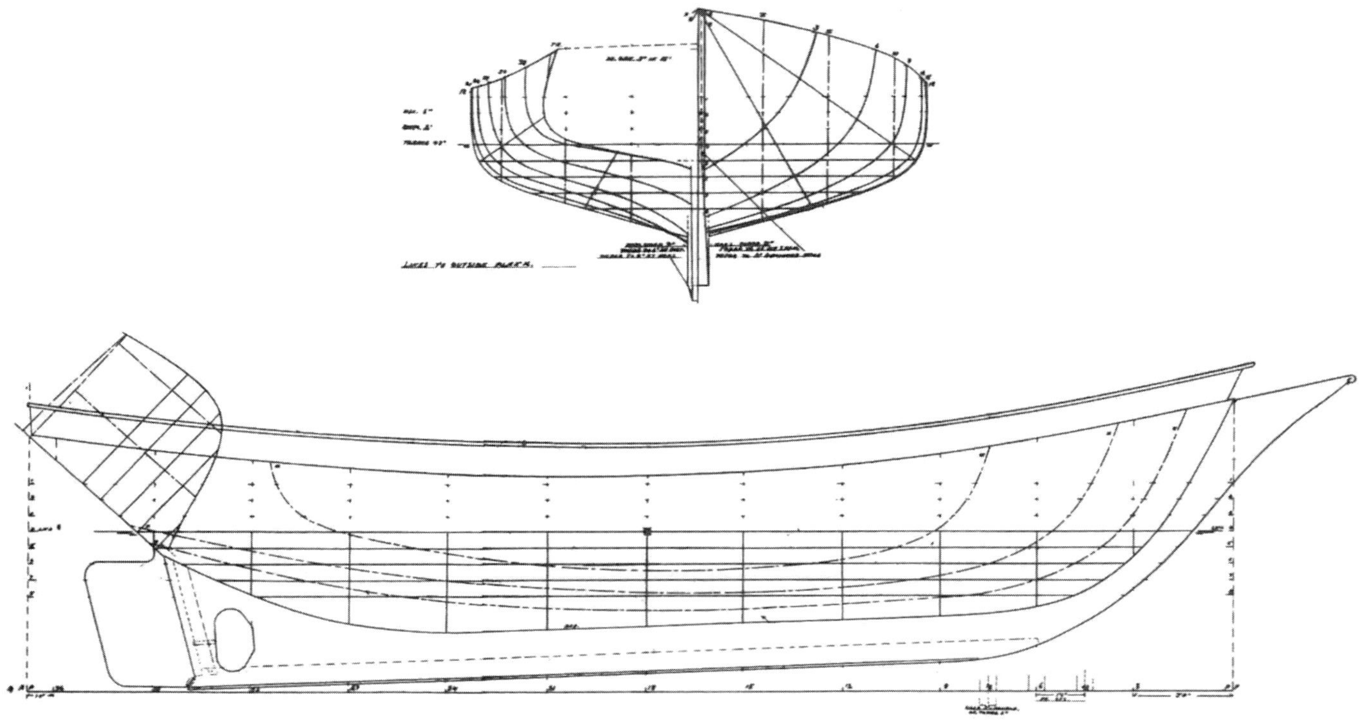

Lines of Pete's *Spray*.

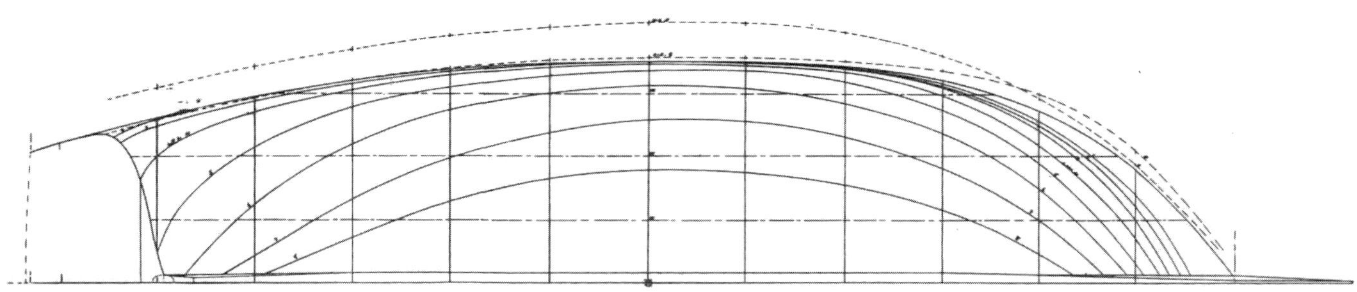

died unexpectedly and Pete inherited title to his *Spray*. For the next 20 years, the first 10 by himself and the remaining 10 with his wife, Toni, *Spray* was home. The vessel never let Captain Pete or Toni down in all the years they sailed her.

Anyone seriously interested in *Spray* (and you must be if you have read this far) should read Captain Pete's book on the vessel: The *Spray*. It's a wonderful story and the closest thing to an autobiography by Pete.

Prior to building the Oxford *Spray*, there were two years of careful research and planning. This thoroughness certainly paid off, since Pete's version has long been considered the best of the *Spray* replicas. Many improvements over the original design were incorporated, including a definite style and beauty.

As mentioned before, Captain Joshua was gone, but his son Victor was very much alive. It was from Victor that Pete obtained the original plans, scaled up to ½ inch to 1 foot. Over the years, there had been a persistent controversy that the lines, as taken off by C.D. Mower, and published in Slocum's book, were not those of the *Spray*. As usual, Pete met this silliness head-on with plain common sense. If the lines of the original, as published, were a fabrication, how was it that Pete's copy behaved with uncanny similarity to the original, as described by Slocum? After 20-plus years with his vessel, Pete was convinced that he had a faithful copy of *Spray*.

And so can you!

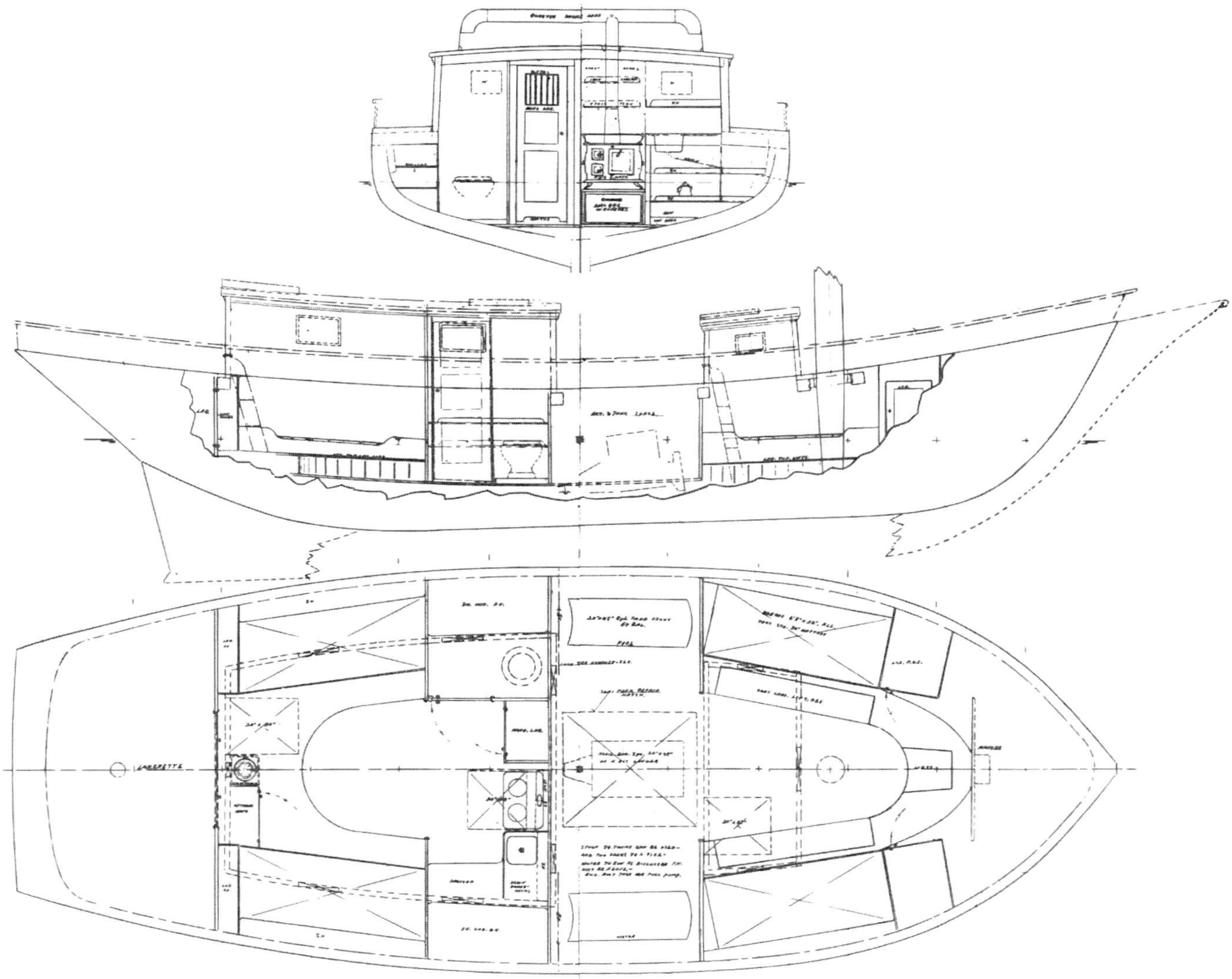

Above and below: Revised plans of the *Spray* adapted by Pete for Hugh Bigelow.

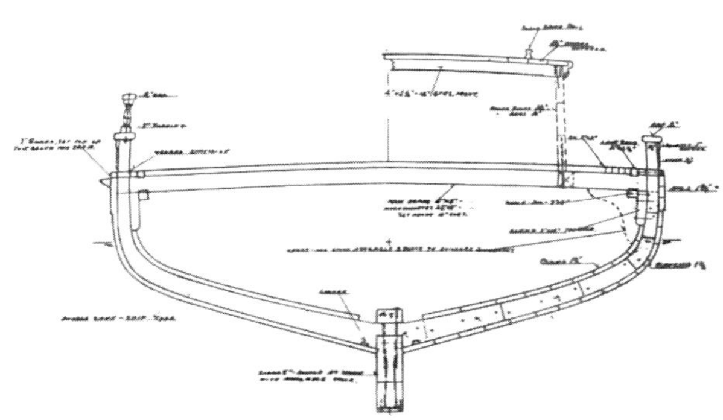

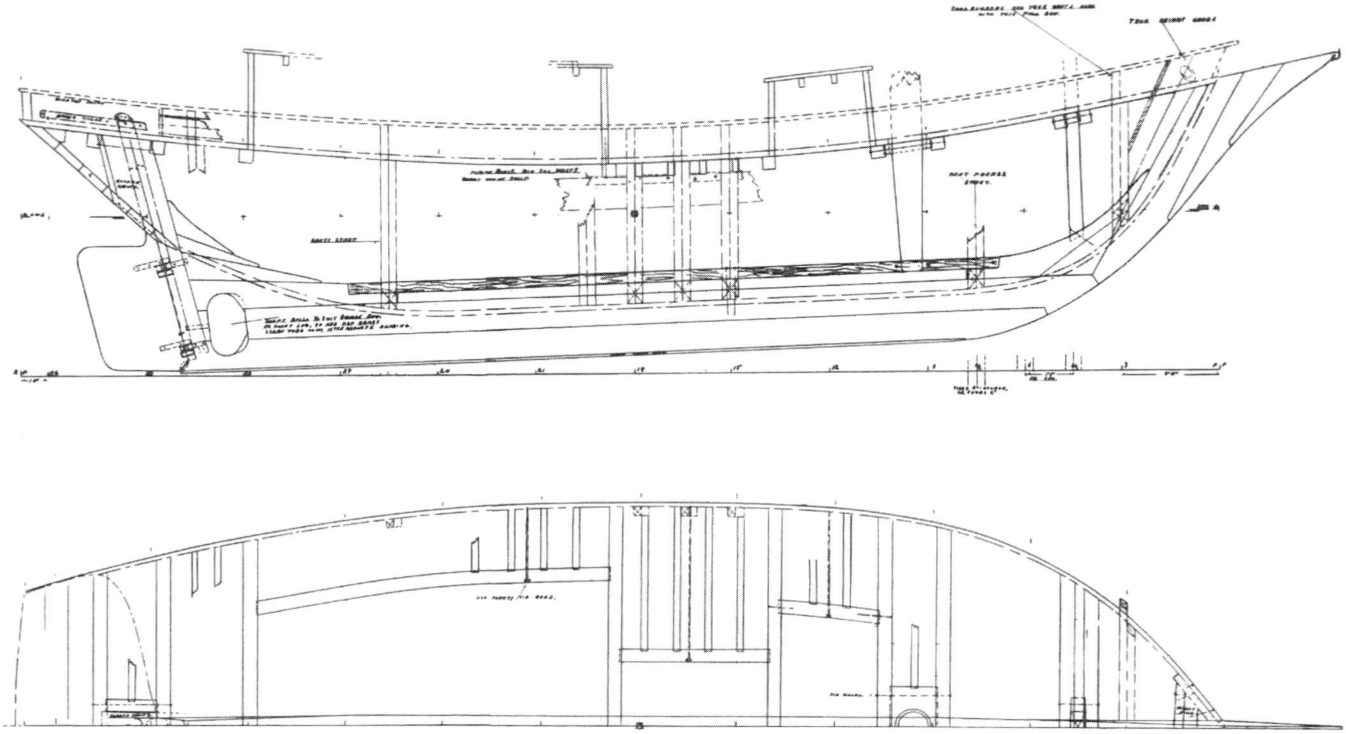

Construction plans of the *Spray* for Hugh Bigelow.

This is the only design in this book that is not Captain Pete's. These plans for *Spray*, as worked up by Pete, are about as complete and faithful to the original as you will find. They include the improvements and simplifications worked out by Pete after long use. These are primarily in rigging leads, ground tackle, her topmast, stern davits, and engine, which Slocum did not have.

As set down in this plan, her cabinhouse is split; that is, there are both a forward and an after cabin, with the engine located amidships. This is interesting. Pete's copy had the engine located in the forepeak and there was a single cabin trunk. The single cabin trunk was an improvement suggested by Captain Slocum in the appendix of his book, *Sailing Alone Around the World*. It was to be considered if the vessel was to be used as a party boat. Captain Pete, knowing he would be doing some chartering as well as living aboard, adopted this single-cabin-trunk arrangement. It worked out well for him.

All the detail included, specifically the construction plan, is a boon to would-be *Spray* builders, for there is a lack of such detail in Slocum's plan. It would be wise to follow this construction. Pete's *Spray* has lasted for more than 50 years, the last half without proper maintenance.

As with most things, there is a wide gulf between dreaming about ships and the sea and doing something about it. Of all of Captain Slocum's literary gems, I have always felt the following to be the best: "For a young man contemplating a voyage, I would say go."

Captain Pete's *Spray*. (George Yater photo)

Length overall: 35 feet 10 inches
Molded beam: 10 feet 10 inches
Draft: 6 feet
Sail area: 956 square feet
Displacement: 11.39 long tons

1840 British Cutter For Bruce Northrup

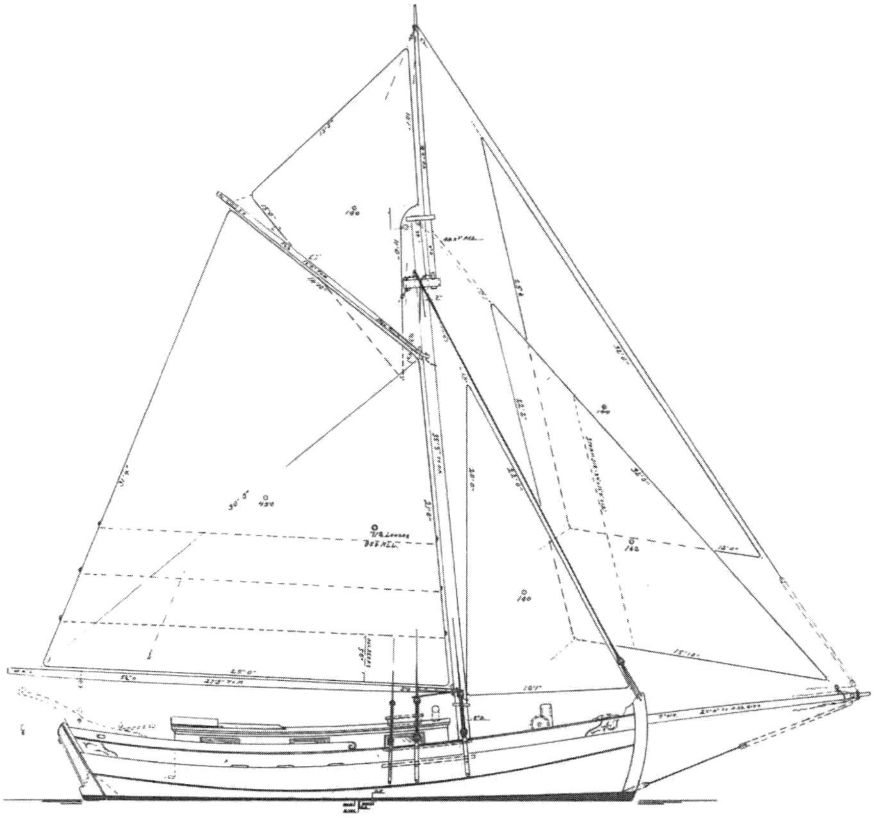

Sail plan of the 1840 cutter for Bruce Northrup.

The cutter rig has always been a favorite of the British sailor. The rig has been used on a variety of types of fishing vessels, pilot boats, and even on sailing barges of the western rivers. It is essentially a single-masted, gaffrigged, twin-headsail—that is, a jib and staysail—arrangement. Invariably, the bowsprit would be offset, as tradition dictated, one side or the other from the stemhead. On this design, it is offset to port. Usually cutters carried a main and a jib topsail in light weather.

The workboat cutter was a different animal, in both hull and rig, from the racing cutters that would later be the rage on both sides of the Atlantic. These working craft, by their very nature, had to carry heavy loads and therefore be burdensome with a rig to match, as well as able and seakindly, with a good turn of speed. This was before the age of power. In other words, the need was for a wholesome craft.

Bruce Northrup had admired the cutters for some time. In 1966, he asked Captain Pete to design this little cutter for him. The decade of the 1960s was a heady time in the Old Man's design career. He was making quite a splash with unique vessels based on

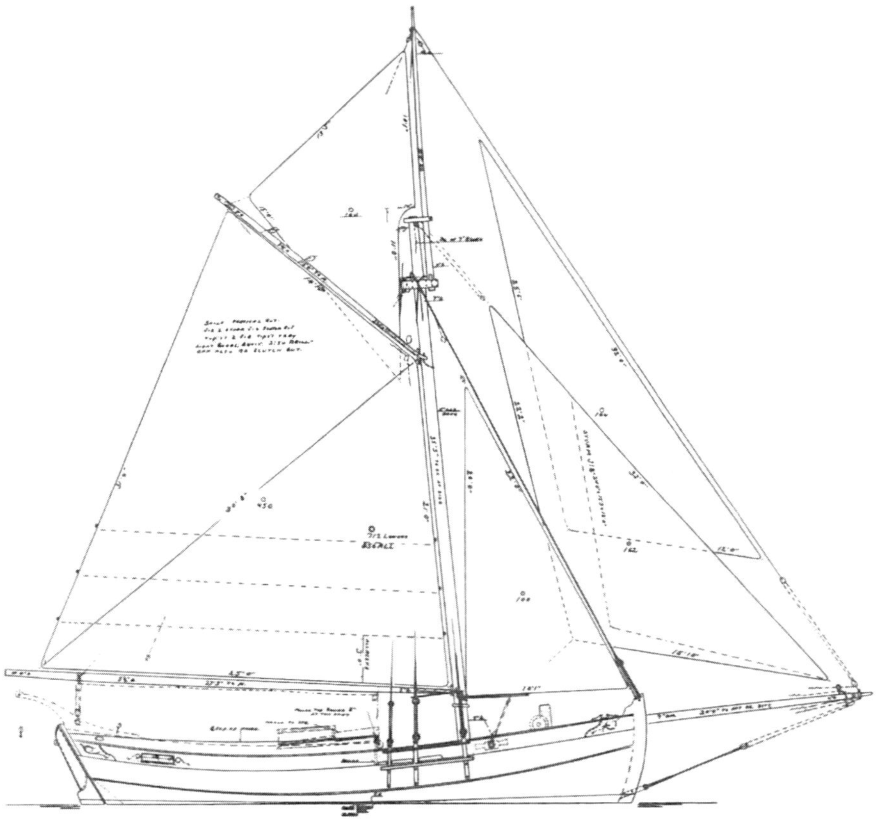

Revised profile of the 1840 cutter.

working watercraft of the past. Pete too was much interested in the cutter type and was happy to take on the project. I think it shows.

This design is a clipper version of the British cutter type prevalent around 1840. The craft is characterized by a radiused stem of stout proportions, ending with a distinct knuckle at the forefoot. The keel is straight with much drag. There is a straight raking sternpost with double transoms and an outside rudder. The vessel steers with a tiller. She has a strong sheer with low bulwarks and good deck area. As burdensome as this vessel is, she has a fine underbody with a good entrance and a very good form of run. The diagonals are nice fair sweeps, ballast would be all inside, and there is plenty of room to stow it.

There are two cabin layouts using the same hull and rig. These were designed at separate times. The initial accommodations used the trunk cabin with engine aft, stove offset to port, and main cabin amidships. There is lots of room here and plenty of cabin sole to walk around on. The engine room, main cabin, and fo'c's'le are separated by bulkheads.

After this design was completed, Northrup did

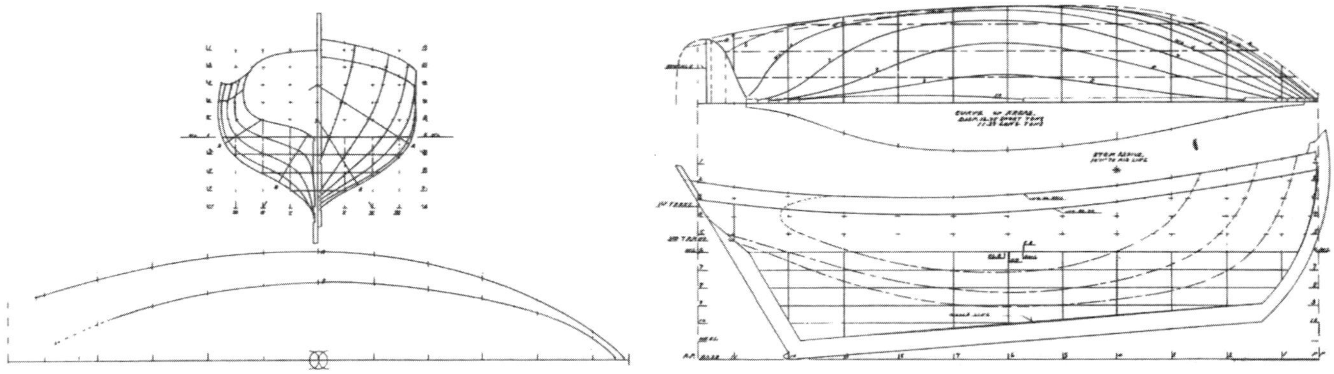

Lines of Bruce Northrup's cutter.

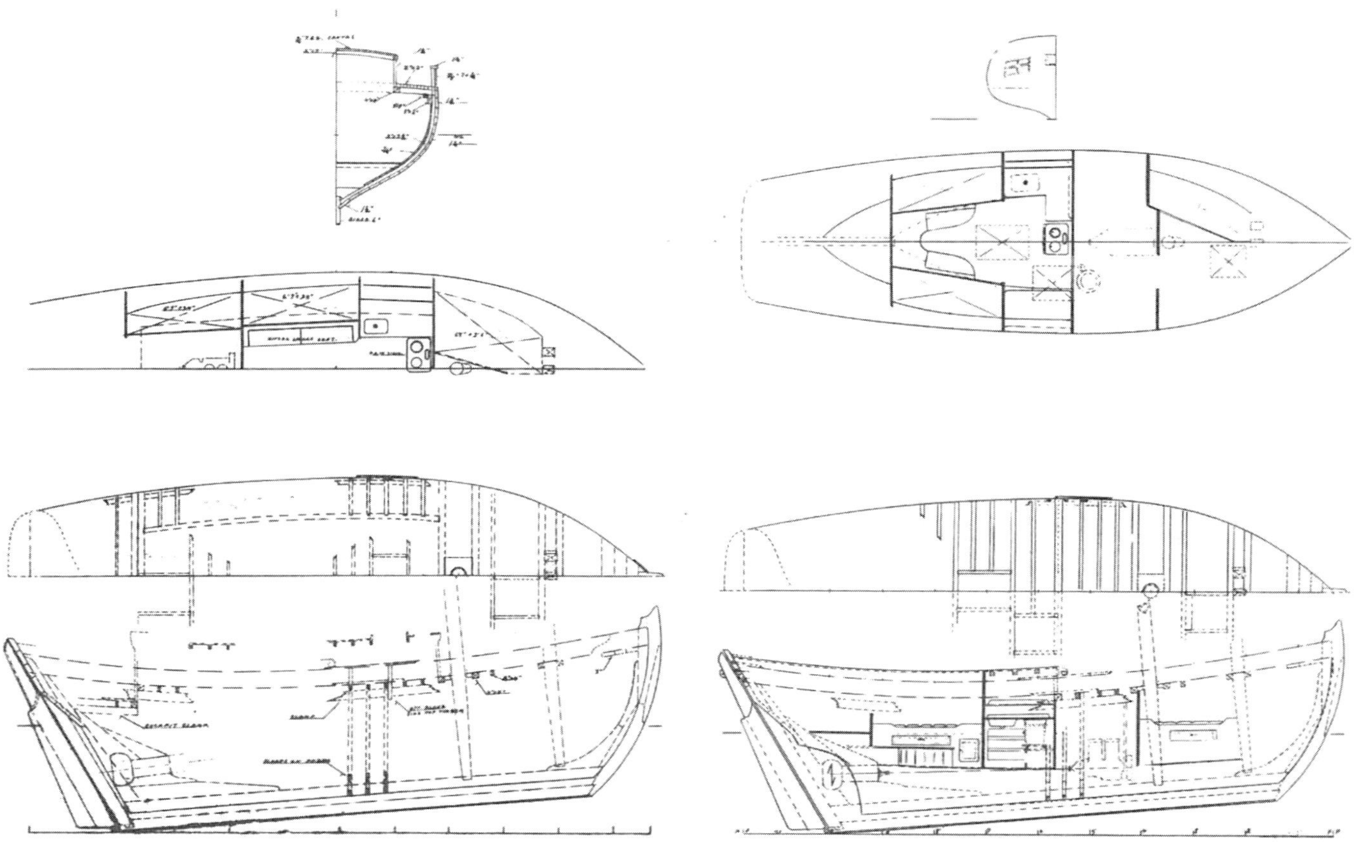

Above: Construction plans and layout of the 1840 cutter.

The 1840 cutter under construction on the West Coast. (Bruce Northrup photo)

some traveling around Europe with these plans tucked under his arm. He found a builder in Greece who completed the hull at a very reasonable cost. Due to illness, Northrup then was forced to sell the boat and return to the United States. He then commissioned Pete to design the Baltimore clipper *Lizard King*, which he and Paul Diack built. This was the first true Baltimore clipper to be built in this country since the Chapelle-Robinson *Swift*.

After a successful sea voyage to the Marquesas, the *Lizard King* was sold; she continues to turn heads wherever she sails. It was then, in 1974, that Northrup asked Pete to redesign the cabin plan on this cutter. This included a great cabin aft with stern windows and quarter ports, which was the fashion on the West Coast at the time. As a sailor, I would be uneasy with those potential breaches in hull integrity, but storm shutters can be rigged. I must agree that the stern cabin would be a marvelous place to sit and watch the knots reel off.

Not all hull shapes are capable of the arrangement shown (steering gear can become horrendously complicated), but this cutter may be better off for it. The new layout allows a lower profile and perhaps better weight placement.

No matter how experienced a designer is, a vessel must be produced—in the flesh, so to speak—before it is known with certainty how correct his judgments were. This design has been built, in both versions. From the knowledge gained thereby, she can be considered successful.

Length between perpendiculars: 35 feet
Beam: 11 feet 6 inches
Draft: 5 feet 6 inches
Sail area: 1,046 square feet

Friendship Sloop Proposals

Length overall: 30 feet 3 inches
Length on waterline: 25 feet 10 inches
Beam: 10 feet
Draft: 5 feet
Sail area: 825 square feet

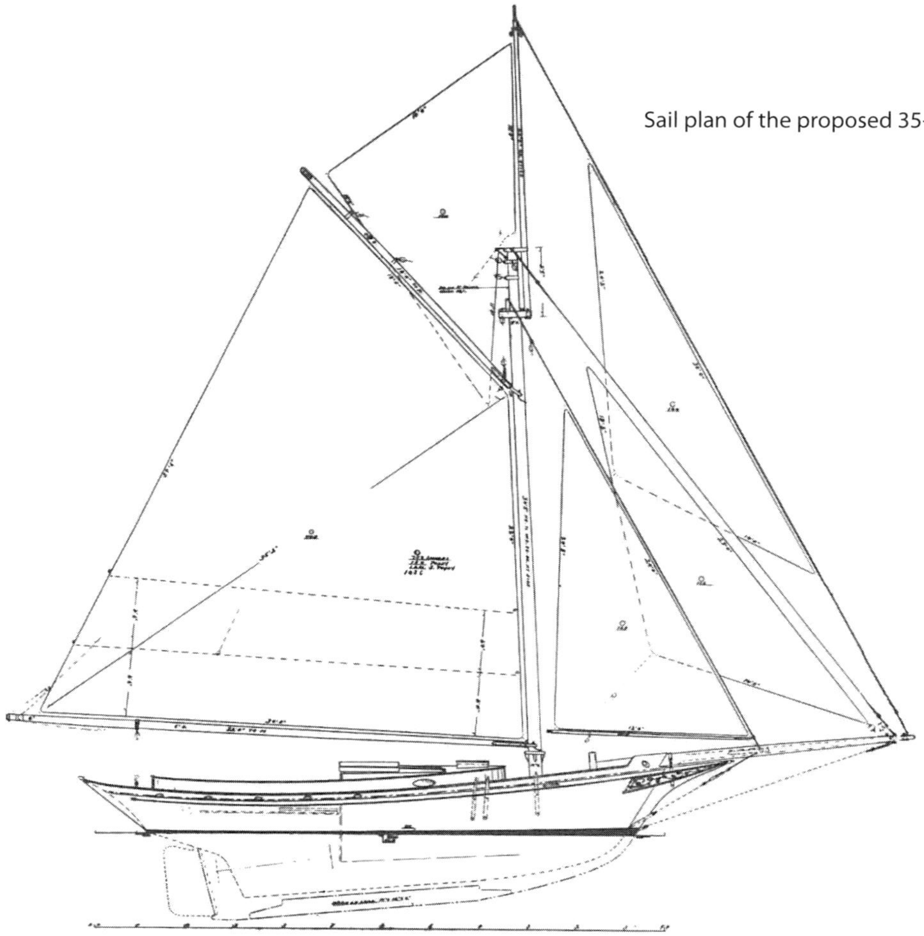

Sail plan of the proposed 35-foot Friendship sloop.

There is an unmistakable quality in Friendship sloops that excites every boat lover's eye. Their high-hatted rigs and sweet-lined hulls exemplify to most what is meant by the term enduring classic. At least this is so when a Friendship is developed by a designer who has the proper feel for and understanding of the type, as Pete did.

Both of these designs use outside ballast. Other than that, they adhere closely to his thoughts on the type that appear with the 22-foot version in the next section.

The accommodations are snug on both, less so on the 35-footer, of course, for this is one of their drawbacks—faults, if you insist. With boats like these, however, I think I could learn to sleep on nails, if need be.

I don't know why these designs didn't proceed, but I wish they had.

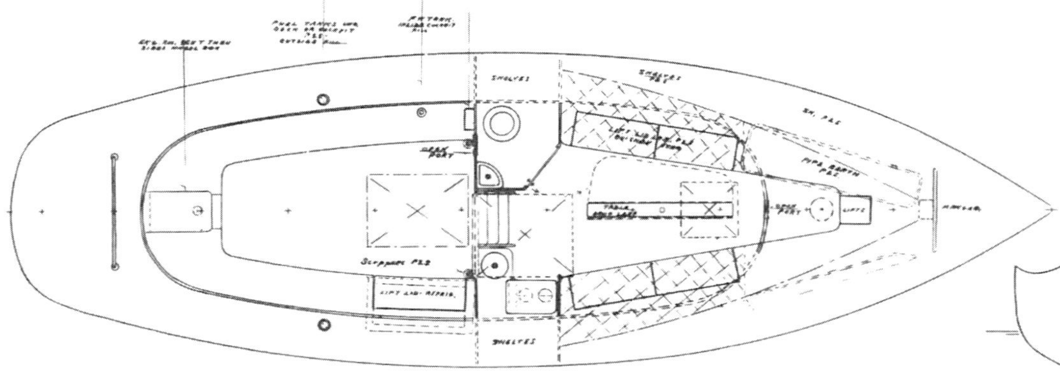

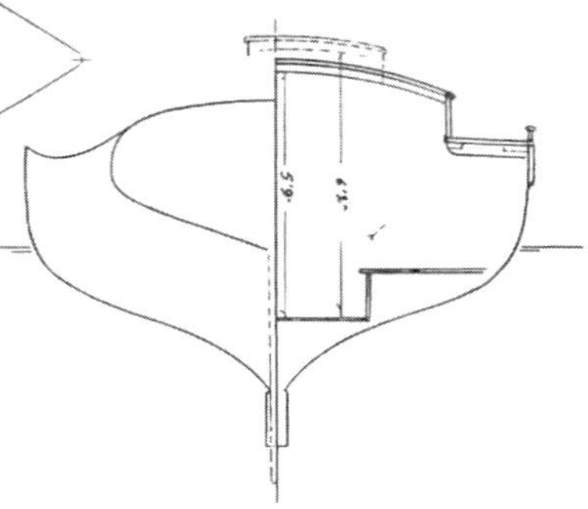

Above: Accommodations of the 35-foot Friendship sloop.
Below: Sail plan of the 30-foot Friendship sloop proposal.
Below right: Layout of the 30-footer.

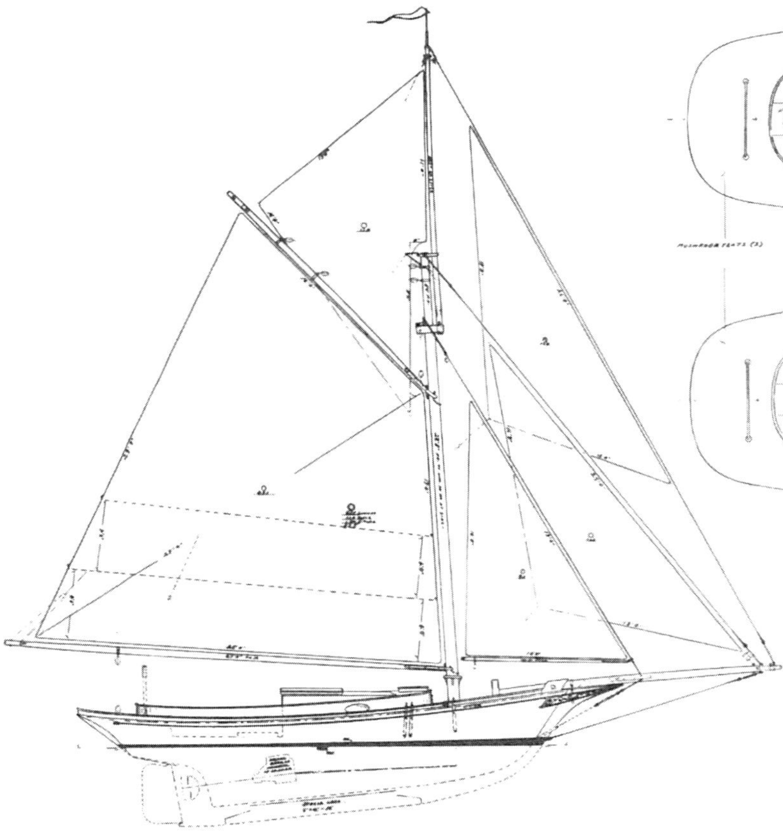

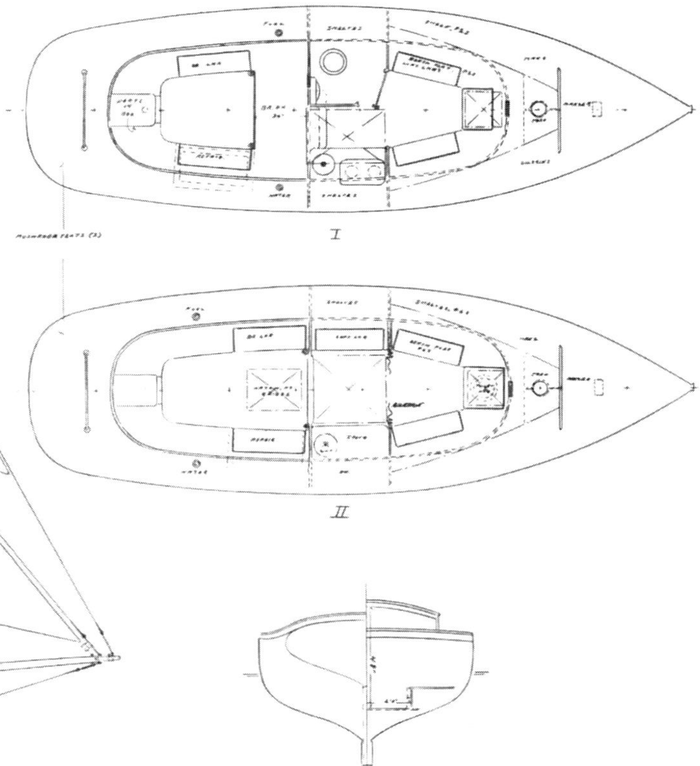

Length overall: 22 feet 4⅜ inches
Length on waterline: 18 feet 7 inches
Beam: 7 feet 3 inches
Draft: 4 feet 5 inches
Sail area: 357 square feet
Displacement: 7,900 pounds

Friendship Sloop For Knight Sturges

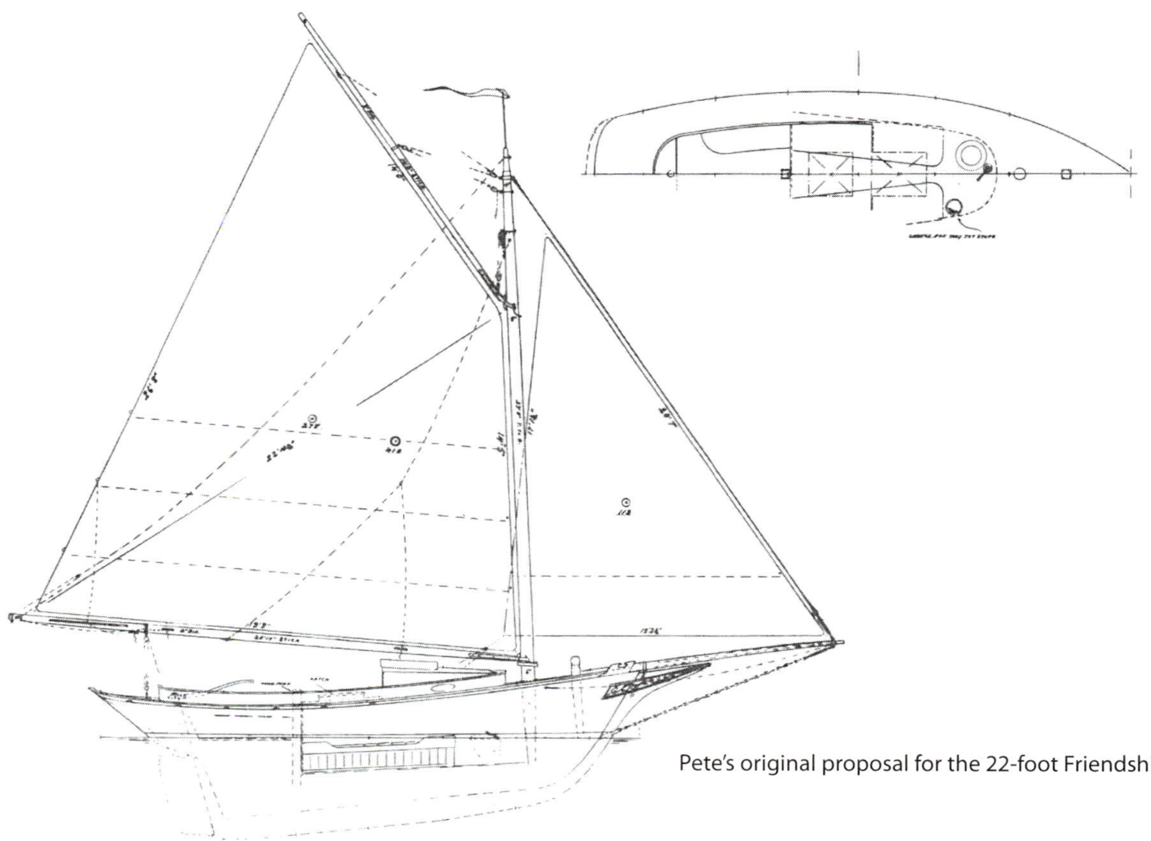

Pete's original proposal for the 22-foot Friendship sloop.

Comments by Pete Culler

The hull of this craft seems a quite powerful and stocky little thing, more so than would be needed if it were not for the room required in the cuddy.

The trim as shown is what I choose to call workboat trim; she could be trimmed somewhat lighter—say, 3 to 4 inches at the load line. True to her type, she will require a lot of ballast—this is a "floaty" model. Inside stone will be best and most seakindly. The design is not really suited to outside ballast. There is no point in using lead inside, unless the room the stone takes up is a problem. I don't think it will be here, as there isn't full headroom anyhow. And bilges, besides winging out some stone under bunks, should take care of the problem—small boats need small stones.

Construction would be just as always on Friendships—stout backbone of oak, flat frames, harpins to hold her together, cedar planking, white pine deck, spruce stick, and so on. All fastenings should be galvanized, including the clinched plank fastenings. Gear and fittings are pure Friendship.

I have reduced the sail area in line with Knight Sturges' thinking, and would not care to reduce it further. In view of the displacement, I feel she is now somewhat undercanvased for light weather.

The Friendship type is a craft of great power—it had to be to do the work intended. The hull requires a large sail area, at least by modern standards, for lightweight sails as we now know them were not handy or economically sound in earlier working craft. Also, the design requires a rig

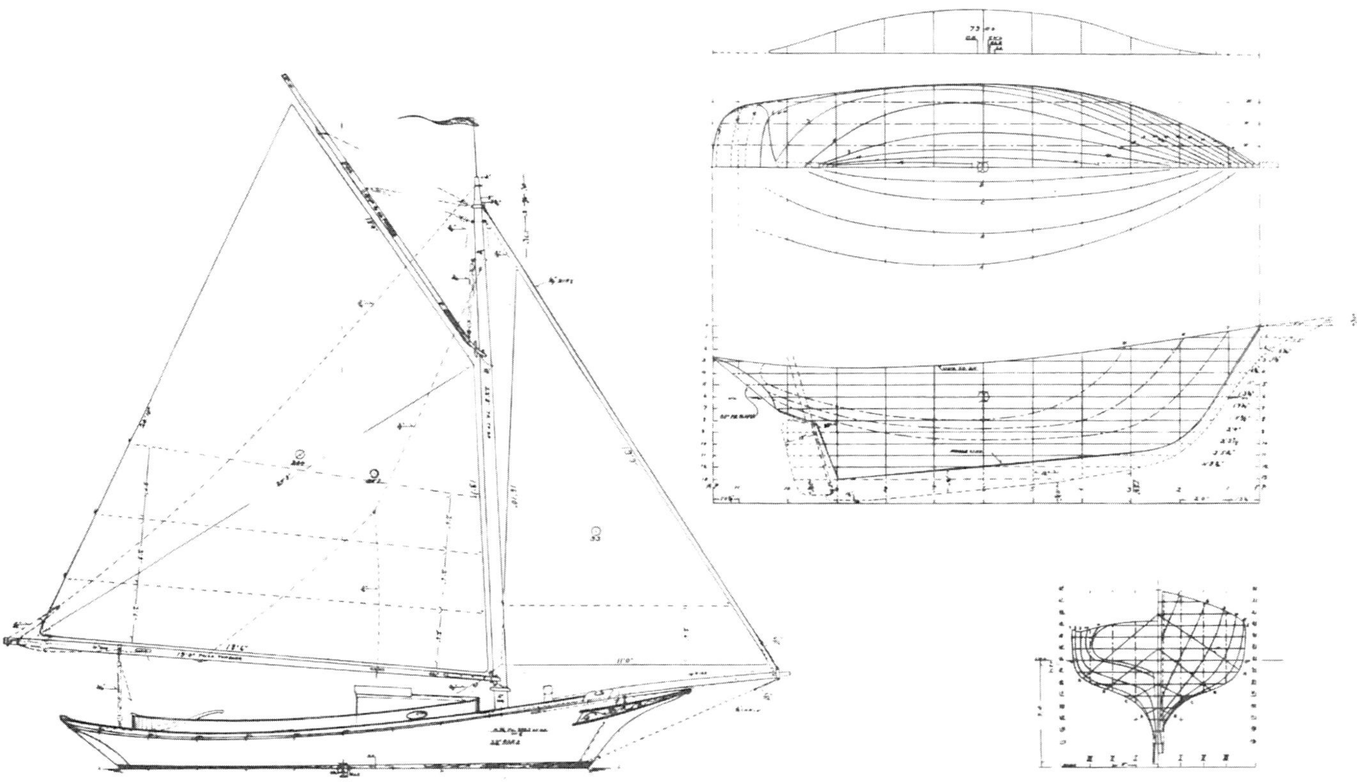

The final sail plan and the lines of the Sturges Friendship.

with a low center of effort—it is not suited to tall, narrow rigs. Any craft that depends on sail alone needs adequate sail area or she will be impossible in light airs. This means that one must become accustomed to reefing when necessary. Reefing these days seems to be misunderstood and much feared. Having personally done both, I much prefer to reef a properly rigged craft than to take in a modern, slippery, light sail. Such sails may be wonderfully efficient, but we are still behind in the development of proper gear to handle them in trying conditions. The old-time reefing methods, on the other hand, are so well worked out that there have been no recent improvements. These techniques are based on working in winter weather; it's just a matter of learning to use them.

In addition, workboat hulls are not of a shape to be sailed on their ears. They do better when on their lines; thus, there comes a time when one must reef for the good of the ship. Proper reefing gear and an understanding of its use make the task not nearly the terrible job most people think it is.

The various centers seem to indicate that the designed balance will be good for this type of craft. I think she will be a very good sail carrier, with the hard bilge and heavy quarters. The run is easy for so bulky a craft, and the traditional slab bow should help her to windward as well as with the ability to carry sail.

Buzzards Bay is often considered a tough body of water. Having sailed it for fun and profit for a good many years, I don't wholly agree. It is primarily an area of large amounts of wind, but also of light air. A boat with a powerful, large rig that is easily reefed is made for such conditions. Anyone who has spent time along the southern coast of Maine will agree that this is a windy, rough area on occasion. This is where Friendships lived and worked, and not always in the summer. Personally, I think the Friendship type is a good choice for Buzzards Bay, where a powerful boat, though a small one, is quite well suited .

There is some comfort in a craft of this type. No matter how one hashes it about, the plainly built, well-tried, simple boat is the easiest to use and the one that does the most sailing. In addition, because one hopes to be able to look at the boat for many years, she should be easy on the eye. I think it would be good to read again what Howard Chapelle has so ably written about Friendship sloops in *American Small Sailing Craft.*

Right: Sailing the 22-footer in Buzzards Bay.

Below: Construction plans of the 22-foot Friendship sloop.

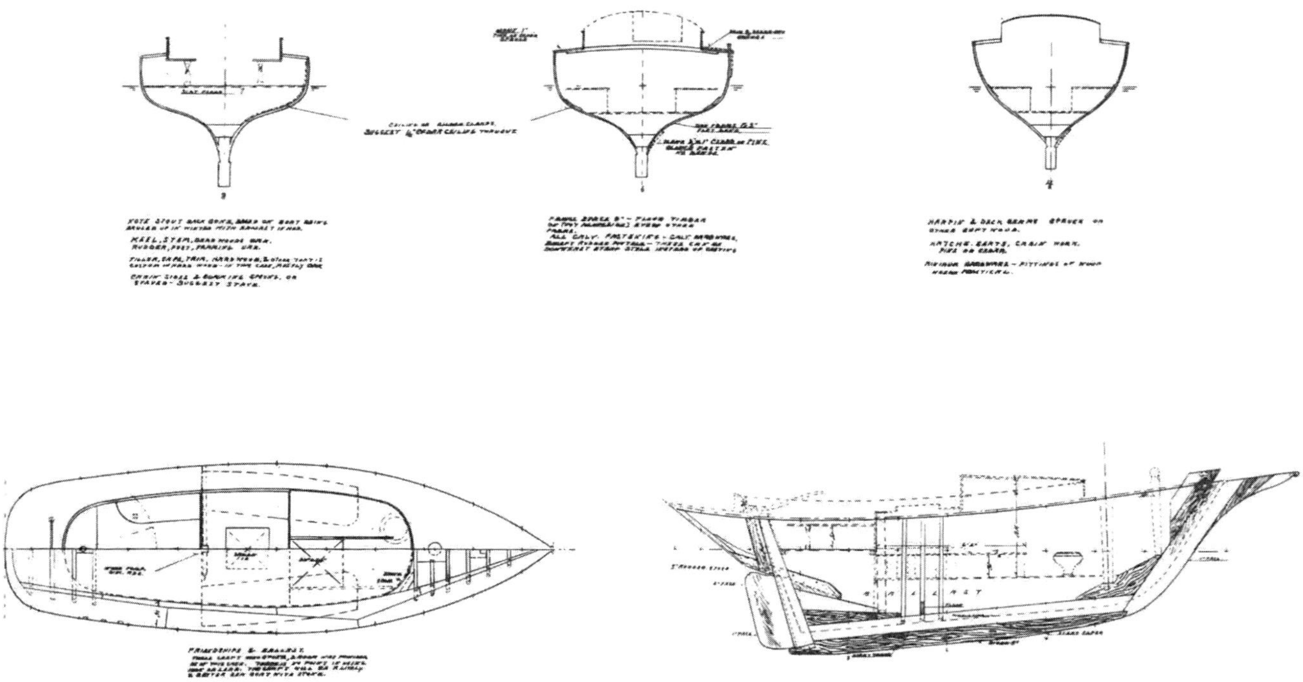

Length overall: 27 feet 10 inches
Length on waterline: 25 feet
Beam: 8 feet
Draft: 2 feet
Sail area: 366 square feet

Roanoke (Croatan) Boat Proposal For Mr. Rogers

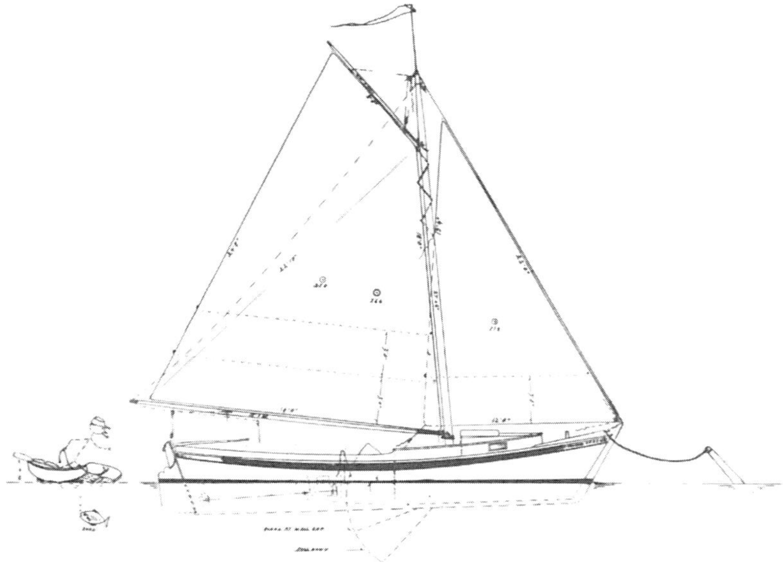

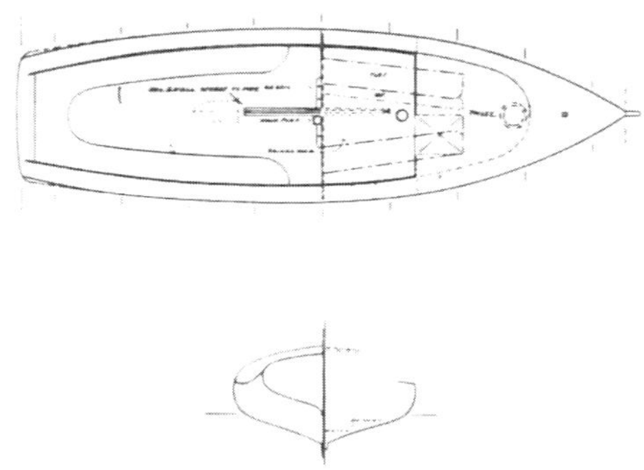

Plans of the Roanoke (Croatan) boat.

Comments by Pete Culler

A brief history of the Roanoke boat type may be of interest. At one time these were the boats of the southern coastal United States. There was some variation, of course, with different builders. Most were built entirely of cedar, with much use of sawn cedar root. Those around Roanoke Island were especially noted for fine design characteristics. Many years ago I was fortunate to be exposed to the boats of that area. They are very good sailers.

This type of craft, in my mind, most nearly fits the requirements stated. The high, raking bow fits in very well for a cuddy, and helps to fit the rig also. The original boats were used to carry a big seine aft, so they were not very fine in the run and generally were burdensome. However, some were more along clipper lines, where excellence under sail was important.

For pleasure use, I've used a midsection much finer than most, with a rabbet line and stern shaped to develop a very fine run, along with a rather hollow forefoot. In other words, this is a fast, able boat of modest displacement. One can only guess at displacement at this stage of a design, but it looks like not much over 2,000 pounds. Note that the hull is skeg-built, like the 17-foot Concordia sloopboats.

I've not used the sails and rigging of a Roanoke boat, yet the profile of the one shown agrees very closely with what these boats carried—low-cut, long-footed jib (rare among workboats), mast well into her, and a rather short-footed mainsail. She still looks like a Roanoke. Structurally, the rig is just the same as on a 17-footer. It has no more parts, except for a jibstay, jib downhaul, and an extra part on the jibsheet because of its size. Two halyards can come to deck leads and to the pinrail like a catboat jib downhaul to cleat alongside the coaming. One can do an awful lot of sail handling and never leave the cockpit. No shrouds are needed. The boat will sail better without them.

The cuddy way forward is made possible by the general shape of the hull and the placement of the mast what headroom there is happens to be there also. The bridge deck is an important part of the boat. It ties her together, provides room for a couple of flats long enough to sleep on, some storage space, and support for the mast and centerboard well. Also, it's just the right width for stretching out on in moderate weather.

Naturally, there is some variation possible in the cockpit seats, coamings, and stove space. From what is shown, more detail can be worked up. As a roomy, smart dayboat, with mug-up facilities, and once in a while an overnight jaunt, she seems good.

Note that with care and common sense, she is quite beachable.

People seem to get unnerved over size. This boat is just 4 feet longer than the original proposed limit of 23 feet, and the difference is less on the waterline. Moreover, her tonnage is no more and possibly a bit less. Therefore, the cost should be no more, and is usually less, than for some misfit that has to be warped and jammed to make do in a reduced size, and that does not sail or handle well, or look the part.

I look for this craft to be quite smart and able and very nice to handle—even with little way on—with the aid of the big jib. She will require some ballast. The sail area seems ample. Note its location a little farther aft than usual—the custom in proud-bowed boats. Her weak point sailing will be dead downwind because of jib blanketing. The simple alternative is to tack downwind, like *Nina* does.

I think that cost can be compared to a 17-footer in direct proportion to the increase in weight, with a little extra for the cuddy and what goes in it. By its nature the backbone is strong, so one could side it 3 inches. The frame could be just a little larger than on a 17-footer, and use ¾-inch planking. Spruce spars and tanned sails would suit her fine.

Cutter For Lars Lindblom

Length between perpendiculars: 28 feet
Beam: 10 feet 11 inches
Draft: 3 feet 2½ inches
Sail area: 556 square feet (proposed),
531 square feet (final)
Displacement: 11,200 pounds

This little cutter was designed for a gentleman from Finland, Lars Lindblom. Lindblom is a traditional sail enthusiast, having previously owned a 90-foot Baltic schooner and a 24-foot Cornish crabber with gaff rig. After reading Captain Pete's *Skiffs and Schooners*, he got the bug to have the Old Man design him a boat. His requirements were: good accommodations for four, an enclosed head, ample galley space, a centerboard, good deck area, self-draining cockpit, a clipper head (of course), maximum draft of 3 feet 3 inches with board up, and maximum length of 29 feet. A pretty tall order.

Pete called her hull shape "sort of a Noank sloop, due to draft limitations." He gave her a cutter rig. I think she turned out pretty well, considering all of the above. So does Lindblom, judging from the following letter.

"Captain Culler: I am very pleased with the plans, and I think she is a most beautiful vessel. When showing the plans to my friends they all get very impressed and enthusiastic about her. But as you probably know, there are few persons who dare go for a vessel like this. Everybody wants to have a racer and pay a lot for extra unnecessary things, though they never will race, nor can race. I think those people will never understand real sailing. They just want to play with expensive things in order to impress their neighbors.

"My grandfather was a captain on square-riggers sailing to Australia. He would, I am sure, be very pleased with this vessel if he could see her.

"We have sailed her almost three months already. I am pleased with her and she is doing rather well beating against the wind. There was a 30-knot wind blowing and she made steadily between 5 and 6 knots. When the wind is aft of amidships, she is excellent. We were once very close to 7 knots, but she reaches 6 knots without trouble.

"She carries full sail without reefing in winds up to 25 knots, and if you are lazy, she stands with full sails 30 knots. But then there will be some water on deck, and her motion is not so comfortable anymore.

"In light airs we have not had any trouble, but of course you feel that she is rather heavy compared to the modern plastic monsters. If you are alone, you can leave the helm and go below deck. She goes steadily like a train.

"Inboard we have a 20 h.p. Danish diesel, which gives her a speed of 6.5 knots, sometimes close to 7. We have had no trouble maneuvering her in narrow places. She does not tack as easily and as

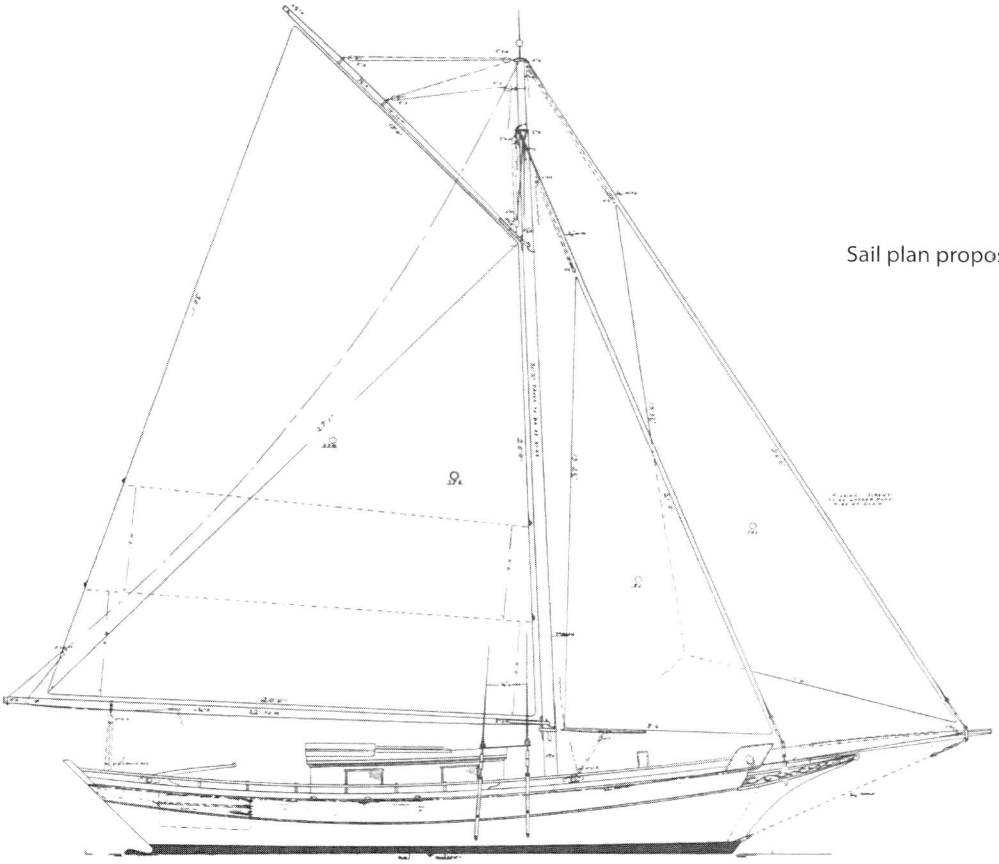

Sail plan proposal for the Lindblom cutter.

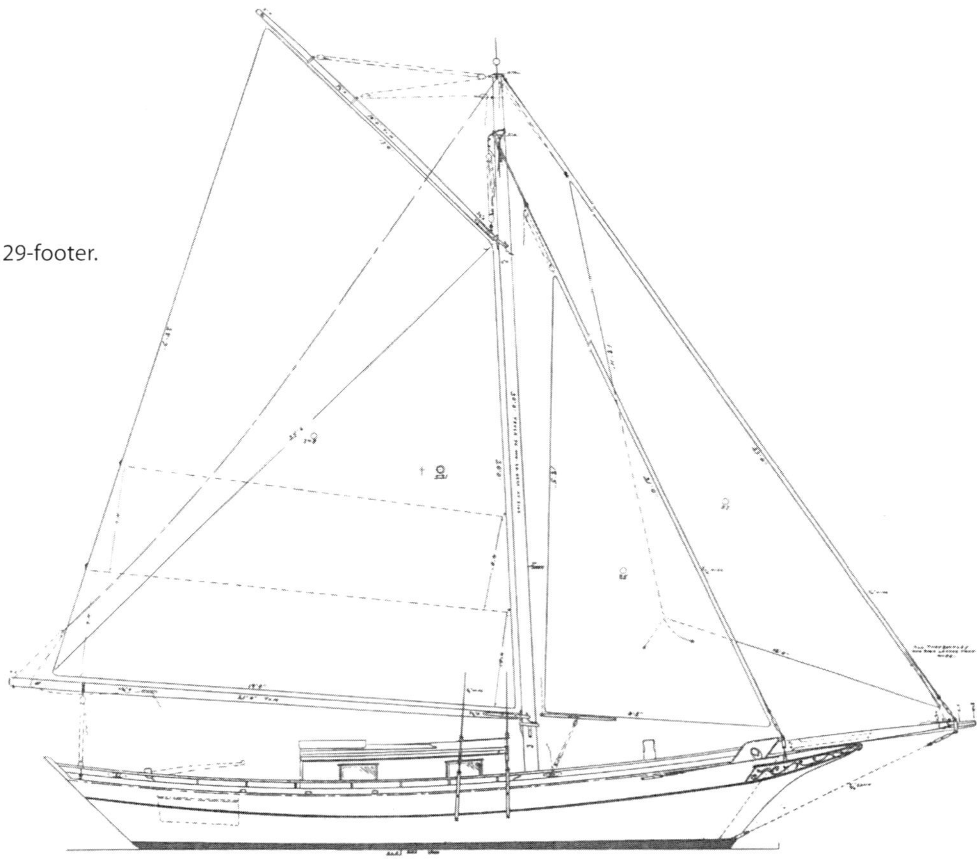

Final sail plan of the Lindblom 29-footer.

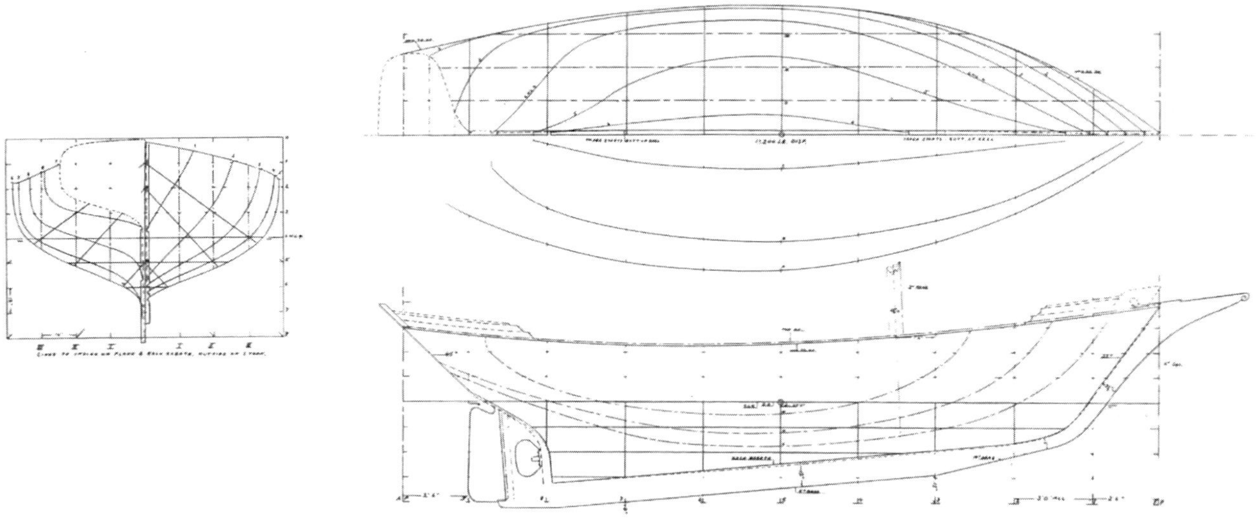

Final lines plan of the Lindblom cutter. The centerboard was dispensed with in the final version.

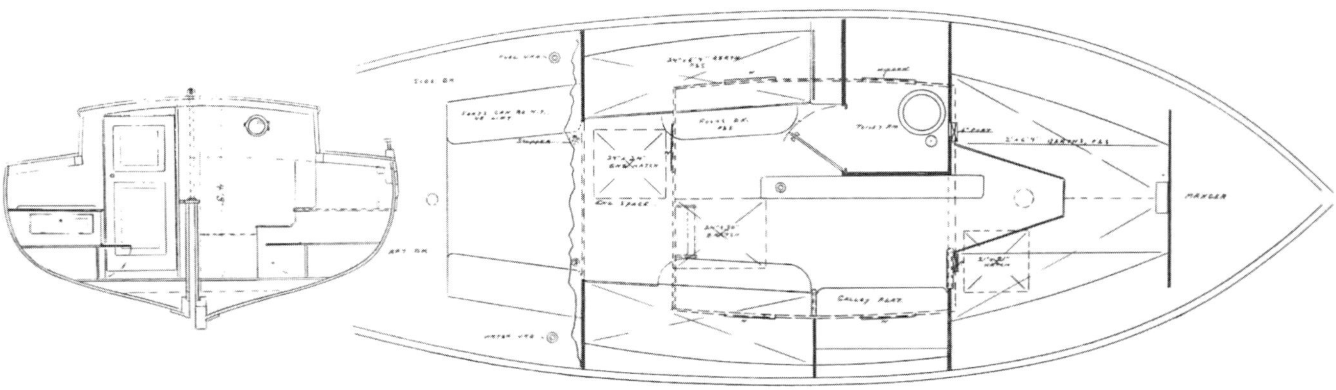

Proposed cabin plan of the Lindblom 29-footer.

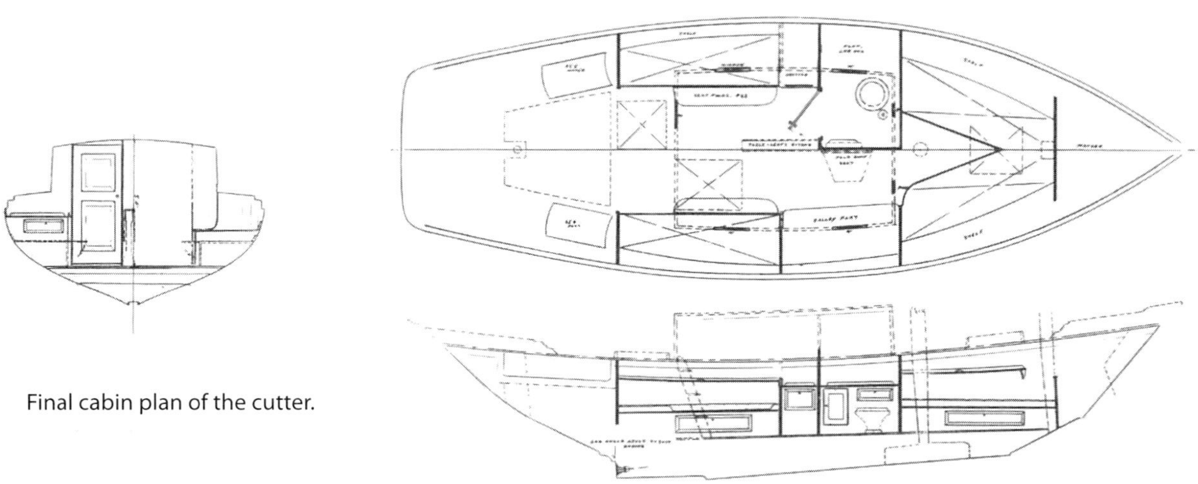

Final cabin plan of the cutter.

Mr. Lindblom's cutter "steaming along like a train." (Photo courtesy Lars Lindblom)

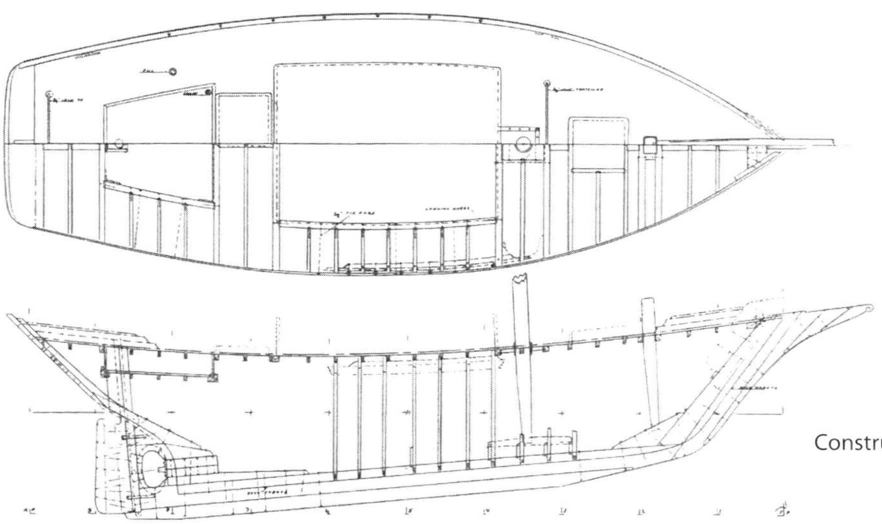

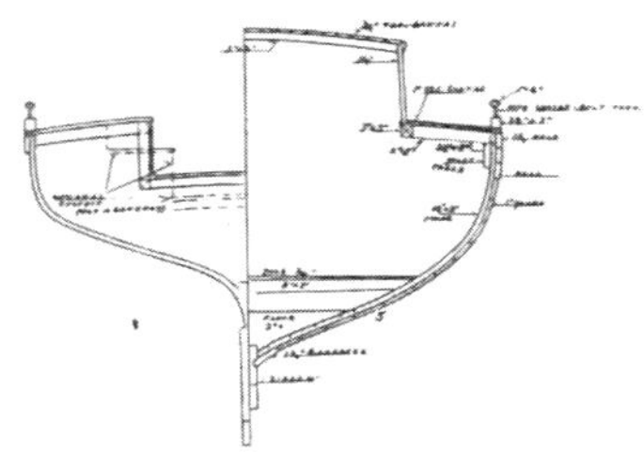

Construction drawings of the Lindblom cutter.

fast as today's racers, but she has never stopped tacking, even with no speed at all. It is just to turn her around and wait. She will go around, but the smallest circle she can turn in is 8 to 10 meters.

"People have been very interested in her. It might be that someone will make an offer that I cannot refuse! "Once again, many thanks for a nice vessel. When I stand on her deck, I feel safe and very happy. People we meet when sailing just don't stop staring at us!"

Catboat Proposals For John Lee

Cat A

Length: 20 feet
Beam: 8 feet 6 inches
Draft: 2 feet
Sail area: 257 square feet

Cat B

Length: 20 feet
Beam: 9 feet
Draft: 2 feet 3 inches
Sail area: 284 square feet

Comments by Pete Culler

First, let me say that these designs are worked up only far enough to give an idea of the particular boat.

Boat number 1 is based on about the simplest and most economical form, yet it retains true cat features. Note that most of the cruising gear has been left out in this case to show a good daysailer with only a sleeping bag and a tent over the boom for overnight cruising. Omitting these very much simplifies construction and cost for a boat that will be used largely as a daysailer.

Simplifying also allows a much finer craft for a given length, for there is no problem of headroom or a large displacement to accommodate a cabin, engine, and other gear. Thus, a self-bailing cockpit to protect the investment in machinery and cabin fittings is not needed.

This allows a smaller and simpler rig to drive what is a rather fine hull for the type. This makes for lighter weight aloft and in working, with a low center of effort, approaching that of the old working cats.

Carrying little weight, though able to stow ballast rather low, this boat is of lower displacement and finer lines than later cats. She should sail quite well and be good in light weather, for there is just a modest amount submerged when at a small angle of heel, yet she should do quite well in fresh winds, as the flaring sides begin to bear. The wide decks and cuddy should allow her to handle considerable amounts of broken water.

At this point I felt it unnecessary to show a lot of detail, but one pictures this craft as built, rigged, and fitted out very much like a Concordia 17-foot sloopboat, with many of the features that have proved good in those craft. Wood buffalo chocks, wood pump discharging into well, tiller through a port, straight coamings aft, and the rather simple gear for the rig come to mind. The traveler shown has proved superior, for it is nonfouling.

The tiller looks long by current standards, but it is proportioned to rudder width, as on working boats. One is often forced into a too-short tiller, or a wheel, when the cockpit is shortened by a long house, engine box, and other cruising considerations. When this happens, a too-short centerboard well also is needed.

As far as this design has been developed, I feel the boat should not be much of a handful, even running off in a breeze. Besides, having no power, she will not be fighting a propeller, which tends to increase the helm in about the same proportion as it slows the boat down.

I feel this boat is suited to a small keel siding, though with good molded depth, and the use of an off-center centerboard similar to the one used on a Concordia 17-footer.

Boat number 2 has about the usual cruising cat arrangement found today. Also, it is closer to the latter-day Cape Cod cat type. This requires little or no discussion, for it is just about what one expects.

Accommodations similar to these have been worked up for boats as short as 18 feet, but this always seems to crowd things, especially the installation of an engine. As it is, a bit more centerboard could be used, though there isn't room to do much more. When a boat has rather good freeboard, and full lines, she should have more board than a finer model.

The rig is quite moderate. In fact, this applies to both boats. I've kept in mind that these days people don't care for a large rig. However, they are quite willing to put in a large engine, to the further detriment

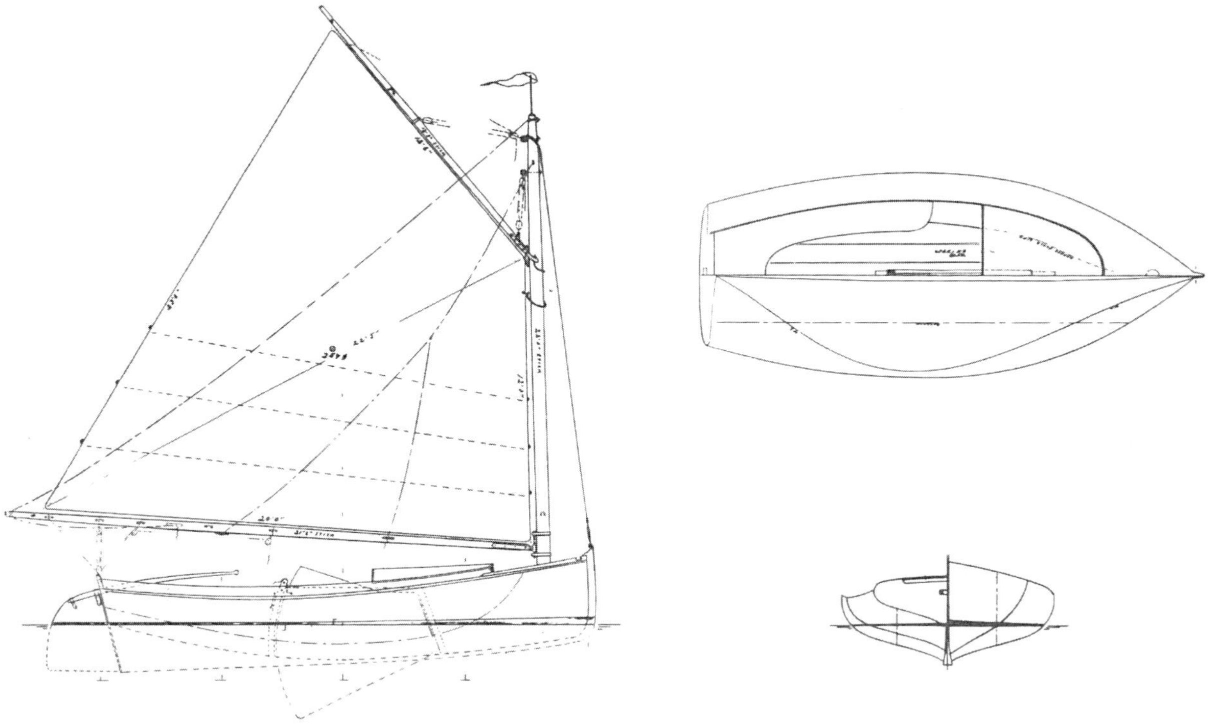

Proposal for a 20-foot catboat (Pete refers to this as "boat number 1"), a dayboat.

of the boat's sailing ability. One wonders sometimes if there is an unwillingness to learn to sail a boat with a large enough rig, together with a lack of understanding of the proper gear to cope with a large rig.

My personal feeling is that cat number 2 should have at least 300 square feet of sail to properly handle her bulk and the drag of a propeller. The rig shown has more lead than cat number 1, for I feel that the fuller hull and prop aperture contribute to an ardent helm. Along this same line, and to allow more room, a wheel will be best. A tiller would have to be quite long to be effective.

As to weight and cost of the two boats, at this point there are not enough ordinates worked up to figure displacement. A rough estimate seems to make cat number 2 at least one quarter more boat. This is in hull and rig only. The cruising layout and all that goes with it is simply not there in cat number 1. Stoves, toilets, cushions, and steering apparatus all add up fast. It costs about as much to buy and install a single-cylinder engine as it does any other. The real engine problem is length; the singles fit best. The self-bailing cockpit is needed in this case. It's a large-cost item, but the boat will be self sufficient when on a mooring, and there is plumbing and machinery to take care of and other gear to tend not found on a dayboat.

Cat number 2 can be quite a cruising boat. Either keep it very simple with a cedar bucket and dishwashing on deck, and a minimum of tankage and bedding, or equip it with the usual plumbing, sink, solid- and liquid fuel stoves, good tank capacity, and a two- or three-day icebox to boot. It's simply a matter of deciding if that much cruising is going to be done, and if the economics make the expenses worthwhile. Also, the boat can be built very much on the yacht style (which it really is not suited for) or in plain but neat workboat finish.

Cat 2 is a powerful boat, as it must be to have much of a cabin. Powerful is not necessarily fast, nor is it always able, though I think this one will be as able as any. She will not be quite as much fun to sail as a sharper boat, but she should do well.

Let me sum up the two boats. Often when there are two somewhat different boats to consider, with

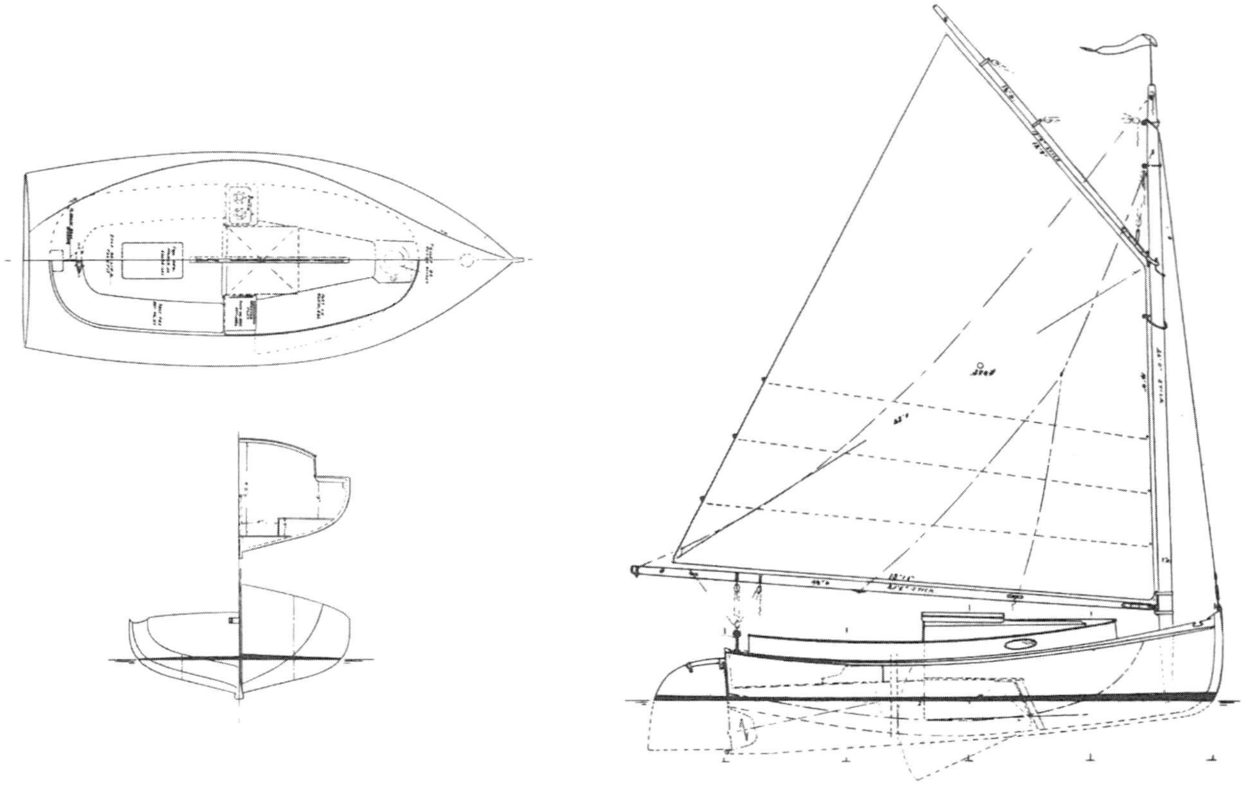

Proposal for another 20-foot catboat ("boat number 2"), a cruising cat.

good and attractive points in each, there is a desire to compromise by using the good in both, forgetting the drawbacks and not realizing that the faults tend to build up rapidly.

Compromise is often called for. Often, too, the more one compromises, the more one is apt to produce a boat that will do nothing really well.

My experience has been that boats used primarily for daysailing, but with some pretensions for cruising, usually cruise much less than is planned, though they may sail a lot otherwise.

Cat 2 seems like a quite workable boat if enough cruising is done to warrant the cost, which could be considerable for her length. The only compromise here would be to simplify the equipment to the minimum, although, if one is to have a cabin and bunks, one needs a certain amount of headroom and length. As mentioned before, I feel she would be better with about 300 square feet of sail.

Cat 1 is what she is, a dayboat with a cuddy that can only be crawled into. A boom tent, air mattresses, open boat galley stowed in a box, cedar bucket, and a camp or picnic cooler would work for overnighting once in a while. I do think sitting out a three-day nor'easter in her at Cuttyhunk would be rather unpleasant. Of course, one could rationalize such an experience by dwelling on the economy of it.

Once again, I feel this boat would be better with an increase in sail area of, say, 25 to 35 square feet in the hoist, for the center of effort is quite low, even for the type. This would tend to move the center of effort forward, which would make up for the slight increase in length of leech.

One must be prepared to reef in a cat—there is no other practical system of sail reduction, nor is the rig suited to light sails. The modern approach of an underrigged boat loaded with light sails is just not practical in a working cat. It's better to have enough sail to move the boat in light to moderate weather, and expect to reef when necessary.

Cat 1, being a lighter boat, requires lighter spars, rigging, and sail. It will be an easy working boat. If power is required, she's most suited to an outboard, for she would push easily. The low stern makes it easier to install the engine, as well as to rig it each time it is to be used. A 5 h.p. British Seagull with a long shaft should be quite satisfactory.

Length: 20 feet
Beam: 8 feet
Draft: 2 feet 6 inches
Sail area: 271 square feet
Displacement: 4,500 pounds

Newport Point Boat For Dr. John Roche

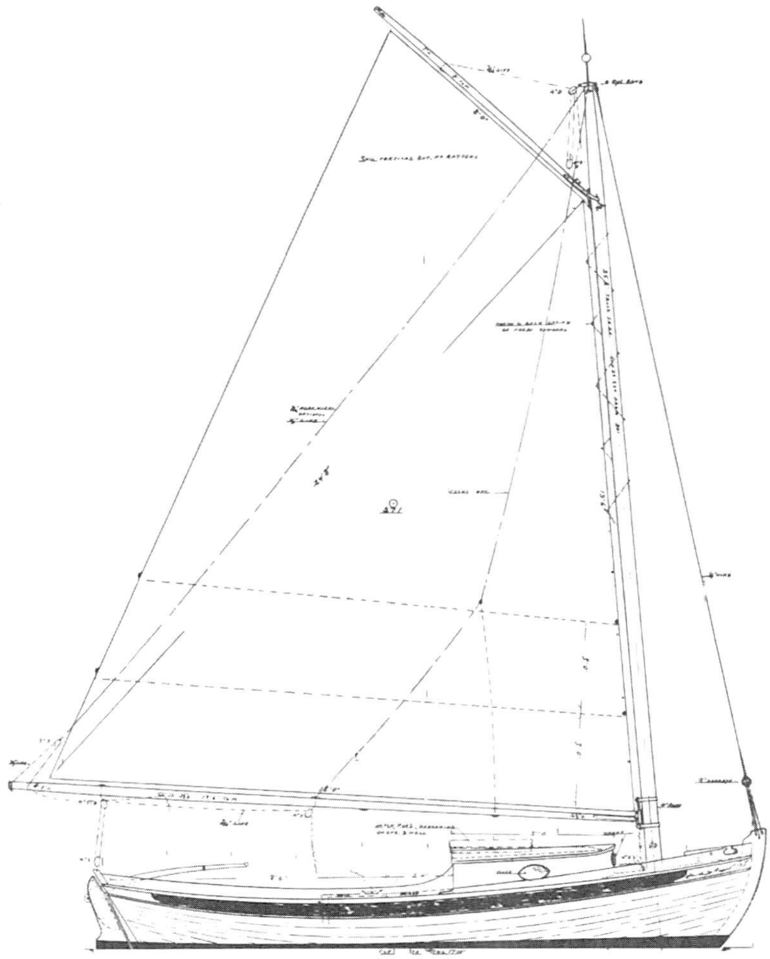

Sail plan of the Newport Point boat.

The seafarers surrounding the shores of Narragansett Bay in Rhode Island have always been an independent sort. Rhode Island is the smallest state in the Union and was anglicized by an outcast, Roger Williams, who chose freedom rather than the strictures of society. He made friends with the Indians, learned their language, and was accepted as one of them.

I have always enjoyed Rhode Islanders. The stoutness of their independent minds is deeply appealing. I married one.

As a distinct minority lying between Boston and New York, Rhode Islanders' efforts largely go unnoticed unless they command attention by sheer merit. For example, consider the sinking of the Gaspé prior to the Revolution, Slater's Mill in Pawtucket, and the Herreshoffs of Bristol. The powers that be were content to summer in Newport, and never mind the rest.

At Newport, a fine deep-water port, a colony of boatbuilders congregated on the Point, a neck of land jutting out from Newport Harbor. Here a

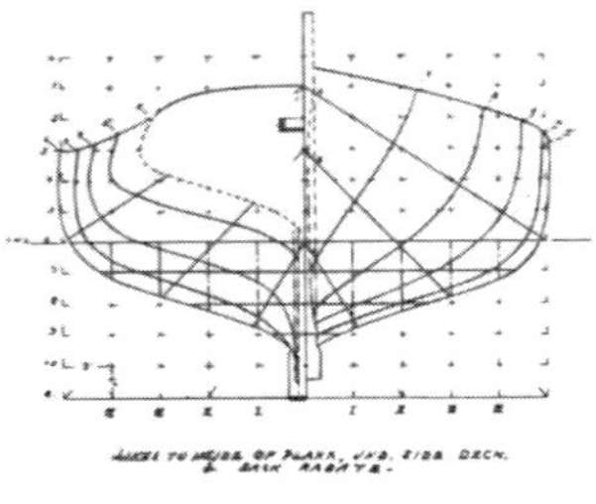

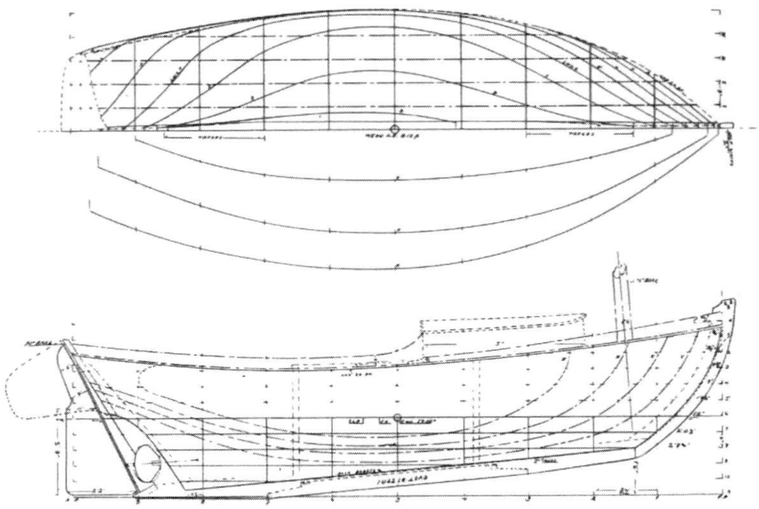

Lines of the Newport Point boat.

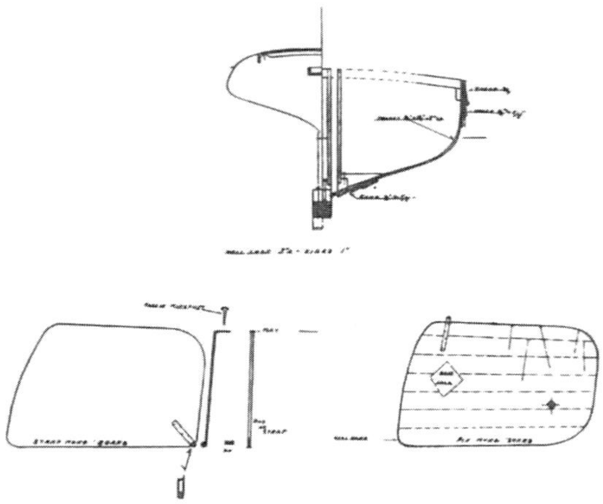

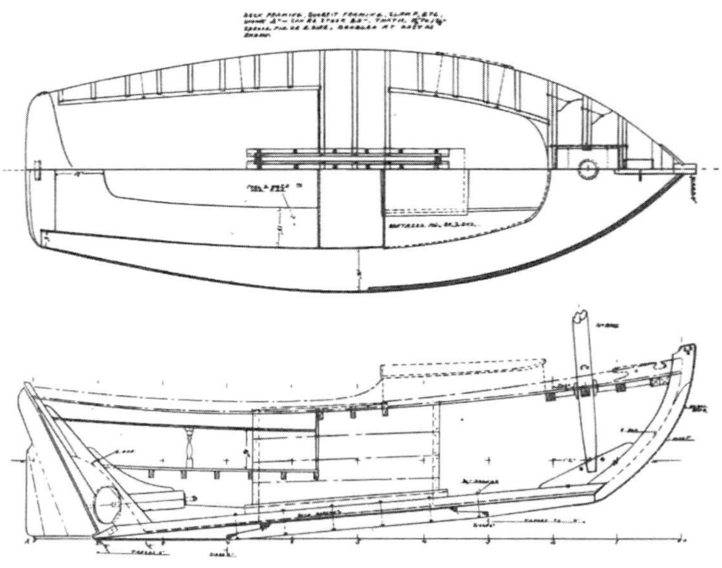

Construction plan of the Newport Point boat.

type of craft was developed that, I think, typifies the inhabitants of the Ocean State. This is the Newport Point boat, or simply the Point boat. It's deep, but not too deep, and big, but not too big. It's powerful and able, seakindly and fast. Point boats are equally at home in the shallow waters of the bay and on the deep rollers off Castle Hill. They are stout and independent.

L. Francis Herreshoff long held that Point boats were the first to carry the cat rig, which, along with the schooner rig, is distinctly American. One story alleges that the name cat was applied to the rig because it is said to have its own mind, being "independent as a cat."

A couple of independents from Cape Cod, Captain Pete and Dr. John Roche, enjoyed discussing the travels of deep-centerboard boats. From later Newport Point types (Is this where Captain Nat got the idea for *Shadow*?) to Muscongus Bay sloops, one of the central themes of these conversations was how the type lent itself to large lapstrake construction. It was decided to put these ideas into form; this design was the result.

Based on the Newport Point boat, this vessel has nice lines, powerful quarters, and a proud bow. Borrowing from the Muscongus Bay sloop,

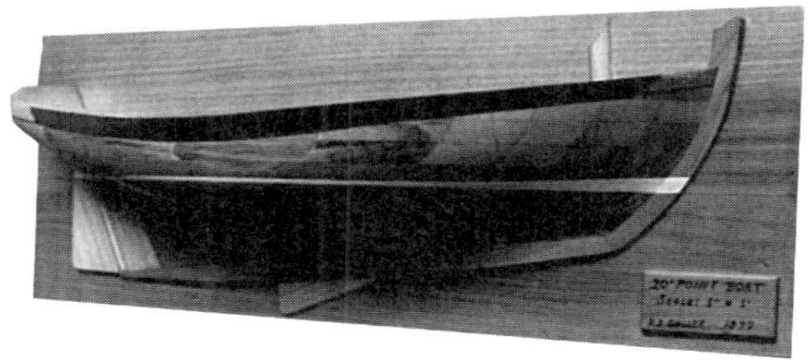

Half-model of the 20-foot Point boat. (R.D. Culler photo)

The Newport Point boat under construction in Dr. John Roche's shop. (Richard Cahoon photo)

her sides have a slight tumblehome. There is an outboard rudder that steers with a tiller through a transom port. Her forestay deadeye and the elliptical ports in the cabin sides are cat trademarks. They certainly add a nice touch to her overall appearance. The cuddy is just right for overnighting, and with a small solid-fuel stove, it would be a snug and comfortable world should you get weathered in.

This powerful and able vessel is cat-rigged. With a short gaff, the total sail area is 271 square feet. With her adequate reefs, she could keep right on driving when others are heading for shore. The mast steps in a massive stem knee. This is stout construction. Should the wind die out entirely, there is inboard power. This vessel, with her economical and simple layout, ample rig, and small auxiliary, would be fiercely independent and thus able to experience the freedom of the seas. She's shoal enough for gunkholing, and there is plenty of ability in her hull, should you decide to visit your favorite island. You have a choice with respect to hanging the offset centerboard. The patent strap hanger, however, has worked very well in the past to provide the most board area if it's needed.

Captain Pete said, "This vessel is a 20-foot catboat like no others today. It's more like a Newport Point boat, only shoaler. It's a deep-centerboarder, with outside ballast, raking mast, short gaff rig, small inboard engine, very small cuddy, and lapstrake construction. The large cockpit makes her an able dayboat for this area in open water. Picture a Herreshoff 12½ blown up, but with less draft, or a Bahama sharpshooter. The idea was that some of the bad features of the usual cat might be overcome. I very much favor the thinking behind it. Certainly there has been nothing like it around for many years. I think the lapstrake should make a dry and lively boat, as well as a handy one for a lone workman."

Choose freedom, build this native of the sea yourself, learn her language, and become one of her crew.

Length overall: 21 feet 8 inches
Length on waterline: 20 feet 9 inches
Beam: 7 feet 2 inches
Light draft: 2 feet 6 inches
Sail area: 234 square feet

Dogbody For Philip F. Volker

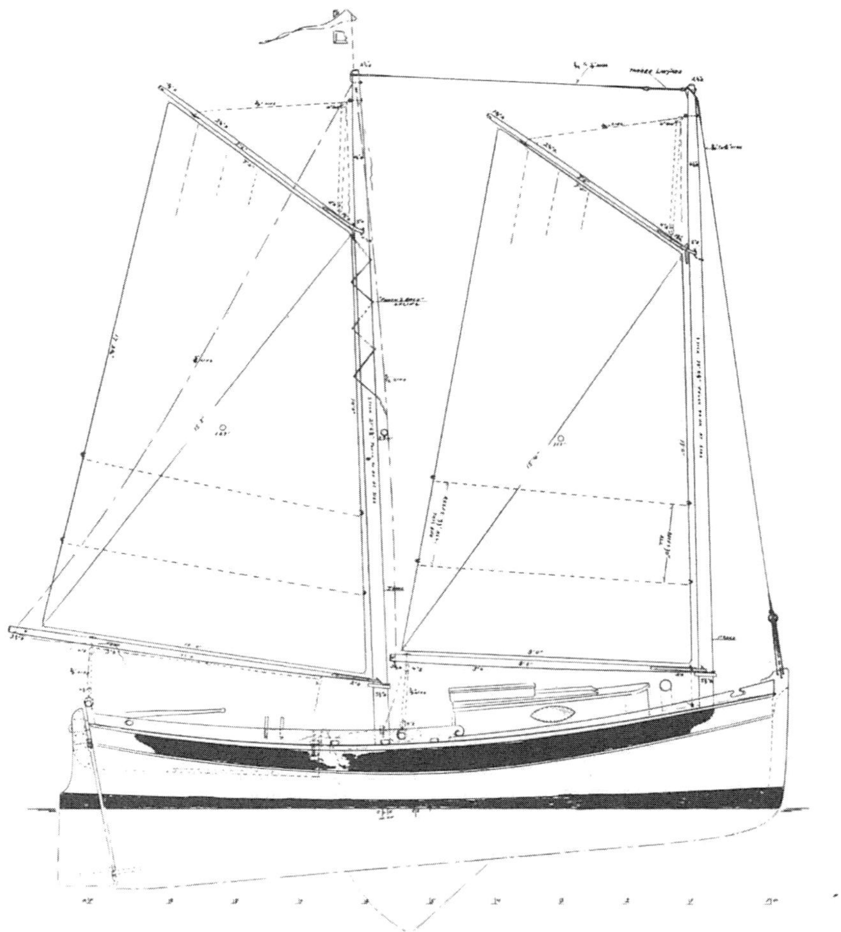

Sail plan of the Volker dogbody.

This is a snug little overnight cruiser based on a very ancient type—the square-sterned Chebacco boat, or "dogbody." This was a two-sail boat of medium size that originated from the smaller shallops, or ships' boats. It originated in Chebacco Parish, which later came to be known as Essex, Massachusetts. The late marine historian W.A. Baker discussed the type in his fine book *Sloops and Shallops.* "Although the sharp or pink-sterned Chebacco boat was the favored model at the time of the Reverend Mr. Bentley's visit (1799), there was also a square-sterned Chebacco boat that was commonly known as a

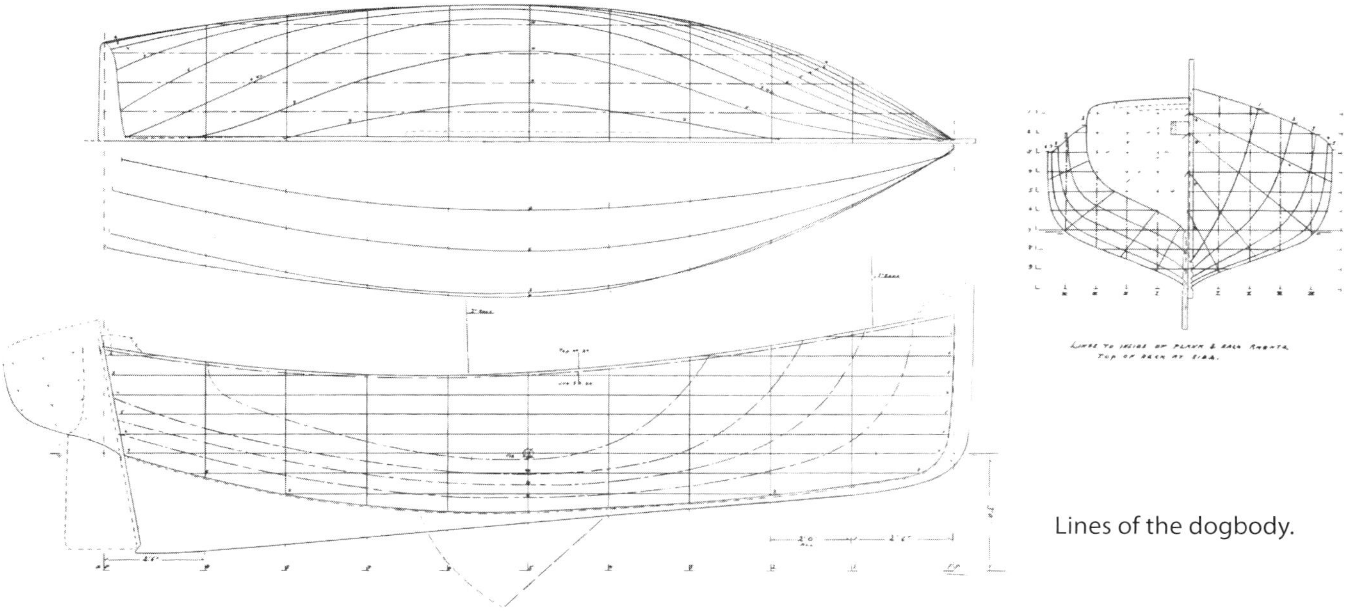

Lines of the dogbody.

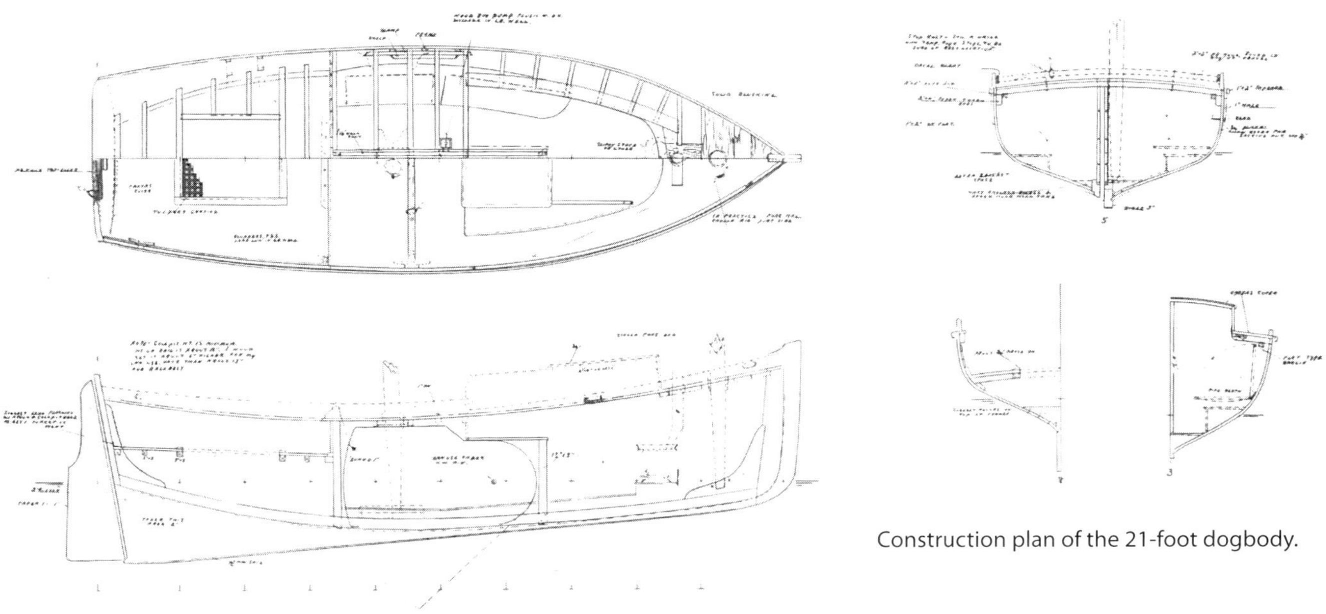

Construction plan of the 21-foot dogbody.

'dogbody.' The origin of this description is lost in time. Generally speaking, dogbodies were a little smaller than the pink-sterned boats, as the square stern gave the same amount of deck room on a shorter length."

There is a lot of boat here for 21 feet, the waterline being nearly the same as her length overall, yet her draft is shoal for alongshore work. Both centerboard and mainmast are offset from the keel, on opposite sides. This is due to her length limitations and is strong construction, if done properly. It should be no problem in practice.

There is a lot of the artistic in this design. The general shape of hull and rig is handsome, particularly the bow profile. The underwater shape is remarkably fine; I would look for her to be a smart sailer.

Here are some comments by Captain Pete: "Conditions that the design will be used in are a beat or a run, winds quite light in summer, quite fresh at times in winter, though the temperature is mild, with much rain, so the cockpit must be self-bailing.

The dogbody under construction by Bruce Northrup. The trunk cabin has not yet been built. (Bruce Northrup photo)

Bow view of the dogbody under construction. (Bruce Northrup photo)

"Yes, she is hollow forward, very much so. In doing a craft so small, with the required capacity, I tend to a catboat hull, like it or not, even though I certainly don't care for cats dead downwind. I think also that crew weight will be aft most of the time. Much can be done with trimming ballast, and if she's down by the head a bit, as most small craft are when the cabin is in use at anchor, it won't matter. Besides, I like to see the ballast a bit aft rather than forward, for I think such an arrangement handles better when so small. I hope, too, that it will go better to windward—not that any really small boat is real hot at it."

There are tholepins for a pair of sweeps when needed. This arrangement should be ample and work well in practice.

Howard Chapelle always felt that this type was particularly well suited for pleasure purposes, and I think Pete has proved it with this design. She is basically a tabloid cruiser.

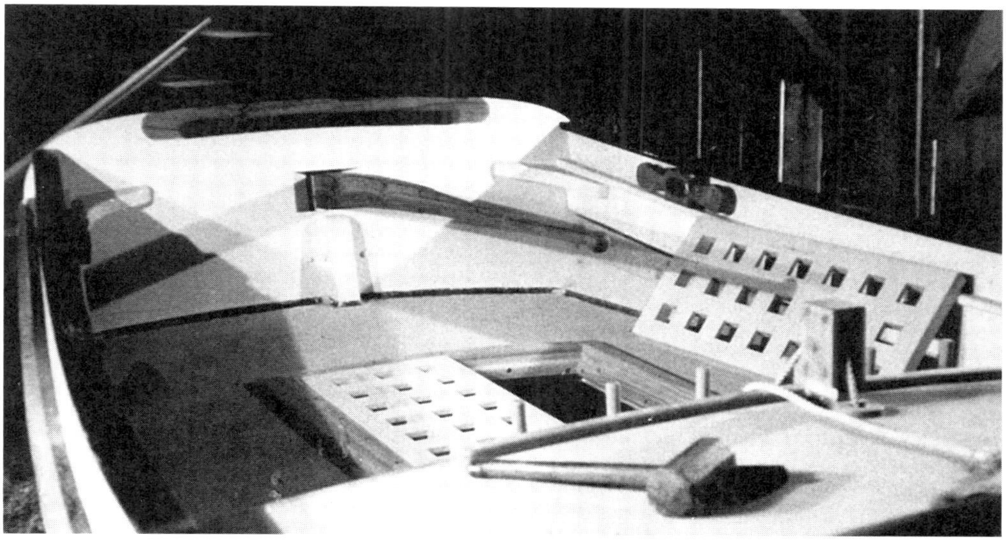

Cockpit construction on the dogbody. (Bruce Northrup photo)

Length overall: 25 feet 10 inches
Molded beam: 7 feet 8½ inches
Draft: 2 feet 7 inches
Sail area: 451 square feet

Sloop Proposal For Bruce Northrup

Comments by Pete Culler

The thinking on this proposal goes like this: shoal, but good body, for ability and room below; a deep centerboarder. Big rig for light going, and an optional topsail based on the short-masthead Polperro gaffers—this rig seems to work on a small boat, and in no way affects the original design. It can always be fitted later—with a couple of extra blocks and a "timonoggy." The use of a lute stern, or double transom, is included simply to make a good outboard setup without disfiguring the boat too much. British Seagull, of course, has the most thrust at low hull speeds. The thing should vent well it has to, or the engine won't run.

I've not included any interior suggestions, not having a finished hull to go by. Using the estimated quarter beam and load waterline, however, there should be no problem with various accommodations, assuming you will be satisfied with sitting headroom.

From a letter to Bruce Northrup
April 10, 1978

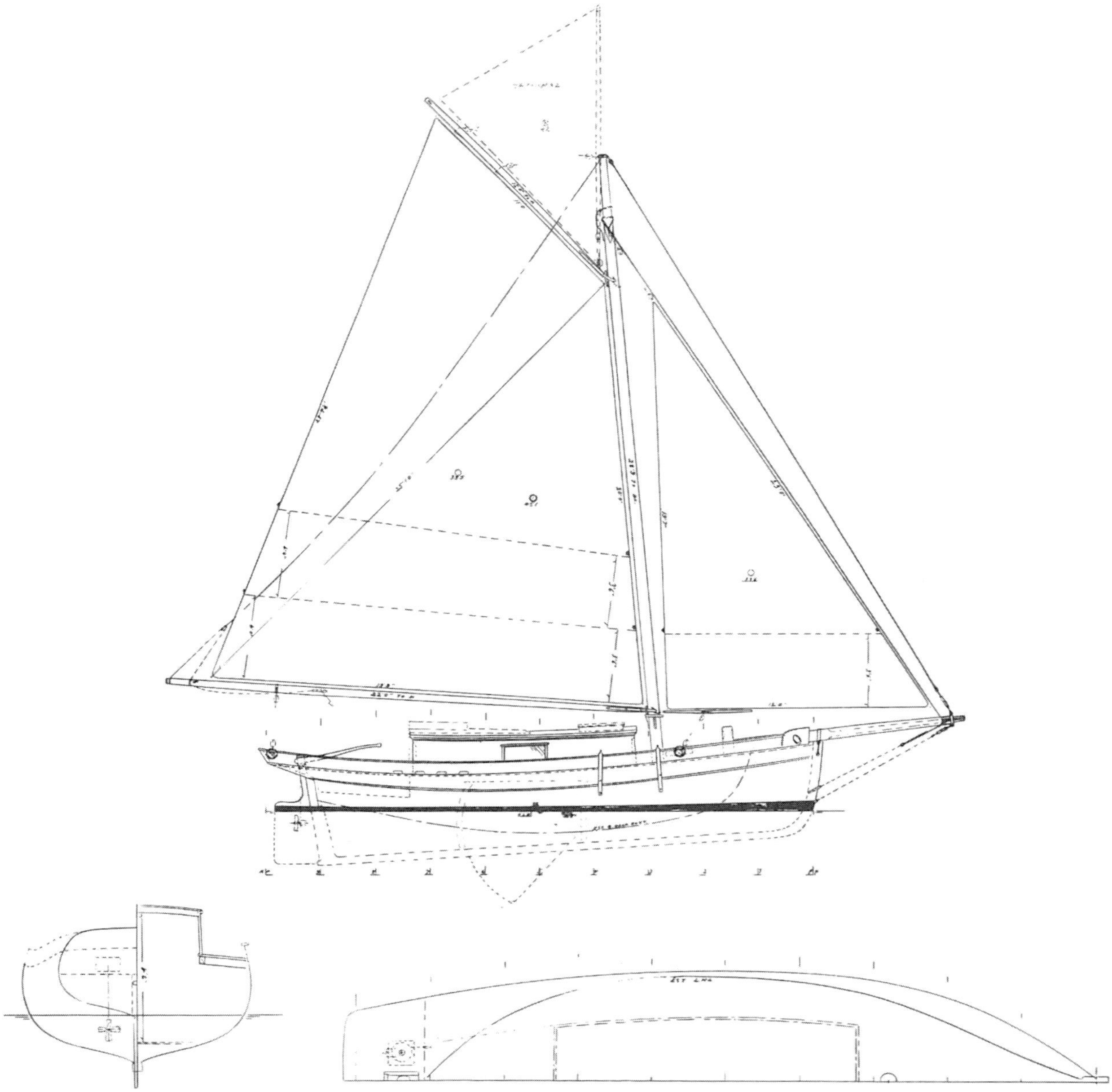

Plans of the proposed 25-foot centerboard sloop for Bruce Northrup.

PART V

Ketches

Length overall: 44 feet 6 inches
Length on waterline: 38 feet 8 inches
Beam: 11 feet 6 inches
Draft: 5 feet 6 inches
Sail area: 1,059 square feet

Ketch Proposal

Although this proposed vessel did not proceed very far, it is sound and sensible in concept, and it serves to illustrate features Captain Pete used in many of his larger designs.

The hull in profile has a pleasing sheer. It is enhanced by the log rail and the cove line, which continues into the transom decoration—a favorite embellishment of Pete's. The transom is of nice shape, slightly immersed, with a deep, thin, outboard rudder. This type of rudder, when coupled with a hull of this shape, is most efficient, and would make for an easy helm. The vessel is deep heeled, with good drag to the keel. The keel is straight for a goodly portion of its length for ease of both construction and haulout.

The stem rabbet is straight, with a well-proportioned clipper head and trailboards. The knightheads are prominent, with hawseholes cut into them. The head of this vessel, as a whole, is characterized by well proportioned simplicity and economy of line. The freeboard and deckhouses are kept low for good appearance, and they allow 6 feet 2 inches of headroom under the house tops. Freeboard was a major concern of Pete's in all of his designs. There is a deck winch forward and davits aft for the small boat, which, when in the slings, becomes a handy platform for tying a reef in the mizzen.

The rig is handsome, and almost schooner-like in appearance. The catchword today might be "shippy." The rig conforms very closely to what Pete says is a sensible ketch rig in his chapter on the rig in *Skiffs and Schooners*. The mizzenmast and foremast are essentially the same height, the difference between the two being just one inch, and there is good rake to both. The sail area is well spread among the three working sails. With the proper number of

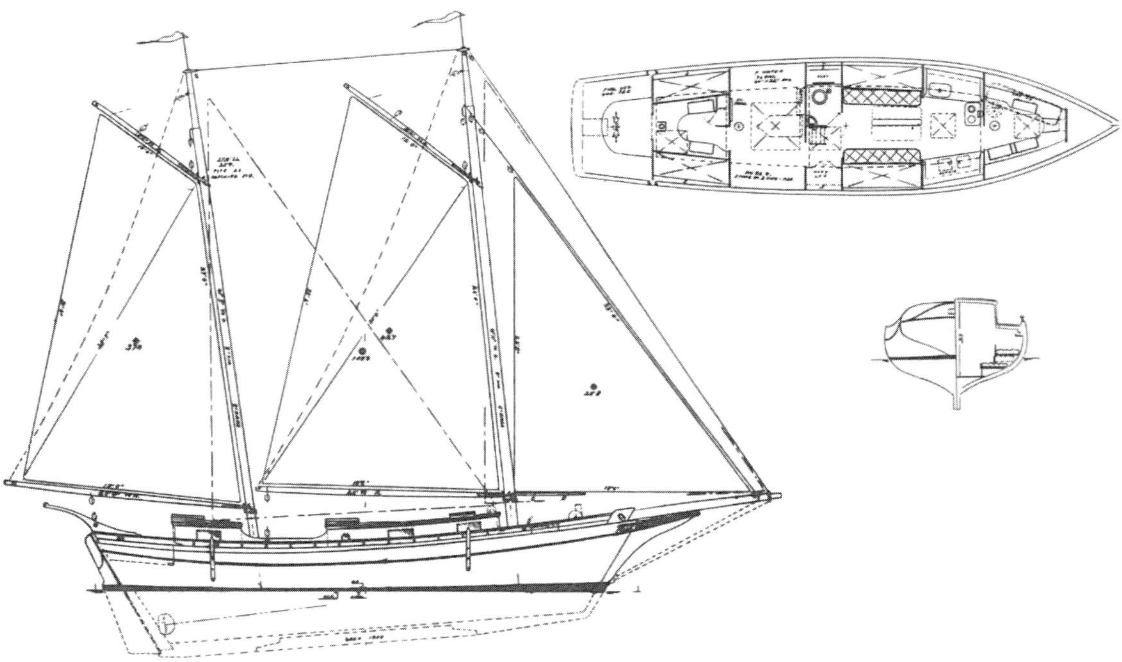

Sail plan and cabin layout of a 44½-foot ketch proposal.

reef bands, this sail plan would balance well under all conditions. The mizzen staysail, which doubles as a reaching jib, is a sail the Old Man used frequently in his ketch designs.

The hull and rig are in harmony. The sharp-lined "slight" hull would have an easy motion and therefore would be easy on the low, lightly sparred rig, which then would require a minimum of gear. This means single shrouds, a springstay, and jib- and forestay with bobstays. Bowsprit side shrouds would be included Ketches 157 mostly for the footropes. This all results in simplicity, economy, and ease of use and repair. Truly, in this rig less is more—that is, less maintenance, less cost, and less difficulty in use mean more sailing!

The cabin layout illustrates Pete's talent for getting the most out of what's available. It's a sensible and somewhat typical arrangement of the Old Man's, and it reflects his long experience with regard to what's workable below decks. Usually the client has a lot to say about the accommodations. Pete, however, was known for his comfortable and livable cabins when he was allowed to point the way.

Pete felt that this size was the limit for the ketch rig. This proposal is his idealized version of it and the hull that should go with it. Beyond this size, he felt, the schooner rig and hull are better suited.

Ketch Proposal For John Kendall

Length between perpendiculars: 40 feet
Length on waterline: 31 feet 8½ inches
Beam: 11 feet
Draft: 5 feet
Sail area: 766 sqaure feet
Displacement: 22,529 pounds

The Old Man was clicking on all cylinders when he worked up this proposal. This is one sweet hull!

These lines were laid down in 1967 for John Kendall. Kendall decided against pursuing the proposal and purchased an L. Francis Herreshoff Nereia ketch instead. I suspect Kendall felt like the man torn between the dazzling new debutante and the reigning belle of the ball. The Nereia ketch has a firm reputation for excellence, but this hull must have been powerfully attractive. It certainly is for me.

In profile, the hull shape is very pleasing. The bow profile and clipper head are just right, and the forefoot is nicely shaped. There is moderate keel drag. There is an inboard rudder and a short counter stern of nice shape that perfectly balances her lines. The waterline is hollow forward, well balanced, easy, and long. The buttocks are very sharp and the run is beautifully shaped and extremely fine.

The sections are nicely modeled, all being of wineglass shape. She is sharp-floored, with high, moderately slack bilges. Her topsides are flared forward and tumble home going aft from amidships. The transom is exquisitely shaped, and the quarters are hard, yet high. When sailing, this transom would produce little drag. On the whole, the hull of this ketch is remarkably well balanced. The vessel is of relatively light displacement. Pete calculated her displacement to outside of plank—a not-too-frequent practice by the Old Man. The lines are to inside of plank, following his procedure of cutting a half-model first. I am afraid that the lines, being two-dimensional, do not fully convey the marvelous character of this hull. If it were possible, I would hand the half-model to you, so you could see, firsthand, her striking shape.

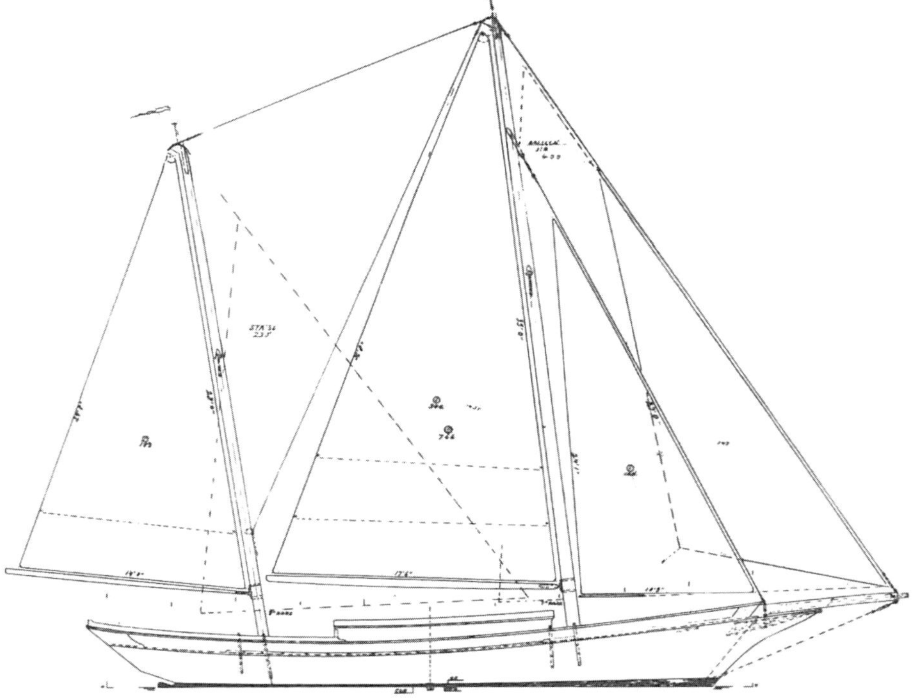

Above and right: Sail plan and lines of the Kendall 40-footer.

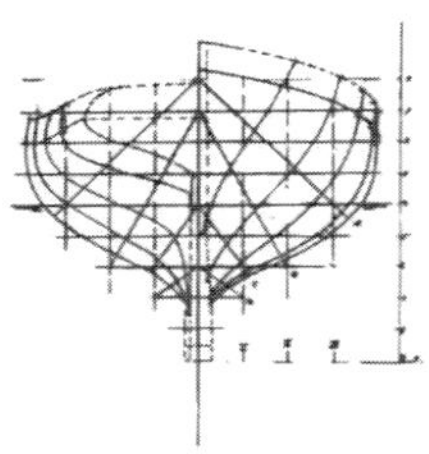

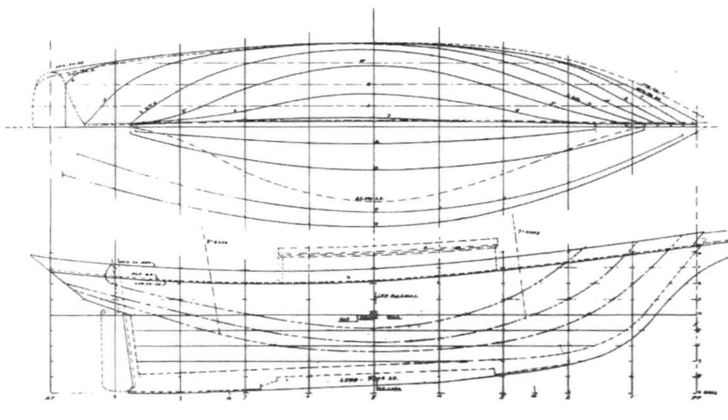

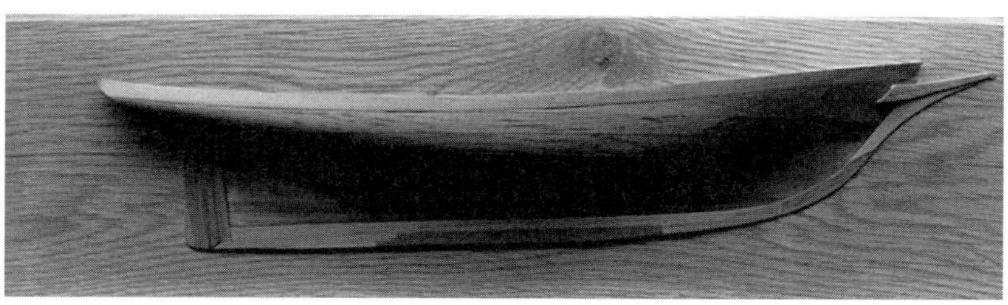

Half-model of John Kendall's 40-foot ketch. (John Burke photo)

Length overall: 38 feet 6½ inches
Length on waterline: 32 feet 1 inch
Beam: 11 feet 1 inch
Draft: 5 feet 6 inches
Sail area: 840 square feet
Displacement: 25,064 pounds

Ketch Proposal For Ted Harper

Howard Chapelle and others have written that 36 to 40 feet is about the length limit for amateur construction. This is definitely sage advice. However, considerations other than length should be accorded equal importance. Displacement, for example, as well as hull construction and complexity of the rig chosen, come to mind. The *Spray* is only 37 feet long, but heavy for her size, weighing in at about 15 tons. Also, her hull construction is somewhat difficult for a lone worker. Granted, she was rebuilt by one man, but Captain Josh was certainly no amateur.

For those who are inexperienced and wish to tackle the construction of a vessel, this ketch is ideal.

When this design was put on paper in 1976, Ted Harper was a 34-year-old ex-banker working in home construction and remodeling. His experience with boats was primarily in cruising in power craft. He was frank to admit that he knew little about singlehandedly building a boat this size. After reading *Skiffs and Schooners,* he chose Pete Culler to design his sailboat. That was smart. In addition, he had a much clearer grasp of the essentials of such a project than most, as his statement attests: "Economy, in building time as well as financially, is very important. I don't want to get into a five-year project, nor do I care about 14 Barient winches and five spinnakers of different cut. What I do care about is a seaworthy hull with a rig that will take advantage of it, and preferably be handled by one or two men."

Economy, simplicity, and ease of use. If these

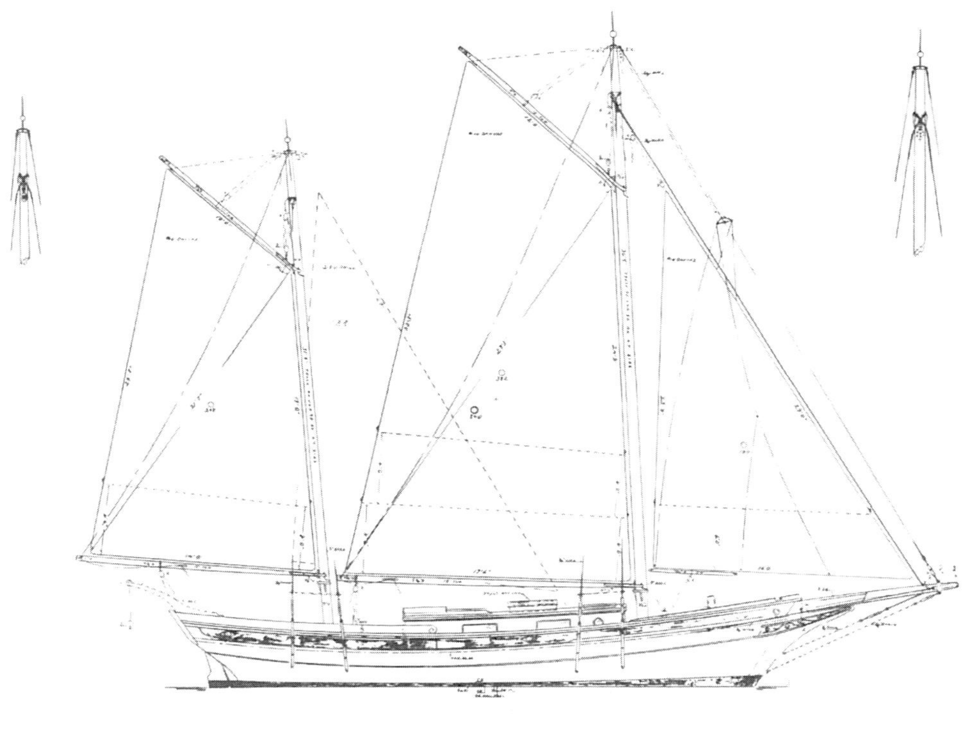

Sail plan of Ted Harper's 38½ -foot ketch .

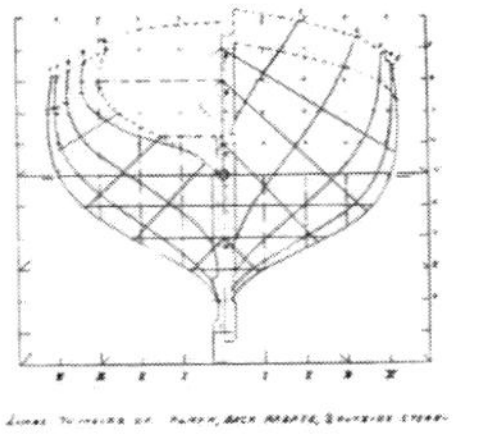

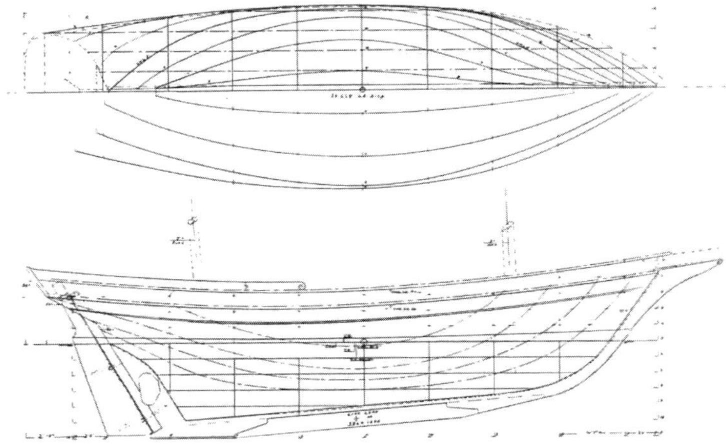

Proposed lines of the Harper ketch.

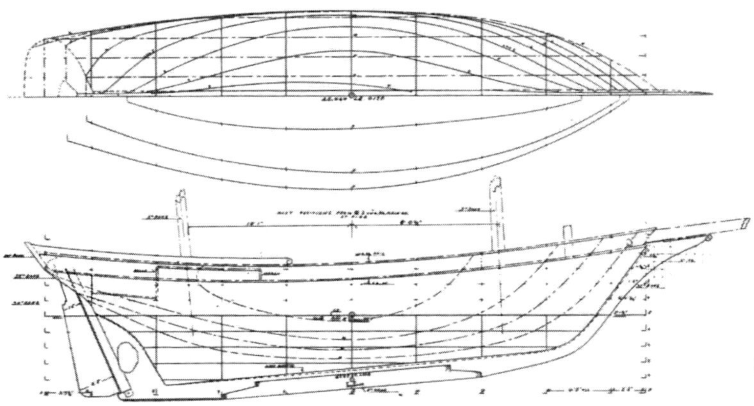

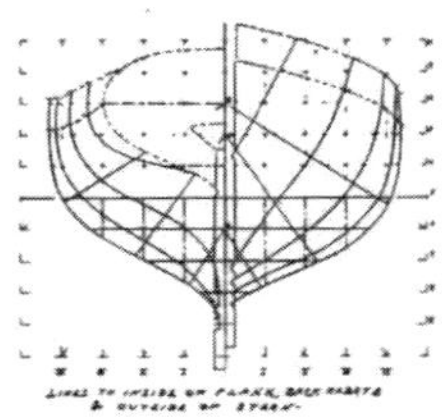

Final lines of the Harper ketch.

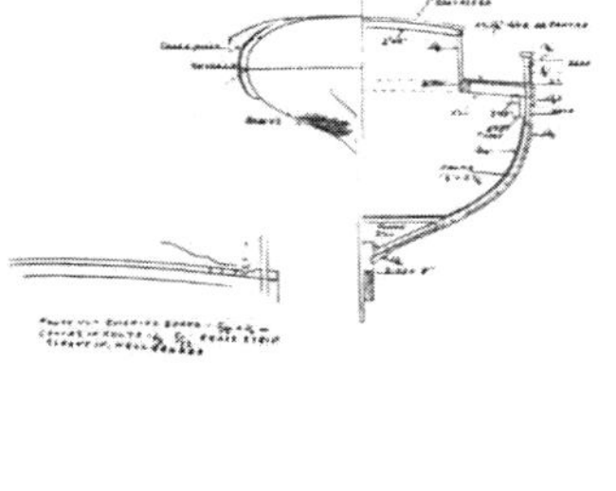

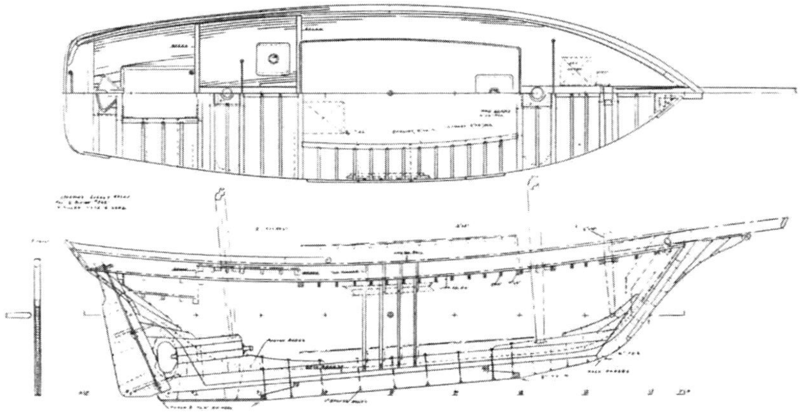

Construction plan of the Harper ketch.

basics were used as cornerstones in backyard building, many more projects would avoid failure. This, of course, was Captain Pete's design philosophy. It shows in Harper's ketch.

At 38 feet 10 inches overall, it is within the 40-foot length limitation for amateur construction. Also, displacement is on the light side, being just over 12 tons. In fact, there are two versions of this hull. The initial proposal was heavier, and Harper asked Pete to lighten her a bit. The hull construction is standard boatbuilding, except perhaps for the stern. This is an exception only because it may be unfamiliar. Pete used the double transom and "rule-joint" rudder because Harper was interested in it, having seen Bruce Northrup's Baltimore clipper *Lizard King*. The various methods of constructing this type of stern are discussed at some length in at least two sources that I know of: Charles G. Davis' *The Built-Up Ship Model* and Howard Chapelle's *The American Sailing Navy*. In my opinion, for certain models the double transom and rule-joint rudder are stronger and easier to build than the radiused transom and counter stern prevalent today.

The rig is simple in construction and easily maintained. It employs the minimum in standing rigging and spars for the sail area it spreads.

This ketch is seaworthy and able. She has an easy motion and therefore is easy on her gear and crew. The rig is exceedingly handsome and allows many sail combinations. The rig is handy to use with the two-part halyards, and the standard Chesapeake pungy jib arrangement has proven itself handy after many years of use on the oyster grounds. Use a Sharrit block on the traveler. The gull chasers on the mastheads are a nice touch. Nice Culler touches are in evidence everywhere on this design. For example, the nicely steeved and hogged-down bowsprit, complementing that beautifully shaped clipper head; the hinged spilling port and Chesapeake-style diamond-shaped cat or fast holes; square ports in the house sides and the break in the deck; the finely shaped quarter rail and wooden davits; the bead on the lower edge of the thick strakes and the striping on the low-sided bulwarks. All of these artistic touches unite harmoniously and add much to the character of the vessel. Pete Culler considered this smart little ketch one of his better efforts. Who would dispute that?

Ketch For Robin Laggeman

Length between perpendiculars: 33 feet 3 inches
Beam: 11 feet
Draft: 4 feet 6 inches
Sail area: 535 square feet

This little vessel reflects much of what Captain Pete felt was sound and practical in a boat. Virtues of economy, simplicity, and good old "boat sense" come right at you from the lines of this sweet-lined, modest, ketch-rigged craft. Due to her forthright nature, this design has acquired the nickname "no-bull ketch." I suppose it fits, for most people remember her as such, although Pete always felt she would have balanced better as a sloop. Robin Laggeman apparently has quite strong opinions when it comes to rigs. However, the ketch sail arrangement is probably best, for some singlehanded sailing was planned. The ketch rig is much handier for the lone sailor.

The hull is of very nice lines, being a shoal-keel type. She would move along very easily with her modest rig. There are no offsets included and no construction plan, but the hull's lines are fully faired and the sail and cabin plan are complete.

There are notes by Captain Pete on the thinking behind this design. Here's the Old Man talking: "Though economy is paramount, nothing is done with that view alone. Every detail is based on experience.

"The craft is a likely model for good sailing, extended cruising, and overnight passages in fair comfort, yet it is not too bulky for day use.

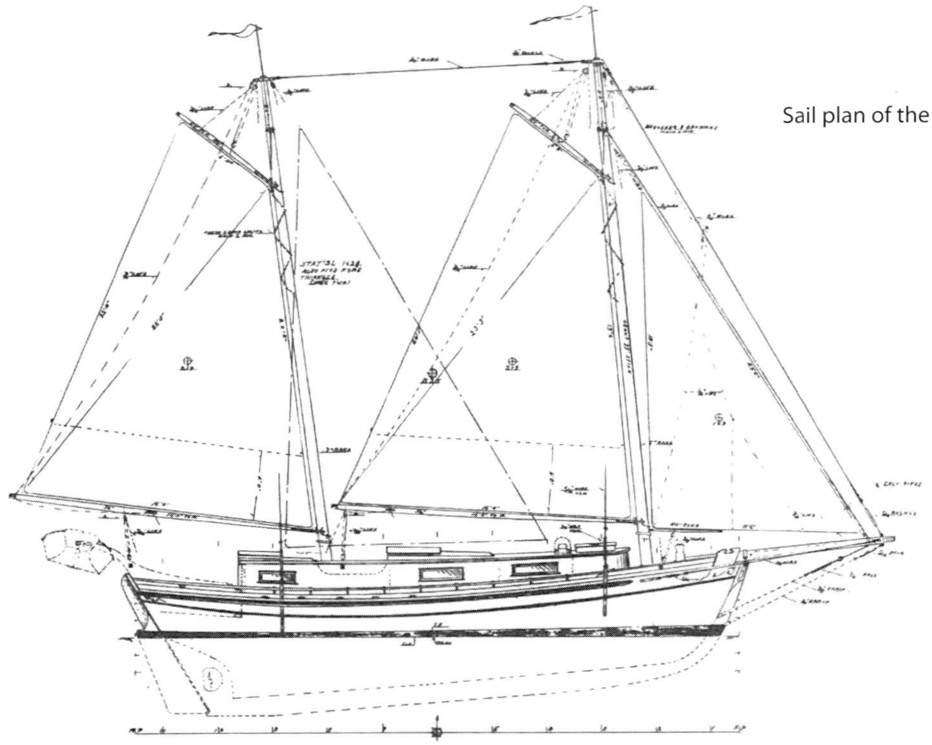

Sail plan of the Laggeman ketch.

"Simplicity is the keynote. There are no gas tanks below; a simple freshwater gravity system, with no pumps and short lines, is used. You'll see an open and accessible engine, preferably with a hand-start magneto. There's little or no electrical equipment.

"Light, air, and ventilation have been carefully planned. Headroom is good for the size and draft. The bunks are planned to be practical for a watch below. Seating is above average. The galley and toilet are far above average—in fact, excellent. Storage space is quite large. No effort has been made to provide a full length hanging locker. It's impractical in a craft this size intended for sea use.

"The joinerwork and finish below are simple and traditional, with much attention to detail. Generally, you'll see white overhead bulkheads to bunk level. The bunk faces, staving, doors, and lockers are to be dull varnish, and there should be rather more varnish used in the galley. She should be trimmed out with black walnut, or another dark hardwood, although it should be used sparingly to avoid a heavy, crowded look. Cabin floors, or sole, should be painted. Forward, this can be barn red; main cabin, emerald green; and aft cabin, prussian blue. It all should be varnished over. This is a good procedure that has been found to be practical.

"Now for some notes on optional gear that in no way really changes the vessel. A number of steering methods are possible. Wheel steering with an Edson rack-and-pinion quadrant is good, but expensive. A wheel drum and tackle is good under sail or power. It has modest cost and is simple to maintain and repair. Or a tiller, the cheapest and easiest, can be used. Even though the craft should steer very well, she is not as handy as some for shorthanded work. "Wood davits are shown, though iron can be used. The wood design gives a slightly more snug cockpit, simplifies the traveler, and makes sheeting the mizzen better. The davits can handle a 9-foot small boat. "Houses are connected by a coaming. This may add to appearance. Also, it makes a safe area and is better for the traveler and for rigging leads. "You can have either windows or ports or a combination of both, if this agrees with cabin layout. The stovepipe can be any style, but the old bay style shown is foolproof and best for a small craft. "The jib sheeting shown is the Sharrit method, about the handiest there is, although a double sheet with a loose foot is OK. A full-length club is not suitable here. Mast hoops can be used, but I see no point in them. They cost more and work no better than lacings. The same is true for large numbers of metal fittings—what is shown works."

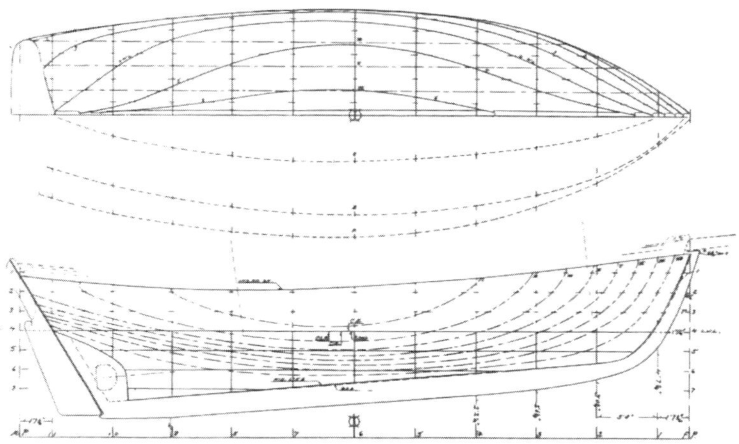

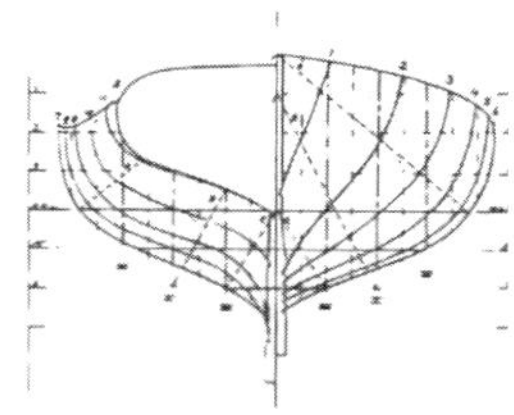

Lines of the 33-foot Laggeman ketch.

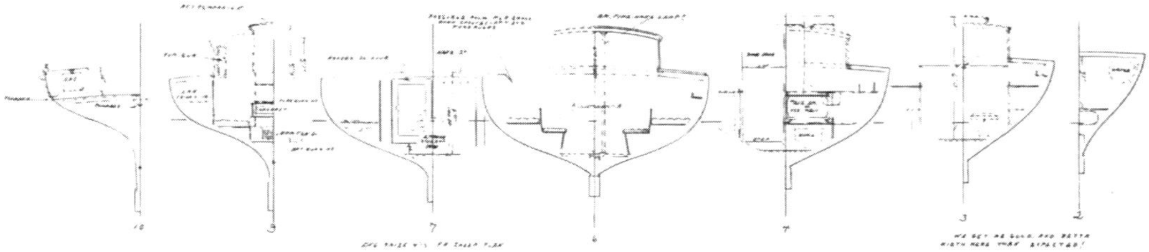

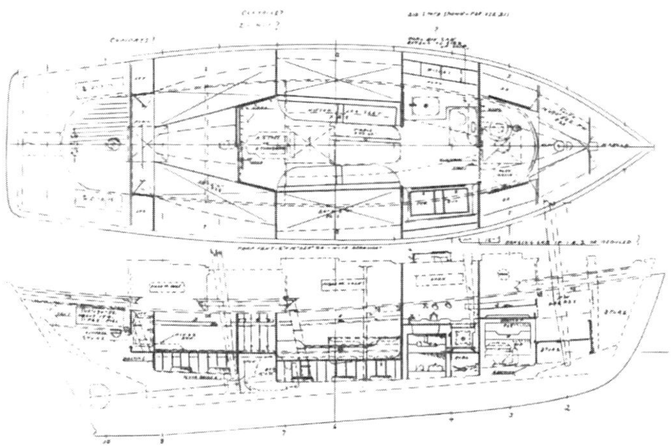

Arrangement plans of the 33-footer.

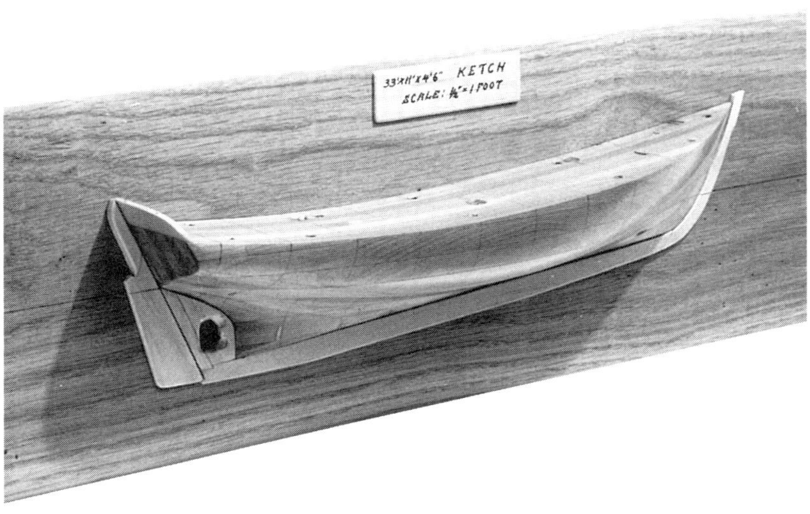

Half-model of the Laggeman ketch.

Wabun-Type Sharpie For Gordon Mott
Presto-Type Sharpie For Admiral J.W. Schmidt

Wabun-Type Sharpie

Molded length: 40 feet 5¾ inches
Molded beam: 11 feet 9 inches
Draft: 2 + feet
Sail area: 747 square feet
Displacement: 13,152 pounds

Presto-Type Sharpie

Length overall: 37 feet 7½ inches
Beam: 10 feet 1 inch
Draft: 3 feet
Sail area: 615 square feet
Displacement: 17,165 pounds

"This is the boat to which my dreams have been led by many years of cruising, followed by a considerable period in which occasional cruises alternated with ample opportunity for memory and hope. She is not the ideal boat, for there are as many ideal boats as there are men and women who love the water. It depends on what you want to do afloat. I want to sail. It is fun." So said Vincent Gilpin, discussing *Wabun*, a design by Commodore R.M. Munroe shown in *The Rudder*, March 1946.

Shoal draft versus deep draft has been a simmering question for many, many years. There are authorities on both sides of the question equally fervent in the defense of their position. Most of those in the deep-draft camp will readily admit the advantages of a shoal cruiser in shallow, protected waters (there are many). It is only when offshore that these people become dogmatic about deep draft.

Almost 100 years ago, Commodore Ralph M. Munroe designed the first of what he chose to call round-bilge sharpies—boats that were slim and of shoal draft. This first craft was named *Presto*; she was to confound those of deep-draft persuasion. She not only sailed the bays and rivers of southeast Florida, but regularly ventured out to sea and frolicked in all sorts of weather. After having done that, she would run the nasty inlets for which that part of the coast is famous—just for good measure. Resoundingly successful, the Commodore designed more boats according to the same principles.

After owning *Wabun* for 19 years and cruising 30,000 miles in her from Florida to Cape Cod in all sorts of weather, Gilpin is qualified to discuss shoal draft. Therefore, I quote again from the article mentioned above.

"This shoal-draft question should be further developed, for it is one of the greatest contributions to fun in cruising. It makes accessible thousands of small harbors that are apt to be the most interesting and comfortable anchorages, not only in New Jersey and Florida, but in many sections where keels predominate, such as in Maine where there are many charming holes and corners with scant depth. Next, a shoal-draft hull, properly designed and built, will take the hammering of rough water with less racking strain; it will rise to a sea quickly and easily without dragging tons of outside ballast up with it. It will not dive headlong into the next sea; to windward or hove-to, it will lightly give way before the blow of a breaking crest, like a boxer, instead of standing anchored to its keel to be pummeled. Further, it can be beached in an emergency, usually without danger to crew or injury to itself, and when it takes bottom, it stands upright without struts or tackles. When accidentally grounded it is easily worked off. Finally, it is cheaper to build, easier to drive, takes less canvas, and is of course lighter to handle."

Gilpin goes on to state, "...I am convinced that one inch draft per foot of waterline length will give a cruiser all the ability she needs; that goes even for hurricanes, given experienced handling." That is a statement of considerable weight.

Captain Pete designed both types, as the designs under discussion here and in the rest of this book show clearly. He fully realized that both types have their merits—and faults, too. All boat design

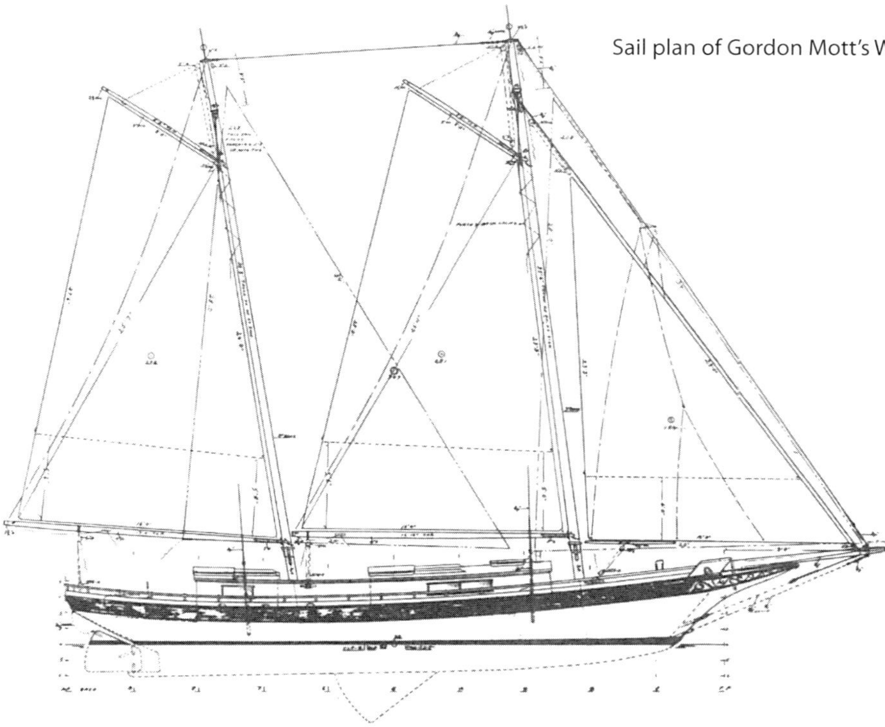

Sail plan of Gordon Mott's Wabun-type sharpie.

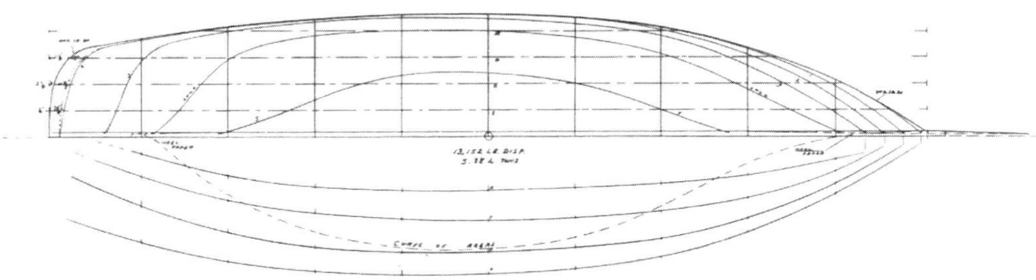

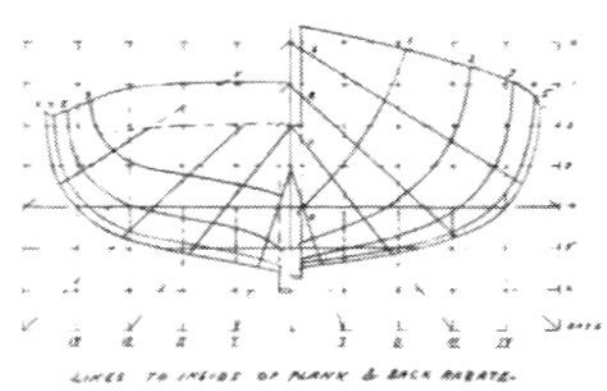

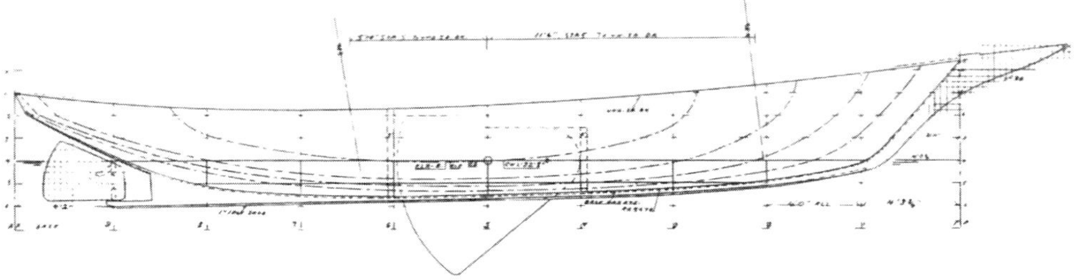

Lines of the Mott sharpie.

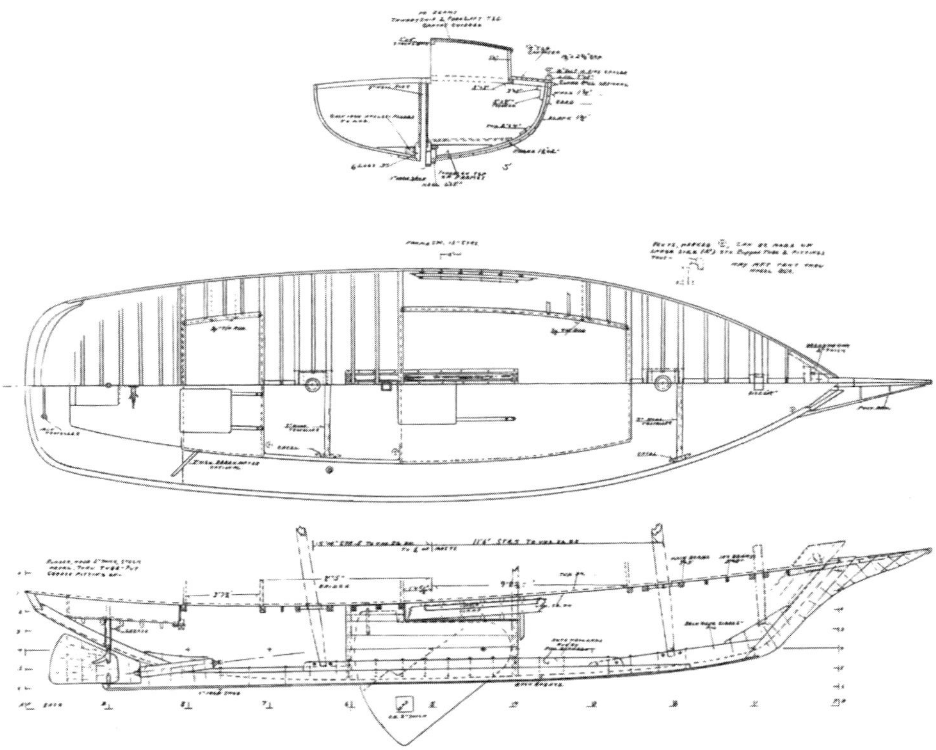

Above and below: Construction and accommodations plans of the Mott sharpie.

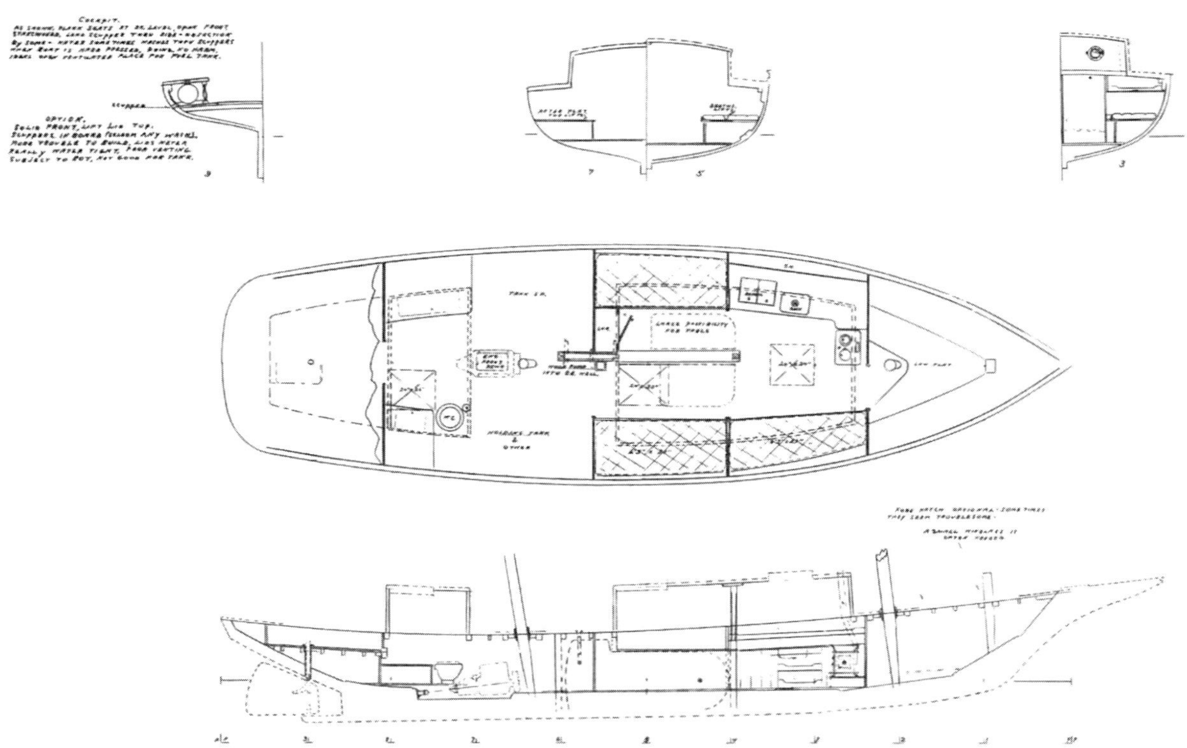

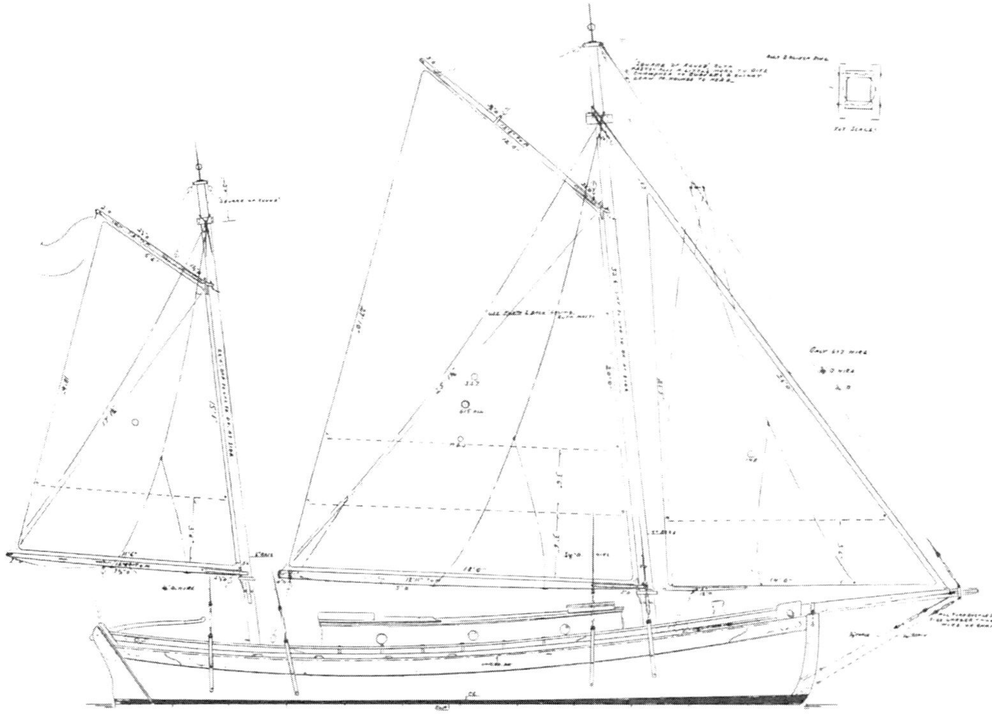

Above and below: Sail plan and lines of the Schmidt Presto-type sharpie.

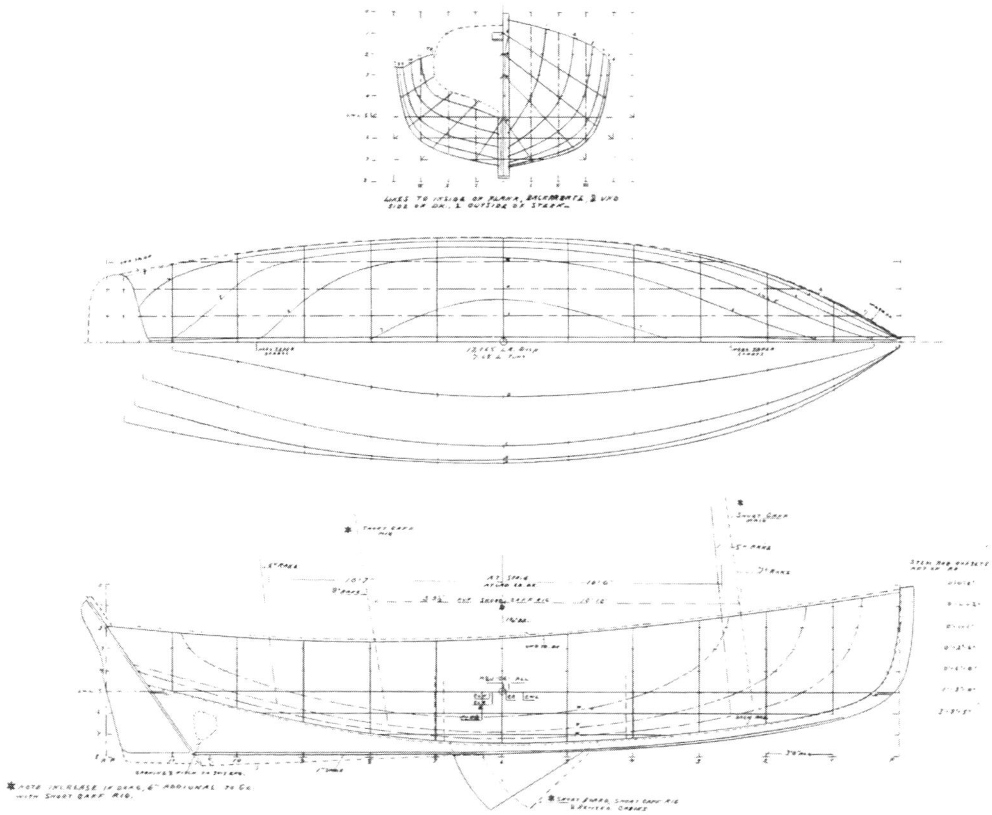

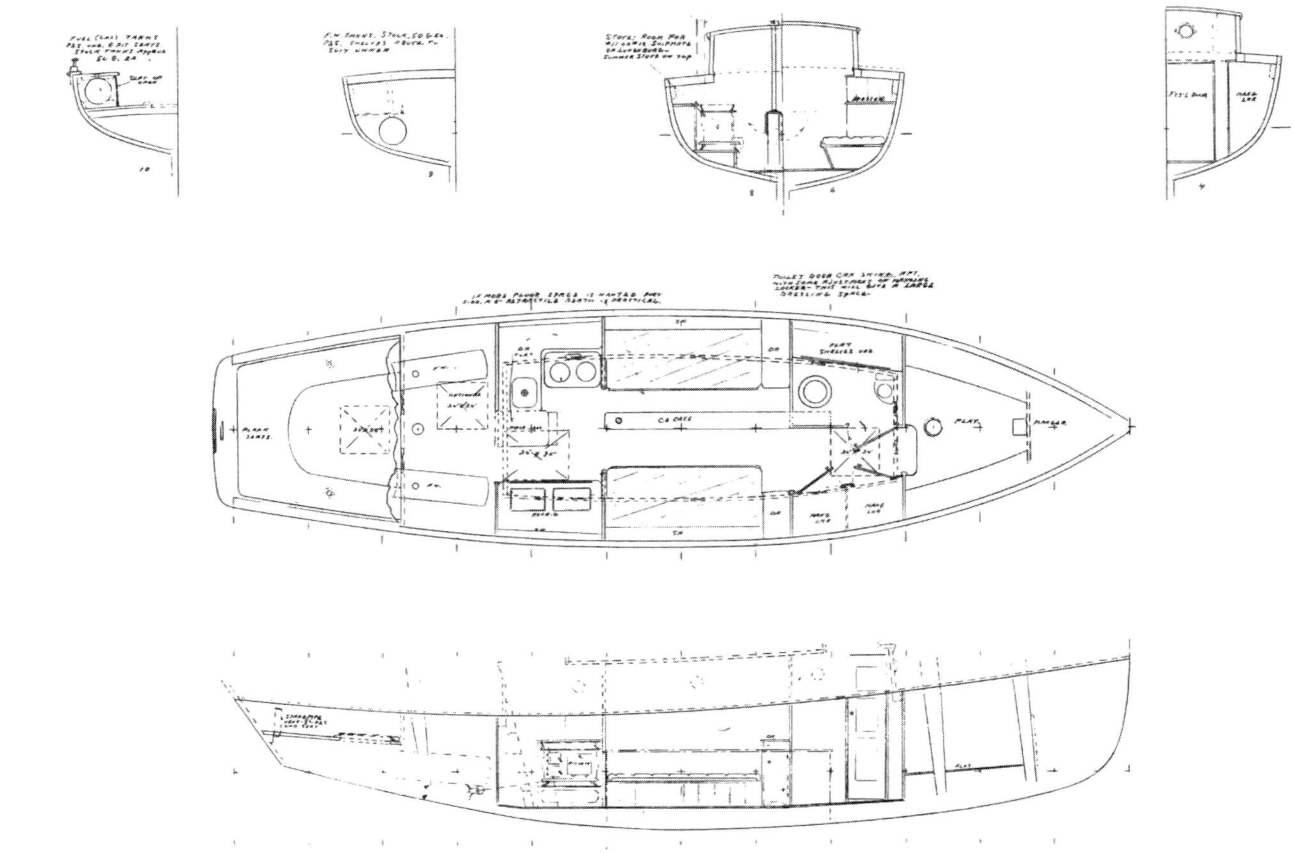

Above and below: Construction and accommodations plans of the Schmidt sharpie.

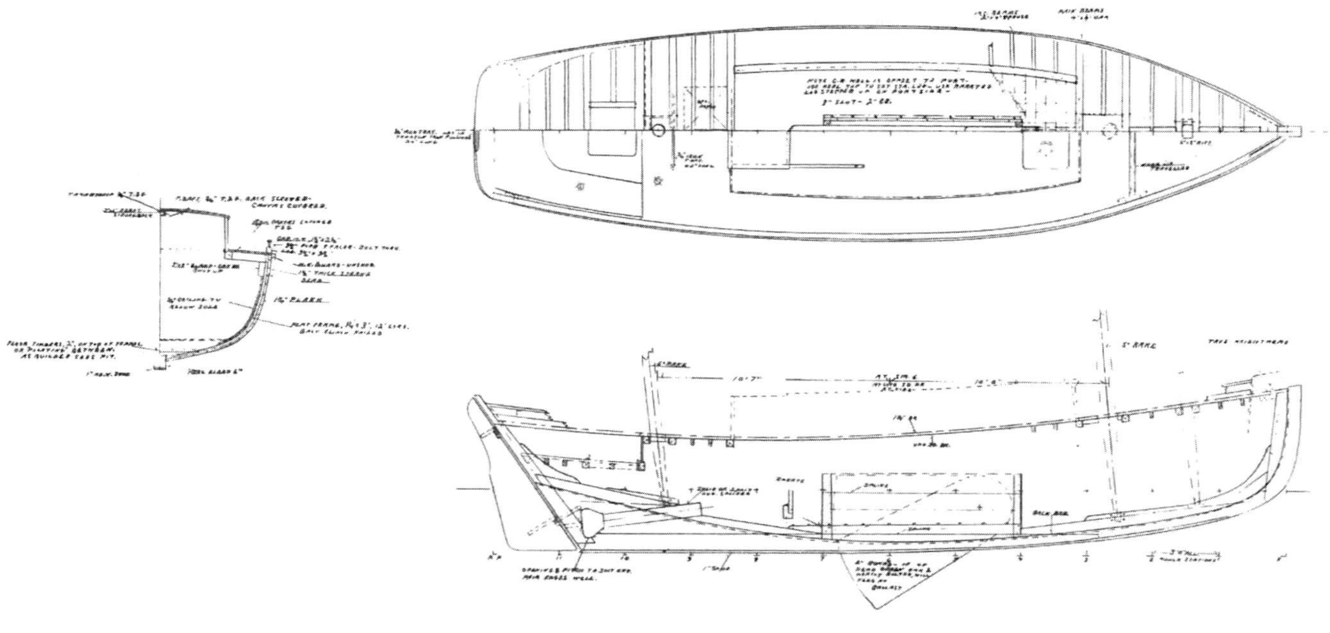

Admiral Schmidt's sharpie ketch *Spray*.
(John Burke photo)

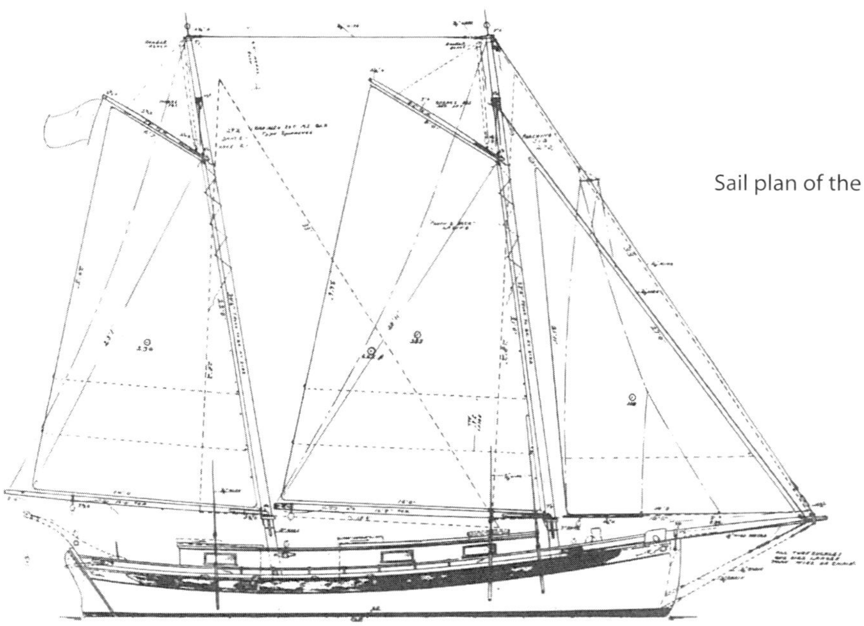

Sail plan of the revised sharpie for Stefan Galazzi.

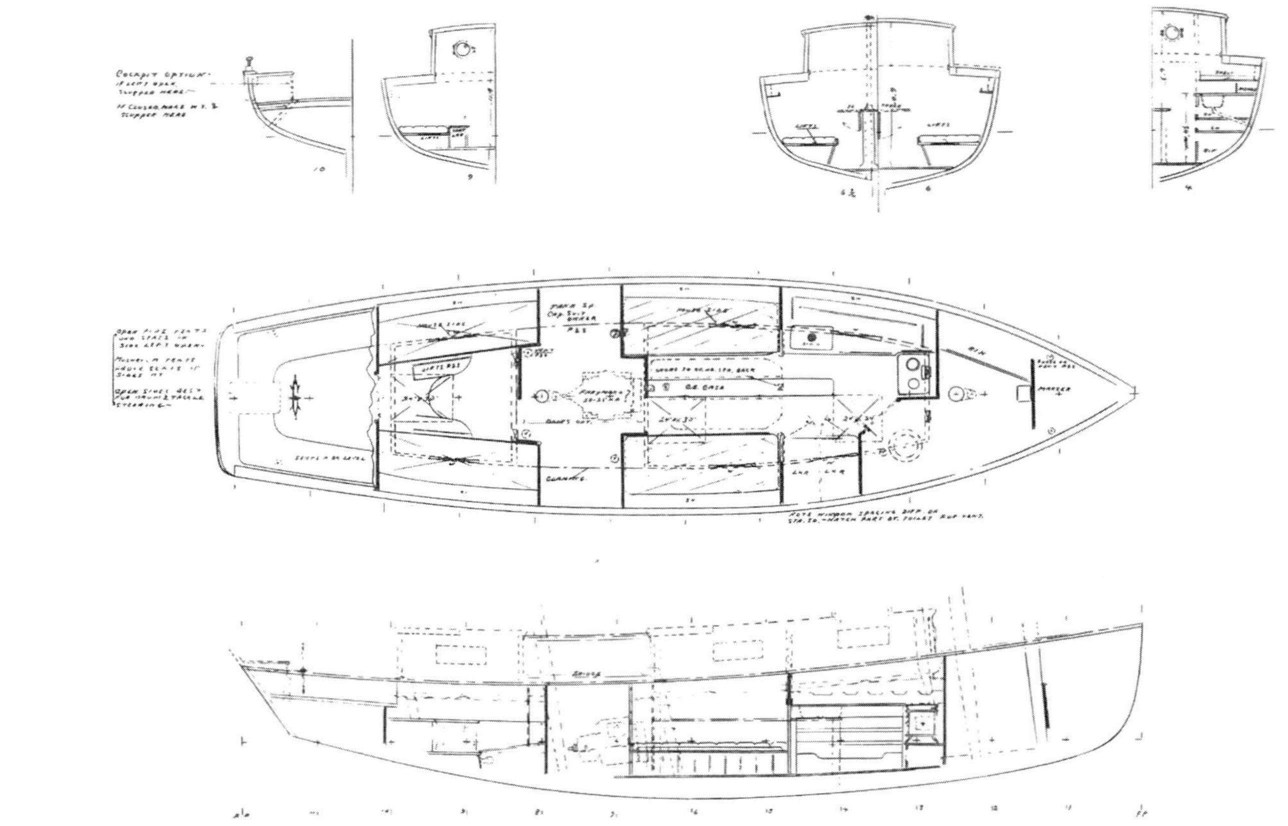

Above and below: Construction and accommodations plans of Stefan Galazzi's version of the Presto sharpie.

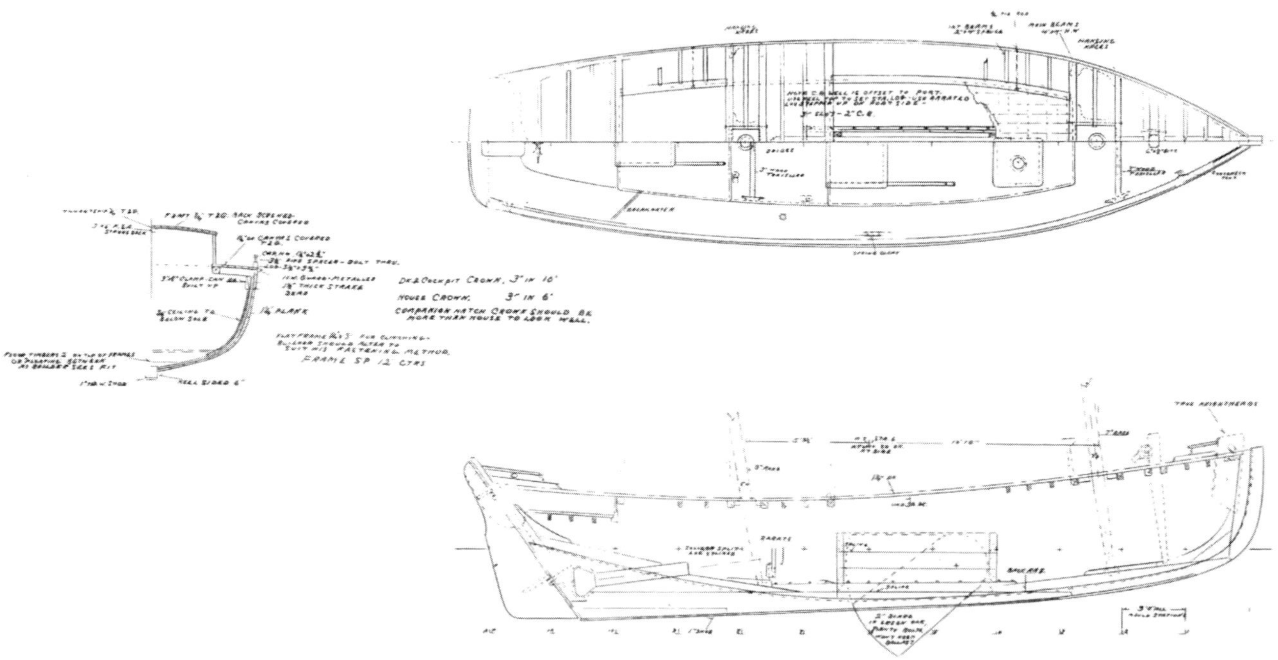

Stefan Galazzi's *Dawn Treader*. (E.L. Boutilier photo)

is a compromise. However, he would definitely disagree with any argument that insisted that if one is good, the other must necessarily be bad.

Captain Pete made this statement in *Skiffs and Schooners*: "Since the beginning of boats, shoal craft have been around, and a study of them from early times to the present shows their record to be remarkably good—just as good, apparently, as that of the deeper vessels. Shoal craft have been everywhere, done everything, and, it seems, made it pay. Captain Bligh made his remarkable 4,000-mile voyage from the Friendly Isles to Java in an open, shoal boat, the *Bounty's* launch. Granted, he was a master at his profession. Many others too have made long cruises in shoal boats, as in Bligh's case, not always from choice. A study of these things makes you aware that the boat, whatever kind she was, did fine. The real problems were grub, water, and exposure. Furthermore, these craft often did a lot of looking after themselves because the crew became incapacitated. If a person is unreasonably afraid of capsizing and of shoal boats, he should stay ashore and take his chances on the highways. Freeways frighten me, for I don't know what I'm doing on them. In trouble with some old shingle of a boat, I may not know what's what either, but if she's let alone, she will usually come through, and the chance of being sideswiped by some nut changing lanes is slim!" Very well said, Captain.

Very well said, indeed.

Perhaps the most succinct statement on the matter can be attributed to Commodore Munroe. Referring to the many shoal-draft cruisers he designed, he said, "None of them were ever capsized, to my knowledge."

I hope the discussion above has helped the reader keep an open mind (if you did not have one already) on these Munroe-type shoal cruisers with distinctive Culler flavorings. I find these two designs very instructive, especially when viewed in conjunction with the originals of the same name.

I trust that those who are truly interested in these boats will research them further in the sources listed in Appendix B. Therefore, I will not elaborate except to emphasize one final point. Those of the sharpie type require ballast. Their performance will be disappointing if they don't have it in the proper amounts, trimmed correctly. The original *Wabun* (smaller than Pete's version) had 1,000 pounds of lead stowed under floors and bunks and about 700 pounds of weight in her centerboard.

Pete felt that these types were of a naturally weak shape, so he designed some of their needed ballast into their construction by increasing the scantlings somewhat. You will need still more. Try to keep all other factors constant while you are adding and shifting this ballast, and try to develop a feel for your craft. For example, in my own sharpie, if the 75-pound anchor is not in place on the bowsprit, her sailing is noticeably different. This applies to the 5-gallon water jug in the forepeak too. We can even tell when it's half full.

Above all, use common sense. Happy sailing!

Length between perpendiculars: 36 feet
Molded beam: 8 feet 6 inches
Draft: 2 feet
Sail area: 517 square feet
Displacement: 8,310 pounds

V-Bottomed Sharpie *Old Glory* For Franklin Parker

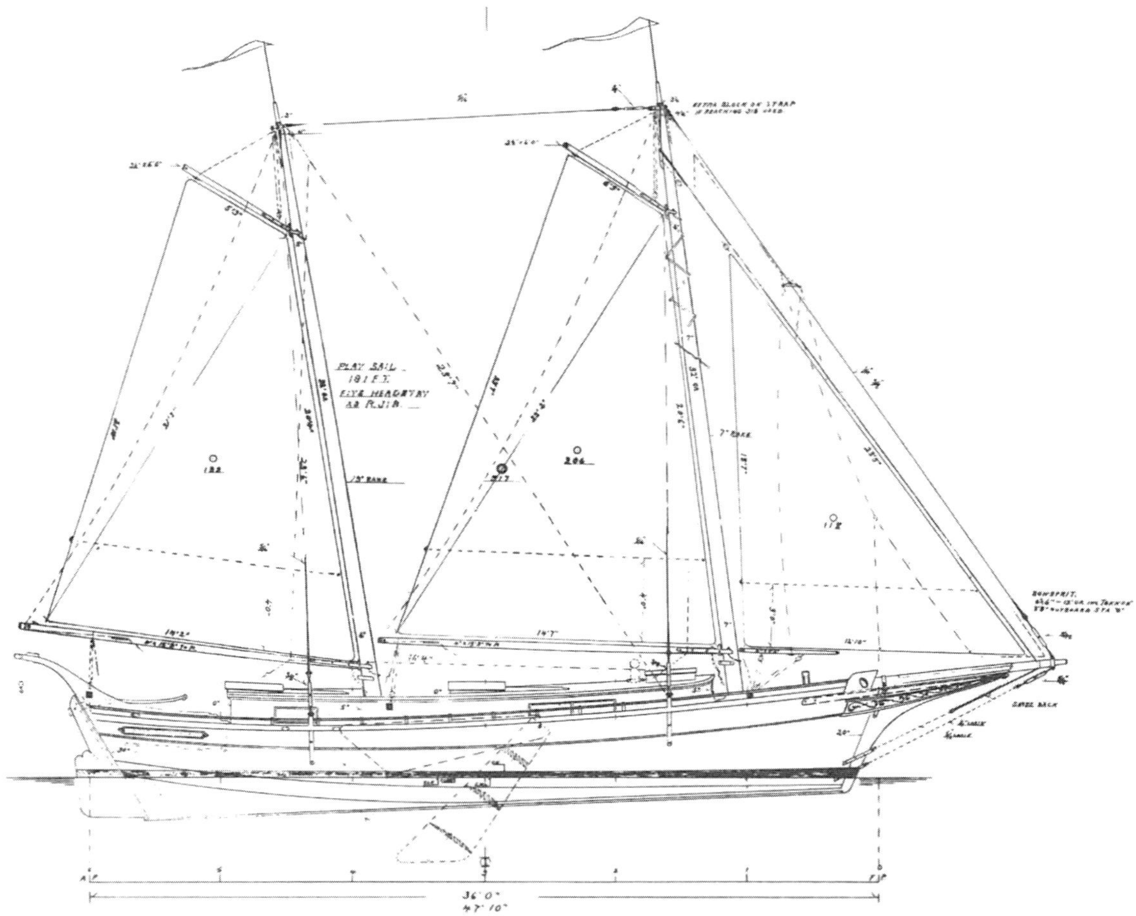

Captain Pete was much enamored of the sharpie model in its many forms. He felt it resulted in a simple, practical, and sensible boat. This attitude was reinforced when L. Francis Herreshoff laid down the lines for *Meadow Lark* in his "How to Build" series in *The Rudder* magazine during the 1950s. Pete felt that this shoal draft, short-gaff ketch with its leeboards was eminently sensible in its approach to the problem of the shallow water cruiser. So much more cruising is available to you if you can follow the ducks up to the shore!

When the opportunity presented itself, Captain Pete used *Meadow Lark* as an inspiration and produced *Old Glory*. Although conceptually similar, they are very different in construction and appearance. *Old Glory* looks like a real little ship!

The hull construction is by the tried-and-true V-bottomed cross-planked herringbone method. With a stout keel, sister keelsons, and strongbacks all tied into chine and side frames, this results in a strong hull that will last if kept clean, well ventilated, and maintained.

By using leeboards, the cabin is kept free of a centerboard box—a great advantage in a minimum-

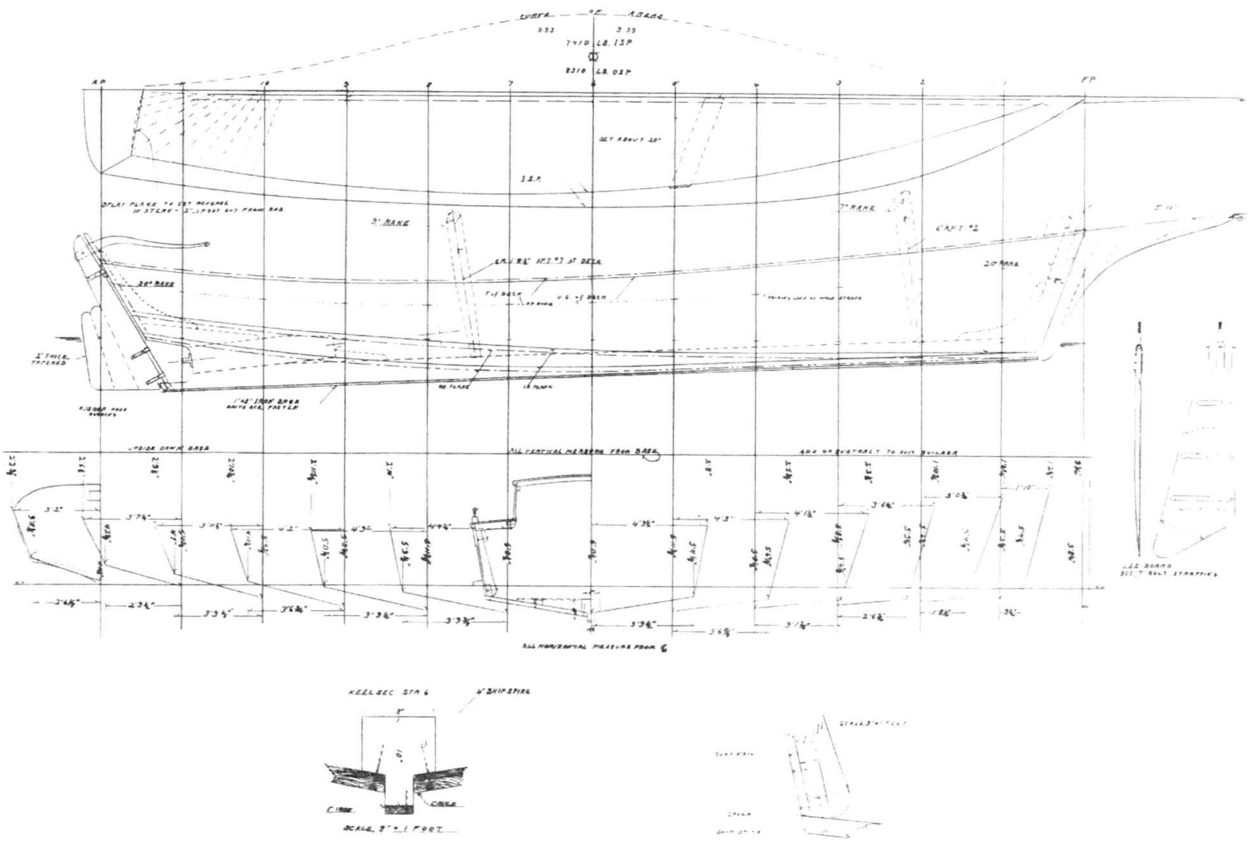

Opposite and above: Sail plan and lines of *Old Glory*.

headroom boat. Together with the keel drag, the leeboards provide all the lateral resistance needed. Many people who are inexperienced with leeboards malign them as too much bother, but those who have used them find just the opposite to be true. With tackles rigged to the cockpit, it is a simple matter when tacking to lower away your leeboard after passing the eye of the wind, and to haul up the high-side board at your leisure. Believe me, it's simple and effective. You will note that on the boards themselves there is a flat side and a convex side. It is important to have the flat side outboard. The convex side works much like an airplane wing, providing lift to windward. The difference is noticeable.

The hull and rig in profile make a handsome craft. The sheer's a nice sweep. It is beautifully enhanced by the fine-looking clipper head with its trailboards and knightheads. The knightheads are a very important part of the vessel's construction. Along with the bobstays, headrails, and gammon iron, they lock the bowsprit in place. Pete always thought that many a good-looking vessel was otherwise ruined by the lack of proper knights.

The transom is raked at 30 degrees, which looks good and allows good rudder area without being deeper than the vessel's heel. The stern davits solve the small boat problem (Pete thought that this was the best possible solution for any craft) and add much to the vessel's appearance.

The rig is low and well spread out, the short gaffs providing good sail area without undue height. The mizzen staysail doubles as a reaching jib, set on the forestay. I would add another reef in the foresail. All of the standing and running rigging is simple and practical and easily owner-maintained.

With the sharpie model, ballast is a must. Stone or brick is best, but if you must, lead will do. Set it down under the floors and bunks. Pea stone poured between side frames and stopped ceiling works very well, and will make the vessel quite stiff. Don't worry about moisture collecting. For some reason, it just doesn't happen. Ventilation still is available.

Once your gear, weights, and ballast are right and you are familiar with the rig, which doesn't take long, this boat will self-steer. With the self-tending jib and running rigging leading to the cockpit, it

Sailing full and by. (R.D. Culler photo)

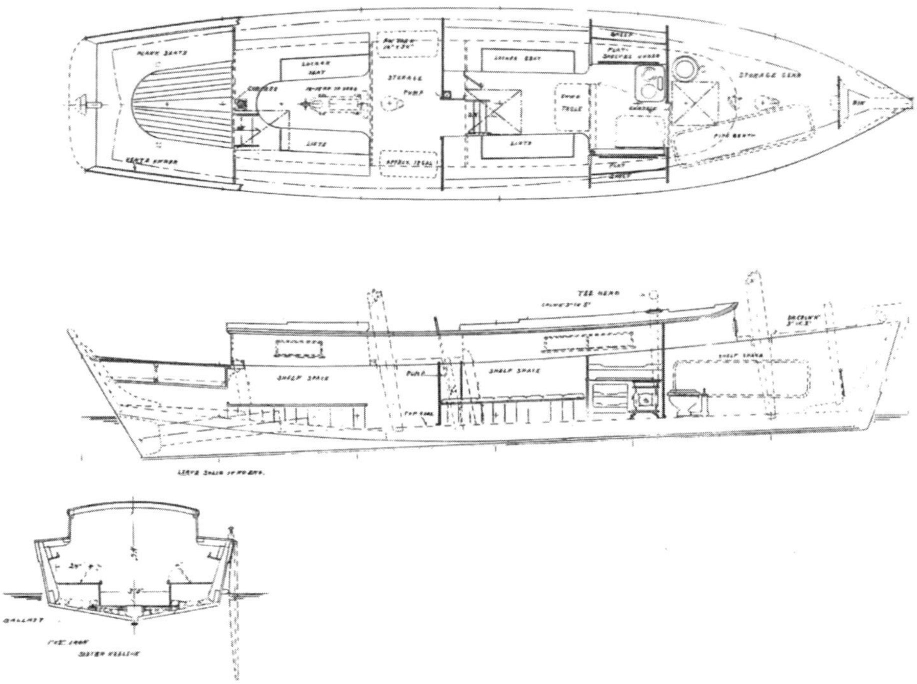

Above and below: Cabin and deck layouts of *Old Glory*.

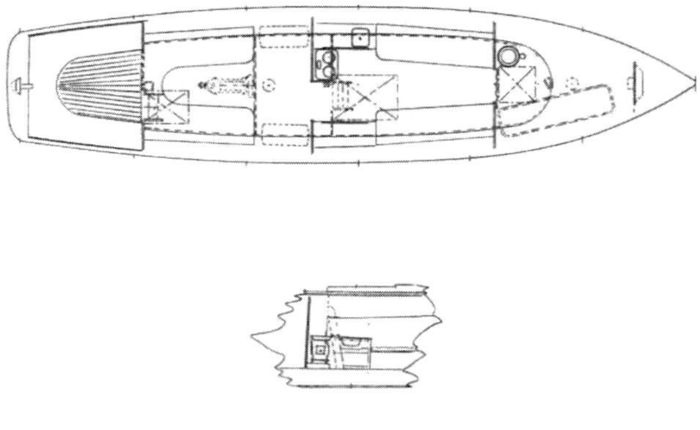

could be singlehanded easily.

The cabin layout is well thought out and should provide all the room needed for a small family or group of friends. The two separate cabins are very handy. The minimum headroom will put off many at first, but the words of Harry Pidgeon still ring true—you don't stand up to eat or sleep. Stand in the forward hatch to pull on your pants. That's why the pot is located there. Of the two layouts, I recommend the one that has the stove forward. You will have fewer draft problems, both with the stove and with the vessel's natural tendency to ventilate. Refrain from boxing in the engine. A clean and properly maintained engine is a much better sleeping companion than some others. Also, if the engine is kept out in the open where problems are easily noticed, headaches will be kept to a minimum.

Pete felt that this design was perfect for Cape Cod waters, and that it would do well in any area that is similar. Yet, the vessel is capable of extended cruising too. The Old Man's good friend Jim Melcher of Orleans, Massachusetts, built a copy, *Triumph*, and took her on an ocean sail from Chatham to Penobscot Bay in Maine. Jim also cruised *Triumph* down the East Coast and through the Caribbean one winter. Intelligent handling and proper planning make such trips safe and comfortable.

I own and sail a smaller version of *Old Glory*, designed and built by George Kelley. I can't begin to tell you how much fun she is. The boat is a joy!

Length: 36 feet
Beam: 10 feet
Draft: 2 feet 6 inches
Sail area: 610 square feet
Displacement: 14,600 pounds

Steel Sharpie For Dr. Robert L. Baxter

Comments by Pete Culler

In recent years, I've watched the performance of many steel craft—some yachts, many others commercial craft—and I suppose they do the intended job quite well. None were handsome, many were ugly, and some were just plain horrible. All seemed to be some form of chined craft with more or less developed surfaces. It's been notable that many of these seemed unable to make up for limitations of design. Some even went through the water like they hated it.

From talking to experienced seamen with much time in all sorts of craft, I drew the conclusion that a fully molded hull would be their choice if it were not for the cost. Any seaman worth his salt likes a good-looking craft. Any designer knows that it's impossible to get a good run, and often a decent entrance on a chined hull that, by its very nature, must be deep bellied.

Dr. Robert Baxter of Hyannis, who has had many boats, had much interest in the Munroe Presto-type sharpie. His son, Hudson, has a professional welding shop. (He worked in a small steel shipyard in the past.) There was plenty of room at the shop, and three strapping grandsons to keep busy. Thus, I was consulted about a design for a Presto in steel.

Not caring to willfully turn out another ugly steel craft, I went at the project with caution and careful study. The round-bilged Presto looked like it could be made to work in steel, yet retain the shape and charm of the type.

Call the result what you want. I call it multi-multi-multi chine or plating by strakes—not very much different from planking. This more or less keeps the round bilge form without hot-forming or compound curves.

Dr. Baxter wanted a fantail stern, and I much approve; it's simply a segment of a cone. Getting the shape of the "strakes" was done by a "fingerspiling batten" that I dreamed up. It worked just fine. A lot of work, a lot of cutting, and a lot of welding, some will say. Maybe so, maybe not, but steel is heavy and the pieces we worked with were for the most part small, so most were more or less bulled into place without a hoist.

Having done considerable lofting and pattern work in advance, Dr. Baxter soon had things ready to set up. The boys worked! A hand-steered power

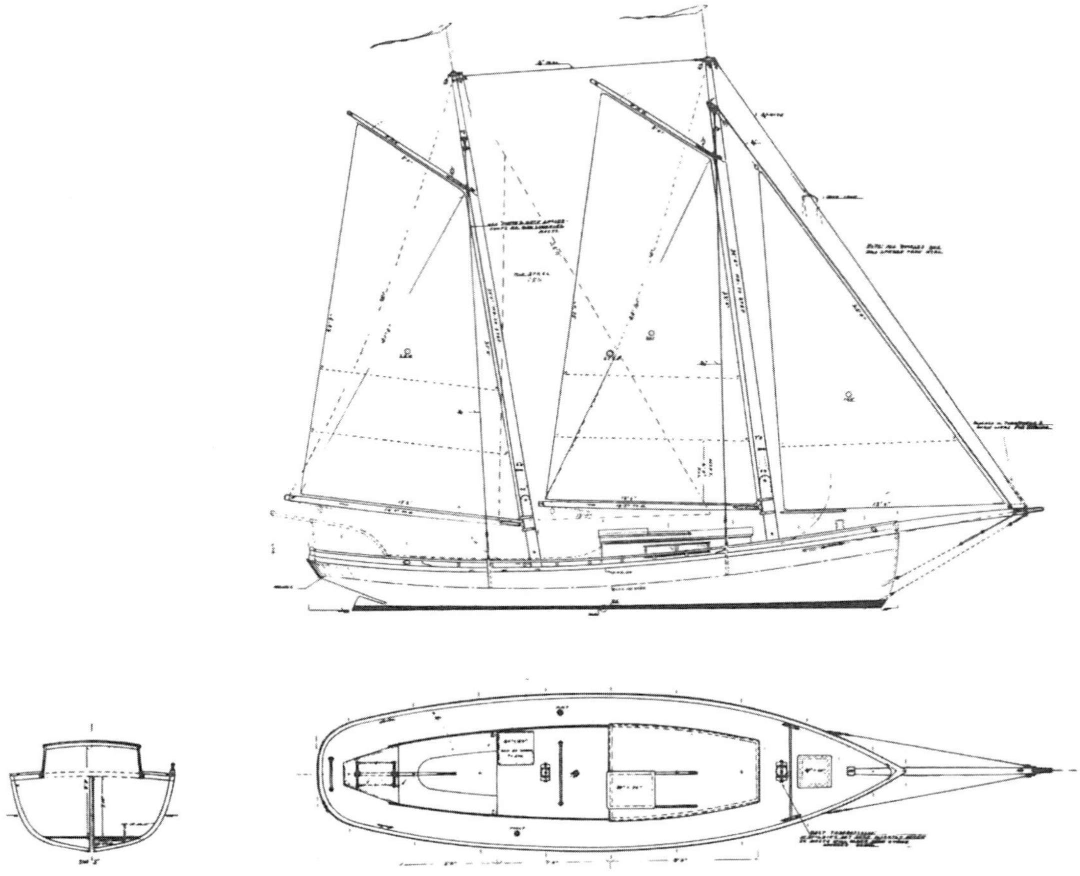

Above and below: Sail plan, deck plan, and lines of the steel sharpie.

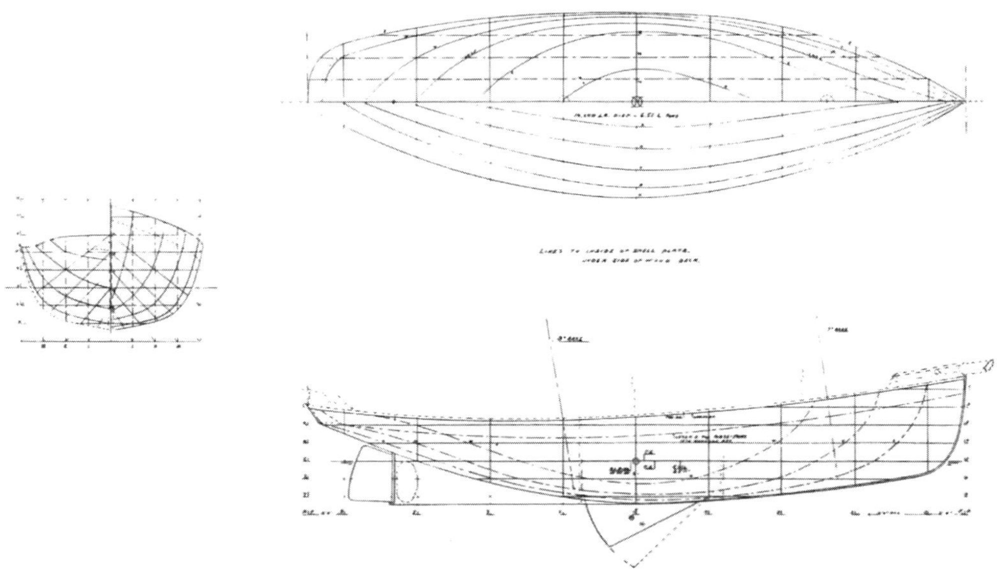

nibbler was acquired, and all plates were soon in place and tacked. It seems she went together quite rapidly. Only a small amount of advice was needed from the pro—and no help, except for tools.

Just how good this approach to steel boatbuilding is, time will tell. It all seemed so practical for this boat that we don't feel it's totally experimental. The molded shape, with no real flats, the rod "chines," a big steel centerboard well, and a thick "garboard strake" make the hull very stiff and strong—so strong that the plate used is lighter than that in many boats of this size. Moreover, frame spacing is rather wide.

We don't expect a big weight problem—the craft has a bit more displacement than a wooden one of about the same size and shape, and the decks and houses will be of wood. The ketch rig will be about like those on the sharpies *Old Glory* and *Triumph*.

I think the boat's assembly was quite rapid. The argument by some that this is the hard way to do it sort of falls on its face. There were preparation and hard work, to be sure, but she's not just another box. Besides, as small steel craft go, she's reasonably fair—not perfect, we all know, but pretty good.

The craft is 36 feet overall, and otherwise proportioned very much like the original Presto. Only slight concessions had to be made to adapt to steel.

Even if this craft were to turn out to be a huge success, she will influence the small steel boat field little, if at all. The urge to use four panels and a lid, using up the scraps to close in the stern, is just too strong.

Length overall: 34 feet
Length on waterline: 29 feet
Beam: 11 feet
Draft: 5 feet
Sail area: 628 square feet
Displacement: 23,408 pounds

Live-Aboard Ketch For Fred Stanton

Comments by Pete Culler

This little craft had rather unusual design requirements, compared with the usual cruising yacht. Basically, it was to be a one-man year-round home, to be used in northern climates. Finding such a craft on the used-boat market is nearly impossible, since few people do this sort of thing.

The ketch rig seemed the best choice. The 34-foot length, according to what one man could handle, and the other details were based on the use intended and the total cost.

The vessel was designed for Fred Stanton of Fairhaven, Massachusetts, and built by the Concordia Company. Her name is *Plover.* She was launched in mid March 1971 with ease and dispatch in the usual raw weather that most of our launchings take place in. Only this time there was no gale.

The hull had to be of large displacement to get the required room—it is bulky, though rather fine underwater for such a chunky craft. This, in turn, required a rather large rig. The one shown gave the best sail area (as long as one stays with the ketch rig) for the money. In my opinion, the marconi ketch rig is entirely unsuited to a hull of this type. The rig must be unduly tall to get the needed sail area, producing the problem of overly narrow sails to set. Besides, the cost, if figured in the current fashion, would be much greater. The rig shown is very much workboat style, as is the rest of the construction.

There is a fair amount of wood in her, for both strength and insulation. The framing is traditional, for the most part all oak, with plank, ceiling, and decks of cedar. The interior is pine. The ceiling is stouter than usual to keep out heat and cold.

The craft is based on inside ballast, though there is a fabricated 6-inch by 6-inch steel shoe about 14 feet long. The idea of fabricating iron ballast keels is not new. With the large thick billets now available in great lengths, modern cutting and welding rigs, and the ability to "metallize," a form of oxyacetylene zinc galvanizing, right on the job, it is practical up to a point. Boring bolt holes is no problem, if

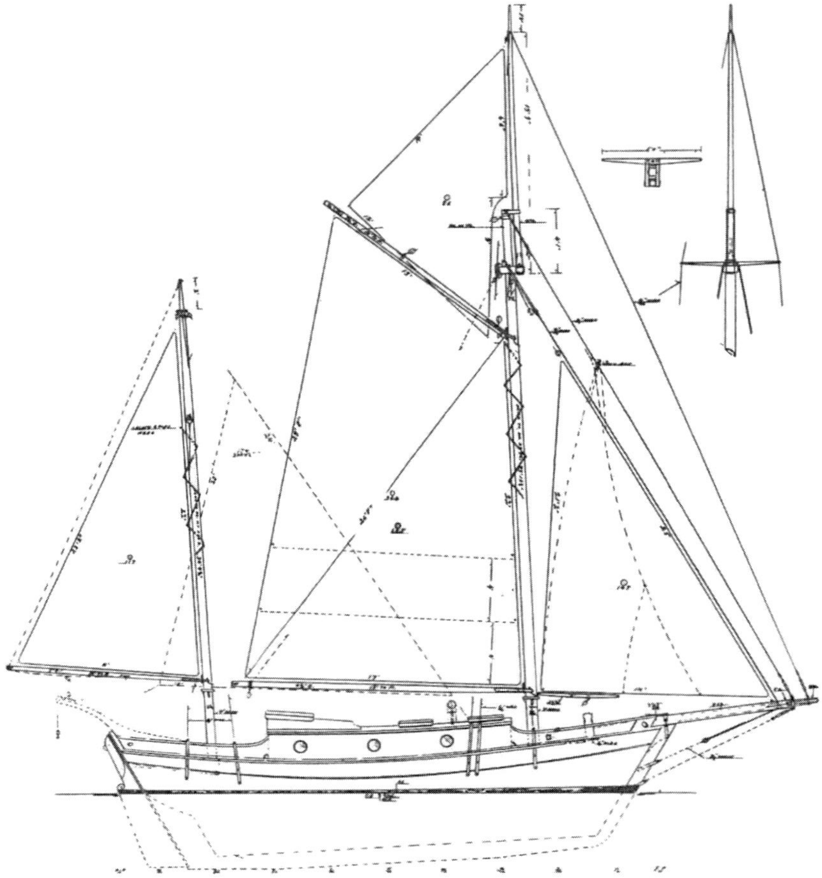

Above and below: *Plover's* sail plan and lines.

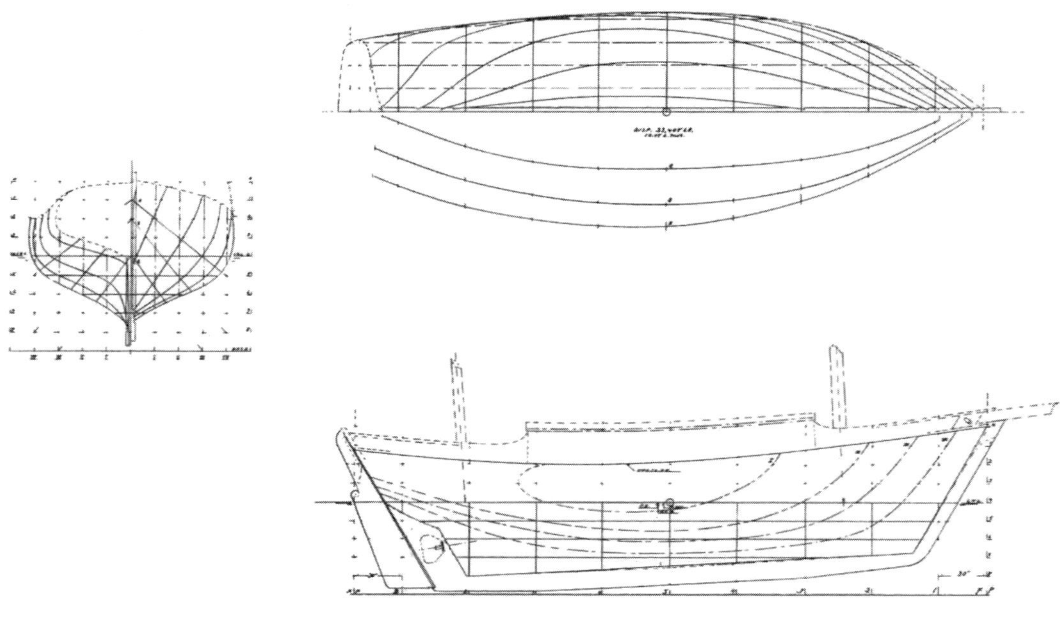

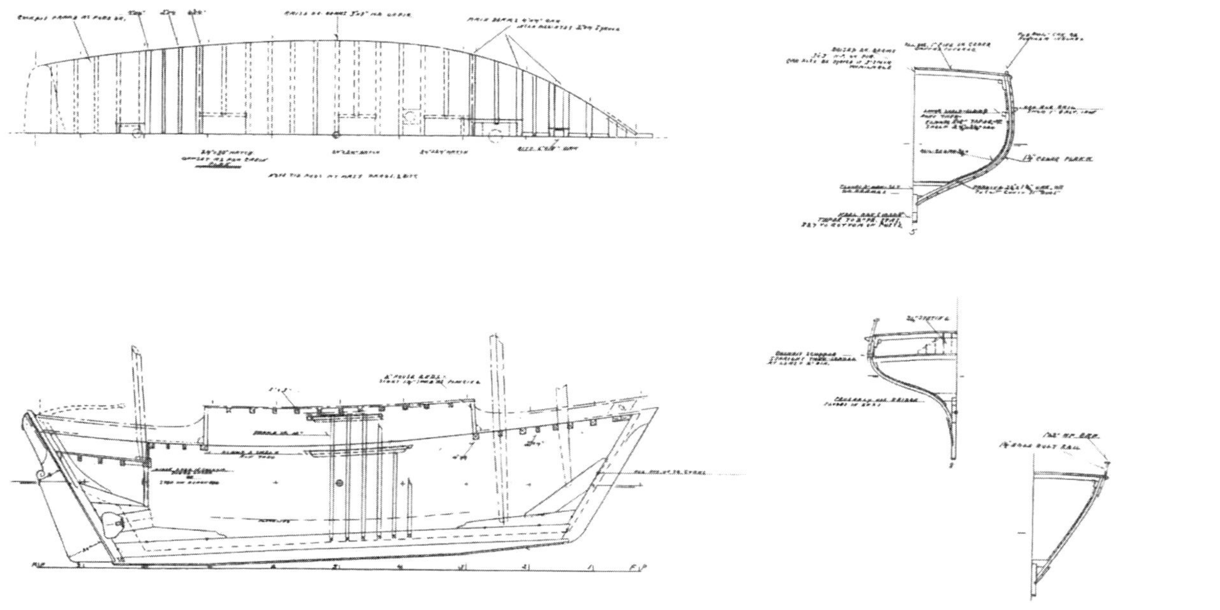

Construction drawings for Fred Stanton's 34-foot ketch.

one plans for it. In these days of high pattern and foundry costs, this is worth considering for each job.

The use of the raised deck was for more room and a feeling of bigness below, as well as for the possibility of lower cost and fewer leaks. Though this was the most practical here, the raised deck in a chunky boat is not very handsome. It is also important that it can be made to look good in a very long and large boat, where it's probably not needed, and that it does give considerable righting moment if the boat is knocked down heavily. Certainly it makes a pleasant cabin in this case, especially in the galley area.

Year-round living aboard, cruising in the usual summer season and to some extent in the off season, require many features not needed in the usual yacht. Some of these are a thick-sided hull and painted surfaces that are easy to restore after the winter's beating; simple snow removal; hatches that can be opened during, or after, an ice storm; a cockpit that has no real scupper problems. In this case the cockpit floor goes from side to side, like on a lobsterboat, the scuppers being large, straight out, and well above water. The floor is rather high crowned and pitched, as is a deck. The fuel tanks are outside in the cockpit. There are large chocks and cleats for mooring during winter gales, and a rig that is relatively simple to dismantle.

Naturally, there is a coal stove, and water tanks placed so they get enough heat to prevent freezing. It's been my past experience that an oil anchor light kept burning in an isolated tank compartment is quite sufficient to prevent freezing if the boat is otherwise kept heated by a coal stove.

The layout is, of course, much to suit the owner; it has many practical aspects. The galley location has proven very good in other craft used for this sort of thing. Besides, it provides better ventilation in the summer than when it is aft. Also, the draft problems for the stack are far less severe, especially if the long T-head stack with elbows, as used in big coasters, is rigged. The cabin is quite light, which is important any time, but more so in winter. The idea of a small vestibule at the foot of the ladder is good. What is needed is a place to shed clothes and drip, meanwhile keeping direct cold drafts out of the cabin. One problem of winter living is cold floors. Here the main working floor is thick pine. The owner will use some removable covering of his fancy for winter insulation.

In the interests of cost, simplicity, easy upkeep,

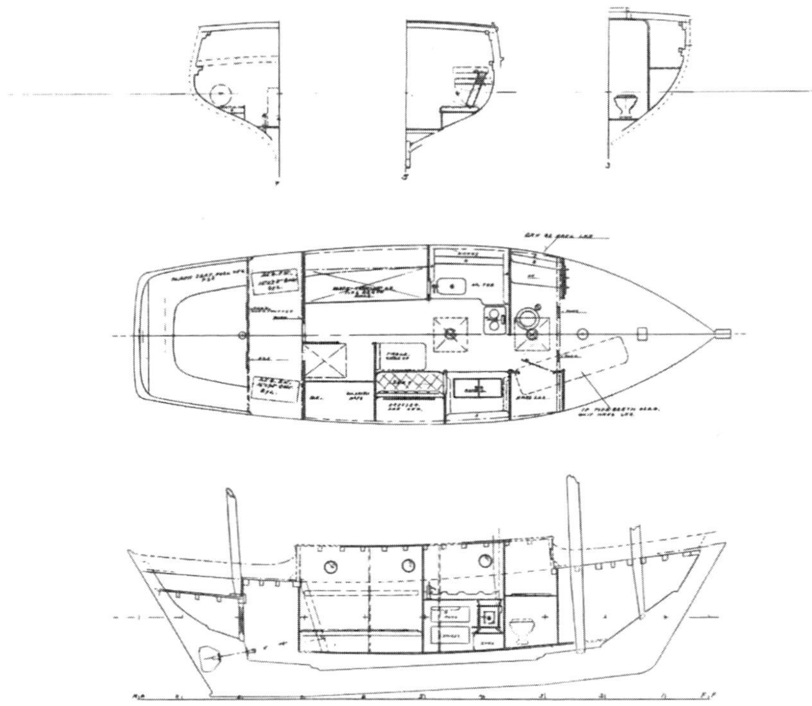

Above: *Plover* rides at anchor. (Pete Culler photo)

Left: Cabin plans for the 34-foot raised-deck ketch.

and so on, electric equipment is about nil, except for the engine, which can be started manually. (She has a Volvo 15 h.p. diesel.) Of course, meeting all the above requirements means concessions. The vessel looks able, which is a prime consideration, and sailing ability is quite good—enough for the use intended. The present great interest in windward ability is less important here. In any event, fulfilling the owner's requirements makes this almost impossible. She is underpowered by some standards, yet in light weather the engine should do quite well. The wheel is quite deep and gets free water.

The owner still thinks a sailing craft is to sail, and the fact that she can't tack 75 degrees is of little matter, for he well knows he can't stick to that sort of sailing very long when alone. A steady helm, ease of working, and maintaining one's strength, in this case, far overshadow the requirements of closed-course or ocean racing.

The boat was launched in a semifinished condition below. The main things were in, including stove and plumbing, and the owner was to take it from there, doing the detail work. This is, no doubt, the most pleasant way.

I'm often asked how much a craft like this costs. Of course, design modifications and complications cost more. Boat costs are figured by the ton or pound, more or less. The more displacement, the more cost. There are also fairly cheap "pounds," and expensive ones too, depending on how fancy one gets. One might say that the cost per pound in this vessel is rather moderate allowing for inflated dollars.

Almost anyone can make an estimate of a boat's cost, simply by getting the cost price of many finished boats (the more, the better) and their displacement and type—gold-plater, workboat, or plain-finish cruiser.

When a boat is built, allow for inflation since the design was done, and estimate inflation to come. This is about how most builders do it, and they underestimate very often. One thing stands out—it will always cost more than you think, and possibly more than it should, but what are you gonna do if you can't live without a boat?

Length on deck: 45 feet 2 inches
Length on waterline: 36 feet 5 inches
Beam: 12 feet
Draft: 6 feet
Sail area: 945 square feet
Displacement: 31,000 pounds light trim

Ketch *Swan V* For William Wood

This ketch, *Swan V*, is perhaps the most yachtlike design the Captain ever produced. An occasional criticism of Culler designs is that they don't have enough "finish." This ketch proves that the Old Man was certainly capable of producing a gold-plater when called upon to do so. It simply was not his nature to strive for this quality. He felt that yacht standards were in no way a prerequisite for enjoyment on the water, and that the rigors of maintaining varnish and glossy paint could be dispensed with, with more time spent sailing. This is not to say that Culler craft must be dull. Only that, as classic vessels, they are more suited to organic paints, pine tar, and oil. With these treatments, they have a patina that is naturally distinctive and proud.

Without dwelling on the above, it hardly needs saying that this sweet-lined ketch is a real gem. Essentially, this ketch is the same as the 40-foot Kendall proposal. The extra length and cutaway forefoot are the primary differences. Captain Pete had this to say about *Swan V*: "Though yachtlike in many ways, she follows the old clipper vessel principles of being very thin-footed and deep-heeled, with a very fine run. She is about 16 tons, and was entirely planked with 1¼-inch native cedar, with 1½-inch garboards and bends. The decks and housetops also are cedar, though canvas covered."

Her rails, caps, bulwarks, hatches, and cabin moldings are bright mahogany. Captain Pete was a longtime admirer of the work of L. Francis Herreshoff; there are some nice Herreshoff style details here, notably the rudderhead and the quarter rail. Coupled with Pete's usual detailing, such as the Chesapeake diamond shaped cat or fast line chocks, they make for an interesting mix.

Speaking of nice details, note how, in profile, all the vessel's fore-and-aft lines (including the booms) sweep gracefully forward to a point just ahead of the bowsprit iron. This is masterful, as there is much more to it than just drawing them in. It all has to work.

The marconi, or jibheaded, rig follows closely the principles the Old Man wrote down in *Skiffs and Schooners*. That is, the ratio of sail hoist to boom length should be no more than two to one; raked masts; a rig long on the base, necessitating a bowsprit; and some overhang aft. Plus light sails to fill it out. If the Old Man had his druthers, he would choose a gaff rig. However, this sail arrangement looks good and has proved successful in use.

In fact, this vessel is now in its second decade of success with her original owner, sailing the waters of southern New England. To me, that says a lot.

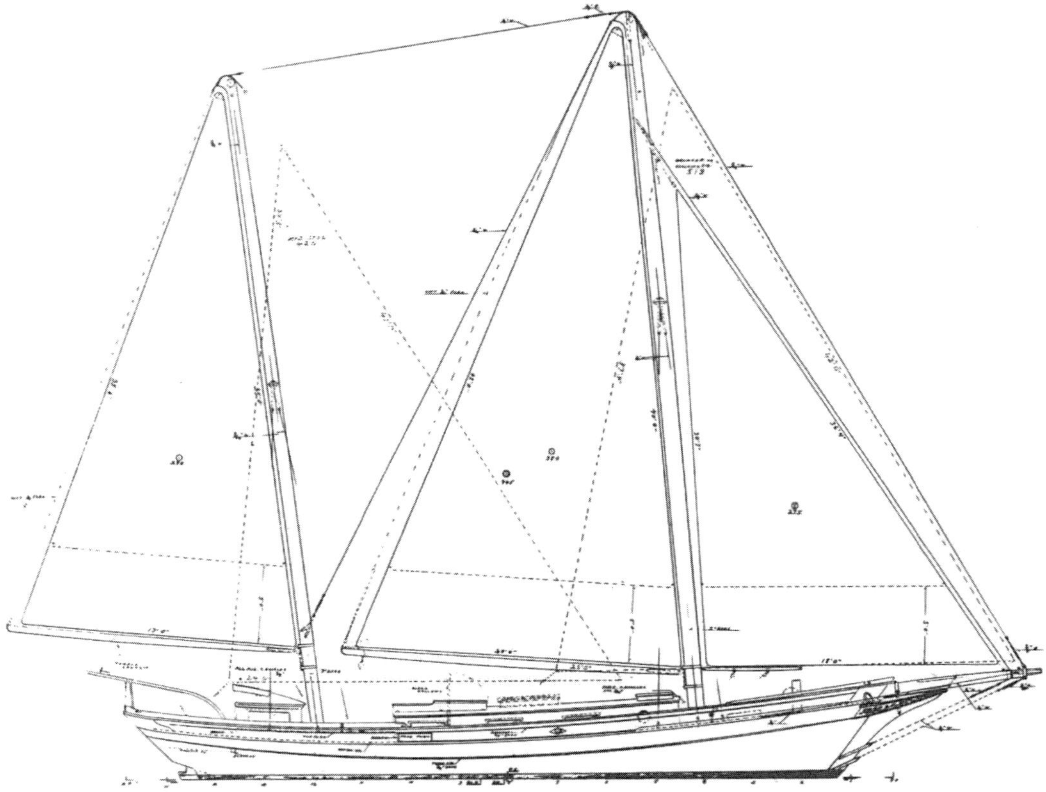

Above and Below: *Swan V,* sail plan and lines.

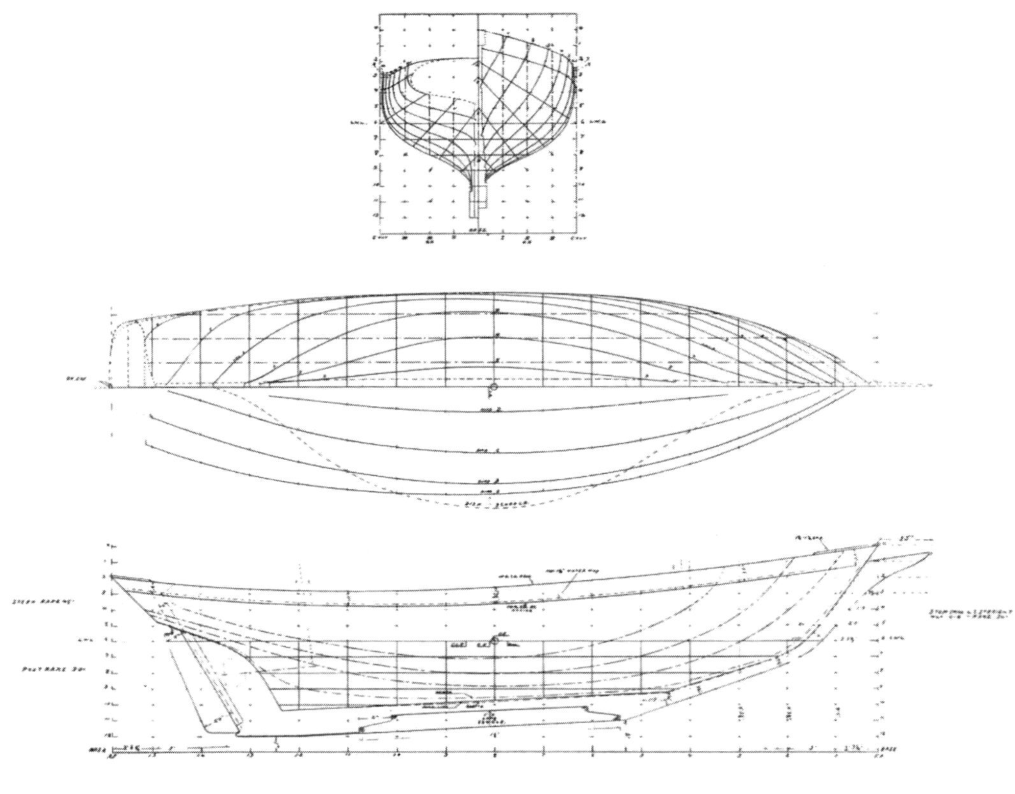

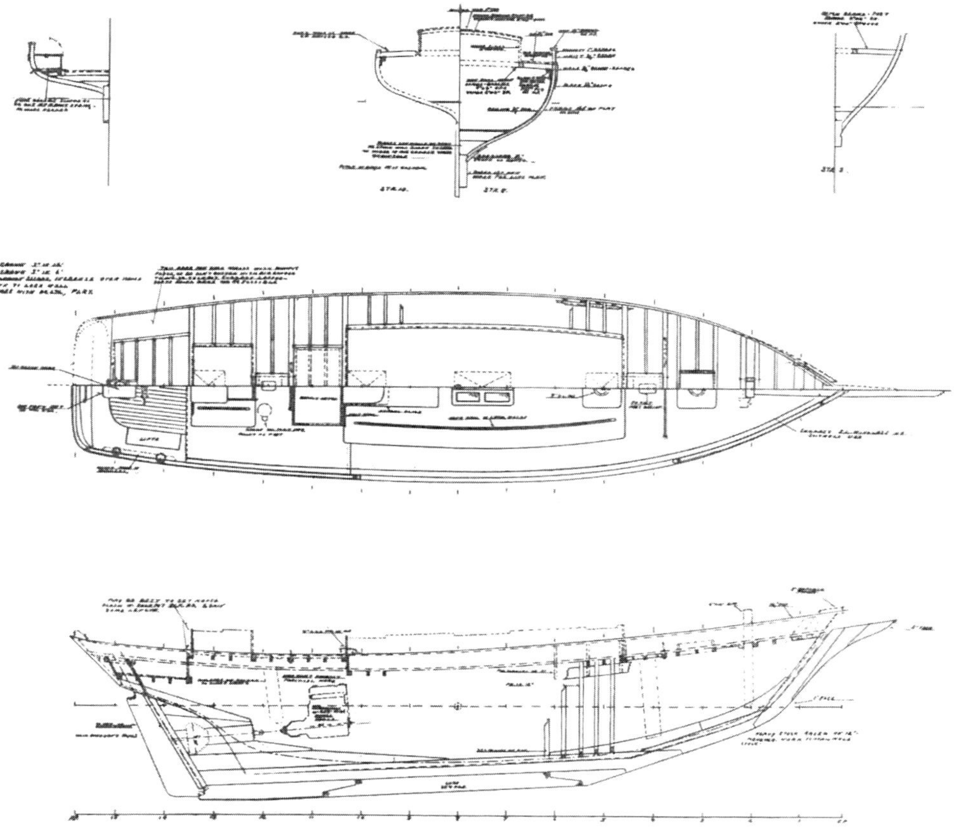

Above and below: Construction and accommodations plans for the 45-foot ketch.

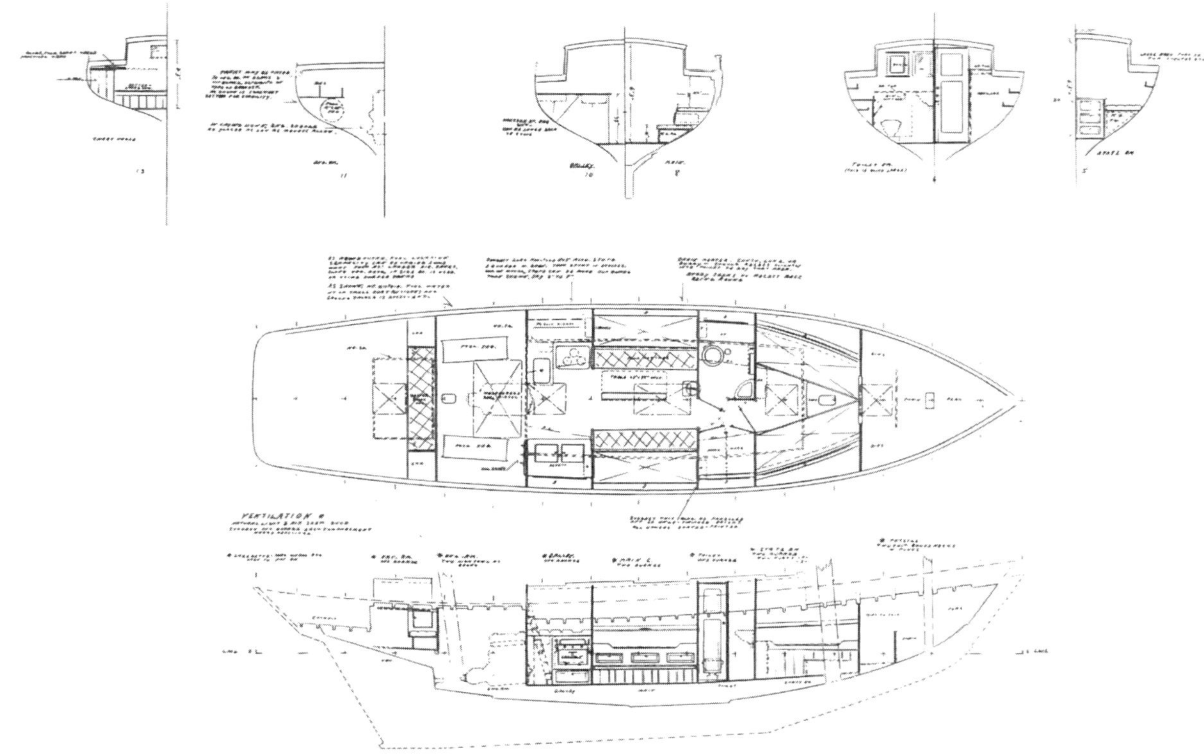

Framed out, her planking begun, *Swan V* takes shape. Fleshed out, this skeleton would become a "gold plater" with a shapely transom and much brightwork. (R.D. Culler photo)

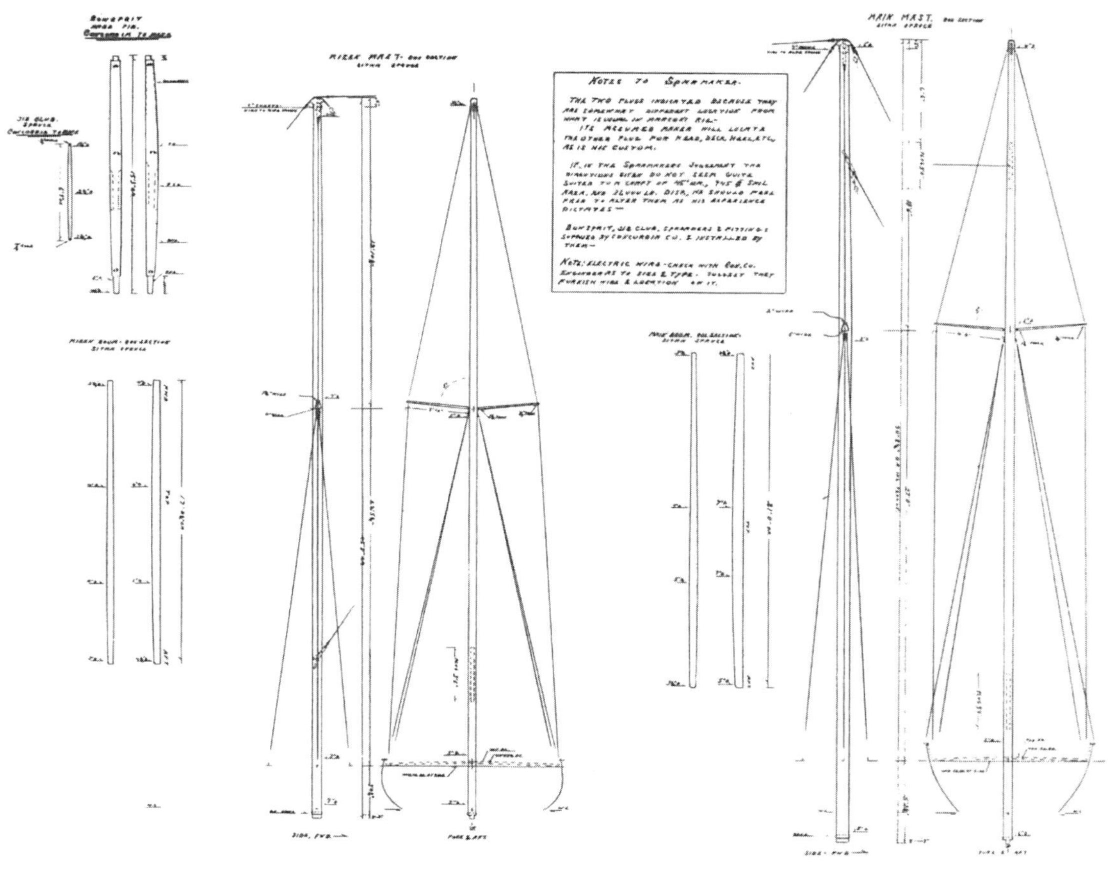

Spar plan for *Swan V.*

Length on deck: 47 feet 10 inches
Length on waterline: 42 feet 4 inches
Beam: 12 feet
Draft: 5 feet
Sail area: 741 square feet
Displacement: 17.22 long tons

Motorsailer *Transition* For Addison Taylor

During one of their many trips together Downeast, Captain Pete and George Kelley stopped in East Boothbay, Maine, to see what builder Sonny Hodgdon was doing, since they had heard that there was a project abuilding. As soon as Pete walked through the shop door, he exclaimed, "Why, that looks like one of Billy Hand's rumrunners!" Indeed, that's just what she was. Hodgdon was using the boat as a model for an offshore lobsterman. That was intelligent—present-day use of an older, existing design.

I retell the story here to show that Pete was very familiar with William Hand's design work (the V-bottomed powerboats in this book also should make that clear), and to illustrate that what was successful in the past has much to offer today. Pete said, "No designer or builder can have full experience in all things pertaining to vessels, but they can and should be very much guided by what worked in the past."

Over 50 years ago, Hand was the designer most responsible for defining the motorsailer type. Starting in 1927 with *Nor'easter* and *Water Witch*, there was a steady succession of these vessels from his design board. Each succeeding one was a refinement of his idea of the type. Instantly famous, they came to be known as 50/50 cruisers.

The astonishing part about these vessels was their extraordinary ability to sail in anything over a fresh breeze. An article in *WoodenBoat* magazine (Number 28) on the Hand motorsailer discussed this feature in *Water Witch*. "She carried inside ballast and a gaff ketch rig. She was hardly over-canvased, the whole idea being to use power in light air. Yet, when it breezed up and the sea began to run (an uncomfortable time for most pure powerboats), *Water Witch*, her sails set and drawing, would settle down and really begin to move. No one had seen anything quite like her."

Although highly respectful of Hand's contribution, Pete never cared for the motorsailer type, feeling that it was for those who could not (or would not) make up their minds.

Nevertheless, when Addison Taylor asked Pete to design him a motorsailer, the Old Man knew where to look for inspiration. The original proposal for this design is very much in the classic Hand style. However, it did not suit Taylor, who wanted a center cockpit with, at most, a folding dodger.

The hull alone follows the principles Hand set down, with some notable exceptions. For her length, she is leaner, and her bilges, although high, are somewhat slacker due to the use of outside ballast. The bilges run all the way aft to the transom, allowing it a minimum of drag. She is very fine ended. This hull is more of a sailer than anything else, yet with that long, essentially flat run, she would be good under power alone or in combination with the sails.

With the deckhouse rejected, Pete was able to keep her profile, and therefore her windage, low. This is good, both for appearance and performance.

One very good result from choosing the motorsailer type is ample room for accommodations. The necessary hull shape produces generous displacement.

This design certainly has plenty of space for owner, guests, crew, and stores, including the hardest-working crewmember on board—the engine. It is always prudent to treat the engine as part of the crew and give it space accordingly. Note the details on the plan for machinery ventilation.

Of course, for every plus there is a tradeoff. Boats cost by the pound. All that space adds up in dollars.

After all was said and done, and the vessel was built and sailing, Pete's verdict was the same as always. He felt she was "good... if you like motorsailers."

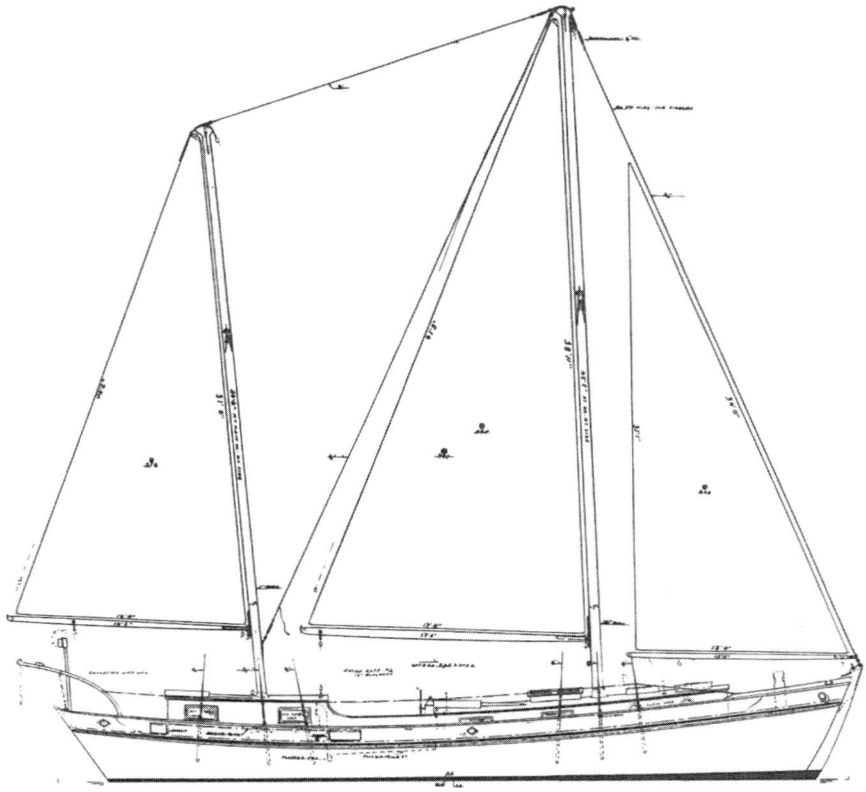

Above and below: Sail plan and lines of Addison Taylor's 48-foot motorsailer.

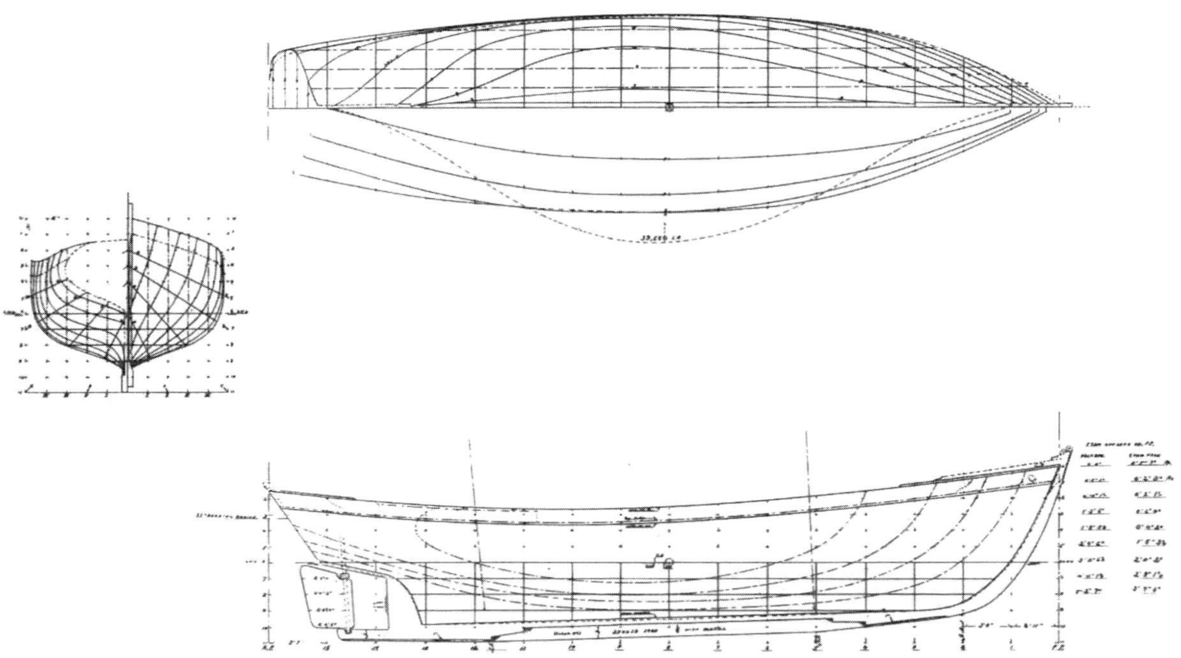

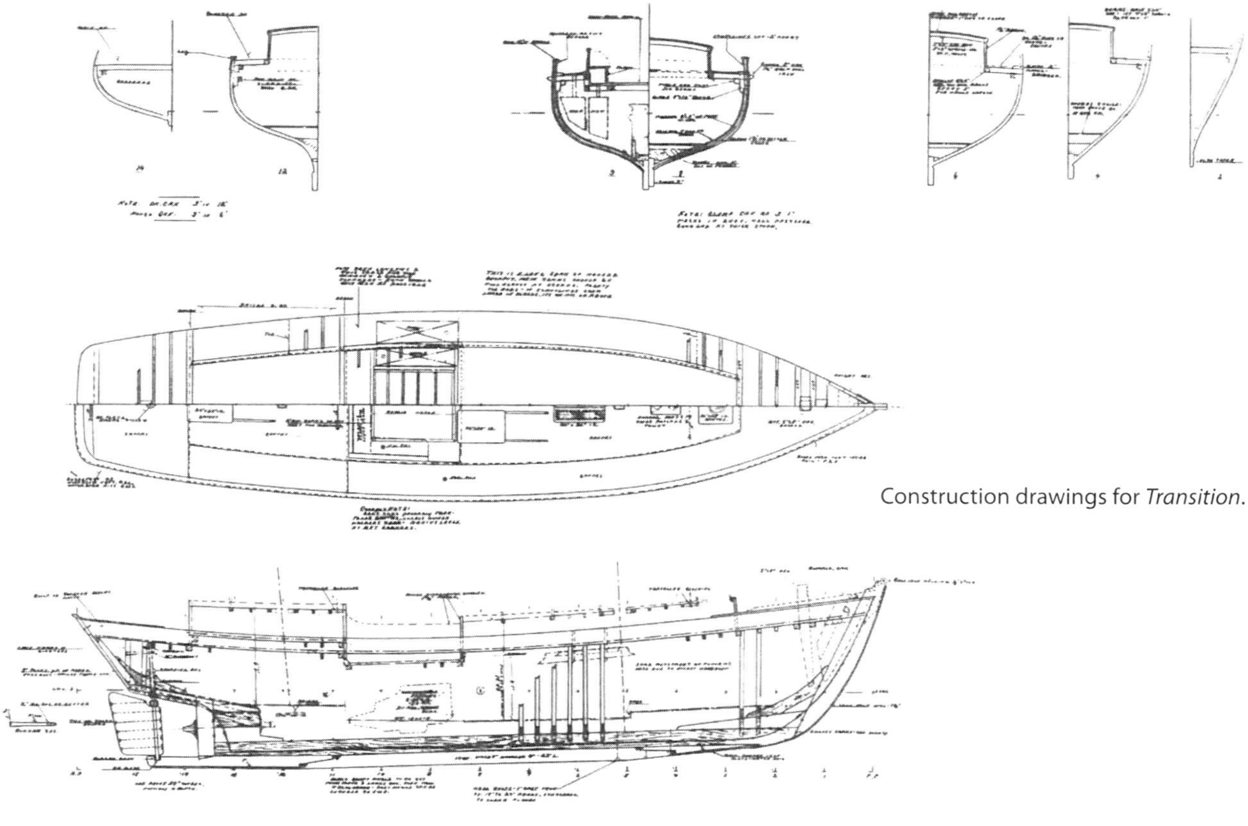

Construction drawings for *Transition*.

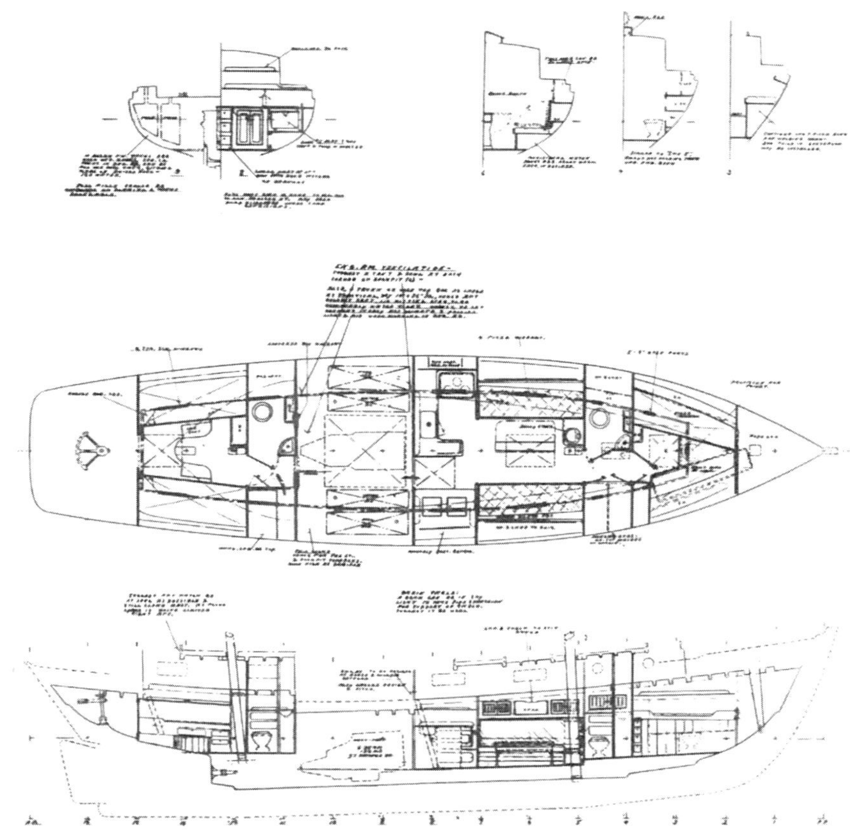

Transition's accommodations.

She floats! (R.D. Culler photo)

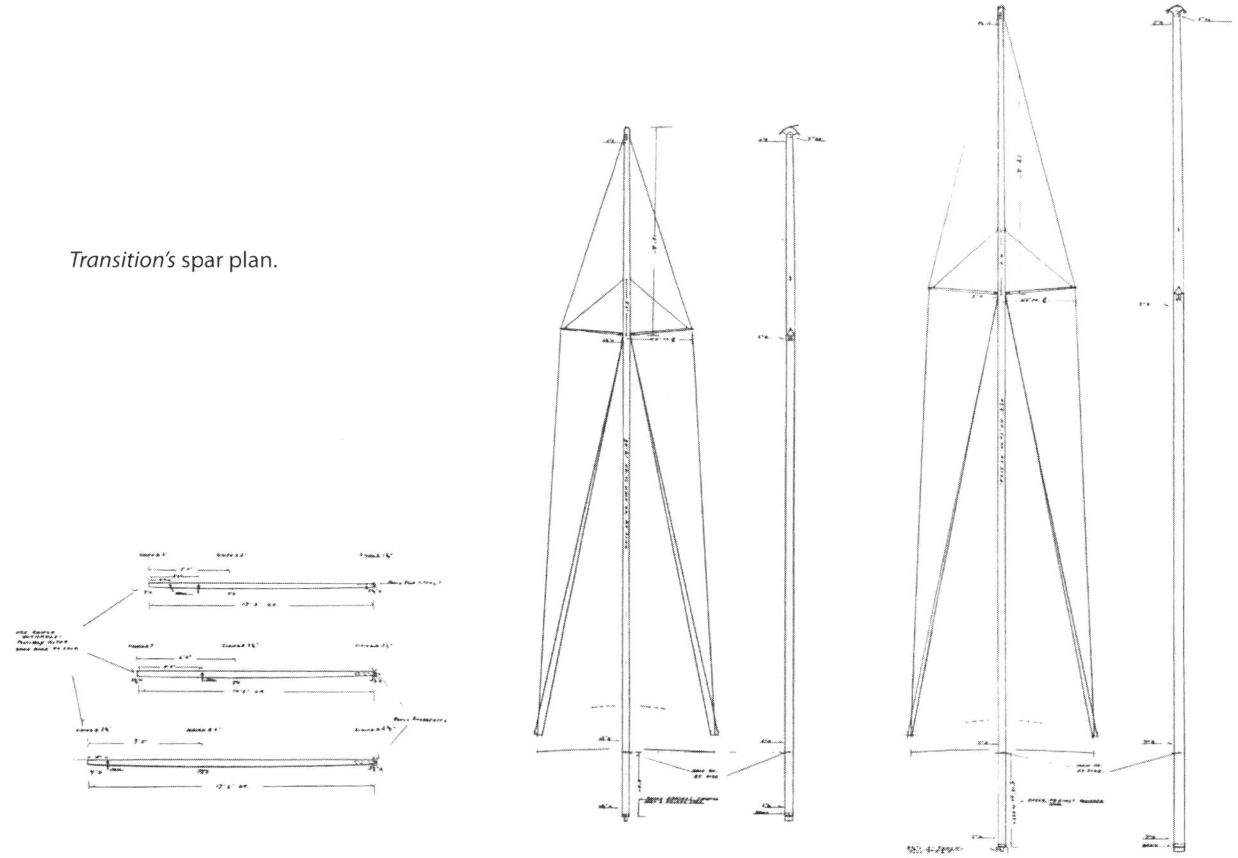

Transition's spar plan.

Cowhorn Dory

Length overall: 26 feet 6 inches
Beam: 8 feet
Molded depth: 2 feet 5½ inches
Sail area: 288 square feet

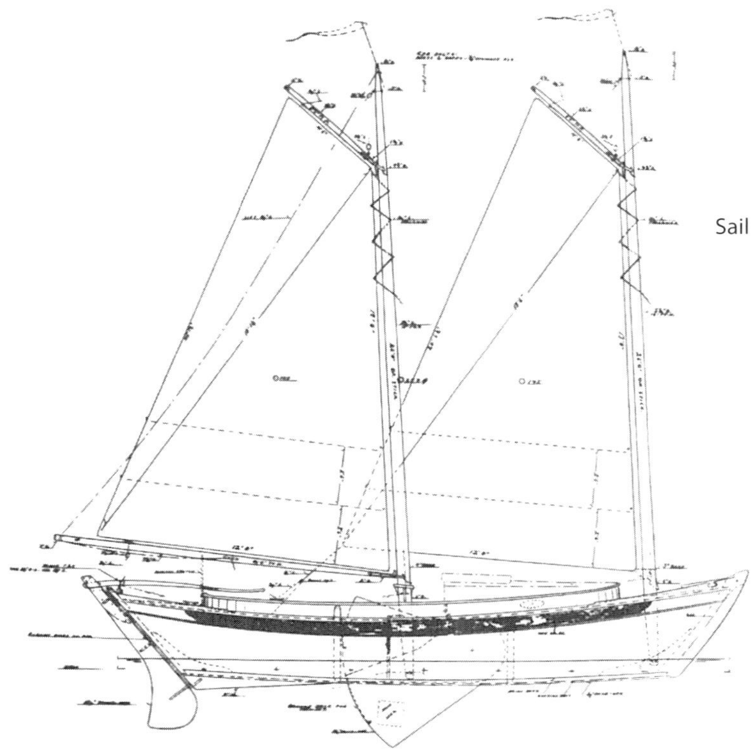

Sail plan of the cowhorn dory.

Comments by Pete Culler

This design in general has seemed to work out very well. It is also about as simple in principle and construction as you can have and still end up with a good, durable boat.

The details and methods shown are what I feel we can do economically at Concordia. There are other methods that might save. If the boat were home-built, for example, many parts could be made. We at the yard usually find it cheaper to use stock stuff than to make every item, due to labor costs. In this case it's not very much in the way of fittings.

The dory looks as though she would be fun to sail, once one gets used to a dory's ways and learns to live with her. The big Newfoundland and the standard Coast Guard dory were used for inspiration, and of course immediately modified to suit. However, the boat is all dory, both in shape and construction. She is very true to a type that has had a lot of development.

Dories, like other types, have their weaknesses, but one can adjust to them. Though excellent sea-boats, they are not boats of great power. The Block Island rig seems to suit. The sail area is good, and the boat will have to be reefed at times. This was true of the real Block Island boats. Though heavier and deeper, they were not hulls of great power. They had no side decks, yet their ability in practiced hands was unquestioned.

Being an ardent dory sailor myself (in my case in a 17-foot 6-inch Swampscott with a large rig), I can say I'm constantly surprised at the ability of the boat. She is even less powerful than the standard dory, being round sided and only 2 feet wide on the bottom. Strangers to the type find her very crank. After much use, I don't find her so at all. When I shift occasionally to a more powerful small boat, I find her dull.

One learns, after much use of a certain craft, some pretty sound conclusions. Dories sail better

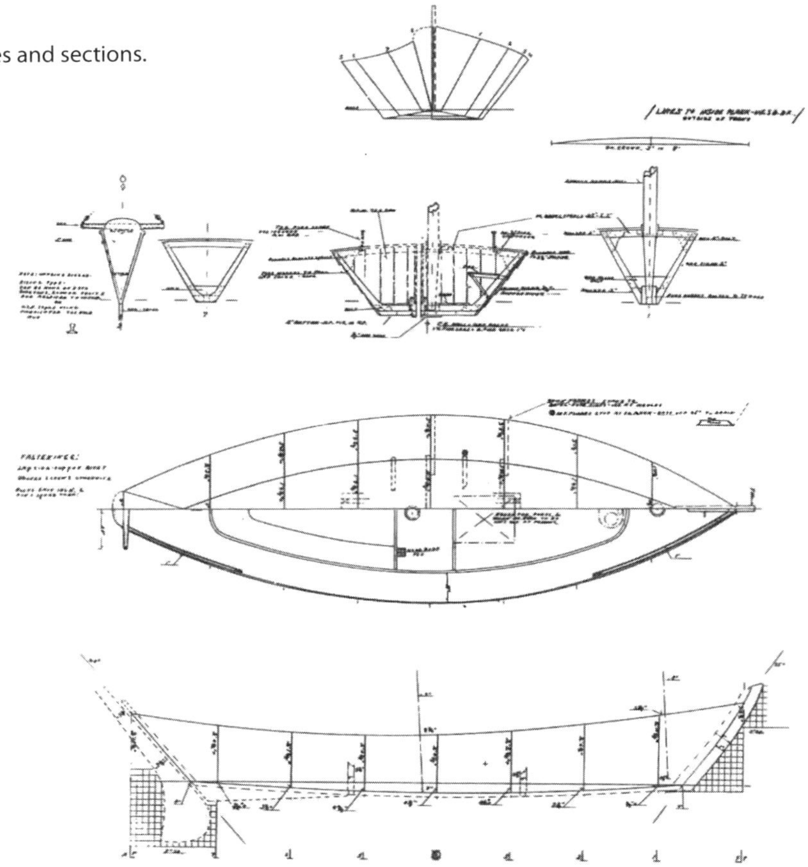

Lines and sections.

at a small angle of heel. They foot and point better, and are drier. This, in a small one, is accomplished by some ballast (90 pounds, in my own boat) and some body English. Larger craft must rely much more on ballast. I don't think anyone can say just how much ballast will be required. When she feels right and sails right, that is the right amount. Dories like weight up to a point. We have a choice of ballast: stone, which is easy to come by in New England and does not rust or affect a compass; sandbags, which I prefer for a small dory; or lead, which costs money but has an advantage in limited space.

I'm aware that this is an open boat, though provided with very wide side decks—perhaps too wide to get the most room. The chances of swamping out in open water should be kept in mind, though I do feel a swamp-out would be due to poor management and a lack of understanding of the type.

The question of flotation always comes up—in these days of molded craft—with good reason. We put it in the 24-foot outboards. I feel they do not need it. No one wants to take the trouble to swamp one out with simulated engine and equipment weights to find out how much is needed. We put it in the 17-foot sloopboats, for they seem to need it with the 400 pounds of lead ballast. One West Coast owner wanted his without flotation, then sent pictures of the boat swamped, full of ballast and several kids.

Flotation costs money to install—we use the block type. If one feels the need of it, he should have it. This dory is very woody. Any flotation should be in the ends and under the side decks, high up. Any boat that will float filled loses much of her stability; there is nothing one can do about it.

I mention the above although I do not think there is a great menace in open boats. Accidents of this sort are rare, assuming proper management. The ones we hear about each summer, and often see, are caused by the most inept management.

On the more pleasant side, I would think this dory might sail very well, though she is slightly on the wide side as dories go. This is the reason live ballast is not very effective in a craft this size. She should be simple to handle and care for—assuming home layup and fitting out. She will haul readily on rollers, need no cradle, and be easy to get on a flat trailer. The rudder is easy to unship, and the centerboard will come out of the top of the well. The pin is above water. The masts are the biggest chore, assuming one uses his own gear. This can be done well enough, however, using an A-frame of, say, standard 4 x 4s and a guy.

The two pump boxes are essential on a flat-bottomed boat to get her really dry, or to pump when heeled. The bulkhead and the bridge deck should be put in, even though the craft is to be used entirely open at first. These are stiffening members. A dory tends to be somewhat limber.

The two reefs in the sails are essential; one should learn to reef when needed. Boats based on the working craft of the past should have good sail area, and a means of shortening sail when needed. The so-called modern thinking of having too little canvas, lugging through conditions unfit for the craft, let alone the abilities of the owner, and the notion that it's sissy to reef (because, in truth, the owner does not know how), is foolish in the extreme, and also is the cause of many accidents. Also, it's a very good way to alienate one's wife and friends forever.

The object of the boomkin for the mainsheet is to allow the rudder to rise should it strike bottom—a bail traveler is not practical over a tiller that might rise. Dories require a center of effort rather far aft by modern standards, but this is not a modern craft, and her centers pretty closely follow what was customary in two-sail workboats. A dory is rather light bowed, and the loose-footed foresail tends to move forward with started sheets, so the old principles of balance work out. Also, on centerboard boats sailing today, very little attention, if any, is given to the adjustment of the board to get the best out of the boat. Usually, it's just put down and forgotten.

The cabintop should provide a fair cuddy. There seems to be room for a very small woodstove, such as a Skippy model, a couple of narrow pipe berths, and a cedar bucket or toilet. One wonders, with the threat of pollution, the use of holding tanks, and whatnot, whether simple boating is soon to be gone forever. On the other hand, the present laws are impractical with regard to small craft. Very small craft just cannot meet the requirements as now written in some states.

As to the craft's gear, I think manila line is quite good enough, and in keeping. Maple Leaf brand (from Canada) fisherman-grade blocks will do. These are first class—there is no point in going into yacht grade. The boat might look very good with tan sails.

The cowhorn dory *Trudi* just after launch. (John Burke photo)

I still prefer cotton sails in a craft such as this Cuprinol treated, tanned or otherwise. For this rig, the sails should be vertical cut without battens, and roped all around. Spruce spars, of course. There is very little other gear to discuss. Boat compass, well-battered chart, and oil lights are appropriate. One should keep in mind that there is a choice with respect to lights, according to the law.

It occurs to me that a light pole lashed from the coaming forward to the mainmast, with a canvas over it to the coamings, might make a decent shelter until a house top was built. With a water jug, grub, Primus, tobacco, and a cedar bucket, one could short-cruise quite well in warm weather. However, a little woodstove would be missed.

Since this boat violates all "yachting standards, "I personally feel this would be a very pleasant little craft to own.

Length overall: 25 feet 10 inches
Molded beam: 8 feet 6 inches
Draft: 2 feet 4 inches
Sail area: 152 square feet

French Dory Proposal For Richard Tatlock

This proposal came about as a result of a series of articles on the St. Pierre dory by John Gardner. The articles appeared in *National Fisherman* in the early 1960s.

Communication and the exchange of ideas are vital in any field of endeavor. Within a forum, concepts can be presented, prodded, and polished with input from many sources. The value of periodicals, when addressed to special interests, is their immediacy. A periodical is as current as the next issue, and it allows input from the men in the field. Writing articles is considerably less time-consuming than writing books. The latter, of course, can be a full-time job. Believe me, I speak from experience!

The primary thrust of the articles on the St. Pierre dory was that the boats are particularly suited to pleasure use as motor craft. They were used around the islands of St. Pierre et Miquelon for motorized open ocean fishing in the North Atlantic. Without the luxury of sheltered harbors, this meant launching and landing on open, exposed beaches. The boats are traditionally inboard powered, usually with the standard two-cycle, make-and-break engine.

These requirements evolved a distinct, burdensome type of dory characterized by great sheer and bottom rocker for ability in both surf and ocean swell. In the articles, Gardner stated that the type was very much suited to a rig. Without giving his modified version any sail, he hoped someone would give it a try. Since that time, many versions have been successful with a wide variety of sail arrangements.

Captain Pete eased somewhat the great sheer and bottom rocker on this proposal. With the addition of the keel/skeg, the great bottom rocker was not required. The beam was increased to add power and better accommodate the sailing rig. More flare was gained in the ends, so the pronounced sheer was not needed either. What this amounts to is a handy little day motorsailer, the rig being very moderate.

The rake of the transom was increased for dryness and ability, in addition to making it look better. This allows the use of an inboard rudder. It brings the rudderhead inboard, to allow steering with a tiller and still have access to the engine controls.

The rig used is the Block Island type—a good choice for a somewhat tender hull. With this rig you can get a fair spread of sail, while keeping the center of effort low and the rig inboard. This rig worked out very well in practice on the 25-foot cowhorn dory. It should prove satisfactory here also, since the hulls are similar.

The deck and washrails give good reserve stability. With a woodstove and a couple of pipe berths in the cuddy, this little motorsailer would make a fine overnighter.

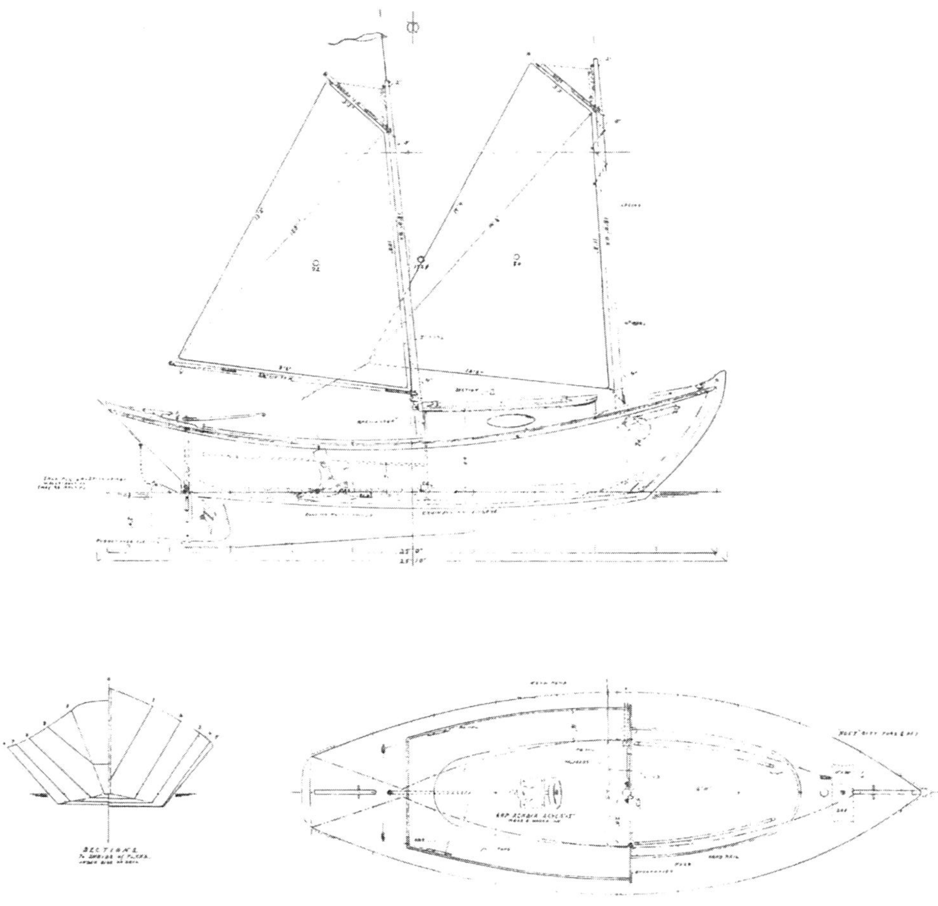

Sail plan, deck plan, and sections of the proposed French dory.

PART VI

Schooners

Schooner For Malcolm Kirkbride
Schooner For Thomas Doyle

Kirkbride Schooner

Length: 32 feet ½ inch
Length on waterline: 25 feet 10 inches
Beam: 10 feet 4½ inches
Draft: 5 feet
Sail area: 524 square feet
Displacement: 17,400 pounds

Doyle Schooner

Length between perpendiculars: 28 feet 2½ inches
Length on waterline: 24 feet 8 inches
Beam: 9 feet 2½ inches
Draft: 3 feet 6 inches
Sail area: 446 square feet
Displacement: 7,900 pounds

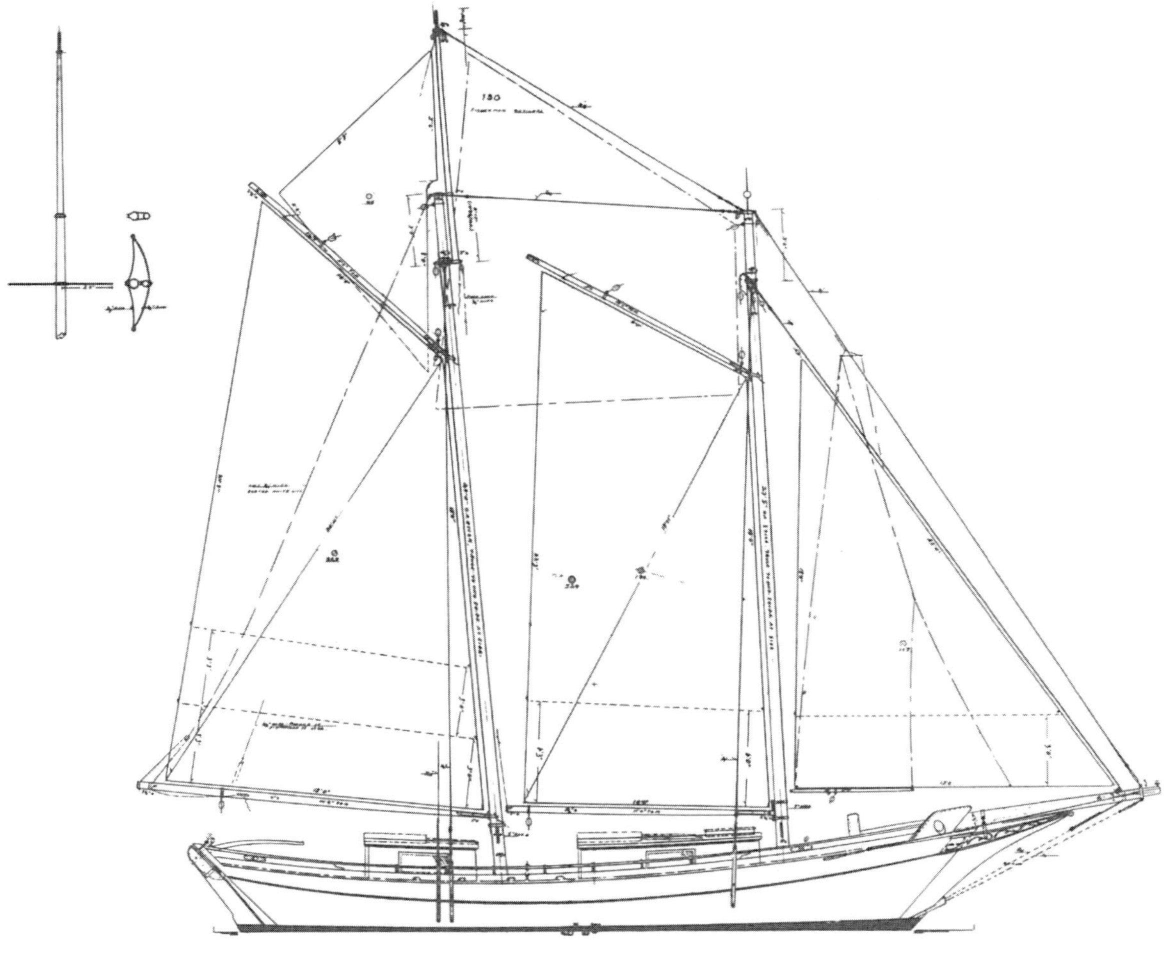

The sail plan of Malcolm Kirkbride's 32-footer.

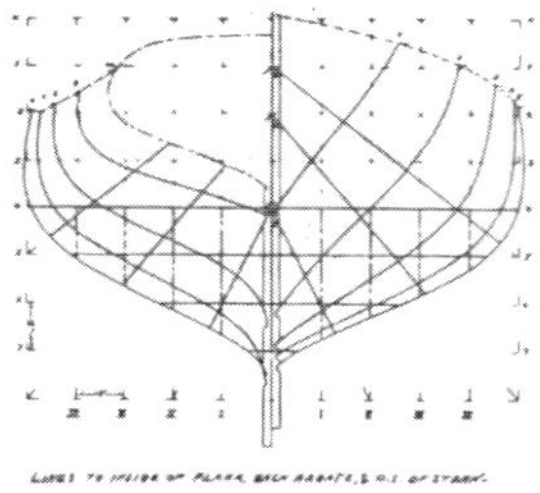

Lines of the Kirkbride schooner design.

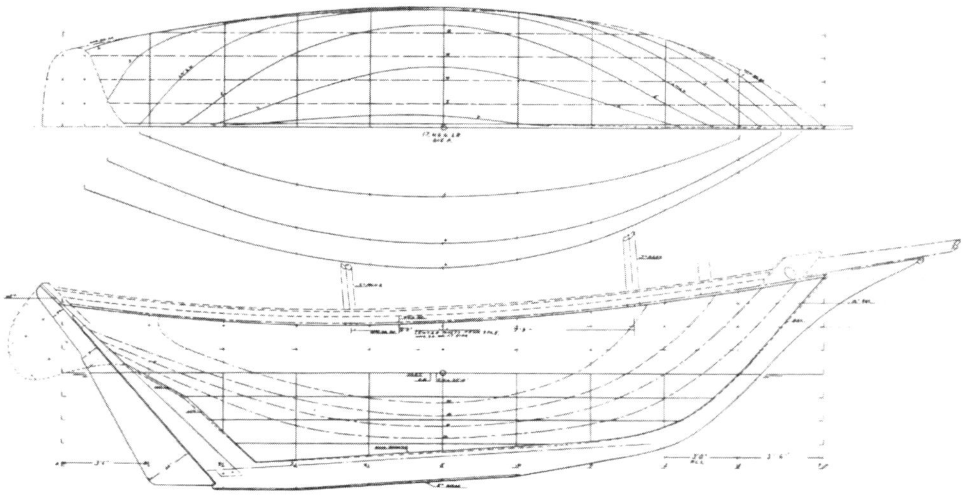

When Captain Pete had the chance to use the schooner rig, and model a proper hull to go with it, his talents were raised a few more notches. Study the designs in this chapter and see if you don't agree. I think they are magical.

People investigating Pete's schooner designs usually gravitate to these two first. Then they discover that these are not much more than "toy" schooners.

Schooner rigs, and for that matter, brigs and ship rigs, are fun to dream about. Most of us can't afford the real thing, so when we find something that appears small enough to be affordable, it sort of catches our eye.

Pete told a story about a time when he was sailing the *Spray* on Nantucket Sound. His eyes fooled him. The day was a bit hazy; suddenly there appeared, way off on the horizon (so it seemed), a full-rigged ship. Sort of dumbstruck (Pete knew of no ships in the area, and certainly none foolish enough to be navigating that section of the Sound), he fumbled for his glasses. As soon as he had the "ship" in focus, he realized what was going on. Just at that moment, the skipper stood up and made an adjustment to the main royal yard! The "ship" was a 16-foot skiff all decked out as a miniature ship. It was complete, right down to a yawlboat in stern davits. As it turned out, she was no more than a mile away.

These two schooners are not in that class of miniature, but they are very good for their designed purpose. However, it must be realized that they are small as schooners go.

The larger boat was designed for Malcolm Kirkbride, an ex-towboatman from Belfast, Maine. Her hull is a smaller version of *Gallant,* and although only three feet longer between perpendiculars than the Doyle schooner, she is a much larger boat, being nearly five tons heavier.

With the extra heft, this vessel can carry considerable sail. This amounts to 524 square feet in her lowers, plus a fisherman and a main topsail. The jib has a club and is self-tending. Note the fore topping lift reeved to the main crosstrees.

There are two cabin plans on the Kirkbride schooner. Both are practical. I favor the split cabins, mostly because this arrangement looks better.

The rails on both vessels are treated the same way. This is a construction method Pete used often on his designs. They start off with a 3-inch by 3-inch base log rail. In the ends, a piece set on edge fills the area between cap and log. In the middle, or

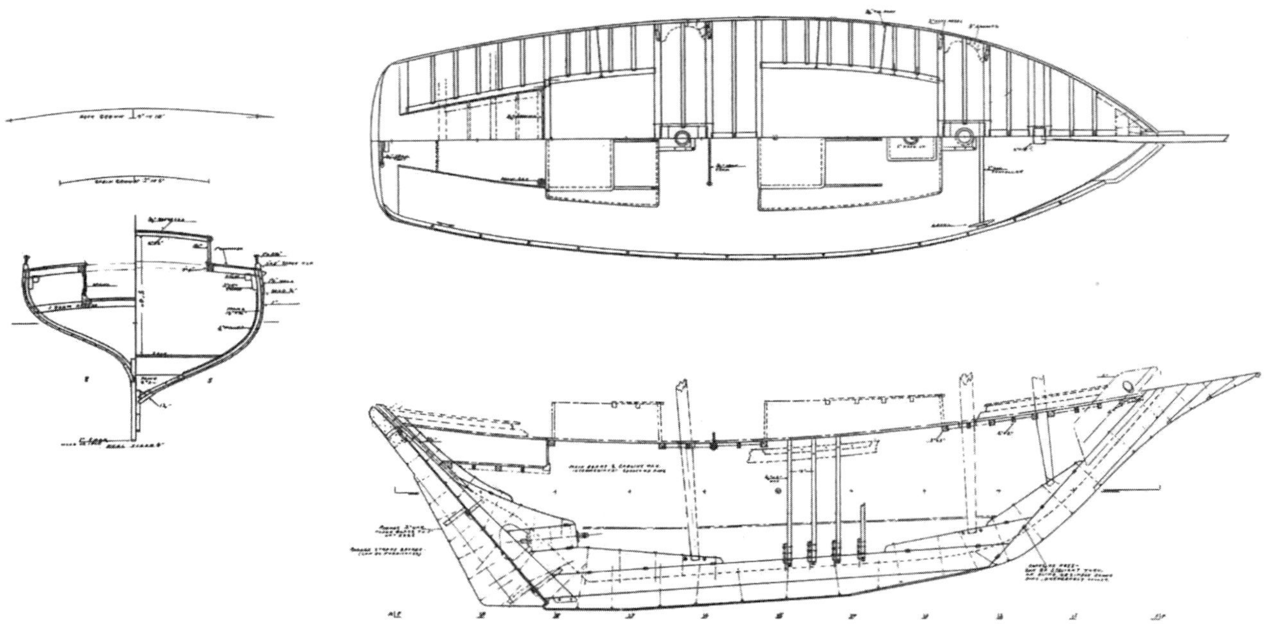

Above and below: Construction and accommodations plans for the 32-foot schooner.

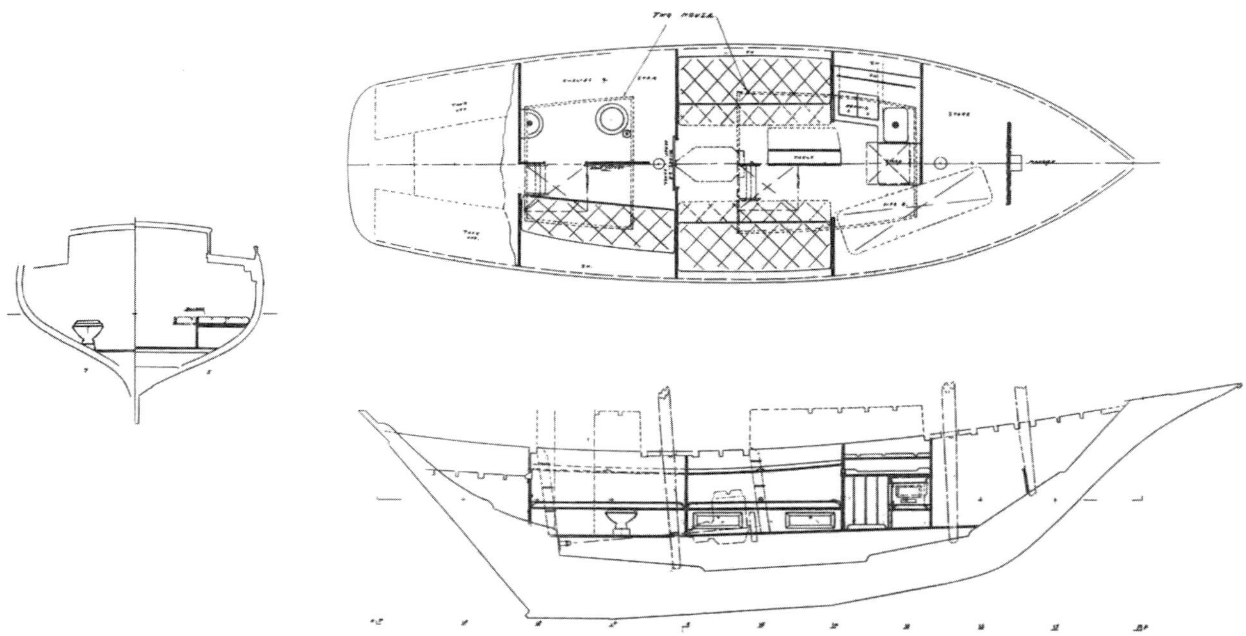

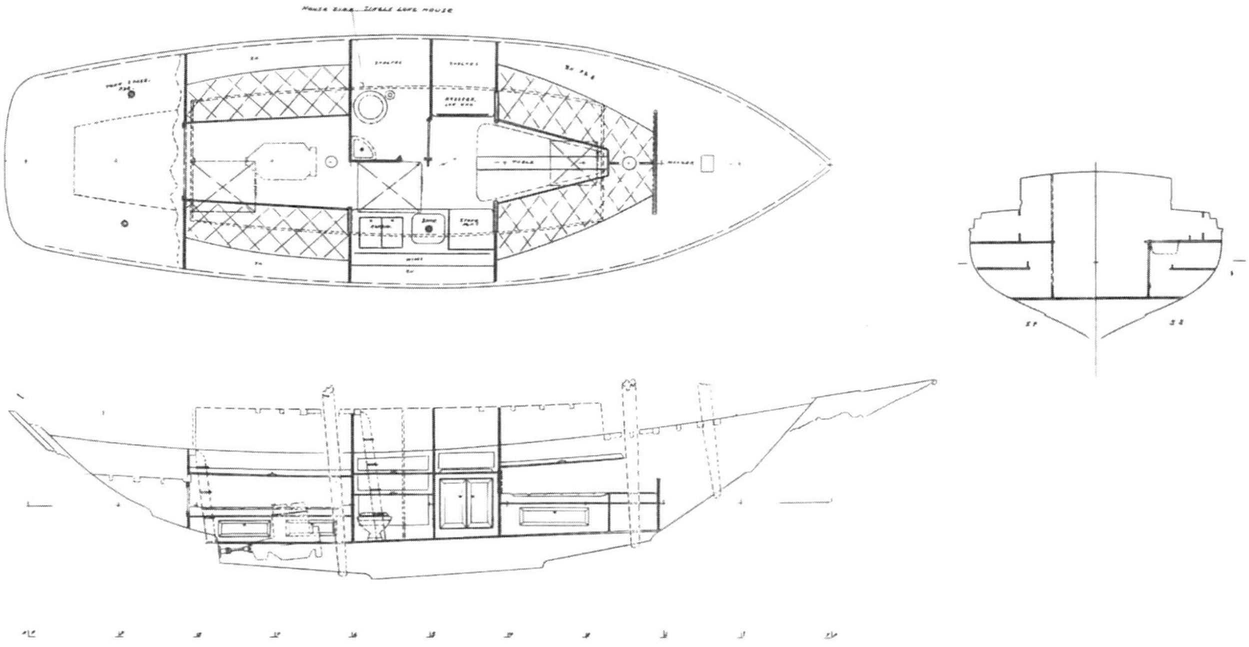

Above: Alternate (single-cabin) accommodations plan for the Kirkbride schooner.

Below: The baldheaded schooner sail plan of Thomas Doyle's 28-footer.

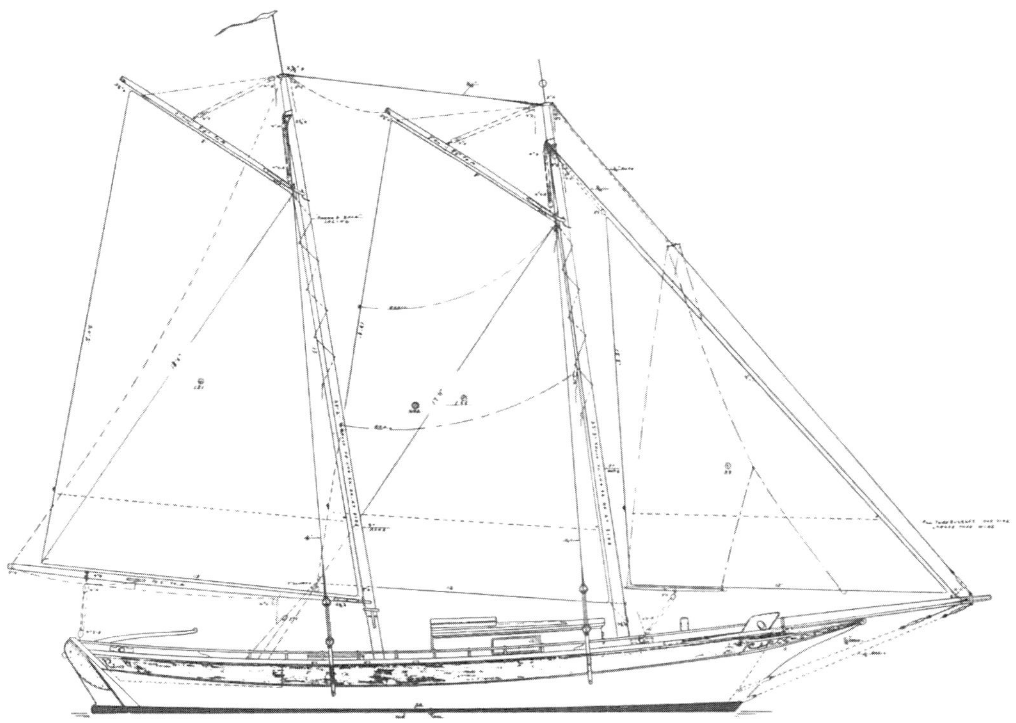

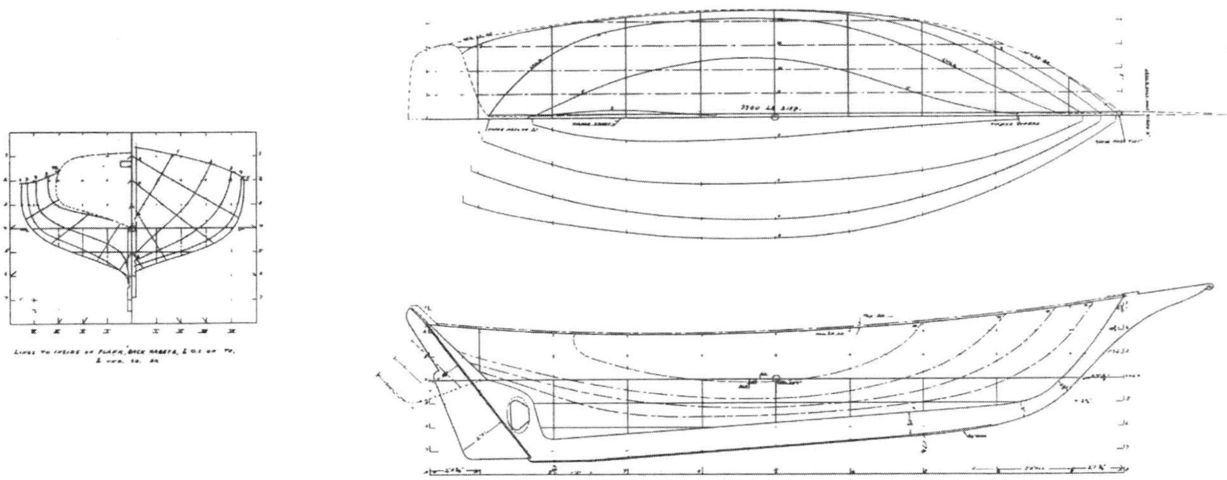

Above and below: Lines and accommodations plans for the Doyle schooner.

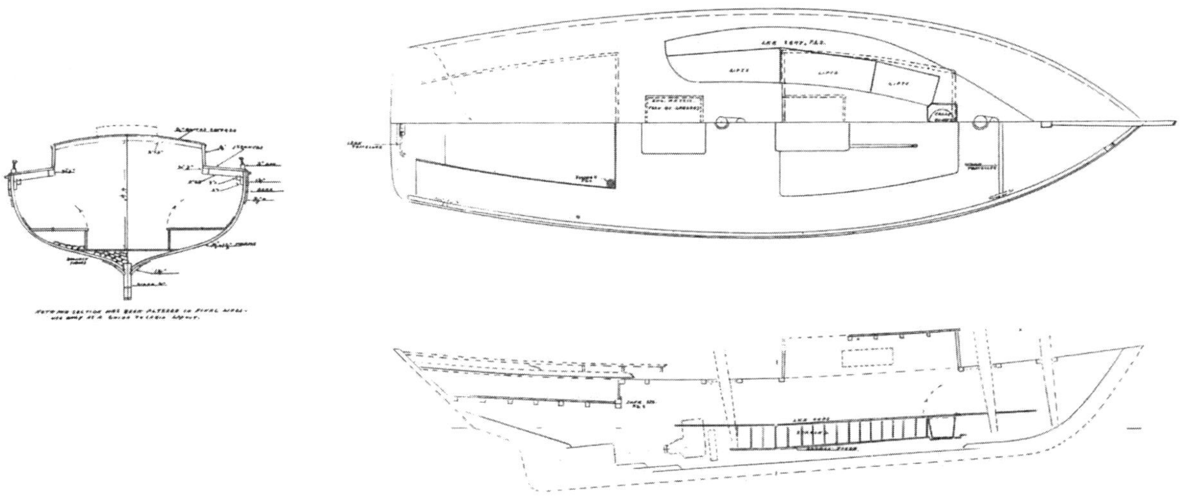

waist, the rail is open. To ensure uniform spacing between cap and log, sections of galvanized pipe are used as spacers, with the lag bolts running through cap rail and spacer, and securely into the lower log rail. The bolt heads are well bedded on top of the cap rail. It works, and it's good looking, too.

The smaller schooner, designed for Thomas Doyle, was intended for daysailing, with occasional overnights, around Block Island Sound, Newport, Rhode Island, and the eastern end of Long Island, New York. She is of light displacement, with a shoal underbody, and has ample beam for her length. The hull is remarkably fine, considering the above.

This little schooner was given an exceedingly handsome rig. Usually, baldheaded schooners don't look quite right to me, but this one does just fine. I suppose it's because of that loose-footed overlapping foresail, large self-tending jib, and not-oversized main. The proportions are just perfect. The foresail is particularly intriguing. This sail laces and brails to the foremast and has two-part sheets (Watch your head!). Note that this is a rare instance where Pete used a vang due to the loose foot. The cuddy cabin is simply a place to stow the cedar bucket and retreat to when the wind blows up. It is large enough for the occasional overnight trip, or if you happen to be weathered in at a foreign port. The deckhouse provides sitting headroom and adds much to the vessel's looks. And it leaves lots of deck area and a spacious cockpit to enjoy the really fine sailing that this craft is capable of. In fact, I think she would be good enough with sails alone so that you could leave out the engine. Although Pete felt the schooner rig was not suitable for craft under 40 feet, I think he proved himself wrong with these two designs. As long as you understand their limitations, these two craft can be practical.

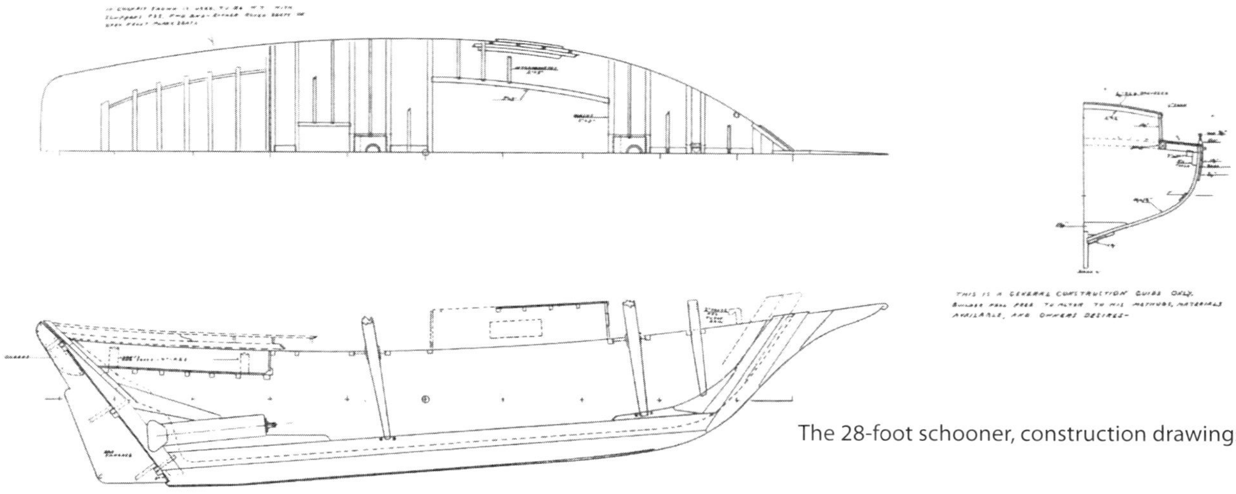

The 28-foot schooner, construction drawings.

Length overall: 38 feet
Length on waterline: 26 feet
Molded beam: 8 feet 8 inches
Draft: 3 feet
Sail area: 747 square feet

Tancook Schooner Proposal For Thomas Hooper

Here is a workboat model of great reputation, modified for pleasure use, but, sadly, only in proposal form. It's a type particularly suited to Pete's design talents. Therefore, to me at least, it is frustrating to see the unfulfilled promise in her lines. The basics are there, however. I hope someone someday will continue where the Old Man left off.

The Captain set forth very easy lines in the hull, staying true to the type. She utilizes a centerboard, offset to port; by tradition, this would be steel. There is an outboard rudder of good size and much external deadwood aft of the sternpost. This allows good water for the propeller. Note that Pete intended her to be planked lapstrake. This will make an able, dry, and lively craft, and also a very good-looking one.

The Old Man gave this vessel a pink stern that is very smart. Coupled with the low rails, it further increases her ability and dryness, in addition to making a cheery and snug cockpit. Her bow profile is handsome, and the knightheads are left prominent, in Pete's style. This vessel will be a good seaboat and have an easy motion with all inside ballast.

The rig is ample. Though these craft are extremely able, their hulls are not powerful, and one must shorten sail in a real breeze. The proposal allows for plenty of reefs. In light airs, she should move right along, for these hulls are very easy moving and famous for speed.

Not long ago, both the ability and speed of these Tancook whaler types were brought home to me in a wild Nantucket Sound gale. The short, steep chop that the area is famous for had built up to 5 to 8 feet out of the southeast. Things were sort of nasty. I was skippering a large passenger ferry bound for

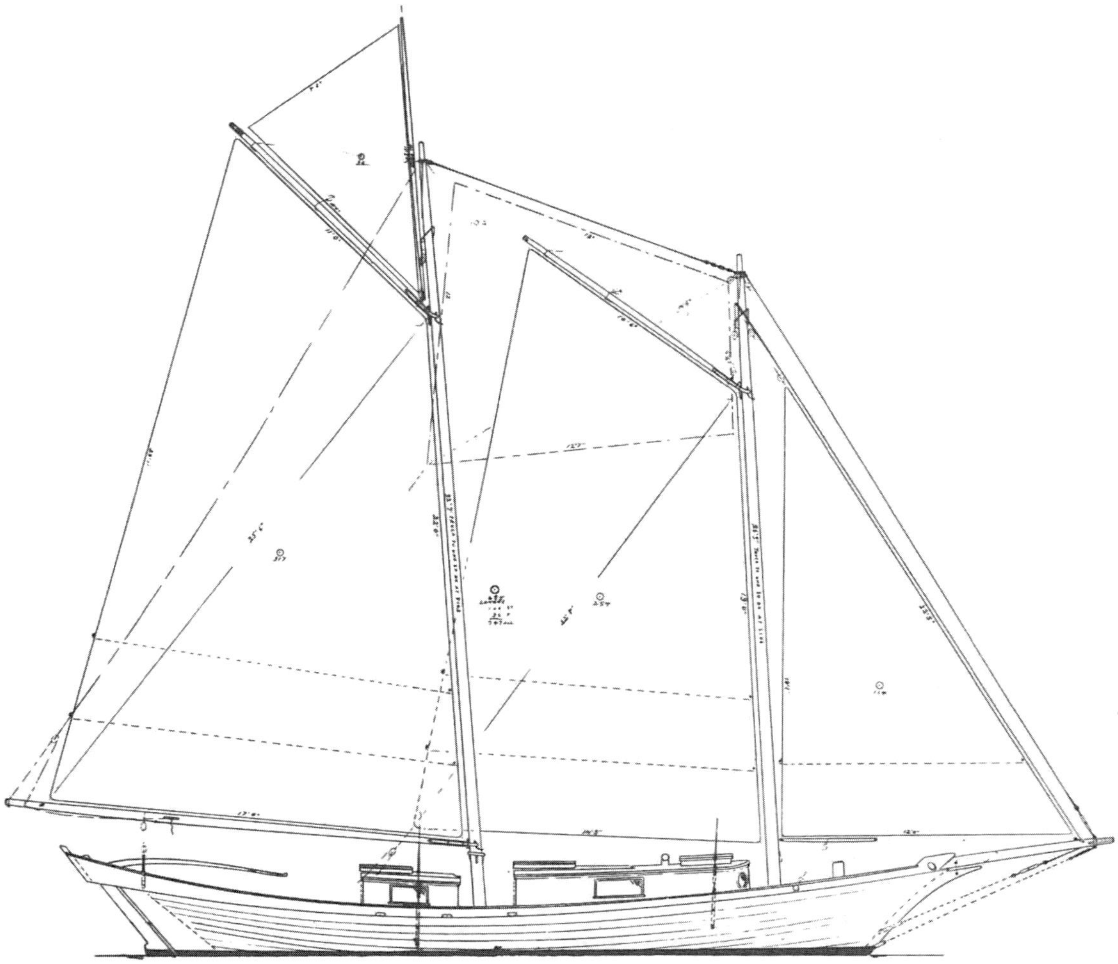

The 38-foot Tancook whaler has 685 square feet of sail in her lowers.

Nantucket Island and therefore slogging right into the wind and seas. Shortly after clearing the Hyannisport breakwater, I noticed a sailing vessel rounding Point Gammon off my port bow. Things were bouncing around a bit, so I eased off the throttles, gave the helmsman a more easterly course, and in the back of my mind began to rehearse rescue procedures for that damn-fool sailboat. With that wind and sea, the whole south side of Cape Cod was a lee shore. From my vantage point, the sailboat appeared uncomfortably close to shoal water. As we approached each other, I recognized her as the *Vernon Langille*, a 35-foot Tancook whaler built by the Apprenticeshop in Bath, Maine. They were hove-to, tying a reef in the foresail, having used the extra sail to round the point. Still not convinced, I fully expected them to run in and anchor behind the breakwater. But no. Their task completed, they eased her off and shot to the west, riding that miserable sea like a duck and moving along at a very good clip. I was impressed, and still am to this day, for I found out later that she made her destination with no problems. The passenger ferry? She is a two-decker, 120 feet long, with a 25-foot beam. That day she received a very thorough saltwater washdown.

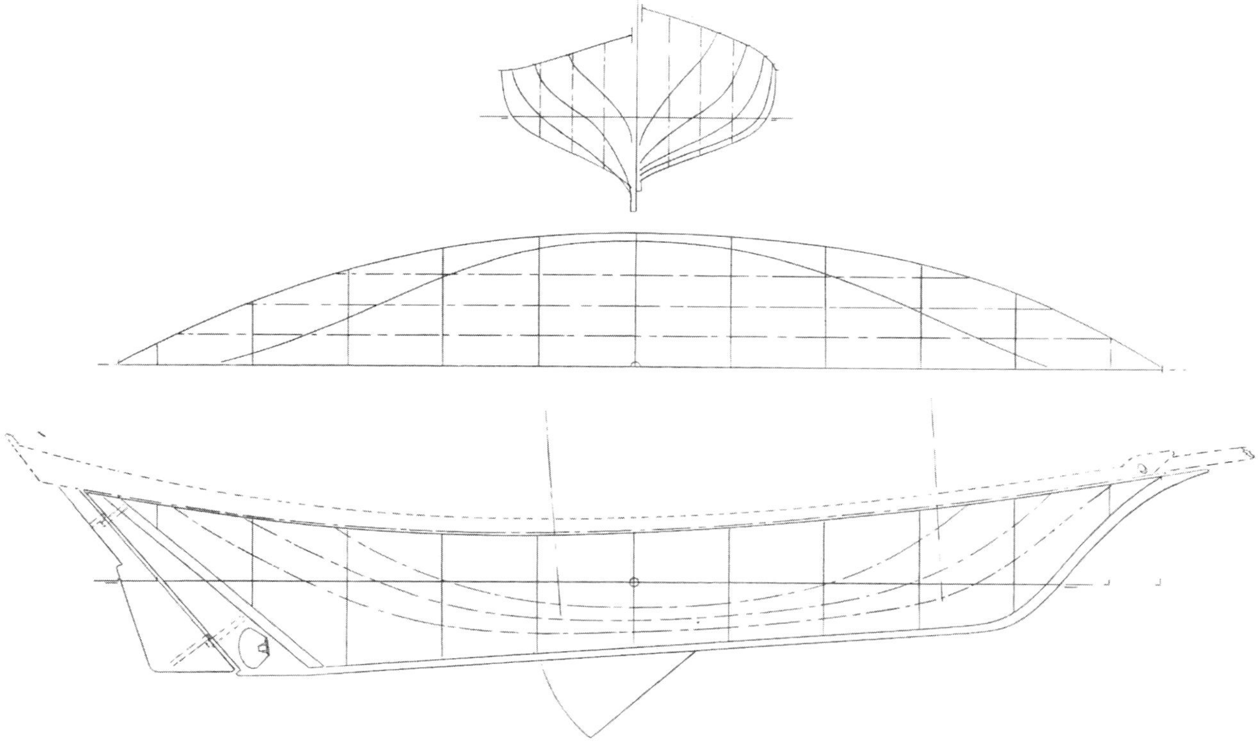

Above and below: Lines and cabin layout of the Tancook whaler.

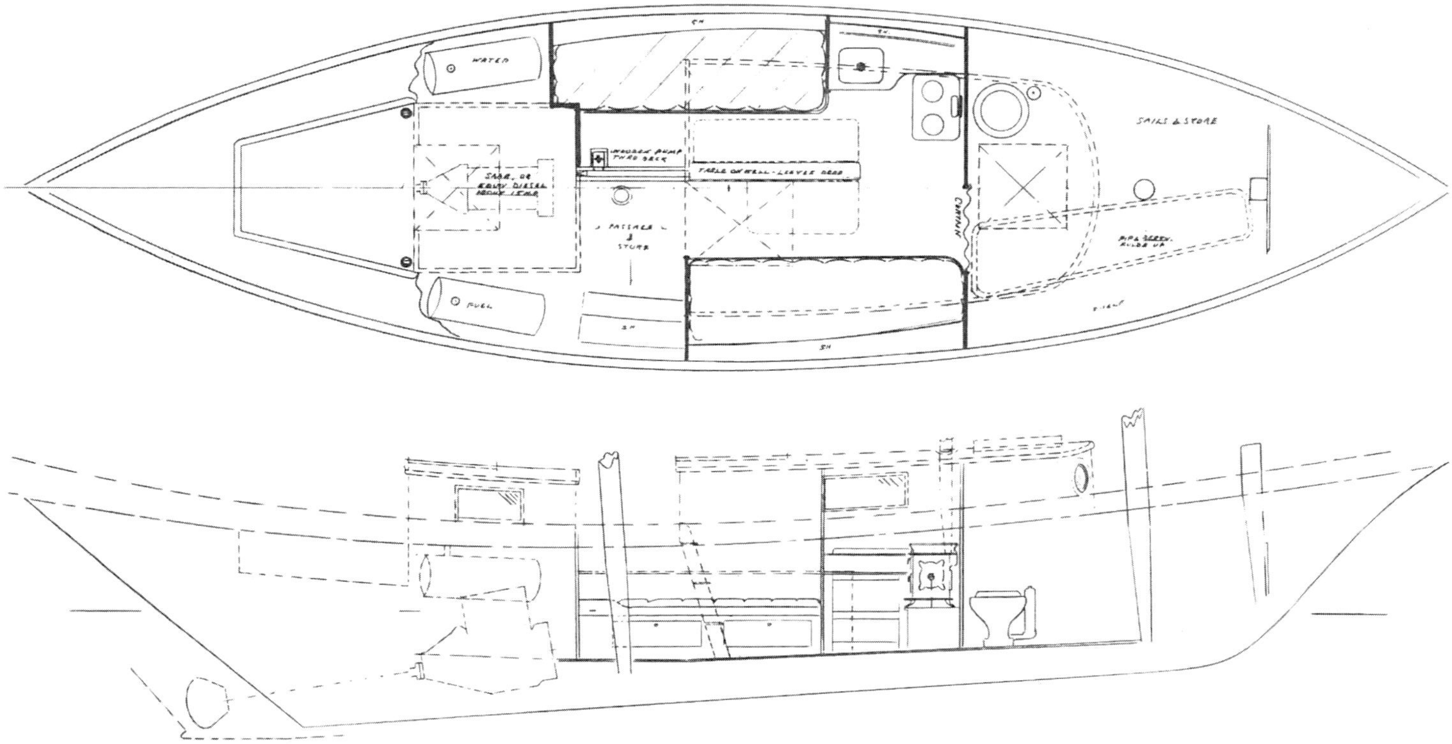

Length on deck: 40 feet 4 inches
Length on waterline: 33 feet 7½ inches
Beam: 12 feet 1 inch
Draft: 5 feet 7 inches
Sail area: 1,407 square feet (with fisherman)
Displacement: 28,000 pounds

Schooner *Gallant* For Richard Tilghman

This little schooner was designed and built for Richard Tilghman in 1966. She is based on the pilot schooner design that was common on Chesapeake waters many years ago. For those who appreciate fine vessels "whose ageless beauty fits the sea," she is lovely, simply lovely.

The shape of this schooner hull is classic Culler. She has wineglass sections throughout with much external deadwood. Her floors forward and in her midsection have plenty of deadrise, then flatten as they approach the large, well-shaped transom, set at just the right angle of rake. The straight raking stem rabbet complements the transom line, and, along with her fine entry, strong sheer, and the wineglass shape, give very sharp buttock lines and a nicely shaped run. All of the above result in high, hard bilges with a very fine underbody shape. Yes, I know; accommodation is less than what's expected these days, but so what! There is enough, and with the Old Man's usual sheer (which "works" and looks good from any angle), there is plenty of deck area to enjoy a real sailing vessel.

With all that lateral plane below, she is easy and steady at sea. The well-shaped forefoot and keel drag are all leading edge—and very efficient, too. Gallant is good on all points of sailing, but off the wind she really kicks up her heels.

Looked at in profile, this vessel, with her sheer, sheer striping, cove lines, clipper head, and steeved bowsprit and jibboom, gives the impression of being ready to leap ahead, right off the page.

Pete gave the vessel a powerful rig to go along with her sweet-lined hull. She is a main-topmast flying-jibboomer. Pete Culler will never be criticized for short topmasts. It's one of his trademarks. A rig like this is a little bit more expensive and difficult (not much) to stay, but it's worth it. You will thank the designer when you can't feel the wind, but notice that the boat is moving along pretty well.

Captain Pete was essentially a subcontractor for Concordia Company. His job was to design vessels and small craft, on commission. The idea was that his design efforts would help keep the yard busy. He did all his designing and custom small craft

Rigging up! Stepping *Gallant's* mainmast. (R.D. Culler photo)

building up to 20 feet in his shop in Hyannis, and was available for consultation and supervision of construction at Concordia, just 50 miles away at Padanaram Harbor, South Dartmouth, Massachusetts.

It so happened, for various reasons, that Pete supervised the building of this vessel, and also did much of her detail work. He built the sternboards, quarterboards, trailboards, and other parts. (The photograph on the back of the jacket on *Skiffs and Schooners* is from that time. I will forever applaud Norman Fortier for taking that photograph.) I bring all of this up as a point of information, and to show that the design details you see in the photographs here and in the Appendix are Culler-inspired. And also to remind you that the following comments are

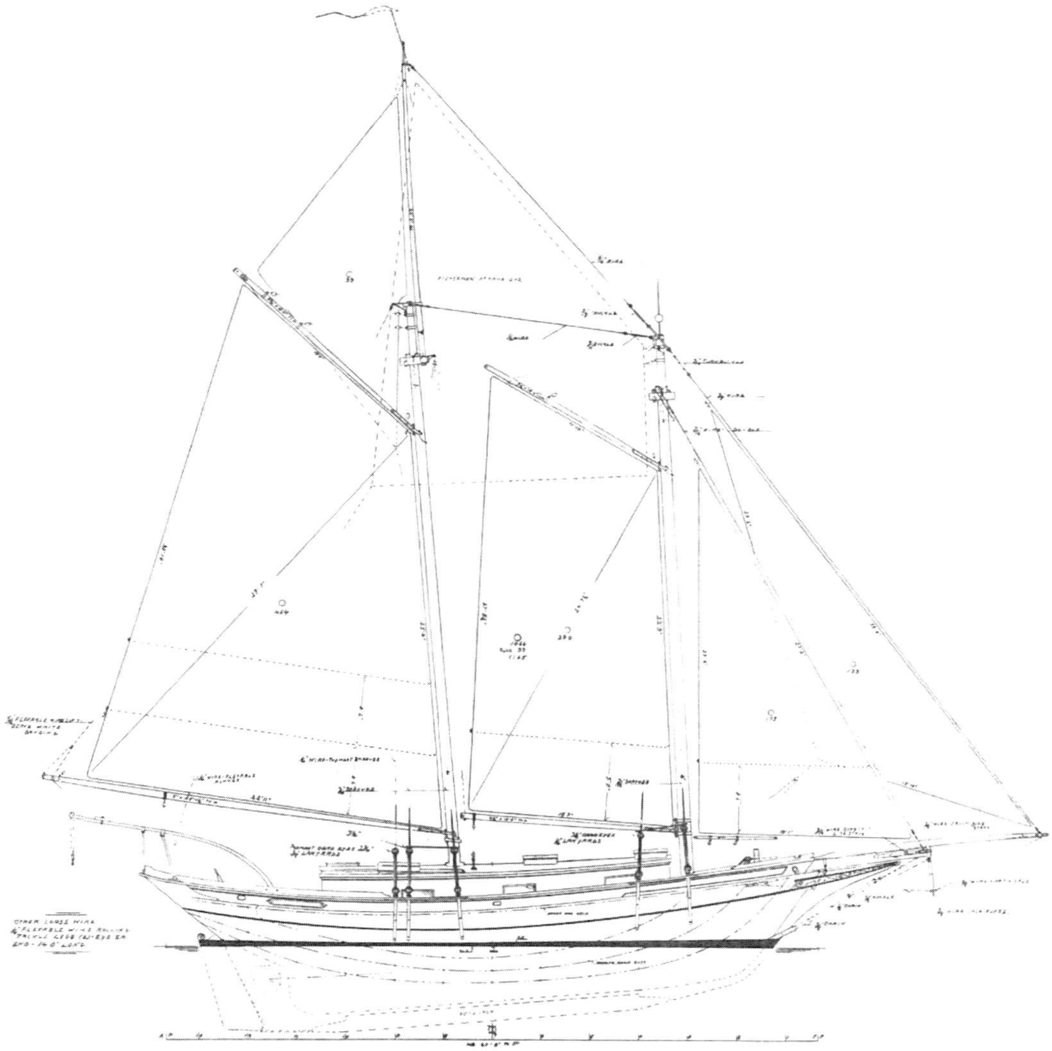

Gallant's sail plan.

from a designer/builder.

Captain Pete said, "One interesting point in construction is the use of a ship keelson, something not generally employed in a sprung-frame vessel or one of this size. We feel this is very good for a long-lasting craft, and make a point of bolting the ballast keel right up through the keelson, as well as stepping the masts in it. This, combined with the ship-type stem, deadwoods, and sternpost, makes a great washer the whole length of the backbone, with her floors sandwiched in between. This also allows the use of thick garboards and room for plenty of fastenings.

"The garboards are of white oak, for the vessel will be afloat winters. Planking will be of southern cedar to the bends, or wale strakes, which, in turn, will be hard pine. The deck will be regular lay, of thick white eastern pine.

"Deck joinerwork will be very old hard pine. We find this makes excellent trim for a painted finish, as the heartwood is as near to waterproof as a wood can be. Ceiling is native cedar, rather thick for added strength (we are still old-fashioned enough to think ceiling is a strength factor) and insulating value, as well as for sound deadening." Maynard Bray has said that these schooners "were designed by a seaman for a seaman." If you feel you belong in that fellowship, take a closer look.

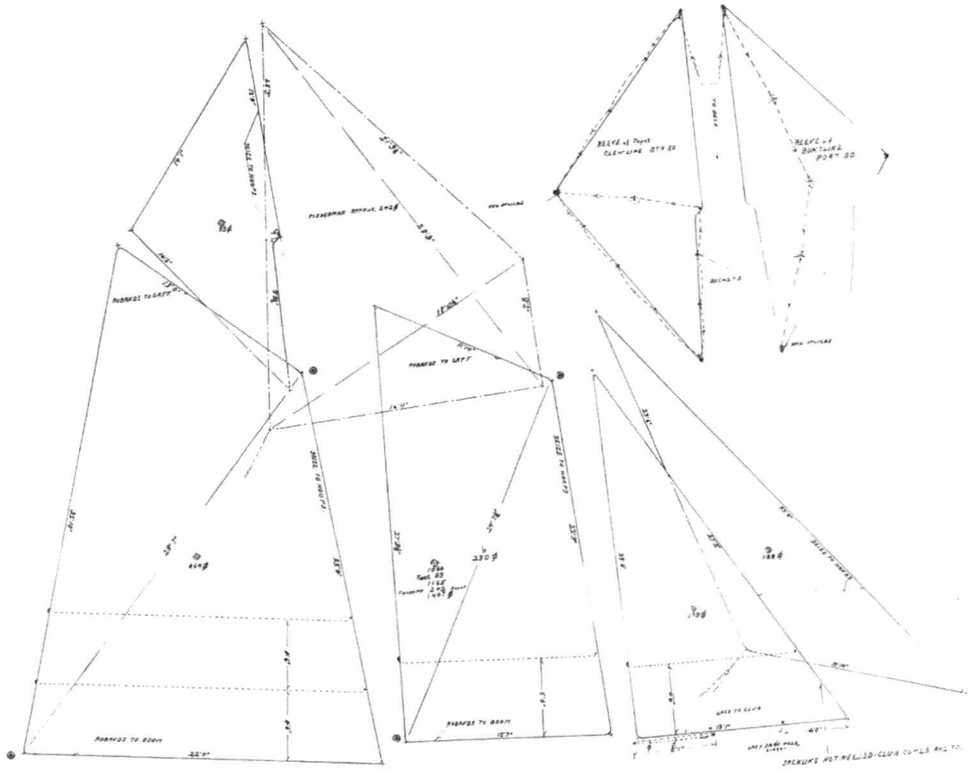

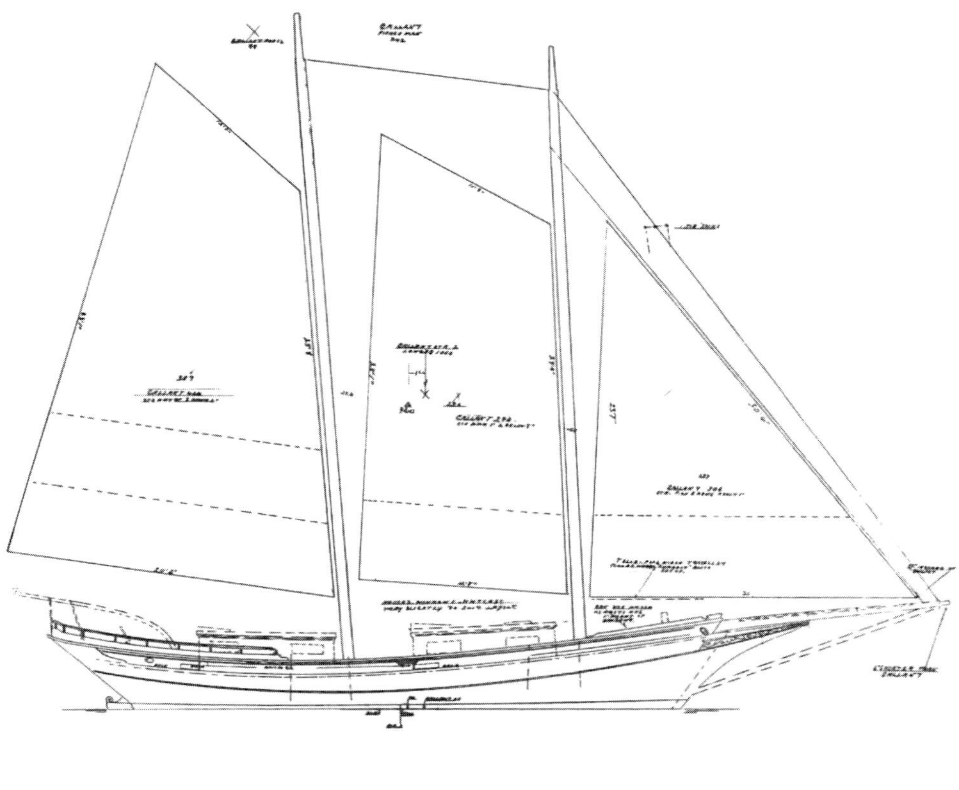

Top: *Gallant*, the sailmaker's plan. **Bottom:** One of several alternate designs considered, showing a modified sail plan and two deckhouses.

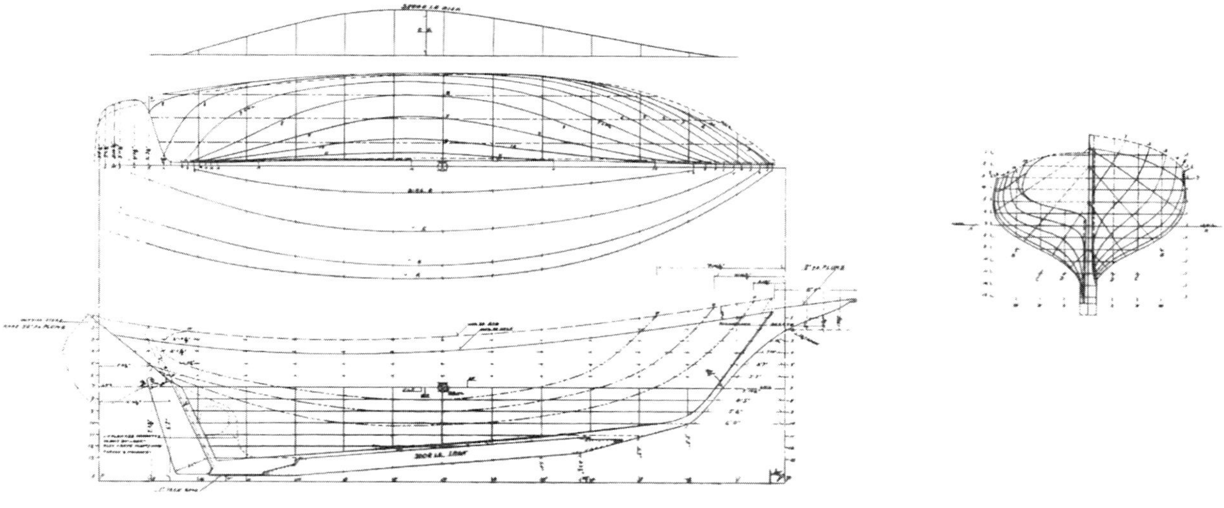

Above and below: Lines, original cabin plan, and sections drawings for *Gallant*.

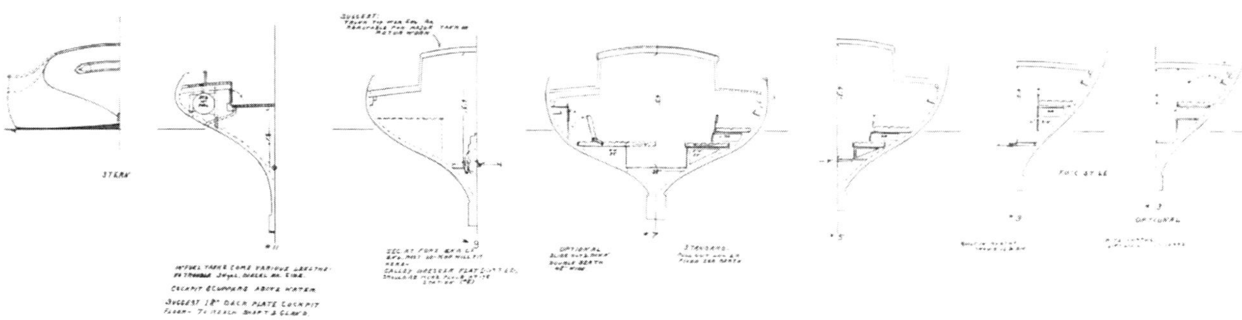

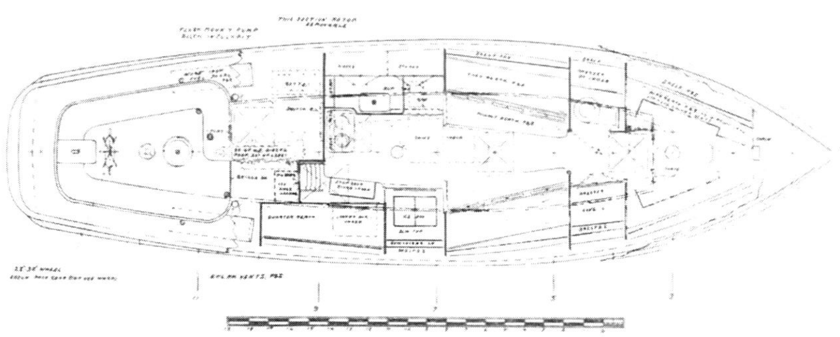

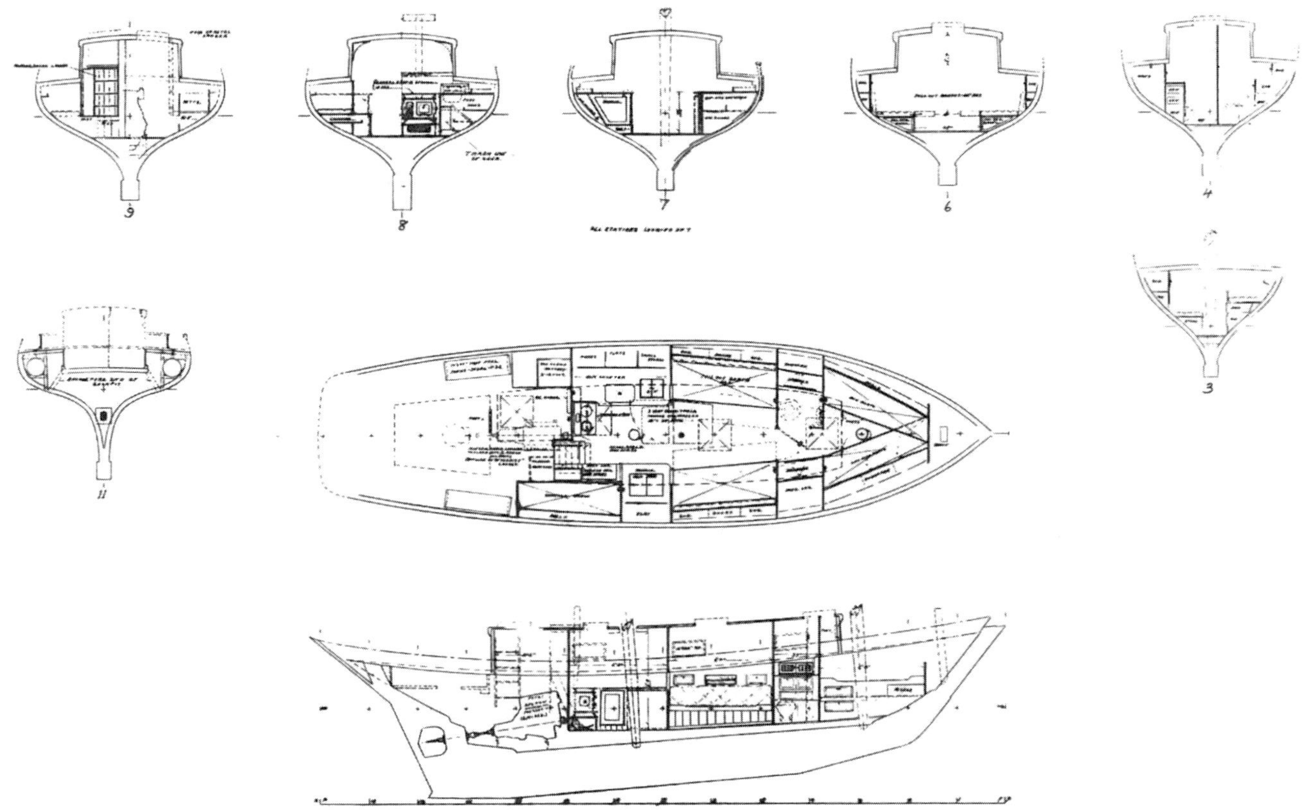

Above and below: A revised cabin plan and construction drawings for *Gallant.*

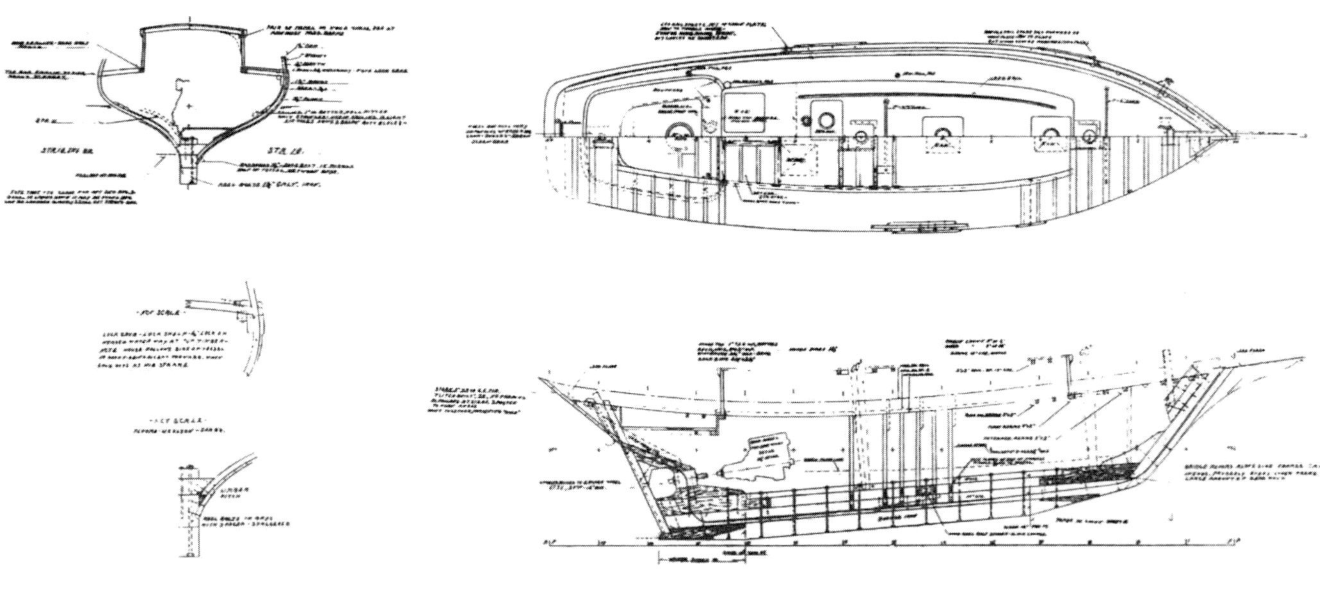

Framed out, battened off, and ready for plank. (R.D. Culler photo)

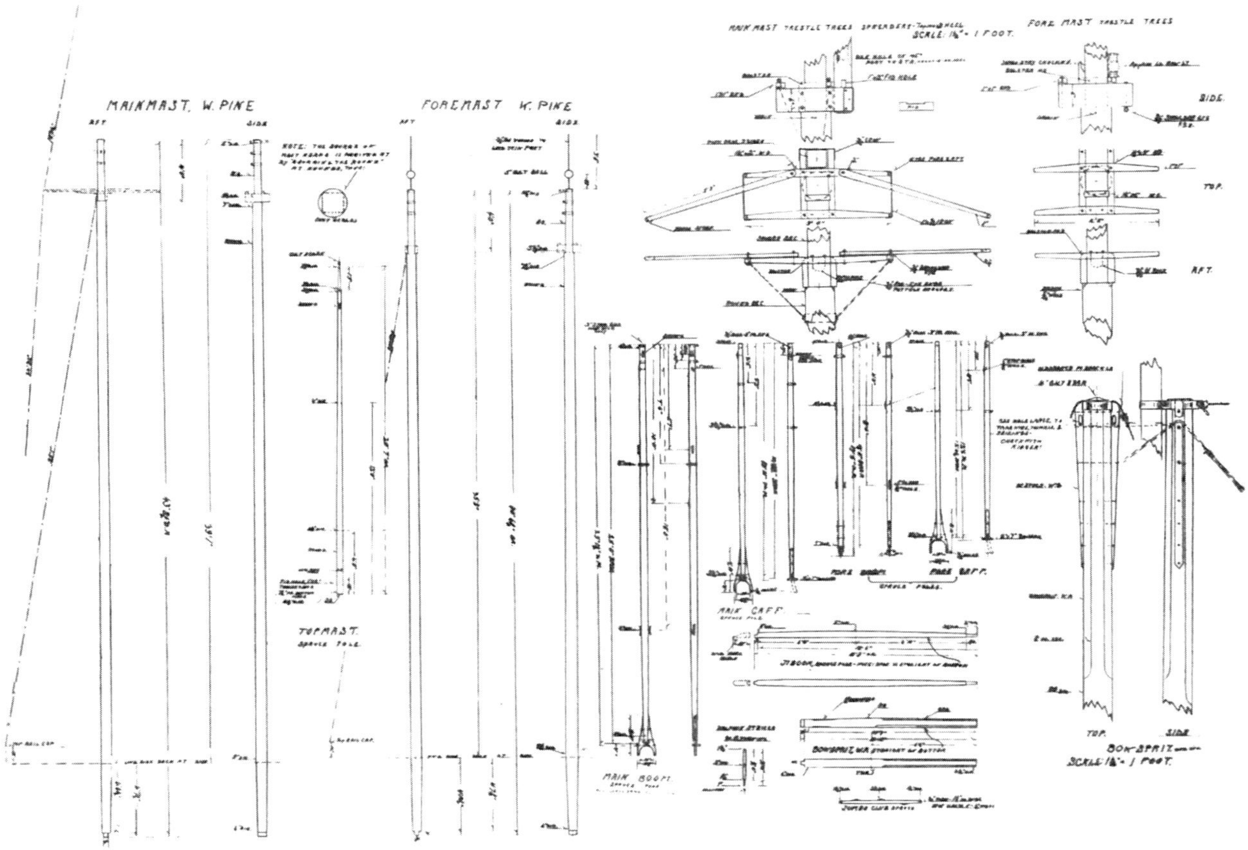

The spar plan for Tilghman's schooner, the *Gallant*.

Length overall: 42 feet
Length on waterline: 33 feet 1 inch
Beam: 10 feet 4 inches
Draft: 6 feet 6 inches
Sail area: 1,086 square feet

Schooner Yacht *Prudence* For David Forbes

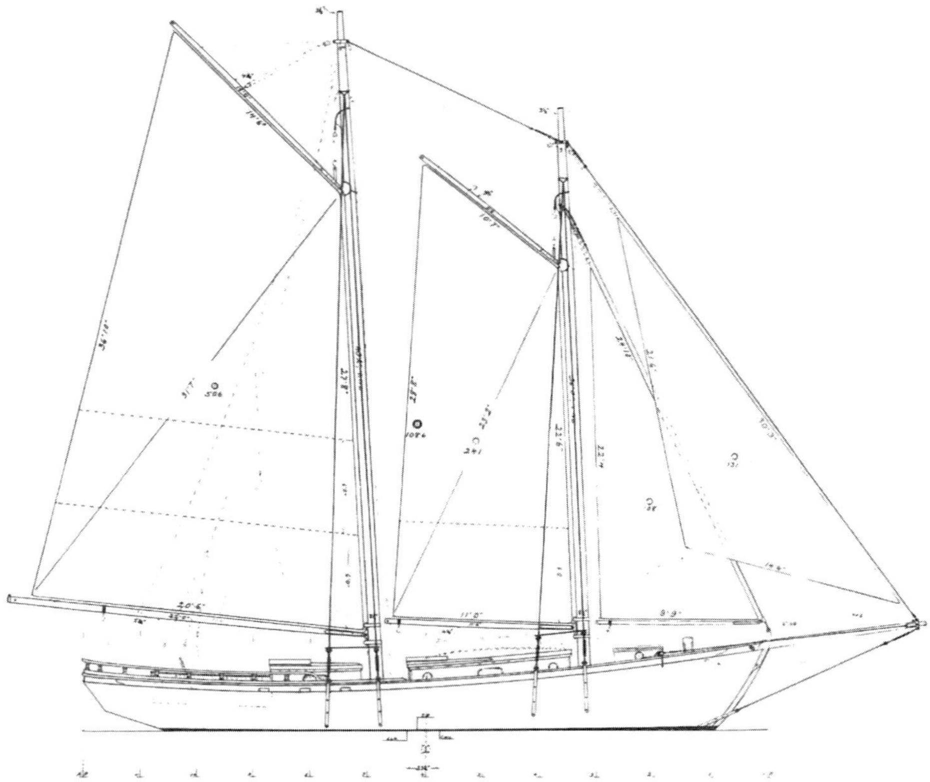

Prudence's sail plan. Atypical of a Culler design in several respects.

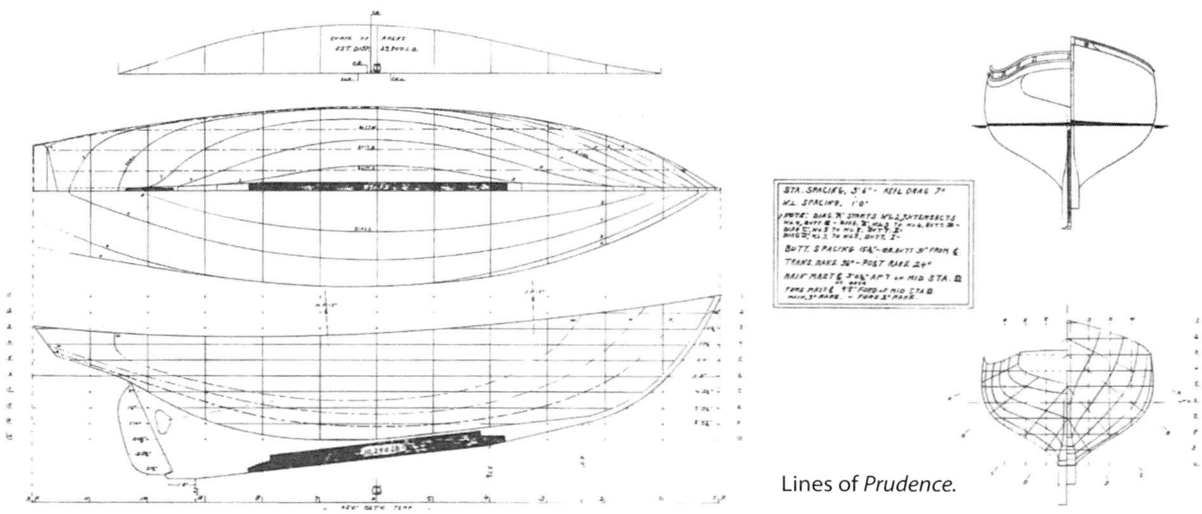

Lines of *Prudence.*

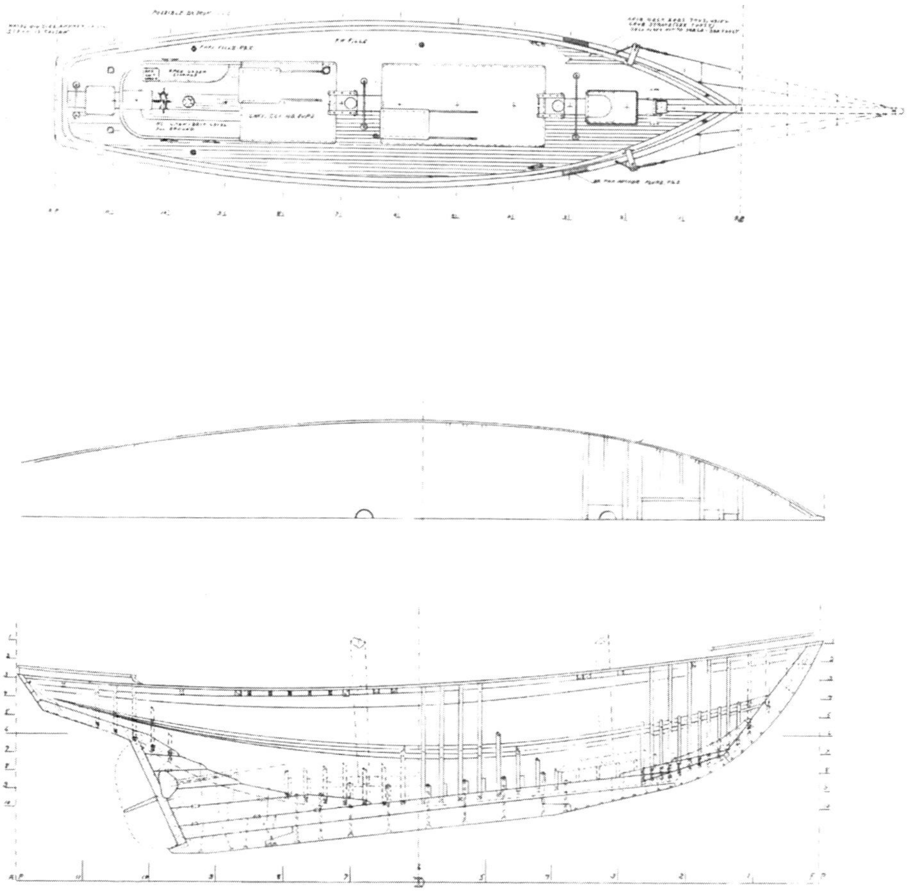

Deck layout and construction drawings for *Prudence*.

This design is interesting for a number of reasons. It was done early in Captain Pete's design career. It was drawn shortly after *Integrity*, which was the Old Man's first big-boat design. Therefore, it reflects his early drafting style. The influence of others, most notably L. Francis Herreshoff, can readily be seen in this early draftsmanship, for Pete had yet to develop the distinctive characteristics that would be called the "Culler touch."

To avoid confusion, I want to add that although *Integrity* was designed earlier, it was later redrawn (1966). The original drawings of *Integrity* were done on tracing paper; they exhibit much the same character as Forbes's schooner. I don't wish to bore you (and you are very patient), but only want to point out that one of the subtle pluses of a design catalog is the opportunity to study the designer's evolving style.

There are clues within these plans that tell me there was much input from the client. Examples are the lack of a clipper head and the baldheaded rig with its large mainsail and small fore, necessitating running backstays on the main. Pete would only use a full-length club on the jib with great reluctance, feeling it was lethal more often than not, especially for anyone sticking a head up through that forward hatch. The staying of the rig is not at all typical, and there is a distinct lack of Culler details.

The lines in the vessel's hull are long, lean, and very sharp, with a nice form of run. It could be said that they are somewhat similar in shape to the later 40-foot ketch and *Swan V*. However, Pete felt this schooner yacht would be somewhat tender, and he readily admitted that the vessel was based on Forbes's ideas.

Periauger Scow; Scow Schooner For Robert Servais

Periauger Scow

Length overall: 32 feet
Length on waterline: 27 feet 8 inches
Beam: 10 feet
Draft: 2 feet
Sail area: 527 square feet

Scow Schooner

Length: 45 feet
Beam: 15 feet
Draft: 30 inches, board up
Sail area: 1,411 square feet
Displacement: 23,618 pounds

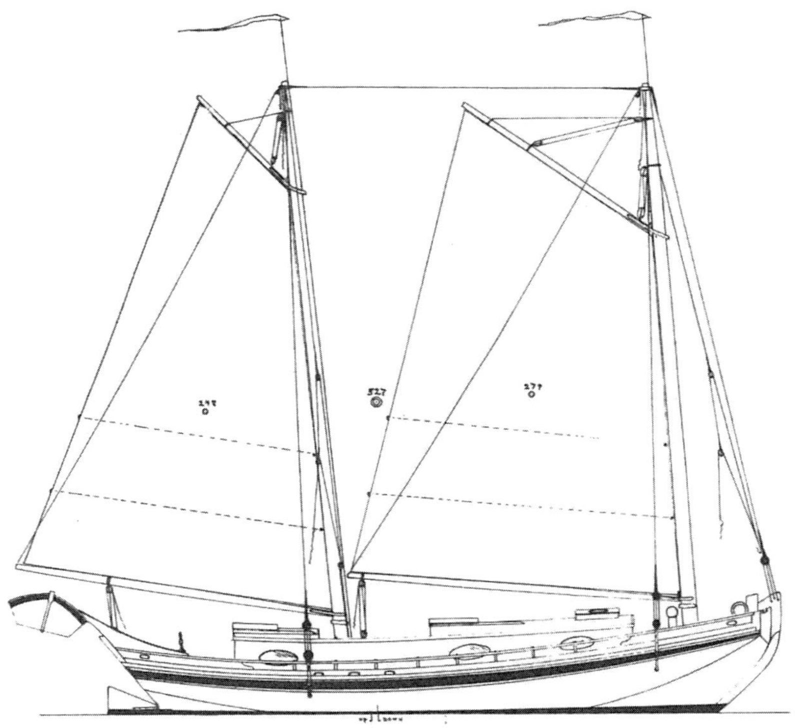

Sail plan of the Old Man's periauger scow.

During the heyday of coasting vessels, the commercial carriers of the time, the scow, or "flattie," hull was perhaps the most common type. Inexpensive in materials, construction, and operation, these could be built rapidly by unskilled labor and had large carrying capacity. These vessels fulfilled a great need when much of the country's trade traveled by water, on rivers and along the coasts.

These two scows are distinctive, not only for their wholesome good looks (It's no small chore to make a box pretty!), but because they represent the first and last major designs Pete put on paper. This, by itself, is thought-provoking.

When Pete sold his beloved *Spray* in the early 1950s, the new owner considerably revamped her and ruined what was fine, snug, and livable below

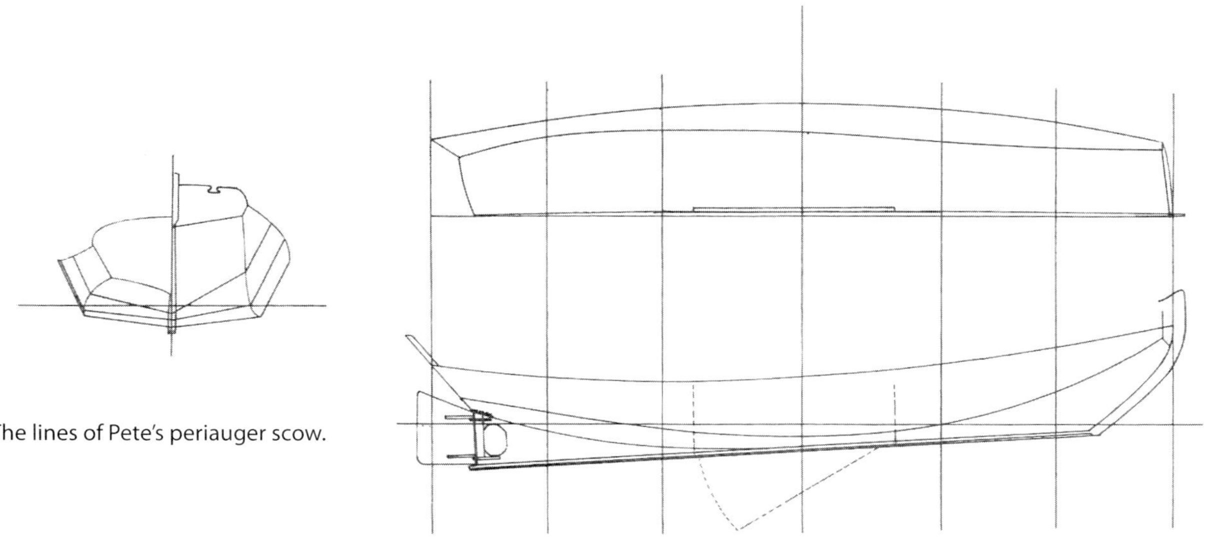

The lines of Pete's periauger scow.

decks. He turned her cabins into cramped, gadget-filled, and horrendously complicated spaces. He hired Pete to oversee this transformation; it must have been terribly painful for him to witness. The only plus from the experience was that Pete was there to appreciate all that good stuff being torn out of her.

Finding himself once again the owner of most of *Spray's* guts, Pete designed the little periauger scow to carry it. Ever practical, he chose the quick-and-dirty scow hull and ancient Dutch periauger rig because the boat was buildable in only the spare time that was available. Pete still had to pursue a living, just like almost everyone else. Although the periauger was never built, Pete had fun designing her. He incorporated numerous items that intrigued him, such as that "eight day" log windlass, so-called because it takes you about eight days to get the anchor up with it!

He was seeking a boat that was straightforward in construction and economical to build, maintain, and operate; this is just what she is—in addition to being handsome in workboat fashion.

The schooner rig is appealing to many, but for most it is beyond reach. In *Skiffs and Schooners* Pete discusses a possible solution. In the Old Man's words: "More often than not, the idea of a schooner is, for many reasons, doomed to always be a dream, yet sometimes there is a way. Usually the stumbling block is money. In the past in working craft, the same problem caused the development of a type, with several variations, that was economical to build out of easily obtained materials without necessarily using highly skilled labor. A cheap schooner of this type might be an enlarged sharpie, a pointed-bow scow schooner, a full scow schooner, or, in effect, just a large flatiron skiff.

"That such craft were practical is shown by the records and pictures of them from various parts of our coast and the Great Lakes. Some of these vessels were sloop-rigged. Many others had the normal coasting schooner rig with slight variations peculiar to each locality. The idea of such craft might be hard to accept nowadays, but once understood, they make sense for use in shoal waters and for their comparative low cost. Some of these flat-bottomed craft were quite good looking in a businesslike way. So they can be today. It's a matter of the designer's ability and the builder's artistic skill.

"Nowadays the sailing ability of a flat-bottomed schooner will be questioned, but many a skipper of a deep-draft boat has found out, quickly and decisively, that with started sheets a scow can leave him behind in short order. By the wind, with much of a sea, these flatties do not do so well, yet with their shoalness and ability to cut corners, many a scow schooner could just lay the harbor on one tack, and was soon in and to a wharf, crew maybe ashore in some local barroom, while the deeper vessel, with maybe better windward ability, had to stick to the deep water and take hitch after hitch to make the same port, often finishing after dark with a failing

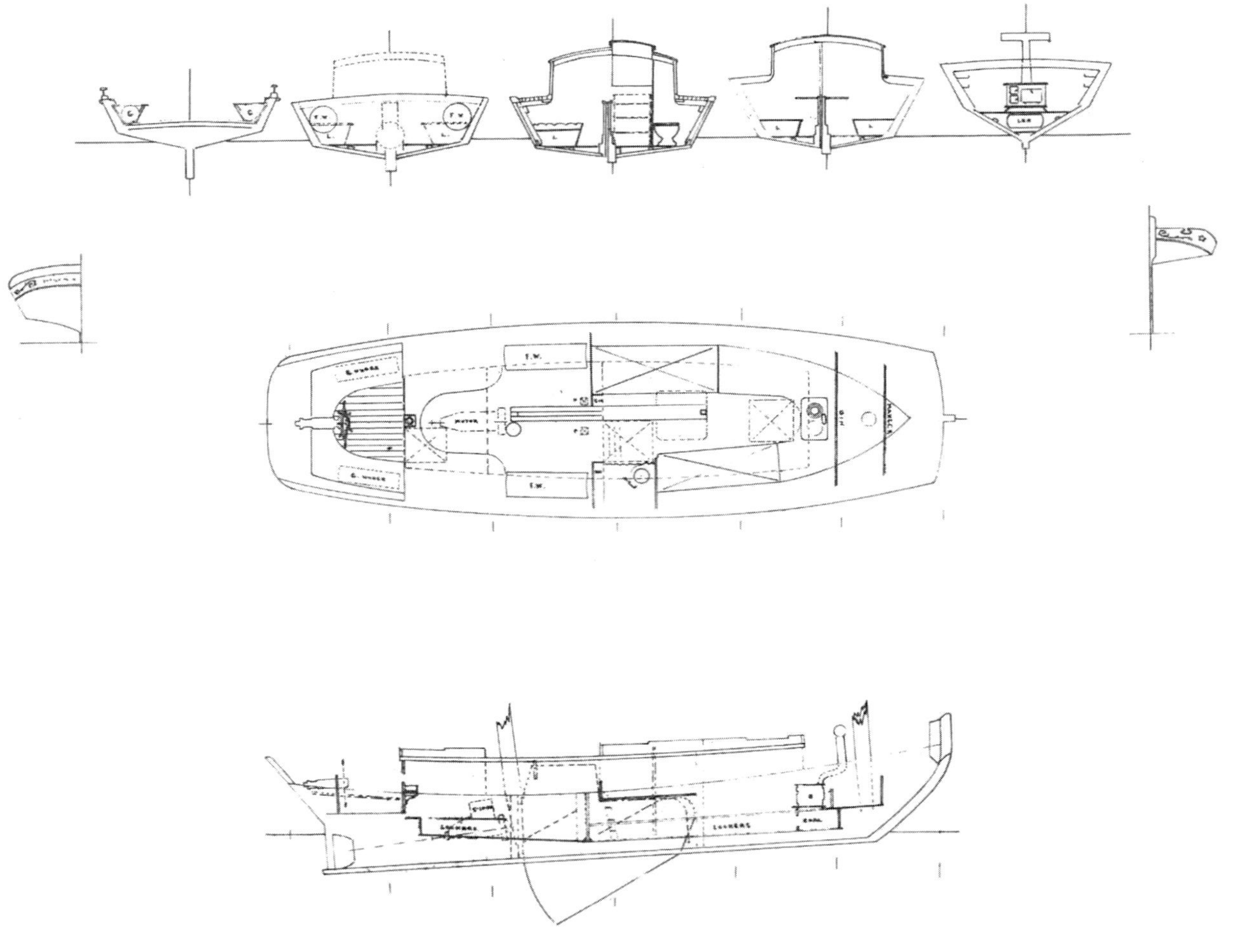

The cabin layout of the periauger scow.

wind. Yes, in waters suited to them, these sharpie and scow schooners got around with dispatch!"

Robert Servais, a frequent visitor to the Old Man's Hyannis shop and a good friend, was looking for just such a solution to his persistent schooner dream. After reading the above, Servais put down some of his hardearned cash and had Pete work up this scow schooner design. As stated before, this was Pete's last completed design. She is graceful, appealing to the eye, and full to brimming with character. It is particularly appropriate that, if and when she is built, Bob intends to name the vessel the *Captain R.D. Culler.*

In profile the design is exceedingly handsome in hull and rig. Repeatedly, I find the need to remind myself that it is a scow I'm looking at. The usual blunt stubbiness of the type has been minimized by the use of nicely raking ends, swept-up sheer, and chine and rabbet lines accented by the cutwater and bow piece. A long nose pole, washrail cove line, and monkey rail and davit shape the after end. Even the rudder shape adds to and harmonizes the overall effect of apparent lengthening and liveliness.

All of this added shape to a flattie hull was not done solely for the sake of appearance, for it allows the bow transom and quarters to be well clear of the water and achieves a good run. What is less than ideal, primarily due to the restricted draft, is a somewhat reduced amount of water for the necessarily large propeller. But, as Pete said, "The way she is, I can't do anything about it. "

There is a world of room on her decks and below. And the deck room is not at all diminished by two large deckhouses with their characteristic Culler square ports.

I have often thought how easily her forward

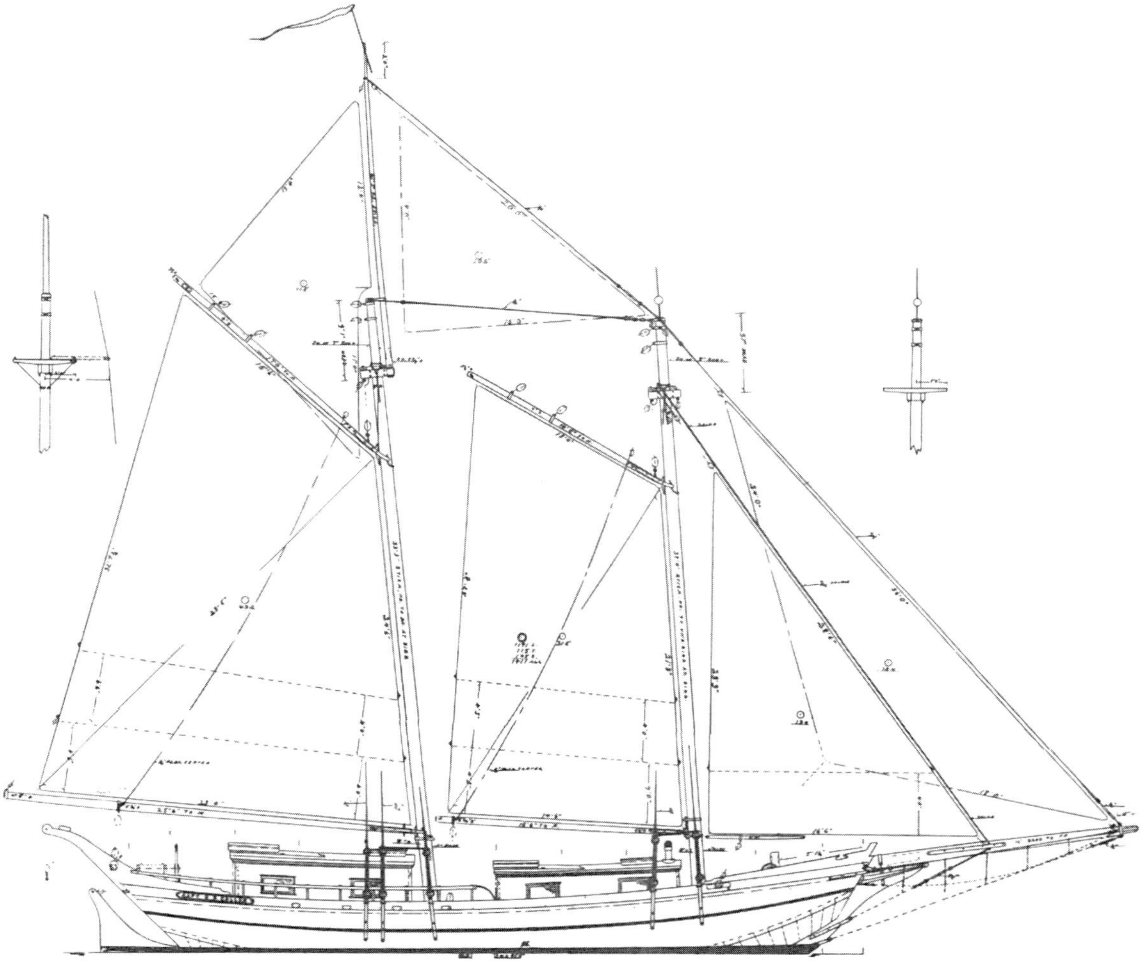

The schooner rig on Robert Servais's scow.

house could become a cargo hatch. I think she could carry a fair amount of cordwood and a good deckload of boards, or perhaps be stacked to the second reefs with hay bales, as on San Francisco scows. If the skipper were clever, the arrangement could be interchangeable. The forward house could be removable, using the schooner's own gear, and with a unitized arrangement below, all could be off and ready for cargo within a few hours. Yes, it would be quite workable.

It's pleasing to see how easy the road travels when you make the right choices. Note how readily that great deck will empty water as a result of the lively sheer. Naturally, the deck has a 3-inch crown. Except in rare cases, any crown in a Culler design is 3 inches, no matter what the length.

Having the schooner rig was Servais's dream, but the scow hull was a concession to affordability. Pete balanced this scow with a handsome rig that is nearly identical, in proportion and area, to that of the Joseph Russell. The big difference is that there is no foreyard and a smaller fisherman staysail, for obvious reasons. Pete was quite pleased with the way this hull and rig evolved; he told me he felt she would prove to be a good sailer and a successful design.

Once again, I quote the Old Man from *Skiffs and Schooners*: "I feel, for the right waters and for the man with the right outlook toward them, these scows or flatties, schooner-rigged for the hell of it and because it makes 'em look very good, have a lot to offer as a cruising boat, or sometime floating home. They're one way of getting about in interesting waters."

If Servais doesn't hurry up and build this vessel, I might beat him to it.

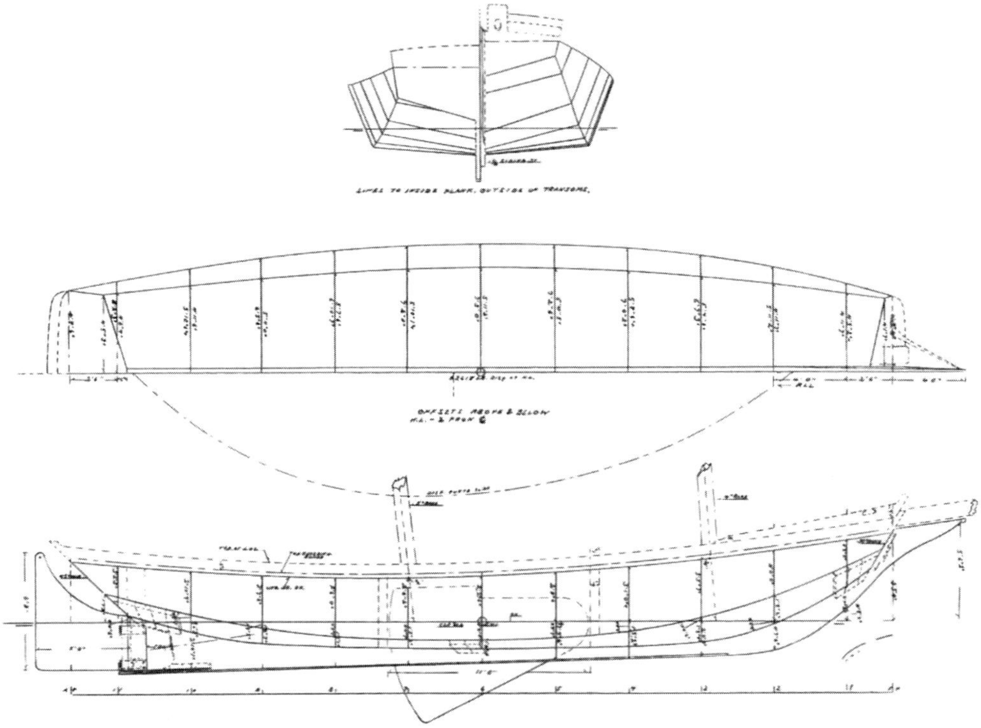

Lines of the 45-foot scow schooner.

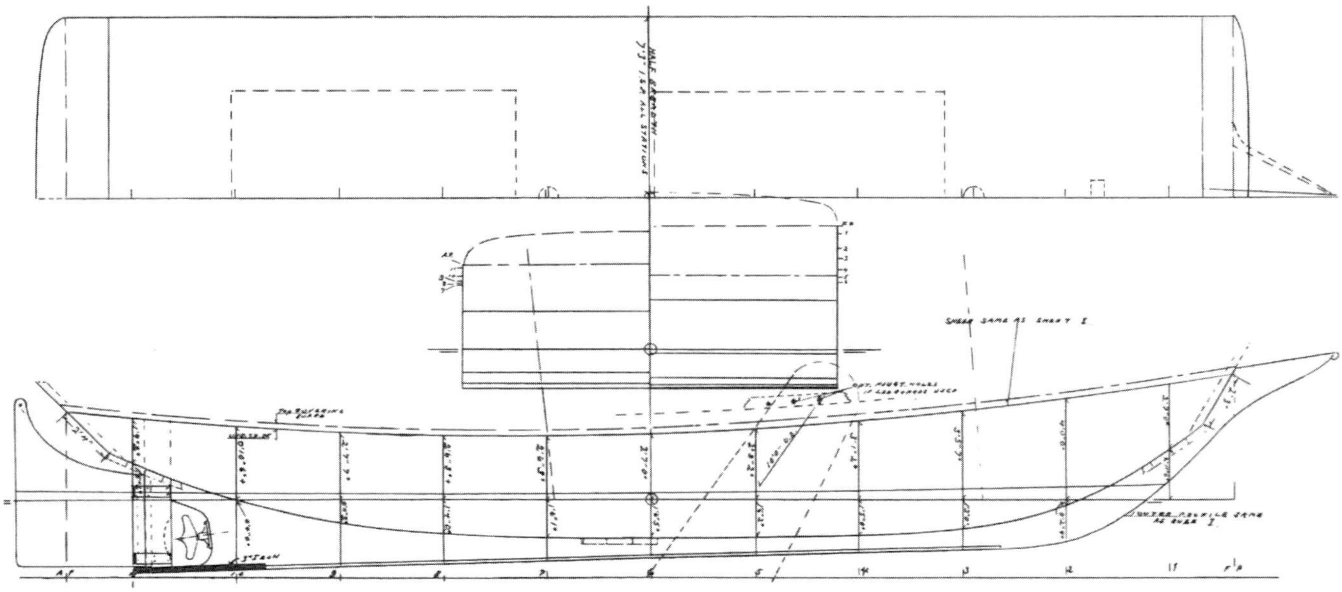

Alternate lines, showing a squared-off deck and no deadrise in the sections.

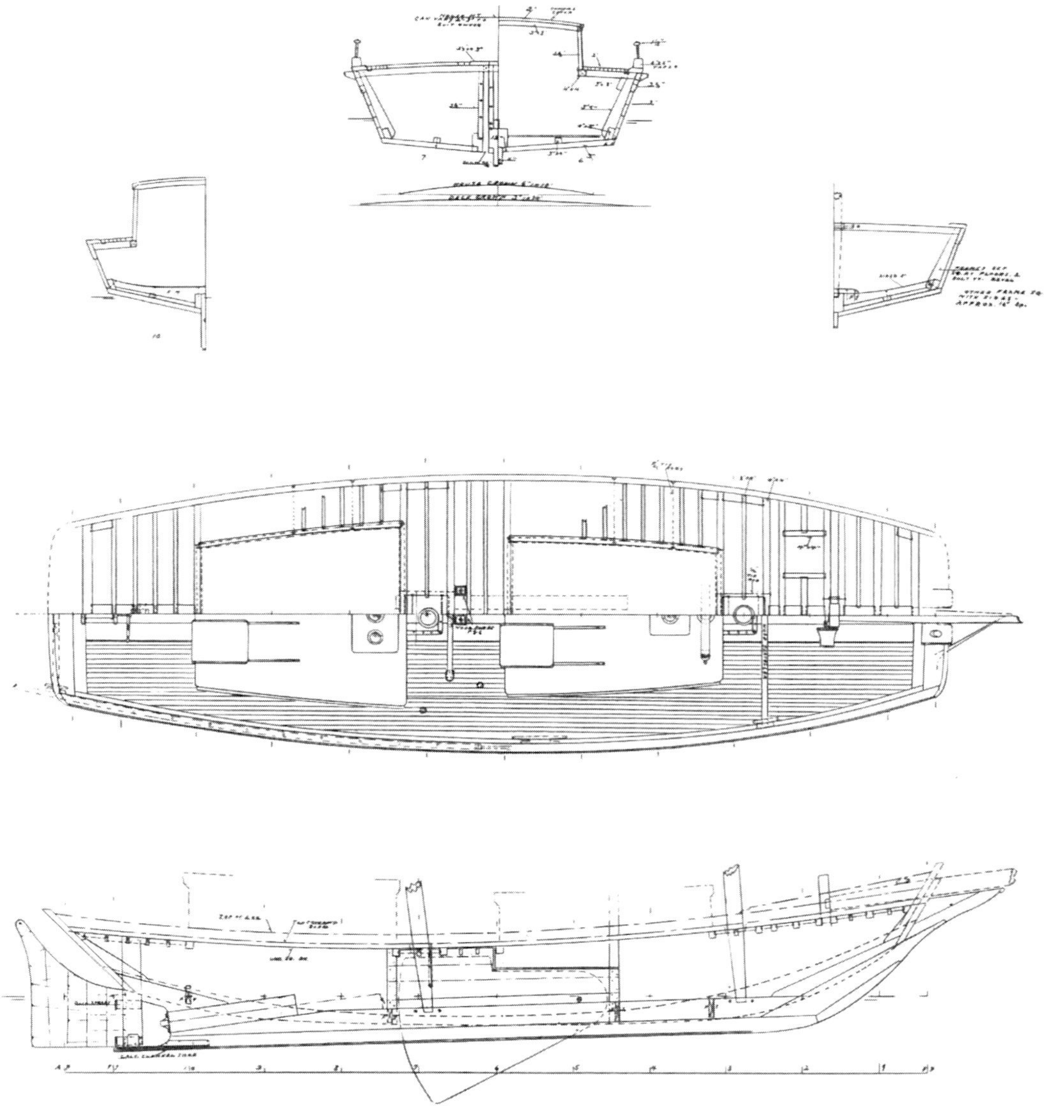

Construction drawings for Robert Servais's schooner.

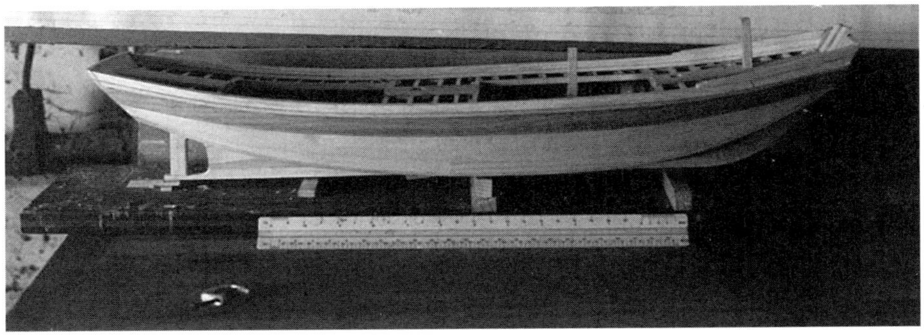

George Kelley constructed this model of the scow schooner. (John Burke photo)

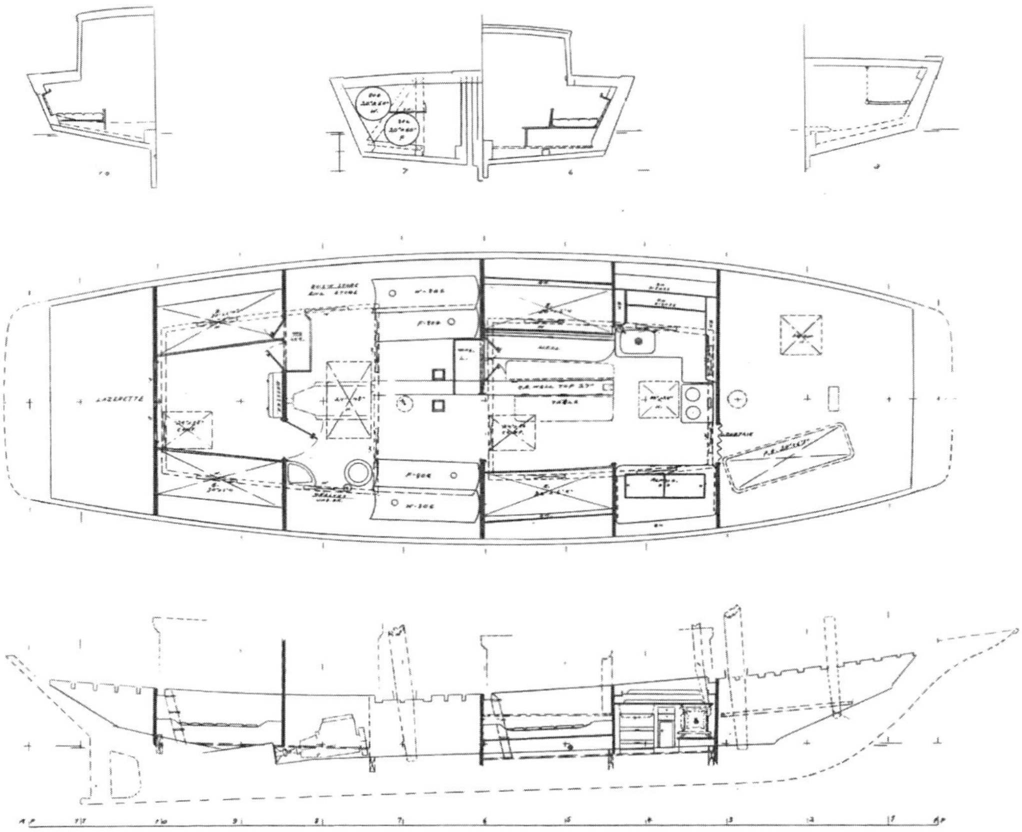

Inboard profile and cabin plans.

The *Fiddler's Green* For Ned Ackerman
The *Joseph W. Russell* For Buzz Garrahan

Fiddler's Green

Length overall: 47 feet 6 inches
Length on waterline: 37 feet 9 inches
Beam: 13 feet 2 inches
Draft: 6 feet 7 ihces
Sail area: 1,553 square feet
Displacement: 47,800 pounds

Joseph W. Rusell

Length between perpendicualrs: 45 feet
Beam: 13 feet
Draft: 6 feet
Sail area: 1,711 square ffet
Displacement: 41,500 pounds

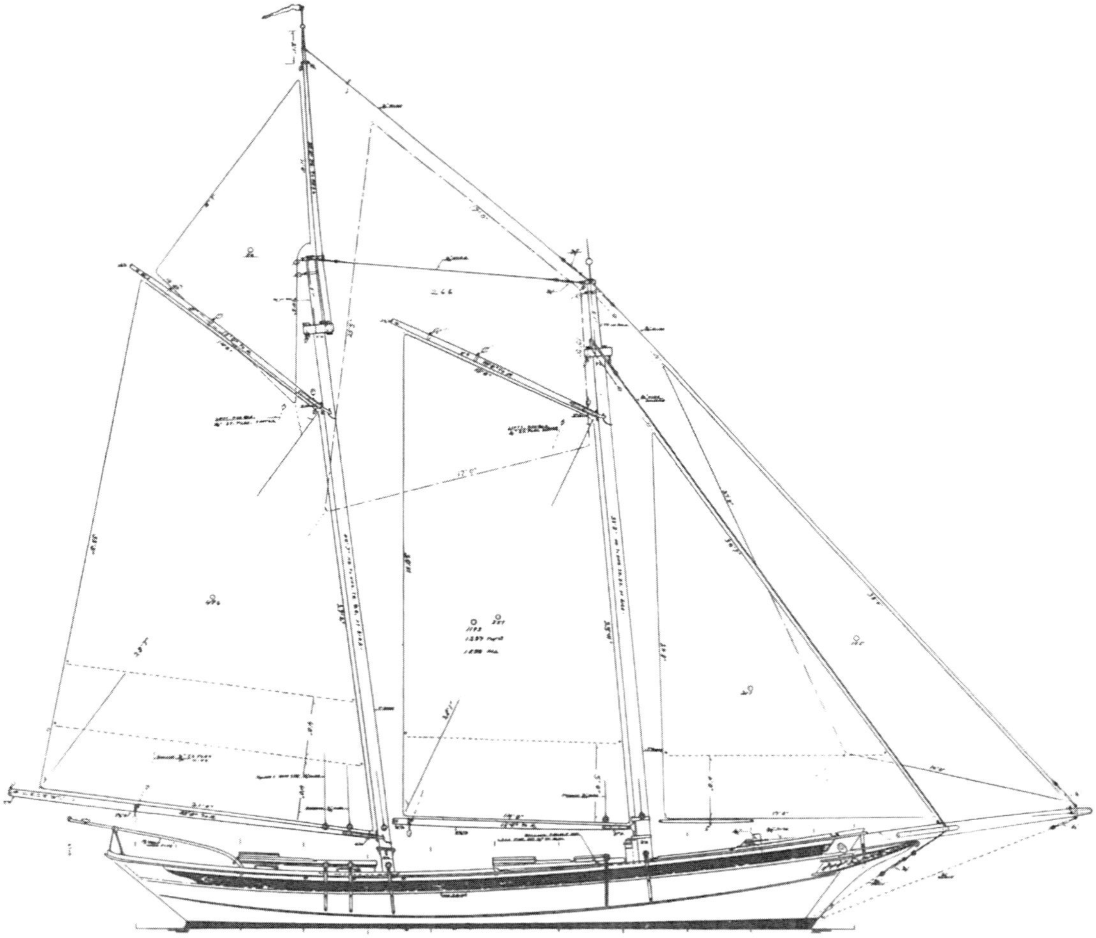

Fiddler's Green, sail plan .

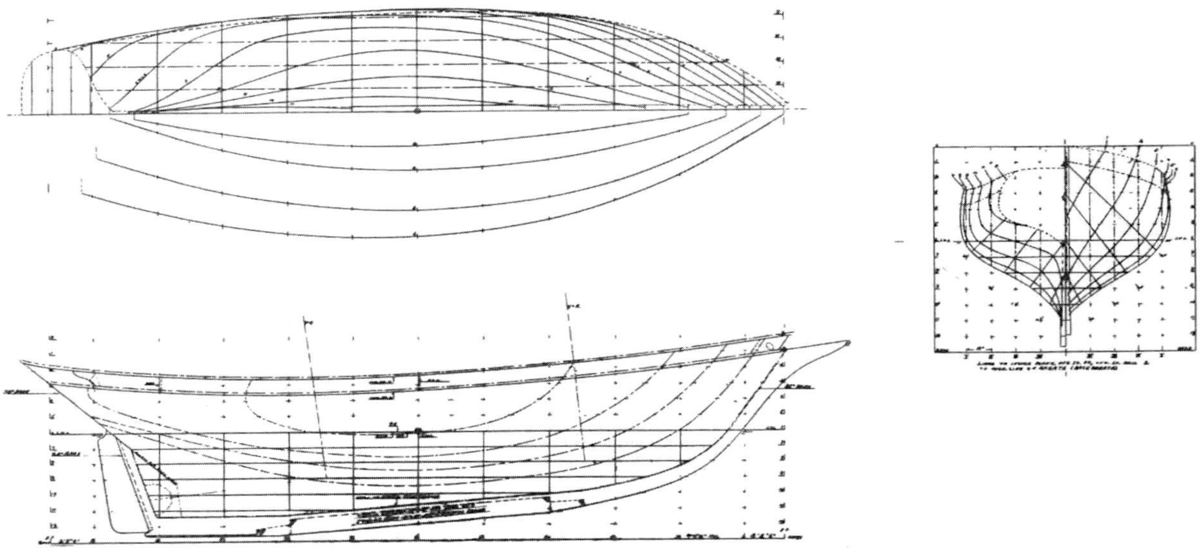

Above and below: The lines of *Fiddler's Green,* and her cabin layout as Captain Pete originally drew it.

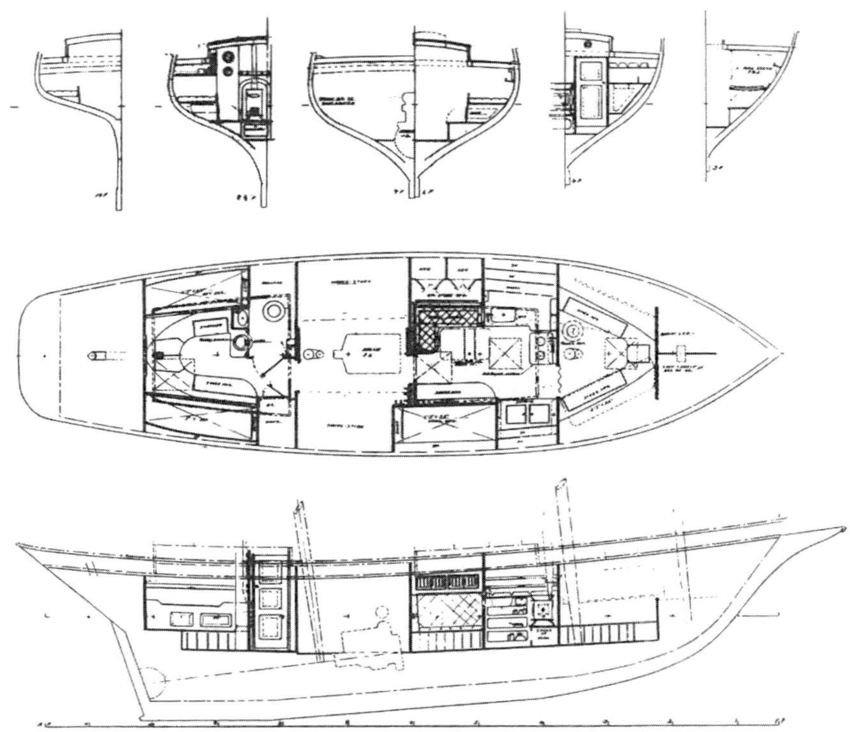

These two schooners are nearly identical and yet they differ in one basic sense. *Fiddler's Green* has deeper draft, slacker bilges, and is somewhat sharper, having been designed to utilize outside ballast. The *Joseph W. Russell* carries all her ballast inside and is therefore less deep, has a harder bilge and less deadrise to her floors. Simplistically, it could be said that *Fiddler's Green* has her ancestry in the pilot boats of Virginia, and the *Russell* in the coaster model. Beyond that, they are very similar in style, appearance, sail plan, and cabin layout. For a variety of reasons, I consider these two vessels to be the

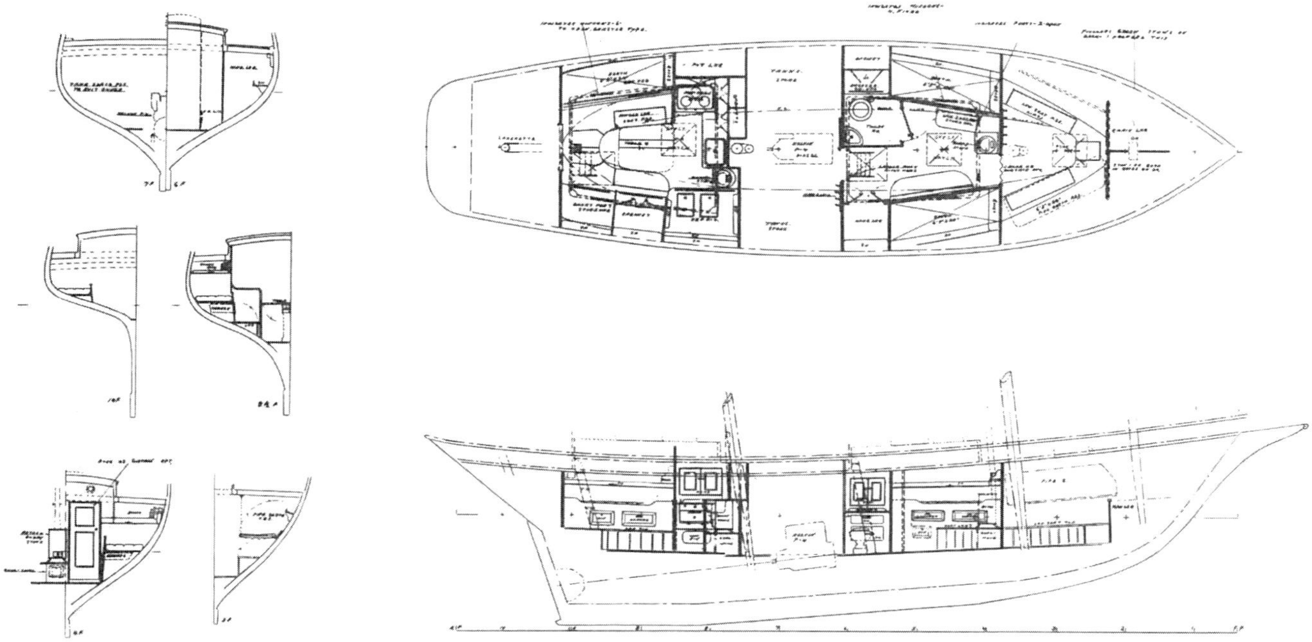

The revised accommodations plan for *Fiddler's Green.*

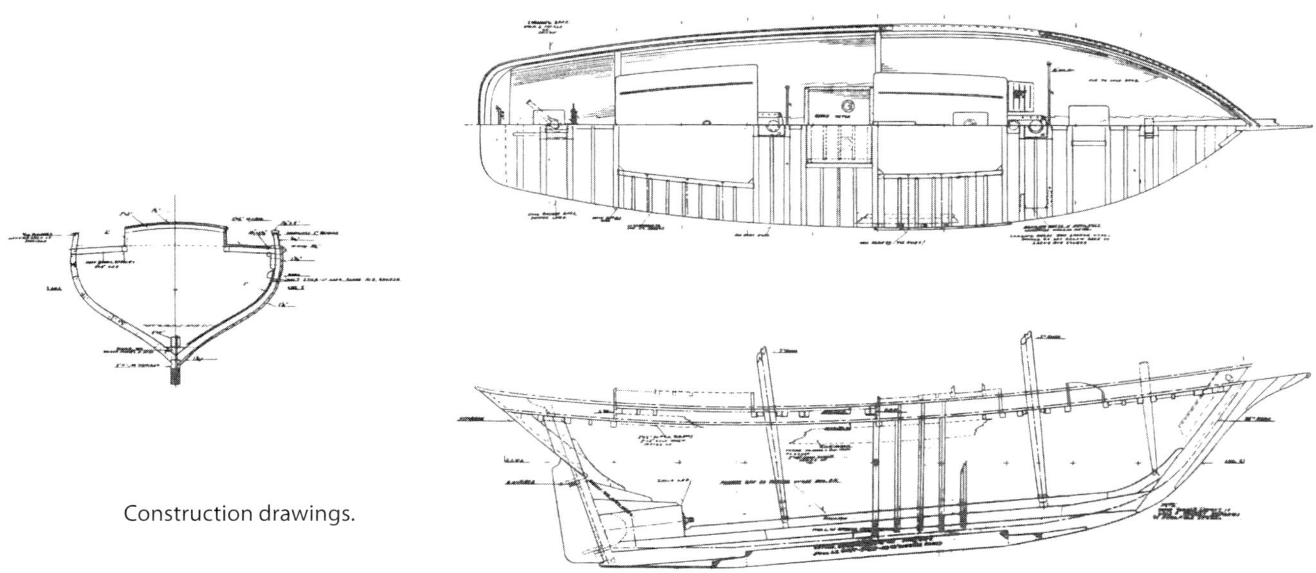

Construction drawings.

core of Captain Pete's schooner designs.

They are both 45 feet between perpendiculars. This is the length at which Pete felt the rig came into its own. However, it is not so large as to be priced out of existence, both in first cost and in yearly maintenance, for those of modest means. *Fiddler's Green* in light condition is 21.3 long tons displacement; the *Joseph W. Russell* is slightly less. These types cost by the pound.

Each of these designs has been built and proved successful in use. This is important. Just prior to his death, Captain Pete estimated that no more than

And here she is. Now the pride of St. Malo, France.
(R.D . Culler photo)

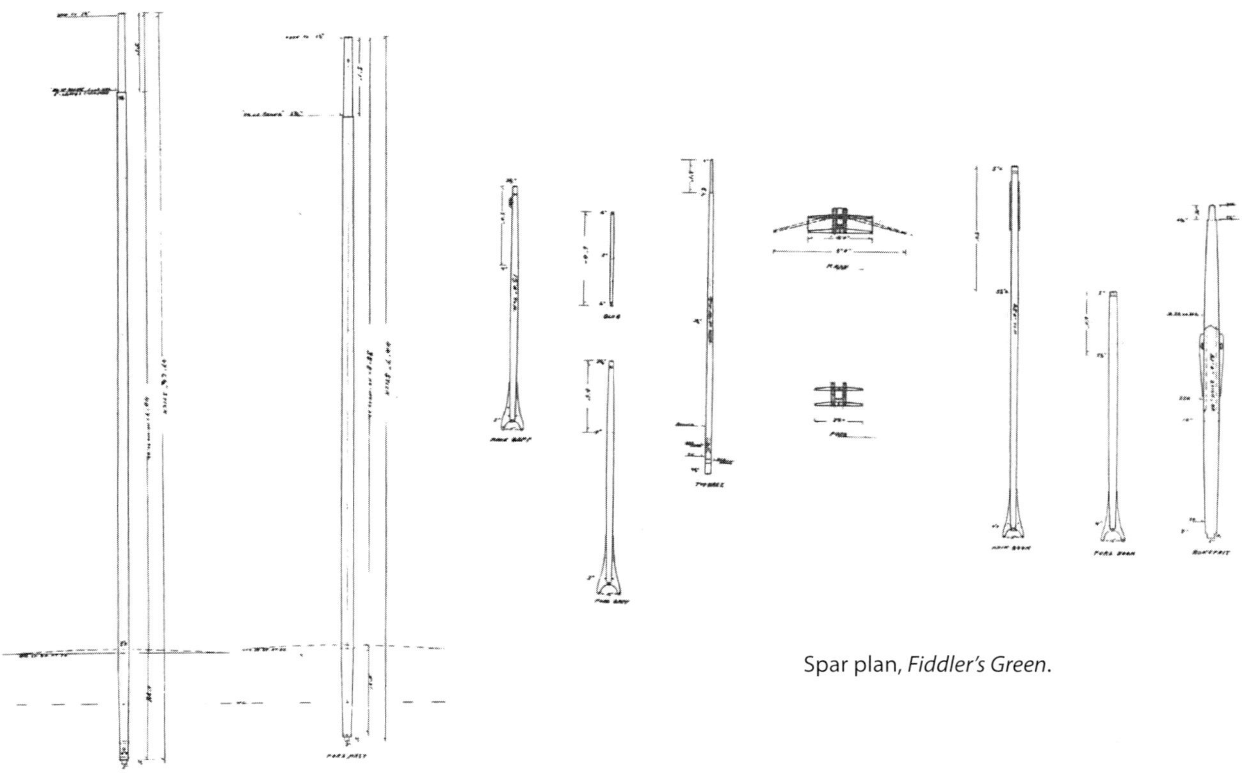

Spar plan, *Fiddler's Green*.

Traditional schooners always have a wealth of detail. Looking forward on the *Fiddler's Green*. (R.D. Culler photo)

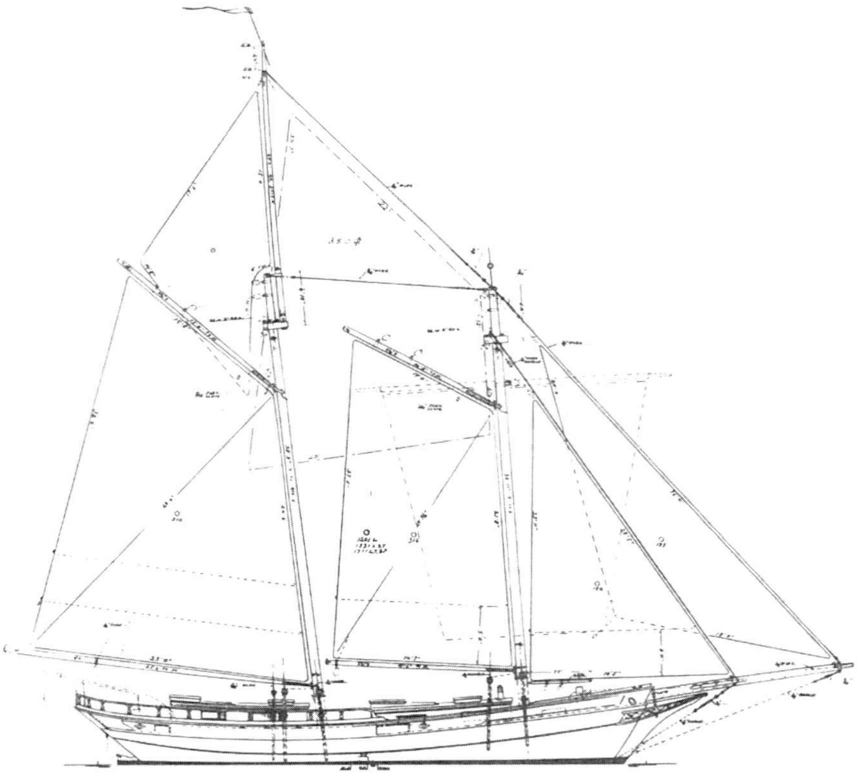

Sail plan of the *Joseph W. Russell*, showing a yard on the foremast.

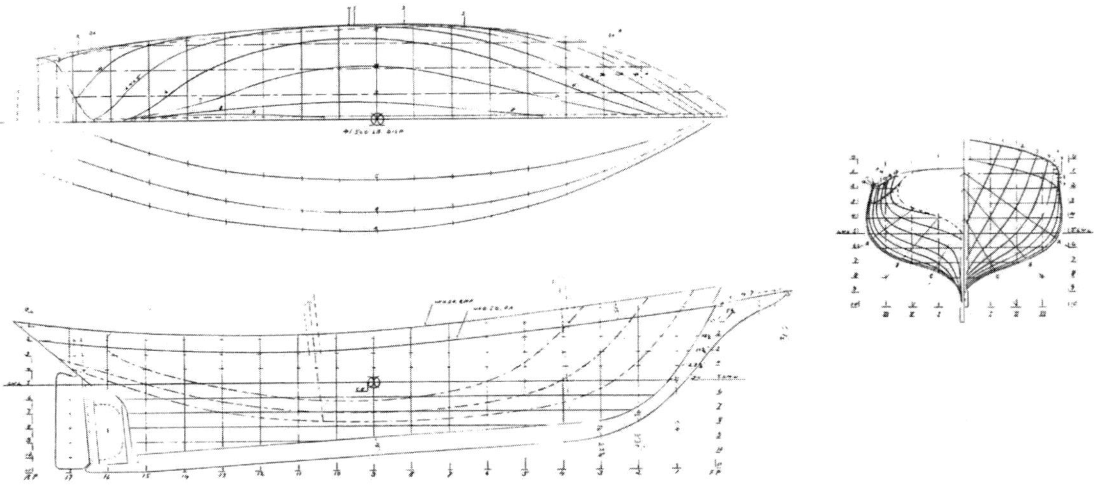

Above and below: Lines and cabin plans for the 45-foot schooner, *Joseph W. Russell.*

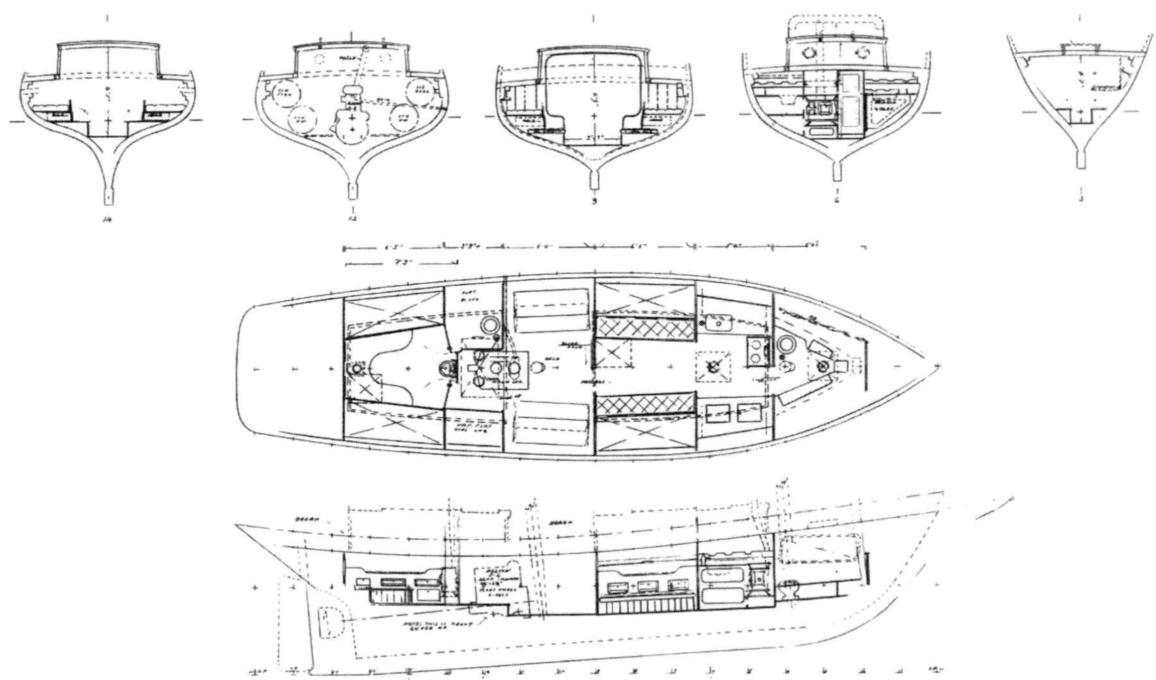

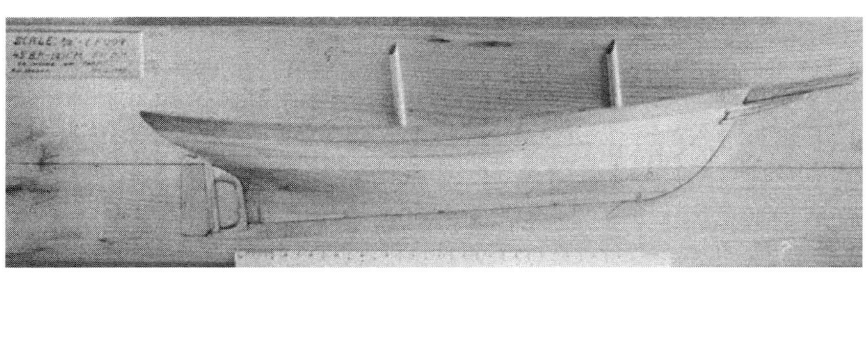

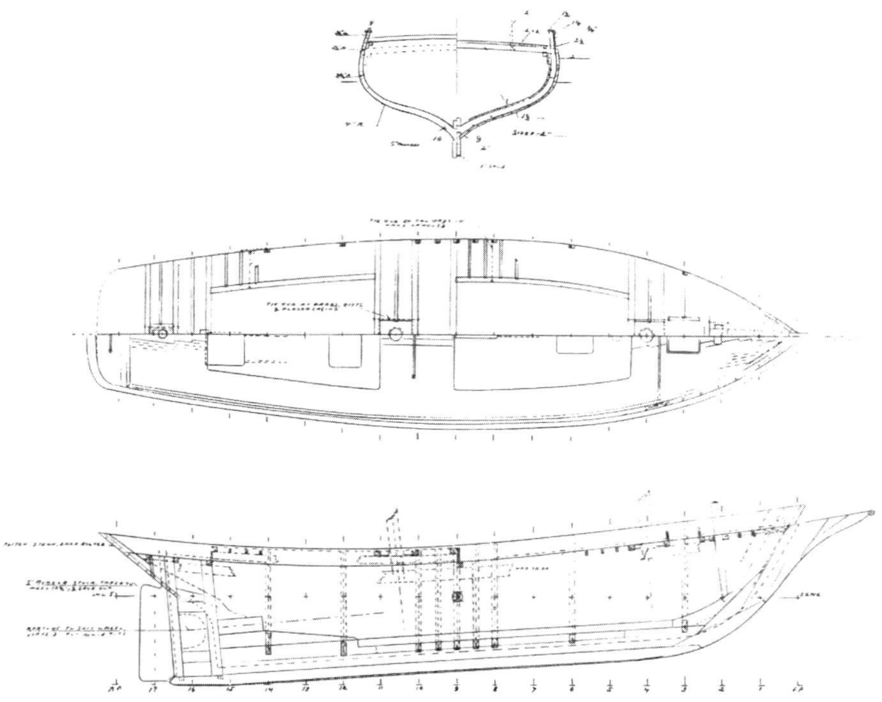

Construction drawings and a half-model (opposite) of the *Joseph W. Russell*, which was built at the Lash Brothers yard in Friendship, Maine, and named after the founder of the City of New Bedford. (R.D. Culler photo)

10 percent of his designs ever were built. This includes his small craft, which raises the percentage somewhat.

These vessels are of a size and type capable of extended cruising, and voyaging, too. The *Russell* has recently been sailing out of St. Thomas, U.S. Virgin Islands, and *Fiddler's Green* crossed the Atlantic and is now homeported at St. Malo, France. She once created a sensation at an international sail gathering in Britain.

Beyond the choice of inside or outside ballast, I feel that these two vessels illuminate clearly Pete's philosophy of adapting traditional working schooner rigs and hulls for today's uses. I quote from his notes on the Russell's plans: "Easy motion, light, air, good stove, clock with a hearty tick, pleasant cabin, and a ship that is good to the feel and sight, seems more satisfactory than one that is only scientifically correct."

Length between perpendiculars: 46 feet 7½ inches
Molded length on waterline: 39 feet
Beam: 13 feet 7 inches
Molded depth: 7 feet 5 inches
Draft: 7 feet 1 inch
Sail area: 1,153 square feet
Displacement: 48,000 pounds

Pinky Schooner For Warren Lemaster

This pinky schooner design is informative in many ways. It serves to show Captain Pete's talent for adapting traditional design features to today's pleasure uses, without losing sight of the original inspiration. In addition, several unique Culler details are shown clearly.

The design came about through Pete's West Coast connection, Bruce Northrup, a capable builder with several fine Culler vessels behind him. He presently builds to his own designs. Warren Lemaster had sailed with Northrup aboard the Culler 54-foot Baltimore clipper *Lizard King*, and was much impressed.

Lemaster desired a clipper pinky. The Bay of Fundy pilot schooner *Dove* was given as an example of what he was after.

The pink stern is an ancient form (some would say old-fashioned), its roots being in the Old World, but its application flourished in the working vessels of New England. The pinky's distinctive tombstone and bulwark arrangement allows greater deck area and ability on a double-ended hull. New England pinkies have a deserved reputation for great ability, capacity, and seakindly motion. As long as one keeps the original character of these types firmly in mind, they are simple, economical, and practical to construct, maintain, and sail. The Old Man felt right at home with this project.

Sharp, deep, and slim, this vessel is very well balanced in hull and rig. Her sections are the wineglass shape that Pete favored in all his designs. A preference for this shape results in fair diagonals for ease of planking, good body for capacity, and a tendency toward sharp lines for speed. This pinky's keel has much drag, and is straight for ease of construction and haulout. It is full length, without scarfs, primarily because the vessel was to be built on the West Coast, where there are still long, thick timbers available. When Bruce Northrup was building *Lizard King*, he asked the Old Man if it was necessary to make the keel out of so many pieces. Pete answered, "No, if you can get a timber long and thick enough, it could be built in one piece." Bruce replied, "Sure, we got timber that size." The Captain chuckled about that one for a week. If *you* can't find timber of sufficient size, by all means scarf the keel.

This pinky has a nicely shaped clipper head, which is balanced by the sharply raking sternpost. The clipper head was used frequently by Captain Pete, especially on his schooners. You will find the shape drawn for this vessel quite similar to those on Pete's other clipper bowed craft. It is beautifully proportioned and well worth the time and expense. At one time, a client for whom Pete had designed three schooners was grumbling about the trouble involved in that clipper bow. He insisted that the next one would have to be without so much headwork. Pete said, "If you want a schooner without a proper head, find someone else to design it."

Although of sharp lines, this vessel's 24-ton displacement is well distributed throughout its length. This usually results in a lack of sensitivity to changes of lead, but Howard Chapelle discovered that wasn't the case in his pinky *Glad Tidings*. I quote from an article he wrote about the vessel in the February 1938 issue of *Yachting*.

"The boat is quite sensitive to longitudinal trim more than I supposed she would be. When by the head, she is somewhat slow and uncertain in stays, particularly when her masts are given little rake. Apparently she handles best where there is a little reverse lead (that is, when the center of effort is abaft the center of lateral plane). When on her designed waterline, and with the proper rake to her masts, she comes around quickly and certainly, carries a small weather helm, and steers easily. She can be made to steer herself close-hauled and reaching when in trim."

Although of finer lines, Lemaster's pinky is somewhat reminiscent of *Glad Tidings* in hull shape. Pete was quite familiar with and appreciative of that vessel.

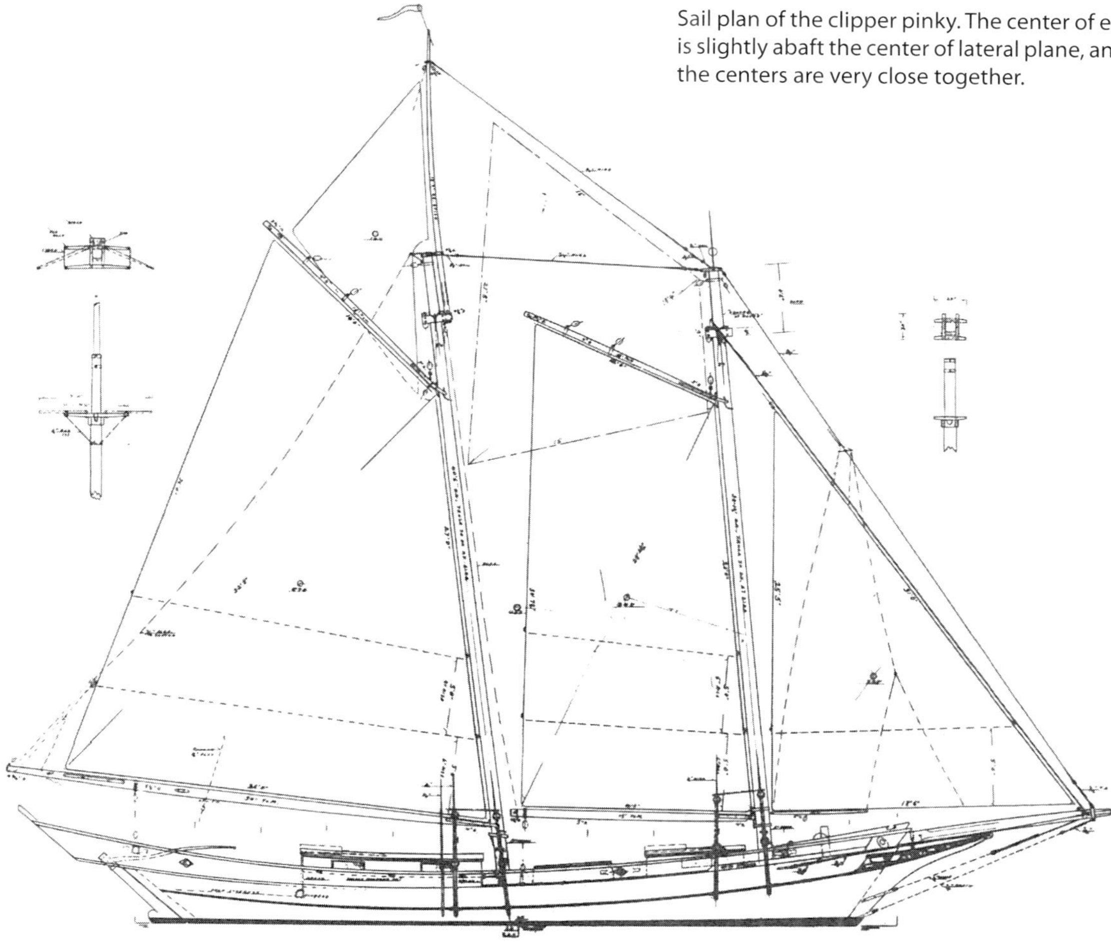

Sail plan of the clipper pinky. The center of effort is slightly abaft the center of lateral plane, and all the centers are very close together.

You will note that the pinky shown here has reverse lead, and that all her centers are very close together. This reminds me of a builder's expression: If, on paper, you can cover a vessel's centers with your thumb, or on the actual vessel with a bucket (no size being mentioned), she will sail (no mention of how well). Now there's a "rule of thumb" for you!

Although the working sail plan for this pinky is somewhat modest (her lowers total 1,154 square feet), with her sharp hull she should be quite a smart sailer. At any rate, the topsail and fisherman too are really working sails. These will pep things up considerably when in use.

Pete used the standard pungy jib arrangement for the headsail. Two headsails will not work. Most pinkies did not have them. It is interesting to note that there is a lot of pungy in this rig, although it is longer on the base. Gear is best kept to a minimum and it is yachtlike, and that characteristic jaunty topmast is well sprung forward. The fore and main should be rigged for lazyjacks with light stuff. With the topping lifts as shown, this will make the rig most manageable.

The vessel's construction methods are those Pete favored for many of his larger designs—double-sawn frames; full-length caulked ceiling; square, plank-laid deck with nibbed ends into kingplank and waterways, these being jogged down into the deck beams; stout shelf and clamp with lodging and hanging knees in way of the mast partners; and plenty of tie rods for the carlins. The knightheads and hawse timbers are prominent and integral to the vessel's construction. Pete suggested the inclusion of catheads, which is good advice. Glad Tidings had them and they worked out well in practice.

The raised quarterdeck is something of a trademark with the Old Man. This allows greater headroom in the wings, is strong construction, and breaks any sea that may come aboard. There are large spilling ports at the forward end of the break. These hang on trunnions, inboard, and will therefore hang closed when not spilling water. Spilling ports

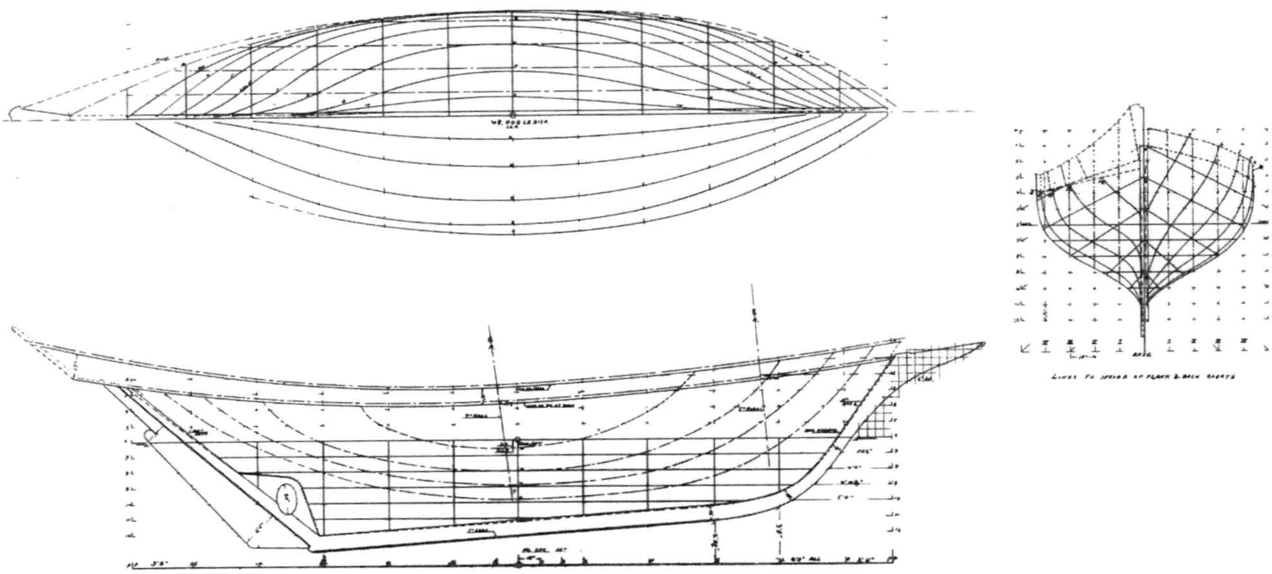

The pinky's lines.

that stay open are irritating to the eye, in my opinion.

The Old Man's arrangement of house windows is distinctive and good looking. He had a definite way of doing it. As he said: "On windows, my practice has been to have them solid on the forward house, with opening ports in the ends of both houses, and opening windows on the after house—with or without wood shutters outside. I like the shutters. How the windows are hung is somewhat hard to describe, but it's a wood trunnion on top, in a slotted side casing, with inside water stop at bottom, and outside stops at sides and top. The windows hinge inboard, so screens, if any, can be left rigged. They are flush so the shutters will work."

This vessel has a hold as designed. The Old Man included a hold, if the vessel was suited to it, whenever a client would allow it. I think they add a lot, and could be useful in many ways. Stop and think about it.

The design calls for cemented bilges and will probably raise a few eyebrows. Before you decide against it, however, allow Pete to comment: "Cemented bilges do not cause rot if the vessel is always afloat. It's standard commercial practice. The only preparation of surface is to have it and ALL CRANNIES clean. Read Claud Worth on how to cement a vessel—he was a most thorough man. Hold off on the cement until the vessel is caulked and payed, This last should not be done till waterways are buttoned down or there is risk of raising the sheer. In fact, I would wait till she could stand a water test with a hose or other means, even though it might be handier to do the cement before. A good water flushing will get her quite clean: have drain holes at the low points, port and starboard. I like to cement the ends, too, so things will drain, and ceil the ends where fustiness starts. Pitch is good if used on a smaller boat that does not want the weight of cement. Personally, I like to cement a boat afloat, as they do in Maine. One can control trim and ballasting to a certain extent. Also, there is less weight to handle in launching. It's not the easy way, but I think the best."

With this method you also get to check for leaks before they get locked in with cement. It's a real drag to break up new cement to get at and fix a leak. With the deep nature of this pinky, there should be no problem keeping the cement from encroaching on the headroom.

Pinkies were developed around the deep and rockbound coasts of Maine, Massachusetts, and the Maritimes. The design is a good choice for the Pacific Northwest, where many of the same conditions exist. If your waters and requirements are similar, consider this fine, clipper-bowed, topsail pinky. I don't think you can go wrong.

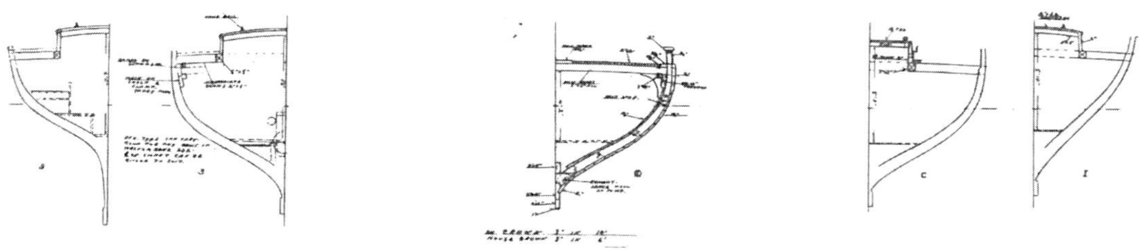

Construction drawings for the pinky.

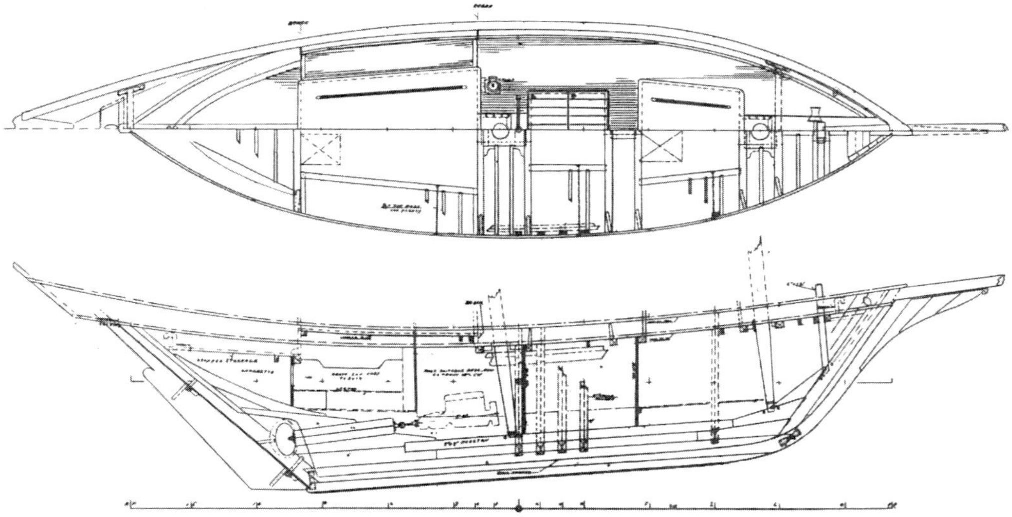

Length between perpendiculars: 52 feet
Molded beam: 14 feet 8 inches
Draft: 6 feet 9 inches
Sail area: 1,511 square feet (lowers)
Displacement: 29.5 long tons

Schooner *Integrity* For Waldo Howland

The *Integrity* was Captain Pete's masterpiece. He had "done the hull of it," from modeling and designing to building and skippering. She is as handsome as they come, and during her day she was considered the finest schooner on the coast.

Her owner, Waldo Howland, named the vessel *Integrity* after witnessing the methods, materials, and craftsmanship that went into her. Under Howland's ownership, maintenance and upkeep too were of the "finest kind." She was kept in pristine condition. From the time of launching, in December 1962, at the former berth of the whaler *Charles W. Morgan* on Colonel Greene's estate, until she was sold to Caribbean interests in 1970, she spread the word all along the Atlantic seaboard and throughout the West Indies that this was the way it was done at Concordia Company. A finer calling card could not have been found.

Integrity proved, over the years, to be a smart, powerful sailer and a very comfortable craft for those who sailed on her. Just prior to being sold, she was chartered, and made a transatlantic crossing to Ireland. From there she sailed to Spain, and then back via the southern trades to the West Indies. She returned to Padanaram having made better-than-average passages and having weathered more than one gale on the long voyage.

The luck in her horseshoe, nailed to the winch post, finally ran out after she was sold to a partnership that intended to use her for chartering in the

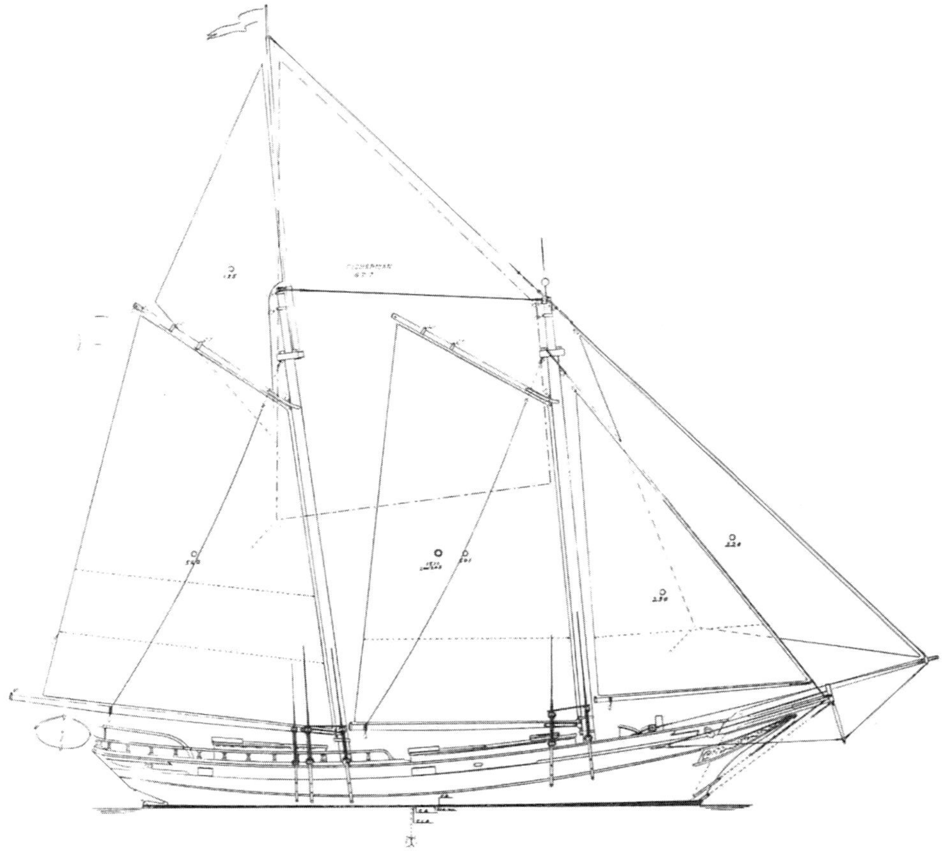

Integrity's sail plan.

Caribbean. She was abandoned in a storm off Cape Hatteras on her way south. Thus began a long, sad story that mercifully ended when she sank while being towed. The person who was towing her, Frank Mulville, has written a book, *Death of the Schooner Integrity*, about her post-Howland life; it makes very interesting reading. *Integrity* now rests on the bottom of the Atlantic Ocean.

Just prior to Integrity's launching in November 1962, an article on her design and construction appeared in *Maine Coast Fisherman* (now *National Fisherman*), with extensive comments by Captain Pete. These follow:

"Mr. Howland wanted a schooner on the coaster model, but he did not require the same carrying capacity, so we worked up a design along the lines of a fast packet schooner of moderate draft and very clean lines.

"Her length is 52 feet overall, 44 feet LWL, with a 15-foot beam and 6 feet 9 inches draft. She'll have a main-topmast, flying-jibboom rig with a rather large foresail, and fairly sharp rise of floor and sharp entrance, although she'll be full on the deck line. Run is extremely long and fine, which meant the use of a longer-than-usual quarterdeck to get the required room below.

"This also allows for a very nice engine room amidships with required tank space that won't affect trim. Unusual in these days of things being built right in place—and wrecking a vessel to get at them later—is the large caulked-up hatch over the engine room.

"The New Bedford area has built many vessels in the past with native materials and labor. We decided to do it the same way, with the only modern concessions being electric power, autos to get to work in, supermarkets to feed our faces, and, of course, modern wages. We also decided to use an iron keel and shoes of 8,000 pounds to 'better massage a rock with,' as one of the workmen so aptly put it.

"Otherwise it's all done the old way, with no use of materials that were not always used in vessels of this class. The construction would not have been thought unusual in the 1880s—but it would be now. It includes all oak framing for anything that is a real strength member.

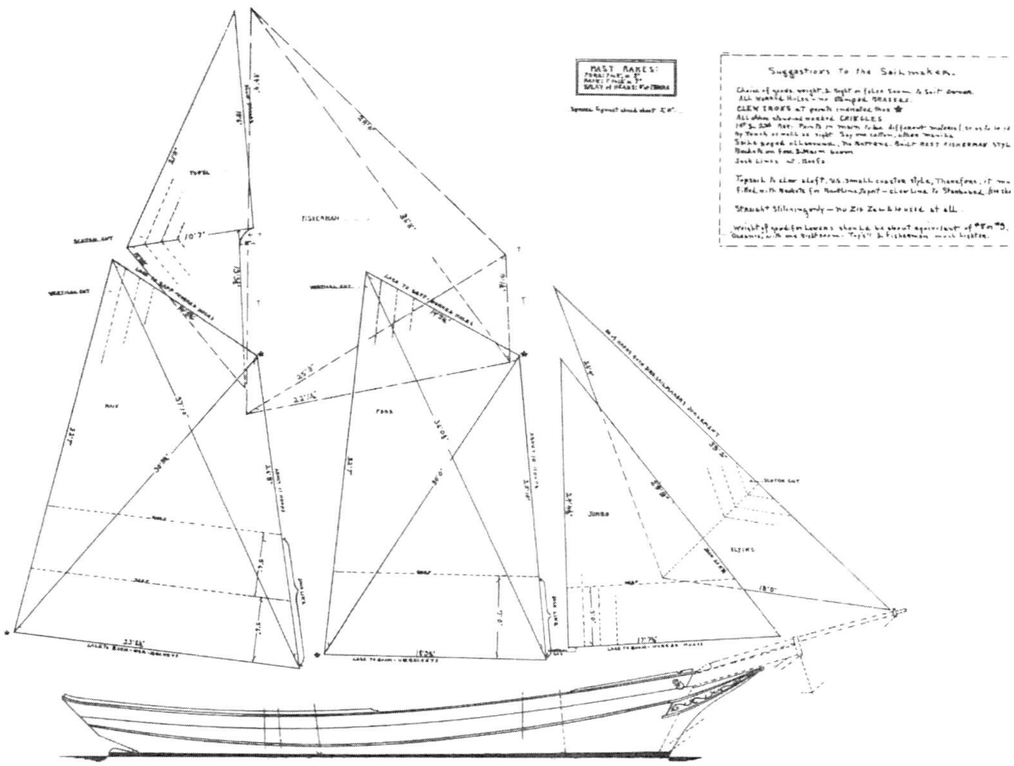

The sailmaker's plan.

"She has sawn frames molded 6 inches by 6 inches at throats, a ship keelson, oak bottom until clear of the sharp turns, then 1¾-inch hard pine, white pine decks, and so on. Suffice it to say, some well-known old-timers familiar with such work pronounced her better than average compared to the days when such things were commonplace.

"Great attention is placed on having a well-built vessel by the old standards, as well as making her handy, smart, and handsome. While she was intended to be plainly finished, we used traditional moldings and beads well suited to the type.

"One is often asked if it's practical to build a vessel of this type today. We think it is. These vessels are very fine and easy seaboats. Questions of weight of stores, storage space, and trim are small matters—this type can carry.

"Of course, the subject of speed comes up right away, and over a closed course under working sail, it is still a moot point as far as I am concerned. The working sail is the joker, as these vessels carry a big rig, some of which could be considered light sails on a less-stiff hull. They tend to be very good drifters in light airs. At sea they can be driven hard over long periods in comparative comfort.

"This particular hull has a long waterline, sharp with good drag, so it can be driven and still steer well—we look for her to be on the smart side. Auxiliary power will be a diesel in the 100 h.p. range.

"To be practical again, all shipbuilding is costly. However, it seems a vessel of this type can be built for less than modern yacht construction of considerably less tonnage.

"Now for a note or two on the design procedure and building. First, a model was cut and hashed around a while, and also approved by the local 'skippers emeritus.' Then lines were lifted and simple calculations made, with slight corrections. It's surprising how well things fall into place by starting with the cutting of a model. So much that is now arrived at by other means just plain works out by the model method, besides giving the feeling of the craft to those working on her.

"Lines were lofted in the usual way, and all bevels and frames were taken off the floor by a form of rising square and then produced in timbers with a tilt-head bandsaw, as of yore."

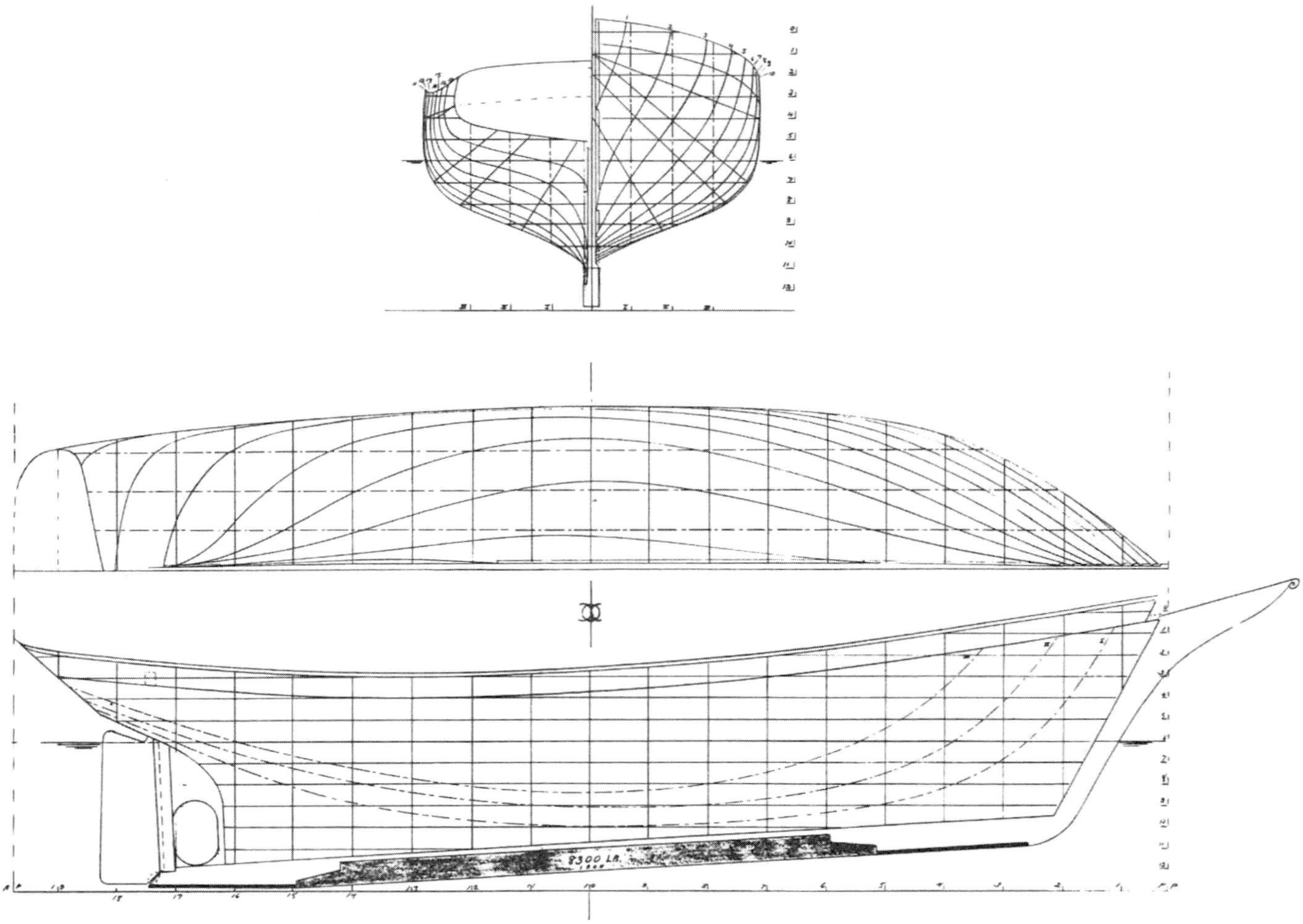

Above and below: *Integrity*, lines and accommodations.

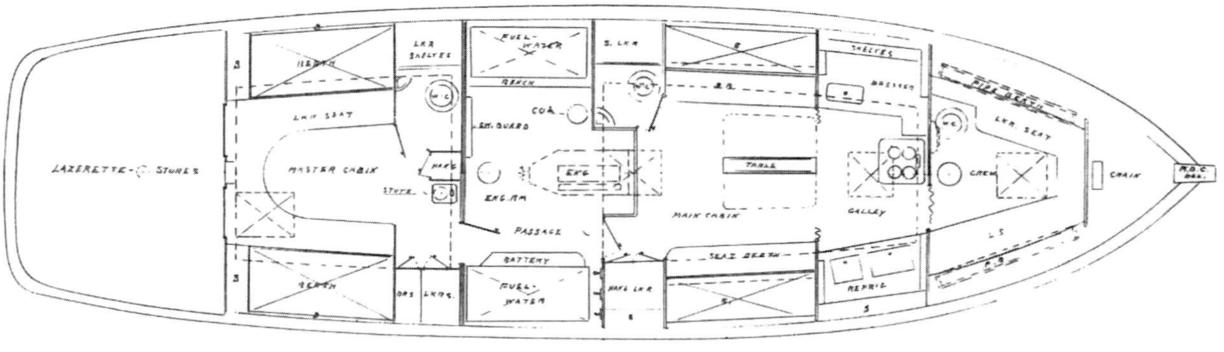

Frames set up. She is a sawn-frame vessel. Each frame, made up of doubled futtocks, is a mold that gives the vessel her shape. The frames are then "dubbed" fair and planked up. (R.D. Culler photo)

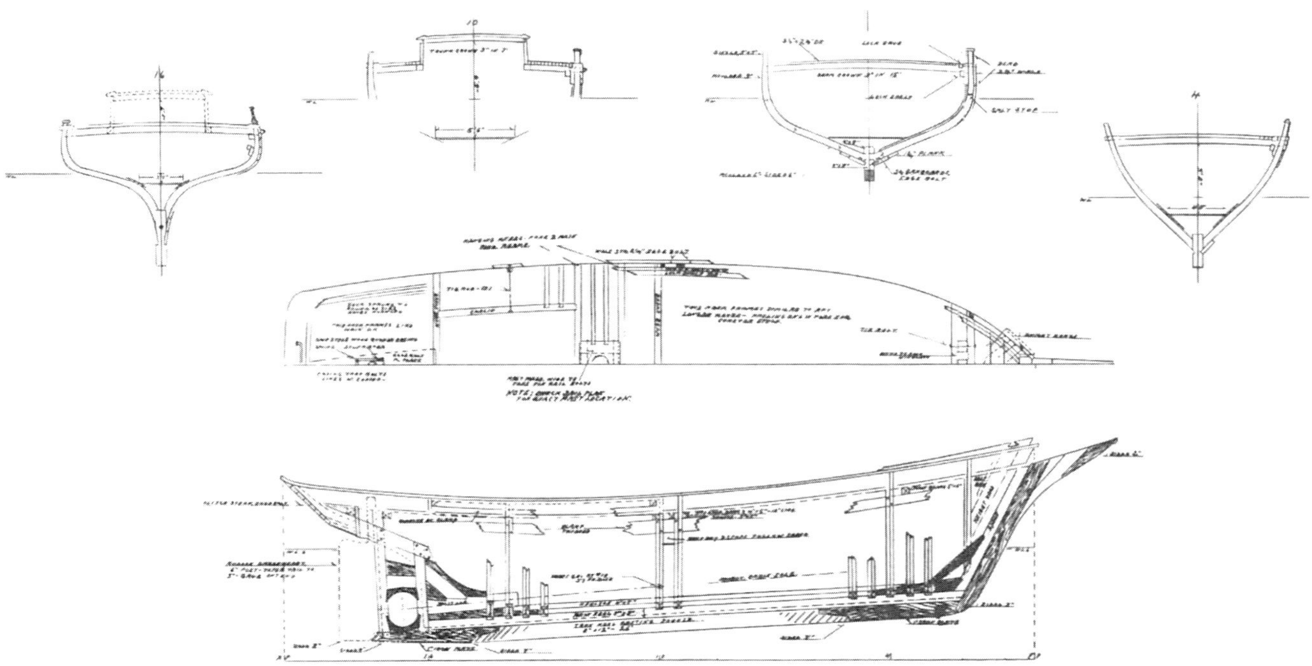

Construction drawings for *Integrity*.

Waldo Howland holds the half-model of his schooner.

An excellent view of the large quarterdeck. (R.D. Cullerphoto)

Integrity underway. Visible are her traditional "coaster T-head" smokestacks. (Norman Fortier photo)

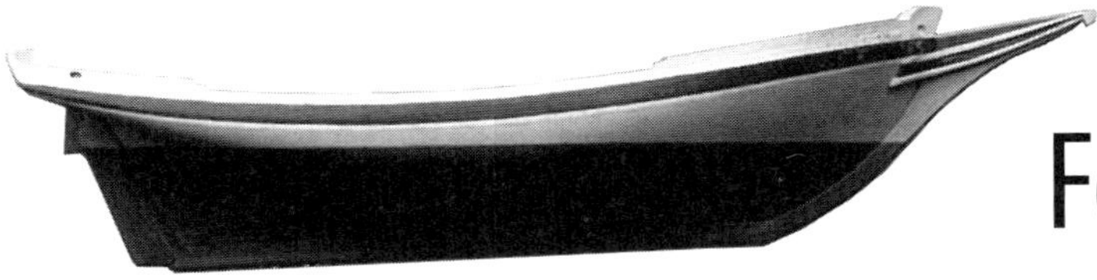

She Pungy Schooner For Captain Eddie Crosby

Model of a "He" Pungy schooner that Pete Culler intended fo his own use. (John Burke photo)

Length between perpendiculars: 45 feet
Molded beam: 14 feet 8 inches
Molded depth: 5 feet 6½ inches
Sail area: 1,546 square feet
Displacement: 42,500 pounds

How do you tell a "she" pungy from a "he" pungy? One has a centerboard case and the other doesn't.

A couple of sailors sat down and put this design together. It certainly shows the influence of two men who knew the sea intimately. She is fast, rakish, and fine ended. There's plenty of sail to push her slippery hull along at an exhilarating clip. As a rule, pungies were good-looking craft, and as Pete has stated, they could be daintily pretty. Every sailor likes a good-looking boat. It is readily apparent from this design that the Old Man and Captain Eddie Crosby pursued this goal intently, seeking primarily a handsome hull and rig and letting other considerations fall where they may. There is not much in the way of accommodations for such a long craft, but oh, what a vessel!

Although speculative on my part, I believe this design began during a discussion between the two men on pungy travels in Cape Cod waters. According to Chapelle, writing in *The National Watercraft Collection*: "In the decade 1845-55 New England fishermen who were seeking faster vessels obtained a considerable number of Chesapeake Bay-built schooners, particularly for the oyster fishery at Wellfleet. These were employed in the summer in the mackerel fishery and in the winter to transport oysters from the Chesapeake Bay to Cape Cod. Some were shoal-draft keel vessels of the pungy type, others were centerboarders... but all had sharp lines and were designed for speed." Chapelle goes on to state that this regional exchange had a marked influence on the introduction of the sharp-model schooner to the New England fishing fleet.

Direct descendants of the Baltimore clippers, the smaller pungies carried out commerce throughout the Chesapeake Bay area, and beyond, until just 40 years ago. With their lean, rakish hulls, the craft were noted for their speed rather than their cargo capacity. Where swiftness was required, these vessels served well. Primarily, this entailed carrying farm goods to city markets and transporting fish and oysters. Some entered the Bahama fruit trade—green-picked fruit ripened en route in the hold. Take too long getting to your destination and you have a worthless cargo.

As the harbors and rivers of the Chesapeake silted up and became shallow, a shoaler centerboard model evolved—the "she" pungy. I don't know what cargo Crosby had in mind for the vessel's hold (perhaps reptilian T-shirts with freshly starched collars for Nantucket preppies), but I very much favor it, for it sets the tone. Nothing yachty, no fooling around. She's a pungy, through and through.

These vessels were characterized by sharp but short entrances, with greatest beam well forward, a sharplined, slight-displacement underbody incorporating long and fine runs, long heads, and high, thin quarters with the typical pungy double transom.

The lower transom set into the sternpost and began as a large chunk of wood. It was then hewed to shape and rabbeted on top to accept deck planking, and on the bottom for the hull plank. Large quarter knees secured it to the bulwarks. The upper transom was built up of edge-fastened planks and was secured to the top edge of the lower transom log. The rudderpost pierced this upper transom; sometimes "fashion pieces" were let into the sides to hide the edge grain. It was usual for the lower transom to be parallel with the load waterline; this gave the stern a distinctive T-shape. Although this may sound difficult, it is not. As Pete said, "The pungy has a rather uncomplicated stern, though it may look fierce to one not used to its construction. Though building this stern takes an artistic eye and some adze work, it eliminates framing and a built-up rudderport, and it also simplifies the

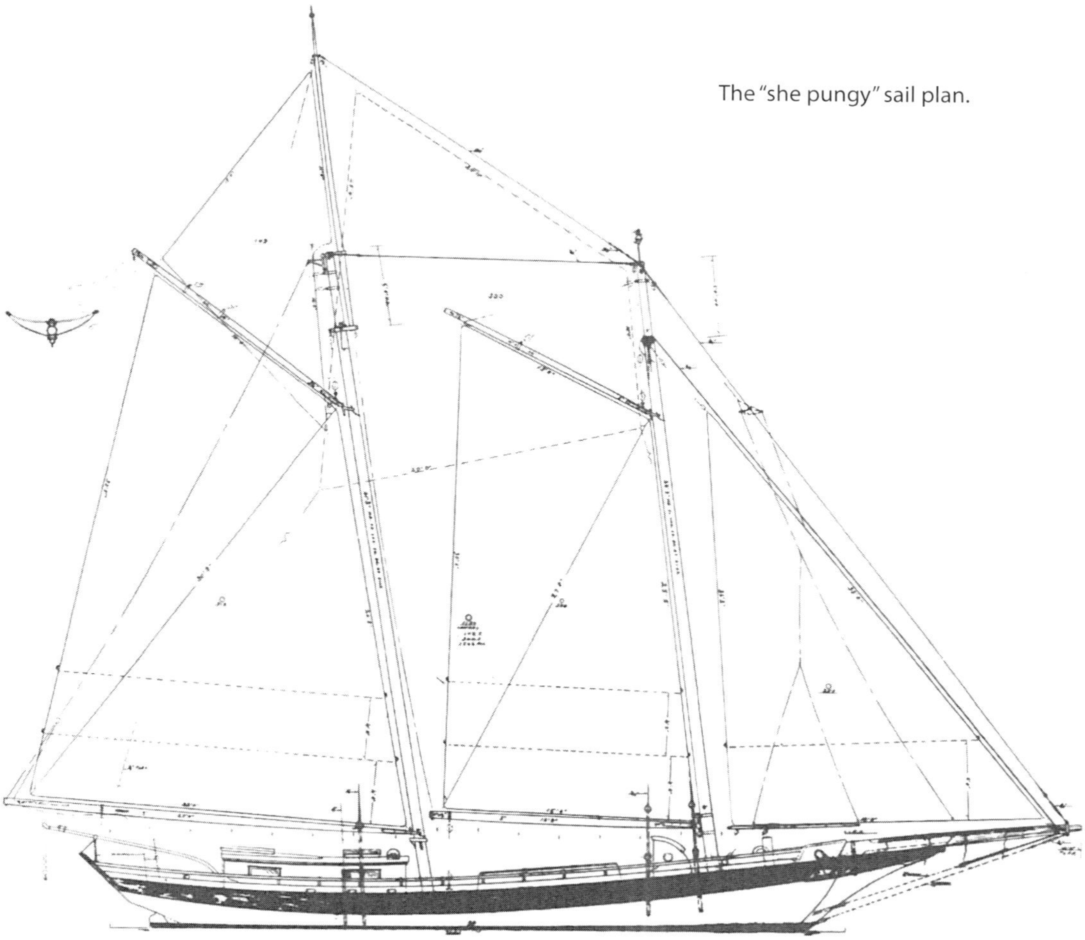

The "she pungy" sail plan.

taffrail work. If properly designed, these craft steer very well, so they are suited to a tiller."

Many pungies were steered with a wheel. Crosby opted for this system, the after house being rather far aft for protection (pungies are wet) and to increase the rather snug accommodations. There are pipe davits for the small boat. This she pungy follows closely in style the deck arrangement of the famous pungy *Amanda F. Lewis*. Forward of the trunk cabin is the mainmast, offset to starboard, with the deck pumps close by, and the main hatch, divided by the offset (to port) centerboard.

The centerboard is lifted by a tackle, with monkey tail rod, reeved through a block at the hounds. Forward of the main hatch is a booby hatch for the fo'c's'le, with deck winches forward of the foremast. The knightheads and hawse timbers are left prominent. These knights and hawse timbers are edge-drifted to each other and to the stem, the drifts being placed carefully so they will be clear of the hawseholes, which are cut after all is in place. Even with careful drift placement, it is not uncommon to find yourself hacking through a drift when cutting the holes.

Here's one method of cutting hawseholes. Determine the diameter and angle by considering the size of your ground tackle and its angle at anchor. Now, even though the hawsehole is a cylinder, its shape on both inside and outside faces of the timber will be elliptical because the angle of the cylinder's axis is not normal or square to the timber face. To get the shape of this ellipse, simulate the cylinder axis by boring a pilot hole through the timber at the proper angle and inserting an iron rod that fits snugly but is free to move both radially and in and out of the pilot hole. An arm is fitted square to one end of the rod. At the end of the arm there is a longish scriber set to the radius of the hawsehole—in appearance it is very much like a circle cutter. Now scribe the timber face by turning the rod, making sure to keep the arm square to it. Repeat on the opposite face, then chisel out the hole. Refer to the catalog of the Lunenburg Foundry of Halifax, Nova Scotia, for making the pattern for the

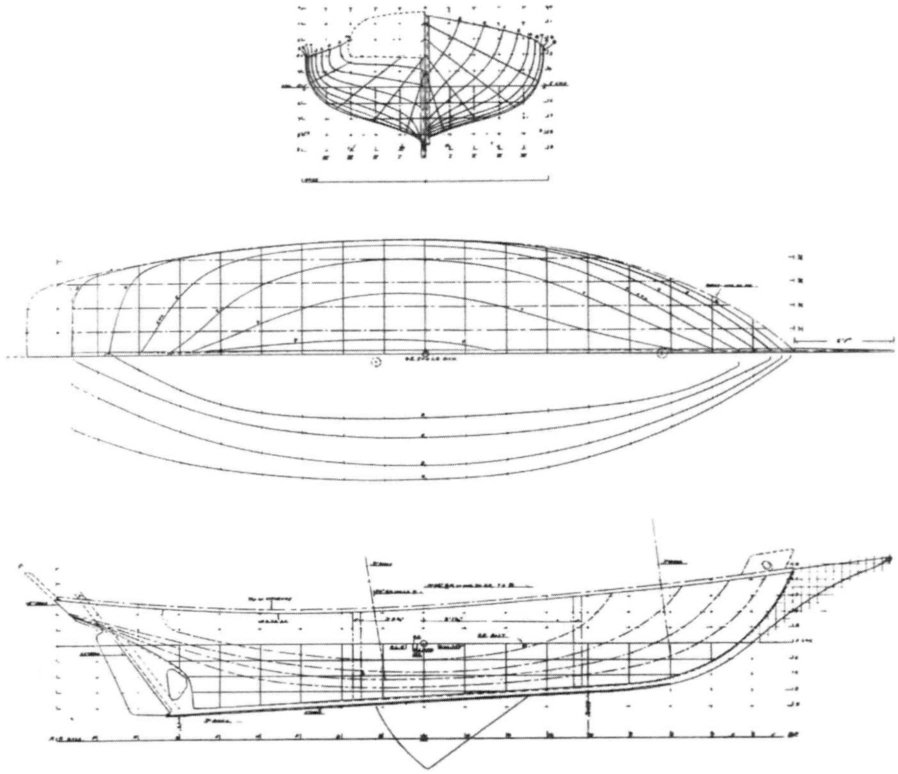

Lines of the she pungy.

hawsepipe. Lunenburg will also cast it for you.

The long head with pole sprit is characteristic of the type, and Pete gave this pungy a beautiful one. Be sure to hog down the steeve of that nose pole.

Pungies were known as much for their rig as for anything else; this one follows the proportions closely. High-hatted and lightly sparred, with a minimum of gear, their ample area drove these clipper hulls at high speed, in any breeze.

Robert Burgess, the noted chronicler of Chesapeake Bay craft, was particularly enamored of pungies. I quote from his fine book, *Chesapeake Sailing Craft:*

"There is always something exciting about the rakish sailing craft of the Chesapeake, particularly the pungies. By rakish I mean the lean hulls with pleasing sheer, fine lines, tall raking masts, with thin main topmast bowed slightly forward. The stout bowsprits, shaped by master shipwrights and unlike the pole-like spars found on most of the schooners and rams, had been fashioned so that their upper surfaces seemed to dip downward slightly as if being pulled by the bobstay chains, straining to hold the craft in leash. This combination of curves and daintiness imparted the feeling of swiftness even if a particular pungy was not noted for smartness."

Many today do not understand the reason for the bowed topmast, which, of course, was a feature seen on craft other than pungies. It simply allowed the topsail to set flat or belly forward according to the lay of the wind and the course.

The traditional pungy color scheme was bottle-green wales and "pungy-pink" topsides, and a yellow bead carried around into the stern embellishments, encompassing the name. The stern itself was often an apple green. White doublings and small spars, and white log rail and waterways. Sounds odd, but for pungies it worked, and was very attractive.

Once again, I'll quote from Robert Burgess: "Even now I can see, in my mind's eye, a pungy drifting into Baltimore on a misty early fall morning. The wind is ever so slight, just barely filling her sails, but her sleek lines and appearance suggest more motion than she is actually making. There is a curl of water around her stem and faint ripples follow in her barely noticeable wake.... If she chooses to continue up the harbor to a dock, she creates a scene purely Chesapeake, harking back to the days when the even more rakish privateers and Baltimore clippers slipped up those very same waters more than a century before."

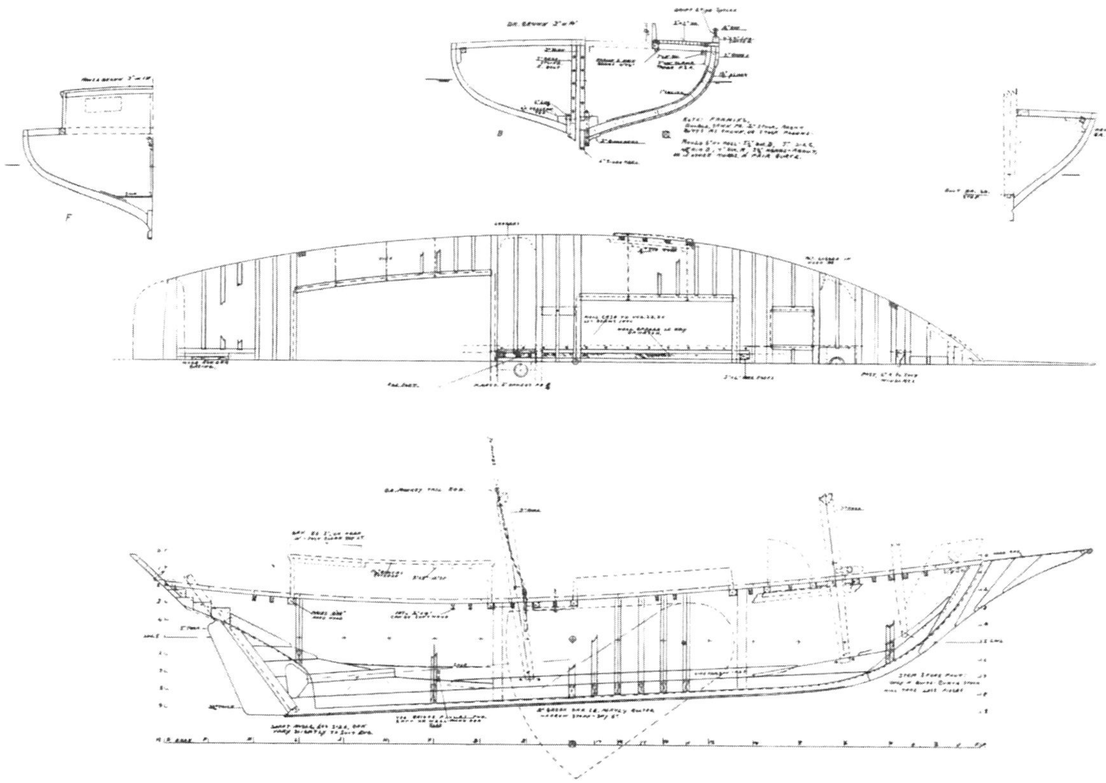

Construction and accommodations drawings for Captain Eddie Crosby's pungy.

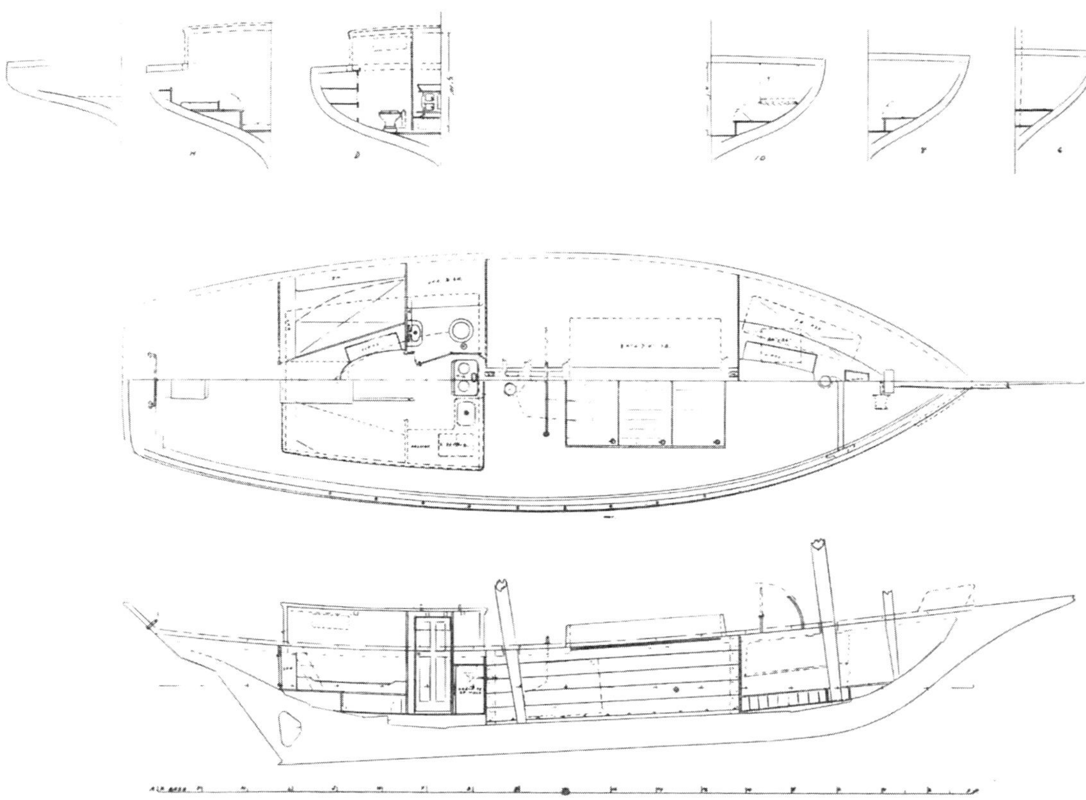

Baltimore Clipper Schooner *Lizard King* For Bruce Northrup

Length between perpendiculars: 53 feet 9½ inches
Molded length on waterline: 45 feet
Molded beam: 14 feet 11 inches
Draft: 7 feet 2½ inches
Sail area: 1,592 square feet (lowers)
Displacement: 56,300 pounds

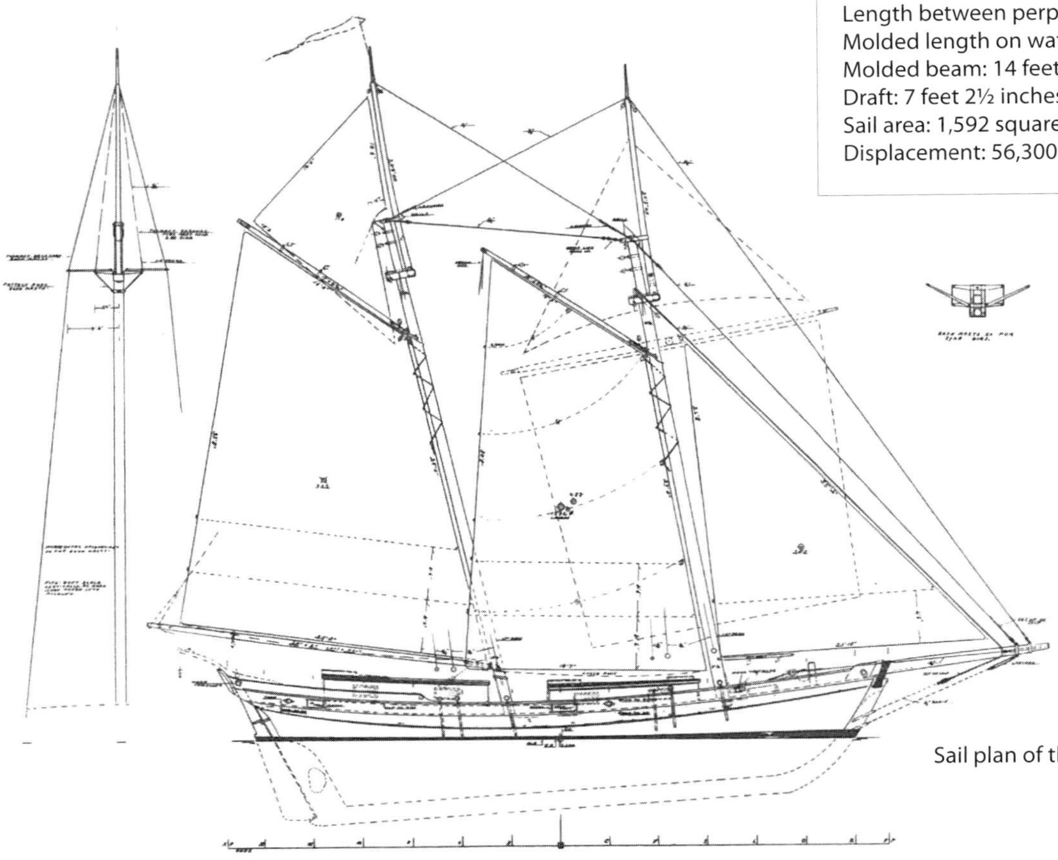

Sail plan of the *Lizard King*.

Comments by Pete Culler

The rig on this vessel is not excessive by some old standards, yet it will provide enough canvas for general use (she might be a bit short for the Slave Trade). It looks as if she will be quite handy under the foresail; I would think she would work very well under it alone.

I don't know just what the spar stock will be, but if there is much choice, use something reasonably light in weight. The dimensions for spars as given are about right for the rig, and would be fine in a light-grade fir, spruce, or, here in the East, white pine—at least for the masts. With a bit of common sense, there should be no problems with this rig. The details shown are in keeping with the type, yet the rig uses some modern-day materials. The rope gammoning you can suit yourself on, though I see nothing wrong with it when properly done. The stem should be well through-bolted fore and aft in that area.

You are no doubt struck by the height of the houses—this is a weakness of the type. These craft are shoal and fine, so there is little actual hull depth. Increasing the freeboard is not the way out, though it's often tried. It just puts all the deck weight high up and increases windage, besides spoiling the looks. The great crown to the houses is not good either, as it adds cost and makes them difficult to work on, stow gear on, or sit on. I find 3 inches of crown, the width of the house, is about right.

There is the matter of room for ballast also. Depending on the weight of construction materials, she might require 10,000 to 15,000 pounds of ballast. Naturally, tanks, engine, and other heavy gear

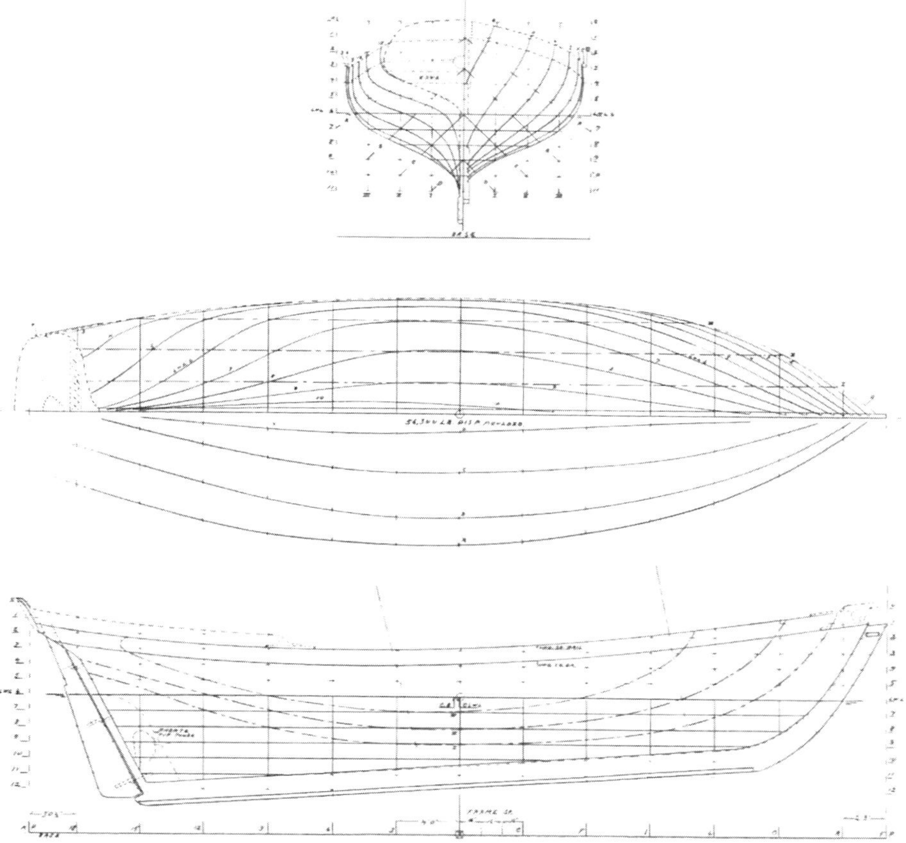

Lines of the *Lizard King.*

make this a variable. I have made an arbitrary floor line, using WL 8 amidships, and 6 inches above that in the middle of the house aft, figuring the house heights from that. One could set lower and still have good floor width, but that crowds the ballast space. One must also consider that the frames will mold about 6 inches plus ceiling, which takes up more room.

Here's an idea I use in building any boats under my supervision, regardless of how much data I may have on the weights to go in her. (You will soon know about what stock, engine, and tankage you will use.) When the vessel is along to the point of starting the houses, mock up a floor, having due regard for ballast room, and see just what you can gain here and there. Mock up a house section, too. I rarely increase house crown, for it's miserable with too much. If I do, it's very little. I usually find I can cut down height a few inches. This headroom business is a source of great bother, for most yachtsmen are headroom-happy. Thus, it's difficult to get them interested in shoal, fast hulls.

The hull seems quite easy and should sail well. A waterline of 45 feet was needed to get the required room; these craft by nature are not very roomy, as they are shoal in hull and fine ended. I feel she will steer and handle very well. Also, she should be an easy seaboat.

I kept her slightly full forward to bear the square yard. She will, however, do quite well as a main-topmaster with no fore topmast or yard.

Note that the stations are such that frames of 16-inch centers can be used—doubled, out of 3-inch or even 4-inch stuff. I think 3 inches is a bit light in fir, though it would be practical if the craft were well planked and ceiled. One could of course use heavy stuff in the lower parts of frames, with lighter stuff above, and in the ends. This was often done in clipper craft.

This design stacks up very well to the *Swift* and other craft of similar size and sharpness. Compared with Waldo Howland's *Integrity*, this vessel is about a foot longer all around, a bit more beamy, with less molded depth, though of greater heel draft, less tonnage, and slightly more sail area. Also, she is generally much sharper.

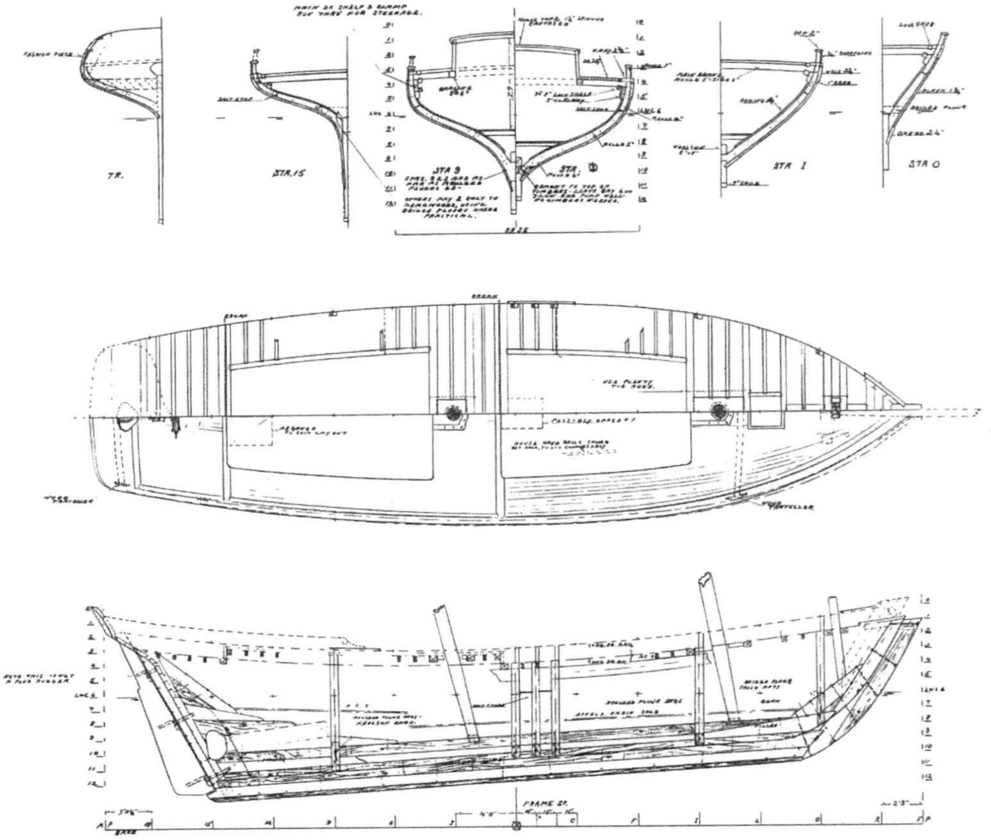

The Baltimore clipper's construction drawings.

I feel she should be a smart sailer, and do well on all points of sailing. Quality sails should make her handy by the wind. I feel one must always build a vessel well, and plenty stout, but in this design much consideration must be given to keeping down the weight of the upper works. Do this by the proper choice of stock, rather than by too-light construction, which could be weak and hard to keep tight.

I did not spend much time on the calculations of various ratios used in the comparison, to keep the hours down, but what I did shows very well against other craft of the same size and general type. The quarter beam is very long and flat for such a small vessel—14:1 ratio, if I remember correctly. This should, along with other factors, produce a vessel that is able to keep speed well under passage conditions.

While this sort of thing is helpful in comparing, I feel a lot of it is the effect rather than the cause of a wellbalanced hull. There have been too many paradoxes in the past to say a certain set of standards always makes a good or a poor boat.

I'm often struck by this when sailing my open Swampscott dory, which is a tiddly craft with a big rig for her power. Naturally, she is smart in light going. However, in blowing weather, under very short sail, she is a match or better for decked craft 10 to 15 times her weight! Just why, I still don't know, though I've given it much study. Possibly, it's not that she's so good, but that the others are poor.

I think this vessel will be a very nice seaboat, steering easily and laying-to well. Properly trimmed and ballasted, she should have an easy motion.

Assuming sawn fir frames, the more I think of the idea of graduating the siding, the more sense it makes. Consider it like this: Mold 6 inches tapering to 3 at the top timbers, which is about standard for this craft anyhow. In the middle three-fifths of the vessel, up to about the waterline, use 4-inch stock. This will, doubled, give 8-inch siding. From the waterline up, use 3-inch doubled, for a total of 6 inches. This will show steps in the frame sides, but no matter, since it planks and ceils over. The end fifths at bow and stern can be 3-inch stuff. This will keep the weight low, somewhat out of the ends, and put more wood in the bottom where ballast works. Also, it will provide a stout bottom for iron ballast.

Lizard King, full and by. (Bruce Northrup photo)

The first true Baltimore clipper built since the 1936 Chapelle-Robinson Swift, *Lizard King* take shape in 1969 under the able hands of Bruce Northrup and Paul Diack. (Courtesy Bruce Northrup)

This should not complicate lofting or framing at all, except in handling and paying for the heavier stock. As to lofting, layout, and molding, also bevels, one works from the center, so thickness does not matter. It's just more labor for man and saw. It's a thing to consider.

A construction plan is never complete enough—one can only do so much on a small scale. This is about as much as I supply for building at Concordia. *Integrity* had much less, though in that case, I was the boss shipwright.

In these days of poor imagination, and often a background that never makes one cope for oneself, I always have trouble getting any plan complete enough. What really seems to be wanted is every item and part to a very large scale, even full size, with the position of every bolt, nail, and screw shown. If by chance one fastener is shown in the way of another, there's always a beef. Naturally, plans so detailed for a vessel this size are economically impractical—they would cost as much as the vessel itself.

I think that what is here, namely, much more than proposed vessels of this type and period ever had, should be sufficient to build and rig her. As shown, the construction is pretty much as it has always been done, and still is done. The scantlings are sufficient, with some margin, for any of the usual shipbuilding woods.

Plenty of bolt iron, clinch rings, and galvanized ship spikes is all she needs—it always pays off to fasten well and closely. The sizes of everything are about standard for the tonnage.

The planking is thick enough to use a choker thread of cotton, then one of oakum. After all is made, and set back (except the garboard, which should be caulked but not made back till last), it can then be hawsed in. This really sets things up.

I would suggest that what few screw bolts are used, mostly odd length, should be made up out of standard bolt iron, using stock nuts, and clinch rings for heads. All ironwork can be galvanized, except for the rudder straps. It's worthwhile to make these out of bronze.

I think the main problem in building this vessel will be handling some of the timber. Yet, a couple of men who know what they are doing, along with some occasional just plain laborers, can make out. After all, a couple of us built Integrity's stern in place, for there was no way of lifting it as a unit. It must have weighed 15,000 pounds, being all white oak, and large anyhow for such a craft. Framing we did with a poor bandsaw, but three of us turned out two a day, from molding to bolting up.

The problem is always the same—how to get the required room in a vessel of a given type. Some additional tonnage, and more often, length, seems to be the only answer.

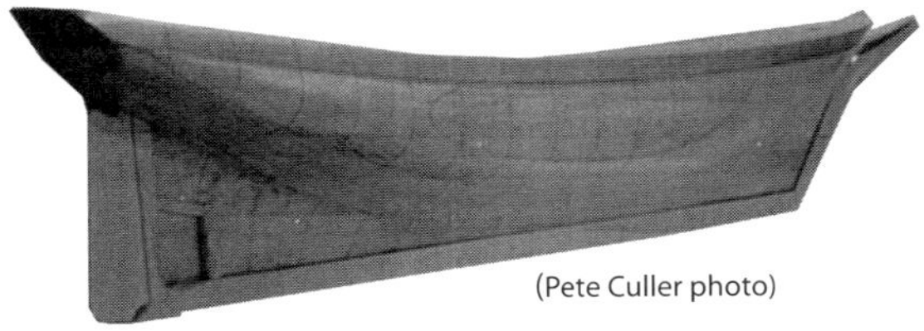

(Pete Culler photo)

Schooner *Gallant Lady* For Roy Grizzle

Length on deck: 60 feet 2 inches
Beam: 17 feet 3 inches
Draft: 8 feet 8 inches
Sail area: 3,125 square feet
Displacement: 53.5 tons

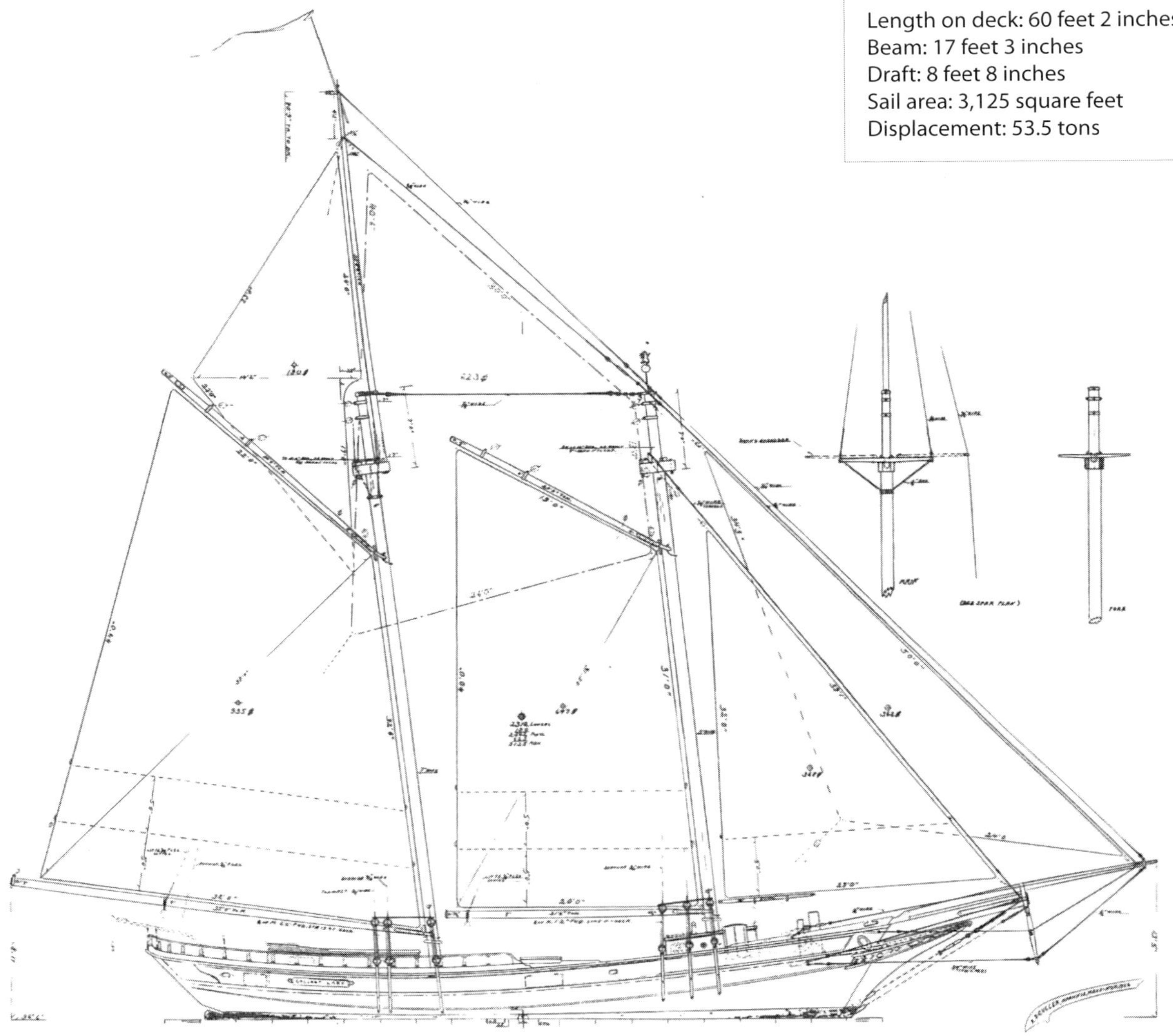

Gallant Lady's sail plan, an ample rig for a powerful hull.

In this schooner we begin to see what is possible with added length and displacement. For most of us, this size and tonnage are out of reach. However, for those who have both the commitment and the means, such a vessel must be exciting beyond description. Indeed, it must.

This is a deep-draft offshore vessel that uses the West Coast sealer type for inspiration. She was designed for Roy Grizzle of San Diego, California, in 1966. The vessel is reminiscent of the *Integrity* in that both serve to show Pete's idea of a proper schooner hull. This includes a straight raking stem rabbet with clipper head; a deep, prominent forefoot; straight keel with drag; a raking sternpost; and a short counter, with a flat, raking transom. Also, generally sharp ends and a good body; and hollow

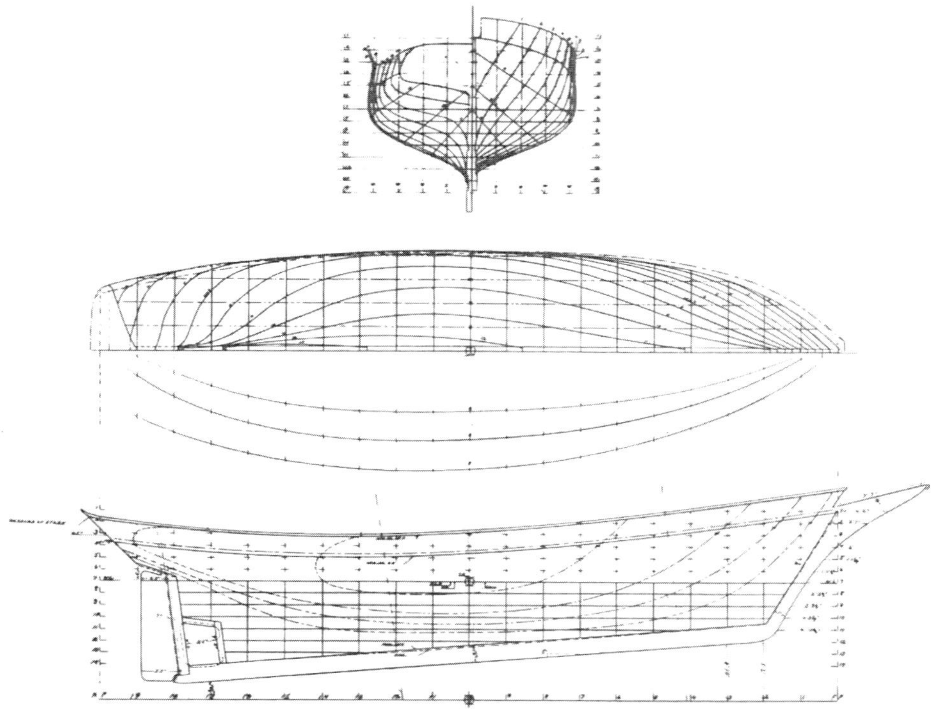

Above and below: Lines and construction drawings for the schooner *Gallant Lady*.

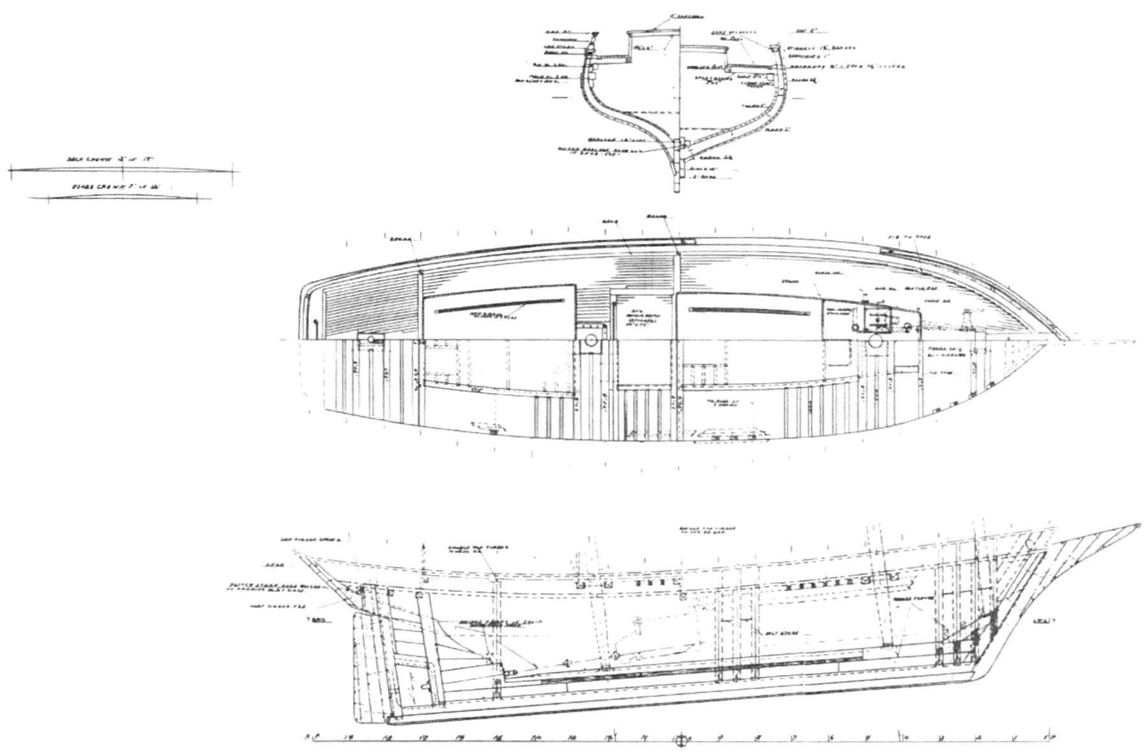

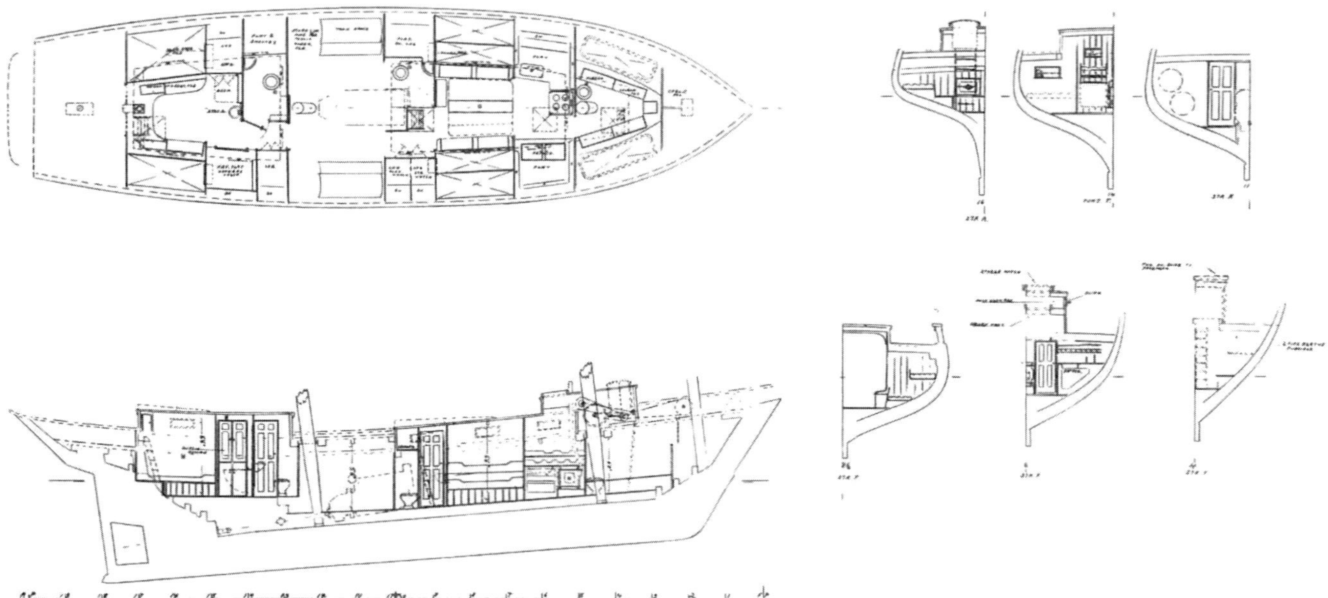

Accommodations and spar plans.

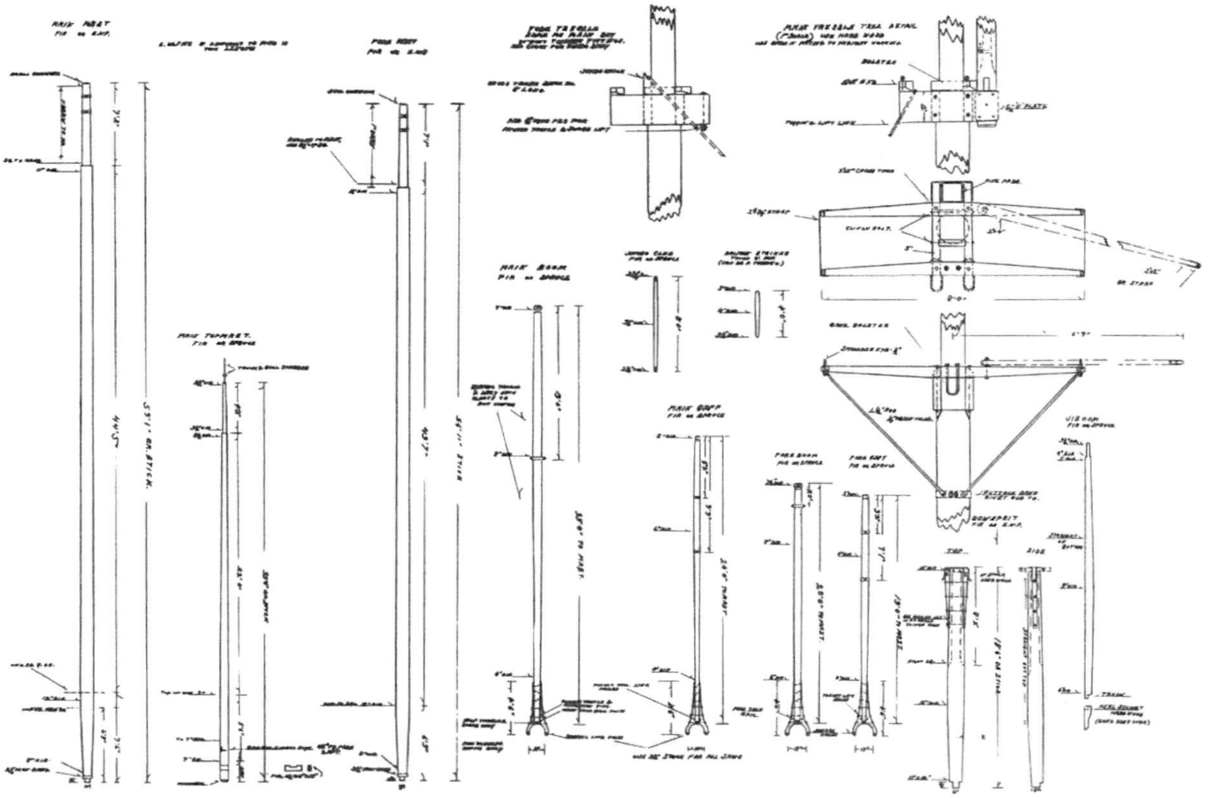

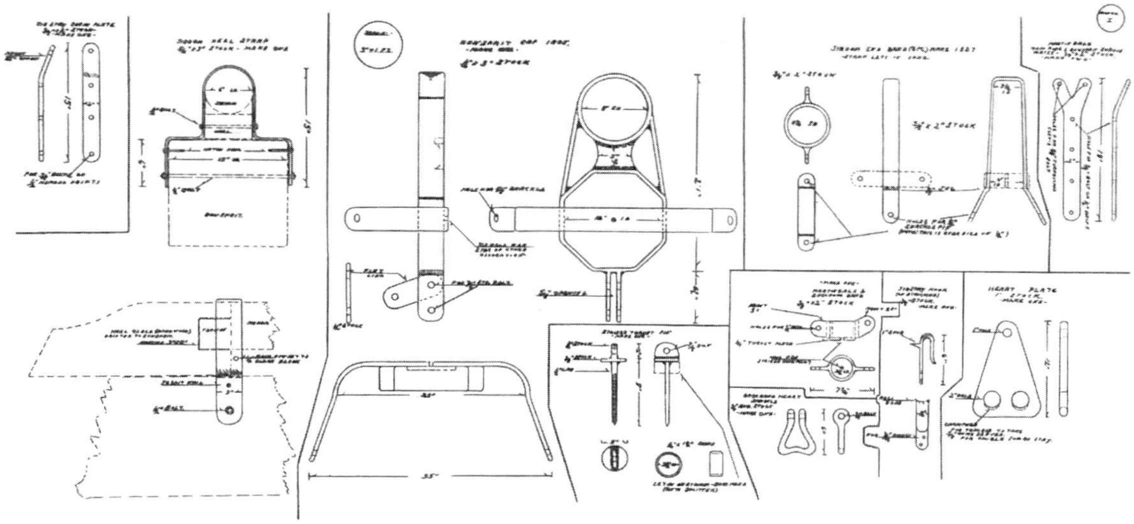

Here and on opposite page: Details of hardware and fittings for the *Gallant Lady*.

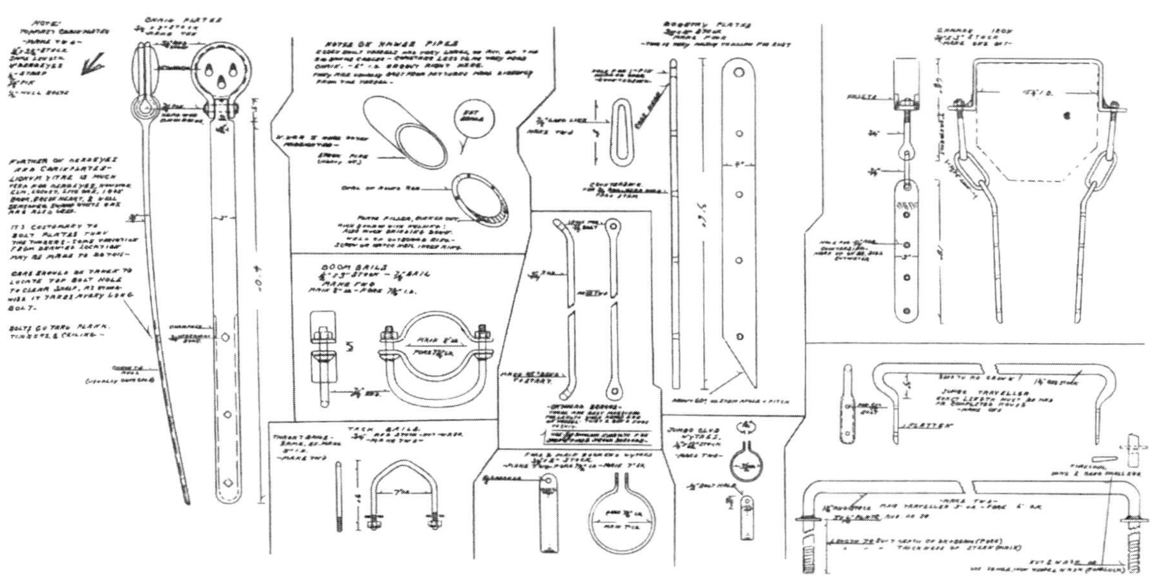

garboards with much wineglass shape worked into her sections. All of the above points to an exceptionally fine run. The topsides have good flare in the bow for dryness and buoyancy, and good deck area. There is tumblehome going aft, ending with high, powerful quarters.

This results in a vessel with more than adequate windward ability and exceptional offwind capabilities. With its great power, this craft stands up and can be driven, yet it will steer well with that long, straight, deep keel.

Haulout is simply done with this vessel, and her construction would not be unduly difficult. The head, stem, backbone, and deadwoods are of large scantling, but straight, which avoids waste. Her framing is stout, being double sawn; this simplifies setting up—no molds are needed. A seagoing vessel, with strong decks and houses, she will withstand a boarding sea. There is a long quarterdeck.

I could stand erect in her cabins! This would be a rare treat for me. Equally pleasing are the cabins themselves. They are fitted out coaster style, with beads, moldings, and panels. Nice!

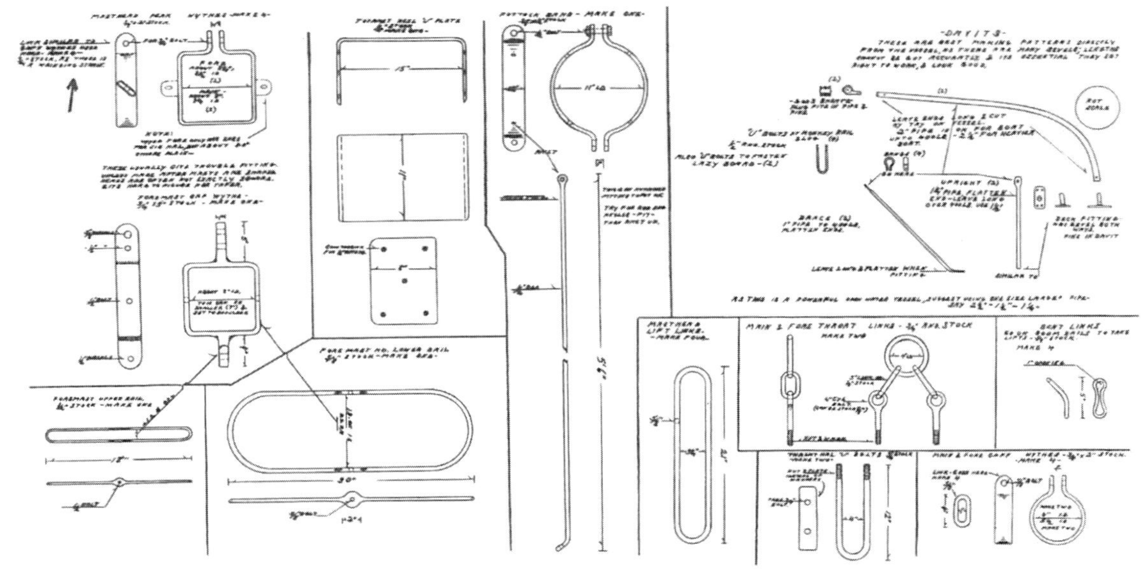

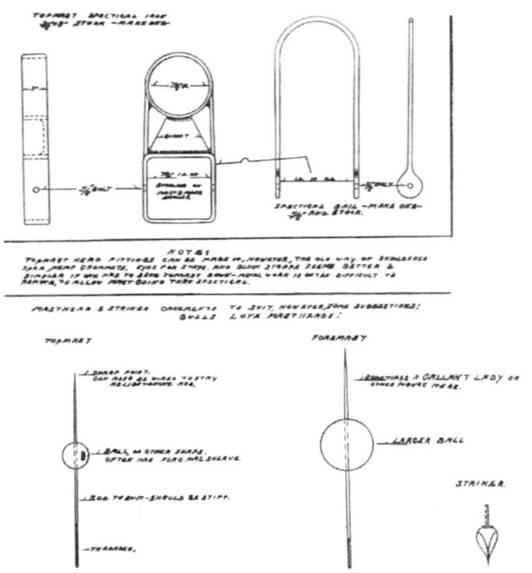

You'll note a double berth in the owner's stateroom, two berths in the saloon, and two pipe berths in the fo'c's'le. Ventilation and light are ample, and access below is well thought out. Note the donkey winch in the forward house, with winch heads port and starboard and a chain-driven windlass.

Those winch heads will be very useful when handling the vessel's high-hatted rig. As designed, this rig will balance well under many shortened-down variations, yet there is ample sail area for light airs. With this sail plan and her fine hull, *Gallant Lady* will be an exceptional ghoster.

There is a full set of ironwork drawings. Pete felt it was important to get this down on paper for posterity, so those who follow can be guided. At one time a person could go to any shipyard town and order a full set of ironworks for a schooner of "so many ton," and have it made rapidly, correctly, and in good style. But not now. For those in need, here 'tis.

West Coast sealers were able, handsome, and fast schooners. This design follows that tradition and would be prideful to own.

Schooner Propsal And Two-Masted Clipper Schooner For Henry Sears

Schooner Proposal

Length overall: 76 feet 9 inches

Two-Masted Clipper Schooner

Length on deck: 82 feet 6 inches
Length on waterline: 69 feet 6 inches
Beam: 19 feet 6 inches
Draft: 9 feet 6 inches (normal trim)
Sail area: 5,082 square feet
Displacment: 87.86 long tons

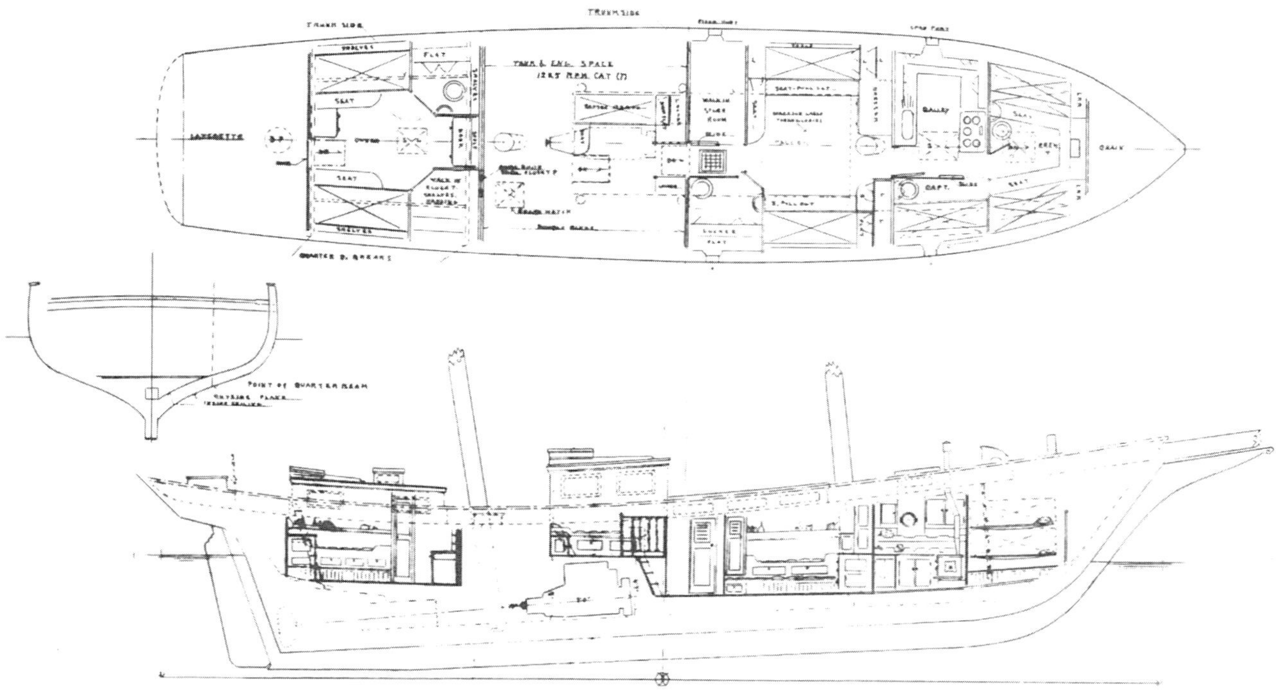

The cabin layout in the originally proposed Sears schooner, which was 76 feet long, cap to taffrail, and 75 feet long on deck.

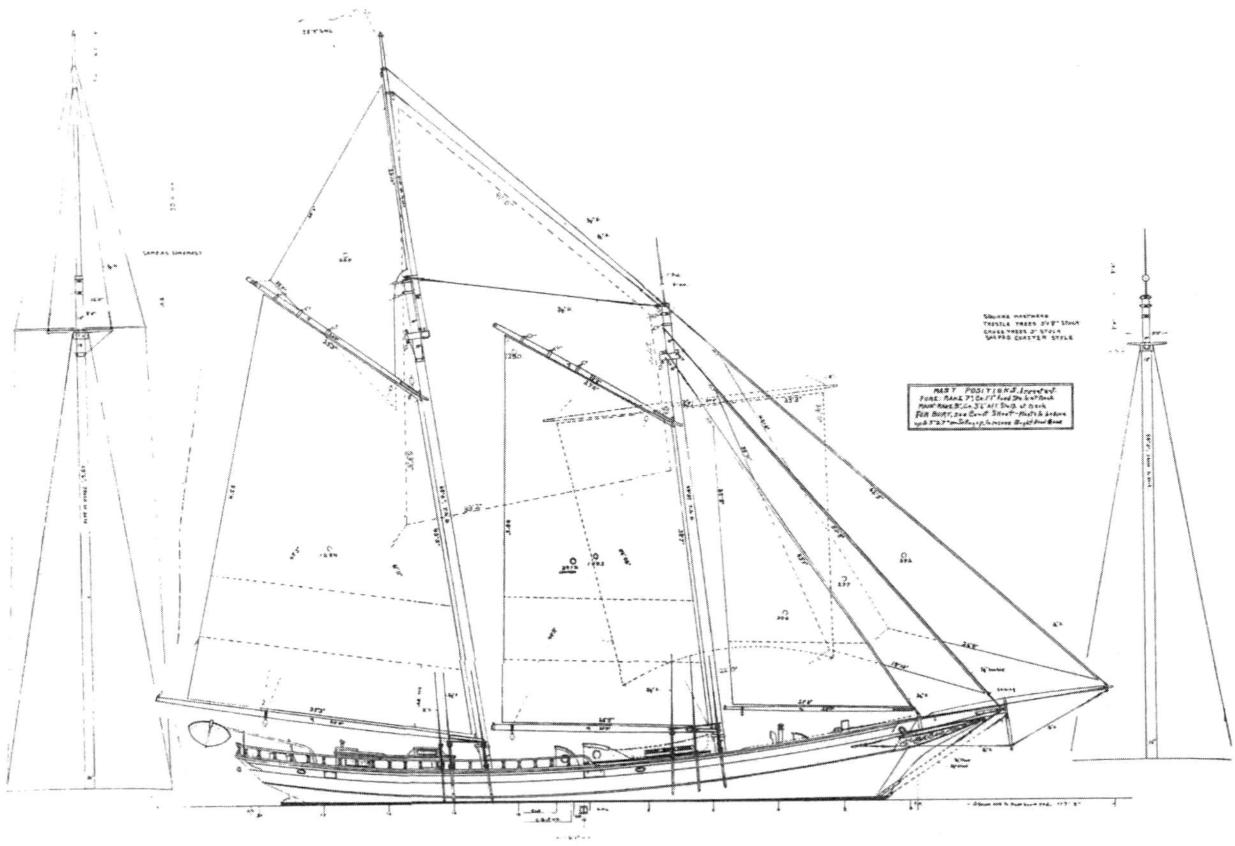

Sail plan of the revised, larger Sears schooner design.

The birth and development of American yachting are inextricably linked with the venerable New York Yacht Club, which was founded in 1846. During those early years of recreational sailing, yachts were based on working clipper models, notably the pilot boats, fast packets, and rakish craft of the Chesapeake—the renowned *Virginia* model.

The Club's early experimentation with speedy clipper designs led the membership to accept an English challenge to build and campaign a vessel during the Queen's Jubilee Celebration in 1851. George Steers was given the commission to design a fast schooner. This became the yacht *America*, a rather notable vessel in many ways. With great good fortune, she managed to win a gaudy silver cup. In the face of many challenges afterward, we managed, with equal good fortune, not to lose it until 1983.

As commodore of the New York Yacht Club during the 1950s, Henry Sears was primarily responsible for changing the cup rules to allow use of 12-meter sloops. The America's Cup Races, which had lapsed for 20 years, were then renewed.

Sears was a satisfied Concordia yawl owner. When Waldo Howland began building *Integrity*, Sears became interested in a fast schooner for himself. Knowing full well the tradition Pete was a part of, Sears commissioned the Old Man to work up a fast schooner. Captain Pete produced a fine, handsome clipper—a two-master based on the fast Chesapeake Bay fruit-runners.

The vessel is long and slim, with her maximum beam well forward. She has great drag, a well-shaped forefoot, sharp entry, and a straight keel. The rabbet line aft fairs into a beautifully shaped counter transom, nicely raked. The sheer is lively, with a proud clipper bow and much flare forward. Fruit-runners were wet sailers. The buttocks are sharp and there is a fine run.

Initially, there was a 75-foot proposal. This, however, was found wanting in accommodations, so the vessel was lengthened. This is the correct (but regrettably infrequent) solution to a common problem. Admittedly, it is a luxurious choice that many could not afford. Yet, if you get to 75 feet, 82 feet

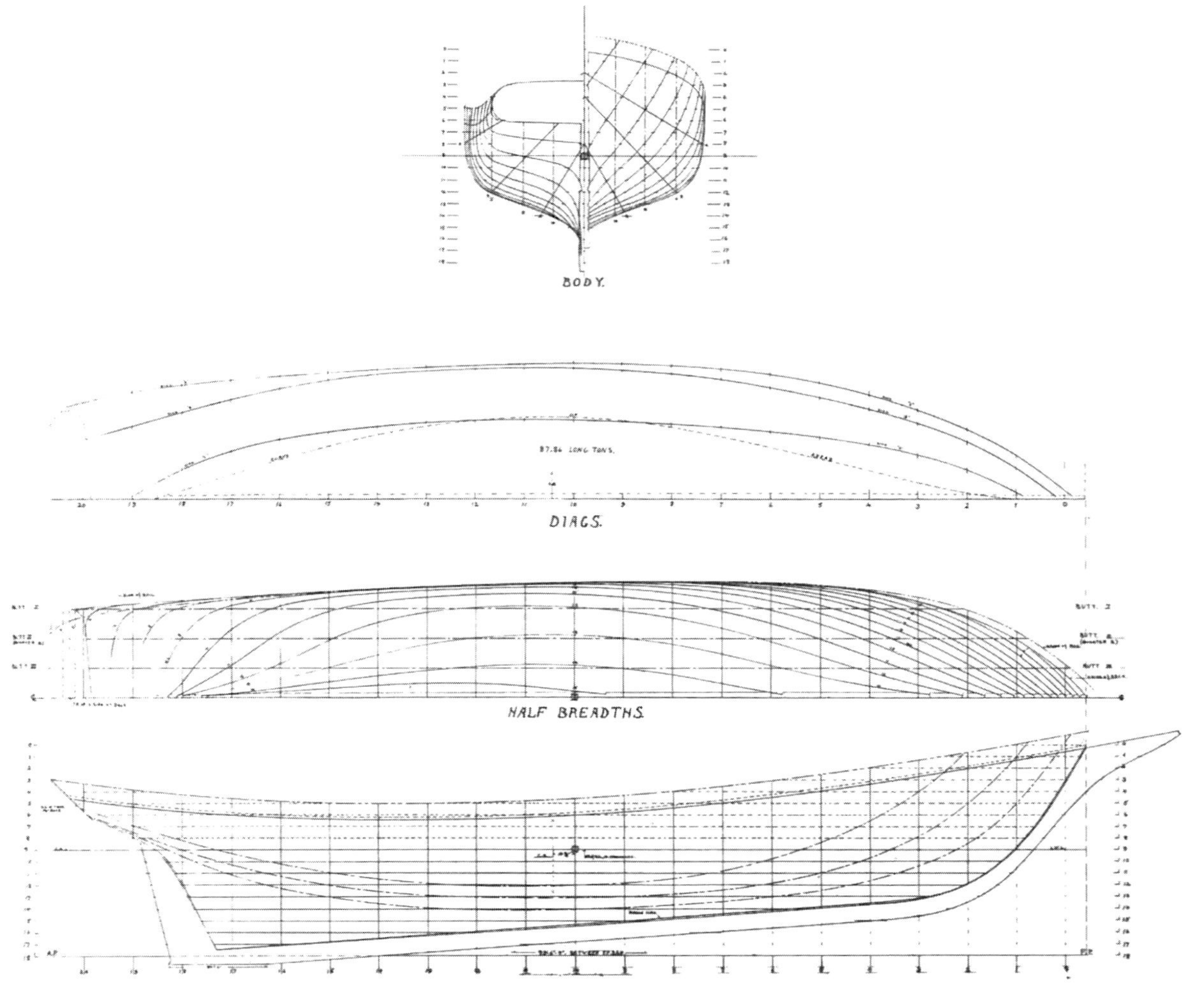

The lines of Henry Sears's proposed 82-foot schooner yacht.

should be within your reach.

The cabin areas are comfortable, but not ostentatious. There is plenty of engine and tankage space located in what would be the vessel's cargo hold. The galley and main saloon are most practical. There are ample lockers, storage, and good accommodations for guests and crew. I must confess that I would rather be in the owner's cabin with that snug stove and classy gun rack. I'm ashamed to admit how many covetous glances I have directed there. Captain Pete indicated that her cabins would all be finished out coaster fashion—that is, with styled beading, moldings, and panels. Ahh, yes!

Coming on deck from below would reveal a sight to take a sailor's breath away. The vessel's masts are towering, her sail area awesome. This clipper would reel off the knots faster than you could count 'em. The lowers alone are 3,412 square feet, and this increases to over 5,000 square feet with her light sails. There is even an optional square course set on the foremast. The distance from the waterline to the main truck is nearly 100 feet.

The spacious decks, deckhouses, and rails will appear to go on forever. There is a sunken poop and an enormous quarterdeck and rail its full length. This quarterdeck will break any sea that washes aboard

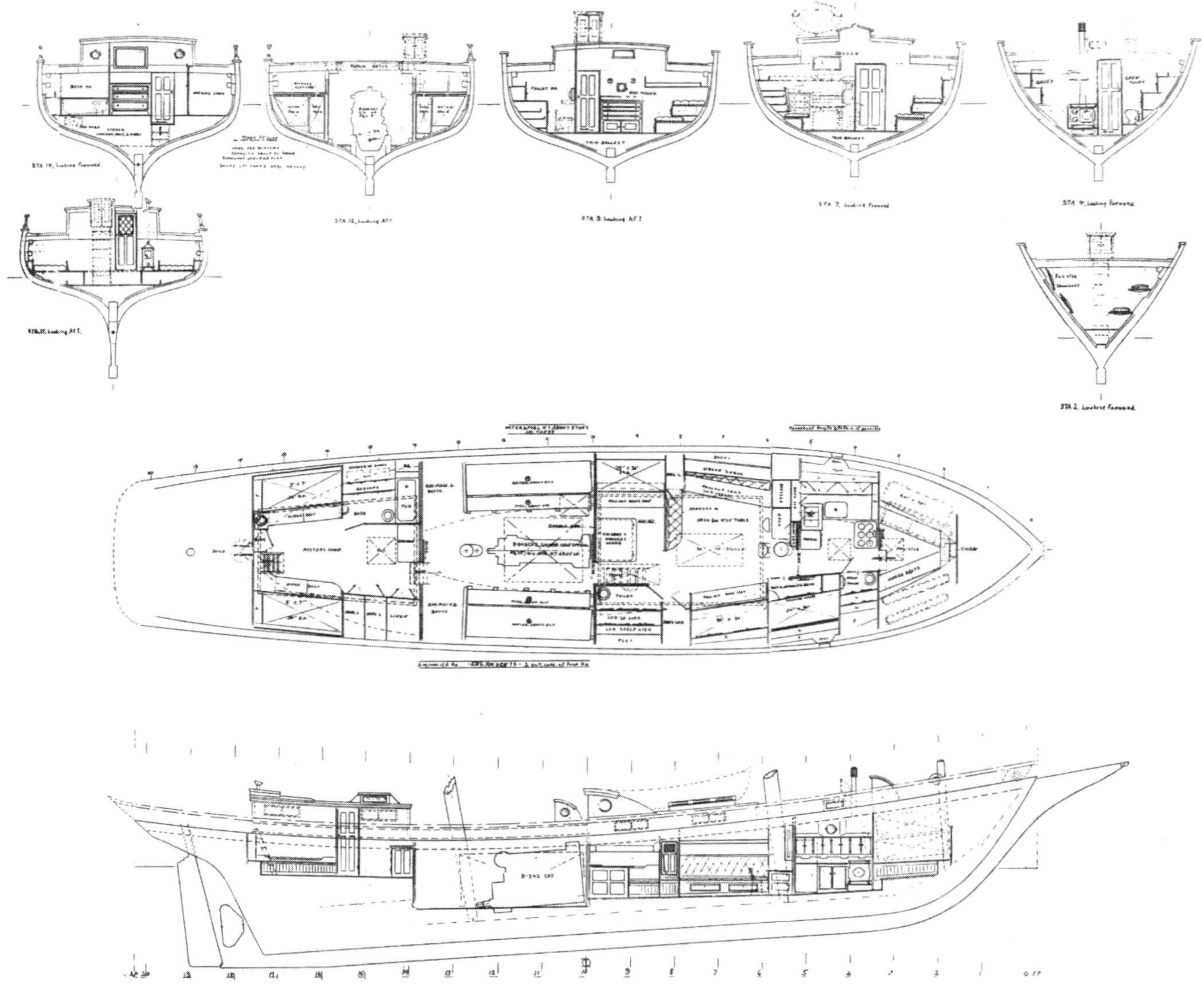

The revised cabin plan.

and provide headroom below. There is room for a jolly boat in davits aft and a smart gig lashed down on the forward housetop. There is ample area forward to handle headsails or anchor. The hatches, skylights, and deck furniture harmonize nicely.

I have had the good fortune to sail a few wooden vessels in the size range of this one, and I can state unequivocally that the experience was priceless. It's impossible to express the thrill of standing on such a vessel's deck, wheel in hand, feeling her "schoon" along at 12-plus knots, all whisper-quiet.

No doubt the person contemplating a vessel such as this, whether or not he has substantial means, will be concerned with the bottom line. To this individual I point out Pete's advice in the construction notes. What is required is first-class fishing vessel, or coaster, construction.

There are builders on both coasts capable of producing this vessel, and for a lot less than you might think.

Concordia Company was all set to build this one right after *Integrity*, but the thought of it turned into a nightmare for Waldo Howland. She was never built. So far, all my dreams about her have been pleasant.

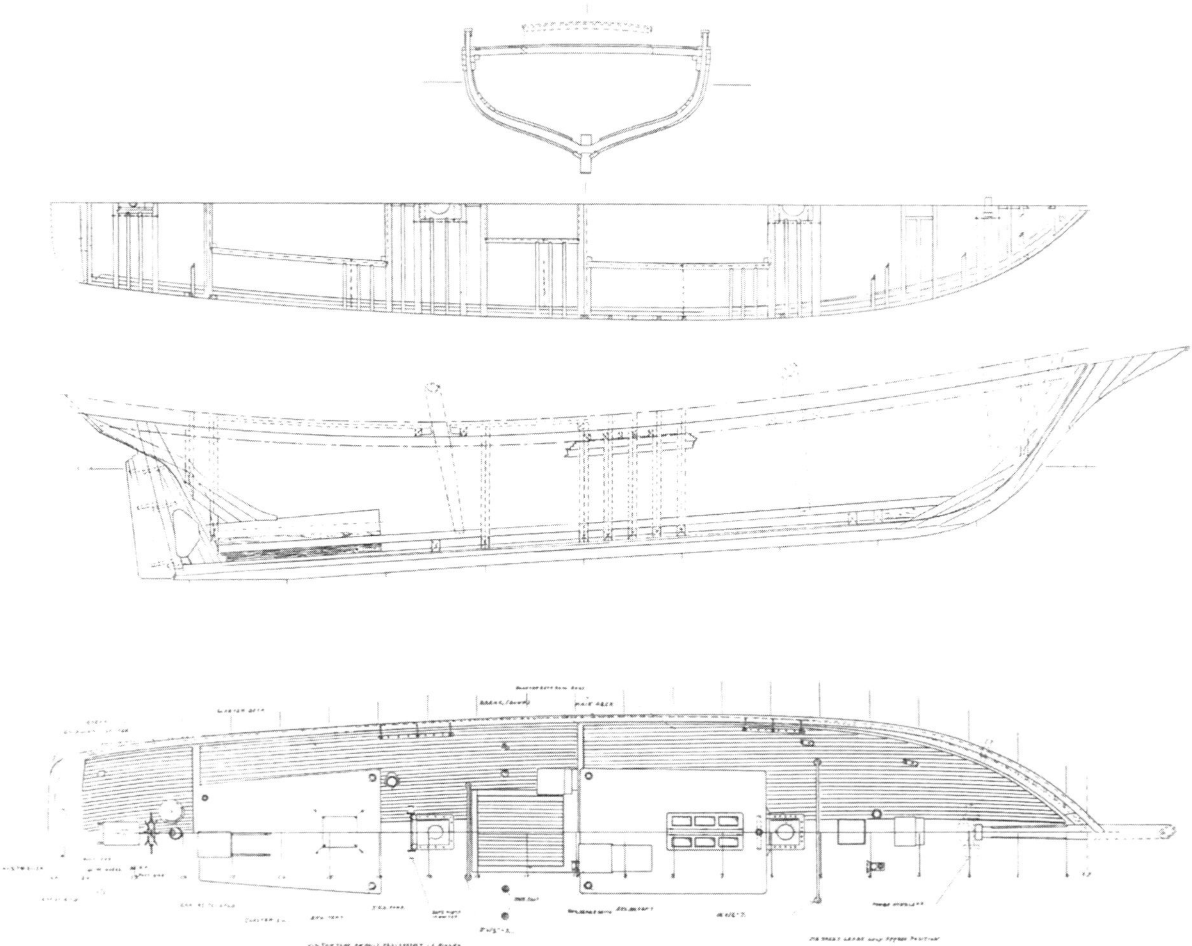

Construction drawings and a half-model for the 82-foot clipper. (John Burke photo)

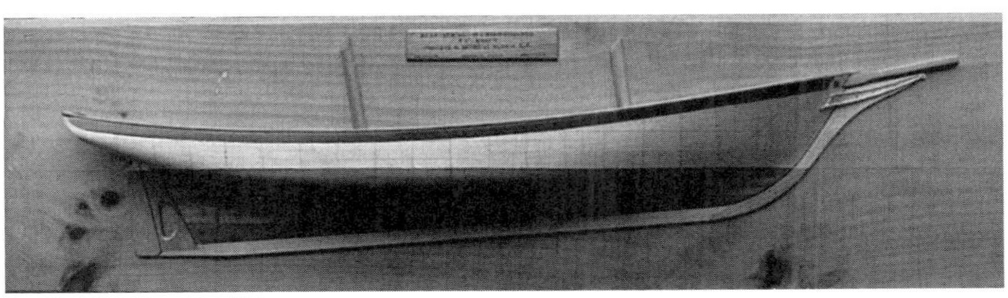

Three-Masted Schooner Propsal For Mr. Currier

Length overall: 96 feet
Length on deck: 90 feet
Beam: 22 feet 8 inches
Draft: 11 feet
Sail area: 5,366 square feet

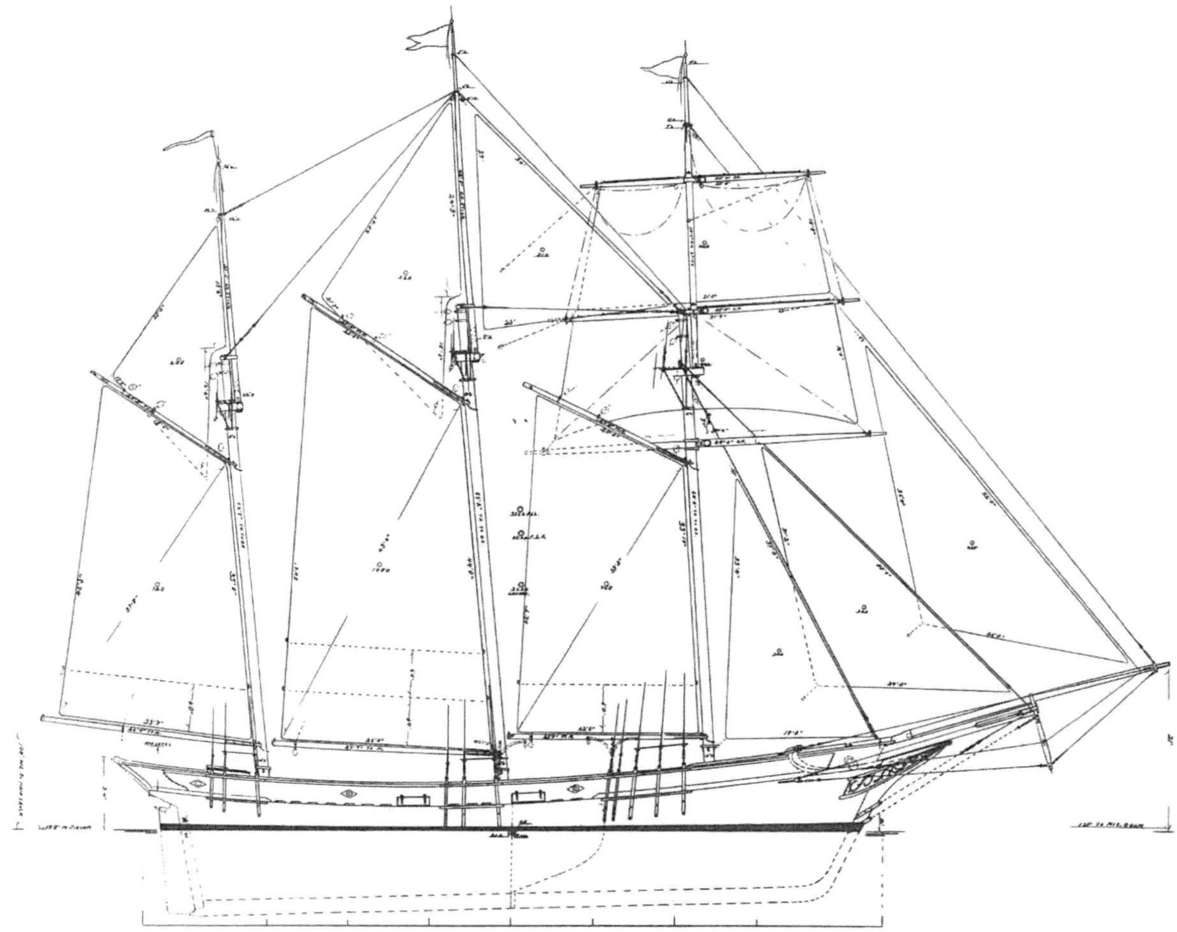

Sail plan of the three-master.

It is a shame this vessel did not proceed beyond the proposal stage, for the design has great possibilities.

In profile the hull shows a well-shaped sheer ending with a nicely raked counter transom and a beautiful clipper head replete with catheads, jibboom, and martingale. The keel has a fair amount of drag to it, and the one midsection drawn in shows that the Old Man had a medium clipper hull in mind. With such a hull, her ample, well-balanced, and handsome sail plan would push her right along. The vessel's rig is the most striking part of this proposal. This schooner would grace any harbor she cared to enter.

Pete's principal reservation was the large auxiliary requirement and the lack of space available for it. The answer is, of course, to use less engine or none at all. I daresay that she would make a good windjammer, for there is ample room for a power yawlboat to be hung in stern davits. People tend to forget there's a lot of power in those sails. With the right captain and crew (say, Irving Johnson, Eddie Crosby, and Sterling Hayden!), she would be able to do most anything with her sails alone. She might serve well as a school ship too. With some slight alterations in the cabin plan, the vessel would make an ideal training vessel. More than one concept is workable. The main point, however, is that the design is too good to remain a proposal.

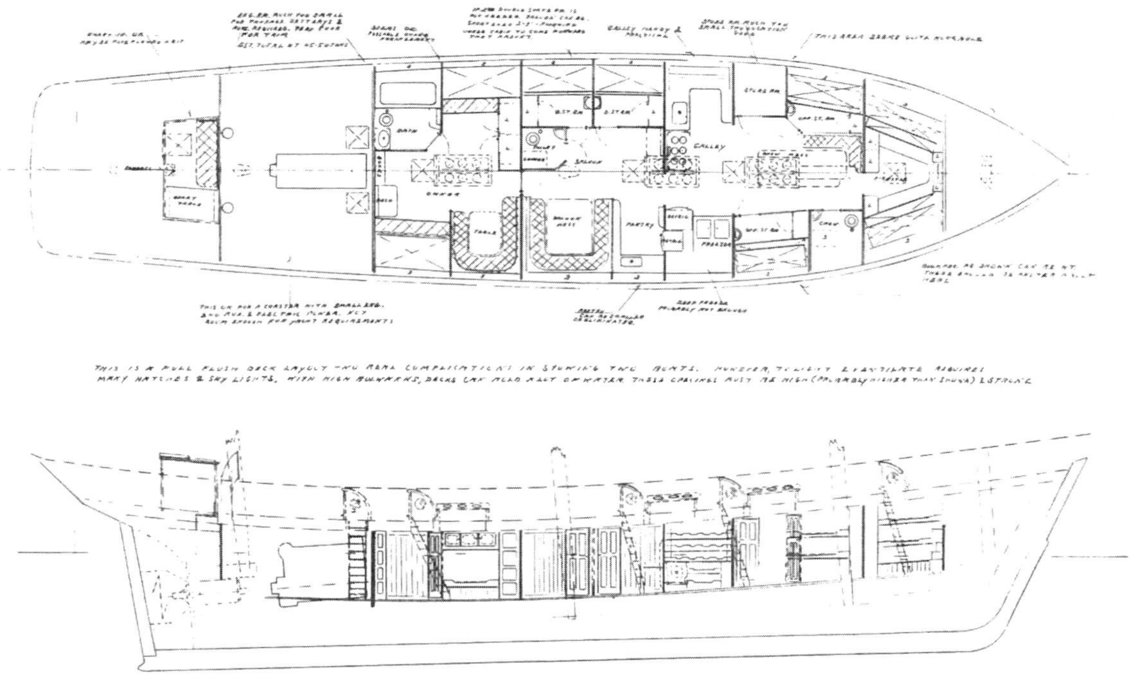

Above and below: Two "exploratory" cabin layouts for the proposed three-masted schooner.

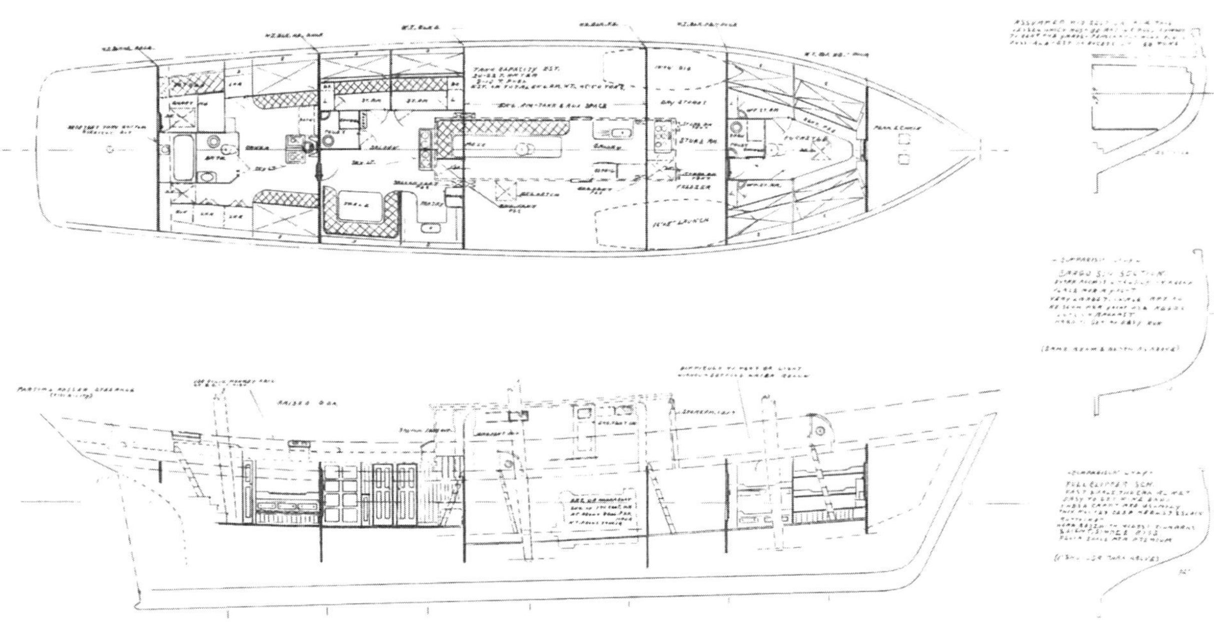

The *John F. Leavitt*, The *Kathy Brown*, Schooners For Ned Ackerman

John F. Leavitt

Length on deck: 91 feet 7¾ inches
Beam: 22 feet 7 inches
Draft: 8 feet 10 inches
Sail area: 4,399 square feet (lowers)
Displacement: 112.35 long tons

Kathy Brown

Length between perpendiculars: 125 feet 6½ inches
Molded beam: 28 feet
Draft: 7 feet 4 inches
Sail area: 6,555 square feet
Displacement: 208 long tons

Throughout this book I have kept an eye on these two designs, much as a sailor is alert to the approach of a tricky stretch of water. The publicity surrounding these two craft—particularly on the building, sailing, and subsequent loss in a 1979 winter storm of the *John F. Leavitt*—has seemingly made experts out of all who wish to express their opinions. In all that has been written and said, however, I have found little that is much more than an opinion.

I readily admit that there is much about these two designs that I don't know. On the other hand, there is some of which I am quite certain. I do know that these two vessels were designed as coasters, and not as yachts. Neither is radical or experimental in any way. I know this because Captain Pete told me so: "No new breakthroughs, just another pair of coasters," he said.

These two designs, together with a third, deep offshore two-master that did not get put down on paper before Captain Pete died, were to be the core of a fleet of windjamming cargo-carriers owned and operated by Ned Ackerman. This is a grand, sensible, and workable idea whose time is now. It would be sheer foolishness to discredit the entire concept of wind-powered cargo carriers because of the tragic loss of one overly publicized vessel.

The two designs shown here are available to anyone who wishes to pursue the idea. I don't know whether Ackerman intends to continue with his dream. I don't know, either, whether there are any other people around with the necessary gumption, courage, and wherewithal to pull it off. Ackerman has already shown these traits by taking the *John F. Leavitt* as far as her maiden voyage. The acid test of success in producing any coaster, of course, is to carry cargo and make her pay. That this test failed was not the fault of the vessel's design.

The *Leavitt* had the shapely, springy, compound sheer characteristic of the best coasters. "Since you expect them to be around a while, why not make them good looking?" Pete said. The thought was that as the years went by and her ends started to droop from hard work and hard carrying, her sheer would still look sweet. Sadly, she did not survive long enough to show this thoughtful bit of planning by her designer.

This style of sheer allows greater deck area forward for the winch housing, more bearing in the deck for the foremast, better staying for the standing rigging, and a natural plank termination for the fine clipper head. (Unfortunately, that fine clipper bow was besmirched with an inappropriate figurehead.)

The crew needed for coasters such as the *Leavitt* was usually smaller than most people assume. In the *Leavitt's* case, one man per mast, plus captain and cook, would have been ample. Traditionally, the cook tended the headsails when tacking—all of 'em. Well thought-out gear, based on years of refinement, made this possible. After all, the primary reasons for the development of the schooner rig, its evolution, and its subsequent near-domination in

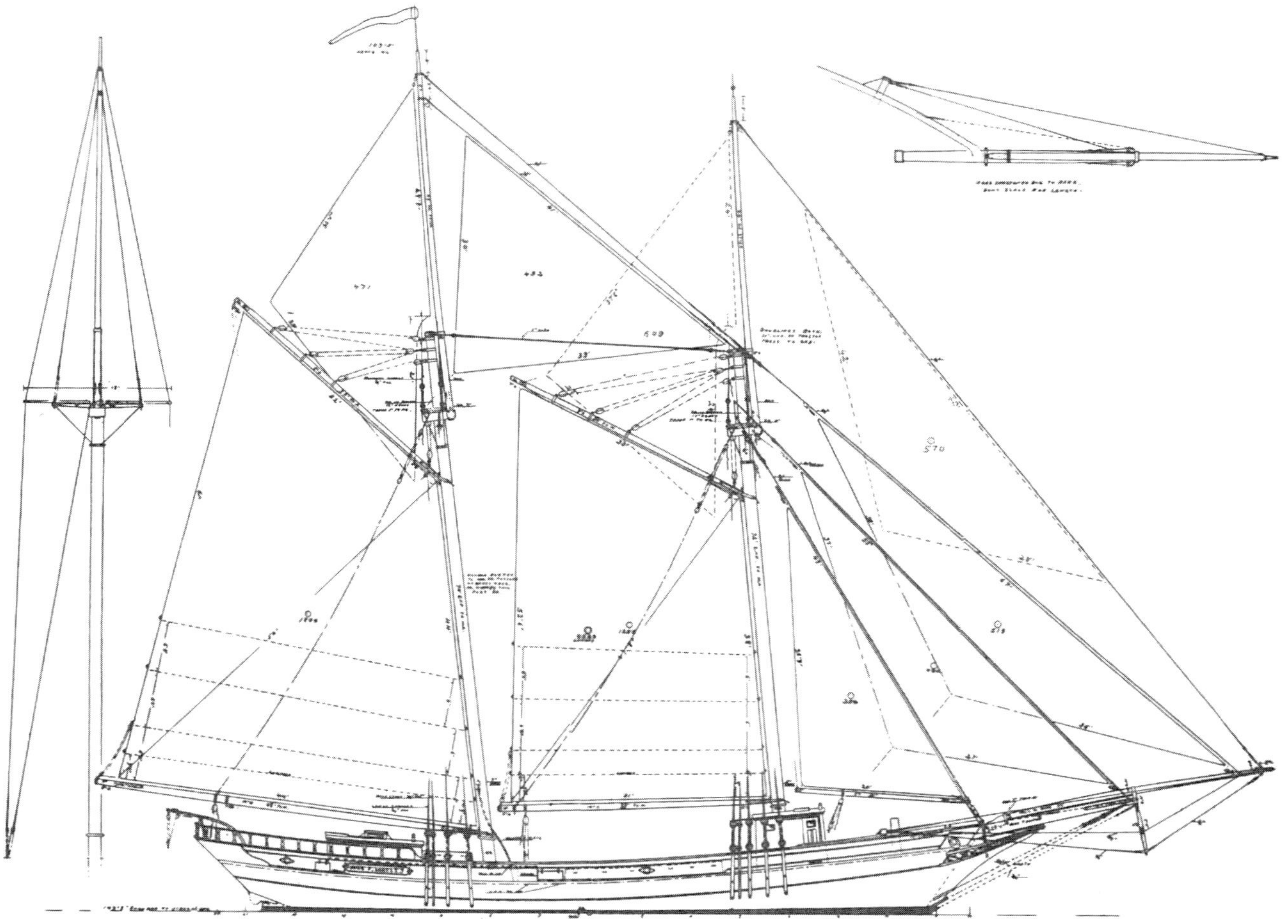

Sail plan of the *John F. Leavitt.*

coasting vessels were its lower operating costs. The bottom line was based on ease of use and repair. Witness the "monkey tail" for raising and lowering the centerboard, the topsail sheeting, and the ample blocking for raising and trimming the lower sails with the aid of the deck winch, as well as the vessel's lazyjacks and topping lifts. All of these items eased the burden of working a vessel the size of the *Leavitt.*

Once Ackerman's two-master was abuilding at the Wallace yard in Thomaston, Maine, he had the foresight to have Captain Pete design him a three-master on the deep centerboard model for future needs, should they arise. This vessel was to be named *Kathy Brown,* after his niece. Ackerman was quoted as saying that, if built, she was to be constructed "quick and dirty"—the scantlings for the *Leavitt,* being a stone-carrier, would do for the three-master. Thus, the construction plan would be a guide for both.

The three-masted schooner was introduced for the same reasons that the schooner rig evolved—the need was to break up an oversize rig as economic demands increased hull length. This kept the rig manageable for a small crew and allowed the hull to remain narrow. In *The History of American Sailing Ships,* Howard Chapelle commented: "As the length of coasting voyages increased, the schooners grew larger. As large two-masted schooners required large crews to handle them, and as the profits of the trade were rarely great enough to warrant this expense, the large schooners were rigged as

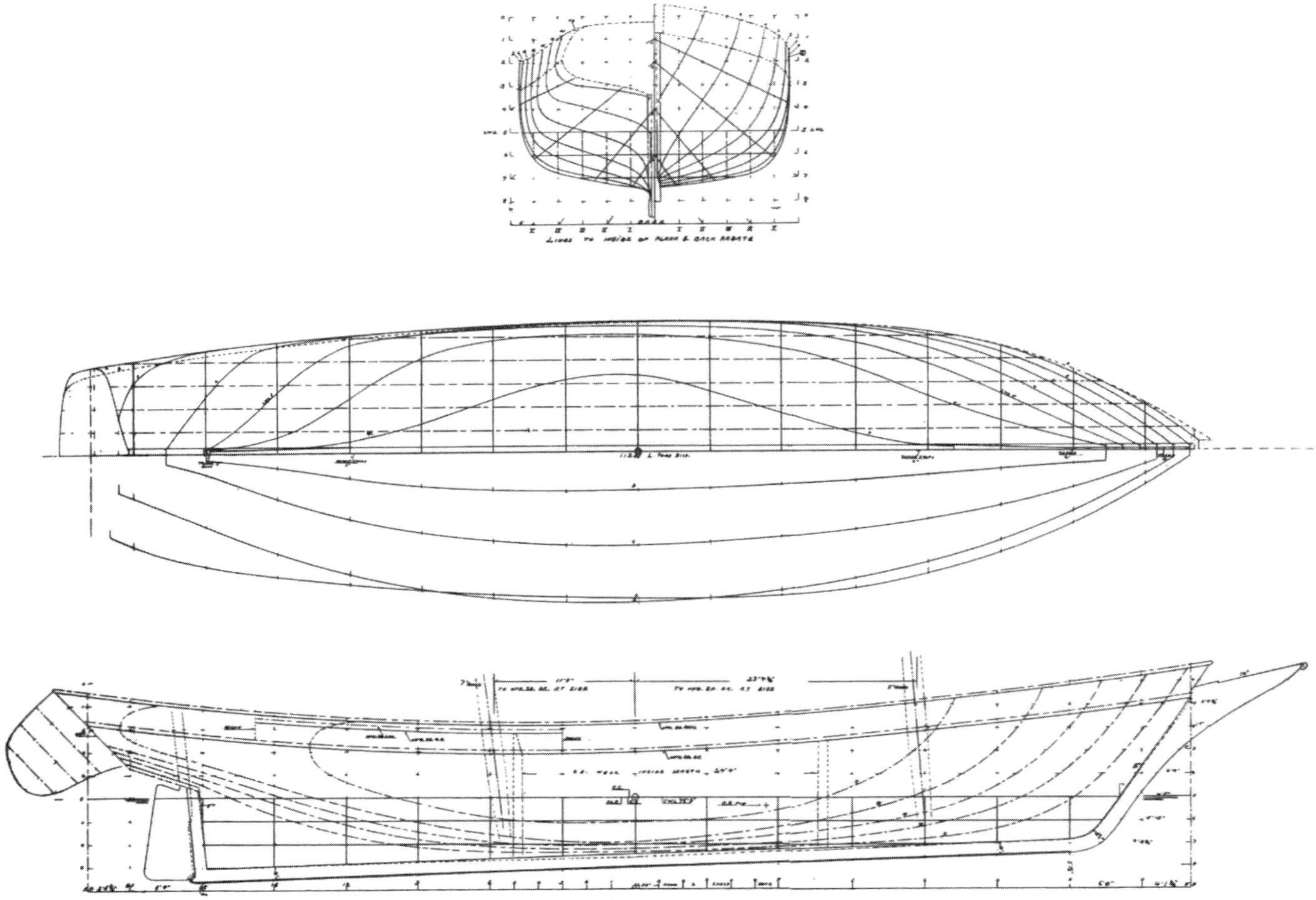

The *Leavitt's* lines.

three-masters. It was found that these schooners could be operated with very small crews and that they also sailed very well. The use of the three-master in the coasting trade seems to have started about 1850, though the rig was employed in seagoing schooners much earlier.

"After the Civil War, the three-masted schooner almost monopolized the coasting trades, particularly the lumber business. There were two types of three-master at this time, a rather deep-draft keel model and a shoaler centerboarder. These were satisfactory for specific trades, but were somewhat unsatisfactory for general work. The keel type was not very reliable in stays when light, and the shoal model did not carry sufficient cargo; there were other objections as well. These difficulties were overcome, in the late 1870s, by the development of the deep centerboarders. These were probably the most satisfactory coasting schooners ever built, for they combined the good features of both the keel and the centerboard model."

The lines and profile for the "tern" schooner *Kathy Brown* are very handsome. Her sail plan is ample, though not outsize. The long quarterdeck was popular when the type developed. This, together with her fine clipper head, makes the vessel look very smart. (Note the "lumber" reefs for when she had a deckload of boards. These vessels excelled in carrying lumber.) Ackerman has stated that, if built, the *Kathy Brown* would be "in response to a known economic situation, rather than to one I was guessing at." We are still waiting to find that out.

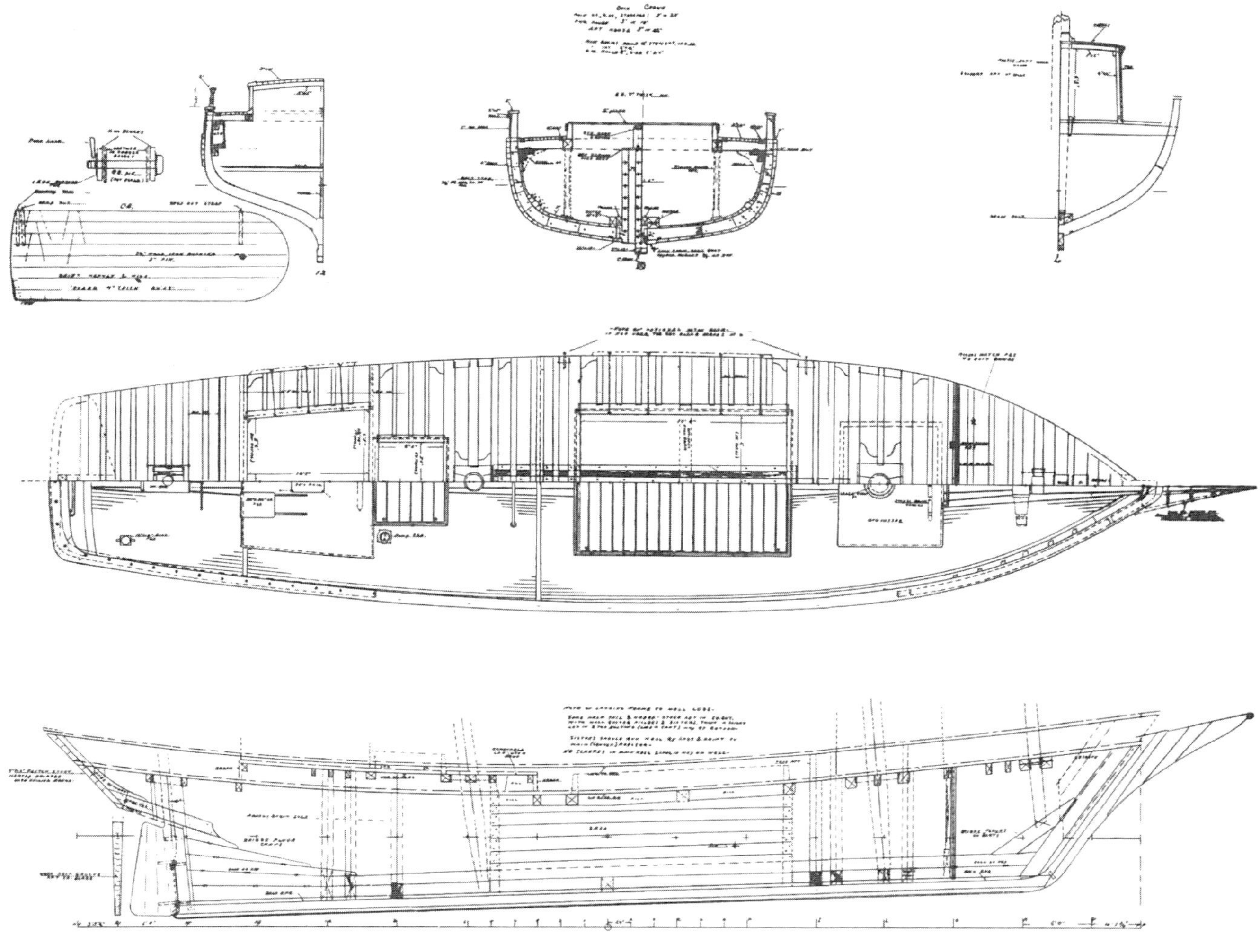

Construction drawings and a tentative deckhouse layout for the *Leavitt*.

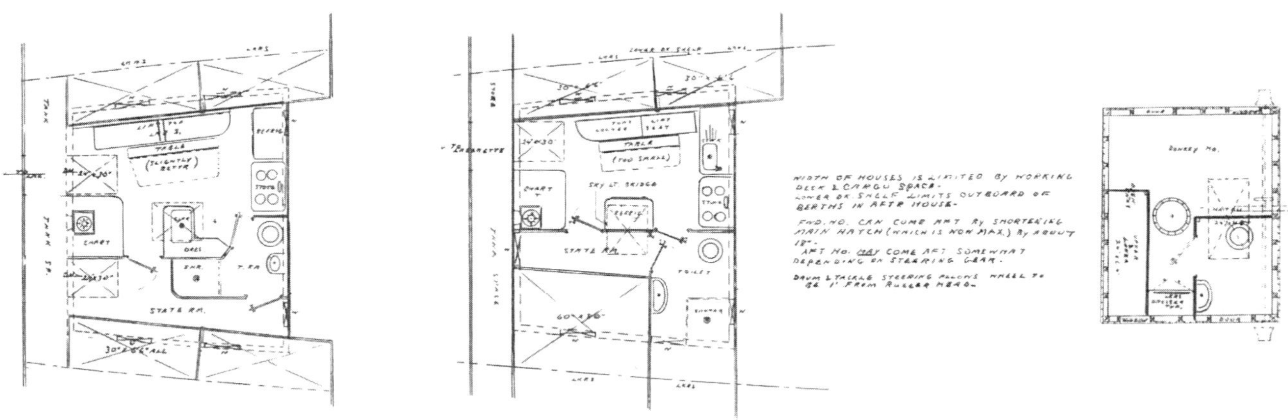

Launch day was a happy occasion. (John Burke photo)

The three-masted schooner *Lucy Evelyn* anchored at Vineyard Haven, Massachusetts, about 1939. She was a deep centerboarder somewhat similar to the *Kathy Brown*. (Photo courtesy Charles F. Sayle)

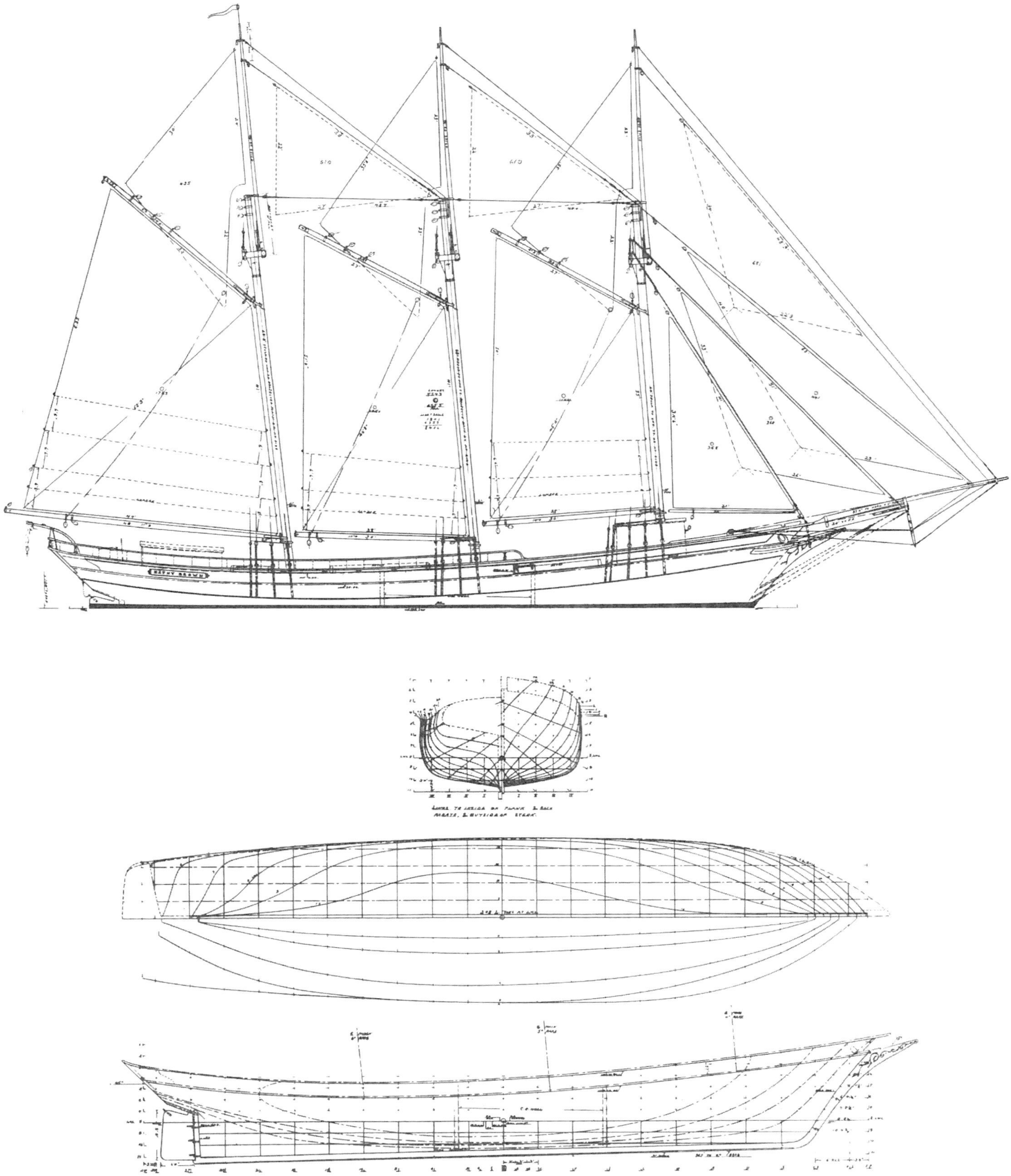

The proposed three-master *Kathy Brown*, sail plan and lines.

Appendix A
Culler Details: From Skiffs to Schooners

With drawings by Kathy Bray

> I think that embellishment is needed to make any boat attractive, and this rests very much with the artistic ability of the builder; nice beading, molding, and other little details, which all of my boats have, certainly spice them up. I can only indicate this detail on a plan; it is up to the builder to carry it out. None of it is expensive, for it's just a matter of the right touch with a tool here and there. This goes for painting, too. The right combination can make or break it.
>
> —Pete Culler

Artistic ability among builders is a highly variable commodity, and this ability, in whatever amount, is not helped by confusion about the designer's intentions. To some, Captain Pete's designs can be maddening in their lack of detail. However, there was a variety of reasons why Pete never felt it necessary to work out on paper every detail of a design. Primarily, it was to restrict the hours, and thereby the cost, to a level of affordability. Additionally, he anticipated that the small boats would be built at his own shop and the larger vessels at the Concordia Company, so detailed drawings would be needlessly redundant. Furthermore, it was against his nature to dictate in an area that lent itself to more than one acceptable solution. Once again, he much preferred to see the builder's artistry flower during a boat's construction.

Nevertheless, many people have asked what constituted these "embellishments" that Pete refers to. This section, through words, photographs, and drawings, will attempt to show some of the "touches" that made Culler craft so appealing.

What this amounts to is a topical discussion of details, primarily through examples on small boats, and how they apply to round-, flat-, and V-bottomed types.

There also is a passing glance at some of the details that made Captain Pete's larger vessels stand out from the crowd. However, due to the size of these vessels, most owners will opt for professional builders, so these details are not discussed in depth.

In fact, none of the following can be considered all-encompassing. The subject of classic boat and vessel details is too vast to cover completely here, or anywhere for that matter: all the works on the subject would fill a large library.

Stems and Stemheads

Let's start with stems and stemheads, since they are common to any small boat, be it V-, flat-, or round-bottomed, Captain Pete preferred thinner siding and deeper molding on his stems than most designers. The greater molding gave strength in the right way and the thinner siding allowed more wood to be left "noble," that is, outboard of the stem rabbet, without becoming chunky in appearance. The stems were relieved further by beveling them at an acute angle from the face back to the outer rabbet line. This angle should always be less than the plank running into the rabbet. This constant bevel ran up from the forefoot and into a "ship-style" or square head. The reasons for leaving the head square were that it allowed good landing for gunwales and any false beads or covings. Running cap rails and inwales into it was easier, too, and, most important, it looks good and will allow a decorative stemhead carving on top. Each plan shows where to start and

The *Owl's* bow, showing: a stem with the thinner siding and deeper molding that Pete preferred; the "ship-style" or square stem head; the decorative stemhead carving on top; the pitched-up angle of the stemhead; the painter spliced around the stem and through hawseholes in the sheerstrakes; the gunwale set down $\frac{1}{16}$ inch from the cap rail; and the bow badge. The leading edge of the bow badge follows the ogee on the sheerstrake.

stop the bevel and square head; simply scale it off and loft it with the rest of the boat.

Now let me give another tip for builders of flat- and V-bottoms: When lofting the boat, be aware that you may need to increase the molding of the stem where the chines run into it in order to give the joint between chine and stem a good landing. To illustrate my point: Cut off a 2 x 4 square, and at an angle; note that the angled cut has much more area to its face than the square one. The same thing occurs with the chine/stem joint. If you keep this in mind, your lofting will make it clear.

Saying this reminds me that after the stem dimensions are transferred from the lofting to the stem piece (use the string-of-nails method), cut your stem-bevel and rabbet on the bench, but leave the stemhead long. Any carving on the back of the stem should be done on the bench, too. This could include chamfering the edges or running a bead down the edge or carving a five-pointed star. The point I am trying to make is that a good lofting job and forethought with common sense as to sequence can make things go a lot more easily. The idea is to finish as much as possible while you have ready access to it. As a further example, consider the stem knee that in sailing models doubles as a mast step. (Flat bottomed, cross-planked boats don't require a stem knee, only a mast-step block.) Your lofting tells you the exact location of those steps on the knee. After the knee is cut and fitted with stem and keel, mark those mast step locations and bore them on the bench. It is much simpler.

Well, you say, if the above is true, why did we leave the stemhead long? Why not carve the sternhead on the bench, too? This brings up the boatbuilder's two most cherished axioms: (1) "Don't make a cut until you have to," and (2) "It's easier to take a little off than to add a little on."

Captain Pete's stemhead designs were directly related to the sheerline and the general cast of the boat being built. He never carved two stemheads quite the same. Stemhead design lends itself to individual expression. Here's Captain Pete talking about stemheads:

"I think different models of boats require different treatment. However, there are a couple of rules that I use. I never cut a stem-top level, nor quite with the sheer; rather, I pitch it up some, the amount depending on the boat, and it looks right. Model, stem profile, stem siding, and sometimes just what wood is available—all enter into my decision. Naturally you treat a heavy, bulky craft much

Knighthead construction on a sharpie.
(R.D. Culler photo)

Knightheads and hawse timbers on a schooner.
(R.D. Culler photo)

Another glance at Pete's " bigboat" methods. this is a clipper head taking shape at Concordia. The hawsehole has been cut and the hawsepipe pattern is in place. Markings have been made for the placement of the trailboards and knees. Note the bead on the lower wale. A guardrail will be placed between the bead and the planksheer. (R.D. Culler photo)

Catheads on a small schooner. (R.D. Culler photo)

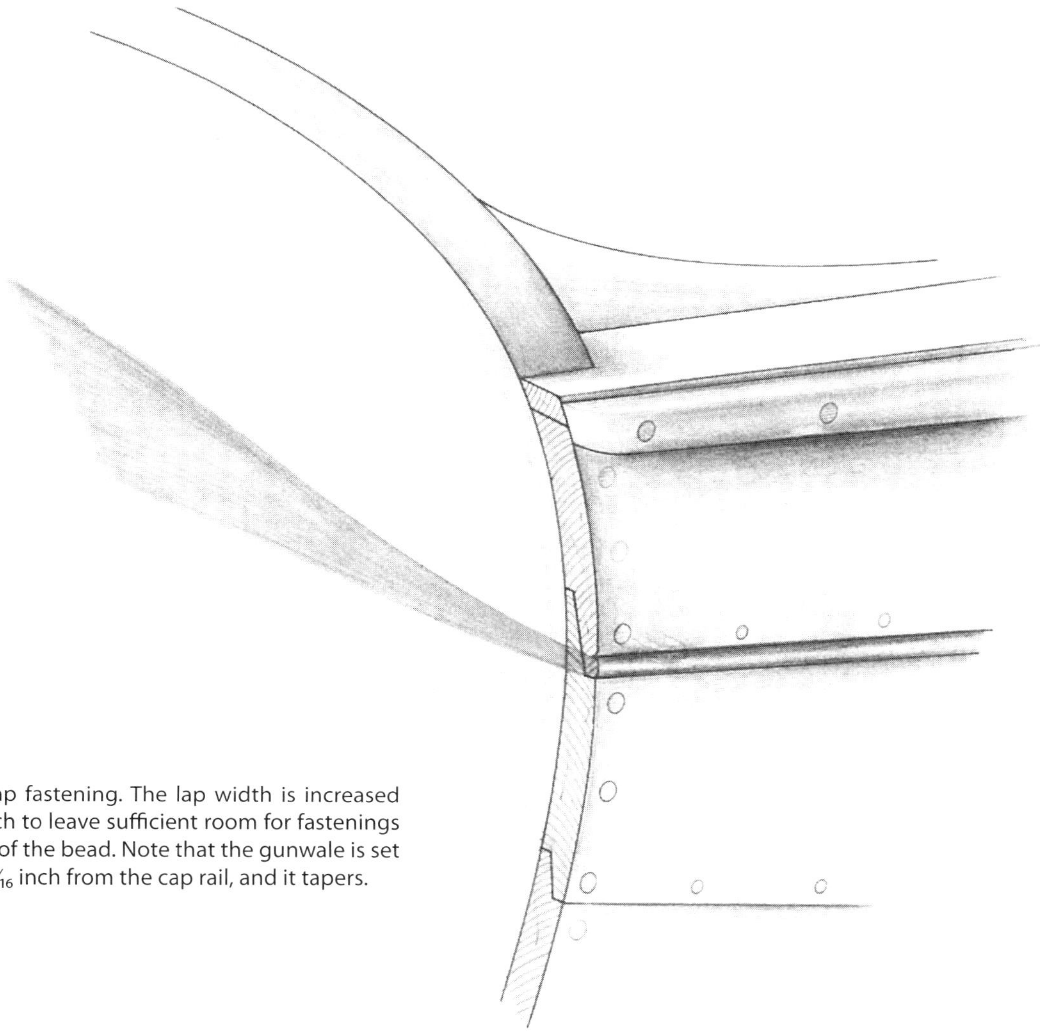

Bead-lap fastening. The lap width is increased to 1 inch to leave sufficient room for fastenings in way of the bead. Note that the gunwale is set down $\frac{1}{16}$ inch from the cap rail, and it tapers.

differently than, say, a wooden canoe."

That part about "just what wood is available" is why the sternhead is left long (and the transom too) until the boat is nearly complete. A more harmonious design is then possible because you have the wood if you need it.

Pete usually accented the bow with a pendant. Almost always this was spliced behind the stem and entered through hawseholes in the sheerstrake, sometimes backed by inside hawse "timbers" (actually, just wood blocks) if the planking was thin. Besides being good looking, this bow pendant was handy for towing, for docking lines, or for a mooring buoy shackle. It was never placed at the waterline, as is the custom today. The hawsehole locations are indicated on the plans, and there is a good photograph of a bow pendant on *Punch*.

The Sheer

Perhaps the most distinctive feature of Captain Pete's design work was his frequent use of the S, or compound, sheer, sometimes called a "powderhorn," which describes it very well. It would, of course, vary some as to model, but it lent itself nicely to the "classic" types Pete preferred to design. In addition to looking right, it "works" when viewed from various angles, and on certain models it allowed good capacity forward and a full deckline. A careful lofting of this line should be sufficient in guiding you. In profile it should be a fair, flowing line; it is sometimes described as "strong" and "springy." This style of sheer was also a trademark of the Alonzo Conley Shipyard, where Pete apprenticed, and I suppose his first lessons in using it were learned there.

Inwale and seat riser. The bead on the lower edge ofthe inwale is the same as that on the sheerstrake. The seat riser follows the sheer, tapers in width toward the ends, and has a bead cut in its lower edge. The chamfer in the lower edge of the thwart ends in a "lamb's tongue."

Using this sheer, Captain Pete employed a variety of methods to highlight its shapeliness. Perhaps his most recognizable technique was to paint the sheerstrake a contrasting color to that of the hull. Sometimes the entire sheerstrake would be painted; other times it would terminate with an ogee short of the ends. Either way, it appears to lengthen any craft and smartens it up nicely. Many times a bead would be cut along the lower edge of the sheerstrake, and this bead would be painted a third color to enhance further the line and the apparent lengthening. As to the color schemes Captain Pete used on his boats, I'll discuss them later.

In using this bead with lapstrake construction (and Pete preferred lapstrake for small boats), you must increase your lap width to allow room for the lap fastenings. For example, if you are using a ¾-inch lap on the boat, with a ¼-inch bead on the sheerstrake, you must increase that lap (that is, the joining lap on both planks) to 1 inch. This allows sufficient room for the lap fastenings, which for Captain Pete were invariably copper clinch nails. He found no weakness in this system, and clinch nails for the lap fastenings are a far easier way to go for the lone worker.

This wider lap technique is no chore mechanically. Simply keep it in mind when you line off your plank initially, and when you spile to get your plank shapes. It helps to use battens that are the width of your lap to line off for plank. After you are satisfied with the line-off, mark both edges of the batten on each mold, and on the stem and transom.

As to the lining-off procedure itself—and it is important with lapstrake construction—read Captain Pete's chapter on lapstrake planking in *Skiffs and Schooners*, where he gives an in-depth discussion of the topic. Naturally, for Culler boats it is the most useful reference available.

It seems I have gotten a bit off course; we were talking about sheers and Pete's methods of highlighting them.

Captain Pete always tapered his gunwales, in both thickness and width, as they approached the ends of the boat. Due to the nature and shape of the sheer, the gunwales were usually made from two or three pieces, joined on the boat with scarfs.

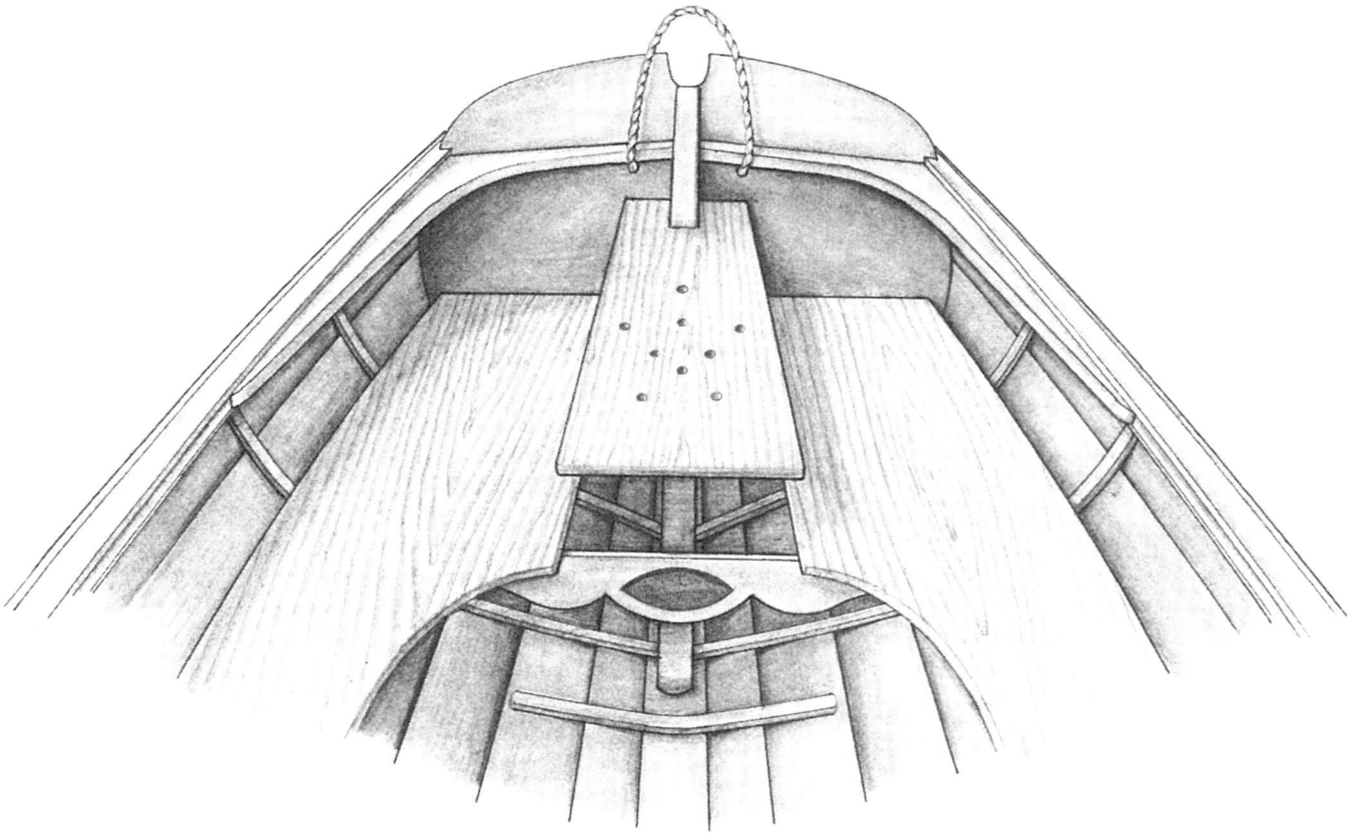

Interior stern layout. The middle section of the sternsheets lifts out. The lower edge of the thwartships member is a good place for a decorative touch, and this member is a handy spot for the builder's plate. Note the two quarter knees.

Save the rippings from the top edge of your sheerstrake and you have the line to follow. If the craft calls for a cap rail, Pete would not attempt to match gunwale and cap rail, but he would set the gunwale down $\frac{1}{16}$ inch from the top of the cap rail. He couldn't explain why, but for some reason it looks better.

A cap rail calls for an inwale, too, and this usually had the same bead on its lower edge as on the sheerstrake. After the frames are in, the inwale goes on first.

Another technique the Old Man used to accent the shape of his boats was to have the seat riser follow the sheer. Only in rare cases would this fore-and-aft member follow a waterline. The seat riser was also tapered in width as it approached the ends, and usually a bead was cut on its lower edge, sometimes on both edges.

Thwarts, Sternsheets, and Mast Partners

Mentioning seat risers brings up that which is placed upon them—thwarts, sternsheets, and mast partners.

Captain Pete always eased the heavy appearance of a thwart by chamfering the lower edges. The chamfer usually ended with a "lamb's tongue" before it crossed the seat riser or centerboard box, if there was one. This lower-edge chamfer always lightened the look of a thwart without detracting from its necessary strength.

This "touch" has a lot to do with proportion. Proportion is something that can't be taught; it must be acquired through careful study of boats and boat plans. Here's Captain Pete on the subject of proportion:

"Proportion in boatbuilding is a very necessary knack to acquire; I don't know of any definite rules for proportion on these classic craft, except that if something looks right, it is right."

Sternsheets are seats in the stern. Pete would usually design the middle section so it could lift out for easy maintenance and allow stowage underneath.

Interior of a round-bottomed yawlboat. The most evident detail is the natural crooks, which were left long and always pinned with a rivet at the end of the long arm. Pete always said "a classic is not a classic until she has some crooked applewood in her." (R.D. Culler photo)

The lower edge of the thwartships member that the sternsheets rest on is a prime spot for some nice art, and it's a good place for your builder's plate.

Forward will be found mast partners if it's a sailing model, or a thwartships member if it is not. You see, these thwarts and mast partners are structural members that help hold the sides together as well as allow you to plop your fanny down, row, or set a mast. Depending on the model, Pete sometimes borrowed from the Cornish gigs and arched or crowned his thwarts, either over a centerboard box or with an upright stanchion underneath set into a keelson. The crowned thwart is an excellent system that allows lightness, flexibility, and ample strength. The stanchion can be artfully turned while avoiding a heavy look.

As structural members, the thwarts and mast partners should be kneed. Pete's knees were always natural crooks. One of his favorite sayings was, "A classic is not a classic until it has some natural apple crooks in her." Using natural crooks is by far the easier, more economical solution. There have been a number of articles written, by Captain Pete and others, on the collection, storage, and sawing out of natural crooks. Try it, you'll like it!

Natural crooks were also employed for quarter knees, breasthooks, stern and stem knees, as well as the stems themselves.

Setting the Mast

I mentioned mast partners before and now would like to discuss Captain Pete's methods of setting small boat masts. For a small boat, say, under 16 feet, this could consist of a single mast hole in the partners, big enough so the mast will rotate freely, and a single mast step. This single mast hole and step is usually sufficient for a mizzenmast, too, or for the intermediate step between mizzen and foremast in a two-sail rig. The mast hole in the partners and step is fixed at a certain rake. However, for ease in setting larger masts and as an aid in tuning and balancing the rig, Pete used a long slot in the partner with a filler block, a swinging mast gate at the after end of the slot, and multiple mast steps. Step locations are shown on the plan, as are the slot size and length. The forward end of the slot has a semicircle cut out slightly larger than your mast radius (remember that you want the mast to rotate freely). The mast gate has the same cutout on its forward side. With the swinging mast gate in its closed position, you have a long slot, slightly wider than your mast diameter, and two radiused cutouts opposite each other. Now picture an upright mast in this slot, free to swing fore and aft. The mast can rest aft against the mast gate or all the way forward at the front of the slot, but in order to do its job (that is, hold up your sail under a press of wind), a filler block is needed to hold the mast in either position. This block, having a radiused cutout on one end and a rounded cutaway on the other, simply fills the space in the slot where the mast isn't. It doesn't matter which position the mast is in; simply turn the filler block end for end. One filler block and two mast steps allow a single mast to be stepped in two locations. Once the idea is grasped, it becomes obvious that two filler blocks and three mast steps give you three locations, and on and on, but three should be the most you would need. It's an ingenious idea, but a very ancient one, being at least a thousand years old. Captain Pete borrowed it from the Norsemen, who had many good ideas on small boat seafaring.

Keep in mind that provisions must be made for keeping the filler block from falling through the slot. Use either a ledge from the underside of the partner for the block to rest on, or a lip on top of the block to catch the top edge of the partner. Either way, a longish toggle on the underside of the block keeps it from jumping out. With a slotted partner, Captain Pete usually set angled stanchions underneath on either side, in addition to stoutly kneeing the partners on top.

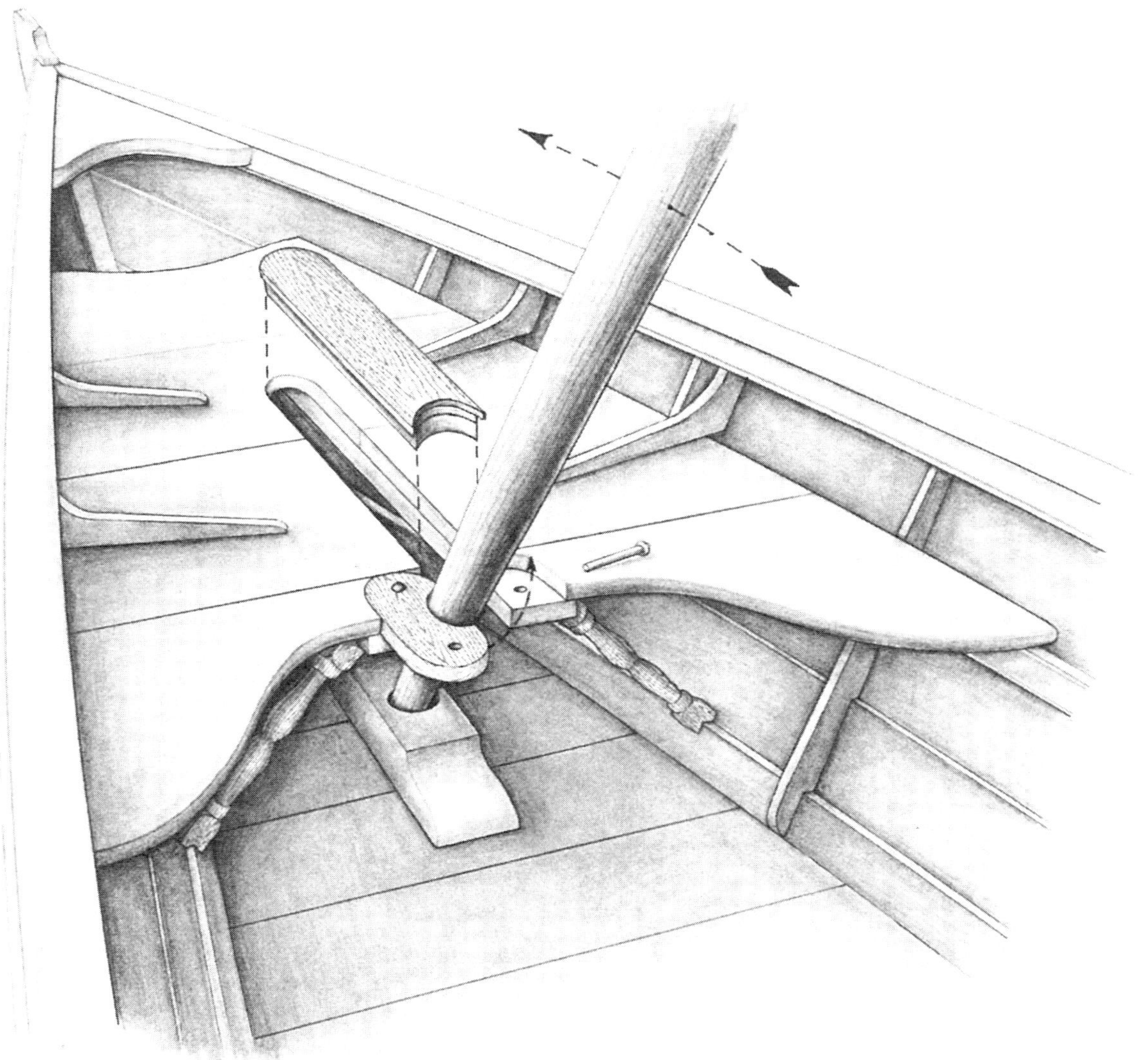

The mast partners, showing: the long slot with the filler block; the swinging gate at the aft end of the slot; the multiple mast steps; the semicircles cut into the forward end of the slot, one end of the filler block, and the forward edge of the swinging gate, these semicircles being slightly larger than the mast radius; the angled stanchions supporting the mast partners on either side; the breasthook; and the natural crook knees for the mast partners.

Sails and Rigs

The subject of masts and mast partners naturally brings to mind sail rigs, and for Captain Pete's small craft this primarily meant the spritsail. In his designing, building, and writing, the Old Man fostered, as much as anyone, the resurgence of this practical, economical, and handy workboat rig. The Captain has written extensively on his methods with sprit rigs (*Mariner's Catalog*, Volume 3, *Skiffs and Schooners*, and *Boats, Oars, and Rowing*), so I only wish to repeat the major dos and don'ts.

Perhaps the most important item to remember is to be sure you allow the mast to rotate. This means you should keep the step and heel round and the mast partners well greased. Tallow is good for this. Also, cleat any halyard to the mast itself. Like any sail rig, the sprit is a system where all of its parts and details are necessary and must work harmoniously to be successful, but if you keep the mast from rotating, it falls right on its face.

The sail should be vertical cut and the panels narrow, roped on at least three of its edges: head, luff, and foot. I prefer cotton, 2:50 boat drill for spritsails, as I think they "draw" and set better. They certainly are easier to handle and are quieter, and cotton is from the spritsail era. I know I will create some controversy by saying this, but my eyes see a difference, and cotton is the winner. The 2:50 boat

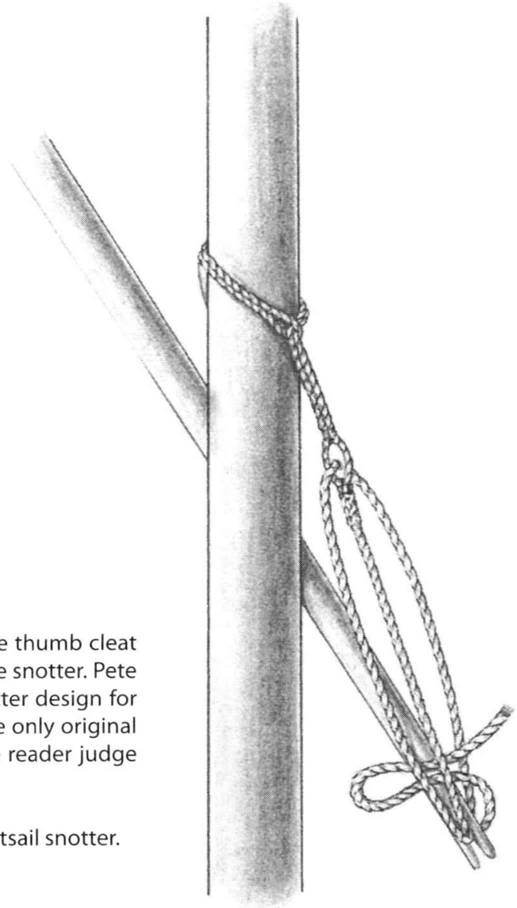

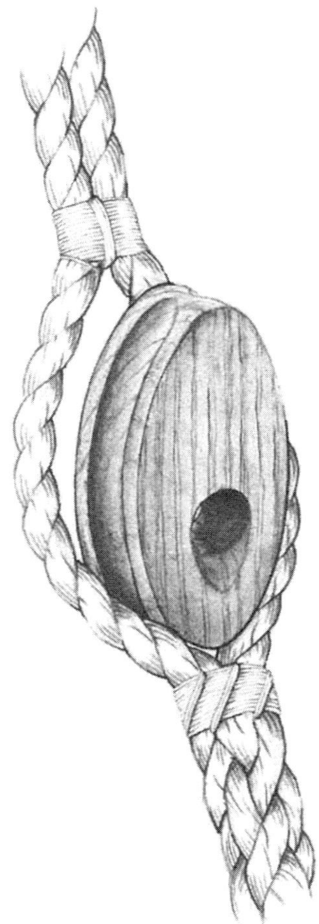

Left: A snotter for a sprit. The thumb cleat is just big enough to hold the snotter. Pete freely admitted that his snotter design for a spritsail may have been the only original item he produced. I'll let the reader judge the truth of that statement.

Right: An oak block for a spritsail snotter.

drill is the same stuff that painter's coveralls are (used to be?) made of.

The snotter is another important component for a successful sprit rig. Captain Pete freely admitted that his snotter design may have been the only original item he produced. Whether that is true or not, rig the snotter so it does not slip down the mast. The best way to do this is with a thumb cleat just big enough to hold the snotter at its correct location on the mast. If the sail has a reef, you will need two thumb cleats. When setting the sprit, take up enough on the snotter so that there are wrinkles in the sail between peak and throat. The sail will then set correctly.

Keep your tack lashing (also held by a thumb cleat) low in the boat and allow your luff to stand somewhat away from the mast by keeping either your robands or your lacings a bit slack. If you use a lacing line, be sure you go "forth and back" so it won't jam.

Sheeting a spritsail is critical because of its loose foot. This takes some trial and error, as proper sheeting depends on the amount of wind and your relative course to it. The best way to allow for this variation is a long pinrail fixed inside the after rails, port and starboard. This allows you a variety of fore-and-aft pin positions. In belaying the sheet to the pin, use the doryman's hitch.

One further item for a spritsail is a peak pennant. Make it longer, rather than shorter. An eight-foot pennant is none too long for a 16-foot boat. Here's Captain Pete on peak pennants:

"I like a long, narrow peak pennant of some colorful, light material, seized or sewn to the peak of the sail. It adds not one jot to the boat's sailing, but I think it dresses things up wonderfully."

Centerboards and Their Trunks

Sail rigs in small boats usually necessitate some form of lateral resistance other than the keel, and generally this means a centerboard. Captain Pete preferred long, narrow boards to short, wide ones.

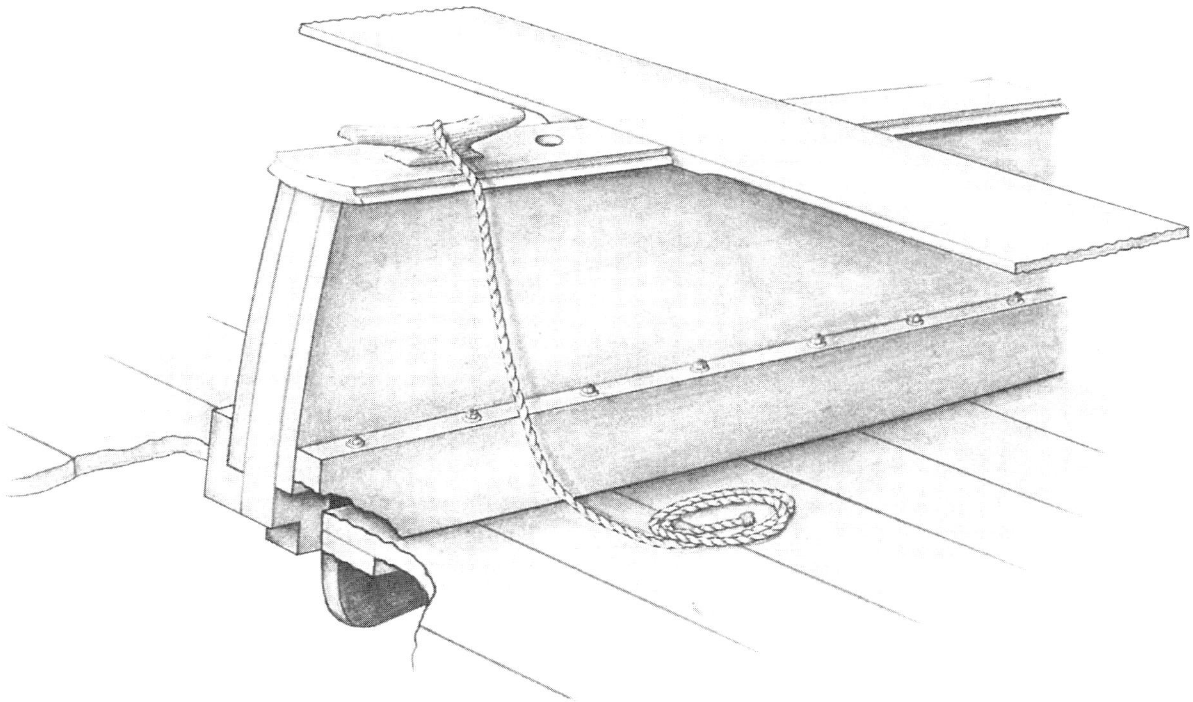

A centerboard trunk, showing: king posts the width of the slot at each end, extending from the bottom of the keel or shoe to the top of the box; thick bedlogs running each side of the king posts the full length of the slot; the sides of the box rabbeted into the bedlogs; and the box finished with a well-cap, the edges of which are beaded. The bedlogs would be set in roofing tar, and the box sides are screwed into the bedlog rabbet and the sides of the king posts. There would be a wicking of marline on the inside slot edge.

In order to get the required depth and lateral area in a short board, he would sometimes pitch up the after top edge. This did the trick when lowered, yet it was still narrow for most of its length, so it would allow a low thwart to cross the top of the box.

When building the board itself, Pete preferred to join two or more narrow planks rather than use a single wide one because of the natural tendency of the wide plank to cup and possibly jam in the box. He would joint the mating edges of the two planks and then fasten them with drifts, "driven wild," that is, at various angles to each other within the plane of the board. This kept the joint from separating. For the drifts he would use galvanized 60D nails with the heads sawn off. A long ⅜-inch drill gives the correct pilot hole and the rough galvanizing grips the hole sides. This system is excellent for any edge joining, including rudders and transoms.

A centerboard must be enclosed, and Pete had a definite way of making the box for small craft. Each plan shows the particulars for that design, but in general it would consist of king posts the width of the slot at each end. The king posts would extend from the bottom of the keel or shoe to the top of the box at the ends. There are thick bedlogs each side of these posts that run the length of the slot and into which the box sides are rabbeted. The box sides are screwed into the log rabbet and to the sides of the king posts. The box was finished with a well-cap, and this usually had a bead worked into both of its long edges. If the box sides were to be made of two pieces, the edge joint was splined and its outside edge was beaded, too. Sometimes.

To get a good fit, the bedlogs should be fitted and shaped to the top of the keel, or inside bottom, before the slot is cut. If there is any movement after the slot is cut, the bedlogs will draw it back when bolted. After there is a snug wood-to-wood joint throughout, all is carefully marked, the slot is then cut, a wicking of evenlay marline is tacked just inside the slot edge, and the area where the bedlogs will set is smeared with roofing tar. The assembled box is then put in place with the king posts now extending down through the slot. Pete made up his own "box" clamps, using ⅞-inch threaded rod with two short lengths of thick flat iron that have a 1-inch centered hole so they are free to move up and down the rod. The rod is placed down through box sides and slot, and nuts and washers are used to draw the flat irons together until they lip the keel bottom and box top, thus making an effective clamp. Take up on the clamps until the bedding is squeezed out all around. You then know the joint is watertight. All that remains is to bore down through the bedlogs, the keel or bottom, and the shoe, then bolt up.

Pete had a system for fastening. He said, "Nail where you can, screw where you must, and bolt where you have to." Centerboard bedlogs are a good example of places where you have to bolt. Stern and stem knees are the others. Perhaps riveted chine scarfs are a close cousin, but for most small boats, that's about it for bolting.

I should have mentioned bottom shoes on flat-bottomed, cross-planked boats before discussing the building of centerboard boxes, but I suppose better late than never. The bottom shoe goes on while the boat is still upside down on the stocks. It's tapered as it approaches the ends and it's fastened (screws or ring nails) from inside out. This is sort of a nasty job, especially if you used a lot of cross-bracing for your molds. If the boat is a sailing model you must keep in mind where the centerboard slot will be cut when you are fastening the bottom shoe, and this is why I should have mentioned it before. Having the cross planks fastened to the shoe keeps them from flopping around when the slot is cut.

Hmmm, let's see... Oh yes! It's easier to fasten the skeg (if there is one) to the bottom shoe before fastening the shoe to the bottom! Use those 60D drifts and screws.

If your centerboard drops through a keel you won't be concerned about flopping bottom planks, but worry about room for the bolts will more than make up for it. If the keel siding is real thin, offset the board and box. It's plenty strong, if done correctly, and doesn't affect the sailing qualities a bit. It was standard procedure on large, commercial deep-centerboarders.

Details of a sloop boat's centerboard box. The board pendant reeves right through the cleat, handy for belaying. The hole through the well-cap is for pushing down with your boathook staff, in case your board gets stuck. The pump alongside empties directly into the box. The cleat at the top of the photo is for a sheet.

The Plank Keel

The real answer, though, for small boats whose model will allow it, is the plank, or "wherry" keel. This is just what the name says: a flat plank keel, narrow at the ends, that gets wider, or "swells ," in the middle of the boat. There's plenty of room to land a centerboard box here. Typical examples of boats that use the plank keel are the Maine salmon wherry and the New Jersey Sea Bright skiff. Where Captain Pete's wherry designs differ from these is in the deadwood of the keel, aft. The Maine wherry and the Sea Bright skiff have hollow, planked-down deadwood areas. Captain Pete's deadwoods are a solid, shaped wedge with a worked rabbet cut into it. The keel rabbet starts out at the heel of the stem and runs straight along the bottom keel plank until aft of amidships, where it starts to rise in a fair sweep until it ends at the base of the transom. Everything below the rabbet aft is solid deadwood that tapers as it approaches the stern, giving it the appearance of a wedge. You make this wedge by starting with a full length lower keel plank, usually out of "two-by" stock (which today translates to 1½ inches thick). In breadth, this lower plank is wide in the middle and tapered at the ends. Remember? From our lofting we find where the rabbet starts to rise from this lower plank and measure from there to the stern, remembering that this "step" needs to be longer than the lower plank because of the transom rake. If you make this new piece out of the same "two-by" stock, the deadwood is now three inches thick, and the top piece is shaped the same as the lower. Find where the rabbet runs out on the second piece, measure to the stern allowing

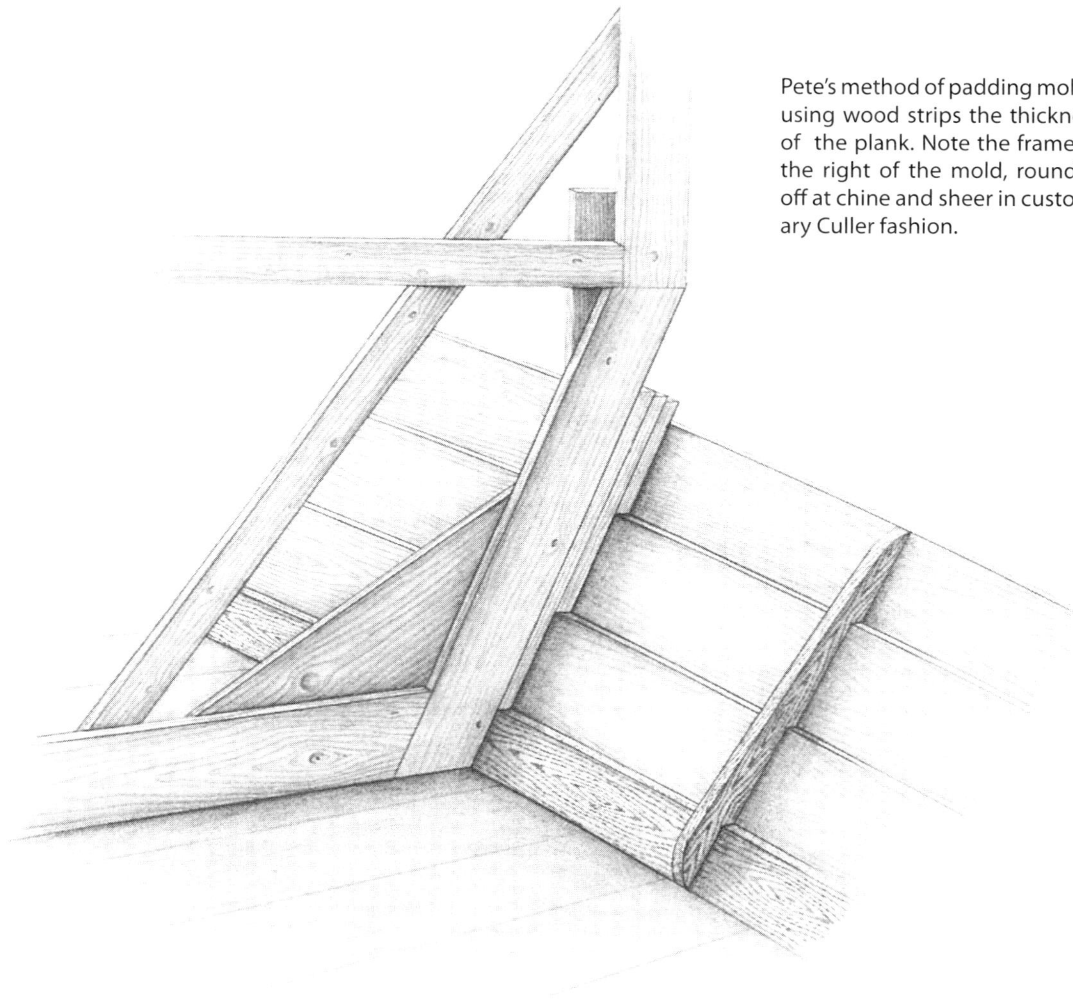

Pete's method of padding molds, using wood strips the thickness of the plank. Note the frame to the right of the mold, rounded off at chine and sheer in customary Culler fashion.

for rake, and then cut out the third piece and place it on top. You now have two steps as each piece of "two-by" gets shorter. Continue in this way until the rabbet reaches the stern. Glue them all together, bolt or lag screw them, and cut the rabbet. I hope you allowed enough wood for a wide bearding, and don't forget the stopwaters.

The keel has always been referred to as the backbone in a boat and the framing as ribs—this metaphor is particularly appropriate because all wooden boats built with integrity have a liveliness and soul that transcends the inanimate. They're alive—and nicely so, too.

Frames and Framing

Rather than install full-length bent frames in his round-bilged craft, Captain Pete made them in two pieces, allowing them to run by each other at the keel and up to the top edge of the garboard on the opposite side. This allowed a slightly smaller frame scantling, gave extra strength where it was needed at the keel, and eliminated a potential fracture point at the keel/frame fastening. Your steam box need only be half as big, too. Between the regular frames he would insert "floating frames." These were steam bent too, and they lay across the first three strakes on both sides of the keel. If there were much shape in the ends, these would be solid floors.

After all the frames were in, the entire inside bottom would be cleaned scrupulously; the area of the inside garboard, keel, and frames would be painted with red lead, and hot pitch would be poured over all. He was a great believer in pitching round-bilged craft.

Bow staving on a V-bottomed boat. In the fore ground is a length of "thick stuff" to be used for a bow stave. In the workman's hand is a nearly completed stave—note the twist in shape. The forward end of the bow has been staved up, and just below the forward mold the change from "butt to lap" can be seen. The power hand planers on the bench are a great aid in shaping the staves. (R.D. Culler photo)

Hard-chine craft, V- or flat-bottom, have straight sides in section. To simplify the framing and give the craft better shape, Captain Pete would pad the molds for lapstrake side plank. The craft is lofted and molds are built, in the normal way, to the designed lines. The molds are lined off for side plank, chines are put on and faired for bottom plank, and the first plank is installed. Now with the second side plank, Pete's method differed from the standard. Instead of "browsing off" or beveling the lap so the second plank hugs the molds, you pad each mold with a wood strip as thick as your plank. (The strip runs from the top edge of the first plank to the sheer mark.) Spile your second plank, cut it out, and lay it on. Then pad out again, from the top edge of the second plank to the sheer mark. Continue in this fashion until you have the boat planked. What results is a craft that is slightly wider and shaplier than the designed lines. Most important, the jogged framing is far easier, as each jog is of uniform depth. Starting in the middle and working toward the ends requires but a single master pattern. Simply mark the jog spacings and cut out your frame. Be sure that the inboard parts of every frame are straight and uniformly thick at chine and sheer so your seat riser will lay fair when fastened to the frames. Round off each frame at the chine and sheer and that's it. Neat and quick.

One point to remember when using the "pad out" method is that the plank will be meeting your stern rabbet and transom at a greater angle than designed. Just keep this in mind when cutting the rabbet and the transom bevels. Plank gains are not affected. Altogether, this "padding out" is neat, effective, and simple, and it results in a handsome craft.

Planking

Mentioning plank gains brings up the fact that Pete had a superior system worked out for these, too. It was designed to avoid the thin, fragile edge of most gain-cutting techniques, which tend to split and ruin otherwise fine planks. At the lap he would divide the plank thickness in thirds. The gain would begin in the usual fashion, then quickly become a rolling bevel that would end angled across the middle third of the plank's thickness. Naturally, the matching gain is opposite, so you get two-thirds of the plank's thickness at the point where most gains tend to split. In joining the plank gains, you should make one longer, or shorter, than the other to avoid the hump you would get if they were the same length. It doesn't really make a lot of difference what length they are; just make sure they are different.

Bow Staving

Having mentioned V-bottoms previously, I would like to attempt an explanation of the construction techniques for bow staving on V- or flat-bottomed boats. Simply put, you need to fill in the area between stem, chine, and keel with individual bottom

Pete's method for deck planking was to cut the plank square. This gives a stout deck and four sides from which to choose the clearest. (R.D. Culler photo)

planks. This is called a "herringbone" bottom. With flat-bottomed planking, it is simple to fill the area of the bottom with individual planks, because both ends of the bottom plank fastened at the chines are in the same plane. A board of uniform thickness will suffice on flat-bottoms. With V-bottoms, the keel rabbet and stem rabbet are on the same plane and the chine is on another, constantly changing plane as it rises, approaches, and meets the stem. With a bit of mental imagery it becomes plain that in order to fasten the flat of one end of the board to the chine and then fasten the flat of the other end to the keel or stem rabbet, the board needs a twist. Right here, think airplane propellers, and I believe you will grasp the idea. Yes? Now most people would think steam to get this twist, but that would be a mistake, because it won't work. The bow staving must begin as thick stuff and the twist is hewed out, so it gives the same effect as an airplane propeller.

There are other slightly different methods to constructing the bow staving on V-bottoms, and Chapelle's Boatbuilding discusses these in some depth. What I have just described was the basic technique that Captain Pete used predominantly on his flat-bottomed boats.

While still on the subject of V-bottom planking, I would like to suggest some tips, hints, or clues that will refine the basic method so that perhaps you can avoid a blind alley or two.

Start planking the bottom forward, never aft. About amidships, the bottom planks should be raking aft about 20 degrees. Because of this, and because the chine at the bow is a longer line than the rabbet, the staves are wider at the chine. Just how wide depends on the boat and the stock you have on hand. Narrow boards shrink less than wide ones, however.

Flat-bottoms are usually built upside down. After molds, keel, stem, and transom (if there is one) are set up, the chine is spiled and bent in place. The chine is then faired down for the bottom, using a narrow board between rabbet and chine. Take your time here. The first side plank is then spiled and placed on the boat with the edge at the chine left full. The bow staving is now begun, and the usual practice is to butt the top of the bow staves to the lower edge of the side plank until the angle of bottom and side plank begins to approach 90 degrees. The bottom plank then runs by, or "laps," the chine and side plank. Depending on the boat's model and how the bow staves are started, this change

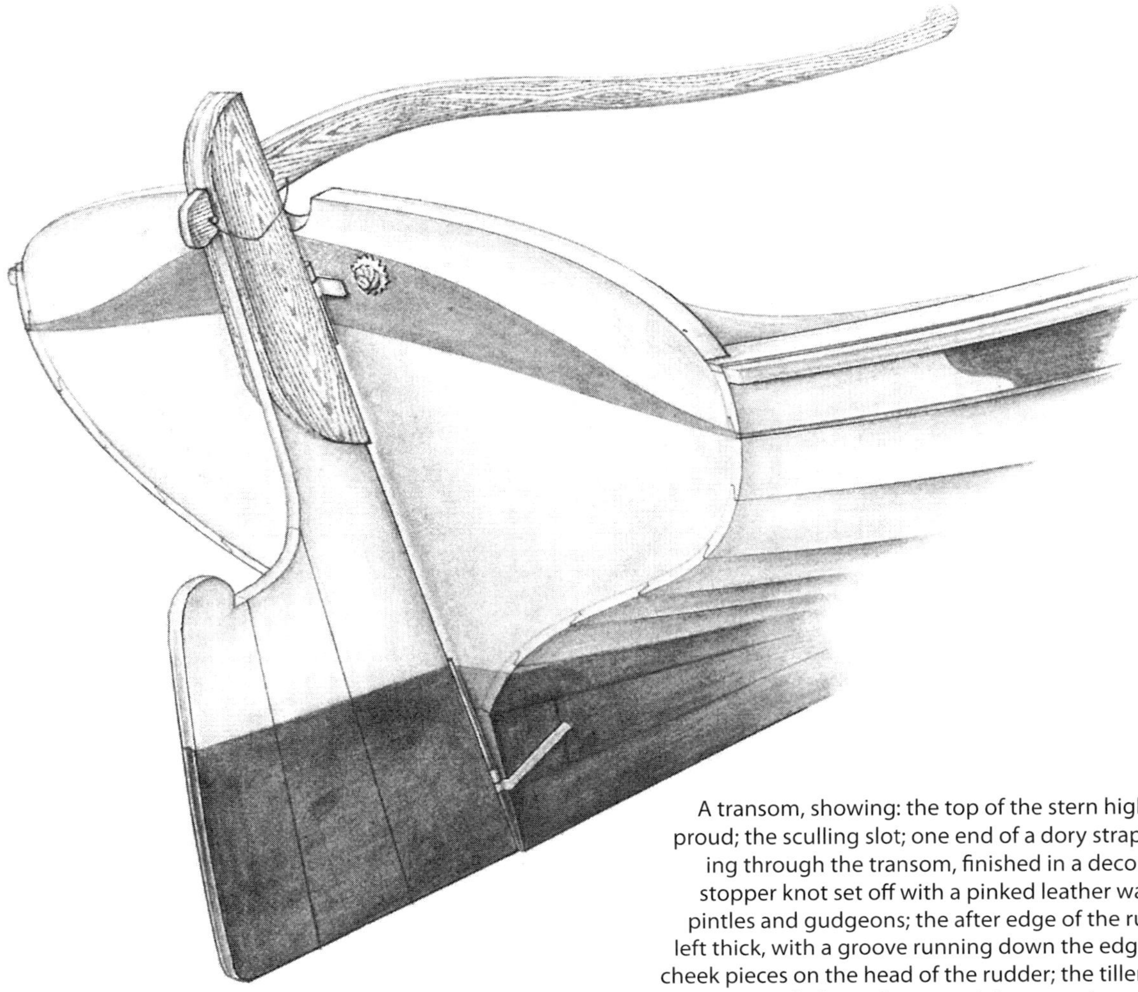

A transom, showing: the top of the stern high and proud; the sculling slot; one end of a dory strap poking through the transom, finished in a decorative stopper knot set off with a pinked leather washer; pintles and gudgeons; the after edge of the rudder left thick, with a groove running down the edge; the cheek pieces on the head of the rudder; the tiller with its powderhorn shape; and the stern decoration.

"from butt to lap" usually occurs somewhere around station 2. The only reason for this "butt/lap" business is to get good fastening at the chine. Keeping your bow staves upright for a bit before beginning to rake them aft results in a hollow forefoot and a sharp entry.

The Stern

That's enough for the forward end; let's go all the way aft and talk a little about small-boat sterns.

Pete drew sterns in all sizes and shapes. The common thread running through all of them was good looks. Unless the boat had a flat bottom, there usually was some reverse down at the rabbet. He also preferred to leave the tops of his sterns high and proud. His standard procedure was to leave plenty of wood, just as the stemheads were left long, and do the cutting and shaping after the boat was nearly complete. The actual height varied some as to model. It mostly had to do with what "looked right."

Invariably, there would be a sculling slot cut somewhere along the top of the transom. Many times he preferred this slot offset to port so a rudder could be used while sculling. Captain Pete considered the ability to scull a vessel just good seamanship.

The Old Man liked to place a dory strap centered below the crown of the stern. This is a bight of line inboard that passes through two holes in the stern with decorative stopper knots on the outboard side. Pinked leather washers set off the knots very nicely. This is a fine place for some seaman's art. A dory strap is also handy for bending a docking line to, it can be used as a lifting ring, and if the knots are placed just so, they pad the rudder cheeks when the tiller is hard over. This is a perfect example of a Culler "embellishment."

The quarter, or monkey rail, on *Integrity*. Many rails nowadays look as though they were bought right out of a furniture showroom. To avoid that "stiff" appearance, each stanchion is set at a different angle so the rail has a slow, rolling tumblehome as it approaches the stern. It then looks "right." (R.D. Culler photo)

In constructing his sterns, Pete kept them as simple as possible. He never used a frame, feeling that they only caused problems by swelling and forcing the plank away from the transom edge. On flat-bottomed craft, chines were butted to the inside transom face, bottom planks were fastened to the lower transom edge, side planks were screwed to the transom sides, quarter knees were fitted, and that was it. Many of his flat-bottomed craft are still around and showing no weakness.

With round and V-bottoms he would add a sternpost and knee. This post was notched deeply into the keel and the transom would be notched into the post. The knee, attached to post and top of keel, holds it all together, along with two, very necessary quarter knees.

Rudders

Sailing models require rudders, and Pete had a definite way of hanging these. He liked to use the English beachboat system. The hardware on the boat consisted of a normal gudgeon on the transom, but the lower fixture on the keel is an inverted pintle with an extended pin. On the rudder, the upper piece is a long pintle mounted normally, and the lower hardware is a pintle with its pin sawn off and a hole bored where the pin normally would be. The pintle on the rudder is not the same length as the "reversed" pintle on the boat, although both are much longer than the usual variety. This system allows you to ship your rudder easily, because even with your weight aft, that lower pintle is above water. With the two pintles of unequal length, you can connect the lower set and then turn your attention to the upper ones, without the need to do them both simultaneously, which can be a chore in a bobbing boat. With this design it is also quite obvious that when you scrape across that just-discovered shoal spot, the rudder will rise considerably without unshipping. The transom rake helps this in the same way that a raking mast allows a sail to slide down easily. This is a most handy system when looked at as a whole, and it is understandable why it developed for beachboats.

Captain Pete made his rudders out of several boards of uniform thickness that were edge-fastened with drifts that are "nailed wild." The after edge of these rudders was rarely tapered thin; more commonly, it was left thick or even thickened, and a groove was run down the after edge so the rudder would have "bite" and provide a steady helm. The trailing part of a rudder, above the waterline, is a prime spot for some individual art.

The Tiller

The main body of the rudder rises to the height shown on the plan and cheekpieces are placed on both sides. The tiller is inserted between the cheekpieces and rests on the rudderhead. You should engineer this so the tiller at rest and in its normal position will just clear the gunwales when swung from side to side.

The tiller is pinned forward and aft of the slot. The forward pin is permanent and the after, removable pin is held to the permanent one by a lanyard. The heads of these pins can be turned artfully, and the removable pin should have a slot cut down its length, like a clothespin, to ease its entry and exit from the hole. The tiller that Captain Pete was fond of using is shaped much like a powderhorn and therefore reflects the sheer that was his trademark. It is wide at the rudder, rising in an arc at the rudderhead and then sweeping downward in a graceful line that tapers all the while to a slight handle. The shape of the rudderhead and the initial part of this tiller accent the height of the stern.

The Boat Name

With all of this detail around and about the stern, many people often wonder where they should place the name. Pete rarely if ever placed a name on the transom, preferring the sheer plank at the bow. Many times he would only indicate the name with a bow badge. His dory *Dancing Feather* is a good example. If the full name was used, it was painted on a very thin name board that was removable. That way, you won't have to paint the name every year.

Many times the name was set off with five-pointed stars. The stern is a good place for five-pointed stars, too. Sometimes these stars would be used in conjunction with a painted stern decoration that would run into the stern from the sheerstrake bead. *Integrity's* yawlboat and the Staten Island skiff are good examples of this.

The Color Scheme

Captain Pete liked to use yellow and sometimes red for the sheerstrake bead. Often he used bottle green for the hull, with a black sheerstrake, yellow bead, and barn red gunwale. He referred to these as "schooner colors." He almost always painted the inside a light or French gray and always oiled his inside skiff bottoms. In a word, you could say he preferred "earthy" colors. Here's Captain Pete on paints and paint schemes:

"As to paints, for 40 or more years I've been doing it about the same on my own boats. I use plain white oil house paint of good grade as a base for most of it. Find something that weighs heavy by the can; this indicates good lead content. I make grays, yellows, buffs, browns, and blues, if light, out of this, using colors ground in oil, or occasionally dry ones. This is a soft paint with little gloss, it wears well, and it is not garish. Others I use are barn (or oxide) red, ready mixed, and black and green. I use a little dark blue at times, though for mixing I like Prussian blue—it fades, but no matter how much, it is always blue.

"That's about all I've ever used, and with some tinting colors (the umbers and siennas) where it fits in, I sometimes add red lead; it's a very good drier when mixed with other paint.

"If you want a flatter paint, mix to suit, then let it set until it settles and oil comes to the top. Pour off some oil and add a little turps. I use very little hard enamel paint for myself, except for trucks and machinery, where the standard tractor paints work well.

"I've done a lot of different schemes for small craft of traditional model. My old sailing dory is attractive. She has buff sails, dark full green (a green that looks green, not black) sheerstrake, and a colonial (cream) yellow hull with raised badges. A little varnish on the tiller and the well-cap set it off.

"Sometimes I make sketches for a new boat and use a cheap watercolor set; this gives mild but contrasting colors. I simply never have cared for most store-mixed paints or the hard finishes. Everybody says I'm nuts, but the boats look good. People think you can't possibly use paint that doesn't have a picture of a speedboat on the can."

I don't know why I feel as though I have rambled on too long and yet have not said enough. I suppose the best thing to say now is—DO IT. Read, look at plans, visit boatyards, seek out knowledgeable people, and then start. Once you get into it, you'll find that a lot of things that seem mysterious begin to make sense, and all the time you are building, you are gaining experience. Right here I'll leave you with another of Pete Culler's favorite sayings: "Mostly, boatbuilding is simply correcting one mistake after the other, and possibly the first mistake is to begin... but it's so much fun!"

Appendix B Bibliography

All of these works have been very helpful to me, so they also ought to be helpful to you. Further reading sources, listed by chapter, follow this selected bibliography.

Abell, Sir Westcott, *The Shipwright's Trade.* Centreville, MD: Cornell Maritime Press, 1948 (reprint). This is an important history of shipbuilding from ancient times to the 20th century. It somehow manages to highlight and explain clearly most of the important details.

Bray, Maynard, *Mystic Seaport Watercraft.* Mystic, CT: Mystic Seaport Museum, Inc., 1979. Second only to Howard Chapelle's *National Watercraft Collection* in wealth of information and therefore very useful. A number of Culler-built boats are pictured.

Bray, Maynard, *Taking Care of Wooden Ships.* Sea Grant Publications, 1979. Describes methods of wooden vessel maintenance. Very important for any wooden boat owner. Much information from Captain Pete; the book is dedicated to him.

Burgess, Robert H., *Chesapeake Sailing Craft - Part I.* Centreville, MD: Tidewater Publishers, 1975. A very good history and record of bay craft written by one of the bay's most noted historians. Captain Pete and the Spray appear on page 50.

Chapelle, Howard I., *American Sailing Craft.* New York: Kennedy Brothers, 1936 (reprint: Bonanza Books). A reprint of articles that appeared in *Yachting* magazine in the 1930s on certain types and their potential use as yachts.

Chapelle, Howard I., *American Small Sailing Craft: Their Design, Development and Construction.* New York: W.W. Norton, 1951. This is the definitive work on sailing workboat types up to 45 feet. Much history of their development and many lines plans are reproduced.

Chapelle, Howard I., *The Baltimore Clipper: Its Origin and Development.* Salem, MA: Marine Research Society, 1930 (reprint: Bonanza Books).

Chapelle, Howard I., *Boatbuilding.* New York: W.W. Norton, 1941. If you have decided to build a design from this book of plans, you're going to need Chapelle's book.

Chapelle, Howard I., *The History of the American Sailing Navy.* New York: W.W. Norton, 1939. Chapelle, Howard I., The History of American Sailing Ships. New York: W.W. Norton, 1955.

Chapelle, Howard I., *The Migrations of an American Boat Type.* United States National Museum Bulletin 228, 1961. A discussion of the sharpie type and its rapid spread throughout the coastal United States.

Chapelle, Howard I., *The National Watercraft Collection.* Camden, ME: International Marine Publishing Co., 1976 (2nd ed.). An extremely useful catalog for those interested in traditional vessels.

Chapelle, Howard I., *The Search for Speed Under Sail 1770-1855.* New York: W.W. Norton, 1967. Analyzes speed factors and their design development in sailing craft. During the mid-1950s, an expanded outline of this book appeared in *Yachting.* A comment on Chapelle's conclusions was made in the September 1968 issue of the late, great *Skipper* magazine, and is worth repeating here:

> Modern yachtsmen may be surprised to learn that their craft are seldom better, and usually poorer, than many commercial vessels of the past two centuries in comparative performance. This is one of the conclusions reached by marine historian Howard Chapelle in his book *The Search for Speed Under Sail.* Chapelle compares performances of different vessels by an index number which is, in fact, a speed-length ratio calculated by dividing highest recorded speed in knots by the square root of the waterline length in feet. Yachtsmen are seeking speed in boats whose qualities are determined by whim, fashion and arbitrary rating rules, Chapelle says. He points out that the current world record for sustained speed under sail, ten days during which the speed-length ratio of 1.29 (the best of the clippers managed 1.25) was set in 1965 by a ketch that rates poorly under all modern handicapping rules. Her hull is characteristic of the best small commercial vessels of the last century. She is, of course, "*Ticonderoga,*" designed by L. Francis Herreshoff and built in 1936.

Chapelle, Howard I., *Yacht Designing and Planning.* New York : W.W. Norton, 1936. This book and *Boatbuilding* were always on Captain Pete's desk, immediately available for ready reference.

Culler, R.D., *Boats, Oars, and Rowing.* Camden, ME: International Marine Publishing Co., 1978. A very tight essay on rowing craft with much illustration and lore.

Culler, R.D., *Skiffs and Schooners.* Camden, ME: International Marine Publishing Co., 1974. The primary source: this book should be studied by all who are interested in Culler craft.

Culler, R.D., *The Spray: Building and Sailing a Replica of Joshua Slocum's Famous Vessel.* Camden, ME: International Marine Publishing Co., 1978. Pete's story of his *Spray*. The closest to an autobiography of the Old Man.

Desmond, Charles, *Wooden Shipbuilding*. New York: Rudder Publishing Co., 1919. Tremendous amount of useful information chronicles the last great boom in wooden shipbuilding.

Estep, H. Cole, *How Wooden Ships Are Built*. Cleveland, OH: Penton Publishing Co., 1918 (reprint: W.W. Norton, 1983). Extremely valuable photographic record, with good supporting text. The final chapter is on lofting (laying down) large vessels. The above two books were almost Bibles for Captain Pete.

Farmer, Weston, *From My Old Boat Shop: One-Lung Engines, Fantail Launches, & Other Marine Delights*. Camden, ME: International Marine Publishing Co., 1979. Captain Pete and Westy Farmer were penpals for many years and shared much the same philosophy regarding boats. I recommend Chapters 2 and 3.

Gardner, John, *Building Classic Small Craft*. Camden, ME: International Marine Publishing Co., 1977. John Gardner is the dean of traditional small craft, and the chapters of this book are revised and updated articles that originally appeared in the National Fisherman. Describes the building, handling, and lore of all manner of small craft. Everyone interested in small craft owes much to John Gardner.

Gardner, John, *The Dory Book*. Camden, ME: International Marine Publishing Co., 1978. The definitive book on the subject by the acknowledged authority on the type.

Getchell, David, Putz, George, Spectre, Peter, *The Mariner's Catalog*, Volumes 1 through 7. Camden, ME: International Marine Publishing Co., 1973-1979. Captain Pete was a frequent contributor to these catalogs . All seven catalogs (none of them repetitious) contain a gold mine of information pertaining to boats and their way of going. Highly recommended.

Griffiths, John W., *A Treatise on Marine and Naval Architecture or Theory and Practice Blended in Shipbuilding*. New York: D. Appleton & Co., 1853 (3rd ed.). Griffiths' prose is difficult to read but there is much written here on shipbuilding and design. Pete used this work frequently.

Herreshoff, L. Francis, *The Compleat Cruiser*. New York: Sheridan House, 1956. After you choose your dreamboat from among the Culler designs, you'll find this book invaluable in guiding you in its cruising. The chapters originally appeared serially in *The Rudder* magazine—a couple of the best chapters were left out of the book.

Herreshoff, L. Francis, *An L. Francis Herreshoff Reader*. Camden, ME: International Marine Publishing Co., 1978. An excellent sampling of the writings of Herreshoff, including a good chapter on half-modeling.

Herreshoff, L. Francis, *Sensible Cruising Designs*. Camden, ME: International Marine Publishing. Co., 1973. Displays some of the Skipper's cruising designs, including Meadow Lark.

March, Edgar J., *Inshore Craft of Britain in the Days of Sail and Oar*, Vols. I and II. Camden, ME: International Marine Publishing Co., 1970. Exhaustive research and detailed history of small craft types in Britain. Pete used these books extensively.

Simmons, Walter J., *Lapstrake Boatbuilding* and *Lapstrake Boatbuilding, Vol. 2*. Camden, ME: International Marine Publishing Co., 1978, 1980. Chapelle's *Boatbuilding* is thin on lapstrake techniques, but these two books will answer most of your questions. Written by a man who is doing it.

Smith, Hervey Garrett, *The Arts of the Sailor*. New York: D. Van Nostrand Co., 1953. Excellent introduction to marlinspike seamanship. My paperback copy (Funk and Wagnalls, 1968) is usually found in my ditty bag. It is an excellent quick reference. The author is an artist by profession and his drawings show it.

Smith, Hervey Garrett, *Boat Carpentry*. New York: Van Nostrand Reinhold, 1965 (2nd ed.). A basic introduction that shows the elementary clearly, with Smith's excellent drawings.

Stephens, W.P., *Traditions and Memories of American Yachting*, Complete Edition. Camden, ME: International Marine Publishing Co., 1981. Primarily a history of American yachting from its beginnings to the 1940s by a man who was there for most of it. Excellent discussions on small craft and small cruisers.

Captain Pete was well versed in all the allied boat trades. In addition to being a boatbuilder and designer, he was an accomplished machinist, sailmaker, and blacksmith. The following three books will help you become familiar with smithing.

Andrews, Jack, *Edge of the Anvil*. Emmaus, PA: Rodale Press, 1977.

The Blacksmith's Craft—An Introduction to Smithing for Apprentices and Craftsmen. Publication #54. London: Rural Industries Bureau, 1952.

Weygers, Alexander G., *The Modern Blacksmith*. New York: Van Nostrand Reinhold, 1974.

Periodicals

The American Neptune, Salem, MA (Vol. I, 1941) A scholarly journal of marine history. At times has very good articles on traditional boat types.

The Ash Breeze, Mystic, CT (Vol. I, 1977) Quarterly newsletter of the Traditional Small Craft Association, of which Pete Culler was a founding member.

The Mariner's Mirror, London (Vol. I, 1914) The

Captain Pete in 1951 with the first skiff he built at his Hyannis shop.

quarterly journal of the Society for Nautical Research. Founded by Dr. R.C. Anderson.

National Fisherman (formerly *Maine Coast Fisherman*), Camden, ME (Vol. I, 1947) In recent years has concentrated more on fishing news. Back issues have much information on traditional craft, including many articles by Captain Pete.

Nautical Quarterly, New York (Vol. I, 1977) A superbly produced magazine that occasionally has articles on small craft.

Rudder (Vol. I, 1890) No longer being published. I recommend issues prior to 1965. These are priceless.

The Small Boat Journal, Bennington, VT (Vol. I, 1978) Concentrates on craft under 30 feet, both power and sail. Soundings, Essex, CT. The most extensive used-boat classifieds available anywhere.

WoodenBoat, Brooklin, ME (Vol. I, 1974) An excellent magazine for the craft shown in this catalog.

Yachting, New York (Vol. I, 1907) Lately has concentrated on the go-fast set but older issues have a wealth of information on traditional boat types.

Further Reading Sources, Listed By Design

Part I

Sharp Wherry

Gardner, John, "Traditional Craft Gather at Mystic Seaport." *Soundings*, July 1976.

Culler, R.D., *Skiffs and Schooners*, p. 52.

Bray, Maynard, *Mystic Seaport Watercraft*, p. 158.
Blandford, Percy, "English River Skiffs." *WoodenBoat* #30, p. 36. A good discussion of details in classic small boats.

Soundings, February 1976.

Fast Gig

Culler, R.D., *Boats, Oars, and Rowing*, p. 142.

March, Edgar, *Inshore Craft of Britain in the Days of Sail and Oar.*

Watts, Simon, "Pilot Gigs of Cornwall and the Scilly

Islands." *WoodenBoat* #25, p. 28.
Taylor, Roger C., "The Great Sliding Seat." *Nautical Quarterly* #18.

Punch
Culler, R.D., *Skiffs and Schooners*, p. 85.
Bray, Maynard, *Mystic Seaport Watercraft.*
Gardner, John, "Traditional Craft Gather at Mystic Seaport." *Soundings*, July 1976.
Chapelle, Howard I., *The National Watercraft Collection*, p.98.

Shallop
Culler, R.D., *Skiffs and Schooners*, pp. 87-88.
Baker, W.A., *Sloops and Shallops.* Barre, MA: Barre Publishing Co., 1966.
Chapelle, Howard I., *American Small Sailing Craft.*
Baker, W.A., "Notes on a Shallop." *The American Neptune*, No.2, 1957.

Clipper Cornish Yawl
See references listed under "Fast Gig."

Sloopboats
Culler, R.D., *Skiffs and Schooners*, p. 122.
Howland, Waldo, "The Concordia Sloopboat." *WoodenBoat* #29, p. 98.
Barnard, W.L., "The Plymouth Lobster Boats." *WoodenBoat* #1, p . 65.
Bray, Maynard, *Mystic Seaport Watercraft*, pp. 72-73.
Chapelle, Howard I., *American Small Sailing Craft.*
Gardner, John, "Kingston Lobster Boats." *National Fisherman*, July 1969.
Soundings, February 1976.
National Fisherman: January 1965, October 1971, and December 1972.
Skipper magazine, May 1969.
Yachting magazine, November 1964, p. 66.

Staten Island Skiff
Culler, R.D., *Boats, Oars, and Rowing*, pp. 140-141.
Simmons, Walter, *Lapstrake Boatbuilding*, Vol. 2.
Guthorn, Peter J., *The Sea Bright Skiff and Other Shore Boats.* Exton, PA: Schiffer Publishing, Ltd., 1982.
Bray, Maynard, *Mystic Seaport Watercraft.* See "The Yankee Skiff," p. 158.

Double-Paddle Canoes
Culler, R.D., *Boats, Oars, and Rowing.*
Manley, H. Atwood, *Rushton and His Times in American Canoeing.* Syracuse, NY: Syracuse University Press, 1968.
Stephens, W.P., *Traditions and Memories of American Yachting*, Complete Edition.
Soundings, February 1976.
The Mariner's Catalog, Volume 4.
Roche, John, "Pete Culler Remembered." *Ash Breeze*, Vol. 5, No.2, Spring 1983.

Sailing, Paddling Canoe
See references listed under "Double-Paddle Canoes."

Yacht America II *Yawlboats*
Culler, R.D., *Skiffs and Schooners*, p, 92.
Gardner, John, *Building Classic Small Craft.* An excellent discussion of Whitehall boats, and the *America II* yawlboats are pictured.

Race Point Surfboat
Culler, R.D., *Skiffs and Schooners*, p. 49.
Stackpole, E.A., *Life Saving Nantucket.* Nantucket, MA, 1972.
Bray, Maynard, *Mystic Seaport Watercraft.* Race Point boats are pictured, with lines, and there is an excellent listing of further reading sources.

Yawl
Culler, R.D., *Skiffs and Schooners*, p. 45.
Chapelle, Howard I., *American Small Sailing Craft.*
Chapman, F.H., *Architectura Navalis Mercatoria.* 1768.
Classic Boat Monthly, July 1974.
Soundings, February 1976.

Wherry Yawl
See references listed under "Yawl."

Concordia Baeteka Pram
Culler, R.D., *Skiffs and Schooners*, p. 5.
Gardner, John, *Building Classic Small Craft.* Chapter on building prams.
Howland, Waldo, "Reflections on Simple Boats." *Ash Breeze*, March 1979.

Part II
Revised Sharptown Barge
Culler, R.D., *Skiffs and Schooners*, pp . 29, 65, 115.
National Fisherman: June 1968, August 1971.
Rudder, November 1952.
Soundings, February 1976.

Sharpie
Culler, R.D., *Skiffs and Schooners*, p, 5.

Swampscott Dory
Culler, R.D., *Skiffs and Schooners*, p. 119.
Gardner, John, *Building Classic Small Craft.*
Gardner, John, *The Dory Book.* A very good discussion of

all manner of dories, including the Swampscott.
The Mariner's Catalog, Volume 3, p. 26.
The Mariner's Catalog, Volume 4, p. 14.
Soundings, February 1976.

Clipper Pulling Bateau Otter
Culler, R.D., *Skiffs and Schooners*, p. 66.
Soundings, July 1976.
Chapelle, Howard I., *American Small Sailing Craft.*
The Mariner's Catalog, Volume 3, p. 26.
The Mariner's Catalog, Volume 4, p. 14.

Clipper Pulling Bateau
See references under "Clipper Pulling Bateau Otter."

Good Little Skiffs
Culler, R.D., *Skiffs and Schooners*, pp. 62-63, 112.
Culler, R.D., *Boats, Oars, and Rowing*, p. 131.
The Mariner's Catalog, Volume 3, pp . 54, 56.
Bray, Maynard, *Mystic Seaport Watercraft.* Culler skiffs are pictured.
Howland, Waldo, "Reflections on Simple Boats." *Ash Breeze*, March 1979.
Soundings, February 1976.
National Fisherman: August 1968, December 1970, July 1971, August 1974.

Catboat
Culler, R.D., *Skiffs and Schooners.*
Culler, R.D., *Boats, Oars, and Rowing.*
Leavens, John, *The Catboat Book.* Camden, ME: International Marine Publishing Co., 1972.

Beachboat Java
Culler, R.D., *Skiffs and Schooners*, p. 82.
National Fisherman, February 1968.

V-Bottomed Pod
Culler, R.D., *Skiffs and Schooners.*
Culler, R.D., *Boats, Oars, and Rowing*, p. 13.
The Mariner's Catalog, Volume 3, p. 55.
National Fisherman: July 1963, August 1967.

Skiffs
Culler, R.D., *Boats, Oars, and Rowing*, pp. 132-134.
WoodenBoat #24, p. 96.
Baker, R., "The Westport Skiff." *WoodenBoat* #32, p. 29. A good discussion of a flat-bottomed skegless type.

Daysailers
Culler, R.D., *Skiffs and Schooners*, pp. 74-75.
Roche, John, "Pete Culler Remembered." *Ash Breeze*, Spring 1983.

Rowing Skiff/Wheelbarrow Skiff
Chapelle, Howard I., *Boatbuilding.*
The Mariner's Catalog, Volume 2, p. 100.
Meras, Phyllis, *A Yankee Way With Wood.* Boston, MA: Houghton-Mifflin Co., 1975. Pete Culler builds the rowing skiff.

Yawlboat for Integrity
Culler, R.D., *Skiffs and Schooners*, p. 57.
Culler, R.D., *Boats, Oars, and Rowing*, p. 24.
National Fisherman, July 1963.
Soundings, February 1976.

Sailing Sampan
Culler, R.D., *Skiffs and Schooners*, pp . 42-43.
National Fisherman, January 1965.

Concordia Yard Butthead
Bray, Maynard, *Mystic Seaport Watercraft.*
Gardner, John, *Building Classic Small Craft.* Punt building.

Part III

Motor Vessel Proposal
Culler, R.D., *Skiffs and Schooners*, p. 100.

Albacore Troller Townes
Brooks, "A Sailing Albacore Troller." *National Fisherman*, March 1977.
National Fisherman, September 1972.
Crowley, Michael, " Better With Age." *WoodenBoat* #16, p.63.
Larssen, A.K., and Jaeger, Sig, *The ABC's of Fo'c'sle Living.* Seattle, WA: Madrona Publishers, Inc., 1976. How-to of working and living aboard a commercial fisherman.
The Mariner's Catalog, Volume 4, p. 71. A Hundested diesel is pictured.

Concordia Novi Motor Cruiser
Mayher, Bill, "The Lobsterboats of Grand Manan." *WoodenBoat* #45, p. 82.
Bray, Maynard, "Understanding a Novi Boat." *WoodenBoat* #45, p. 88.

Steam Launches
Culler, R.D., *Skiffs and Schooners*, pp. 94-96.
Durham, Bill, *Steamboats and Modern Steam Launches.* Berkeley, CA: Howell-North Publishing Co., 1973.
National Fisherman: August 1972, February 1973.

V-Bottomed Fantail Steamer
See references listed under "Steam Launches." Also see the May-June 1962 issue of *Steamboats and Modern*

Steam Launches. Captain Pete wrote about a "Deadrise Fantail Steamer."

Fast Outboard Launch

Culler, R.D., *Skiffs and Schooners*, pp. 78-79. *Motorboat*, April 1970.

National Fisherman: July 1963, January 1969. *Yachting*, July 1969.

Tug

Reid, George H., *Primer of Towing*. Centreville, MD: Cornell Maritime Press, 1975.

Mowat, Farley, *Grey Seas Under*. New York: Bantam Books, 1982. If you are interested in tugs, read the above two books, preferably in order. You'll be hooked.

Fast Outboard

Culler, R.D., *Skiffs and Schooners*, pp. 36-37.

National Fisherman: July 1963, December 1966.

Fantail Motor Launch

Martin, Fred W., *1901 Album of Designs*. Mount Prospect, IL: Altair Publishing Co., 1980.

Outboard Fishing Workboat Long John

Kelley, George, "Rhode Island Box." *The Mariner's Catalog, Volume 1*, p . 31

Classic Boat Monthly, July 1974.

National Fisherman: July 1963, January 1970, November 1971.

Motor Yawlboat for a Schooner

Olson, Stephen, "Yawlboats Aren't For Sailing." *The Small Boat Journal* #17.

Yard Tug

Culler, R.D., *Skiffs and Schooners*, pp. 26-27.

Reid, George H., *Primer of Towing*. Centreville, MD: Cornell Maritime Press, 1975.

National Fisherman, January 1973.

Part IV

Joshua Slocum's Spray

Culler, R.D., *The Spray: Building and Sailing a Replica of Joshua Slocum's Famous Vessel*. Highly recommended.

Slocum, Joshua, *Sailing Alone Around the World*. New York: Sheridan House, 1954. The prime source.

Slocum, Victor, *Captain Joshua Slocum*. New York: Sheridan House, 1952. Much additional information on the Spray and her captain.

Maynard, Mary, "Sailing Together Around the World." *WoodenBoat* #21, p. 58.

Slack, Kenneth, *In the Wake of the Spray*. New York: Sheridan House, 1981.

Culler, Toni, "Spray is our Home." *The Rudder*, April 1940.

Culler, R.D., "Going South." *The Rudder*, February 1946.

Friendship Sloops

Chapelle, Howard I., *American Sailing Craft*.

Barnard, W.L., "The Maine Sloops." *WoodenBoat* #2, p. 15.

Bray, Maynard, *Mystic Seaport Watercraft*. The further reading sources listed for Friendship sloops in this book are the most extensive I've seen.

Roanoke (Croatan) Boat

Wooden Shipbuilding and Small Craft Preservation. Washington, DC: The Preservation Press, 1976. On the cover, a Roanoke boat is pictured abuilding.

Catboats

Barnard, W.L., "The Cape Cod Catboat." *WoodenBoat* #3, p. 51.

Leavens, John, *The Catboat Book*. Camden, ME: International Marine Publishing Co., 1972. The sharper cat proposal is based on the Jersey cats and the more burdensome proposal on the Cape Cod cat. Both types are treated extensively in Leavens' book.

Chapelle, Howard I., *American Sailing Craft*. Chapelle gives an in-depth discussion on the Cape Cod cat.

Chapelle, Howard I., *American Small Sailing Craft*. Good discussion of New York types.

Newport Point Boat

Herreshoff, L. Francis, *The Compleat Cruiser*.

Leavens, John, *The Catboat Book*. Camden, ME: International Marine Publishing Co., 1972. Stephens, W.P., *Traditions and Memories of American Yachting*, Complete Edition. Roche, John, "Pete Culler Remembered." *Ash Breeze*, Spring 1983. Dogbody Baker, W.A., Sloops and Shallops. Barre, MA: Barre Publishing Co., 1966.

Chapelle, Howard I., *The National Watercraft Collection*, p. 181.

Part V

Ketch

Chapelle, Howard 1., *The History of the American Sailing Navy*.

Davis, Charles G., *The Built-up Ship Model*. Largo, FL: Edward W. Sweetman Co., 1980 (reprint).

Ketch
National Fisherman, May 1967.

Wabun-Type Sharpie
Gilpin, Vincent, "My Dream Boat." *The Rudder*, March 1946.
Gilpin, Vincent, *The Good Little Ship*. Lititz, PA: Sutter House, 1952.
Bebee, R.P., "Wabun: A Shoal-Draft Cruiser." *The Rudder*, February 1951.

Presto-Type Sharpie
Culler, R.D., *Skiffs and Schooners*, pp. 155-157.
Griffiths, Maurice, *Little Ships and Shoal Waters*. London: Conway Maritime Press, 1972.
Taylor, Roger C., *Good Boats*. Camden, ME: International Marine Publishing Co., 1977.
Gilpin, Vincent, and Munroe, R.M., "The Commodore's Story." *Classic Boat Monthly*, July 1974.
National Fisherman, September 1977.

V-Bottomed sharpie Old Glory
Culler, R.D., *Skiffs and Schooners*, pp. 102-105. Melcher, Jim, "Triumph." *National Fisherman*, April 1973.
MacNaughton, Dan, "The Sharpie: Flat is Back." *WoodenBoat* #25.
National Fisherman: January 1965, May 1965.

Steel Sharpie
See references listed under "Presto-Type Sharpie."

Live-Aboard Ketch
Culler, R.D., *Skiffs and Schooners*, p. 30.
Coffey, Burton, "Heavy 34' Concordia-Built Ketch Designed to Accommodate One Man." *National Fisherman*, October 1971.

Ketch Swan V
Culler, R.D., *Skiffs and Schooners*, pp. 124-127.
Motorboating and Sailing, November 1973.

Cowhorn Dory
Culler, R.D., *Skiffs and Schooners*, p. 6.
Taylor, Roger C., *Good Boats*. Camden, ME: International Marine Publishing Co., 1977.
Holle, Beverly, "The Block Island Cowhorn." *WoodenBoat* #22.
National Fisherman, May 1970.

French Dory
McMillan, Bruce, "Emme." *WoodenBoat* #35.
White, Mark, *Building the St. Pierre Dory*. Camden, ME: International Marine Publishing Co., 1978.
National Fisherman, September 1963.

Part VI

Tancook Schooner
Much material on the Tancook has been compiled by the Apprenticeshop and Lance Lee of Sea Street, Rockport, Maine. Contact them for information.
Nation, John, "The Building of a Tancook Whaler," *WoodenBoat* #5, #7.
Day, Jane, "The Return of Working Sail." *WoodenBoat* #31.
Taylor, Roger C., *Good Boats*. Camden, ME: International Marine Publishing Co., 1977. A good discussion of Tancooks and Ralph Wiley's *Mockingbird*. Wiley and Pete Culler were very good friends.

Schooner Gallant
"A Pilot Schooner for Traditionalists." *National Fisherman*, March 1966.

Periauger Scow
Herreshoff, L. Francis, *The Compleat Cruiser*.

Scow Schooner
Servais, Robert, Capt. R.D. Culler—A Scow Schooner's Dream." *WoodenBoat* #30.
Fetesoff, B., "San Francisco's Alma." *WoodenBoat* #3.
Chapelle, Howard I., *American Small Sailing Craft*, p, 33. Sea Letter. San Francisco Maritime Museum, December 1967.
Yachting, October 1942.

Schooners Fiddler's Green *and* Joseph W. Russell
Culler, R.D., *Skiffs and Schooners*, pp. 136-138, 139.
Culler, R.D., "Fiddler's Green - Finest Kind." *National Fisherman*, October 1973.
Ackerman, E.A., "Rediscovering Hackmatack." *WoodenBoat* #9, p. 44.
Taylor, Roger C., *Good Boats*. Camden, ME: International Marine Publishing Co., 1977. These two vessels are similar in style and appearance to Murray Peterson's Coasters.
Soundings, February 1976.

Pinky Schooner
Chapelle, Howard I., *American Sailing Craft*.
Chapelle, Howard I., *The National Watercraft Collection*, pp. 182-185.
Chapelle, Howard I., "The Return of the Pinky." *Yachting*, February 1938.
Brewer, E.S., "The Pilot's Pinky *Dove*." *WoodenBoat* #3, p.65.
Krotenko, Linda, "*Reliance*, A Pinky Schooner." *WoodenBoat* #18, p. 46.

Taylor, Roger C., *Good Boats.* Camden, ME: International Marine Publishing Co., 1977. Chapelle's pinky *Glad Tidings* is highlighted.

Schooner Integrity

Culler, R.D., *Skiffs and Schooners,* pp . 180-181.

Howland, Waldo, "The Other Man's Boat." *Yachting,* November 1965.

National Fisherman: November 1962, December 1962.

Gann, Ernest K., "Gems of the Ocean." *Rudder,* November 1970.

Mulville, Frank, *Death of the Schooner Integrity.* Boston: Charles River Books, 1981.

She Pungy Schooner

Steinlein, Eric, "Pungy Boats of the Chesapeake." *WoodenBoat* #45, p. 56.

Chapelle, Howard I., *The National Watercraft Collection,* pp. 193, 194, 197, 205.

Burgess, Robert H., *Chesapeake Sailing Craft.*

Baltimore Clipper Schooner

Culler, R.D., *Skiffs and Schooners,* pp. 150-151. Baltimore Clipper is reborn.

National Fisherman, June 1969.

Culler, R.D ., "Boatbuilding: The Philosophy of an Approach." A number of pictures of *Lizard King* are shown. *WoodenBoat* #4.

Gillmer, T.C., "The Emergence of *Pride,* A Baltimore Clipper." *WoodenBoat* #14, p. 16.

Chapelle, Howard I., *The Search for Speed Under Sail.*

Chapelle, Howard I., *The Baltimore Clipper: Its Origin and Development.*

Three-Masted Schooner

Culler, R.D., *Skiffs and Schooners,* p. 144.

Schooners John F. Leavitt *and* Kathy Brown

Any local newspaper of August 9, 1979.

Hartley, Peter, "Vessel's Loss Needs Second Look." *Cape Cod Times,* January 6, 1980.

Day, Jane, "The Return of Working Sail." *WoodenBoat* #31, p, 18.

Spectre, Peter, "North Atlantic Shakedown: The Abandonment of the *John F. Leavitt.*" *WoodenBoat* #33, p, 20.

Leavitt, John F., *Wake of the Coasters.* Mystic, CT: Mystic Seaport Museum, 1970. According to Ned Ackerman, this is the book that started it all.

Chapelle, Howard I., *The History of American Sailing Ships.* A good discussion of coasting types, both two and three masts.

National Fisherman, October 1979.

Smith, E.W., *Workaday Schooners.* Camden, ME: International Marine Publishing Co., 1975.

Coaster, Atlantic Films. A film of the building and subsequent loss of the *John F. Leavitt.* Captain Pete is not mentioned once during the film, nor is his name mentioned in the interminable credits at the end of the film. Why not?

The Ways of Wallace and Sons, Allegra May, May Day Films. The building of the *John F. Leavitt* from the perspective of those who worked on her. This film is available from Mystic Seaport.

Details

A listing of further reading sources on this topic could go on forever; therefore I find the need to be concise.

Culler, R.D., *Skiffs and Schooners.*

Culler, R.D., *Boats, Oars, and Rowing.*

The above two books when studied will give the most information on Culler details available anywhere.

Getchell, David, Putz, George, and Spectre, Peter, eds., *The Mariner's Catalog,* Volumes 1-7.

Captain Pete was a frequent contributor to *The Mariner's Catalogs.* I especially recommend "What Makes Classics Real," Volume 3, p. 52, and "Old Ways Work," Volume 1, p. 96.

Putz, George, "Profile of a Master Boatwright." *Sea,* March 1978.

Editors, "Pete Culler's Workshop." *WoodenBoat* #27, #28.

Soundings, February 1976.

Pete giving a demonstration of the use of natural crooks in boatbuilding.
(Mystic Seaport photo by Mary Anne Stets)

Appendix C
Boats Built at Pete Culler's Shop

(Richard White photo)

Captain Pete and his wife, Toni, came ashore at Hyannis in October 1948. They bought an ancient Cape Cod house with a small barn in back, right across the street from my family's homestead.

To utilize space better, and I suppose to hark back to his apprentice days at the Conley Shipyard in Maryland, Pete arranged his shop in the loft of that barn and housed his vehicle on the lower level. In those early days, access to the shop was from the inside via a ladder and a trap door.

As a young boy I used to play in the Cullers' yard. My memories of that time, however, are not of Captain Pete, but of Mrs. Culler's homemade cookies! During one of those playtimes I found the barn door open, and, being very young and very curious, I began to explore. I was halfway up the ladder when Mrs. Culler pounced on me like a cat. "Don't you go up there," she scolded. "Don't you ever go up there. That's the Captain's shop!" I was promptly led away by the scruff of the neck and the door was refastened. Well, it took me another 20 years, but I finally got inside Captain Pete's shop.

It was a wonderful place.

For a young aspiring boatbuilder, the shop was an answer to questions, a clear and simple inspiration, and a measure of what could be. It was that kind of place because of the man who worked there. From his fertile mind and through his talented hands came glorious creations. There were tools and inventions, both general and specific, finely proportioned models and artistic designs, both large and small, and there were boats and boats. Some of these were simple, but they all had exquisite character.

Captain Pete was always "doodling" with small craft. He was only about 16 when he produced his first skiff. For all of that, he didn't design a vessel until he was 50, when he drew Integrity. This was for the simple reason that he didn't feel he knew enough about it until then.

As can be seen in the following list, Pete's boatbuilding in Hyannis was slow to take off. He produced 14 boats during the first 17 years. Of course he was busy with other pursuits during this time, chartering and skippering being chief among them. However, starting in 1967, and until illness slowed him down in 1976, he averaged four boats a year. This may not seem like much, but it must be remembered that he was a lone worker, all construction was traditional, and every job was a custom one. Even boats built to the same design were often different in styling and detail. And, except for two, Captain Pete designed the boats he built. The bulk of his design work, both large and small, was produced during this period too. Look back at the designs in this catalog and you will realize the industry of these years.

Captain Pete had two lists of boats built, and unfortunately they do not jibe. Therefore, some extrapolation was necessary. This was done carefully with all that research, memory, and intuition could bring to bear, but there may still be some errors, which I will gladly correct if they are brought to my attention. Additionally, there are some informational gaps as to weights and owners. Boat names and original color schemes would be a nice addition to the list, too. I would be most appreciative of any assistance that can be offered by readers.

—John Burke

Above : Captain Pete's boatshop.

Below: Captain Pete ponders the beginnings of the $10\frac{1}{2}$-foot wherry yawl. (Richard White photos)

Right: The blacksmith shop. (Mystic Seaport photo by Claire White Peterson)

Below: The design quarters of Captain Pete's shop. (Mystic Seaport photo by Claire White Peterson)

Hull #	Type/Model	Weight	Place/Owner/Vessel	Year
		Boats Built 1950-1966		
1	14′ skiff		Holbrook	
2	V-bottomed 16′ motor skiff		Athern	
3	11′ skiff—varnished transom			
4	13½′ V-bottomed outboard for open water		Musata	
5	1st 11′ sampan		own	
6	11′ V-bottomed pod		Paul Glaser	1958
7	15½′ fast outboard, 25 knots		Eaton	
8	15′9″ V-sail beachboat		Waldo Howland—*Java*	1958
9	12½′ V-bottomed sailing yawlboat		for schooner *Integrity*—W. Howland	
10	9′ V-bottomed butthead		sternboat for *Gallant*—Tilghman	
11	11′ varnished sampan		Ewing	
12	8½′ sampan		Norton	
13	15½′ V-bottomed outboard skiff, 16 knots			
14	11′ yard sampan			
		Boats Built 1967-1977		
15	13′ yard skiff		Sturges, Noank	1967
16	13′ yard skiff		South Dartmouth	1967
17	11′ stock sampan		to M.V. Fletcher	1967
18	12′ lightweight sampan	120	to Orleans	1967
19	15½′ West Coast sailing skiff	302	R. Laggemann, Barnstable	1968
20	Sharptown barge		R. White, West Barnstable	1968
21	15½′ V-bottomed sailing beachboat		Museum of the Sea, Savannah	1968
22	15½′ V-bottomed sailing beachboat		Museum of the Sea, Savannah	1968
23	8′ Herreshoff Nereia pram	135	John Kendall—Nereia ketch	1968
24	10′ work punt		Tony Scott, Mishaum Point	1969
25	17′ clipper wherry	300	Dr. Freydber—Marth'a Vineyard	1969
26	9′ Concordia pram		Morgan Brown—Concordia yawl	1969
27	16′ V-bottomed fast outboard	415	John Hallett—Portsmouth, NH	1969
28	11′ sailing sampan	274	Wm. Wood—*Swan V*	1969
29	10½′ New England yawlboat	180	Forbes, Nashawena Island	1970
30	10′ work punt		Mystic Seaport	1970
31	17′ clipper wherry	300	John West, North Haven, ME	1970
32	18½′ gentleman's gig	243	Glenn MacNary, North Falmouth—*Punch*	1970
33	17½′ Concordia sloopboat		Brown, Boston	1971
34	18′ V-bottomed outboard work skiff	455	R. Thomas, Barnstable—*Pintail*	1971
35	18½′ flat-bottomed sailing skiff	347	W. Howland—*Dixie Bell*	1971
36	17½′ pulling bateau	92	*Otter*	1971
37	9′ butthead punt		Stanton—*Plover*	1972
38	15½′ outboard skiff			1972
39	16½′ Atkin skiff		Texas	1972
40	16′ V-bottomed outboard skiff		Conco - Pinney (?)	1973
41	16′ Race Point lifeboat	262	Caldwell, Nantucket—Coskata	1973
42	10½′ ship's yawl	178	*Stormsvala*	1973
43	16′ fast V-bottomed outboard		Kaufmann, Sakonnet	1974
44	17½′ Staten Island skiff	302	Hovey, Manchester	1974
45	10½′ wherry yawl	178	Ackerman—Fiddler's Green	1974
46	12½′ double-paddle canoe	39	*Butternut*	1974
47	19′ Swampscott dory	399	Capt. Charlie Sayle, Nantucket	1975
48	10′ sampan	151	schooner *Welcome*	1975
49	18′ V-bottomed outboard skiff		Linhares	1975
50	18½′ flat-bottomed sailing skiff		McManus	1976
51	18′ fast gig	152	Dr. Freydberg—*Quitsa Pilot*	1977
52	19′ Swampscott dory	375	Wentz, New York	1977

Appendix D
Boat Plans By R.D. Culler

If Pete said it once, he said it at least a thousand times. "If you can't afford the plans, you can't afford the boat!"

It was decided, when planning this book, that a considerable amount of determining data would be included on the plans. This has been done with the knowledge that a few people will attempt to build a boat from these study plans. While plans reproduced in a book may be satisfactory for model makers, they are usually not the best way to tackle a full-size boat. I can guarantee that such builders will run into unforeseen problems. No, it is much easier to cough up the cash and receive properly sized drawings. All of these designs are reasonably priced. Spending the money marks commitment.

I want you to be excited by these plans. There can be no finer memorial than to build a designer's boats.

The following boat plans by R.D. "Pete" Culler are available at the Daniel S. Gregory Ships Plans Library, Mystic Seaport. This is George Kelley's list of Culler's plans. All editorial comments are George's. Please inquire for current prices and a list of specific sheets of plans within each design. Daniel S. Gregory Ships Plans Library, Mystic Seaport Museum, Inc. 75 Greenmanville Ave. Mystic, CT 06355. 860-572-5360. collections@mysticseaport.org

Catalog #	Description	# of Sheet Sets
	Vee- and Flat-Bottom Open Boats	
128.1	10'2" Concordia yard butthead. A utilitarian, square ended work punt.	2
128.2	11' sailing sampan *Jade Arrow*. A very good tender. Rows and tows well.	3
128.3	11'6" vee-bottom pod for Paul Glaser. Very small one man tender. Similar to 15'9" beachboat. No offsets.	1
128.4	12'6" vee-bottom yawlboat for *Integrity*. Powerful, able carrier. Rows and sails well.	2
128.5	13' 6" original Good Little Skiff. Popular boat. Sails, rows and tows well.	2
128.6	14' 6" rowing skiff for Dr. James Wallace. Rows well.	1
128.7	14'6' wheelbarrow skiff for Dr. James Wallace. Centerboard is a wheel.	1
128.8	14'9" vee-bottom day boat similar to 17' 7" daysailer, more vee. Also for Dr. Roche.	1
128.9	15'8" flat-bottom sailing skiff. The mid-sized of the three Good Little Skiffs. Uses construction plan for the 13'6" version.	2
128.10	15'9" vee-bottom, double ended beachboat *Java and Cruz del Sur*. No offsets.	1
128.11	16' 8" vee-bottom catboat for W. H. Hagan, Jr.	3
128.12	17'4" clipper pulling bateau *Otter* built for Pete's own use. 92 lbs.	1
128.13	17' flat-bottomed skiff for Maynard Bray. No skeg for backing on beach.	2
128.14	17'9" flat-bottomed skiff for Anne Bray. No skeg for backing on beach.	2
128.15	17'7" vee-bottom daysailer for Dr. Roche. Shallow draft, Bahama rig.	3
128.16	18'6" flat-bottom sailing skiff *Dixie Bell* for Waldo Howland. Biggest of the Good Little Skiffs.	2
128.17	18'8" Swampscott dory for Charles Sayle. Fast, able, and handsome.	3
128.18	20' fast pulling bateau for Dr. James Eldredge. Flat-bottom, no rig, one to three people. A big Otter.	1
128.19	20' sharpie proposal for John Parkinson. One sail or two. Lack of lines requires guessing.	2
128.20	24' Sharptown barge. Centerboard, flat-bottomed, fast.	2
	Round-Bilged Open Boats for Sail and Oar	
128.21	9' Concordia Baeteka pram, lines only, no rig shown, no construction drawings. (Also inquire about Ships Plans catalog #130.1 for additional plans and specifications.)	1
128.22	10'6" wherry yawl for Ned Ackerman's schooner *Fiddler's Green*. Plank keel with rig.	3
128.23	10'6" New England yawlboat for Stephen Forbes. Known as the "sheep boat." No rig.	1
128.24	13' canoe. Pete's own *Butternut*. Double paddle and lapstrake, one man.	1
128.25	16'4" yawlboat for yacht *America II*. Similar to a Whitehall.	3
128.26	16'7" Staten Island skiff for Richard Hovey. Split rig, handsome, able, and powerful.	2
128.27	16'8" Race Point surfboat *Coskata* for Robert Caldwell. Lapstrake.	1

Catalog #	Description	# of Sheet Sets
128.28	16'11" clipper wherry *Seaman's Friend* designed for Nicholas Freydberg.	3
128.29	17' canoe. Dr. Roche's *Cymba*. Double paddle and lapstrake, two man.	2
128.30	17' two sail, double paddle canoe for William Pinney.	2
128.31	17'8" Concordia sloopboat. Minimal construction drawings.	5
128.32	I7'8" Kingston lobsterboat. A "reverted" Concordia sloop with shallop rig.	3
128.33	18'8" Buzzards Bay sloop *Beaver*. Based on Concordia sloop but more powerful, able. Lapstrake .	5
128.34	18' fast Cornish pilot gig for Nicholas Freydberg. No rig shown. High performance, light (151 lbs), a really way-out craft. Needs spoon oars.	1
128.35	18'6" clipper pulling boat *Punch*. Fast, three rowing positions, not a sailboat.	1
128.36	19'6" shallop for George Putz. Lute sterned.	4
128.37	20' fast Cornish yawl for Clayton Lewis. Small rig, no centerboard, high performance.	2

Inboard and Outboard Power Boats

Catalog #	Description	# of Sheet Sets
128.38	15'6" shipyard work boat/tow boat *Gracie III*. Vee bottom, powerful and heavy.	4
128.39	15' motor yawlboat for schooner *John F. Leavitt*. Very stout.	3
128.40	18' and 16' vee-bottomed outboards. Similar to 24' outboard for Chubb. A set.	2
128.41	21'9" outboard fishing/work boat *Long John* with small sprit rig. Motorwell and rudder.	2
128.42	24' fast outboard work boat or pleasure boat with variations in layout for Percy Chubb.	5
128.43	24' fantail motor launch with pilot house for Peter Burling.	3
128.44	25' light motor skiff proposal for Mr. Hankinwell.	1
128.45	25' heavy motor skiff proposal for Mr. Hankinwell.	1
128.46	28'9 " round-bottomed launch proposal for Commodore Percy Chubb.	1
128.47	21' vee-bottomed tug for Mark Marting. Complete, an enlarged "*Gracie III*"	3
128.48	30' fast vee-bottomed outboard launch. Needs at least 120 h.p.-two 85s or better with one 150.	5
128.49	32' vee-bottomed fantail steamer.	3
128.50	32'8" original proposal for Hovey's steam launch.	1
128.51	34' fantail steam launch for Richard Hovey. Really handsome.	4
128.52	35'10" power boat *Susan A*.	2
128.53	39'8" Concordia Nova Scotia motor cruiser. Light and easy moving.	5
128.54	55' fast express cruiser proposal for Drayton Cochran. 1925 style, modern power.	2
128.55	70' motor vessel proposal for Mrs. Brooks. A study only.	2

Cutters, Sloops, Yawls, and Shallops

Catalog #	Description	# of Sheet Sets
128.56	20' proposal for light daysailer catboat. No lines.	1
128.57	20' proposal for heavy cruising catboat. No lines.	1
128.58	20' Newport Point boat for Dr. John Roche. Deep centerboard, single cat-rigged sail, lapstrake.	4
128.59	21' dogbody for Philip Volker. Two sails, offset mainmast and centerboard. An overnighter.	3
128.60	22' Friendship sloop for Knight Sturges.	5
128.61	25' Friendship sloop *Pemaquid*, mostly redrawn from Chapelle. Complete, a much copied design.	4
128.62	25'10" sloop proposal for Bruce Northrup. No lines.	2
128.63	27' Roanoke/Croatan boat proposal for Mr. Rogers. No lines.	1
128.64	28' cutter for Lar Lindblom. Sleeps four very well, built in Finland.	8
128.65	30' Friendship sloop proposal. No lines.	2
128.66	35' Friendship sloop proposal. No lines.	2
128.67	35'10" British cutter for Bruce Northrup. Two versions: conventional cabin and "stern window" cabin.	5
128.68	36'9" replica of Slocum's *Spray*. Detailed construction drawings with layout slightly altered for Hugh Bigelow.	7

Catalog #	Description	# of Sheet Sets
128.69	46'5" cutter for Wayland Purmont. A powerful fisherman with 7-ton hold.	5

Ketches

Catalog #	Description	# of Sheet Sets
128.70	25'10" French dory proposal for Richard Tatlock. A bit of imagination required to use this plan.	1
128.71	26'6" cowhorn dory.	1
128.72	33' ketch for Robin Laggeman. Trunk cabin, shoal keel, nice hull.	3
128.73	34' live-aboard ketch *Plover* for Fred Stanton. Main topmast. Raised deck makes nice, comfortable one-person boat.	8
128.74	36' vee-bottomed sharpie *Old Glory* for Franklin Parker.	4
128.75	36' multichine steel sharpie for Dr. Robert Baxter.	2
128.76	37' 7" Presto-type sharpie for Admiral Schmidt.	4
128.77	37'7" Presto-type sharpie *Dawn Treader* with slight variations in rig and cabin plan for Stefan Galazzi.	4
128.78	38'6" seagoing, short gaffed ketch for Ted Harper.	4
128.79	40'6" Wabun-type round-bilge sharpie for Gordon Mott. Very attractive, shoal draft.	7
128.80	40' ketch proposal for John Kendall. Lines and sail plan only.	2
128.81	45' marconi ketch *Swan V* for William Wood. Handsome , able, and successful.	6
128.82	43'10" ketch for Taylor. Sail plan only.	1
128.83	44'6" unfinished ketch proposal. Could be good. Handsome.	1
128.84	48' marconi rigged motorsailer *Transition* for Addison Taylor.	9
128.85	55'5" albacore troller for Wes Wickham. A sail-assisted fishing vessel with ketch rig.	5

Schooners

Catalog #	Description	# of Sheet Sets
128.86	28' schooner for Thomas Doyle. A real toy boat.	5
128.87	32' schooner with loose footed foresail for Malcolm Kirkbride.	5
128.88	32' Periauger scow. A very sketchy idea Pete had for his own boat, which he never completed.	3
128.89	38' Tancook whaler proposal for Thomas Hooper.	4
128.90	40' main topmast schooner *Gallant* for Richard Tilghman. Fast and hand some with flying jibboom.	15
128.91	42' schooner yacht *Prudence* for David Forbes. Somewhat tender.	5
128.92	45' she pungy (Chesapeake) schooner for Eddie Crosby. Fast and rakish.	5
128.93	45' vee-bottomed scow schooner *R. D. Culler* for Robert Servais.	5
128.94	47' schooner *Joseph W. Russell* for Buzz Garrahan. Fast and able.	5
128.95	47'6" schooner *Fiddler's Green* for Ned Ackerman. Nearly identical to *Joseph W. Russell*.	7
128.96	46' main topmast pinky with fish-hold for Warren Lemaster.	4
128.97	52' schooner *Integrity* for Waldo Howland. A powerful vessel considered to be Pete's masterpiece.	8
128.98	53'10" Baltimore clipper *Lizard King* for Bruce Northrup. Fast, handsome, but no offsets.	3
128.99	60'2" deep-draft offshore West Coast sealer *Gallant Lady* for Roy Grizzle.	10
128.100	82'6" main topmast clipper for Henry Sears. Based on fast fruit runner.	3
128.101	96' three mast topsail schooner, proposal only for Mr. Currier.	3
128.102	91' coasting schooner *John F. Leavitt* for Ned Ackerman. Another fast carrier. Scantlings for the *Leavitt* would do for *Kathy Brown* so the construction plan would be the guide for both.	5
128.103	125' three mast centerboard coasting schooner *Kathy Brown* for Ned Ackerman. A fast, handsome vessel.	3